Guns in America

Guns in America

A Reader

EDITED BY

Jan E. Dizard, Robert Merrill Muth, and Stephen P. Andrews, Jr.

New York University Press

NEW YORK AND LONDON

NEW YORK UNIVERSITY PRESS
New York and London

Library of Congress Cataloging-in-Publication Data
Guns in America : a reader / edited by Jan E. Dizard, Robert Merrill
Muth, and Stephen P. Andrews Jr.
p.   cm.
Includes bibliographical references and index.
ISBN 0-8147-1878-7 (cloth : alk. paper). — ISBN 0-8147-1879-5
(pbk. : alk. paper)
1. Gun control—United States.   2. Firearms—United States.
3. Firearms—United States—History.   I. Dizard, Jan E., 1940–
II. Muth, Robert M.   III. Andrews, Stephen P., 1959–
HV7436.G878   1999
363.3'3'0973—dc21   98-47896
CIP

New York University Press books are printed on acid-free paper,
and their binding materials are chosen for strength and durability.

Manufactured in the United States of America

10   9   8   7   6   5   4   3   2   1

Contents

Acknowledgments

The editors wish to thank the Trustees of Amherst College for their generous help in defraying the costs of preparing this volume for publication. We would also like to acknowledge the assistance of the students enrolled in Robert Muth's seminar in Social Conflict and Natural Resource Policy, many of whom contributed provocative and helpful ideas on the gun controversy when this project was in its infancy. Martha Mather also gave us sage advice throughout the shaping of this volume.

Finally, without Beth Muramoto's guidance in the ways of the Web, her good cheer, and her inventiveness, this project would have taken much longer and would have been a good deal more arduous.

Part I

The Rise of Gun Culture in America
Introduction: Guns Made Us Free — Now What?

The assassination of President John F. Kennedy in November 1963, set off a national debate over the place of guns in our society that has continued, virtually unabated, to the present. There is no end in sight. In fact, Kennedy's assassination did not start the debate so much as it rekindled passions that had lain dormant for several decades. The essential elements of the debate were framed well over three hundred years ago in England and brought to these shores by the English colonists. The issue was straightforward: should the right to possess, control, and use firearms be solely vested in the state? If the authorities were the only ones armed, how could the people protect their rights, persons, or property (Malcolm, 1994)? As in so many other cases, common origins have given way to divergent paths. England, over time, has sharply restricted the private ownership of guns and established the tradition of an unarmed constabulary. Indeed, in 1997 Parliament voted to ban outright the private ownership of all handguns. In the United States, gun ownership became widespread and the police, at all levels, became conspicuously armed — though, interestingly, police forces did not begin to embrace service revolvers until early in the twentieth century (Gilmore, 1975). Which society is freer? In which are citizens' rights more secure?

Proponents of gun restrictions point to Great Britain's low crime rate, especially its minuscule rate of homicide, to suggest that not only are Britains as free as Americans, they are also safer because so few guns are in private hands there. But the correlation may be deceptive. In Switzerland, all adult males are required to serve in the Swiss equivalent of our National Guard. As a result, all must possess a military weapon and maintain minimal proficiency with it until they reach fifty-five years of age. For all practical purposes, this means that there is a firearm (indeed, what we would regard as an "assault weapon") in nearly every household in Switzerland. Crime rates in general and the homicide rate in particular are even lower in Switzerland than in Great Britain. Might this suggest that if everyone is armed, few dare commit a crime? Some gun advocates do indeed draw this lesson. Whatever the lesson, it is clear that no simple relationship exists between gun ownership and political freedom, or between gun ownership and crime.

The passion guns evoked strongly suggests that the debate is at least as much about the symbolic meanings we attach to them as it is about guns themselves. So, for example, gun advocates have successfully turned away repeated efforts to ban so-called Saturday Night Specials—small, easily concealed pistols that are cheaply made and inaccurate beyond point-blank range—even though no serious shooter or collector would deign to own one. But while those attempting to ban handguns focus on the mayhem they are capable of creating, gun advocates focus on the rights they feel are forged into the very metal of each and every gun, regardless of its pedigree or the uses to which it might be put. Guns made us free and have kept us free, one side says; the other side rejects guns as instruments of domination, lawlessness, and terrorism. The conflict rages on because both sides are right. Guns *are* instruments of violence, and there is no guarantee that they will be deployed only on the side of the good. Extreme gun lovers and gun haters aside, the rest of us are left with an uneasy ambivalence, our attitude toward the private possession of firearms contingent upon circumstances. This is as much so today as it was when the Pilgrims landed at Plymouth.

The Puritans who sailed for the New World were convinced that they would be greeted by hostile natives, quite possibly the Devil's own people. Accordingly, they were well armed. Their leaders had urged all men to acquaint themselves with their muskets and steel themselves for combat with savages. Once here, the authorities in fact required men to be armed. In 1632, the Massachusetts Bay Colony began to require that each householder "have . . . a sufficient musket or other serviceable peece for war . . . for himself and each man servant he keeps able to beare arms" (Kruschke, 1985, 14). The fact that the natives were not immediately hostile did not alter things much. After a brief time of relative accord, more the result of the colonists' near helplessness than of their pacifism, the Puritans launched a campaign of aggression that forced the natives to fight back, thereby confirming the colonists' worst fears and fueling in God-fearing whites a paroxysm of murderousness that still staggers the imagination (Lepore, 1998).

Given this almost entirely self-imposed predicament, the leaders of the colony needed the colonists armed. The colonists also depended upon game, initially for food, but quite soon the products of the hunt became an important part of their commerce with England. Hides and pelts, as well as meat, were highly prized in England, and the colonists were only too happy to pay their bills from the success of the hunt (Cronon, 1983). This further established the need for an armed citizenry.

But even at this early date, an armed citizenry posed problems for those intent on maintaining hierarchy and internal order. The problem was complicated. First, there was the obvious risk that discord might escalate into lethal violence, whether within the domestic circle or between neighbors. Further, an individual or group of individuals, emboldened by their arms, might be tempted to defy constituted authority. Finally, there was the threat of secession. Given the intense demand for order built into Puritanism and the close scrutiny of the most minute details of daily life to which the colonists were subjected, each of these threats loomed large and was magnified by the very precariousness of the fledgling settlement.

The theocratic leaders of the Massachusetts Bay Colony were thus on the horns of a dilemma: for reasons of maintaining strict obedience and observance, they no doubt would have preferred an unarmed and thus more easily controlled population. But they were too fearful of hostile natives and too dependent upon hunting to restrict access to firearms. The dilemma was further intensified because the availability of vast amounts of land and abundant game served as constant temptation to those whose faith wavered. Being armed made it possible for the disaffected to strike out on their own, thereby weakening the still-fragile community.

Though the preachers who led the community had a propensity for imagining threats and fearing for the rectitude of their flock, the threats posed by dissenters were not imaginary. At the very outset, the Puritan authorities were challenged by one Thomas Morton, who, with several other *Mayflower* passengers, set up camp apart from the main settlement and quickly befriended the natives, with whom they were soon trading briskly and frolicking with energy and enthusiasm. Miles Standish led a party of enforcers to arrest Morton and his followers, which they succeeded in doing after a scuffle that included a few harmless shots. Morton was held prisoner and sent packing on the next ship bound for England (Zuckerman, 1977).

Hunters posed a less ideological risk, but a risk nonetheless. Errant shots understandably worried folks. Very quickly, settlers began complaining about hunters shooting too close to dwellings or across heavily traveled trails and roads. But options were few, given their circumstances. The authorities forbade the discharge of weapons on the Sabbath, as part of the comprehensive package of "blue laws" they imposed to ensure devoutness, and promulgated rules aimed at reducing the risks associated with firearms. Given the Puritans' determination to thwart activities that were so absorbing as to deflect concentration from religious contemplation, it seems reasonable to guess that guns and hunting were looked upon as necessary evils they would have been only too willing to sharply restrict had they not needed guns for defense and for procuring valuable game. Thus was established the tradition of widespread ownership of firearms with which we are still contending.

By the time the Constitution was framed, this tradition was embedded in daily practice as well as in the fast unfolding story of national destiny. Every schoolchild in the United States is taught about how "ordinary Americans" defeated the better armed and better trained British. The famed shot "heard 'round the world" was fired from the musket of a Concord farmer. The impression has long been that privately owned guns were commonplace in the colony. Yet militia commanders routinely complained about lack of arms and of arms in such poor repair as to be all but useless. These sorts of complaints persisted well into the nineteenth century. Of course, one could discount this as a standard ploy to get more resources for one's company, much as the Pentagon today pleads helplessness when it suits its weapons procurement dreams. But tax rolls reveal that rarely more than a third of the households reported guns to the tax authorities. Even if we assume tax dodging deflated reports of taxable property in guns, it may well be the case that many fewer colonists owned guns, at least guns in working order, than our popular national mythology would suggest.

There is a straightforward reason why guns may have been less common than we think: they were expensive, so ownership was probably restricted to prosperous landowners. Muskets were also easily ruined by careless use or neglect. All but the most minor repairs were prohibitively expensive and slow. These material realities made guns hard to come by, which probably increased the desire to own one. So even though they were far from widespread, they were sought after. This demand kept prices high, thus reinforcing limited ownership. The relatively narrow base of ownership, however, did not seem to diminish the strength of the principle that the citizenry should be armed, a principle that Joyce Malcolm (1994) convincingly shows was directly linked to the ideal of liberty and the desire to have a popular check on arbitrary authority.

Even without the French and Indian War, the War of Independence, and the War of 1812, the ideology of expansionism that fueled a steady push westward would have been reason enough to accept, with whatever reservations, the practical necessity of an armed citizenry. But make no mistake: there were reservations. Despite Jefferson's bold assertion of the fundamental right of the people to revolt—even more, despite his observation that such revolt should occur with some regularity—those who would lead the new nation were not indifferent to the threat of disorder inherent in an armed citizenry. Indeed, Jefferson's wish to leave industry in Europe so that Americans could remain wedded to the soil grew out of his desire to prevent the formation of a class of abjectly poor laborers in the New World, not out of an opposition to the industrial revolution per se. An armed working class would be even worse. But like the Puritans a century and a half earlier, those who gathered to frame the constitution were stuck: like it or not, the new nation needed to be armed against both external foes and the natives who were not about to passively accept European expansion into their territories.

Making this dilemma even more palpable was the Founding Fathers' concern that the central government they were creating become too powerful. The most potent symbol of this power was a standing army. Rejecting a professional standing army left no alternative but to permit the private possession of firearms to provide for a citizens' army. Fears of an armed citizenry were thus trumped by the recognition of the need for a citizenry capable of defending the nation at a moment's notice. This dilemma is no doubt one of the reasons why the Second Amendment, over which we still argue, was framed so vaguely. It was not sloppiness or inadvertence in an otherwise tightly drawn document; it was the same sort of ambivalence with which we, over two hundred years later, still contend.

While legislators, jurists, and legal scholars wrestled with the muddle of the Second Amendment, technological advances all but settled the matter at the practical level. When the Second Amendment was being drafted and debated, guns were still individually crafted, each one a unique piece. If a gun was broken, the original maker was typically the only one able to make the necessary repairs, if they could be made at all. At best, repairs were slow and costly. Cheaply made guns turned out to be no bargain. Armies dealt with this fact by laboriously and painstakingly training soldiers in the proper care and handling of muskets and restricting access so as to keep repairs to a minimum.

An American inventor, John Whitney, helped change all this forever, and in the process, fundamentally altered the course of the industrial revolution and America's role in it. Ironically, Jefferson, the foe of homegrown industry, played a key role. As president, he recognized the need to build the nation's armory, which had fallen into a sorry state after the War for Independence. The cost of importing weapons from Europe was prohibitive, and there was concern that dependence on European arms would leave the country vulnerable to embargo should hostilities arise. Whitney approached the Army with the novel idea of manufacturing guns that would be both relatively cheap and easily repaired and found a receptive audience (Smith, 1981). Whitney, fresh from the triumph of his cotton gin, thought he could devise machines that would make interchangeable parts from a single pattern. Each gun would be less expensive than its hand-crafted counterpart and, as importantly, could be repaired quickly by almost anyone capable of mastering a few common operations. With such guns and a supply of spare parts, an army could function quite well with little or no elaborate training in or supervision over the use and care of weapons. This would give a largely volunteer force more equal footing with professionals, thus avoiding the need for the dreaded standing professional army that was synonymous with monarchy and tyranny.

The idea was too risky to attract sufficient private capital, which is why Whitney approached the government. Backed by a large order from the U.S. Army, Whitney had little difficulty drumming up investors and the American arms industry was born. Though Whitney encountered more difficulties than he had anticipated and his endeavor proved less than a success, his idea turned out to be brilliant. It fell to others to make the idea of mass production and interchangeable parts work. By the 1840s, all up and down the Connecticut River valley, machine shops were producing both long guns and pistols using Whitney's basic ideas. None was more successful at this than the fabled Samuel Colt, who was part inventor, part promoter. Colt's pistols became more legendary than the man himself. Colt and his imitators made reliable and durable guns that virtually everyone could afford. The door to widespread private ownership of firearms was thrown fully open.

Attempts to shut this door have been largely unsuccessful. The most anyone has been able to accomplish is to narrow the opening ever so slightly. The closest we have come to a general prohibition on ownership were the laws in the South that kept slaves from owning guns. Aside from this, until recently regulation was directed more at limiting use than at restricting access or ownership. Early on, most cities passed laws forbidding or sharply circumscribing the discharge of firearms within the city limits. Some establishments, particularly saloons, required patrons to check their weapons upon entering. Many states adopted laws proscribing the carrying of concealed weapons, and virtually all forbade transporting loaded weapons and shooting across roads or near dwellings.

The first ban on a class of weapons came in response to the rise of organized crime during Prohibition: fully automatic weapons (machine guns) and sawed-off shotguns were made illegal. In the wake of President Kennedy's assassination, it became somewhat more cumbersome to purchase a firearm—a buyer could no longer get one through the mail and there were more forms to fill out. Purchasers from that time forward have had to attest that they are not a convicted felon and do not have a history of mental illness or drug use, each of which is a disqualification for ownership. Efforts to ban the sale of various handguns, most notably the Saturday Night Special, have failed and bans on assault weapons have become a political football at both the federal and state levels. All told, proponents of gun control have little to show for their efforts. The Brady Bill passed after years of wrangling and merely mandates the imposition of a background check (which required local law enforcement personnel to do the checking, a provision the Supreme Court invalidated in 1997) and a waiting period between purchase and delivery. The door to gun ownership remains virtually as wide open as ever.

Indeed, it may well be that gun control is a moot issue. Whatever the courts, legal scholars, or legislators decide, the inescapable fact is that there are so many guns in circulation that any attempt to assert meaningful control would require a virtual police state. No politician in his or her right mind would even seriously contemplate the effort. Once Whitney's invention proved workable and guns became so widely distributed, the strictly constitutional debate became irrelevant for everyone but scholars and ideologues. On the ground, as it were, Americans had won the right to own guns, if not as a matter of constitutionally guaranteed principle then as a politically irreversible *fait accompli*.

Guns are woven into the warp and woof of our nation's history. No one has demonstrated how thoroughly guns have permeated our culture more convincingly than the historian Richard Slotkin (1973, 1985, 1992). In his exhaustive trilogy, Slotkin shows how violence in general, and firearms in particular, have been at the core of our national narrative. From the Puritans' embrace of guns to beat back the devilish Indian to our delight in the extralegal exploits of Dirty Harry, Americans have relied on the gun to right wrongs, real and imagined. Slotkin guides us painstakingly from early settlement to the present, showing how virtually every surface in which we can see ourselves reflected reveals a gun—the Minuteman's muzzleloader, the Colt revolver ("the gun that won the west"), the Sharps rifle (the weapon of choice of those who slaughtered the buffalo), the Enfield that troops carried with them in America's first combat on foreign shores (and, as surplus, became widely used by American deer hunters after World War II), and, of course, the service revolver that, until recently, was the standard of virtually every police force in the nation.

Many of the iconic figures in our history are men who made their mark with a gun—generals, adventurers, hunters, outlaws, gangsters, and "peace officers."

Our history cannot be told without acknowledging the centrality of guns in our national experience. This is by no means simply an abstract point. The history of which we speak is not a "dead" history. Despite our reputation for having little or no sense of history, many thousands of Americans each year flock to reenactments of historic battles fought at such sites as Concord and Gettysburg. Dressed in period costumes, brandishing antique or replica weapons, they replay history. Others assemble to relive for a week or two the lives of early trappers, "mountain men," and explorers. Dressed in skins, they try in as many particulars as possible to replicate the slice of the past that appeals to them. Still others practice year round for contests in which, dressed in western garb, they try to beat one another to the draw. Thousands of Americans trade in antique weapons, modern replicas, and related memorabilia, with each war or weapon or artifact boasting its own world of aficionados. Each of these hobbies sustains at least one nationally circulated magazine devoted to promoting interest and participation. Encampments, gun shows, and black powder musket competitions (who can shoot and reload fastest, who can be most accurate at distances up to 400 yards) bring like-minded people together.

Understandably, people at such gatherings talk about the specifications and comparative performance of various weapons. Much like baseball fans eternally arguing over who was the best player or team, so, too, do gun enthusiasts argue endlessly over the merits of their favorite gun or cartridge load. But it is a mistake to think this is a purely technical dispute, even when the level of technical detail gets daunting. At the core of such debate is the symbolic meaning attached to guns: guns made and keep us free. What such gatherings do, among the other obvious things, is provide a forum for the reaffirmation of traditions that embody our hard-won freedoms—freedoms that seem beleaguered to many, whether or not they own guns. Guns embody the pioneering spirit, the love of liberty, individualism, and self-reliance. From this vantage point, anyone who would jeopardize gun ownership must not appreciate democracy and the need to defend individual rights.

The crucial role guns have played in our nation's history is hard to deny. But gun enthusiasts' interpretation of our history is obviously not the only one available, any more than their definitions of liberty or freedom are the only ones in play. The story of our nation's founding and growth is problematic. It is a story of much bravery and heroism, to be sure, but also of much deceit, outright theft, and, of course, an ocean of spilt blood, most of it set flowing by musket balls and bullets. This revisionist interpretation is by no means a recent creation, some creature of political correctness. As we have already seen, from the beginning Americans have worried about their gun-toting neighbors. Disgruntled farmers in western Massachusetts appear to have taken Jefferson at his word when they launched an insurrection known as Shays' Rebellion in 1786–87, before the smoke of the War for Independence had time to clear. Twentieth-century Americans have lionized the likes of Daniel Boone and Davey Crockett, but their contemporaries were far less enamored of them. Historians have discovered that Boone's neighbors, for example, were constantly irritated by his unruliness and his indifference to his wife and brood, as well as the condition of his land (Faragher, 1992).

Crockett was similarly regarded by his contemporaries. He headed off to glory at the Alamo, leaving behind much irritation and exasperation. Few who knew him likely shed a tear when news reached them of his demise. And so it goes. General Custer was a vain strutting dandy who sacrificed his men's lives to his own ill-considered ambitions. Indeed, the massacre of his force at the Little Bighorn was unusually brutal because the Sioux sought retribution for Custer's razing of a Sioux encampment only weeks earlier. Had he been less genocidal, he and his men might well have been treated less murderously. In the same vein, it appears that folks on the frontier and in the towns and cities that spread across the landscape were at least as fearful of their peace officers as they were of ruffians and outlaws (White, 1991). Indeed, the line between the two was blurred and crossovers were by no means uncommon. It would seem that many of our gun-wielding heroes had feet of clay (which may be why they preferred to die with their boots on) and many of the glorious chapters in our legendary struggles to advance freedom and defend democracy are marred by villainy, gratuitous violence, and brutal repression. The guns that liberated some are the same guns that terrorized others.

This double-sidedness is remarkably persistent. A single reading of our history is no more possible than a single response to firearms. Such conflicting responses to our own history make it clear that the debate over the private ownership of guns is another battlefield in the "culture war" that has characterized our society at least since the 1960s. The result is a polarization much like that over the issue of abortion. As James Davison Hunter (1994) has demonstrated with respect to abortion, this sort of polarization obscures the remarkable stability of views of the majority in the middle, who would prefer a world in which abortions were not performed because they were not necessary, but who also recognize that we do not live in such a world and that banning abortions will not get us there. The question is not whether there will be abortions but whether abortions will be legal and safe or illegal and unsafe.

Much the same can be said about guns. Public opinion polls repeatedly show a large majority of Americans in support of restrictions on guns, especially handguns and assault-type weapons. But this consensus masks more complex and nuanced feelings. Most people, for example, would agree that everyone has the right to defend themselves and their loved ones from an attacker. We would prefer a world in which such threats did not occur, but most of us recognize that that is not the way things are. In certain circumstances the possession of a gun makes sound sense. Personal defense aside, many firearms in private possession are hunting and target guns. Little interest exists, even among anti-gun forces, for restricting ownership of these weapons. But this raises an immediate and intractable problem—the line separating the two classes of weapons, those for personal protection and those for recreation, is anything but clear or straight. Certainly intelligent and reasonable lines can be devised. But in the polarized atmosphere in which we currently find ourselves, the nuance and reasonableness needed to come up with such distinctions have virtually no public voice. The prospects for sensible regulation of ownership and use are continually frustrated by the impassioned shouts from the pro-gun and anti-gun extremes.

Our democracy is weakened when we persist in framing issues in terms that admit no nuance, contingency, or compromise. Thus, as the 1996 elections approached, the National Rifle Association (NRA) leveled a steady barrage of broadsides against most Democratic candidates, heedful only of the most narrow of litmus tests—do they favor or oppose the Brady Bill and the federal ban on assault weapons? These two pieces of legislation were arguably flawed, perhaps even misguided. Indeed, the Supreme Court, by a 5-to-4 majority, invalidated the section of the Brady Bill that required local law enforcement officials to conduct the mandated background checks on prospective gun buyers. This now forces the federal government to put in place a computerized data bank enabling gun sellers to run background checks quickly and cheaply. Ironically, the NRA has been urging just such a move for several years. But the NRA was not thinking of such details when it urged members to vote only for those who oppose all restrictions on gun ownership. Why do guns provoke such relentless, single-minded partisanship?

We have already sketched the outlines of an answer to this question. gun advocates and their opponents think they are arguing over guns, but what gives the argument such passionate intensity is an underlying clash of cultural values and competing visions of our past and future national identity. Guns function much like lightning rods in an electrical storm. In effect, the rapid social and cultural change that has characterized our society more or less continuously for the past century and a half has created the charged atmosphere in which the debate over guns takes place. The historical moment that most nearly mirrors our present situation, the late nineteenth and early twentieth centuries, reveals how social change can give rise to culture wars. It is worth reflecting for a moment on that period.

After the Civil War, the United States underwent nothing less than a sea change. Industrial giants came to dominate the economic and political landscape. Rail lines, the telegraph, and then the automobile linked Americans to one another as never before, laying the basis for a truly national culture. At the same time, immigration reached unprecedented proportions such that by 1910, on the eve of World War I, roughly 15 percent of the American population was foreign born. As war broke out, America ceased being a nation dominated by its rural and small town population. For the first time, most Americans lived in cities. Each of these developments, taken one at a time, would have required significant adjustment. But they did not come one at a time—they came as a package, and together they hit with the force of a tornado. Local cultures began to give way to attitudes and styles established in remote, even exotic places, as national advertising, national radio networks, and the movie industry brought new ideas into every nook and cranny of America. Small businesses were upstaged by giant corporations, sending local elites into panic, not only because their livelihoods were placed in jeopardy but also because their cultural dominance was threatened (Wiebe, 1967).

Adding to these fears of displacement were urban political machines, virtually all of them unabashedly corrupt, that were busy mobilizing the immigrant masses into electoral majorities whose attachment to prevailing political alignments was less than reassuring to the Protestants who then dominated Congress and most state legislatures. Fears of papal conspiracies mixed with fears of anarchism and socialism in a most unsettling way. In short, an entire way of life seemed under siege: the culture of thrift and responsibility was giving way to the clarion call of an emergent consumption-oriented economy. The transportation and communications revolutions made rootedness seem quaint ("how you gonna keep 'em down on the farm after they've seen Paree?"). The easy virtue of the city threatened the straightlaced propriety and probity of the small town Protestant elite.

The "old guard" struck back in defense of its cherished notions of virtue and its former cultural, economic, and political influence. One might expect that the reaction would have been direct, a counterattack aimed at the source of threat. There were such counterattacks. Teddy Roosevelt went after the "bad trusts," those corporations whose behavior was most egregiously rapacious. Patronage, the lifeblood of the urban machines, was limited to a degree by civil service reforms. An intense and broad campaign of Americanization was launched to counter the perceived threats of immigrant disloyalty. The Pure Food and Drug Act and other regulatory legislation helped to protect Americans from unscrupulous businesses. Together, reform impulses such as these gave the decades just after the turn of the century the label "the Progressive Era." As important as these reforms have proven to be, however, it must be said that they did little to rescue the old local elites from the oblivion they faced. These reforms did not speak to their central fears and aspirations. Prohibition did (Gusfield, 1963).

The temperance movement began amid a welter of Protestant moral reform fervor in the nineteenth century. It gathered support rapidly after the Civil War, when supporters linked drink to every manner of vice and evil. Drink ruined families, made workers agitate for higher wages (so they could drink more, presumably), made immigrants the willing dupes of political bosses. Put alcohol behind us, the Prohibitionists urged, and a new day would be ushered in and greatness restored to our nation. The Eighteenth Amendment was passed in 1919 and people awaited the dawn of a new era. They were in for a surprise. Drink was not abolished, it just went underground. A lucrative business fell into the laps of the very elements small town America most loathed and feared. In one of the greatest ironies in our history, moralists became unwitting supporters of organized crime. Absent Prohibition, it is likely that figures such as Al Capone and Bugsy Siegel would have remained minor hoods known only to local cops and ambitious local prosecutors. As fate would have it, the revenues from booze catapulted them and many of their counterparts into the national limelight. Germane to our focus on guns, it should be noted that Prohibition and its unintended effects also spurred the first modern debates over guns in this century. Gangland slayings and the exploits of such notorious (and partially idolized) criminals as Bonnie and Clyde and John Dillinger helped to create a sense that society was at the mercy of thugs armed more heavily than the police charged with corralling them. Thompson submachine guns ("tommy guns") and sawed-off shotguns seemed best to epitomize the threat and, as noted earlier, legislation was enacted at both state and federal levels to make possession or sale of these firearms illegal. Many states also passed laws making the carrying of concealed weapons illegal in a further effort to enhance public safety.

These legislative actions aside, alcohol, not guns, was the lightning rod in the early part of this century. The connections between alcohol and the anxieties that arose from the rapid changes were, of course, symbolic. Though people felt passionately about drink, and some may have really been convinced that sobriety was the linchpin of a more perfect order, no serious observer believed that the traditional order would be rescued once the gin mills were shuttered. Temperance came to represent the whole complex array of anxieties that rapid change had produced; working to advance the cause gave people a sense that they were doing something tangible to bring the world back into some semblance of its former order. Of course, hindsight shows that no such thing occured: virtually everything, from the most intimate of private matters to the most public expressions of social values, was irrevocably altered by changes that continue to transform our society to this day. Alcohol or its absence was not going to affect the pace or the direction of economic and cultural change. This is not to say that people were wrong to be alarmed by rapid change, but they were deluded to believe that banning alcohol would save the society from chaos. The strong effects they hoped for did not obtain because the links between drink and social dislocation were so complex and so indirect, when they were not illusory, as to have little or no measurable effect on the sociocultural change that was in motion.

Temperance did change the culture, but not in ways its advocates intended. Joseph Gusfield (1963) called the temperance movement a "symbolic crusade," destined from the start to lead to disillusionment because the hopes and aspirations that advocates pinned to the struggle to create a dry nation were too weighty to be borne by so frail a vessel. The same can be said about guns.

Like our counterparts in the Progressive Era, we are being buffeted by change, much of it a direct continuation of the changes that bedeviled them. The economy is shifting beneath our feet, creating opportunities for some and ruin for others, while most people cling uncertainly to their jobs and plans for the future. Family life has been utterly transformed. The high divorce rate is only one aspect of this transformation. More and more parents report having too little time to spend together, making them more dependent upon people and agencies outside the home. Children are less closely supervised and in many cases seem not to be supervised at all. The young flout this autonomy with all manner of outlandish garb, hairdos, tattoos, and body piercings. Even as crime declines in our nation's large cities, the suburbs and rural areas seem less and less safe havens. Those who can afford it are flocking to gated communities, currently the fastest-growing type of real estate development. Despite recent sharp declines, violent crime continues to dominate the daily news, including crimes that are stupefyingly vicious. It is not hard to understand why so many Americans feel as though we have lost the way, that something has gone profoundly awry. Prohibition is again before us, though this time around drink is not the target. In complex, overlapping, and even contradictory ways, we are being urged to prohibit, among other sorts of presumed evils, abortion, drugs, and guns as paths to restored virtue and "normalcy" (Wagner, 1997). Like their precursors, these moral reform movements encourage participants to see the world in the stark oppositions of good and evil.

This is where the commonality ends, however. While there are a number of fronts in the current culture war, each one is driven by its own agenda and made up of a distinct set of supporters. For example, gun control advocates are predominantly drawn from urban and suburban populations and are disproportionately middle and upper middle class. Foes of legal abortion, by contrast, are drawn from the lower middle and working classes and from small towns and cities. The former are politically liberal while the latter are politically conservative. As a result, the prohibitionist impulses of the gun controllers and the opponents of legal abortion are unlikely to coalesce. We are thus likely to continue to be wracked by intensely divisive clashes between groups who have quite different ideas about how society ought to function, none of whom can achieve sufficient support to carry the day. The result will be more of what we have seen in the past two decades: relatively small and highly dedicated groups endeavoring to harness one or the other political party to their single cause, distorting broader discussion and debate that might otherwise produce policies which all but the most extreme elements could accept. Political leaders who might otherwise appeal to a majority can see their base cut to ribbons if they get caught in the buzz saw set in motion by single-issue zealots.

The political costs of pressing for gun control might be worth risking if guns really were at the root of violence in our society. But this is a question that is far from settled. As improbable as it may seem, given the steady stream of reports of gun-related violence, accidents involving guns have steadily declined over the past thirty years, while the number of guns in private hands has roughly doubled over this same period. Americans must be using their guns more responsibly. A similar story can be told about hunting. Statistics reveal that hunting has among the lowest accident rates of any outdoor recreational activity. Despite all the horror stories, the woods are a far safer place to be than bike trails or beaches.

As for crimes committed with guns, the story is somewhat more complex—but by no means does it offer a uniform indictment of guns. A large number of the "criminal" fatalities associated with guns are suicides, the most rapidly rising component of which are suicides committed by older males. Remove these crimes and guns look far less ominous a threat to public order than many imagine them to be. If we further deduct the murders associated with urban gang warfare (the rationale for this deduction is that this sort of violence would not stop even if guns magically vanished—knives, chains, fists, or clubs would do), the lethality largely disappears. In fact, gun homicides were higher, per capita, in the 1920s and 1930s than they are today, again despite the far larger number of guns in private possession today. As terrible as our national rates of violence are, as tragic as the murders are, the facts make it hard to support the notion that we are in the midst of an epidemic of gun violence.

Despite these trends, there is a widespread sense that gun violence is running off the charts. Why is this so? We can round up the usual suspects and point our finger at the media—sensationalist journalism, Hollywood's celebration of mayhem, TV dramas rivaling Hollywood for graphic portrayals of violence. No doubt these contribute to the sense of siege that many Americans share. But this is just part of the story. Another part of the story is the culture war over guns. Both pro-gun and anti-gun forces promote a sense of precariousness. The pro-gun folks portray a nation on the verge of anarchy that requires law-abiding people to arm themselves in self-defense. The anti-gun folks portray a nation awash in guns, held hostage to the impulsive acts of unstable people; or burglars who, if unarmed, would be upsetting but not life-threatening; or the carelessness of a gun owner whose unsecured gun falls into the hands of a child. Paradoxically, the pro-and anti-gun extremists feed each other's fears. The consequences of this not only harden the opposition but also help to reinforce the pervasive sense of danger that grips so many Americans.

Independent Yeomen, Enterprising Manufacturers, and Manifest Destiny

Chapter One

The Origins of Gun Culture in the United States, 1760–1865

Michael A. Bellesiles

An astoundingly high level of personal violence separates the United States from every other industrial nation. In 1993, when the number of murders in Canada reached a high of 630, the United States (with nearly ten times the population) experienced 24, 526 murders, out of a total of nearly two million violent crimes. The weapon of choice in 69.6 percent of those murders was a gun, and thousands more are killed by firearms every year in accidents and suicides.[1] More people are killed with guns in the United States in a typical week than in all of western Europe in a year. It is now thought normal and appropriate for American urban elementary schools to use metal detectors to check students for firearms.

We are familiar with the manifestations of American gun culture; the sincere love and affection with which our society views its weapons pours forth daily from the television and movie screens. Every form of the media reinforces the notion that the solution to your problems can be held in your hand and provide immediate gratification. Since the United States does not register guns, we have no idea how many there are or who actually buys them. The FBI (Federal Bureau of Investigation) estimates that there are 250 million firearms in private hands; an additional 5 million are purchased every year. The National Sporting Goods Association estimates that 92 percent of all rifles are bought by men (94 percent of the shotguns). Most of those men fall into the 25-to 34-year-old age group, make between $35,000 and $50,000 annually, and do not need to kill animals for their survival.[2]

The consequence of this culture is also very familiar. To select just a few more statistics as indicators: The chief of police and mayor of New York City were nearly euphoric that the number of murders in the city dropped below two thousand (to 1,995) in 1993; it reached a contemporary low of 1,581 in 1994. Yet the total number of murders in New York City in those two years exceeds by over 500 the 3,000 killed in Northern Ireland since the beginning of the "Troubles" in 1969.[3]

It is assumed that the nation's love affair with the gun is impervious to change,

Reprinted from *Journal of American History* 83 (2) (September 1996): 425–55. Copyright © 1996 by *Journal of American History*.

since its roots are so deep in our national history and psyche. The origin of this culture of violence is routinely understood to lie in our frontier heritage. With guns in their hands and bullets on their belts, the American frontiersmen conquered the wilderness and created modern America. In the imagined past, "the requirements for self-defense and food-gathering," as Daniel Boorstin has said, "had put firearms in the hands of nearly everyone."[4] The almost universal ownership of guns in the eighteenth century was enshrined in the Second Amendment to the Constitution, and its continuation is defended with ferocity by the National Rifle Association today. That frontiers elsewhere did not replicate our violent culture is thought irrelevant. The frontier experience simply required that every westward migrant carry a gun. The result was a deep inward faith that, as Richard Slotkin so eloquently put it, regeneration came through violence. In short, we have always been killers.[5]

Such statements are often presented as logically obvious. An examination of the social practices and cultural customs prevalent in the United States in the late eighteenth and early nineteenth centuries, however, will show that we have it all backwards. Before we accept an individual right to gun ownership in the Second Amendment, we must establish who were "the people" who were allowed to "keep and bear arms." Did they in fact own guns? What was the popular attitude toward firearms? Did such perceptions change over time? We will find that gun ownership was exceptional in the eighteenth and early nineteenth centuries, even on the frontier, and that guns became a common commodity only with industrialization, with ownership concentrated in urban areas. The gun culture grew with the gun industry. The firearms industry, like so many others, relied on the government not just for capital development but for the support and enhancement of its markets. From its inception, the United States government worked to arm its citizens; it scrambled to find sources of weapons to fulfill the mandate of the Second Amendment. From 1775 until the 1840s the government largely failed in this task, but the industrialization of the arms industry from 1820 to 1850 allowed the government to move toward its goal with ever-increasing speed, though against residual public indifference and resistance.

Probate Records

The evidence for this contrary thesis began with the dog that did not bark. In Sir Arthur Conan Doyle's "Silver Blaze," the Scotland Yard inspector asked Sherlock Holmes, was there "any other point to which you would wish to draw my attention?" Holmes responded, "To the curious incident of the dog in the nighttime." "The dog did nothing in the night-time." "That was the curious incident."[6]

While studying county probate records (inventories of property after a death) for a project on the legal and economic evolution of the early American frontier, I was puzzled by the absence of what I assumed would be found in every record:

TABLE 1.1
Percentage of Probate Inventories Listing Firearms

	1765–1790	1808–1811	1819–1821	1830–1832	1849–1850
Frontier[a]	14.2	15.8	16.9	20.4	32.9
Northern coast, urban	16.1	16.6	17.3	20.8	27.3
Northern coast, rural	14.9	13.1	13.8	14.3	18.7
Southern	18.3	17.6	20.2	21.6	39.3
National average	14.7	16.1	17.0	20.7	30.8

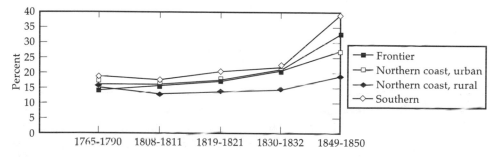

SOURCE: Probate records for the following 38 counties (modern names): Bennington, Rutland, Windham, and Windsor, Vermont; Luzerne, Northampton, Philadelphia, Washington, and Westmoreland, Pennsylvania; Litchfield and New Haven, Connecticut, Essex, Hampshire, Plymouth, Suffolk, and Worcester, Massachusetts; Burlington, New Jersey; Kent, Delaware; Anne Arundel and Queen Anne, Maryland; Fairfax, Spotsylvania, Chesterfield, Charlotte, Halifax, Mecklenburg, Brunswick, and Southampton, Virginia; Orange and Halifax, North Carolina; Charleston, South Carolina; Baldwin, Chatham, and Glynn, Georgia; Jefferson and Knox, Indiana; Adams and Washington, Ohio.

[a] Frontier counties moved into other categories with each new time period.

guns. An examination of more than a thousand probate records, which listed everything from acreage to broken cups, from the frontiers of northern New England and western Pennsylvania for the years 1765–1790 revealed that only 14 percent of the inventories included firearms; over half of those guns (53 percent) were listed as broken or otherwise dysfunctional. A musket or rifle in good condition often drew special notice in the probate inventories and earned a very high valuation. Obviously guns could have been passed on to heirs before the death of the original owner. Yet wills generally mention previous bequests, even of minor items, and they list only a handful of firearms.

Integrating Alice Hanson Jones's valuable probate compilation into this general study and examining counties in sample periods during the eighty-five years from 1765 to 1850 reveals a startling distribution of guns in early America. Probate records are not a perfect source for information, and there has been a long, instructive debate on their reliability as historical sources.[7] Nonetheless, they do provide much information on common household objects and can be used as a starting point for determining the level of gun ownership. Stated briefly, the probate inventories reveal that gun ownership was more common in the South and in urban centers than in the countryside or on the frontier, and that it rose slowly up to the 1830s; it increased to half again as much over the next twenty years. By 1849–1850, guns appeared in nearly one-third of all probate inventories.[8]

Almost all of the probate inventories studied are for white males. Most states had laws forbidding blacks to own guns, and no woman's inventory lists a gun. The inventories, therefore, are from the people most likely to own guns. The figures indicate that few people actually had guns in their possession, at least at the time of death. White males older than fifteen made up just under a quarter (23.8 percent) of the population in 1820; if we dare to include women and blacks in our definition of Americans, it would appear that at no time prior to 1850 did more than a tenth of the people own guns.

Militia Records

Looking at militia records can also provide some sense of gun ownership in early America. Militia units were based in their home communities or counties, but they existed under state authority. "All adults" (white, Protestant, non-immigrant, property-owning males) were expected to serve, with exceptions for those with specific jobs; in time, the list of those expected to serve expanded, as did the list of exceptions. Age and other requirements varied widely with time and place.

In the colonial period, the militias drew their authority from colonial legislatures operating in the name of the king. After the ratification of the Constitution, the authority was in the state governments as authorized and regulated by Congress (Article I, Section 8). On several occasions states and communities ordered censuses of the firearms in the possession of their citizens. Militia records also sometimes include accurate counts of the total number of guns in the possession of those eligible for militia service. Such records are scattered, but they do provide a sampling of the number of firearms and a reflection of the public attitude toward them.

The old myth of the military effectiveness of the militia has taken a battering over the last twenty years as historians have studied its performance more carefully. Military historians have debated the utility and commitment of the militia, and they generally doubt both. Those scholars have noted the absence of a well-armed and efficient militia in the period from the French and Indian War through the War of 1812.[9] Those findings are strongly supported by extant military records, though the period of militia ineffectiveness should be extended into the 1850s. Right up to the beginning of the Civil War, nearly every militia officer's report, even from the frontier, complained of the shortage and poor quality of the weapons available and the routine failure of their rank and file to care for the weapons they did possess. Regular army officers noted this same paucity and inferiority of firearms and commented often on the recruits' unfamiliarity with guns. Such comments ran right up the chain of command. For instance, Capt. Charles Johnston reported to the New Hampshire Provincial Congress in June 1775 that his company was "in difficult circumstances; we are in want of both arms and ammunition. There is but very little, or none worth mentioning—perhaps one pound of powder to twenty men, and not one-half our men have arms." On the top of the military hierarchy, Gen. George Washington complained incessantly about his lack of arms. Every volume of *The Papers of George Washington: Revolutionary War Series* has dozens of letters with such complaints as "Being in the greatest distress here for Arms without the most distant prospect of obtaining a Supply." The shortage of guns and ammunition even led Washington to dismiss troops he could not arm. He concluded that he and his officers were but "amusing ourselves with the appearance of strength, when at the same time we want the reality."[10]

A quarter century later, the situation remained unaltered. In 1801, Gov. William Claiborne of Mississippi Territory informed James Madison that the settlers did not have guns, nor could they acquire any. Six years later, as governor of Orleans Territory, Claiborne reported that he had 126 muskets for 4,971 members of the militia. That same year, three of Delaware's five regiments had no serviceable firearms at all; Gov. Nathaniel Mitchell told the legislature that the militia was effectively unarmed and that it was ridiculous to expect the people to arm themselves.[11] During the interminable Seminole wars of the 1830s, Gen. Winfield Scott discovered that the Florida militia was essentially unarmed, and he frantically sought firearms from Washington for those frontier militia companies.[12]

Quantitative evidence supports the views of those officials. In the first official inventory of American arms in 1793, Secretary of War Henry Knox found that 37 percent of the 44,442 muskets owned by the government were unusable, and an additional 25 percent were either archaic or in serious need of repair and cleaning. The following year Knox estimated that there were 450,000 militia members in the United States, of whom no more than 100,000 either owned or had been supplied with guns.[13] A decade later Secretary of War Henry Dearborn conducted a more precise census of the militia and its arms. Counting weapons both privately and publicly owned, Dearborn discovered that 45 percent of the militia bore arms. His census of weapons, which was certainly incomplete, indicated that just 4.9 percent of the nation's population was armed, or 23.7 percent of its white adult males. In 1810 Secretary of War William Eustis, in what was probably the most thorough and exact of all the studies, found that almost nothing had changed: 45.4 percent of the militia bore arms; the total number of guns recorded was sufficient for 4.3 percent of the American population, or 20.9 percent of the white adult males. Ten years later, John C. Calhoun found some slight improvement, with 47.8 percent of the militia bearing arms, and enough guns for 4.7 percent of the American population, or 19.9 percent of the white adult males (down a point). But Calhoun found it rather disturbing that several states had simply ceased bothering to issue militia returns; their governments just no longer cared if their militia carried guns or not. In 1830, Secretary of War J. H. Eaton found that just 31 percent of America's militia bore arms. With only enough arms for 3 percent of the population (12.5 percent of the adult white males), the militia was obviously no longer able to defend the United States—if it ever was.

By comparison, the current figures, based on FBI estimates, indicate enough firearms for 102.5 percent of the total population, 334.9 percent of the adult white

TABLE 1.2
Census of American Militia Members and Firearms, 1803–1830

	1803[a]	1810[b]	1820[c]	1830
Militia members	524,086	677,681	837,498	1,128,594
Muskets	183,070	203,517	315,459	251,019
Rifles	39,648	55,632	84,816	108,036
Other[d]	13,113	49,105	0	0
Total arms	235,831	308,254	400,275	359,055

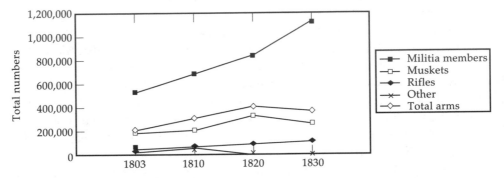

SOURCES: Frederick Bernays Wiener, "The Militia Clause of the Constitution," *Harvard Law Review*, 54 (Dec. 1960), 181–219.

[a] In 1803 Tennessee, Delaware, and Maryland did not respond to Secretary of War Henry Dearborn's request for information. Population is based on the 1800 census, producing an overstatement in percentages since the population had grown in the intervening three years. On the other hand, Dearborn's study would not have indicated those instances in which an individual owned several firearms, nor the arms of those avoiding the militia officers who conducted this survey (though there is no evidence of anyone doing so).

[b] The 1810 returns from Michigan, Orleans, and Illinois territories were incomplete and are therefore not included.

[c] By 1820 statistics were becoming significantly less reliable. The adjutant general noted that Delaware last made a return in 1814, Maryland in 1811, South Carolina in 1815, Mississippi in 1812, Arkansas never, Alabama's return left out sixteen regiments, and the District of Columbia's returns vanished. Most surveys were actually conducted in 1821. The 1820 census was used for population figures, leading to a slight overstatement in percentages.

[d] *Other* includes pistols, fowling pieces, blunderbusses, and other curiosities. From 1820 on, such pieces are included with *muskets*.

male population, and 49,765.8 percent of the militia (the current National Guard, which has 512,400 members, or 0.2 percent of the population). Under Article 1, Section 8 of the Constitution, only congressionally regulated militia can be the legal militia of the United States. Since the Dick Act of 1903, the National Guard, and only the National Guard, has held that status.[14]

The early national audits depended on the willingness and ability of the states to count accurately the number of firearms within their borders. With several states ignoring the whole procedure, the results cannot be considered entirely reliable. The complete absence of any debate within the state legislatures over the right of the national government to conduct these censuses is surprising; nor were there external protests. Apparently the public did not question government action on this issue.

Massachusetts made concerted efforts to determine the level of its gun ownership. On several occasions the state government counted all privately owned guns. As their findings indicate, at no point prior to 1840 did more than 11 percent of that state's citizens own firearms (30 percent of the adult white males);

Total Firearms as a Percentage of Selected Populations, 1803–1830

SOURCES: See table 2.

and Massachusetts, together with Connecticut, was the center of arms production in the United States.[15]

In 1812, a similar census in Pennsylvania found that there were 30,366 guns, both publicly and privately owned, for the 99,414 men in the militia (30.5 percent, or 3.7 percent of the population). An 1837 census in New York revealed that of 84,122 state troops, 30,388 (36.1 percent) had neither private nor public arms in their possession, and 15,500 (18.4 percent) of those who had guns had no flints. Even in the heavily armed and deeply paranoid state of South Carolina, militia officers continually expressed shock over the shortage of firearms. In 1825 Gen. Robert Y. Hayne reviewed Charleston's 2,060 troops, finding that 509 had no arms at all. Of those who had guns of some kind, the majority bore muskets "in bad order." The following year, one militia company rejected a shipment of arms from the government as inadequate; its commander wrote to the governor, "I have taken the sense of my company and they refuse to make use of such arms."[16]

Improperly armed, the militia could not do its duty. During Nat Turner's rebellion in Southampton County, Virginia, in 1831, newspapers reported that the local militia were "very deficient in proper arms, accoutrements and ammunition." Gov. John Floyd spent weeks trying to acquire arms and ammunition to supply these units, and he continued to do so even after the rebellion had been repressed. Similarly, militia units on both sides of the Dorr Rebellion in Rhode Island in 1842 lacked sufficient arms to exercise effectively their political will.[17] Given that the supposed purpose of the militia was to protect American liberty and order, it is ironic that neither the state nor the rebels were well armed. As New York's general J. Watts dePeyster said of his own troops in 1855, "We always associate the term militia with the rag-tag and bob-tail assemblages armed with broomsticks, cornstalks and umbrellas."[18]

Statistics alone give no indication of the condition of these firearms nor of the ability of the citizenry to employ them. Practically every adjutant general and militia commander in the United States in the antebellum period complained of the indifference with which Americans treated their weapons, and many state

TABLE 1.3
Private Gun Ownership in Massachusetts

	Number of Privately Owned Muskets or Rifles	Population	% of Population with Guns	
			Total Population (%)	White Males 16 or Older (%)
1789	27,619	475,327	5.81	23.00
1795	34,000	524,946	6.48	25.60
1808	50,000	675,509	7.40	28.70
1812	49,000	482,289	10.16	27.80
1815	50,000	497,664	10.05	29.80
1824	32,128	557,978	5.76	19.40
1839	21,760	724,931	3.00	9.50

SOURCES: Adjutant General, annual Return of the Militia for Massachusetts, Commonwealth of Massachusetts Military Division, Military Records (National Guard Armory, Natick, Mass); Quartermaster General's Letter Book 6, p. 9, ibid.

NOTE: Population estimates are based on per year increase during the decade. The adjutant general tended to round up the number of muskets in the state.

governments discovered that their armories were full of useless firearms.[19] Unlike today's glistening beauties, firearms in the eighteenth and nineteenth centuries were made mostly of iron and, as a consequence, required constant attention to keep them from rusting. Most people who owned guns brought them forth but once a year, on muster day; it is little wonder that those who did not have servants tended to let their weapons rot. In 1817 Virginia's adjutant general, G. W. Gooch, warned that the state's militia companies did not keep their arms "in good order—indeed, I might say, [not even] to preserve them from ruin." Gooch tried issuing orders demanding greater attention to the care and maintenance of the militia's weapons, but he found such efforts worthless; he finally ordered that all public arms be collected and stored in a single location. An awareness of this lack of enthusiasm for firearms by the public led a House special committee on the militia, chaired by William Henry Harrison, to propose in 1818 that the government keep its arms in armories under federal control and maintenance rather than giving them directly to the people. The committee felt that the nation's guns, so grossly abused by the public, should be left in the care of experts who could keep them operational. Their recommendation was ignored, only to be repeated time and again over the next twenty years. In 1838, Secretary of War Joel R. Poinsett complained to Congress that military expenses were nearly four times what they should be, largely because the militia did not seem capable of caring for their arms. The following year he reported that "when mustered, a majority of [the militia] are armed with walking canes, fowling pieces, or unserviceable muskets."[20] Nothing had changed.

Even those with arms lacked experience in their use. Musters were, after all, usually held but once a year; parading, drinking, and partying clearly took priority over target practice; and uniforms evoked far more passion and interest than musket fire.[21] For example, the militia records of Oxford, Massachusetts, which begin in 1755, devote more space to uniforms than to any other subject. The company argued over the color of their pantaloons (white or blue) from just after the Revolution until 1823, and of their plumes (white or black) until 1824. They spent a year debating whether to require each member to powder his beard when appearing at muster, voting in May 1821 to so require, repealing that act in October. There were instances of companies disbanding because of a change in uniform. In 1819 Charles K. Gardner wrote an instruction manual for use by militia companies after discovering during the War of 1812 that "so many militiamen . . . are not skilled in the use of the Rifle or Musket." Drills in muster books involved marching, not shooting. The Oxford, Massachusetts, militia voted for the first time in May 1819 to meet once a year "for the purpose of fireing at a mark." In 1823 they voted 35–5 to stop this annual target practice in order to avoid public humiliation.[22]

Target-shooting contests, which began in the 1820s, were often major embarrassments. When the Second Company of New York's Seventh Regiment held their first target-shooting contest in 1825, it was a miserable show. As the company's official historian admitted, it was "not a very brilliant exhibition of sharp shooting"; but then very few members had ever fired a musket before. When the prestigious New Haven Grays held its first target-shooting contest in 1822, forty-three men fired 172 shots at a target six feet high by twenty inches wide at one hundred yards. Only twenty shots (11 percent) hit any part of the target. The winner, Frederick T. Stanley, admitted that he had "but little experience in the use of firearms, and have neither before or since owned a pistol, rifle, musket, or fowling piece." His gun was on loan from the state arsenal. In 1826 the Grays shortened the distance to one hundred feet, which improved their ratio to 65 hits out of 198 shots fired (33 percent). Shortening the distance again over the next several years raised their percentage of successful shots as high as 48 percent in 1827. As a Pennsylvania newspaper unkindly said of one company's effort at target shooting: "The size of the target is known accurately having been carefully measured. It was precisely the size and shape of a barn door." The prize went to the man "who came nearest to hitting the target."[23]

Several historians have suggested that proficiency with a gun carried a necessary definitive power for manliness.[24] If so, we must wonder what it means that American men were generally such terrible shots. There are instances of militia units shooting their officers, bystanders, and one another during target practice. Even that man's man, Robert E. Lee, could bag but four birds in a pigeon shoot (a captured pigeon is placed in a black box, shaken, and released, whereupon the shooter raises his gun and hopes to blow the bird away) that lasted all afternoon and was outshot by his British opponent.[25]

It is not surprising that the militia entered a period of rapid decline after the War of 1812. Many people opposed the very institution of the militia, some because they were idealistic pacifists, others because they found no utility in the institution now that the United States was not threatened by any external foe. To the contrary, many Americans feared that the presence of the militia could encourage a democratic government to declare an unnecessary war—a fear seemingly confirmed by the Mexican War in 1846.[26] *Brother Jonathan*, a popular magazine, described a militia muster as "useless and unseemly," its members "obstructions of humanity" and "extraordinary looking individuals, with . . . rusty muskets dangling at the end of their arms . . . waiting with an indifference certainly highly praiseworthy in professional soldiers." This journal, at least, felt that "this shamefully ridiculous practice has continued too long already, and should be abolished forthwith. What is the object—what the utility of it?" T. L. Hagood, a company commander, described the militia to New York governor William Bouck as "mere *mobs* of half-drunken men." Even children's books derided the militia. In one from the mid-1820s, a boy described seeing a militia muster: "I saw many drunken men. One was crawling on his hands and feet like a dog, being too much intoxicated to walk upright. Two of them were fighting; the blood ran down their faces, and they looked like furies." Not much of a role model for young men and patriots.[27]

Militia companies reflected this public sentiment; many made a deliberate mockery of the whole enterprise. Officers were often elected specifically on their promise that they would not call musters. Jean Baptiste Beaubien was elected colonel of Chicago's militia every year from 1834 to 1847, calling only one muster during that entire period. The ever-pained William H. Sumner, adjutant general of Massachusetts, complained in 1834 that "The records of my office are disgraced with returns of persons of infamous character to honorable places,—of town paupers, idlers, vagrants, foreigners, itinerants, drunkards and the outcasts of society" elected militia officers. Most militia companies died from inattention or hostility by the early 1830s.[28]

When the members of a militia did not mock themselves, the crowds would. Locals, including many who should have been taking part in the exercises, often gathered to make fun of the militia. The crowd's favorite target was the poor marksmanship of the militia. Some state legislatures attempted to outlaw heckling the militia; for instance, in 1835 South Carolina passed a law fining any person who heckled or disrupted a militia muster $50. In 1841 the legislature added to the fine a five-day jail sentence. Both efforts apparently proved ineffective.[29]

In the years after the War of 1812, avoidance of militia duty reached crisis levels. Much of it was perfectly legal, as state laws exempted ever more citizens from the need to serve. The South Carolina act of 1833 excluded from militia duty most government officials, clergymen, teachers, students, doctors, pilots, ferrymen, sheriffs, and jailers; toll bridge, grist mill, and forge operators; canal, railroad, bank, and lunatic asylum employees; arsenal and lock keepers; toll collectors and all federal officials; and, most significant, all members of volunteer fire companies. In South Carolina, as in nearly every other state, fire departments proved the premier method of avoidance—indicating that antebellum American males would rather run around with hoses than guns.[30]

Generally individuals were saved the trouble of fabricating excuses to avoid militia duty as state governments themselves undermined the entire militia structure. Several states followed the lead of Delaware, which passed "An Act to Repeal Military fines for non-attendance on days of parades" in 1816. With the state then lacking any coercive power to enforce attendance, scores of militia companies vanished within a few years, leaving the militia effectively dormant in Delaware. In 1827, the legislature attempted to reverse direction by enacting a new militia law that carried heavy fines for nonattendance. The response of the public was immediate: they turned out most of the old legislature and voted in a new governor, Charles Polk, who led the drive to repeal the offending act. In 1829 the legislature repealed all fines and penalties, and the state issued no new commissions for the next seventeen years. Delaware's militia ceased to exist, leaving only a few scattered private volunteer companies. In 1846, Delaware was unable to respond to President James K. Polk's call for militia to fight Mexico. Fifteen years later Gov. William Burton responded to yet another presidential call for a regiment of militia by stating that Delaware did not have one.[31]

Hunting

This widespread rejection of the militia was paralleled in public attitudes toward hunting. From the time of the earliest colonial settlements, frontier families had relied on Indians or professional hunters for wild game, and the colonial assemblies regulated all forms of hunting, as did Britain's Parliament.[32] Also as in England, most hunters were actually trappers, finding the use of traps more efficient and less expensive than the time-consuming process of tracking animals with guns. Most Americans in the seventeenth and eighteenth centuries got nearly all their meat from domesticated animals, and it was rather unusual to use a musket to slaughter a cow or pig. From the start, hunting was an inessential luxury. In the first decades of the nineteenth century, hunting was held up to ever-increasing ridicule as a waste of time, money, and resources and mocked as the play of insufficiently grown-up boys. In the popular press, hunting had become both exotic and foolish. Hunters themselves were often portrayed as little more than tedious bores looking for any opportunity to tell the same tired story of the glorious hunt.[33] An 1825 article in the *Atheneum* described the incredible number of animals killed by various aristocratic hunters, the thousands of deer, ducks, and rabbits, and expressed amazement at the pride that those aristocrats took in totting up such statistics: "A magnificent list of animal slaughter carefully and systematically recorded as achievements." Another article warned that citizens of Philadelphia interested in a walk in the country should "go a considerable distance from the city, to avoid the showers of shot" sent skyward by a few overenthusiastic bird hunters.[34]

Judging from the popular literature of the day, the public seemed completely uninterested in firearms. In 1843, the first book to lavish attention on the details of gun production, part of the Marco Paul's Adventures series for children, closes with a long condemnation of the gun. Carrying weapons makes men "fierce in spirit, boastful, and revengeful." Men with guns are like little boys with sticks, bound to hit each other with them.[35]

Even western magazines showed a decided coolness toward hunting and militarism, with occasional opposition to both. For instance, the *Western Monthly Magazine* of Cincinnati stated, "We aspire to be useful"; yet it found no need to publish anything on guns, hunting, or the military or militia, being much more concerned with education. In its first three years, 1833–1835, it published thirty-six issues and 356 articles; there was one article on hunting, one on a shooting match, and four on Indian wars—and not a single other article on any gun-related themes. Likewise, the *Western Miscellany* published 300 articles in its first year, 1849, but only two were hunting articles. An article "On Western Character" in *Western Miscellany* describes westerners as marked primarily by autodidacticism and ingenuity, insisting that respect for the law and the avoidance of violence were far more notable in the West than in the East. While these magazines were, in part, promoting the West, their observations that eastern and European cities were more violent are valid. In those few instances when guns appeared in articles, it is surprising how often firearms prove useless in combat. Again and again in these and other magazines, hunters and soldiers fire and miss. After the first errant shots, battle descends to tomahawks and knives, the real weapons of frontier combat. Sometimes the descriptions border on the comic, as in one historical account of the siege of Ft. McIntosh, Ohio, in 1782. Volley after volley is exchanged without anyone getting injured. Finally a relief column appears, the Indians run away, and the "battle" is over.[36]

The most famous frontier novel is James Fenimore Cooper's *The Pioneers*, first published in 1823. This book begins with an unusual meeting between Cooper's representative of frontier mores, Leather-Stocking, and that of the cultivated elite, Judge Temple. The judge, shooting his fowling piece from the seat of his carriage, believes he has hit a deer, which Natty Bumppo has claimed for himself and his protégé, Oliver Effingham. Bumppo contemptuously rejects the judge's "pop-gun" as a toy rather than a tool. The reader soon learns that Judge Temple actually shot Effingham, while it was the frontiersman, with his plain but utilitarian long rifle, who has hit the deer. Of the two archetypes of frontier gun owners, the gentleman and the hunter, only one knows what he is doing; only one really deserves to carry a gun.[37]

Murder Methods

As a final measurement of the marginal role of guns in American life prior to the Civil War, it should be noted that the gun was not then the preferred weapon for murder, as it is now. It is difficult to build up a compelling statistical base on this issue since murder was so rare in the antebellum period. For instance, during Vermont's frontier period, from 1760 to 1790, there were five reported murders (excluding those deaths in the American Revolution), and three of those were politically motivated.[38] A study of 685 nineteenth-century murders indicates that prior to 1846 the gun was the weapon of choice in just 17.2 percent of the murders committed; for the years from 1846 to 1860, that figure nearly doubled, to 32.6 percent; for the remaining forty years of the century, it climbed to 47.5 percent. Prior to the Mexican War, the knife was the weapon of choice. By the end of the century, guns were being used three times as often as knives. Samuel Colt's own brother, John C. Colt, preferred an ax to one of his brother's revolvers when he murdered a rival in 1841. Samuel Colt did take advantage of the

TABLE 1.4
Nineteenth-Century Murder Methods

	1800–1845	1846–1860	1861–1899	Total
Beating, drowning, and strangling	92	36	59	187
Stabbing	53	31	48	132
Using an ax	33	11	21	65
Using a gun	41	46	145	232
Using poison	15	14	22	51
Other[a]	5	3	10	18
Total	239	141	305	685

Nineteenth-Century Murder Methods by Percent

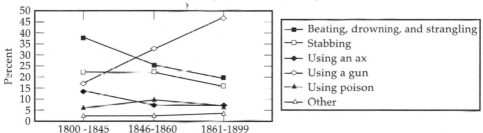

SOURCES: 501 cases are drawn from Thomas M. McDade, *The Annals of Murder: A Bibliography of Books and Pamphlets on American Murders from Colonial Times to 1900* (Norman, 1961); an additional 184 cases were drawn from the following newspapers and magazines: *Baltimore Weekly Magazine; Niles' Weekly Register,* Baltimore; *Boston Gazette; Southern Patriot,* Charleston, S.C.; *Western Monthly Magazine,* Cincinnati; *Western Miscellany,* Dayton; *Connecticut Courant,* Hartford; *Southern Recorder,* Milledgeville, Ga.; *New York World; New York Tribune; Graham's American Monthly Magazine,* Philadelphia; *Pennsylvania Packet,* Philadelphia; *Southern Literary Messenger,* Richmond; *Vermont Journal,* Windsor.

NOTES: The execution of rebellious slaves has not been included in these statistics, though they certainly were unjustifiable homicide. The beating deaths of slaves have been included, though the law did not consider them murder. Also excluded from this data are all Civil War-related murders and deaths in the New York City draft riot of July 1863.

The year 1846 has been chosen as a demarcator because of Colt's introduction of the revolver into the mainstream of American life.

[a] *Other* includes abortion, cannon, bomb, and chloroform.

publicity surrounding the trial to give a shooting display in the courtroom, convincingly demonstrating the superiority of his revolver to his brother's ax as a murder weapon.[39]

Gun Production

Until the 1830s, guns were tools, luxury items, or broken relics. Guns were either mass-produced for the military or handmade for specific customers rather than for general sale. A truism, repeated "by the best gunmakers," ran that no two guns were alike, not even the double barrels of a shotgun.[40] The few gunsmiths in colonial America seem to have enjoyed a brisk business, but their production remained minuscule. The first known gunsmith in colonial America, Eltweed Pomeroy of Windsor, Connecticut, established a family business in 1630 that lasted until 1849, yet this family enterprise rarely produced more than two dozen guns per year. There were a few successful efforts to found larger operations, most notably those of Hugh Orr in Bridgewater, Massachusetts, and William Henry in Lancaster, Pennsylvania, in the mid-eighteenth century. But even at these forges, each gun was an individual product, handmade by a highly skilled artisan. Hand cranks, foot treadles, treadmills, and water wheels supplied the power for such crude machinery as the pole lathe and rifling bench, and all metal parts had to be imported from Europe. At both those establishments, axes and scythes made up the greater part of their business, and the demand for guns dropped to almost nothing at the end of the Revolution.[41]

Most communities lacked gunsmiths and had to rely on blacksmiths to make the necessary repairs to guns—and they did not always know what they were doing. Even qualified gunsmiths often found far more work available in more general smithing. For instance, David Reese, the first gunsmith in Buffalo, had a sign in the shape of a large ax and took pride in his ax-making skills. Reese did repair several firearms, but he made no guns from 1800 to 1825. Oddly, there did not seem to be much of a market for guns in this frontier town. In 1817 M. D. Mann arrived in Buffalo, announcing that he would commence making and repairing guns. In 1819 he declared bankruptcy and closed his shop. The same fate awaited Peter Allison, who opened his gun shop in May 1825 and was gone by the end of the year.[42]

Guns of any quality tended to be either rugged and serviceable, made to order for those who made their living from hunting, or beautifully crafted, to grace the study and, on special occasions, the hands of a member of the elite. The overwhelming majority of guns in circulation were poorly cared for; they were passed on from generation to generation as family heirlooms and not kept in operational order. The consequence was that most states made frantic efforts at the beginning of military campaigns to get their militias' guns into working order.[43]

The federal government had been trying to overcome these resistances since 1775 in an effort to arm its citizens, but the nation just simply did not have the productive capacity. Throughout the colonial period, Americans had relied almost entirely on Great Britain for firearms, yet they never really had enough even for their most immediate defensive needs; even those who wanted them could not get them. Frontier settlers commonly petitioned their assemblies for firearms during time of war, as they neither owned nor could they purchase guns, but they were not alone in having a shortage. Assemblies were hesitant to expend the necessary funds, but they often gave way to pressure and sent agents to England to try to purchase guns for private and public use.[44] Throughout the seventeenth and eighteenth centuries, Americans had been almost entirely dependent on Europe for arms and ammunition. Locks (firing mechanisms), the most important parts of firearms, were not made in America; gunpowder too was imported from Europe. During the American Revolution, the United States acquired 80 percent of its firearms and 90 percent of its gunpowder from France and the Netherlands. Most of the remaining 20 percent of the firearms had been supplied by Britain during the French and Indian War. Not surprisingly, the

British Parliament imposed a complete embargo of firearms and gun parts on its rebellious colonies in October 1774.[45]

After the Revolution, Congress attempted to bolster the supply of American arms by outlawing the export of firearms and removing all import duties on foreign-made guns. In 1792, Congress, fearing war with France, ordered the purchase of 7,000 muskets. By 1793 the United States government, paying above market prices, had only been able to acquire 400 guns from American manufacturers. As a consequence, Congress voted to purchase arms from Europe. In 1800, 6,000 used muskets arrived, eight years late and still 500 muskets short. Every effort to promote domestic arms production seemed to end in failure. In 1819, G. Gregory's *A New and Complete Dictionary of Arts and Sciences* argued that the "manufacture of fire-arms is now carried to such a degree of perfection by different European nations, that it may perhaps be justly doubted whether any farther improvement . . . can be made." There was therefore almost no reason to try to make firearms in the United States.[46]

Congress's most notable effort came in 1808, when it voted to devote a large proportion of the federal budget every year "for Arming and Equiping the whole body of the Militia of the United States." Like the colonial and revolutionary legislatures, Congress understood that most militia members could not afford to provide for themselves what they saw as an expensive luxury. The members of Congress intended to accomplish what colonial and state legislatures could not: arm their constituents. With an initial appropriation of $200,000 per year, Congress hoped to see every adult white male in the nation in possession of a firearm; arms were allotted to each state based on population, with the firearms remaining the property of the state. Drawing upon the two major arsenals in Springfield, Massachusetts, and Harpers Ferry, Virginia, as well as private companies throughout the United States, the government absorbed the vast majority of guns produced prior to 1840, and still it was not enough. The government made every conceivable effort to promote production, not just at its own arsenals but in privately owned gun shops as well. No shop was too small to escape the government's efforts at financial encouragement. Yet even with these efforts, Congress failed to fulfill its constitutional mandate of arming the militia in any year prior to the Civil War.[47]

Production levels in the United States just could not keep up with congressional demands. The 1808 congressional call for 170,000 firearms was only half fulfilled by the beginning of the War of 1812, and most of them were channeled to the federal army instead of to the states. By 1813 Massachusetts had received none of the promised 5,688 muskets. The state government responded by withholding taxes from the federal government in order to try and purchase arms elsewhere. This extortion actually worked; Massachusetts received 2,300 muskets in five shipments, but it did not receive its full 1808 allotment until 1817. Allotments were never large enough to meet state needs. For instance, in 1818, New Hampshire reported 23,399 men in the state militia, a quarter of whom needed guns; the federal government supplied 750 stands of muskets. New York re-

TABLE 1.5
*Average Yearly Arms Production at the Harpers
Ferry and Springfield Armories, 1795–1870*

	Harpers Ferry	Springfield
1795–1800		2,102
1801–1810	3,107	5,099
1811–1820	7,318	10,473
1821–1830	11,855	14,770
1831–1840	10,264	13,047
1841–1850	8,551	12,603
1851–1860	8,081	12,586
1861–1870[a]		90,992

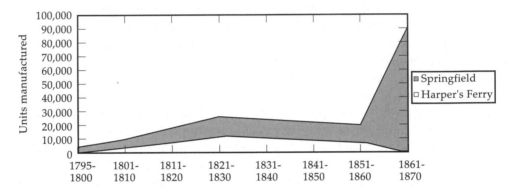

SOURCES: Merritt Roe Smith, *Harpers Ferry Armory and the New Technology: The Challenge of Change* (Ithaca, 1977), 342–47; Felicia J. Deyrup, *Arms Makers of the Connecticut Valley* (Northampton, 1948), 233.
  NOTE: The statistics include all firearms made at these armories (muskets, rifles, pistols, carbines, and pattern arms).
  [a]Confederate troops destroyed most of the armory at Harpers Ferry in June 1861.

ported 40 percent of its adult white males, or 109,990 men, in need of arms and received 3,522 stands.[48]

The individual states also attempted to fill their armaments needs by entering into contracts large and small. At the beginning of the War of 1812, the Massachusetts quartermaster general reported the state's total ordnance as "177 spears . . . 35 muskets 'out of repair', and 124 firearms, good." During the crisis of the War of 1812, Massachusetts gun makers (excepting the Springfield Armory) could produce just over a thousand muskets a year. With state and federal governments competing for guns, few American-made arms were left for the public market.[49]

The first hindrance to arming the nation was swept away in the 1840s as American arms manufacturers reached new heights of productivity. Industry created the supply and encouraged the demand for firearms. Production took off in the late 1840s and 1850s with the organization of a series of large gun manufacturers: Colt, Sharps, Remington, Robbins and Lawrence, Smith and Wesson, and Winchester. But the government's participation was vital in this as in many other early industries; the federal government provided capital, patent protection, technological expertise, and the largest market for guns.[50]

Gun Promotion

The increased production fed a gradual expansion of interest in and appreciation for guns. Hunting became increasingly popular with an urban middle class seemingly desperate for the instant status granted by possession of a gun. Largely through the efforts of John Stuart Skinner's *American Turf Register and Sporting Magazine*, which began publication in 1829, and William T. Porter's *Spirit of the Times*, first published in 1831, hunting became an appropriate enterprise for would-be gentlemen.[51] It is extremely difficult to find an article published in either of those journals or a gun advertisement in any newspaper that did not use the word "gentleman" in describing a hunter. Amateur hunters looked for legitimacy to the British aristocracy, modeling their notions of sportsmanship, hunting styles, clothing, appropriate game, and even patterns of speech after the British elite. The very portraits of hunters the magazines published mimic the style of those available in British sporting journals. Porter and his colleagues sought to rescue hunting from public disdain and to translate it into "the very corinthian columns of the community," the mark of the true gentleman and of a real man. The magazines pushed for the acceptance of the idea that "our rifles and our liberties are synonymous." Owning and using a firearm is therefore "a moral decision."[52]

There is much in mid-nineteenth century hunting literature that we would recognize. The male bonding and the deep romantic affection for a favorite gun stand out. In the 1830s the first loving descriptions of every detail of firearms appear in print. No longer is it sufficient simply to say "He held a musket in his arms." From this date the dedicated author of hunting articles must have the precise name and maker of the piece noted, with sensual descriptions of the well-oiled stock and the long, gleaming barrel, as well as the delicate intricacies of the lock. The gun is no longer held; it is now "cradled," "caressed," "hugged," and ultimately "grasped with firmness" in order to fulfill its "deadly purpose." Real men hunt, while "the effeminate young man may die at home, or languish in a dead calm for the want of some external impulse to give circulation to the blood."[53]

On the other hand, the magazines sought to separate the participants in their luxurious sport from hoi polloi. Thus there are constant references to servants almost as necessities of the hunt. Close attention is paid to the quality of the dogs, horses, food, and spirits appropriate for a fruitful hunt. The decadence of this elite romanticism is savored by connoisseurs, those with the education and intelligence to appreciate the deeper meanings of this close contact with nature.[54] The mixture of nature, sociability, and killing comes together perfectly in one of the many hunting songs popular at the time:

> The cordial takes its merry round,
>   The laugh and joke prevail,
> The huntsman blows a jovial sound,
>   The dogs snuff up the gale;

> The upland hills they sweep along,
>   O'er fields, through breaks they fly,
> The game is roused; too true the song,
>   This day a stag must die.[55]

Samuel Colt initially appealed to these gentleman hunters with his elegant revolvers; but his ambitions demanded a broader market. Colt had hit on the perfect weapon for a gun culture: his revolvers were relatively inexpensive; fired several rounds quickly, negating the need for skill; were perfect for urban life, being easy to conceal; had no function other than "self-defense," being useful in neither hunting nor militia service; and, in short, were clearly intended for personal use in violent situations. Unable to discover a large demand for such weaponry, Colt tried to create one through the cleverest advertising yet seen in America. He engraved his guns with heroic scenes, such as a man protecting his wife and child against a pack of savage Indians, armed only with a Colt revolver. He filled eastern newspapers with advertisements identifying his revolver with the romance of the West, commissioning Currier & Ives to craft beautiful portraits of Colt hunting buffalo with a revolver. His most ingenious move was to include instructions, carefully printed on the cleaning rag that came with every Colt firearm; he realized that most Americans did not actually know how to use a gun.[56]

Despite the subtle cultural shifts exemplified by Skinner and Porter, and despite the efforts of Colt and his fellow gun makers, the vast majority of Americans remained apathetic toward guns and what they represented. The complete lack of interest on the part of most states in taking advantage of the federal government's arms giveaway program is stunning. In order to receive firearms from the federal government, a militia company simply needed to file a return listing its current membership. Yet in 1839, 230 of the 490 militia companies in Massachusetts did not bother to make returns. In 1851 the United States Army Ordnance Office informed Congress that only *seven* states had made militia returns in 1850. In fact, seven states and the District of Columbia itself had made no returns for the previous decade. Ironically, the one state that took advantage of the disinterest of the others to maximize its armaments was the Quaker State. Pennsylvania paid a penny for each name enrolled on the militia lists and was thus able to return the largest number of militia. As the New York Senate complained, even though Pennsylvania's "population is less by at least one million than our own," that state continually reported more militia to the federal government and received more arms.[57]

Incredibly, even when they took federal arms, states rarely expended any money for the maintenance of these weapons, and Congress made no provisions for the verification of numbers or for the storage of weapons. States were thus entirely free to do what they would with the weapons, perhaps most commonly just letting them rot in inadequate storage facilities. State militias almost never repaired broken weapons, rarely discarded obsolete ones, and simply stored the vast majority of weapons without regular servicing in the most inappropriate locations. Certainly this official lack of interest reflected the general population's inattention to military and firearms concerns.[58]

What the government needed was a constituency for its arms program. It found that support in middle-class militarists. The same people who revived hunting in the 1830s breathed new life into the militia in the 1840s. But just as they sought to separate hunting from its plebeian American roots, so urban militia companies rejected the traditional republican ideal of universal citizen service and embraced the notion of elite volunteer companies, creating for the first time a gun subculture.[59]

The volunteer movement got off the ground in Massachusetts. The state legislature finally got tired of trying to make its tradition-bound but nearly invisible militia system work, so in 1840 it created a volunteer militia. A new "active militia" of no more than ten thousand soldiers would form the core of this reorganized structure; all other adult males were theoretically in the inactive "enrolled militia."[60] The state also acknowledged its other key problem of arming its soldiers by no longer requiring each soldier to supply his own musket; the new volunteer militia companies were to apply to the Adjutant General's Office for arms, which they were required to maintain. The volunteers were thus not only better armed than the old militia but they kept their arms in good repair—a drastic innovation. Volunteer companies attracted those who valued guns and enjoyed the military style, and the state rewarded them with all the arms they needed. Within four years the state had issued more than 10,000 of its 17,000 muskets to the active militia.[61]

There were dangers in these better-armed volunteer militia units. The companies included a small minority of their communities, were usually organized along ethnic and class lines, and demonstrated a disturbing willingness to use their guns. The Philadelphia riots of 1844 devolved into a battle between nativist, Irish, and state militias that ended with twelve deaths. In 1849, the Astor Place riot in New York City culminated with the Seventh Regiment firing on a crowd and killing twenty people. For the first time, American militia opened fire on unarmed fellow citizens.[62]

And volunteer companies effectively began the greatest carnage in American history: the Civil War. As Southern states were seceding through the winter of 1860–1861, volunteer militia companies around the South seized federal property; from Harpers Ferry in Virginia to Fort Moultrie in South Carolina to the United States Arsenal at Apalachicola in Florida, they grabbed all the federal armaments they could. It was a wise move; the South lacked a single gun manufacturer other than Harpers Ferry, which they destroyed. In Texas, volunteer companies forced the regular United States Army forces under Gen. D. E. Twiggs to abandon the state and all United States military property. When war came in April 1861, South Carolina turned first to the volunteers, not calling out the regular militia until May 27.[63]

North and South, volunteers rushed to do battle. North and South, state governments discovered that most of these new soldiers—except those in volunteer companies—owned no arms and that the state arsenals were empty. In

Ohio, 30,000 volunteers sprang forth to fill the state's quota of 13,000 troops. But George McClellan reported that the state arsenal contained only a few boxes of rusty muskets, leaving the state no choice but to send its first two regiments to Washington without guns. An Indiana inventory in 1861 found 3,436 firearms "of sixteen different kinds, but of uniform inferiority." In 1860 Maryland's adjutant general reported that the state's three arsenals held 780 muskets and 19 rifles that were "tolerable good," plus an additional 700 that desperately needed repair, 44 condemned rifles, and 687 condemned and entirely worthless muskets. Mississippi found that the state arsenal contained 110 rifles and 234 muskets in fair order. Like other Southern states, Mississippi responded by calling for contributions of arms, and many wealthy planters exchanged personal arms caches for field commands. Northern states turned to the federal government for their weapons.[64]

The Civil War

The Civil War dramatically accelerated the slow cultural shift that had been instigated by the increase in arms production in the 1840s. By 1865 it would seem that most Americans believed that the ability to use a gun made one a better man as well as a patriot more able to defend the nation's liberties—they certainly showed a willingness to act on that assumption. Technological innovation coupled with government support had powerfully altered the national character and sensibilities within a single generation. The Civil War established these attitudes permanently by demonstrating the need for one American to be able to kill another. In 1865 the army allowed Union soldiers to take their firearms home with them. The government had finally succeeded in arming America.[65]

The initial consequence of all those guns is easy to guess: a rising murder rate. It was not simply that the number of murders increased; the very nature of the crime shifted dramatically. The rare prewar murders had been seen in the public imagination as outbursts of madness or acts of demons. After the war, murder took on an air of calculation or anonymity. The gun itself changed the workings of murder. The face-to-face fury of strangling or the ax attack gave way to the bullet in the back of the head.[66] Prior to the war, the emerging middle class viewed with disdain the ugliness of personal confrontation and violence, though workers tended to find some defining manliness in the ability to fight well. Yet resorting to violence in antebellum America rarely involved the use of firearms. That attitude changed considerably after the war, most especially in the cities, with revolvers now small enough to fit in a coat pocket. Inexpensive and readily available guns changed many social equations, as the Ku Klux Klan demonstrated in their terror campaigns in the South, most notoriously in Louisiana's Colfax Massacre of 1873.[67]

Despite the war's end, firearms production levels remained high, while prices fell. Coupled with the expansion of advertising that built on Samuel Colt's antebellum equation of firearms possession and manly security, high levels of production led to the wide distribution of guns, both geographically and socially. It was now possible for anyone to own a gun. But the production of firearms is not in itself sufficient to create a gun culture; otherwise Britain would have developed such a culture sooner than did the United States. There needed to be a conviction, supported by the government, that the individual ownership of guns served some larger social purpose; for instance, that they preserved the nation's freedom or the security of the family. The advertising campaigns of all the gun manufacturers played up those two angles, with the added incentive of low prices. Having finally succeeded in arming its citizens, the government generally maintained a benign neutrality in the further promotion of the gun culture, with one exception: subsidies to the National Rifle Association (NRA).

The very existence of the National Rifle Association is a testament to the absence of a widespread gun culture in the antebellum period. Many former Union officers recalled their soldiers' lack of familiarity with firearms and hoped to avoid that situation in the future. The NRA's founders, the veterans William Conant Church and George Wood Wingate, sought to maintain widespread familiarity with firearms in times of peace. Doing so required teaching a new generation of American men to shoot. Church and Wingate understood that accuracy was irrelevant with the traditional muzzle-loading musket, while the new mass-produced breech-loading rifle offered the opportunity to develop sharpshooting skills. But American men had to own guns and use them regularly to develop these skills. With support from the state of New York—monetary backing that would later be taken over by the federal government—the NRA opened its first target-shooting range at Creedmore in 1872. The NRA's influence, along with its emphasis on individual gun ownership, spread west from Long Island.[68]

These developments may appear, and have generally been treated as, arcane historical details. But recently, the arguments of scholars have spilled over into more public forums. In looking back over the nation's obsession with firearms, historians, political scientists, and politicians usually come to rest at the Second Amendment. Those who adhere to the self-described "standard model" of the Second Amendment insist on their understanding of the original intent of the Framers. Looking to the second half of the amendment—"the right of the people to keep and bear Arms, shall not be infringed"—adherents of the standard model argue for an individualist reading of the amendment. The Framers intended free access to firearms for every American. The historical roots of this right lie deep in the British heritage and drew intellectual validation from Niccolò Machiavelli and the British commonwealth writers. Good republican citizens did not bear arms simply for the protection of the state; there was also the presumption of a right to self-protection and even armed insurrection—despite the Constitution's treason clause in Article III, Section 3.[69] But as Garry Wills and others have pointed out, the second is the only amendment with a preamble establishing its purpose, clearly stated to be "a well regulated Militia" preserving national security and civic order. The context for the amendment was the antifederalist fear that the Constitution diminished state power, particularly in granting

Congress authority to "provide for organizing, arming, and disciplining the Militia" (Article I, Section 8). The debates addressing the Second Amendment demonstrate that no one cared about an individual right to bear arms; they were concerned with the fate of the militia. James Madison formulated this amendment as a political response to the anti-federalists, guaranteeing state control of the militia yet promising federal support.[70]

The point this article seeks to make is that Madison attempted to deliver on that promise. Since the passage of the Second Amendment, the federal government has worked to arm and regulate the militia. The first and most persistent problem was that there just were not enough guns available for the militia to arm itself, or even for the government to provide free to the militia. The government also ran into resistance—not from adherents of states' rights, for the southern states actually took greater advantage of federal largess than did the northern and western states—but from the people at large. It took seventy years of government and industrial efforts to produce sufficient firearms for the American market and twenty years of promotion to convince even a proportion of the public that private gun ownership was a necessity. The Civil War finally presented the federal government with the opportunity to fashion a well-regulated militia. The war brought home the idea that firearms were necessary for social control and order: guns preserved the Union and, in the Reconstruction years, helped to reestablish white supremacy in the South. And, perhaps most important, the war's end brought guns into the home, making them part of the domestic environment and an unquestioned member of the American family.

NOTES

1. In 1990 there were 36,866 deaths involving firearms in the United States. The high point for American murders so far was 24,703 in 1991. In 1993 there were 22,526 murders and 1,932,270 violent crimes reported; in 1994, 1,924,188 violent crimes. U.S. Department of Justice, *Uniform Crime Reports for the United States, 1993* (Washington, 1994), 10, 13; *The World Almanac, 1994* (Mahwah, 1994), 936–64, 967; *Statistics Canada, 1995* (Ottawa, 1995).

2. *Atlanta Constitution*, June 18, 1992.

3. *New York Times*, Jan. 3, 1994. Jan. 2, 1995.

4. Daniel J. Boorstin, *The Americans: The Colonial Experience* (New York, 1958), 353; see also, for instance, Richard Maxwell Brown, *Strain of Violence: Historical Studies of American Violence and Vigilantism* (New York, 1975); Robert Elman, *Fired in Anger* (Garden City, 1968); and John Hope Franklin, *The Militant South, 1800–1861* (Cambridge, Mass., 1956), 20–25.

5. Richard Slotkin, *Regeneration through Violence: The Mythology of the American Frontier, 1600–1860* (Middletown, 1973).

6. Arthur Conan Doyle, *Memoirs of Sherlock Holmes* (1893; Garden City, 1990), 23.

7. Alice Hanson Jones, *American Colonial Wealth: Documents and Methods* (3 vols., New York, 1977), I, 13–24, III, 1847–59. On the value of probate records, see Gloria L. Main, "Probate Records as a Source for Early American History," *William and Mary Quarterly*, 32 (Jan. 1975), 89–99; Daniel S. Smith, "Underregistration and Bias in Probate Records: An

Analysis of Data from Eighteenth-Century Hingham, Massachusetts," ibid., 100–110; Lois Green Carr and Lorena S. Walsh, "Inventories and the Analysis of Wealth and Consumption Patterns in St. Mary's County, Maryland, 1658–1777," *Historical Methods*, 13 (Spring 1980), 81–104; Peter Benes, ed., *Early American Probate Inventories* (Boston, 1989); and Carole Shammas, *The Pre-Industrial Consumer in England and America* (Oxford, 1990), 18–46, 95–112.

8. No differentiation is made between functioning and dysfunctional firearms.

9. Don Higginbotham, *War and Society in Revolutionary America: The Wider Dimensions of Conflict* (Columbia, S.C., 1988), 106–31; George D. Moller, *Massachusetts Military Shoulder Arms, 1784–1877* (Lincoln, 1988), xi; Donald R. Hickey, *The War of 1812: A Forgotten Conflict* (Chicago, 1989), 33–34, 221–23; Kenneth O. McCreedy, "Palladium of Liberty: The American Militia System, 1815–1861" (Ph.D. diss., University of California, Berkeley, 1991). The entire militia system has been blamed for the debacle of the War of 1812: Emory Upton, *The Military Policy of the United States* (Washington, 1907), 91–106; and Harry L. Coles, *The War of 1812* (Chicago, 1965), 265.

10. Frederic P. Wells, *History of Newbury, Vermont* (St. Johnsbury, 1902), 72–73; George Washington to Artemus Ward, June 26, 1776, in *The Papers of George Washington: Revolutionary War Series*, ed. Philander D. Chase (5 vols., Charlottesville, 1993–), V, 111; Washington to James Clinton, July 7, 1776, ibid., V, 232. For a later period, see, for instance, Worcester County Regiment of Cavalry, Records, 1786–1804, Local Records (American Antiquarian Society, Worcester, Mass.); Oxford, Mass., Militia Muster Records, ibid.; and Records and Orderly Book of the Boston Rifle Corps, ibid. All three companies found that the majority of their members did not own guns.

11. Mark Pitcavage, "Ropes of Sand: Territorial Militias, 1801–1812," *Journal of the Early Republic*, 13 (Winter 1993), 485, 494; *Delaware Archives, Military Records* (5 vols., Wilmington, 1911–1919), IV, 155–56, 271–76, 307–9.

12. Winfield Scott's inspection of the militia was validated by numerous observers, including Gov. John Eaton. U.S. Congress, *House Document 78*, 25 Cong., 2 sess., 1839, 52, 145, 334, 420; U.S. Congress, *Senate Document 278*, 26 Cong., 1 sess., 1840, 126, 179; *Niles' Weekly Register*, July 2, 1836, pp. 309–10; *Florida Herald* (St. Augustine), March 14, 1839; Clarence E. Carter, ed., *The Territorial Papers of the United States* (28 vols., Washington, 1934–), XXV, 299. The citizens of Key West bought guns for their militia from the Spanish in Havana: *Key West Inquirer*, Feb. 3, 1836. For nearly identical concerns about the Michigan militia during the Black Hawk war, see Gen. John R. Williams to Lewis Cass, May 27, 1832, in "The Black Hawk War, Papers of Gen. John R. Williams," ed. Burton, in *Collections and Researches Made by the Michigan Pioneer and Historical Society*, XXXI, 388–89; and Williams to Stevens T. Mason, May 31, 1832, ibid., 397–98.

13. Henry Knox, "Return of Ordnance, Arms, and Military Stores," Dec. 16, 1793, in *American State Papers: Documents, Legislative and Executive, of the Congress of the United States*, class V: *Military Affairs* (7 vols., Washington, 1832–1861), I, 44–60, 70. Censuses of firearms for the militia generally ignored fowling pieces, which were not considered to have any military value.

14. Frederick Bernays Wiener, "The Militia Clause of the Constitution," *Harvard Law Review*, 54 (Dec. 1960), 181–219.

15. Felicia J. Deyrup, *Arms Makers of the Connecticut Valley* (Northampton, 1948), 115–23.

16. "Pennsylvania Militia," *Niles' Weekly Register*, Dec. 12, 1812, p. 240; *Army and Navy Chronicle*, 6 (1838), 168, Census of Troops in Charleston, 1825, in Williams-Chestnut-

Manning Families Papers, Caroliniana Collection (University of South Carolina, Columbia). Capt. John Mathis to Governor Manning, Nov. 27, 1826, ibid.

17. Henry I. Tragle, ed., *The Southampton Slave Revolt of 1831: A Compilation of Source Material* (Amherst, 1971), 43, 255; Marvin E. Gettleman, *The Dorr Rebellion: A Study in American Radicalism: 1833–1849* (New York, 1973), 107–38.

18. *Eclaireur*, 2 (March–April 1855), 116. See also Henry Bushnell, *The History of Granville, Licking County, Ohio* (Columbus, 1889), 162; John Borden Armstrong, "General Simon Goodell Griffin's Account of Nelson and the New Hampshire Militia," *Historical New Hampshire*, 21 (Summer 1966), 43; Charles Edward Banks, *History of York, Maine* (2 vols., Boston, 1935), II, 218; Everett Newton Dick, *The Dixie Frontier* (New York, 1948), 268–69; Maud Carter Clement, *The History of Spotsylvania County, Virginia* (Lynchburg, 1929), 215; David Turpie, "The Pioneer Militia," *Indiana History Bulletin*, 38 (Jan. 1961), 48; Raymond W. Albright, *Two Centuries of Reading, Pennsylvania, 1748–1948* (Reading, 1948), 153; David Duncan Wallace, *The History of South Carolina* (3 vols., New York, 1934), III, 148; and Ernest C. Hynds, *Antebellum Athens and Clarke County* (Athens, 1974), 39.

19. For instance, in 1843 Massachusetts determined that 6,649 (47.5%) of the 13,994 muskets in the Cambridge Armory were useless and sold them over the next several years for less than $3 each: Annual Report of the Massachusetts Adjutant General, 1840, p. 30, Commonwealth of Massachusetts Military Division, Military Records: Annual Report of the Massachusetts Adjutant General, 1849, p. 32, ibid; Quartermaster General's Letter Book 3, p. 76, ibid. See also Adjutant General to Gov. Pierce M. Butler, Nov. 27, 1837, Military Affairs Committee Files, Legislative Group (South Carolina Department of Archives and History, Columbia); Frederick Townsend, "Annual Report of the Adjutant General of the State of New York, Transmitted to the Legislature March 20, 1857," *Assembly Document #15* (Albany, 1857), 9; Doc. 36, *Documents Accompanying the Journal of the Senate of the State of Michigan, at the Annual Session of 1841* (2 vols., Detroit, 1841), II, 83–86; *Annual Report of the Adjutant General of the State of Michigan for the Year of 1856* (Lansing, 1857), 3–5, 21; *Annual Report of the Adjutant and Quarter Master General of the State of Michigan for the Year 1858* (Lansing, 1859). 15–16.

20. G. W. Gooch to Commanding Officer, 3d Regt., Orange, Sept. 20, 1817, Barbour Family Papers, p. 919 (Virginia Historical Society, Richmond); Gooch to Regimental Commanders, March 7, 1818, sect. 58, ibid., p. 923; *American State Papers*, class V: *Military Affairs*, I, 675; *Army and Navy Chronicle*, 6 (1838), 263–64; U.S. Congress, Senate, "Report of the Secretary of War," Nov. 30, 1839, *Senate Journal*, Serial Set 354, 26 Cong., 1 sess., 1839, 44. See also *American State Papers*, class V: *Military Affairs*, I, 318; Thomas H. McKee, comp., *Reports of the Committee on the Militia, House of Representatives* (Washington, 1887), Report 584, 26 Cong., 1 sess. Calls for reform came from the states as well: see, for instance, H. A. S. Dearborn, Annual Report of the Adjutant General for 1839, Commonwealth of Massachusetts Military Division, Military Records.

21. *Militia Laws of the United States and Massachusetts* (Boston, 1836), viii–ix, 33–37; Jerome B. Lucke, *History of the New Haven Grays* (New Haven, 1876), 29–30; D. A. Winslow, "The Old Vermont June Training," *Vermonter*, 6 (1901), 250; J. Trasker Plumer, "The Old Times Muster," *Manchester Historical Association Collections*, 3 (1902–1903), 176; John L. Sibley, *History of the Town of Union* (Boston, 1851), 350–86; E. G. Austin, "Memorandum of the Boston Light Infantry from Its Foundation in 1798 to 1838," Military Records (Massachusetts Historical Society, Boston).

22. Members of the New Haven Grays each fired four shots at the annual muster: Lucke, *History of the New Haven Grays*, 15–17, 26, 29–31, 44, 47, 107. Charles K. Gardner,

Compend of the United States System of Infantry Exercise and Maneuvers (New York, 1819), 247; Oxford, Massachusetts, Militia Muster Records, Local Records (American Antiquarian Society); Regimental Orders, 75th Regt., New York State Infantry, 1815–1820, June 22, 1816, Military Records (New-York Historical Society, New York); Minutes of the Charleston Washington Light Infantry, April 21, 1841, Caroliniana Collection; *American State Papers*, class V: *Military Affairs*, I, 20–21, 26, II, 314–19, 329–37, 389–95, 527–29; Gayle Thornbrough, *Outpost on the Wabash* (Indianapolis, 1957), 125, 155; Arthur St. Clair, *A Narrative of the Manner in Which the Campaign against the Indians, in the Year 1791, was Conducted* (Philadelphia, 1812), 199; William Guthman, *March to Massacre: A History of the First Seven Years of the United States Army, 1784–1791* (New York, 1975), 93, 105–6; Ebenezer Denny, *Military Journal of Major Ebenezer Denny* (Philadelphia, 1860), 344.

23. William H. Zierdt, *Narrative History of the 109th Field Artillery: Pennsylvania National Guard, 1775–1930* (Wilkes-Barre, 1932), 67; Emmons Clark, *History of the Second Company, Seventh Regiment, New York State Militia* (New York, 1864), 62, Lucke, *History of the New Haven Grays*, 30–31, 50–51. By 1833, with the target back at 100 feet, one-third of the company was hitting the target: ibid., 79–80.

24. Edmund S. Morgan, *American Freedom, American Slavery: The Ordeal of Colonial Virginia* (New York, 1975), 239–40, 377–79; Bertram Wyatt-Brown, *Southern Honor: Ethics and Behavior in the Old South* (New York, 1982), 357–60; Franklin, *Militant South*, 14–62.

25. Fred Anderson, *A People's Army: Massachusetts Soldiers and Society in the Seven Years' War* (Chapel Hill, 1984), 75–76; Anthony Marro, "Vermont's Local Militia Units, 1815–1860," *Vermont History*, 40 (Winter 1972), 28, 31; *American Turf Register and Sporting Magazine*, 1 (1829–1830), 338–39, 359. Outside the pages of fiction, hunters miss more often than they find their targets. See also *Western Monthly Magazine*, 3 (1835), 65–66; *Brother Jonathan*, 6 (1843), 43.

26. Edward B. Bourne, *The History of Wells and Kennebunk* (Portland, 1875), 698; Maud Burr Morris, "William A. Bradley, Eleventh Mayor of the Corporation of Washington," *Records of the Columbia Historical Society*, 25 (1923), 130–33; Wells, *History of Newbury, Vermont*, 289–90; Marro, "Vermont's Local Militia Units," 32; *Principles of the Non-Resistance Society* (Boston, 1839); New England Non-Resistance Society, *National Organizations* (Boston, 1839); William Little, *The History of Weare, New Hampshire, 1735–1888* (Lowell, 1888), 383; William H. Kilby, ed., *Eastport and Passamaquoddy: A Collection of Historical and Biographical Sketches* (Eastport, 1888), 472.

27. *Brother Jonathan*, 6 (1843), 186; T. L. Hagood to William C. Bouck, Dec. 15, 1843, box 3, William C. Bouck Papers (New York Historical Resource Center, Olin Library, Cornell University, Ithaca, New York); *Ten Dialogues on the Effects of Ardent Spirits* (n.p., c. 1826), 6–7. A favorite phrase for the militia seems to have been "a promiscuous assemblage"; see, for example, Adjutant General A. C. Nevin, *Report of the Adjutant General for 1843*, New York Senate Doc. #5, Jan. 4, 1844 (American Antiquarian Society). See also Johnson Jones Hooper, *Adventures of Captain Simon Suggs, Late of the Tallapoosa Volunteers* (n.p., 1845), 65–103; Augustus Baldwin Longstreet, *Georgia Scenes, Characters, Incidents, &c., in the First Half Century of the Republic by a Native Georgian* (New York, 1840), 145–51.

28. A. T. Andreas, *History of Cook County, Illinois* (Chicago, 1884), 206–7; *Report of the Adjutant General and Acting Quartermaster General Accompanying the Annual Returns of the Militia of Massachusetts*, Senate Document #27 (1834), p. 91, Commonwealth of Massachusetts Military Division, Military Records. See also Joseph J. Holmes, "The Decline of the Pennsylvania Militia, 1815–1870," *Western Pennsylvania Historical Magazine*, 57 (April 1974), 208; Charles W. Burpee and Charles F. Chapin, "Military Life Since the Revolution," *in*

The Town and City of Waterbury, Connecticut, ed., Joseph Anderson (3 vols., New Haven, 1896), III, 1186; Randall Parrish, *Historic Illinois: The Romance of the Earlier Days* (Chicago, 1905), 368; Oxford, Massachusetts, Militia Muster Records, Local Records (American Antiquarian Society); *American State Papers*, class V: *Military Affairs*, II, 320.

29. Turpie, "Pioneer Militia," 48; Richard W. Musgrove, *History of the Town of Bristol, Grafton County, New Hampshire* (2 vols., Bristol, 1904), I, 187; David J. McCord, ed., *The Statutes at Large of South Carolina* (10 vols., Columbia, 1836–1841), VIII, 2650, XI, 2856.

30. McCord, ed., *Statues at Large of South Carolina*, VIII, 2650; William H. Sumner, "Massachusetts Adjutant General's Report of 1834," 39 (American Antiquarian Society).

31. McCreedy, "Palladium of Liberty," 185–87; J. Thomas Scharf, *History of Delaware, 1609–1888* (2 vols., Philadelphia, 1888), I, 816–17; Upton, *Military Policy of the United States*, 228. For similar patterns in other states, see McCreedy, "Palladium of Liberty," 187; Everett Stockpole, *History of New Hampshire* (New York, 1916), 93, 159; Marro, "Vermont's Local Militia Units," 29–39; "Military Reports and Recommendations, 1830–1831" (microfilm: reel 64), Commonwealth of Massachusetts Military Division, Military Records; "Militia Reports and Recommendations, 1834," ibid.; "An Act supplemental to an act to organize the Militia," Jan. 15, 1831, in *Laws of a Public and General Nature of the State of Missouri, 1824–1836* (2 vols., Jefferson City, 1842), II, 237–39; and "An Act supplemental to the several acts to organise the Militia," Jan. 14, 1833, ibid., 320–22.

32. To take just one example, see Bernard Bush, ed., *Laws of the Royal Colony of New Jersey* (5 vols., Trenton, 1980), II, 294–95, III, 181, 189–90, 253, 489–90, 580, IV, 52–53, 237, 326–27, 582–85, V, 52–53, 69–72, 162–63. In general, see Paul C. Phillips, *The Fur Trade* (2 vols., Norman, 1961), I, 377–430; Thomas E. Norton, *The Fur Trade in Colonial New York, 1686–1776* (Madison, 1974), 60–82.

33. See, for instance, *Atheneum*, 2d ser., 7 (Boston, 1827), 29–34, 53–59, 167–68, 276–77, 408, 426–27; ibid, 3d ser., 1 (1828), 207–8; *Godey's Lady's Book*, 2 (1831), 150; *Army and Navy Chronicle*, 5 (1837), 59–60; *Anglo-American*, 5 (1845), 200–201, 390–91; *Brother Jonathan*, 6 (1843), 43; *Eclectic Magazine*, 33 (1854), 563; Norton, *Fur Trade in Colonial New York*, 83–99; Patrick Malone, *The Skulking Way of War: Technology and Tactics among the New England Indians* (Lanham, 1991), 60–66; Sarah F. McMahon, "A Comfortable Subsistence: The Changing Composition of Diet in Rural New England, 1620–1840," *William and Mary Quarterly*, 42 (Jan. 1985), 26–65; Henry M. Miller, "An Archaeological Perspective on the Evolution of Diet in the Colonial Chesapeake, 1620–1745," in *Colonial Chesapeake Society*, ed. Lois Green Carr, Philip D. Morgan, and Jean B. Russo (Chapel Hill, 1988), 176–99.

34. "Sporting," *Atheneum*, 2d ser., 2 (1825), 444; *Ariel*, 3 (1829), 94.

35. Jacob Abbott, *Marco Paul's Adventures in Pursuit of Knowledge* (Boston, 1843), 111–12. Some children's books and magazines questioned the necessity for violence at all, even in the American Revolution: Increase N. Tarbox, *Winnie and Walter's Evening Talks with Their Father About Old Times* (Boston, 1861); Joseph Alden, *The Old Revolutionary Soldier* (New York, 1849); *Evils of the Revolutionary War* (Boston, 1846); *Parley's Magazine*, 3 (1835), 17, 81; Henry C. Wright, *A Kiss for a Blow: or, A Collection of Stories for Children* (Boston, 1842.

36. *Western Monthly Magazine*, 1 (1833), 2–3, 49–55, 238–39, 318; ibid., 2 (1834), 268; *Western Miscellany*, 1 (1849); Robert S. Dykstra, *The Cattle Towns* (New York, 1965), 112–48; Luc Sante, *Low Life: Lures and Snares of Old New York* (New York, 1991), 197–235; Elliot J. Gorn, " 'Good-Bye Boys, I Die a True American': Homicide, Nativism, and Working-Class Culture in Antebellum New York City," *Journal of American History*, 74 (Sept. 1987), 388–

410; Paul A. Gilje, *The Road to Mobocracy: Popular Disorder in New York City, 1763–1834* (Chapel Hill, 1987), 235–64; Carl E. Prince, "The Great 'Riot Year':Jacksonian Democracy and Patterns of Violence in 1834," *Journal of the Early Republic*, 5 (Spring 1985), 1–19; David Grimsted, "Rioting in Its Jacksonian Setting," *American Historical Review*, 77 (April 1972), 361–97.

37. James Fenimore Cooper, *The Pioneers: or, The Sources of the Susquehanna* (1823; Albany, 1980), 20–25.

38. Vermont Superior Court records (County Courthouse, Rutland, Vt.). In a study of 559 criminal actions in North Carolina from 1663 to 1740, murder accounted for 43 cases (7.7%): Donna J. Spindel and Stuart W. Thomas Jr., "Crime and Society in North Carolina, 1663–1740," in *Crime and Justice in American History: The Colonies and Early Republic*, ed. Eric H. Monkkonen (2 vols., Westport, 1991), II, 699–720. A study of Ohio County, Virginia, 1801–1810, found a total of 240 criminal indictments, 3 (1.2%) of which were for murder: Edward M. Steel, "Criminality in Jeffersonian America—A Sample," ibid., 721–26.

39. *An Authentic Life of John C. Colt, now imprisoned for killing Samuel Adams* (Boston, 1842); William B. Edwards, *The Story of Colt's Revolver* (Harrisburg, 1953), 139–75, 191–275.

40. N. Bosworth, *A Treatise on the Rifle, Musket, Pistol, and Fowling Piece* (New York, 1846), 106; G. Gregory, *A New and Complete Dictionary of Arts and Sciences, Including the Latest Improvement and Discovery* (3 vols., New York, 1819) defines a musket as a tool of war, "a fire-arm borne on the shoulder, and used in war"; s.v. "musket."

41. M. L. Brown, *Firearms in Colonial America: The Impact on History and Technology, 1492–1792* (Washington, 1980), 224–89, 371–81; James B. Whisker, *Arms Makers in Colonial America* (Selinsgrove, 1992), 9–22; S. N. D. North and R. H. North, *Simeon North, First Official Pistol Maker of the United States* (Concord, N. H., 1913), 10–36; Merrill Lindsay, *The New England Gun: The First Two Hundred Years* (New Haven, 1975).

42. *Niagara Journal*, July 1, 1817, p. 4; ibid., March 6, 1819, p. 3; *Buffalo Emporium*, May 14, 1825, p. 3; Robert W. Bingham, *Early Buffalo Gunsmiths* (Buffalo, 1934), 13–18. See, for instance, the account books of Emerson Bixby, Barre, Mass., blacksmith, 1824–1855, Account Books (American Antiquarian Society); Jonathan Haight, rural New York, blacksmith, 1771–1789, ibid.; Elihu Burritt, Worcester, Mass., blacksmith, 1839, ibid.; Janes & Shumway, West Sutton, Mass., blacksmiths, 1833–1835, ibid.

43. See, for instance, Whisker, *Arms Makers in Colonial America*, 17–19; Moller, *Massachusetts Military Shoulder Arms*, 35–56; Solomon Van Rensselaer, *A Narrative of the Affair at Queenstown: In the War of 1812* (New York, 1836), appendix, 36–53; and George C. Bittle, "In the Defense of Florida: The Organized Florida Militia from 1821 to 1920" (Ph.D. diss.. Florida State University, 1965), 213–14.

44. The records of every colony contain complaints of the shortage of firearms and frantic searches to complement scarce resources in arms and ammunition. See, for instance, Bush, ed., *Laws of the Royal Colony of New Jersey*, II, 15–16, III, 8–9, 503–4, 525–28, IV, 495; *The Public Records of the Colony of Connecticut* (15 vols., Hartford, 1859), III, 252–54, 429–33; J. H. Easterby, ed., *The Colonial Records of South Carolina: The Journal of the Commons House of Assembly*, vol. V: *February 20, 1744–May 25, 1745* (Columbia, S.C., 1955), 355–56, 370–71, 429–31, 434, 445–46, 460, 538, 560; R. Nicholas Olsberg, ed., *The Colonial Records of South Carolina: The Journal of the Commons House of Assembly*, vol. X: *23 April 1750–31 August 1751* (Columbia, S.C., 1974), 441; Terry W. Lipscomb, ed., *The Colonial Records of South Carolina: The Journal of the Commons House of Assembly*, vol. XIV: *November 20, 1755– July 6, 1757* (Columbia, S.C., 1989), 388–89, 445, 463–66.

45. Arcadi Gluckman, *United States Muskets, Rifles, and Carbines* (Buffalo, 1948), 44–48; *American State Papers*, class V: *Military Affairs*, V, 519; Jenny West, *Gunpowder, Government, and War in the Mid-Eighteenth Century* (Woodbridge, 1991); Harold Leslie Peterson, *Arms and Armor in Colonial America, 1526–1783* (Harrisburg, 1956), 7–52, 159–225; Brown, *Firearms in Colonial America*, 1–111; Carl Parcher Russell, *Guns on the Early Frontiers: A History of Firearms from Colonial Times through the Years of the Western Fur Trade* (Berkeley, 1957), 1–141.

46. Gregory, *A New and Complete Dictionary of Arts and Sciences*, s.v. "gun-smithery"; North and North, *Simeon North*, 19; James E. Hicks, *Notes on United States Ordnance* (2 vols., Mount Vernon, 1940), I, 14.

47. Moller, *Massachusetts Military Shoulder Arms*, 19; Hicks, *Notes on United States Ordnance*, I, 11–14, 42–43. The armories at Springfield, Mass., and Harpers Ferry, Va., were the most productive gun manufacturers in the United States. As can be seen, Springfield was rather consistent in its production, not deviating far from its average 13,252 guns produced per year between 1821 and 1860.

48. Moller, *Massachusetts Military Shoulder Arms*, 49–51; "Militia Returns for the Year 1818," p. 17, entry 117, Records of the U.S. Army Ordnance Department, RG 156 (National Archives, Washington, D.C.).

49. Amasa Davis to Gov. Caleb Strong, Oct. 6, 1812, quoted in Moller, *Massachusetts Military Shoulder Arms*, 39; see also ibid., 47, 49; Account of Powder, Arms, Accoutrements, Standards & Music Delivered, Commonwealth of Massachusetts Military Division, Military Records.

50. On this new productivity, see Deyrup, *Arms Makers of the Connecticut Valley*, 115–215; Michael S. Raber, "Conservative Innovators, Military Small Arms, and Industrial History at Springfield Armory, 1794–1918," *Journal of the Society for Industrial Archeology*, 14 (no. 1, 1988), 1–21; David A. Hounshell, *From the American System to Mass Production, 1800–1932* (Baltimore, 1984), 46–50; Robert A. Howard, "Interchangeable Parts Reexamined: The Private Sector of the American Arms Industry on the Eve of the Civil War," *Technology and Culture*, 19 (Oct. 1978), 633–49.

51. The first issue of the nation's first hunting magazine states that hunting as a sport is just beginning to attract the attention of American men: *American Turf Register and Sporting Magazine*, 1 (1829), 1.

52. *Spirit of the Times*, 7 (1837), 4; Bosworth, *Treatise on the Rifle, Musket, Pistol, and Fowling Piece*, 64, 97; see also *Spirit of the Times*, 5 (1835), 1; ibid., 9 (1839), 1; *American Turf Register and Sporting Magazine*, 1 (1829–1830), 240, 441; ibid., 5 (1834), 371–73, 474–75, 615.

53. *Army and Navy Chronicle*, 6 (1838), 209–11; *American Turf Register and Sporting Magazine*, 1 (1829–1830), 79, 338–39.

54. See, for instance, *American Turf Register and Sporting Magazing*, 1 (1829–1830), 88, 238, 400, 443–45; ibid., 5 (1834), 298–99; *American Penny Magazine*, 1 (1845), 387; *Ariel*, 3 (1829), 117; *Army and Navy Chronicle*, 6 (1838), 209–11.

55. *American Turf Register and Sporting Magazine*, 1 (1829–1830), 352. See also ibid., 447–50, 595–96; *Ariel*, 5 (1832), 308–9; *American Penny Magazine*, 1 (1845), 388.

56. James E. Serven, *Colt Firearms, 1836–1958* (Santa Ana, 1954), 99–159.

57. New Jersey, Delaware, Maryland, Georgia, Mississippi, Tennessee, and Indiana made no returns. "Report of The Colonel of Ordnance," Oct. 28, 1851, *U.S. Army Ordnance Office* Serial Set, 611, Department of War (Washington, 1851), 452; Charles W. Hall, *Regiments and Armories of Massachusetts* (2 vols., Boston, 1899), I, 120. "Report of Commissioners and the Adjutant General to codify and amend [the Militia Laws], April 1, 1853,"

Senate Document #66, Collections of the New-York Historical Society (New-York Historical Society).

58. See, for example, *Annual Report of the Adjutant and Quarter Master General of the State of Michigan for the Year 1858*, 15–16; G. W. Gooch to Commanding Officer, 3d Regt., Orange, Sept. 20, 1817, Barbour Family Papers, Sect. 58: 919; Gooch to Regimental Commanders, March 7, 1818, ibid., Sect. 58: 923; Martin K. Gordon, "The Militia of the District of Columbia, 1790–1815" (Ph.D. diss., George Washington University, 1975), 301–3; Ebenezer Stone, *Annual Report of the Adjutant General of the Commonwealth of Massachusetts for the Year Ending Dec. 31, 1852*, Senate Document #8 (Boston, 1853), 31; *Florida Senate Journal* (Tallahassee, 1859), appendix, 7–8; Frederick Townsend, *Annual Report of the Adjutant General of the State of New York*, Assembly Doc. no. 15 (Albany, 1857), 9; "Report of Committee on Volunteer Companies," Sept. 18, 1856, Military Affairs Committee Files, Legislative Group (South Carolina Department of Archives; and History, Columbia); "Petition of Volunteer Companies of St. Philip's and St. Michael's" [1849], ibid.; George Bomford to Lewis Cass, Jan. 19, 1832, in *American State Papers*, class V: *Military Affairs*, IV, 829.

59. One sign of that new subculture was the creation of urban pistol galleries: Bosworth, *Treatise on the Rifle, Musket, Pistol, and Fowling Piece*, 82, 101.

60. This proposal replicated the suggestions of Henry Knox and George Washington back in the 1790s. There had been a few such "select militia" units in the colonial period, but they had died out in the years after the War of 1812. *American State Papers*, class V: *Military Affairs*, I, 7–8; McCreedy, "Palladium of Liberty," 16–46; Lyle D. Brundage, "The Organization, Administration, and Training of the United States Ordinary and Volunteer Militia, 1792–1861" (Ph.D. diss., University of Michigan, 1958), 52–55, 142–47.

61. See, for example, "Report of Committee on Volunteer Companies," Sept. 18, 1856, Military Affairs (South Carolina Department of Archives and History, Columbia); "Petition of Volunteer Companies of St. Philip's and St. Michael's" [1849], ibid. Committee Files, Legislative Group; Annual Report of the Massachusetts Adjutant General, 1840–1844, Commonwealth of Massachusetts Military Division, Military Records.

62. McCreedy, "Palladium of Liberty," 267–324; Michael Feldberg, *The Philadelphia Riots of 1844: A Study of Ethnic Conflict* (Westport, 1975); Richard Moody, *The Astor Place Riot* (Bloomington, 1958).

63. McCreedy, "Palladium of Liberty," 371–72, 375; T. R. Fehrenbach, *Lone Star* (New York, 1968), 352.

64. Stephen W. Sears, *George B. McClellan: The Young Napoleon* (New York, 1988), 70; McCreedy, "Palladium of Liberty," 394; Joseph A. Parsons Jr., "Indiana and the Call for Volunteers, April, 1861," *Indiana Magazine of History*, 54 (March 1958), 2; N. Brewer, *Report of the Adjutant General of Maryland to the General Assembly* (Annapolis, 1860), 7–8; Jack Gunn, "Mississippi in 1860 as Reflected in the Activities of the Governor's Office," *Journal of Mississippi History*, 23 (Oct. 1960), 185–86; Terry L. Jones, *Lee's Tigers: The Louisiana Infantry in the Army of Northern Virginia* (Baton Rouge, 1987), 3–4.

65. Officially, Union soldiers had to purchase their firearms before taking them home. But the army did not make a concerted effort to collect this money. Even most Confederate soldiers took guns home with them when the war ended. See Noah Andre Trudeau, *Out of the Storm: The End of the Civil War, April–June, 1865* (New York, 1994), 379; Edith Abbott, "The Civil War and the Crime Wave of 1865–70," *Social Service Review*, 1 (1929), 212–34.

66. Abbott, "Civil War and the Crime Wave of 1865–70"; Sante, *Low Life*; Waldo L.

Cook, "Murders in Massachusetts," *Journal of the American Statistical Association*, 3 (Sept. 1893), 357–78; Harry G. Nutt, "Homicide in New Hampshire," ibid., 9 (1905), 220–30.

67. Michael Kaplan, "New York City Tavern Violence and the Creation of a Working-Class Male Identity," *Journal of the Early Republic*, 15 (Fall 1995), 591–617; Eliot J. Gorn, *The Manly Art: Bare-Knuckle Prize Fighting in America* (Ithaca, 1986), 129–47; Elizabeth Pleck, *Domestic Tyranny: The Making of American Social Policy against Family Violence from Colonial Times to the Present* (New York, 1987), 49–66; Jerome Nadelhaft, "Wife Torture: A Known Phenomenon in Nineteenth-Century America," *Journal of American Culture*, 10 (Fall 1987), 39–59; Ted Tunnell, *Crucible of Reconstruction: War, Radicalism, and Race in Louisiana, 1862–1877* (Baton Rouge, 1984), 185–202; *United States v. Cruikshank*, 92 U.S. 542 (1876); Ralph L. Peek, "Lawlessness in Florida, 1868–1871," *Florida Historical Quarterly*, 40 (Oct. 1961), 164–85.

68. There is surprisingly little historical study of the National Rifle Association (NRA): one dissertation, Russell S. Gilmore, "Crackshots and Patriots: The National Rifle Association and America's Military-Sporting Tradition" (Ph.D. diss., University of Wisconsin, 1974); an official history, James Trefethen and James Serven, *Americans and Their Guns: The National Rifle Association's Story through Nearly a Century of Service to the Nation* (Harrisburg, 1967); and a biography, Donald N. Bigelow, *William Conant Church and* The Army and Navy Journal (New York, 1952). On the modern NRA, see Osha Gray Davidson, *Under Fire: The NRA and the Battle for Gun Control* (New York, 1993).

69. Glenn Harlan Reynolds, "A Critical Guide to the Second Amendment," *Tennessee Law Review*, 62 (Spring 1995), 461–512. This entire issue of the *Tennessee Law Review* is an uncritical celebration of the "standard model." See also Robert J. Cottrol, ed., *Gun Control and the Constitution: Sources and Explorations on the Second Amendment* (New York, 1994), ix–xlviii; Joyce Lee Malcolm, *To Keep and Bear Arms: The Origins of an Anglo-American Right* (Cambridge, Mass., 1994); Don B. Kates, "Handgun Prohibition and the Original Meaning of the Second Amendment," *Michigan Law Review*, 82 (Nov. 1983), 204–73; Stephen Halbrook, *That Every Man Be Armed* (San Francisco, 1984); Robert E. Shalhope, "The Ideological Origins of the Second Amendment," *Journal of American History*, 69 (Dec. 1982), 599–614.

70. The finest critique of the "standard model" is Garry Wills, "To Keep and Bear Arms," *New York Review of Books*, Sept. 21, 1995, pp. 62–72. See also Lawrence D. Cress, "An Armed Community: The Origins and Meaning of the Right to Bear Arms," *Journal of American History*, 71 (June 1984), 22–42; Roy G. Weathrup, "Standing Armies and Armed Citizens: An Historical Analysis of the Second Amendment," *Hastings Constitutional Law Quarterly*, 2 (Fall 1975), 961–1001; and Dennis A. Henigan, "Arms, Anarchy, and the Second Amendment," *Valparaiso University Law Review*, 26 (Fall 1991), 107–29.

Chapter Two

Guns, Gun Culture, and the Peddling of Dreams

William Hosley

God created men; Colonel Colt made them equal.
—Frontier Saying

A musket is an old established thing; it is a thing that
has been the rule for ages; but this pistol is newly
created.

—Sam Colt, 1854

Economy and necessity made Texas vigilant to choose
the most efficient arms, and she had chosen Colt's.
—Report from the Secretary of the Navy, 1840

I am proud of the results of my exertions, and can
paddle my own canoe.

—Sam Colt, 1854

Gun-making is a heck of way to make a living. For as long as there have been people willing to sell arms, there have been critics ready to condemn them. More than a century ago, even in a city made rich through the sale of armaments, critics described the "gun lobby" as "always inventing trouble" and being anxious to "keep the public mind on war, not because they fear war, but because they have cannons to sell."[1] Epitomizing the qualities that have made social pariahs of arms merchants for generations, the character of armorer Andrew Undershaft in George Bernard Shaw's play *Major Barbara* explains his philosophy of good government:

> You will make war when it suits us, and keep peace when it doesn't. You will find out that trade requires certain measures when we have decided on those measures. When I want anything to keep my dividends up, you will discover that my want is a national need. When other people want something to keep my dividends down, you will call out the police and military. And in return you shall have the support

and applause of my newspapers, and the delight of imagining that you are a great statesman.[2]

Repeatedly accused of bribery, of fomenting war scares, and of conspiring with each other to raise prices, arms manufacturers accept as an occupational hazard that few will ever be grateful for their contributions to national defense. More often they will be vilified.[3] Why would anyone bother? Progress and morality, the twin peaks of Victorian culture. Sam Colt personified the evangelical strain of thought often apparent among gun-makers certain they are making the world safer and more secure by arming the weak and just against the strong and predatory. As Sam Colt put it, "The good people of this wirld [sic] are very far from being satisfied with each other & my arms are the best peacemakers."[4]

The middle third of the nineteenth century brought the most rapid period of technological innovation in the history of armaments and warfare. Much like the computer revolution of today, the pace of change was quick, and "innovation . . . appeared almost endless" as each season brought forth new, lighter, faster, less expensive, and more powerful weapons. Whether in the scientific press, reports from the War Department (a branch of government we now call Defense), or the Hartford newspapers, all concurred that "in no branch of scientific industry have there been greater strides in improvements. . . . Few branches of manufacture have received so much attention as . . . weapons of destruction." As witnesses described how, what "five years ago . . . had been scarcely heard of . . . already we have grown to consider . . . obsolete," it became increasingly apparent that "weapons of destruction" were at the center of a revolution not only in the character of technology but in the pace of technological change.[5] For a generation wrestling with the tension between scientific rationalism and religion, the idea that "progress is observable in *everything*" helped reconcile seemingly antithetical tendencies, propelling the notion of perfectibility ever forward. The concept of evolution, a watchword in science and biology even before Charles Darwin's revolutionary *On the Origin of Species* (1859), was applied to all sorts of things, no less to firearms, where the image of the "match-lock, the wheel-lock and the flint-lock," giving "way to the percussion lock," giving way "to the copper cartridge" validated the progressive impulse and in its steadily increasing pace of change hinted that the biblically charged idea of endtime known as the millennium was imminent.[6] "The end," such as it was, passed without notice as science and secular rationalism chipped away at the euphoria of religious expectation, demolishing hope of an impending moment when society, politics, and technology would complete the progressive march to the promised land of a perfect world. But during the middle third of the century, as the two great ships of religion and science passed in the night, *anything* seemed possible.

For those who imagine science operating in a vacuum, history furnishes few better examples of the enormous multiplier effect that occurs when science and technology are in open dialogue with the forces of religion and culture. As religion and science danced to the rhythm of "progress," the nation worked itself into a millennial frenzy, fueling tremendous economic growth, while mowing down incompatible peoples and ideologies in its path. It was not a very pretty picture, and it is almost impossible now to imagine our society, or any society less single-minded than theirs, tackling problems as big and divisive as, to name one of many, slavery. Americans used to be intense. Indeed, if they could see us, they'd likely make it their duty to conquer us. But they'd fail. We now have better weapons.

The United States in the age of Colt was preachy, judgmental, inflexibly moralizing, aggressive, and young. The missionary zeal evident among the machine builders and city-makers of the age was fueled not only by a belief in the miracle of the nation's successful War for Independence against Britain but also by the evidence, interpreted as God's favor, of the unparalleled growth and expansion that followed. Guns, technology, and the campaign of western expansion were overlapping layers of the same progressive tendency. Each fed and enabled the other, amplifying the perception that Americans were a chosen people.

Issues of race, guns, and violence had special meaning in the 1840s and 1850s, one of the most violent and adventuresome eras in the nation's history. Although nostalgia for the Civil War era would be misplaced, in an odd and sadly heroic way, it is, or was, our Golden Age. It was our youthful adolescence, and there is hardly a feature of national character that did not come into focus at that time. Americans have never grappled with the meaning of nationhood more passionately. Violent, idealistic, and proud, never before or since has American society embraced guns with such a vengeance, nor sanctioned violence on so grand a scale. Die for your country? They signed up in unprecedented numbers. The age of Colt was the age of the gun, an age when a youthful nation first dreamed of glory and empire.

Manifest Destiny—the phrase defines an era. The author was John Lewis O'Sullivan. The year was 1845. The place was the *United States Magazine and Democratic Review*, the house organ of the empire builders and western expansionists. If Emmanuel Leutze's *Westward the Course of Empire Takes Its Way* (1862) was its image, and Horace Greeley's "go west, young man, and grow up with the country" its slogan, O'Sullivan's *United States Magazine and Democratic Review* was the intellectual vortex of the age of empire. As a journalist, diplomat, and expansionist, O'Sullivan epitomized the political sentiments that brought forth the Mexican War, made Sam Colt's achievements possible, and set the stage for the war of values that was our Civil War.[7]

What came first, the zeal for guns and glory or the campaign of Manifest Destiny and western expansion? Both were symptomatic of the age. The *Hartford Daily Times* opened the decade of the 1850s by announcing how our "young Republic has advanced steadily in the bright pathway of glory and renown" toward a "future" in which the "progress of the race" is "assured. . . . Despotism will die. . . . Liberty and order will become the common blessings of mankind. . . . Our own beloved country . . . will advance . . . to National glory. . . . Onward! then, brethren, in the campaign of 1850!"[8]

The cult of progress and the mantra of Manifest Destiny guided national life in what historians have dubbed the Young America Movement. Combining the qualities of rampant Anglo-Saxonism and expansionism, one of the central ambitions of the intensely nationalistic Young America Movement was the vision for a slave empire stretching west to the Pacific and south to the Caribbean, including Central America, Mexico, and California.[9] Why not? Progress, in the mind's eye of 1850, consisted of pressing onward to create "new empires of trade and wealth . . . in regions . . . shut against the world for ages by the iron door of heathen prejudice and custom."[10] Rarely has the rhetoric of national life been more florid and melodramatic than during this period nor, in retrospect, more embarrassing for those uneasy about the way the United States achieved its wealth and power.

To varying degrees, many got into it. Secretary of War Jefferson Davis believed that the acquisition of Cuba was "essential to our prosperity and security."[11] Pumped up with pride after a lopsided victory in a war of aggression against Mexico, even more sober voices like Daniel Webster's assumed a bombastic and moralizing tone, sure that the events of the nation's past and present proved the superiority of republican institutions. For the first time, the United States adopted an aggressive foreign policy, based on the perception of moral superiority and a willingness to judge the virtue of foreign governments.[12] Sounding the part of a nation unaccustomed to respect, the *Hartford Daily Times* boasted in 1851 of how "every encroachment and every insult of any foreign power would be speedily met and punished," a policy described as the "practical Monroe Doctrine."[13]

Gun lust and western expansion were symptoms of a young nation stretching to define its identity as it climbed onto the stage of world affairs. Issues of race, cultural and political sovereignty, and national destiny churned the waters made muddy by the burden of expectations of a generation eager to experience the martial glory of their Revolutionary ancestors. Science, by providing a veneer of respectability to the racist notion of genetic hierarchy, helped validate the disposition to read America's success as a triumph of the Anglo-Saxon race as well as its republican institutions.[14] By assuming its superiority, the partisans of Manifest Destiny lay the foundation for a campaign of expansion that, peppered with a sense of religious mission, transformed alien peoples—blacks, Native Americans, and Mexicans, primarily, but also other Europeans, notably the Irish—into "barbarians" and "savages" whose only options were annihilation or conquest.

The culture, particularly its newspapers, was brimming with testy proclamations of racial destiny. Indeed, the Civil War was the last phase of an intense and divisive national debate that perplexed Americans during the twenty years leading up to it. Perplexity and confusion are what make this unsettling episode in the nation's history so intriguing. The United States was pumped up with a sense of destiny; slavery was the stain on an otherwise "perfect picture" of a nation rightfully proud of its political institutions and anxious to "spread the principles of Americanism" throughout the West and beyond.[15] So long as slavery blighted the nation's reputation, a full-throttle assault on the West—with all that entailed—was impossible.

In a work deeply emblematic of the progressive impulse, Neil Arnott's *Survey of Human Progress* explained how "the human race, unlike the lower animals . . . has gradually but greatly advanced from . . . savage to various degrees of civilization," a "fact of progressive civilization . . . little suspected . . . until . . . advances in general science," disproved the "Greeks' and Romans' . . . opinion, that mankind had degenerated from . . . a golden age."[16] Or if you prefer C. Chauncey Burr's take on the matter, the "Caucasian race were never barbarian or savage. . . . All races who ever were savages, are so still. . . . Is it better to exterminate the Indian, or to civilize him?"[17] These were the straight-faced questions of the day. For those committed to, as the expansionists saw it, spreading good government, commercial prosperity, and Christianity throughout the American continent, there was abundant, widely published, public testimony that foretold "the period when the extinction of the Indian races must be consummated."[18]

Consider the image of Sioux Indians "taking an infant from its mother's arms . . . drawing a bolt from the wagon, driving it through the body and pinning it to the fence," leaving it "to writhe and die in agony," while she watched in "speechless misery," until the "gloating" Indians "[chopped] off her arms and legs leaving her to bleed to death"; or of the "womb of a pregnant mother ripped open, the palpitating infant torn forth, cut into bits and thrown into the face of the mother."[19] Before long, this combination of anecdote and ethnology had so totally dehumanized the opposition that the destructive march of progress could not only proceed but also claim a moral victory over the forces of barbarism and evil.

While the progressive impulse was as evident among northern industrialists as southern conquistadors, the way West was guided by the South's martial spirit. Curiously, the only Northerners to occupy the White House during the campaign of Manifest Destiny (1845–60) were Democrats with decidedly pro-Southern sympathies, who appointed Southerners to their cabinets. It was New Hampshire's Franklin Pierce who appointed the future president of the Confederacy, Jefferson Davis, as secretary of war. From John Tyler to James Buchanan, the South dominated electoral politics and was primarily responsible for restoring the government's role as an aggressive agent of expansion when, in 1846, President James Polk provoked the attack that led to the Mexican War.

The Mexican War, although as controversial in the nineteenth century as Vietnam was in the twentieth, restored the nation's martial spirit, tipped the scales away from the peace policy that followed the War of 1812, and provided new impetus for arming the nation. This was nothing new in the South, where violence was much more readily accepted as a part of life. With its duels, chivalry, and martial tournaments, its unbroken history of Indian warfare, and the constant fear of slave uprisings, the South had a long tradition of military preparedness and was well suited to lead the campaign of western expansion.[20]

As the nation armed itself in the years leading up to the Civil War, the reputation of improved gunnery as a deterrent to war took hold. The concept of weapons as "peacemakers," revitalized in the rhetoric of the Strategic Defense Initiative and arms buildup of the 1980s, played an important role in antebellum America in the debates about arming a nation with a deep aversion to standing armies and a limited capacity for self-defense.[21] As a concept, it offered hope for reconciling the conflicting ambitions of the expansionist South and the antimilitarist "peace movement" advocates in the North, still vigilant in recalling the costly and seemingly pointless War of 1812 and still convinced that a "chosen people" of virtuous citizens did not need expansive armaments.[22]

An 1841 description of Cochran's repeating gun, Colt's first significant competitor, as "an American peacemaker" is one of the earliest American references to the peacemaking attributes of improved gunnery.[23] The USS *Princeton*, the nation's first propeller-driven warship, was mounted with a twelve-inch iron cannon known as the Peacemaker, made infamous when it exploded in testing before a military commission in 1844, killing the secretaries of state and navy.[24] But it was Sam Colt and his revolvers that brought the peacemaker mythology to the fore, introducing a line of argument that remains controversial and no less effective a century and a half later.

As early as 1852, the *Hartford Daily Times* described Colt's invention as "not without its moral importance." Citing the argument about the invention of gunpowder diminishing "the frequency, duration, and destructiveness of wars," the *Times* concluded that "men of science can do no greater service to humanity than by adding to the efficiency of warlike implements, so that the people and nations may find stronger inducements than naked moral suasion to lead them towards peace."[25] Jabbing at the resistance of pacifists, whose language and institutions it nonetheless adopted, the peacemaker lobby soon grafted the rhetoric of progress and millennialism onto their cause, describing gunnery as a "humane improvement" and arguing that "when a man can invent a process by which a whole army could be killed . . . the Millennium will arrive, and the lion and the lamb will lie down together."[26] "If a machine were invented and could be readily used, by which a few men could instantly . . . destroy a thousand lives, wars among civilized nations would cease forever. . . . The inventor of such a machine would prove a greater benefactor of his race, than he who should endow a thousand hospitals."[27] And finally, the most famous line from the Brooklyn evangelist and antislavery crusader Henry Ward Beecher, whose description of the Hartford-made Sharps breechloading rifle as containing "more moral power . . . so far as the slave-holders were concerned than in a hundred Bibles," earned them the nickname Beecher's Bibles in the bloody Kansas war of 1856.[28]

The 1850s was the decade when issues of public protection and defense triumphed over the nation's deep-seated resistance to anything like a standing army. The Revolution and the Constitution valorized the notion of a citizen-army. Then as now, amid the strident debate about gun-control and the Second Amendment protection of the "right of the people to keep and bear arms," the image of a citizen-army achieved the status of national icon. Steeped in the literature of political philosophy and history, and fundamentally distrustful of

central government, the founding fathers believed that the greatness of the Roman republic was based upon its citizen-army and that its decline coincided with
the creation of a standing army of professionals. From Machiavelli they learned
that a government of armed citizens was the most effective defense against
foreign enemies and the most likely to be united, virtuous, and patriotic.[29] Civilian militias were covered with glory at the Battle of Bunker Hill in the Revolution
and in the Battle of New Orleans in the War of 1812, when Andrew Jackson's
backwoods riflemen, armed with Kentucky rifles, annihilated a much larger army
of British professional soldiers.[30]

Throughout the country, private, civic, and state militias proliferated during
the 1850s. In Hartford, the most famous was the Putnam Phalanx, formed in 1858
and named after the hero of Bunker Hill, Connecticut general Israel Putnam.[31]
More gentlemen's club than military unit, the Putnam Phalanx was part of a
larger campaign by Hartford's upstart Democrats to wrap themselves in the
mantle of patriotism. Nevertheless, its formation reflected the growing martial
fervor of the period. Sam Colt—a man who loved the glory of a good parade no
less than the smell of gunpowder—was a member of the Phalanx. In addition,
he successfully lobbied for an appointment as lieutenant colonel in the state
militia, rehabilitating and then leading the First Company Governor's Horse
Guard in 1853 and five years later sponsoring a private militia company, the Colt
Armory Guard.

At the same time, cities across the country campaigned to transform the
archaic constable-watch system into a modern uniformed police force that, increasingly and with great controversy, became armed with guns.[32] Initially the
police were resistant to the use of firearms, it being contrary to a macho culture
that relied on brawn and fists. However, beginning in New York (1845), then in
Chicago (1851), New Orleans and Cincinnati (1852), and in numerous cities
across the country, especially following the urban riots and an epidemic of crime
that erupted during the economic panic of 1857, uniformed police were for the
first time allowed, albeit not authorized, to carry concealed firearms.[33] One of the
last products introduced by Colt's firearms before its founder's death in 1862
was dubbed the New Model Police Revolver, a lightweight and powerful .36-
caliber six-shooter with a short, three-and-a-half-inch barrel, easily concealed and
relatively inexpensive (today about $660), designed and marketed to appeal to
the first generation of police professionals forced to acquire arms at their own
expense.[34] From the New York draft riots of 1863, when policemen used revolvers
against armed mobs for the first time, to the increasingly horrifying labor riots of
the later nineteenth century, the gentle age of the night watchman had clearly
passed.[35] Gatling guns were perched on Wall Street during the Great Strike of
1877.[36]

By midcentury, firearms ownership was rapidly losing whatever moral stigma
had previously been attached to it as the gun came to be seen not only as a
means of ensuring security but as a status symbol and source of entertainment.
In New York City, in 1844, it was noted that "the gunshops and hardware stores
where firearms are to be found, have had a most extraordinary increase in

business," and it was noted the following year that at a high society party in New York "four-fifths of the men were armed with pistols for protection against thieves" and, no doubt, for flaunting their ownership of an instrument typically costing the equivalent of two thousand dollars and more.[37] In 1851 Newport, Rhode Island, was already famous for its "shooting-pistol galleries" and, in what sounds like a scene out of the Wild West, its "pistols . . . popping at all hours" as an aspect of the "fashionable season."[38] Throughout the 1850s, the reports of Hartford's annual Fourth of July celebrations reveal gun-toting revelers and pistol fire as an annual and uncontrolled nuisance. In 1866 the Hartford press, citing the "hundreds of explosions of pistols . . . everywhere" reported, matter-of-factly, a "4th of July celebration mishap," in which "Harriet Beecher Stowe's daughter Eliza" was "accidentally shot."[39]

Not surprisingly, shooting sports and recreational marksmanship became increasingly popular. Imported at first by immigrants pouring into the United States from Germany after the failed Revolution of 1848, the sport of marksmanship emerged as an entertainment in firearms manufacturing communities like Springfield, Hartford, and Ilion, New York, where Remington's workers participated in an American marksmen's shooting match in nearby Fort Plain in 1853, one of the earliest American shooting contests outside the German American community.[40] The German Schutzenbunde, featuring uniformed marksmen, became a popular component of New York social life almost from the moment large concentrations of Germans arrived, while turkey shoots emerged as a social custom in smaller towns around New York and New England.[41] Untrained at marksmanship, the American soldier often proved inept at handling the more accurate rifled muskets and breechloaders that came into use during the Civil War. In 1871 the National Rifle Association was founded, not to argue about Second Amendment rights but "to turn the [National] Guard into sharpshooters," which they accomplished by sponsoring target-shooting competitions.[42] Later in the century, celebrated hunters, marksmen, and western heroes such as Frank Butler, Annie Oakley, and Buffalo Bill became national celebrities whose touring displays of fancy gunwork provided crowd-gathering entertainment.[43]

As the demand for guns intensified and the moral argument against them lost force, Sam Colt was well positioned to make the most of the opportunities at hand. Indeed, Colt's greatest invention was not repeating firearms—he had plenty of competition—but the system he built to manufacture them and the apparatus of sales, image management, and marketing that made his gun—and not the equally viable products of his competitors—the most popular, prolific, and storied handgun in American history. Colt was the Lee Iaccoca of his generation, a man whose name and personality became so widely associated with the product that ownership provided access to the celebrity, glamour, and dreams of its namesake. What Colt *invented* was a system of myths, symbols, stagecraft, and distribution that has been mimicked by generations of industrial mass-marketeers and has rarely been improved upon. If we are today drowning in the muck of overhyped, oversold merchandise, thank Sam Colt for lighting the way.

Even now, the French word for a handgun is *le Colt*, in the same way that one might describe a photocopy as a "xerox" or a cola as a "coke." This is the stuff Madison Avenue dreams are made of. When one of Colt's congressional allies defended his petition for a patent extension by describing Colt's central ambition as "not so much to amass wealth as to build up for himself fame," he unveiled the central impulse behind Colt's relentless drive.[44] "Colt's idea," it was later said, was "making the world aware that he was in it."[45]

To advance his reputation and the reputation of his invention, Colt drew from an extraordinary grab bag of tactics. First, he drew a bold line between "mere capitalists" and inventors, and carefully crafted his reputation as the latter, even though his legacy at amassing, investing, and deploying capital was more impressive. Colt helped pioneer the theory and practice of American patent law by surrounding himself with attorneys and threatening to sue and outflank his many competitors. Colt used direct advertising as skillfully as any manufacturer of his generation, expanding both the character of the message and the means of delivering it. Colt sought, bought, and gained the recognition of "expert" authorities in the military and scientific communities, and never blinked (or asked permission) before exploiting a testimonial once provided. Colt was a sensationalist who cultivated controversy, virtually coining the practice that led to the cliché "there is no such thing as bad publicity."

Colt adopted the policy, today called creative destruction, of cannibalizing his own product line to stay ahead of the competition by always offering something "new." Aware of the complexity of his product, he also pioneered the use of users' manuals. And, with astonishing similarity to the personal computer market of today, he was relentless in his drive to lower prices and thus scare off or bankrupt potential competitors. He used commission sales agents, lobbyists, consignments, and quantity discounts skillfully and, while tame by comparison with what passes for influence peddling today, was not averse to bribery and blackmail to accomplish his goals. Finally, and to the enduring affection of firearms collectors then and now, Colt used art to bolster the prestige and soften the associations of a product that was, after all, designed to kill people. Colt translated personal glamour and celebrity into sales. When one of his admirers wrote that "Col. Colt is himself a 'Patent Revolver'—is always loaded, and ready for action!" he described the image in the mirror for generations of (primarily) men eager to be like Sam Colt, a man "ready for action."[46] The man and the gun converged toward a single identity. Colonel Colt, as he liked to be called, had become his generation's Marlboro Man.

Colt lived and worked at the beginning of the American industrial era, and one of his great triumphs was inventing a persona that reconciled the tension between the conflicting ideals of the agrarian tradition of the freeman farmer—the symbol of American liberty—with the promise of technology and mass production. How, in a system that required stifling conformity and regimentation, could one preserve the traditions of self-reliance and individualism? By cultivating a persona as a "genius" and "inventor" and a "restless boy . . . [who] preferred working in the factory to going to school," Colt's gift of insight and vision could be understood as a reward for suffering and perseverance.[47] With this persona, Colt helped invent a model of the heroic industrialist, whose success became the embodiment of, rather than a repudiation of, the American dream. For Colt, who adopted the personal motto Vincit Qui Patitur (he who suffers is victorious), the gift of genius was a reward for suffering. For without genius there was no gift. And without the gift—a veritable sign of God's favor—Colt would have been like the corporate predators he avidly distanced himself from. In the closing argument of an 1851 lawsuit for patent infringement against the Massachusetts Arms Co., Colt's attorneys decried the spectacle of "a corporation . . . exerting itself . . . to break down one of the most meritorious inventors our country has ever seen" and concluded that this "contest is between a meritorious and important inventor . . . and . . . a corporation. Their very name imports a being that can have no merit as an inventor. They can only be the purchasers of the ingenuity of others." In the jury's verdict, "that heroic boy" Sam Colt triumphed over the corporation.[48]

Colt's persona was cut straight from the fabric of the ardently populist social and political discourse of his age. From Ralph Waldo Emerson and Walt Whitman to Abraham Lincoln, the American dream was sustained by an abiding faith in the power of individualism and self-reliance, which was soon translated into a cult of self-expression and self-determination. Prior to the emergence of the industrial, corporate, and urban landscape of the 1850s, Americans had less cause to worry about issues of civic and personal identity. Tied more to family, place, and tradition, the uncertain future was mostly a continuation of a more certain past. But with the rapidly escalating pace of change, the need for self-definition intensified. Walt Whitman's *Song of Myself*, published the same year Colt's Armory began operations on Hartford's South Meadows, elevated personal experience and self-determination almost to the level of a national secular religion by celebrating the intensely existential quality of the *now* and the *new*. "I celebrate myself," Whitman began.

> You shall no longer take things at second or third hand . . .
> You shall listen to all sides, and filter them from your self.
> . . . I am satisfied—I see, dance, laugh, sing:
> . . . What is commonest, cheapest, nearest, easiest, is Me;
> Me going in for my chances, spending for vast returns,
> . . . I dote on myself—there is that lot of me, and all so luscious;
> Each moment, and whatever happens, thrills me with joy.
> . . . O I am wonderful!
> What is known I strip away; I launch all men and women forward with me
> into *the Unknown*.[49]

From the beginning, Sam Colt recognized the euphonic appeal and symbolic potential of his name. "Sam Colt" has all the snap and crackle of the pop icon he became. It was an age of Sams, Andys, and Abes—Sam Houston, Uncle Sam, Andy Jackson, "Honest Abe" Lincoln—not Samuels, Andrews, and Abrahams. The symbolism of the colt was also not lost on Sam who adopted a "rampant" (a synonym for erect, excessive, and dominant) colt as a personal and corporate trademark. It superseded a more benign version, featuring paired colt heads used as ornamentation on the earliest Colt firearms.

By 1856, with a worldwide reputation, having been hosted and toasted by kings, and roasted in verse by the British press as "Colonel Colt, a thunderbolt," and in the midst of building Armsmear, a visionary and idiosyncratic dream house, Sam Colt ruled an industrial empire, conceived as a monument to the rehabilitation of his "good name." Pomp and ostentation, far from undermining his common-man persona, merely confirmed that in America, uncommon courage and virtue, hard work, and free enterprise were bountifully rewarded. On the meadows below was Coltsville, with Colt's Armory crowned by an onion dome, surmounted by a bronze statue of the rampant colt dancing on the globe. With Colt's Guard practicing its drills to the marching beat of Colt's Armory Band, the commercial schooner *Sam Colt* plying the Connecticut River and Long Island Sound, Sam Colt had successfully transformed his name into an icon.[50]

Anxious to validate his reputation as an inventor, Sam Colt joined prestigious organizations, presented papers before engineering colleagues, competed for awards at city, state, regional, national, and international expositions, and sought appointments that conferred prestige and recognition. The purpose of this activity was, in Colt's own words, to "help make up the reputation of my arms."[51] Evidence of technical research and study is less apparent than diligence at reputation building. Colt's one "scientific paper"—"On the Application of Machinery to the Manufacture of Rotating Chambered-Breech Fire-Arms"—as well received as it appears to have been, is almost comical in its avoidance of the stated subject, dwelling far more on the attributes of the invention than the innovative methods used in manufacturing. Britain's prestigious Institution of Civil Engineers nonetheless elected Colt a member and soon installed a bust of Sam Colt in its Hall of Honor.[52]

Colt participated in dozens of industrial fairs, and while he coveted international awards, he rarely failed to participate in the annual exhibitions of the Hartford County and Connecticut agricultural societies. Colt earned his first gold medal from the Hartford County Agriculture Society "for design of pattern, beauty of work, finish and perfection" in 1849.[53] He was awarded gold medals by the Connecticut State Agricultural Society in 1852 and 1855.[54] In 1853 the Hartford Society praised Colt's "revolving pistols . . . mounted with ivory, cacao wood, and other handles, ornamented with silver" and awarded him more gold medals in 1856 and 1857.[55] Colt continued to participate in Connecticut industrial and agricultural fairs as late as 1858.[56] Colt was also involved in the Hartford Arts Union, an organization "composed of mechanics, manufacturers, artisans and all others interested in the advancement of the Arts," organized in 1848 and dedicated to the "acquisition, and diffusion among its members of . . . scientific and useful information" and to acquiring a "suitable room . . . for the reception and exhibition of inventions, models, drawings, designs, and all such articles and specimens of ingenuity, skill, or taste."[57]

The first organization to anoint Colt's inventions was the American Institute in New York. Inspired by the French, the American Institute began mounting industrial exhibitions in 1828, and by 1836, the year Colt first participated, had become the most prestigious organization of its type in the United States.[58] Colt was awarded American Institute medals for inventions including guns, waterproof cartridges, and his submarine battery, in 1836, 1837, 1841, 1844, 1850, and 1855. As early as 1837, Colt volunteered for and received an appointment on the committee that organized its annual exhibition.[59]

Colt accumulated numerous awards and appointments during the 1850s. He was awarded a silver medal at the annual fair of the Massachusetts Charitable Mechanics Association in 1853. He was elected a member of the New-York Historical Society in 1838, the National Institute for the Promotion of Science in 1840, and the Connecticut Historical Society in 1854.[60] In 1851 Colt was appointed to a committee of arrangements that oversaw Connecticut's contribution to the Great Exhibition in London, where he won a bronze medal, and in 1855 he was appointed to a state commission for the Universal Exposition of Industry and Art, Paris, where he won three medals.[61] To rally support for Connecticut's participation in the French World's Fair, Colt urged "manufacturers, inventors, and other citizens of Connecticut who are desirous of contributing to the Great Exhibition . . . [that will] exceed in splendor the Great Exposition of 1851 in London" to step forward and boost the "reputation of Connecticut as an industrial and manufacturing commonwealth."[62] Colt was awarded medals from industrial fairs in London in 1854 and from London's Universal Society for the Encouragement of Arts and Industry in 1856. After his death, he received a final award from London in 1862. Colt's medals were displayed in a trophy case at Armsmear, as a living memorial to his quest for recognition.[63]

Colt's fame and the steady work available providing contract services to Hartford's arms industry attracted the talent needed to sustain a reputation enlarged, to some extent, by smoke and mirrors. Ultimately the message and the messenger became so indistinguishable that it no longer mattered who made what first or when, or whether trumped-up claims were immediately verifiable. Colt was a visionary who achieved excellence and consistency enough to overshadow all competitors and set the standard for an industry. Having used personal celebrity and style to propel his dreams to the point of viability, Colt proved endlessly resourceful in protecting his hard-won advantage.

From its inception, as defined in the Constitution, the U.S. Patent Office was conceived to "promote the Progress of Science and the useful Arts, by securing for limited Times to Authors and Inventors the exclusive Right to their respective Writings and Discoveries," or as Colt's advocates stated plainly while defending his patent rights, "to benefit the community by giving encouragement to men of genius."[64] American patent law essentially defined invention as a "flash of genius."[65] But the law had not always functioned effectively, and it was not until Colt's era that culture and legislation converged in a crescendo of public support and acclaim for inventors, another expression of the new glorification of individuality. Indeed, at the height of the patent medicine craze of the 1830s, when "scarcely a wholesale or retail druggist . . . [was] not consciously selling spurious drugs which were a menace to human life," patents and inventors rather reeked of scam and fraud.[66]

When Colt's victory over the Massachusetts Arms Co. was announced, the *Hartford Daily Times* pronounced it was "about time . . . the law protected inventors."[67] Indeed, inventors and artists were increasingly lionized as romantic heroes of the industrial age. In 1849 the National Gallery of the Patent Office in Washington was visited by 80,000 people, and in 1850, 2,193 patents were filed and 995 issued, up from a couple hundred just a decade earlier.[68] By 1854 the number of patents issued had doubled to almost 2,000. Concerned that the tide of public opinion was against them, the defendants in the lawsuit Sam Colt brought against the Massachusetts Arms Co. urged that the jury not fall for the "devise of ingenious counsel" in representing his client, Sam Colt, as belonging to an "aggrieved and persecuted class of men." The defendant's attorney noted that "when there was less of science applied to the subject, when invention was undertaken rather by adventurers and fallen into by accident, there was a feeling less favorable to inventions than at the present day . . . a feeling of hostility . . . [and] a disposition to disbelieve improvements and to follow the old path," where today, he cautioned, "the public mind has now swung to the other extremity; not a new thought comes in, however absurd, which does not find followers."[69]

Sam Colt used patent law to protect the value of his invention, and few people have ever argued more persuasively or convincingly on behalf of the inventor struggling against the odds. But ultimately, Colt's main weapon against "infringers" was the fame of his product and the pricing advantage he created through volume production. He never fully blocked imitators and, in fact, went to considerable pains to license production in Europe and set up manufacturing facilities in London as an obstacle to European copyists he could not stop by legal means.

The patent secured Colt's reputation as an inventor and, if not quite a seal of approval, was at least a seal of originality at a time when public opinion strongly favored originality and creative genius. Nonetheless, Colt spent ten years in a frenzy about being robbed of his invention. When, within nine months of beginning arms manufacturing in Hartford, Colt "discovered . . . that two of my principal workmen are engaged with several other persons in getting up a repeating pistol . . . [with] hope of avoiding my patents," he flew into a rage, accusing the Ordnance Department in Washington of a "conspiracy" against him.[70] In 1851 the lawsuit he brought against these "workmen" and "other persons," then incorporated as the Massachusetts Arms Co., was widely reported and involved a battery of prominent attorneys. Figuring that Colt would make bushels of money with or without their verdict, the jury awarded him one dollar in damages and the right to serve notice on potential competitors. His attorney Edward Dickerson immediately issued a broadside warning firearms dealers to "desist . . . from the sale of any Repeating Firearms in which rotation or locking & releasing are produced by combining the breech with the lock . . . except . . . as are made by Col. Colt at Hartford. . . . All rotary arms . . . are in plain violation of Col. Colt's patent; and I shall proceed against you."[71] It was show business as usual.

Colt's experience giving laughing gas demonstrations on the lyceum circuit, his close study of the patent medicine industry's use of expert testimonials and sustained direct advertising, and the triumph of packaging over content in the presidential campaign that sent Tippecanoe (Gen. William H. Harrison) and Tyler Too to the White House in 1840, made Colt an early convert to the new art of advertising and mass marketing. A decade after Colt's earliest forays into mass marketing, the *Hartford Daily Times* editorialized on the virtues of advertising: "Extensive advertising is morally certain to work a revolution in trade, by driving thousands of the easy-going out of it and concentrating business in the hands of the few who know how to obtain and keep it," it preached. "He who neglects advertising . . . bestows the spoils on his . . . rivals."[72]

Sam Colt was always on jovial terms with reporters, cultivating their favor, contributing to their pet political causes, and ever ready to present a gift revolver for a good story—a not inconsequential gesture, considering that even the cheapest ones were worth today's equivalent of about a thousand dollars. After Colt succeeded in securing volume sales to the British military, a journalist wrote of how he had been "introduced by a brother member of the press to Colonel Sam Colt . . . [who was] sagacious enough to know that one line in the [London] Times would do him more good than a column in any other paper. . . . [He was] ready to pay any sum. . . . [I] told Colt that I would make an effort . . . [if he would] show me his new armory. . . . I at once sent this letter to the *Times*, asking if it was fair to the British sailors that they should still be limited to the old horse pistol and cutlass. . . . [The] letter was published . . . [and] Colt flourished."[73]

Colt recognized that a good secondhand story or a testimonial was better advertising than the direct approach. How much was paid to place such stories and exactly when he adopted the tactic of buying "good copy" is uncertain, but the stories that appeared in the *New York Times* in 1839 about "A gentleman in New Jersey" who had "lately killed thirteen English snipe, in one day, with one of Colt's repeating fowling-pieces" and of the "17 black ducks [that] were shot on Long Island with a single round from one of Colt's repeating duck-guns" were almost certainly bought and paid for.[74]

In 1839 another newspaper reported that "with one of Colt's pistols . . . Catlin, the artist . . . recently shot three deer in succession while traveling through . . . Pennsylvania," a story that marked the beginning of a relationship between the Colt and the celebrity artist, sportsman, and adventurer George Catlin.[75] Almost twenty years later, Colt commissioned Catlin to produce a series of twelve paintings and six mass-market lithographic prints illustrating his adventures on the frontier using Colt's repeating rifles. The prints, published later by Day and Son of London with such captions as "Catlin the celebrated Indian traveller and artist firing his Colt's repeating rifle before a tribe of Carib Indians in South America," "Catlin the artist & sportsman relieving one of his companions from an unpleasant predicament during his travels in Brazil," and "Catlin the artist & hunter shooting buffalos with Colt's revolving rifle," represent perhaps the earliest pictorial use of celebrity endorsements in product marketing. Catlin, whose trip to Brazil and South America in 1855 was reportedly financed by Sam Colt, emerged as the personification of the adventurous, westward-bound American male, hunting, riding, shooting, and glorying in the freedom of the open plains.[76]

Once Colt's revolvers gained acceptance, Colt was happy to discover unsolicited news stories that he could excerpt, reprint, and repackage. In 1854, at the height of the Crimean War, he wrote of "searching the papers to see new incidents at the Crimea of the gallant use of my repeaters."[77] In 1860 he wrote his secretary J. Deane Alden, then stationed in Arizona on company business, about searching the newspapers for "notices of Sharp[s] & Burnside Rifles & Carbines, anecdotes of their use upon Crisley Bares [sic], Indians, Mexicans, & c. . . . When there is or can be maid [sic] a good storrey [sic] of the use of a Colt's Revolving Rifle, Carbine, Shotgun or Pistol . . . the opportunity should not be lost. . . . [With any published] notices . . . send me 100 copies . . . give the editor a Pistol . . . [and] Do not forget to have his Colums [sic] report all the axidents [sic] that occur to the Sharps & other humbug arms."[78] That, in a nutshell, was Colt's media policy. Even if they had to make it up, Colt demanded good copy, and he wasted no opportunity to make the competition look bad.

The manufacturers of Colt's firearms have chased military contracts, typically the largest but least stable share of the gun market, with unbending determination for 160 years. Colt doted on military officers, especially those who, like himself, were adventuresome, spirited, and hungry for glory. Before the company even had arms to sell, Colt was in Washington wining and dining military and Ordnance Department officials. Lavish and conspicuous spending, personal charm, and an unfaltering confidence in the rightness of his every utterance made Sam Colt the kind of person who—love him or hate him—one never forgot. Despite his wife's later characterizations of him as practically a teetotaler and a person "who never used tobacco in any form," it is hard to imagine how a man who bought cigars by the thousand, was once accused of appearing drunk before a committee of Congress, and whose liquor bills and wine cellar inventories were enormous, was not also something of a lush.[79]

Sam Colt was a glutton for publicity, especially, but not exclusively, for the kind that advanced the reputation of his firearms. Believing, as he once said, that "government patronage . . . is an advertisement, if nothing else," Colt was dogged in his pursuit of government contracts, a fact that quickly strained his relations with the desk soldiers in Washington he grew to despise.[80] Tests and testimonials were the instruments Colt most relied on to secure government contracts. In the first go-around, Colt's revolvers had fared poorly in government tests conducted at the U.S. Military Academy at West Point during the summer of 1837. Unwilling to accept rejection, Colt exhibited the pattern of impulsive misjudgment and ethical sleight of hand that would follow him throughout his career. He planted a story in the West Point newspaper stating how Colt's gun, which fires "18 charges in the incredible short space of 58 seconds, . . . must be invaluable . . . for an Indian campaign."[81] The same day, writing as "your old school fellow," Colt petitioned one of the cadets for a favorable endorsement.[82]

Military tests were never as valuable to Colt as combat testimonials from officers in the field of battle. Colt's determination to secure battlefield testimonials led him to the front lines of the Seminole War in Florida, where he personally delivered a consignment of revolving rifles during the winter of 1838.[83] Florida produced Colt's first military contracts and endorsements, though he later complained that the success of his repeaters brought the war to a quick end, thus destroying his market. Having failed to gain approval from the Ordnance Department, Colt issued a report, in the style of an official government document, complete with statistics on the arms' accuracy, power, rapidity of fire, safety, and water resistance. The report featured an endorsement by Lt. Col. William S. Harney, the officer whose Florida dragoons were the first to use Colt's firearms in battle. Addressing his superior officer, Gen. Thomas Jessup, Harney testified that Colt's revolving rifles had earned the "greatest honor to the inventor" and that he preferred Colt's over "any other Rifle."[84] Quick to capitalize on even a vague and indirect endorsement (it is not clear if Colt had permission to cite the letter), Colt circulated an announcement crediting "the Gallant Colonel Harney" who "with less than one hundred men armed with Colt's Patent Repeating Rifles . . . terminated the Florida war."[85] Years later Harney declared that "I honestly believe that but for these arms, the Indians would now be luxuriating in the everglades of Florida."[86]

It was through Indian warfare, first in Florida and eventually throughout the contested zone of contact between whites and Indians, that the Colt revolver found its market and identity as a tactical necessity for the new style of warfare that emerged in the West. It is not clear that even Sam Colt at first understood the tactical significance of his invention. Throughout the era of the Patent Arms Manufacturing Company in Paterson, New Jersey, Colt's manufacturing and marketing emphasized long arms, not pistols. In Florida, Colt observed firsthand how repeating firearms could revolutionize warfare. This was especially true in what was euphemistically called the "irregular" guerrilla warfare practiced with such terrifying competence by Native Americans and other "savage" peoples, no more respectful of white codes of honor than the whites were of their sovereignty and independence.

As early as 1840, reports from the Florida war zone confirmed that "no man in Florida is safe in his own house" and described the rifle, and especially "Colt's repeating rifle," as the best and "only obstacle to the butchery of his family."[87] By the mid-1850s Colt had successfully appropriated the rhetoric of his frontier testimonials as he described the conditions that made his repeating firearms a necessity. In addressing London's Institution of Civil Engineers in 1851, Colt described the United States as "a country of most extensive frontier, still inhabited by hordes of aborigines." Colt cited "the insulated position of the enterprising pioneer and his dependence, sometimes alone, on his personal ability" for defense, concluding with an account of "the model of attack by the mounted Indians," who would "overwhelm small bodies of American soldiers by rushing down on them in . . . superior numbers, after having drawn their fire."[88] This concept of warfare had tremendous resonance for a British public then in the midst of war with the "savage tribes of the Cape of Good Hope."[89] As described by the London Institution of Civil Engineers, "The tactics of the Kaffirs were to tease an outpost sentry, at a distance, until they had drawn his fire, and then to spring on him before he had time to reload. . . . Nothing could be more perfectly adapted to meet these tactics, than the revolvers."[90] As "savage" and "civilized" societies clashed in the age of colonial expansion and empire, Colt's revolver gained an almost sacred identity as a factor in the triumph of Christian civilization over the forces of darkness, whatever and wherever they might be. Henry Barnard described the new calculus of warfare in terms of mathematical risk noting that as "every man armed with one of [Colt's] weapons was armed sixfold . . . [the] savages . . . would have seen that . . . the first man of them who rushed forward with the tomahawk would rush on certain death. . . . A force so concentrated . . . cannot but 'demoralize' antagonists."[91]

After a second test in 1840 failed to result in the general adoption of Colt's repeaters by the armed services, Colt petulantly petitioned the secretary of the navy, James Paulding, for reconsideration, citing the "wrong conclusion" that had been reached and the "great difference of opinion" held by "those who have used them most." Colt provided additional testimony, this time from the sergeant in charge of drilling Harney's second dragoons in the use of his guns, who claimed that "in passing through Indian country, I always felt myself safer with one of your rifles . . . than if I was attended by a body of ten . . . men armed with the common musket."[92]

Conceived in the North, baptized in the South, Colt's arms reached maturity in the unique climate of the American West. In the years that followed, Colt managed to obtain testimonials from dozens of prominent military officers, enough to cover almost every context and contingency. For the pioneer in Indian Territory and on the Texas frontier there was C. Downing writing in 1840 that "any man of nerve, of coolness, of determined resolution, on the inside of his house . . . would find Colt's rifle a safer reliance in an Indian midnight attack than ten men . . . with an ordinary gun."[93] On the eve of the Civil War, Colt printed an eight-page promotional brochure stating that during the past twenty years his arms had been "tested as no other arms have ever been" and citing the "following distinguished officers" as certifying its "superiority." The list of almost one hundred names is a veritable *Who's Who* of Mexican War heroes, political luminaries, Ordnance Department officials, and past and future U.S. presidents and executive cabinet officers, including 1848 presidential candidate, secretary of state, and U.S. senator Lewis Cass; secretary of war, U.S. senator, and future president of the Confederacy Jefferson Davis; major general and U.S. president Zachary Taylor; Mexican War generals Gideon J. Pillow and David E. Twiggs; brigadier general and U.S. president Franklin Pierce; U.S. senator from

California, western adventurer, and 1856 presidential candidate Col. John C. Frémont; Ordnance Department chief inspector Maj. William A. Thornton; and Mexican War and Japan Expedition hero Commodore Matthew C. Perry.[94]

Of all the endorsements Colt received, none was more significant than that of the legendary Texas Rangers. Founded in 1836 by Connecticut Yankee Steven Austin, the Republic of Texas was a melting pot that played a significant role in the shaping of the American character. Here, in this vast, seemingly unlimited space, plantation lord and Yankee, Native American and Mexican converged to create a civilization different from that found in either the North or the South, one shaped more by the conditions of environment than by race or inheritance.

The new man forged in the crucible of the West, the liberated sovereign individual of Walt Whitman, was epitomized by the Texas Ranger. Bursting onto the stage of American popular culture, guns a-blazing, the rangers emerged as folk heroes during the Mexican War when their exploits and skill were widely reported in the press. Was this truly a new kind of man? In 1846 the *Hartford Daily Times* ran an article with the title "The Texas Rangers—Who Are They?" The newspaper answered with the story of Col. John Coffee Hays of San Antonio, who held a "high place . . . in the hearts of the people of the United States" since moving west to Texas in 1839 after bold and heroic service in the Indian wars in Florida. Having already earned a "reputation for coolness, judgement, courage, energy, and a knowledge of frontier life," in 1840 Hays "induced the government of Texas to tender to him the command of its first company of rangers." Under the leadership of this man who "thinks much and speaks little, and that little always to the purpose," the rangers quickly gained renown as a new breed of mounted soldier "willing . . . to live on parched corn, ride 70 or 80 miles without dismounting" and as the "best light troops in the world."[95] Served up at the dawn of the campaign of Manifest Destiny, romanticized for his skill at horsemanship, marksmanship, and freelance tactical warfare, the Texas Ranger was the poster child of the new West.[96]

It was one of Colonel Hays's men, Capt. Samuel H. Walker, who first linked the celebrity of the Rangers to the name of Colt. In November 1846 he wrote a testimonial letter better than any Sam Colt ever paid for. Recounting the widely publicized episode known as Hays's Big Fight, a clash between fifteen Texas Rangers and some eighty Comanches in June 1844, Walker registered his high opinion of Colt's "revolving patent arms" (in this case the New Jersey–made five-shot model) and reported that "people throughout Texas are anxious to procure your pistols."[97] According to Walker, the superior firepower of Colt's repeaters intimidated the Indians into negotiating a treaty and canceling attacks on new settlements along the Texas frontier. Walker concluded by asserting that "with improvements I think [your revolver] can be rendered the most perfect weapon in the world for light mounted troops," an emerging branch of military service championed by Walker as the "only efficient troops that can be placed upon our extensive Frontier to keep the various war-like tribes of Indians & marauding Mexicans in subjection."[98]

Colt reaped a publicity bonanza in Samuel Walker, a natural ally who shared

Colt's fascination with new technology and new modes of warfare. Together they entered into a collaboration that resulted in a much-improved generation of Colt revolvers and a government contract large enough to sustain Colt's dream of building an arms manufacturing empire. Walker was already a national celebrity when he visited Hartford in 1847 to consult with Colt on design modifications for his handgun.[99] In addition to recounting Walker's service in the Seminole Indian wars and his key role in Hays's Big Fight, the local press described a confrontation in which he recovered after being "pierced through the body by the spear of an Indian, [which] pinn[ed] him to the ground!" In another incident, he had allegedly been captured by Mexicans and "tortured" before escaping to the mountains, where he "suffered greatly from hunger" before being "recaptured by the Mexicans" and subjected to Santa Anna's suicide lottery. Later, Walker had been awarded a captain's commission in the Mexican War Regiment, the first U.S. troops to test the mode of warfare that eventually earned Colt's revolvers notoriety as the Gun that Won the West.[100]

Tales of breathtaking adventure served as the inspiration for the decorative scenes Colt had engraved on the cylinders of his revolvers.[101] The scenes included a rendering of Hays's Big Fight, a pioneer and Indian fight, a deer-hunting scene, and an 1843 encounter between the Texas and Mexican navies, described by commanding officer Commodore E. W. Moore, who wrote Colt that the confidence "your arms gave the officers and men under my Command . . . opposed to a vastly superior force is almost incredible."[102] These distinctive engravings reinforced the link in the popular imagination between Colt's revolvers and the fabled Texas Rangers, as did the occasional visits to Hartford by these bona fide western heroes that Sam Colt hosted throughout the 1850s. It was an association destined to make Colt rich, particularly when the gunmaker's Texas allies began to exert their will in Washington.

By the early 1850s, the former president of the Republic of Texas and, following annexation, its first U.S. senator, Gen. Sam Houston, had become one of Washington's most influential advocates of modern weaponry. Houston and Texas colleague Sen. Thomas Rusk lobbied Secretary of War William Marcy and President James K. Polk "unasked for" on behalf of Colt's revolvers. Rusk reported to Colt that they had urged Marcy and Polk "to arm every soldier upon the frontier with your pistols and prevent a general Indian war."[103] Elated with an unsolicited endorsement from such high-ranking authorities, Colt wrote Houston to say "that your recommendation will contribute vastly more to the successful introduction of my armes [sic] . . . than the . . . opinion of a hundred military men who have had no expereance [sic] in their use in the field." Colt described Texas as his "first patrons" and acknowledged that "Texas has done more for me & my armes [sic] [and has] a better knowledge of their use" than the rest of the country combined.[104]

Colt treasured the collection of "distinguished names" who endorsed his arms for military purposes, carefully preserving them "in the book I keep for that purpus [sic]."[105] The collection, which also included thanks and acknowledgments for the gifts of presentation pistols, contains letters received from Italian freedom fighter Giuseppe Garabaldi, Sardinian nationalist King Victor Emanuel, Hungarian freedom fighter Louis Kossuth, religious exile Brigham Young, California Gold Rush testimony from T. Butler King and William M. Given, and field service testimony from Indian fighter Major O. Cross and Texas Rangers Maj. G. T. Howard and Capt. I. S. Sutton, who praised Colt's revolvers as "the greatest improvement in small arms of the age . . . the only weapon which has enabled the frontiersman to defeat the mounted Indian in his own peculiar mode of warfare . . . [and] the arm which has rendered the name of Texas Ranger a . . . terror to . . . our frontier Indians."[106]

As testimony piled up in Washington, D.C., former Texas war secretary Thomas J. Rusk urged the "government to introduce" Colt's revolvers, claiming "that one hundred cavalry armed with the repeating pistol would be, at least, as efficient as 300 armed in the ordinary way." Lt. Bedney F. McDonald, who was in Huamantla, Mexico, the day Captain Walker was killed there, testified that he had "seen Col. Hays hold in check more than 500 Mexicans, with 30 men armed with these pistols." With the Mexican War over, testimony shifted to frontier defense where it was noted that those "who have used" Colt's revolvers in "Mexico, and elsewhere" regard them as "the most efficient, and economical arms that can be employed in all Indian territory, and on our extended line of frontier."[107] Although sales to the American armed services languished throughout the 1850s, by the time of the Civil War, the question was no longer whether to adopt Colt's revolvers, but how fast could they be supplied.

Colt's factories became another of his successful instruments of publicity. It was in London that Colt discovered the appeal of a behind-the-scenes look. Tours of his armory became so popular that he issued tickets of admission.[108] Mounted on top of Colt's London factory, adjacent to Parliament, was a fourteen-foot-long sign reading "Col. Colt's Pistol Factory."[109] Brash and outrageous, Colt was eventually ordered to remove the sign, but not before it stirred controversy and heightened his fame.[110]

As soon as his Hartford armory, mansion, and worker housing were fully operational, Colt bought himself one of the most expansive "news" stories written about an American industrial concern before the Civil War. In May 1857 Colt paid the publishers of United States Magazine $1,120 (today equal to $61,439) for copies of a flattering, twenty-nine-page illustrated feature story that appeared in the magazine's March issue under the title "Repeating Fire-Arms: A Day at the Armory of 'Colt's Patent Fire-Arms Manufacturing Company.'"[111] Representing a genre of industrial profile that became a staple of the prestigious Scientific American during and after the Civil War, "A Day at the Armory" set a new standard for length, quantity of illustrations, and sycophancy in industrial reporting. It also provides the most detailed account, and the only illustrations released during Colt's lifetime, of the inner workings of Colt's Armory. Colt traded access, hospitality, gift pistols, and the personal attention of a recognized "great man," for glowing coverage. Two years later, Boston journalist John Ross Dix actually wove Colt's unique form of hospitality into the text of his narrative tour of Colt's Armory, lauding the Colonel as a man "as noted for his hospitality as for his genius" and transcribing Colt's letter accompanying a gift revolver inviting the writer to "accept in order that you may examine its structure and finish at your leisure."[112] A connoisseur was no doubt born that day.

In addition to testimonials and news stories, Colt developed a national network of retail commission sales representatives to whom he offered quantity discounts and provided printed advertising broadsides.[113] The best of the many versions of Colt's printed broadsides combined price and model information with wit and visual imagery. Although Colt's broadsides are today very rare, a bill from 1854 documents the printing of 30,700 "pistol directions" and 20,000 "pamphlets," which Colt distributed through his sales agents, retail outlets, and lobbyists.[114] At least 9 different illustrated broadsides were produced during Colt's lifetime. The first, published about 1848 to promote the new .44-caliber, six-shot army pistol, features an image of a cocked revolver with illustrations and descriptions of its use and component parts, printed as if written in the inventor's hand, signed in cursive scrawl, Sam Colt, and so personalized: "I . . . will be glad to attend any cash orders addressed to me in New York city, or at my armory in Hartford, Conn."[115] The world would know that this man's signature was his bond.

Texas and the West may not have generated the majority of Colt's sales, but its aura and associations were soon adopted as key elements of Colt's marketing strategy. An 1857 broadside addressed to the Pioneers of Civilization noted that Colt's "pistols, rifles, carbines and shot gun" were "sold by all respectable dealers throughout the world." Colt probably drafted the text, which described the "Simple Reasons for preferring Colt's Arms to all others." In a curiously defensive, fourteen-point rebuttal of the many criticisms leveled against his invention, Colt noted that "They do not stick fast, refusing either to open or shut without the aid of an axe when heated, as do the guns which open like molasses gates or nut crackers. . . . They leave no burning paper in the barrel after a discharge, to blow the next cartridge into your face, as do the guns which open from behind. . . . They are simple in construction, and easily taken care of, as any ranger or cavalry soldier will tell you. Treat them well, and they will treat your enemies badly. . . . They are always worth what they cost—in the Far West much more, almost a legal tender! If you buy anything cheaper, your life, and that of your companion, may balance the difference in cost. . . . If you buy a Colt's Rifle or Pistol, you feel certain that you have one true friend, with six hearts in his body, and who can always be relied on."[116]

The most artistic of Colt's broadsides, published about 1854, substitutes artwork for text and simply describes the product, illustrated with a break-apart view of the components, as "Colt's Patent Repeating Pistols. . . . Orders . . . may be addressed to me at Hartford, Conn., or New York City. [signed] Sam Colt." The illustrations feature the three most popular cylinder scenes of Colt's arms in action, an innovative convention of Colt's marketing since the Paterson days. Scenes of Hays's Big Fight, the 1843 engagement between the Texas and Mexican navies, and a stagecoach robbery are flanked by patriotic vignettes of the Battle of Quebec and "man the hunter" triumphantly mounting the head of a lion with

Colt rifle in hand. No more alluring use of images and symbols exists in American advertising before the Civil War.

Colt's broadsides typically accomplished several purposes. Some conveyed price information. Some created allure. All attempted to demystify an instrument of considerable complexity. Parallels with today's computer-based communications revolution are striking. For all the attention given to the arms industry's success in mastering uniformity of parts and volume production, firearms still demanded complex care and maintenance. Guns tended to malfunction and break. It was a challenge to convince people to part with almost a month's wages for an instrument that was not wholly dependable. By the time he revived his arms factory, Colt had clearly internalized the criticism heaped on his Paterson-era revolvers for "getting out of order." Today, when we are able to operate our televisions and radios (and increasingly, automobiles) with little or no maintenance, it is easy to take for granted the hard-won qualities of low maintenance, then almost unprecedented in the history of complex things. By persistently illustrating and writing about the working parts of his firearms, Colt chipped away at the subconscious resistance and eventually succeeded in convincing people that this gun was "simple in construction, and easily taken care of," words spoken as corporate mantra in the dogged pursuit of ever-greater refinements and simplifications. But for those still confused, Colt also produced users' manuals, broadsides, and cleaning cloths, reiterating over and over again the principles of gun use, construction, and maintenance. Where modern industry struggles with engineers and specialists interested in dazzling their peers (and the inevitable gadget freaks) with bewildering options, Colt virtually pioneered the field of ergonomics, or user-centered design aimed at product usability.[117]

Colt also mastered the techniques of display and presentation as few arms manufacturers have, before or since. In London he urged dealers and sales agents to arrange his firearms in eye-catching window displays.[118] Colt's display at London's Crystal Palace was described as a "military trophy" that attracted crowds intrigued by the colorful character of its host and the spectacle of its "symmetrically arranged" collection of pistols.[119] Colt served favored guests cigars and brandy. One journalist noted how Colt "liberally indulged" the "sense of touch," letting guests cock and aim pistols that, he assured them, were not loaded. This was a more carefree attitude than was then common in the sale and display of such costly items.[120] At the New York Crystal Palace in 1853, "Col. Colt's Revolvers were arranged in the form of a shield and presented a beautiful appearance." Some years after Colt's death, this tradition of showmanship was perhaps in mind when the company arranged an "exhibit . . . [with] a little bedstead made of pistols," with two "soundly sleeping . . . beauties, all mother-of-pearl silver," beneath a "satin [coverlet]" for the 1876 Centennial Exhibition in Philadelphia.[121]

Even before establishing manufacturing capacity, Colt lavished considerable attention on the appearance and presentation of his guns, hiring engravers and carvers to decorate barrels, grips, and frames, and purchasing presentation cases made of hand-crafted exotic woods.[122] While in Austria in 1849, Colt commissioned "an artist" to make "pistol cases of a peculiar description of inlaid work called by the Austrians 'Buhl,' " which he adopted as part of the packaging for the finest and most artistic of his engraved and gold-inlaid presentation revolvers.[123] At its height, Sam Colt's Armory tapped an international pool of skilled artisans—mostly German Americans—who provided custom decoration and a jewel-like quality of finish that belied the fact that Colt's revolvers were machine-made.

Far from destroying qualities of art and artisanship, machine production increased the share of total cost that could be practically devoted to embellishment. Between the expectations of the "gentlemen" for whom expensive hand-crafted ornamentation and workmanship was an inherited taste and critics afraid that qualitative compromises accompanied volume production, Colt's use of ornamentation and packaging helped secure the reputation of his arms among purists and skeptics. To Frederick Stegmuller of Newark, New Jersey, he turned for mahogany cases.[124] Colt was one of the first to develop a commercial application for Waterman L. Ormsby's patented "grammagraph," a device for roll-die engraving on steel, used to create the "cylinder scenes" on Colt's revolvers. Ormsby, whose work is one of the most distinctive features of Colt's firearms, was a National Academy of Design–trained artist and inventor and the most prolific bank note engraver in America during the 1840s and 1850s.[125] For superb custom decoration, Colt relied on Gustave Young, an immigrant engraver who boasted of having "been engaged in Col. Colt's Establishment . . . [for] twelve years in the highest walks of art" producing "splendid presents" for "Crowned Heads . . . [and] illustrious personages," arms engraved and inlaid in gold, steel, and silver.[126] Christian Deyhle, Carl Helfrecht, Augustus Grunwald, Herman Bodenstein, and John Most, all immigrant German craftsmen, were the most prominent of the skilled artisans who engraved steel, and carved ivory and wood pistol grips, and thus helped shape Colt's reputation for beauty and artistic finish.[127]

Colt also realized that the easiest way to make a product user friendly was to make it affordable. The failure to achieve competitive pricing has led to the failure of many a great invention. Colt, having been stung by accusations that his Paterson arms were a bad value, devised a two-pronged strategy for preserving a dominant share of a rising market. One almost wonders, given the outcome, if all Colt's noise about patent protection was partly aimed at taking the competition's eye off the ball of cost containment. Where business often falls into the trap of basing its price on costs, Colt was determined to do the opposite, to keep his costs consistently at or below a level that would maximize sales volume and below the cost his competitors could match and still survive. He knew from constant haggling with government officials what price would optimize volume. For a product that entered the market at $50 (now about $3,875) and bottomed out in 1859, wholesaling for as little as $19 (now about $1,250), Colt ended up with a better and more reliable gun at about one-third the original price.[128]

In 1854, while clamoring for a patent extension, Colt's advocates and attorneys inadvertently revealed his quest of price-based market dominance. The chairman of the Committee on Patents acknowledged that Colt's goal was to "perfect his armory by the increase and subdivision of machinery, [so] that he will be able to furnish . . . a perfect arm at a price which will defy . . . spurious imitations" and further that "manufacturers of spurious imitations will not find the profit sufficient to encourage the business." Colt's attorney and friend Edward Dickerson noted that "every day . . . his manufacture is improving, and the price diminishing," to the point where "no one today can make a genuine Colt's pistol and compete with him in the market."[129] Both attempted, unsuccessfully, to mask Colt's pursuit of market dominance and profits behind the rhetoric of patent protection. Colt's also became famous for frequent model changes and the most extensive catalog of styles, patterns, sizes, and surface finishes in the arms industry, an accomplishment that stymied the attempts of competitors to gain a toehold in the market.[130] Only by missing a couple of key shifts in firearms technology—notably the adaptation of metallic cartridges—did Colt squander the advantage created by his superior manufacturing capacity, thus providing Smith and Wesson of Springfield and Winchester in New Haven with a share of the market.

Advertising and competitive pricing were the least controversial of Colt's marketing techniques. The presentation gun was the most. Imagine Ford Motor Company giving cars to the purchasing agents of corporate and municipal fleets coast to coast and you get some idea of how Colt used the presentation revolver. For a product that ranged upward from the equivalent of $1,500, it was no small token to receive a pistol "compliments of Col. Colt" or "compliments of the inventor." And where the conflict of interest was most flagrant, as with an infamous gift to former Virginia governor and then U.S. secretary of war John B. Floyd from "the Workmen of Col. Colt's Armory," Colt simply masked the source.[131]

The presentation gun, specially decorated, handsomely cased, and engraved with an honorific inscription, was a convention Colt adapted from a tradition of presentation swords that began during the War of Independence and flourished during the War of 1812 and Mexican War.[132] The difference was that sword manufacturers like Nathan P. Ames were not usually the presenters. Although many of Colt's deluxe presentation-style revolvers were purchased for gift purposes by others, most of the couple of hundred presentation guns known were gifts made by Colt to curry favor. Colt surely did not invent this form of inducement. But no one developed it further or achieved more sensational results. Colt's presentation arms are today prized by collectors of American arms and represent the greatest accomplishment of artistic virtuosity by Colt's workmen, rivaling in painstaking ornamentation, skillfulness, and beauty any form of decorative art produced in America before the Civil War.

How do we understand a man whose hostility toward government officials was so great that he once wrote that "to be a clerk or an office holder under the pay and patronage of Government, is to stagnate ambition. . . . You had better blow out your brains at once & manure an honest man's ground with your carcass than to hang your ambition on so low a peg"?[133] This same man practically wrote the book on courting influence with those same government officials. The triumph of pragmatism over ideals has rarely proved more decisive, and yet Sam Colt can hardly be accused of setting the rules of the game. It was because of the duality of his character—his "flexible patriotism" and situational ethics— that Colt was able to flip-flop so deftly between the worlds of art and industry, handicraft and machine-based uniformity, personal expression and militaristic workplace discipline. Colt's style of lobbying switched back and forth between a tradition of relationship-based friendship networks and purchased influence, and a rigid obsession with merit-based testing and fair play. In all, Colt was as much a victim as a victimizer, and it was probably as a victim that he first discovered how the game might be played. Never one to abide limits, Colt stretched the rules to the point where he became the target of a congressional investigation for bribery.

For a democratic paragon, Colt was ironically addicted to courting favor with men of influence and high social status. His most expensive and impressive gifts were bestowed on European monarchs, whose recognition he craved even more than arms sales. His presentation at the Court of Czar Nicholas in 1854, and the corresponding gift of gold-inlaid presentation pistols, by most standards a relatively insignificant event in a life filled with accomplishment, was singled out for commemoration in a final memorial—Hartford's Colt Memorial Statue—conceived by a doting wife who knew well the passions that made her husband proud. Was it really necessary that a third visit to Russia in 1858 include a "set of his military arms . . . elegantly ornamented . . . presented to the Russian Court" including "large cases . . . containing samples of all the arms made by Col. Colt . . . elegantly engraved . . . [and] gold mounted . . . for the Crown Princes Constantine, Michael and Nicholas"?[134] And what of the dozens of revolvers provided for Commodore Matthew C. Perry's Japan Expedition, to be liberally bestowed on, among others, "the emperor and several of the princes of Japan, the governor of Shanghai, the King of Lew Chew, and the king of Siam," in 1855? Few of these gifts, worth today's equivalent of nearly one hundred thousand dollars, prompted sales.[135]

At home, scores of gift pistols were presented to military officers and Ordnance and War Department officials.[136] Couched in terms of seeking testimonials, these guns helped create the sympathetic and progressive atmosphere that eventually triumphed over the Ordnance Department's resistance to new weaponry. Once the government contracts began to flow, they provided one of Colt's largest sources of revenue.

On certain occasions Colt used outright bribery to lower the Ordnance Department's resistance. In 1839, with his fortunes sagging in Paterson, Colt proposed bribing ordnance officials, to which his uncle and company treasurer Dudley Selden recoiled in shock, insisting that "I will not become a party to a negotiation with a public officer to allow his compensation for aid in securing a contract with the government. The suggestion with respect to Col. Bomford is dishonorable [in] every way."[137]

In 1851 the plaintiffs in Colt's lawsuit for patent infringement complained that

"Mr. Colt . . . has made his threats that he has $50,000 to expend against us." In 1852, in a sneering comment on the way business was conducted with government officials, Colt wrote to his agent in London, "I rejoice to find you have at last closed arrangements with the government & c. & that you have treated the Babes of the Woods & Forests with a small specemin [sic] of sivilization [sic] in the shape of a Dinner," and who knows what else, "at my expense [sic]."[138]

Playing cat and mouse with government officials was Sam Colt's idea of sport. Eventually it caught up with him. Although he was acquitted, the bribery accusation that was most damaging to Colt's reputation led in 1854 to a congressional investigation "to inquire whether money has been offered to members . . . or other improper means used to induce members to aid in securing the passage . . . of a bill to extend Colt's patent."[139] Colt applied for an extension of his patent in January 1854. The Patent Office advised approving Colt's application, but it became mired in debate in the House of Representatives. By July charges that "money has been offered to induce persons to cause members by solicitation to vote for this bill" were out of control.[140] On July 10 a special committee was appointed to take testimony involving the Colt bribery charges. By August it was a national news story, with *Scientific American*, although unfavorable to patent extensions in general, calling Washington a "den of corruption" and basically exonerating Colt, whose crime appears to have been little more than entertaining "the honorables" in the same lavish style he had been doing for twenty years, in this case supplying members' wives with fancy "kid gloves."[141]

Colt's most controversial "marketing" technique involved combinations of bribery, blackmail, bullying, and baiting. Realizing that gun sales thrive in an atmosphere of fear, Colt discovered the value of playing on the fears of adversaries. Although earnestly and fiercely patriotic, Colt's loyalty was more to ideals than institutions, even when the institution was the government of the United States. It is impossible a century and a half after the fact to know what truly motivated certain words and deeds. The record paints a picture of a man deeply conflicted and easily angered by the slow pace of political decision making. Colt discovered that men react more swiftly in fear than in faith. Angered, in 1841, when the government failed to adopt his invention for a system of harbor defense based on submarine explosives, he sulked and suggested that if his own country did not have sense enough perhaps the governments of Europe might.[142] Frustrated after ten years of trying to convince the military to adopt his revolvers for use by the armed services, he boasted that "the Mexicans offered $100 apiece . . . during the war," and he sent agents to Mexico as soon as the war was over to make arms sales to the defeated enemy.[143] Accused by the British of aiding the Russians during the Crimean War, Colt defended himself ambiguously noting that "it is not true that I have furnished arms . . . to the Russian government; . . . since my armory has been established in London, both it and my own skill have always been at the service of the Government. . . . It is not my fault if all my facilities are not now devoted to the British Government."[144]

Having lobbied actively and publicly as a pro-Union, pro-Southern, antiabolitionist Democrat, Colt responded to John Brown's Raid on Harpers Ferry in 1859 not by cutting back on arms sales to a militant and rebellious South but by sending an agent "to the western and south western states [meaning the Deep South and Texas] . . . for the purpose of introducing and making sales of Colt's revolving shot guns and rifles."[145] Colt's sales to Alabama, Virginia, Georgia, and Mississippi in 1860 alone were at least $61,000 (today's equivalent of about $3.35 million).[146] In May 1860 the governor of Virginia sent a delegation to the Connecticut Valley to buy arms and machinery from Colt's, the U.S. Springfield Armory, and Ames Manufacturing Company.[147] For Colt, these sales were not only living by the letter of the law—trade with the South was condoned and unrestricted until the winter of 1861—but an act of faith that arming the South might serve as a deterrent to war. Of course, then and now, interpretations of conduct vary widely and are relatively subjective.

Two weeks after the attack on Fort Sumter, the *New York Daily Tribune* launched an assault against Colt suggesting that "the traitors have found sympathizers among us, men base enough to sell arms when they knew they would be . . . in the hands of the deadly enemies of the Union. . . . Col. Colt's manufactory can turn out probably 1,000 a week, and has been doing so for the past four months for the South. . . . That . . . stopped, . . . he resorts to the only means left him to carry his purpose, and puts up the price of his arms to a figure hereto unheard of. A power so ill used should be taken at once . . . out of the hands of so bad a citizen. . . . Every man who makes arms should be watched, and if he will not work for a fair equivalent for the Government, his manufactory should be taken away from him."[148]

The *New York Times* was no less critical of its industrial neighbor to the north, accusing Colt of "treason," noting that "the Constitution declares *treason* to consist . . . of 'giving aid and comfort to the enemies,' as is done daily, constantly and by contract, with individuals in Connecticut."[149] Describing the accusations as libelous and "absurd," Colt's friends at the *Hartford Daily Times* rallied behind the Hartford arms industry noting that a recent order Colt received from Tennessee "of course was not filled," and that Sharps' Rifle Company and Hazard's Powder Company, in neighboring Enfield, "will not sell a weapon to the enemies."[150] Colt supplied the *Hartford Daily Times* with a letter he allegedly wrote to his sales agents in January instructing them "not to sell to [South Carolina] or any other State which you know to be in open hostility to the Federal Government" and, while not denying that prices had been effectively raised, explained that doing so was necessitated by the rising costs of sales and distribution.[151] Distrustful, his Republican enemies at the *Hartford Daily Courant* wrote of how "Salmon [sic] Adams . . . superintendent of the new armory in Richmond, Virginia, arrived at Springfield . . . after his successful visit to Colt's Armory" where he was "purchasing large quantities of arms from private manufacturers in this vicinity for Virginia and the seceded states."[152]

The facts do not reflect well on Sam Colt. But Colt was a man motivated at least as much by personal political conviction as by profit, convictions shared by many of New England's protrade libertarian industrialists and by almost half of Connecticut's voters, who gave Abraham Lincoln the narrowest margin of victory of any Northern state in the election of 1860. In hindsight it is easy to condemn them for shortsightedness and profiteering while averting their eyes from the suffering of others. In the context of the time, however, these were deeply perplexing issues rife with uncertainty and a bewildering array of bad and good consequences.

What speaks most of Colt's character is his hyperactive brand of opportunism. By temperament, Colt was the sort of man who instinctively marched to the sound of guns, be it a parade around the block or an impending war halfway around the globe. And once on stage, Colt was not averse to making his presence felt. On more than one occasion, he willfully intervened to intensify conflict in some contested battleground. In 1851 Colt allegedly played a role in arming a soldier of fortune, Narcisco Lopez, and his fellow annexationists, in a failed invasion of Cuba.[153] Kansas, still reeling after a year of armed conflict between extremists on both sides of the slavery issue, was a suspicious destination for three of Colt's top aides, who traveled there on unspecified business in 1857.[154] Stirring up controversy or, as Colt might have viewed it, aiding disputants in their right to self-defense was all part of a day's work.

With the outbreak of the Civil War, Sam Colt's behavior and reputation waffled between extremes. Was he a patriot or a traitor? One thing was sure, Colt had no intention of waiting on the sidelines for direction. The war was not two weeks old when Colt seized the moment and "offered to raise a regiment, and arm it with revolving breach rifles of his own manufacture."[155] As a prelude to forming Colt's Armory Guard, Sam Colt had sponsored a grand regimental encampment on the South Meadows in Coltsville in 1858, in which eight hundred or more members of the "first regiment of Connecticut Militia" amassed for two days of drills, marches, and activities.[156] This time it was for real. But Sam Colt was now at the end of his rope and, true to form, his behavior was bizarre and self-destructive.

Colt began amassing a regiment—not a company, not a marching band, but a full regiment—before being authorized to do so. It was vintage Colt. Surely, only Colt's money and Connecticut's desperation prompted the Republican governor to grant a commission to arm troops to the state's richest, staunchest, and most outspoken Democrat.[157] He soon regretted it. By May 18, Colt's Rifle Regiment was full, with "four or five companies [100 men each] now in rendezvous at the meadows," who "sleep in Colt's depot . . . and dine in the Armory Hall." Company A of the 3d Regiment, known as the Mechanics Rifles and composed primarily of men "enlisted from . . . Colt's and Sharps'," envisioned themselves as a prestigious "flank regiment . . . detailed for skirmishing" and caused a fracas when they refused "to take the U.S. muskets given them at the arsenal."[158] Testy and vigorous, Colt, whose entire career and life was a case study in the value of "picked men" and "skirmishing," soon announced that the "Barracks . . . on Huyshope Ave. . . . [would receive] no men under 5'7."[159] The First Connecticut Rifles, or Col. Colt's Rifle Regiment as it was known, aspired to be the best armed and most elite corps on the field of battle. Once again, Colt was marching to the beat of his own idiosyncratic drum, and before long the Republican newspapers were poking fun at "Col. Colt's ... regiment of Potsdam grenadiers," an obvious reference to the Germanic atmosphere and amenities Colt had created in the village community around Colt's Armory.[160]

By the end of the month, Colt's Rifles was in trouble. First by enforcing its exclusionary standards of height, the regiment rejected "members of the New Haven fire company ... as too small."[161] Next, Colt rankled his own men by lobbying to make Colt's Rifles a regular unit of the U.S. Army, violating their patriotic loyalty to Connecticut. Within two weeks of the regiment's encampment on the South Meadows, the governor revoked Colt's commission and dispersed its members. Most entered the regular army as a rifle corps in the 14th Regiment of Infantry; others, as members of the 5th Connecticut Regiment under Col. O. S. Ferry, and the 12th Connecticut Regiment's Company I, known informally as the Colt Guard Company.[162] Although Colt's dream of a full regiment of the U.S. Army armed with Colt's revolving rifles came to naught, members of the two flank companies of the 14th Regiment were apparently armed with Colt's rifles and may have been the first U.S. soldiers so armed in battle when Connecticut troops shipped off for Manassas, Virginia, the following month.[163]

Most of us will never know what it is like to be in the grip of a dream so consuming and overpowering that you would give anything, your life even, to achieve it. Sam Colt was a brinksman who skirted convention, invented and reinvented himself to meet the needs of the occasion, and rarely missed a beat when opportunity knocked. Sam Colt began crossing the lines of good taste and propriety as a boy, and never stopped hungering for the limelight, even when doing so involved almost senseless risk. A man who mingled easily with and celebrated the virtues of commoners, Colt craved and gained the attention of royalty, making him a sort of rich man's working-class hero. Colt wrote, "If I can't be first I wont be second at anything. . . . However inferior in wealth I may be to the many who surround me I would not exchange for these treasures the satisfaction I have in knowing I have done what has never before been accomplished by man."[164] Colt was an opportunist in the best sense of the word. His vision was irrepressible, and in the end, Colt came as close as anyone of his generation to inventing the modern industrial system and acting out the dramatic issues of his age.

NOTES

1. *Hartford Daily Times*, June 30, 1885.

2. George Bernard Shaw, *Major Barbara*, in *Selected Plays* (New York: Dodd, Mead, 1948), 417.

3. Basil Collier, *Arms and the Men: The Arms Trade and Governments* (London: Hamish Hamilton, 1980) 1, 5.

4. Sam Colt, Hartford, to Charles Manby, London, May 18, 1852, Colt Collection, CHS.

5. "The Volcanic Repeating Rifle," *Frank Leslie's Illustrated Newspaper*, October 9, 1858, 291.

6. *Hartford Daily Times*, September 9, 1874.

7. *Dictionary of American Biography* (New York: Charles Scribner's Sons, 1934), 14:89.

8. *Hartford Daily Times*, January 1, 1850.

9. James M. McCaffrey, *Army of Manifest Destiny: The American Soldier in the Mexican War, 1846–1848* (New York: New York University Press, 1992), 31.

10. *Hartford Daily Times*, January 2, 1860.

11. Shearer Davis Bowman, *Masters and Lords: Mid-Nineteenth Century United States Planters and Prussian Junkers* (New York: Oxford University Press, 1993), 114.

12. Donald S. Spencer, *Louis Kossuth and Young America: A Study in Sectionalism and Foreign Policy, 1848–1852* (Columbia: University of Missouri Press, 1977), 33, 40.

13. *Hartford Daily Courant*, January 14, 1851.

14. Summarizing contemporary scientific literature on matters of race, Lionel Tiger recently wrote that "all of contemporary population genetics and molecular biology underscores the notion of races as discrete and different entities as false," and urged that we "stop using 19th century biological concepts as a platform for 21st century social policies" ["Trump the Race Card," *Wall Street Journal*, February 23, 1996].

15. Spencer, *Louis Kossuth and Young America*, 12–14.

16. Neil Arnott, *A Survey of Human Progress from the Savage State to the Highest Civilization Yet Attained* (London: Longman, Green, Longman and Roberts, 1861), 5, 24.

17. *Hartford Daily Times*, December 10, 1866, May 25, 1882.

18. Reginald Horsman, *Race and Manifest Destiny: The Origins of American Racial Anglo-Saxonism* (Cambridge: Harvard University Press, 1981), 1–3. Quotation is from Charles DeWolf Brownell, *The Indian Races of North and South America* (Hartford: Hulbut, Scranton, 1864), 159.

19. Brownell, *Indian Races of North and South America*, 709, 718, 720.

20. Marcus Cunliffe, *Soldiers and Civilians: The Martial Spirit in America, 1775–1865* (Boston: Little, Brown, 1868), 339–40.

21. "Our assumptions about deterrence . . . for the past 20 years . . . [have been the] basic idea that if each side were able to . . . threaten retaliation against any attack and thereby impose on an aggressor costs that were clearly out of balance with any potential gains, this would suffice to prevent conflict" ["The Strategic Defense Initiative," *Special Report No. 129* (Washington, D.C.: U.S. Department of State, 1985), 1].

22. Cunliffe, *Soldiers and Civilians*, 22. Given the intensity of the debate around this issue—it is at the core of pro– and anti–gun control arguments—it is surprising that the history of the "peacemaker" defense has not been studied. Although there is little evidence of its currency in the United States before 1840, the French penal reform theorist Cesare Beccaria wrote in 1764 that "laws that forbid the carrying of arms . . . disarm those only who are neither inclined nor determined to commit crimes" [Gary Kleck, *Point Blank: Guns and Violence in America* (New York: Aldine De Gruyter, 1991), 144].

23. Gen. James Tallmadge, *Address before the American Institute . . . 26th of October 1841* (New York: Hopkins and Jennings, 1841), 14.

24. Bernard Brodie and Fawn M. Brodie, *From Crossbow to H-Bomb* (Bloomington: Indiana University Press, 1973), 140.

25. *Hartford Daily Times*, January 5, 1852.

26. Patterson, *Colt vs. the Massachusetts Arms Co.*, 11.

27. Howe, *Adventures and Achievements*, 149.

28. Frank T. Morn, "Firearms Use and the Police: A Historic Evaluation of American Values," *Firearms and Violence: Issues of Public Policy*, ed. Don B. Kates Jr. (San Francisco: Pacific Institute for Public Policy Research, 1984), 494.

29. Stephen Halbrook, "The Second Amendment as a Phenomenon of Classical Political Philosophy," ibid., 372–73.

30. Cunliffe, *Soldiers and Civilians*, 52.

31. *Hartford Daily Times*, November 8, 1860.

32. Eric H. Monkkonen, *Police in Urban America, 1860–1920* (Cambridge: Cambridge University Press, 1981), 42, 45.

33. Sidney L. Harring, *Policing a Class Society: The Experience of American Cities, 1865–1915* (New Brunswick, N.J.: Rutgers University Press, 1983), 30–31, 107; Morn, "Firearms Use and the Police," 501.

34. Price List, Colt PFAMC, January 1, 1861, illustrated in R. L. Wilson, *The Arms Collection of Colonel Colt* (Hartford: Wadsworth Atheneum and Herb Glass, 1964), xxii.

35. Morn, "Firearms Use and the Police," 491, 503.

36. Harring, *Policing a Class Society*, 107.

37. Morn, "Firearms Use and the Police," 500.

38. *Newport Mercury*, July 26, 1851; *Newport Daily News*, August 19, 1851.

39. *Hartford Daily Times*, July 4, 1866.

40. Rosenberg, *The American System*, 127–28.

41. Russell S. Gilmore, "'Another Branch of Manly Sport': American Rifle Games, 1840–1890," *Hard at Play: Leisure in America, 1840–1940*, ed. Kathryn Grover (Amherst: University of Massachusetts Press, 1992), 93–95.

42. Osha Gray Davidson, *Under Fire: The NRA and the Battle for Gun Control* (New York: Henry Holt, 1993), 22–23, 30–32. The NRA's turn away from its role as a representative body for hunters and target shooters began in 1868 with the passage of the first gun-control legislation and culminated in what is known within the organization as the Cincinnati Revolt of 1977.

43. Morn, "Firearms Use and the Police," 495; Buffalo Bill's Wild West Show first toured Hartford in 1883 and in 1884 attracted an attendance of eight thousand to its "show at Charter Oak Park" [*Hartford Daily Times*, July 31, 1884].

44. Testimony on House Bill No. 59, "for the relief of Samuel Colt," *The Congressional Globe* (33d Congress, 1st Session, July 8, 1854) (Washington, D.C.: John C. Rives, 1854), 1651.

45. Barnard, *Armsmear*, 160.

46. *Hartford Daily Times*, October 4, 1854.

47. McCabe, *Great Fortunes*, 343.

48. Patterson, *Colt vs. the Mass. Arms Co.*, 287–88.

49. Walt Whitman, *Walt Whitman (Song of Myself)*, in *The Walt Whitman Reader* (1855; reprint, Philadelphia: Courage Books, 1993), 29–105.

50. Colt PFAMC, Cash Book A, January 1856–March 1864 (May 29, 1861), 225. The schooner, possibly built at S. Belden and Son's shipyard near Colt's Armory, may not have been built much before its first documented reference in these account books.

51. Sam Colt, Vienna, to Elisha Colt, Hartford, July 18, 1849, as cited in R. L. Wilson, *Colt Engraving* (1974; reprint, Bienfield Publishing, 1982) 22.

52. *London Evening Sun*, August 11, 1852, as cited in Colt PFAMC, Scrapbooks, nd., np. CSL, box 56. The medal is in the Wadsworth Atheneum's Colt Collection and is illustrated in Barnard, *Armsmear*, 121.

53. *Hartford Daily Times*, October 20, 1849.

54. In 1852, the year this organization was chartered by the general assembly, Sam

Colt offered the use of a piece of land on the South Meadows where he was building his armory [*Transactions of the Connecticut State Agricultural Society* (Hartford 1852), 16].

55. *Hartford Daily Times*, October 13, 1853.

56. Colt PFAMC, Cash Book A, January 1856–March 1864 (October 29, 1858), 129, private collection, Colt Archives, Wadsworth Atheneum.

57. *Hartford Daily Times*, November 21, 1849. Although the activities of this organization are not well documented, its founding leadership was dominated by several of Colt's closest business associates, including James H. Ashmead, Samuel Woodruff, E. C. Kellogg, and James G. Batterson.

58. Daly, *Discourse Delivered at the 35th Anniversary of the American Institute*, 16–30. In spite of the greater attention given to Britain for its Great Exhibition of 1851, the French are credited with originating industrial exhibitions in which manufacturers competed for awards, having mounted thirteen such displays between 1798 and 1855. This report notes that the French industrial fair of 1844 was "such as no other nation but France could have made" and the inspiration behind Britain's exhibition, which attracted a record-setting attendance of about 6 million in 1851. The first U.S. industrial exhibition took place in Pittsfield, Massachusetts, in 1811, but it was not until the 1830s that organizations like the American Institute and the Massachusetts Charitable Mechanics Association began holding annual exhibitions on a considerably larger scale. Although claiming that the Hartford County Agricultural Society fair of 1853 "far exceeds that of any previous year," Hartford boosters noted that the 1853 Massachusetts Mechanics fair had been attended by more than 100,000 people, due in part to its emphasis on industrial more than agricultural matters [*Hartford Daily Times*, October 15, 1853].

59. *Charleston Courier*, February 19, 1836, as cited in Colt PFAMC, Scrapbooks, "Records of Colt Company Property," February 1836–June 1852, np. CSL, box 63. No medal for 1836 has been found, but the medals for later years are included in the Wadsworth Atheneum's Colt Collection; Colt's appointment to a committee of the American Institute is recorded in a letter [American Institute, New York, to Sam Colt, Paterson, N.J., 1837, Colt Collection, CHS].

60. New-York Historical Society to Sam Colt, New York, December 12, 1838, Colt Manuscripts, Wadsworth Atheneum; National Institution for the Promotion of Science, to Sam Colt, Washington, D.C., August 22, 1840, Colt Collection, CHS; Connecticut Historical Society to Sam Colt, Hartford, June 7, 1854, Colt Manuscripts, Wadsworth Atheneum.

61. Appointment to the Local Committee for the State of Connecticut at the World's Fair in London, 1851; Appointment to the Connecticut Commission for the Exhibition in Paris, 1855, Colt Manuscripts, Wadsworth Atheneum.

62. *Hartford Daily Times*, February 20, 1855.

63. Certificate of Honor, Universal Society for the Encouragement of Arts and Industry, London, June 30, 1856, Colt Manuscripts, Wadsworth Atheneum. The medals cited are contained in the Colt Collection at Wadsworth Atheneum; several are illustrated and described in Barnard, *Armsmear*, 121–27,

64. "Committee on . . . petition of Samuel Colt for an extension of letters patent," *Reports of Committees of the Senate of the United States*, 707, no. 279 (33d Congress, 1st Session, May 23, 1854), 2.

65. Robert Friedel, "Perspiration in Perspective: Changing Perceptions of Genius and Expertise in American Invention," in *Inventive Minds: Creativity in Technology*, ed. Robert J. Weber and David N. Perkins (New York: Oxford University Press, 1992), 11. The annals of American invention are filled with legends of heroic struggle and divine inspiration.

From Charles Goodyear, for whom rubber was "a divine mission . . . his passion, mistress and Holy Grail" [Grant, *Yankee Dreamers and Doers*, 210–11], to Thomas Edison, the Wizard of Menlo Park, with his reliance on random probing and his contempt for "the-or-retical science" [Wachhorst, *Edison: An American Myth*, 35], the story of invention has been told as a heroic quest composed of a set structure leading from heroic persistence to an unexpected chance encounter or clue, culminating with the gift of insight [David N. Perkins, "The Topography of Invention," *Inventive Minds*, 239].

66. Gustavus Myers, *History of the Great American Fortunes* (1907; reprint, New York: Modern Library, 1936), 399–400.

67. *Hartford Daily Times*, August 8, 1851.

68. Ibid., January 12, 1850; *Report of Commissioner of Patents, for the Year 1850*, part 1 (Washington, D.C.: House of Representatives Printers, 1851), 6.

69. Patterson, *Colt vs. the Mass. Arms Co.*, 34.

70. Sam Colt, Hartford, to Gen. Thomas Rusk, Washington, July 19, 1848, Colt Collection, CHS.

71. Broadside, Edward N. Dickerson to Arms Dealers, November 12, 1852, as cited in Edwards, *The Story of Colt's Revolver*, 1001.

72. V. B. Palmer, "Hints for Business Men," *Hartford Daily Times*, October 22, 1851.

73. "How Colt Got His Pistols Adopted by the British Government," *Scientific American*, January 16, 1864, 34.

74. *New York Times and Commercial Intelligencer*, October 15, 1839, as cited in Colt PFAMC, Scrapbooks, "Records of Colt Company Property," February 1836–June 1852, np. CSL, box 63.

75. *New York Evening Post*, October 18, 1839, as cited in Colt PFAMC, Scrapbooks, "Records of Colt Company Property," February 1836–June 1852, np. CSL, box 63.

76. George Catlin, *Episodes from Life among the Indians and Last Rambles*, ed. Marvin C. Ross (Norman: University of Oklahoma Press, 1959); Wilson, *Book of Colt Firearms*, 94, 179. Catlin's departure for South America was reported by Colt's friends at the *Hartford Daily Times*, who described his mission in seeking "a race who have not yet been changed by the march of civilization" [*Hartford Daily Times*, March 6, 1855]. Nine of the twelve paintings were included in the inventory of Sam Colt's estate in 1862. By the time of Elizabeth Colt's death in 1905, she had dispersed the pictures to family members; today they are scattered among museums and private collections [Estate Inventory, Col. Samuel Colt, 1862, Hartford Probate District Court Records, CSL]. Nine Catlin pictures, appraised at $27 (today's equivalent of about $1,500), were in the billiard room at Armsmear.

77. As cited in Bern Keating, *The Flamboyant Mr. Colt and His Deadly Six-Shooter* (Garden City, N.Y.: Doubleday, 1978), 164.

78. Sam Colt, Hartford, to J. Deane Alden, Arizona, February 23, 1860, Colt Collection, CHS.

79. Colt, "Memoir," *Armsmear*, 307; Testimony on House Bill No. 59, "for the relief of Samuel Colt," *The Congressional Globe* (33d Congress, 2d Session, February 3, 1855) (Washington, D.C.: John C. Rives, 1855), 550; Bill of Sale, J. Morgan Hall, Washington, July 18–31, 1837, Colt Collection, CHS; Bills of Sale, Edward Simms, Washington, January 8, 11, 18, 25, February 9, 17, March 5, 8, 1939—during the three months Colt spent in Washington lobbying to secure a patent, existing bills record the purchase of about 85 bottles of brandy and sherry costing $75.37 (today's equivalent of almost $5,000). At the time of his death Colt's wine cellar at Armsmear contained $2,715 (today's equivalent of almost $150,000) in liquor including 100 gallons of whiskey, 90 gallons of brandy, 1,428 bottles of

port wine, 939 bottles of sherry, and "15 Boxes Champaign [*sic*]," plus 5,400 cigars, appraised at the equivalent of almost $2,000 [Estate Inventory, Col. Samuel Colt, 1862]. Astonishingly, the "wine cellar at [the] Armory Office" contained almost two and a half times as much. Its contents were appraised at $6,379 (today, almost $350,000) and included 109 dozen-bottle cases of champagne, 1,102 cased-bottles of "old pale Brandy," claret, cider, madeira, gin, scotch, Jamaica rum, cherry brandy, and 650 bottles of "25 year old brandy," which, at $2.66 per bottle (almost $150 today), was the most expensive item on the shelves. It is hard to imagine a larger private inventory in the country at that time. Colt was no collector. His liquor was for gifts and for entertaining on an enormous scale.

80. Barnard, *Armsmear*, 366.

81. *West Point Courier and Enquirer*, June 29, 1837, as cited in Colt PFAMC, Scrapbooks, "Records of Colt Company Property," February 1836–June 1852, np. CSL, box 63.

82. Sam Colt, Paterson, to William A. Brown, West Point, June 29, 1837, Colt Collection, CHS.

83. Rohan, *Yankee Arms Maker*, 93.

84. *Report on Patent Arms* (Paterson, N.J.: Colt Patent Arms Manufacturing Co., 1838), CSL, box 63. Harney wrote Colt in February 1839, providing the most optimistic prognosis received during the Paterson years. The lieutenant colonel's comment that "the Rifles of your invention . . . have surpassed my expectations (which were great) in every particular . . . [and in] my honest opinion . . . no other guns . . . will be used in a few years," proved premature [Lt. Col. William S. Harney to Sam Colt, Washington, D.C., February 6, 1839, Colt Collection, CHS].

85. *New York Times*, January 18, 1841, as cited in Colt PFAMC, Scrapbooks, "Records of Colt Company Property," February 1836–June 1852, np. CSL, box 63.

86. William S. Harney to Sam Colt, Hartford, January 14, 1848, Colt Manuscripts, Wadsworth Atheneum.

87. J. K. Paulding, "Report from the Secretary of the Navy," *Reports of Committees of the Senate of the United States* (May 18, 1840), as cited in Colt PFAMC, Scrapbooks, "Newspaper Clippings," February 1836–June 1852, np. CSL, box 63.

88. Cited in "Repeating Fire-Arms: A Day at the Armory," *United States Magazine*, 229.

89. *Hartford Daily Times*, January 5, 1852.

90. *Minutes of Proceedings of the Institution of Civil Engineers*, vol. 11, session 1851–51 (London: Institution of Civil Engineers, 1852), 53–54.

91. Barnard, *Armsmear*, 160.

92. P. W. Henry to Sam Colt, February 22, 1840, cited in "Report from the Secretary of the Navy . . . in relation to the adoption of the improved boarding-pistols and rifles invented by Samuel Colt," *Public Documents of the Senate of the United States*, 360, no. 503, 6, 11–12.

93. C. Downing to Gen. Waddy Thompson [ca. February 1840], cited in "Report from the Secretary of the Navy . . . in relation to the adoption of the improved boarding-pistols and rifles invented by Samuel Colt," *Public Documents of the Senate of the United States*, 360, no. 503, 13.

94. This document, from a private collection, is reprinted in R. L. Wilson, *The Colt Heritage* (New York: Simon and Schuster, 1979), 36.

95. *Hartford Daily Times*, November 11, 1846.

96. Ibid., May 3, 1847. For a readership hungry for news of this exciting new fighting force, the *Times* ran a story describing how "at San Antonio once, when Hays wished to impress the Comanches," he staged an exhibition in which "man after man rode round a

hat at full speed . . . shooting into it five bullets in succession from his revolving pistol." The story concluded by describing the "Texas Ranger," as "a picked man" who had "left the old States," and whose "reckless and undaunting courage, . . . genial and hospitable" disposition, and "natural love of wild independent life," signified the possibility of rebirth through western migration.

97. John L. Davis, *The Texas Rangers* (San Antonio: University of Texas Institute of Texan Cultures, 1991), 21–22. Important to Colt, this was also one of the primary stories in the legend of the Texas Rangers.

98. Capt. Samuel A. Walker to Sam Colt, New York, November 30, 1846, Colt Collection, CHS.

99. *Hartford Daily Times*, February 19, 1847. Although Colt's Walker revolver was first manufactured in New Haven, Colt was in constant motion between New York, New Haven, and Hartford during this formative period and was apparently in Hartford, perhaps at his father's home, when Walker visited.

100. Ibid., November 15, 1847.

101. Ibid., February 24, 1849. One of the most hair-raising of these stories appeared in the Hartford newspapers in 1849, in the story of "A Texian [*sic*] Ranger, Dan Henrie," who was pursued by Comanches through the desert for days on horseback. The details read like an episode of Indiana Jones, complete with wild narrow escapes, quick wit, dashing "through fire," being "chased by wolves and Indians who'd killed his companions," having a "horse [which he "shot and ate"] torn to bits by wolves," and after "a week of almost incredible suffering," dashing across the country to "Hartford . . . to procure some of Colt's Repeaters."

102. Edwards, *The Story of Colt's Revolver*, 96.

103. Sen. Thomas J. Rusk, Washington, D.C., to Sam Colt, Hartford, December 27, 1848, Colt Collection, CHS.

104. Samuel Colt, New Haven, to Gen. Samuel Houston, Washington, D.C., February 24, 1847, Colt Collection, CHS.

105. Ibid. Many of the approximately one hundred letters selected for special care and bequeathed as part of the Colt Collection to the Wadsworth Atheneum in 1905 are testimonials that may once have been bound and maintained as a documentary portfolio.

106. G. Garibaldi to Samuel Colt, January 15, 1860; Victor Emanuel to Samuel Colt, July 24, 1860; Louis Kossuth to Col. Samuel Colt, March 27, 1853; Thomas Addis Emmet to Samuel Colt, May 28, 1852; T. Butler King to Gen. James Wilson, February 26, 1850; William M. Givin to Andrew Ewing, February 26, 1850; Maj. G. T. Howard and Capt. I. S. Sutton to Samuel Colt, February 26, 1850; Maj. O. Cross to Samuel Colt, February 26, 1850, Colt Manuscripts, Wadsworth Atheneum.

107. "Committee on Military Affairs . . . relative to 'Colt's repeating fire arms,' " *Reports of Committees of the Senate of the United States*, 512, no. 136 (30th congress, 1st Session, April 25, 1848), 3. Serving on this committee was Thomas J. Rusk, senator from Texas and the secretary of war of the Republic of Texas, who was one of Colt's staunchest allies.

"Report . . . relative to 'Colt's repeating fire arms,' " *Reports of Committees of the Senate of the United States*, no. 296 (30th Congress, 1st Session, February 12, 1849).

108. Lord Palmerston to Colonel Colt, December 21, 1853, Colt Manuscripts, Wadsworth Atheneum.

109. *Hartford Daily Times*, May 6, 1853.

110. Jabez Alvord, London, to George Alvord, Winsted, Connecticut, August 1, 1853, Alvord Papers, CSL.

111. Colt PFAMC, Cash Book A, January 1856-March 1864 (May 1, 1857), 47, private collection, Colt Archives, Wadsworth Atheneum.

112. Dix, "A Visit to Hartford in 1859," 70–71.

113. Among Colt's more prominent retail distributors were A. W. Spies and Co., "importers of guns, pistols, rifles," John Moore and Son, and Smith Young and Co., New York; B. Kittredge and Co., "importers of guns & sporting apparatus," Cincinnati and New Orleans; Tryon and Bro., Philadelphia; Palmers and Bachelders, Boston; Jasper A. Maltby, Galena, Illinois; James Canning, Mobile, Alabama; and Jerome B. Gilmore, Shreveport, Louisiana [Colt PFAMC, Ledger, 1856–62 (February 28, 1861), 180–520, private collection, Colt Archives, Wadsworth Atheneum].

114. A. E. Burr, Bill of Sale, September 2, 1854, Colt PFAMC, Bills and Receipts, CSL, box 63.

115. Wilson, *Book of Colt Firearms*, 76.

116. Ibid., 68.

117. John Sedgwick, "The Complexity Problem," *Atlantic Monthly*, March 1993, 96–104. Noting that "Americans' deficiencies in programming the VCR are so well known that they have become a staple of comedy," this article outlines how rapidly the "warfare" among manufacturers trying to outdo their competitors by loading their products with options escalates to the point where users, in a state of "cognitive overload," are left with a "machine from hell" that makes them feel stupid; not exactly the best marketing strategy.

118. Joseph G. Rosa, *Colonel Colt in London: The History of Colt's London Firearms. 1851–1857* (London: Arms and Armour Press, 1976), 33.

119. *Hartford Daily Times*, June 16, 1851.

120. *Punch*, July 5, 1851, as cited in Rosa, *Colonel Colt in London*, 15.

121. *Hartford Daily Times*, September 12, 1853, September 22, 1876.

122. Sam Colt, Richmond, to John Pearson, Baltimore, January 16, 1835. In working up models, Colt instructed his gunsmith to "go to a good cabinet maker & agree with him to make a handsome case with apartments [*sic*] in it to receive the gun & each of the several parts, . . . have it lined with green baize to prevent chafing, . . . [and] have the corners of the box tipt [*sic*] with brass and a small silver ornitment [*sic*] . . . in the senter [*sic*] of the lid." Colt instructed Pearson to have the "lid suitable for ingraving [*sic*] the name of the owner . . . [and to have] the ornament on the stock ingraved [*sic*] . . . [with] the Colts heads, in the center of which I want my name (S. Colts PR) engraved" [Sam Colt, Richmond, to John Pearson, Baltimore, January 23, 1835].

123. Sam Colt, Vienna, to Elisha Colt, Hartford, July 18, 1849, Colt Collection, CSL, as cited in R. L. Wilson, *Samuel Colt Presents* (Hartford: Wadsworth Atheneum, 1962), 236.

124. Colt PFAMC, Journal A, 1856–63 (February 20, 1861), 347, private collection, Colt Archives, Wadsworth Atheneum.

125. Ormsby produced half a dozen "cylinder scenes," beginning as early as 1839, illustrating a deer and Indian; a stage coach robbery; Texas navy's engagement with Mexico at Compache, 1843; a frontier pioneer defending his cabin; and Hays's Big Fight, showing western mounted horsemen chasing Indians [Wilson, *Book of Colt Firearms*, 52, 104, 107, 123, 152]. Ormsby graduated from the National Academy of Design in 1829, practiced in Albany and Lancaster, Massachusetts, before relocating in New York where he invented a ruling machine, a transfer press, and a grammagraph, a device for engraving on steel directly from medallions [Mantle Fielding, *Dictionary of American Painters, Sculptors, and Engravers* (1927; revised, Poughkeepsie: Apollo Book, 1986), 683]. A copy of his *A*

Description of . . . Bank Note Engraving (New York: W. L. Ormsby, 1852) was in Colt's library.

126. Newspaper advertisement from 1864, cited in Wilson, *Colt Engraving*, 124.

127. *Hartford Daily Courant*, March 10, 1864; Wilson, *Colt Engraving*, 53–55.

128. Barnard, *Armsmear*, 200; Wilson, *Book of Colt Firearms*, 20, 158; Wilson, *Colt Heritage*, 56. Although models and accessory packages are not identical, this comparison was made between the .34-caliber, five-shot Paterson pistols and the .36-caliber 1851 "navy" model, or "belt pistols," Colt made throughout the 1850s and is based on advertised price lists. During the Paterson era, Colt emphasized rifles and carbines, and his first government contract for one hundred rifles, purchased during the Seminole War, were priced at ninety dollars, then the equivalent of almost seven thousand dollars. Small wonder they weren't flying off the shelves.

129. "Committee on . . . petition of Samuel Colt for an extension of letters patent granted . . . 25, February 1836," *Reports of Committees of the Senate of the United States*, 707, no. 279 (33d Congress, 1st Session, May 23, 1854), 2; Testimony on House Bill No. 59, "for the relief of Samuel Colt," *The Congressional Globe* (33d Congress, 1st Session, June 19, 1854) (Washington, D.C.: John C. Rives, 1854), 1426, Edward N. Dickerson, New York, to *New York Herald*, January 19, 1854, as cited in "Reports of . . . committee . . . to inquire . . . whether money . . . offered members . . . to extend Colt's patent," *Reports of Committees of House of Representatives*, 353 (1854) (33d Congress, 1st Session, August 3, 1854), 41.

130. Bishop notes that by 1864 Colt produced 44 different styles of pistol, in 6 patterns, 11 lengths, and 27 finishes [*A History of American Manufacturers*, 2:741]. Ten years later the *Hartford Daily Times* [January 9, 1874] asserted that "No company . . . has produced so many styles and varieties of cartridge pistols."

131. Wilson, *Samuel Colt Presents*, 246–49. This gift, which featured top-of-the-line engraved decoration, three pistols, a rifle, and a shoulder stock, was worth the equivalent of about nine thousand dollars, based on price list quotations for guns and engraving.

132. Donald S. Ball, "Presentation Swords," *Man at Arms*, 2, no. 2 (March–April 1980), 10–17.

133. Sam Colt, New York, to William Colt, Hartford, July 21, 1844, cited in Edwards, *The Story of Colt's Revolver*, 153.

134. *Hartford Daily Times*, August 3, 1858.

135. In 1852 Colt offered to provide the Japan Expedition with the 500 revolvers on hand after the default of a contract with the Brazilian government [Sam Colt, Hartford, to Commodore Matthew C. Perry, Washington, D.C., March 10, 1852, Colt Collection, CHS]. The *New York Daily Times* [April 7, 1855] reported the value of the consignment at $1,400, consistent with a quantity of between 50 and 75. Commodore Perry appears to have distributed the arms liberally on his journey, and it is unclear if Colt actually donated the guns or was paid something by the Navy Department [Commodore M. C. Perry, Washington, D.C., to Sam Colt, Hartford, April 25, 1857, as transcribed in Barnard, *Armsmear*, 354–55].

136. Wilson, *Samuel Colt Presents*, 283–88, 291–92. This is the most complete list of gifts presented by Colt during his lifetime. It is, however, only a partial list of the gifts he made. A systematic analysis of Colt's gift strategy has yet to be conducted. Among the well-known military recipients are Mexican War officers Maj. Benjamin McCulloch, Col. Thomas H. Seymour, Col. Charles A. May, Gen. Franklin Pierce, Gen. Zachary Taylor, Commodore John Nicholson, Gen. Thomas Jessup, Lt. Col. William S. Harney, Col. David

E. Twiggs, and Col. John C. Hays, and Civil War generals George B. McClellan, William S. Rosecrans, Francis McDowell, Joseph K. F. Mansfield, Thomas West Sherman, Thomas F. Meagher, and Andrew Porter.

Wilson, *Book of Colt Firearms*, 572. Among the well-known Ordnance Department recipients are Col. Charles A. May, Maj. George D. Ramsay, and Col. James W. Ripley. War Department and other political officials who received gift pistols from Colt include Jefferson Davis, William Faxon, John B. Floyd, and Gov. Andrew B. Moore of Alabama.

137. Dudley Selden, New York, to Sam Colt, Washington, D.C., January 6, 1839, Colt Collection, CHS.

138. Patterson, *Colt vs. the Mass. Arms Co.*, 34; Sam Colt, Hartford, to Manby, London, June 22, 1852, Colt Collection, CHS.

139. "Colt Patent, & c., & c.," *Report No. 353 of the House of Representatives* (33d Congress, 1st Session, August 3, 1854), 1.

140. Testimony on House Bill No. 59, "for the relief of Samuel Colt," *The Congressional Globe* (33d Congress, 1st Session, July 8, 1854) (Washington, D.C.: John C. Rives, 1854), 1642.

141. "The Colt Patent in Congress," *Scientific American*, August 19, 1854, 389.

142. Keating, *The Flamboyant Mr. Colt*, 49.

143. *Hartford Daily Times*, October 25, 1848.

144. *London Times*, December 28, 1854, as cited in Colt PFAMC, Scrapbooks, July 1854–November 1860, CSL, box 28.

145. Contract, Amos H. Colt, New York with William W. B. Hartley and Colt's Fire-Arms, Hartford, October 11, 1859, Colt PFAMC, Papers, CSL, box 44.

146. Colt PFAMC, Ledger, 1856–62 (May 15, 17, July 9, 16, August 30, October 11, November 30, December 6, 1860), 381, 389, 396, private collection, Colt Archives, Wadsworth Atheneum. Private armorers in the Connecticut Valley and U.S. armories in Springfield and Harpers Ferry all supplied weapons on a massive scale to the South during 1859 and 1860. President Buchanan's war secretary, John B. Floyd, a Virginian, ordered Springfield to ship 65,000 muskets to Southern arsenals in 1860 and 85,000 from Harpers Ferry in 1859 and 1860, ordered Springfield to share manufacturing data and technology with Southern ordnance experts, and then considered closing Springfield altogether [Hallahan, *Misfire*, 106–8].

147. *Hartford Daily Times*, May 16, 1860. The *Times* described the South as "preparing for the worst."

148. *New York Daily Tribune*, April 27, 1861. Thanks to Ellinor Mitchell for tracking down this citation.

149. *New York Times*, January 14, 1861.

150. *Hartford Daily Times*, April 19, 20, 22, 25, 29, 30, 1861.

151. Sam Colt to Sales Agents, January 17, 1861, as cited in the *Hartford Daily Times*, April 22, 1861. The *Hartford Daily Times* responded (April 30, 1861) to a *New York Times* editorial that "alleged . . . [Colt] has advanced the price of his arms" by insisting that only the "commission heretofore allowed to New York houses has been withdrawn" and that the price would remain the same. Whether or not Colt continued to ship arms to the South after January, the company accounts record two enormous payments ($6,250 [$368,000 today] and $18,750 [$1.1 million today]) in March and April for arms received in New Orleans by Colt's old friend and Texas Ranger Gen. Benjamin McCulloch [Colt PFAMC, Journal A, 1856–64 (March 28, April 9, 1861), 353, 355, private collection, Colt Archives, Wadsworth Atheneum, 922–23].

152. *Hartford Daily Courant*, April 22, 1861. This astonishing story involved Solomon Adams, a "former inspector at the United States Armory in Springfield" and eventually the master armorer for the Confederacy, who was in town ten days after the attack on Fort Sumter. It ended with Adams evading "his pursuers . . . Union men of Springfield . . . in disguise."

153. *New York Times*, September 27, 1851, as cited in Colt PFAMC, Scrapbooks, July 1854–November 1860, CSL, box 28; *British Army Dispatch*, as cited in *Hartford Daily Times*, October 24, 1851. Colt may have been recruited by Mississippi governor John A. Quitman to help Lopez raise money and arms for an invasion of Cuba. Repelled in a first attempt in 1850, they tried again in 1851 and were captured and executed [James M. McPherson, *Battle Cry of Freedom* (New York: Oxford University Press, 1988), 104–7].

154. Elizabeth Hart Colt, Hartford, to Thomas H. Seymour, St. Petersburg, December 1, 1857, T. H. Seymour Collection, CHS; Colt PFAMC, Cash Book A, January 1856–March 1864 (November 30, December 23, 1857), 77, 81, private collection, Wadsworth Atheneum, Colt Archives, 878. J. Deane Alden, Frederick Kunkle and Mr. Brace traveled to St. Louis and Ft. Leavenworth, Kansas, on Colt business.

155. W. A. Croffut and John M. Morris, *The Military and Civil History of Connecticut during the War of 1861–65* (New York: Ledyard Bill, 1868), 73–74.

156. *Hartford Daily Times*, September 22, 1858.

157. Commission, First Connecticut Rifles, Gov. William A. Buckingham to Colonel Samuel Colt, May 16, 1861, Colt Manuscripts, Wadsworth Atheneum.

158. *Hartford Daily Times*, May 18, 1861.

159. Ibid., May 21, 1861.

160. *Hartford Daily Post*, May 21, 1861.

161. *Hartford Daily Times*, May 31, 1861.

162. Ibid., June 15, 1861; James L. Mitchell, *Colt: The Man, the Arms, the Company* (Harrisburg, Pa.: Stackpole, 1959), 12. A Colt carbine in the collection of the Museum of Connecticut History is engraved on the barrel as a gift from Colt to a member of "Company I, 12th Regiment, Colt Guard Company."

163. John D. McAulay, *Civil War Breechloading Rifles* (Lincoln, R.I.: Andrew Mowbray, Inc., 1987), 13–19.

164. Sam Colt, New York, to William Colt, Hartford, July 21, 1844, cited in Edwards, *The Story of Colt's Revolver*, 153.

Chapter Three

The Cowboy Subculture

David T. Courtwright

The twentieth-century image of the cowboy, the most evocative of America's mythic figures, is that of a hero, a knight-errant with a horse and a gun. The gun, and his skill with it, make the cowboy a deadly antagonist, but only against rustlers, bandits, and renegades. In formulaic narratives the cowboy hero may shoot more people than all the outlaws combined, but his killings are justified and self-confidently right.

The men behind the heroic myth were less appealing figures. Journalists in western towns described cowboys as dependable and hard-working when sober but vicious menaces when drunk. Cowboys on sprees shot up towns, terrorized tenderfeet, squandered their wages on gambling and whores. "Nobody then thought of them as romantic," recalled a Montana rancher's wife. "They were regarded as a wild and undesirable lot of citizens." President Chester A. Arthur, in his annual message to Congress in 1881, complained that "a band of armed desperadoes known as 'Cowboys' " was making trouble in the Arizona Territory, "committing acts of lawlessness and brutality which the local authorities have been unable to repress." "Morally, as a class," the *Cheyenne Daily Leader* commented the following year, "they are foulmouthed, blasphemous, drunken, lecherous, utterly corrupt."[1]

The more candid memoirs are equally unflattering. The rancher Bruce Siberts remembered that most of the itinerant cowhands he saw in South Dakota in 1894 "were burned out with bad whiskey and disease." During the winter about half "were pimps, living off some cheap prostitute in Pierre. . . . Most of them had a dose of clap or pox and some had a double dose. All in all, most of the old-time cowhands were a scrubby bunch." Even the cowboys' celebrated freedom has been dismissed. "The cowboy in practice," observes the western writer Wallace Stegner, "was and is an overworked, underpaid hireling, almost as homeless and dispossessed as a modern crop worker, and his fabled independence was and is chiefly the privilege of quitting his job in order to go looking for another just as bad. That, or go outside the law, as some did."[2]

The realistic image of the cowboy as a hired hand with a borrowed horse, a mean streak, and syphilis may be at odds with the heroic myth. But it is not at odds with the argument that the age and gender characteristics of a place or group in conjunction with its social institutions and norms determine the amount of violence and disorder. The cowboys of the Great Plains were young, male, single, itinerant, irreligious, often southern-born, and lived, worked, and played in male company. In the most expansive and violent years of the range cattle industry, the late 1860s and 1870s, many cowboys were combat veterans and almost all carried firearms. The nature of their work precluded drinking on the job, but they made up for it in payday binges. Those who survived the bad liquor and shooting scrapes found themselves back in the saddle, penniless, doing a job that was almost as dangerous as the whiskey mills themselves and in which few lasted for long.

Cowboys, in short, were lower-class bachelor laborers in a risky and unhealthful line of work. They were members of a disreputable and violent subculture with its own rules for appropriate behavior. The word "subculture" is, I realize, a loaded one, connoting to some a radical rejection of all values and virtues of the dominant culture. That was not true of cowboys. Their politics were usually conventional, as were the courtesy and deference they showed to respectable women. And they certainly worked hard. But much else in the cowboy code was unconventional, and therein lies the point of the term. The unwritten rules which governed their lives and which they passed on to new hands were often at odds with the norms of the Protestant core culture. For the cowboy to become a symbol of the American experience required an act of moral surgery. The cowboy as mounted protector and risk-taker was remembered. The cowboy as dismounted drunk sleeping it off on the manure pile behind the saloon was forgotten or transmogrified into a rough-edged, heart-of-gold fellow who liked an occasional bit of fun.

Origins and Character

The American cowboy subculture, like most frontier cultures, blended elements from different ethnic groups. Its deepest roots, however, were Spanish. It was the Spanish who introduced horses and cattle into the Americas and who perfected the techniques of mounted ranching, such as lassoing cattle from horseback. And it was the Spanish who first brought cattle to Texas and Alta California, two remote provinces on their northern frontier. Americans who settled in Texas in the nineteenth century combined Carolina cattle traditions with Spanish ranching techniques, equipment, and stock and added a few innovations like the chuck wagon. After the Civil War they spread themselves and their cattle into the vast grasslands formerly occupied by the bison, whose great herds were being systematically destroyed by professional buffalo hunters. The expansion of the range cattle industry reached its peak in 1885, with perhaps 7.5 million head feeding on the Great Plains north of Texas and New Mexico. The industry thereafter rapidly declined, owing to a combination of overgrazing, harsh winters, westward expansion of farming, and barbed-wire fences. By the early twentieth century the cowboys were fast diminishing, surviving more in the realm of legend than in occupational fact.

The tasks associated with the range cattle industry—rounding up cows, branding calves, castrating bulls, breaking horses, and trail drives to railheads or northern pastures—required youth, strength, endurance, and cool courage. Texas cattle were easily spooked creatures whose impressive horns and heft could kill a man in seconds. Cowboys on the trail had to be constantly alert not only for stampedes but for human and animal predators. They made do with little sleep and indifferent food, were continually exposed to foul weather, and, like soldiers in the field, had to learn to live with discomfort and minor injuries. That, or quit. Of the roughly 35,000 men who accompanied herds up the trails from 1867 through the 1880s, only a third participated in more than one drive.[3] As in gold mining, disillusionment and accidents quickly thinned their ranks. The constant attrition kept cattle herding a young man's game. The average age of cowboys in 1880 was twenty-three or twenty-four years.[4]

Many of the early cowboys were Texans or Texas immigrants, typically Confederate veterans ("TNT dressed in buckskin") or their sons who migrated to the state after the Civil War. The majority of cowboys were Anglos, though by some accounts a seventh were black men, mainly ex-slaves from Texas ranches. Perhaps another seventh were Mexicans. White southern, African-American, and Mexican-American cowboys had at least one thing in common, apart from mutual dislike. All came from cultures that stressed the desirability of decisive action to redress insult or injury. Texas-born cowboys were particularly notorious for their willingness to resort to guns to settle personal disputes, a trait which contributed to the high level of homicidal violence (32 per 100,000 in 1878) in the state in the decades after the Civil War.[5]

If cowboys were concerned with their standing in the eyes of their peers, they cared little for conventional social institutions. Few had wives or lived with their parents, unless they happened to be working on the family ranch. Their outlook was this-worldly, not so much antireligious as irreligious. "After you come in contact with nature you get all that stuff knocked out of you," explained "Teddy Blue" Abbott. "You could pray all you damn pleased, but it wouldn't get you to water where there wasn't water."[6]

A preacher who could "get to water," who could rope a calf or face down a bully, commanded the cowboys' respect. After Daniel Tuttle, the Protestant Episcopal Bishop of the Diocese of Utah, thrashed a stage driver for swearing in the presence of a woman, ranchers, miners, and even an occasional sporting man traveled from miles around to have a look at the fighting clergyman. Pugilistic Christianity was fine with cowboys. They were indifferent to the more peaceable sort and regarded regular churchgoing as unequivocally in the feminine realm. Though a few professed to worship in the "outdoor church of nature" and others claimed to have "got religion," orthodox Christianity was fundamentally at odds with the cowboys' masculine self-image.[7]

What was in keeping with their self-image was a gun. With the exception of professional hunters, cowboys were the most heavily armed civilians anywhere in post–Civil War America. They carried repeating rifles and revolvers, typically large-bore, military-issue weapons whose .44- or .45-caliber bullets did considerable and often fatal damage. Prior to 1880 these weapons were a necessary evil, given the possibility of encountering hostile Indians, robbers, rustlers, rattlesnakes, bears, and the like. But whatever the cowboys' guns bought in the way of deterrence and emergency use was paid for by an increase in accidental death and injury. Cowboy and noncowboy alike died when guns tipped over, dropped from pockets, or fell from blankets. The *Caldwell Post*, a Kansas cattle-town newspaper, estimated that five cowboys were killed by accidental gun discharges for every one slain by a murderer. Those who survived accidents were often horribly injured, living out their lives with shattered knees or shot-away faces.[8]

The other evil associated with gun toting was the increased incidence of unpremeditated homicide. "I always carried a gun because it was the only way I knew how to fight," Abbott admitted. "That was the feeling among the cowpunchers. They didn't know how to fight with their fists. The way they looked at it, fist fighting was nigger stuff anyhow and a white man wouldn't stoop to it." Abbott, whose memoirs are unusually self-revealing, explained how his trigger-happiness led to a shooting:

> I was really dangerous. A kid is more dangerous than a man because he's so sensitive about his personal courage. He's just itching to shoot somebody in order to prove himself. I did shoot a man once. I was only sixteen, and drunk. A bunch of us left town on a dead run, shooting at the gas lamps. I was in the lead and the town marshal was right in front of me with his gun in his hand calling, "Halt! Halt! Throw 'em up!" And I throwed 'em up all right, right in his face. I always had that idea in my head—"Shoot your way out." I did not go into town for a long time afterwards, but he never knew who shot him, because it was dark enough so he could not see. He was a saloon man's marshal anyway and they wanted our trade, so did not do much about it. That was how us cowboys got away with a lot of such stunts. Besides, the bullet went through his shoulder and he was only sick a few days and then back on the job. But they say he never tried to get in front of running horses again.

Here youthful irresponsibility and intoxication combined with the need to demonstrate courage to produce a violent confrontation, the standard formula for a male group disaster. Had the bullet entered a few centimeters in and down, the hapless marshal would have been killed, dead because a drunken boy was acting out a subcultural fantasy of shooting his way out of trouble.[9]

Cowboys used their guns to act out any number of roles, the deadliest of which was *nemo me impugnit*, "no one impugns me." Harry French, a Kansas railroad brakeman, witnessed a fight between cowboys riding in the caboose of his cattle train. It began during a card game when one man remarked, "I don't like to play cards with a dirty deck." A cowboy from a rival outfit misunderstood him to say "dirty neck," and when the shooting was over one man lay dead and three were badly wounded.[10]

This was a classic scenario for homicide. Then as now most killings arose spontaneously in a group situation involving alcohol, gambling, or some other vice in which socially marginal men suddenly turned on one another with deadly weapons in response to an insult, curse, jostle, or dispute over a small sum of money. From our vantage the disputes seem trivial, though the cowboys undoubtedly viewed them differently, as crucial if dangerous tests of their mettle. "That was one thing that got many a man," Abbott conceded, "that foolish sensitiveness about personal courage."[11]

Cattle-Town Sprees

This sort of hot-tempered gunplay seldom erupted when cowboys were on the trail. Drinking and rambunctious behavior were not tolerated in a situation where an impulsive act could kill or maim innocent men and destroy thousands of dollars worth of cattle. Cowboys in the saddle were sober employees who assumed large responsibilities and discharged them well.[12] Journalists and writers who knew this side of their life often defended the cowboys from their detractors, publishing favorable accounts of their colorful and sometimes heroic activities—breaking broncos, turning a stampeding herd, thwarting rustlers. These stories of cowboy competence and courage, suitably embellished, formed the basis for the heroic myth.

Journalists and writers who only saw the cowboys when they came to town formed a very different impression. Like sailors in port, a simile that often occurred to them, they saw young men mad to spend their accumulated wages. This was especially true at the end of long cattle drives, around which rituals of pent-up consumption, pleasure, and status developed. First a visit to the barber to remove several months' growth of hair and beard, then a trip to the dry goods store for a new hat, clothes, and fancy boots. Then a meal featuring delicacies unavailable on the trail: oysters, celery, eggs. Then on to the saloon, gambling room, theater, dance hall, and brothel, perhaps ending the night by shooting out the street lights or "taking the town." The latter was a sure way to impress peers and earn a reputation, a large consideration for the greenest cowboys, who seem to have been more prone than the experienced hands to go wild.[13]

Cowboy sprees had three important consequences, all undesirable from the standpoint of individual well-being and social order. They made the cowboy's life even more dangerous and unhealthful. They kept many cowboys impoverished, dependent, and unable to marry. And they attracted vice predators, who, as on the mining frontier, heightened the level of violence and disorder.

In the heroic myth cowboys are the very picture of sinewy health. The geologist David Love, who grew up in Wyoming in the early twentieth century, recalled that they were "lean, very strong, hard-muscled, taciturn bachelors," mostly in their twenties or early thirties, who worked without complaint from daylight to dark. But he also saw something else, something left out of the myth:

Most were homely, with prematurely lined faces but with lively eyes that missed little. . . . Many were already stooped from chronic saddle-weariness, bowlegged, hip-sprung, with unrepaired hernias that required trusses, and spinal injuries that required a "hanging pole" in the bunkhouse. This was a horizontal bar from which the cowboys would hang by their hands for 5–10 minutes to relieve pressure on ruptured spinal disks that came from too much bronc-fighting. Some wore eight-inch-wide heavy leather belts to keep their kidneys in place during prolonged hard rides.

The damage done by bucking animals, accidents, frostbite, and lightning storms was compounded by a monotonous and inadequate diet. Cowboy grub was long on meat, flour, and beans. It was short on fresh fruit and, ironically, dairy products. In the early years the cowboys did not even have milk for coffee, which they called "blackjack" or "bellywash" and drank hot and strong. This imbalanced, calcium-deficient diet may have contributed as much to their celebrated bow-leggedness as did long hours in the saddle.[14]

When these rickety young men rode into town they hit the saloons, false-fronted palaces full of smoke, gamblers, tubercle bacilli, and spittoons. There they used their hard-earned wages to treat themselves and their comrades to round after round of drinks, or what they took to be drinks. Liquor dealers commonly watered whiskey to maximize profits, concealing their chicanery and restoring the kick by adding stimulants like strychnine and tobacco. Cowboys drank this stuff neat and became extravagantly intoxicated, not so much drunk as on a polypharmaceutical jag, their bodies full of several different kinds of poisons.[15]

The end-of-trail binges often ended in the red-light district. The name originated in Dodge City from the railroad brakemen's custom of leaving their red lanterns outside the door to avoid interruption. Cowboys were equally avid customers of cattle-town prostitutes, some of whom were as young as fourteen years. Commercial prostitution was tolerated because of its profitability and because of the common belief that it provided a safety valve for working-class men who might otherwise sexually assault respectable women—which assaults were, in fact, rare.[16]

The social rationalizations on behalf of prostitution did nothing to alter the fact that it was a leading cause of venereal disease. Studies undertaken in the early twentieth century showed that the majority, in some instances 90 percent or more, of prostitutes harbored gonorrhea or syphilis; that prostitution was a prolific source of venereal infection; and that unmarried men were more likely to be infected than married men. The greatest venereal risk to cowboys who visited prostitutes was undoubtedly syphilis. Known to doctors as "the great imitator," the disease often returned later in life in the form of paresis, locomotor ataxia, or aortic aneurism, fatal souvenirs of their youthful encounters with whores.[17]

Sprees destroyed savings as well as health, reinforcing what was transparently a two-class system. A cattle*man* was a capitalist and employer, generally married, who lived in a ranch house built on his own land. A *cowboy* was an employee, unmarried, who tended cattle marked with another man's brand and who lived in a bunkhouse ("doghouse," "shack," "dump," or "ram pasture") built on another man's land.[18] The bunkhouse was not destiny. Cowboys who saved their wages, a dollar or at most two a day, could eventually acquire a small ranch and herd, slender but sufficient means for starting their own families. But those who kept spending their money on liquor, gamblers, and prostitutes could not achieve the stake necessary to escape their status as hirelings. Without property of their own they were not in a financial or social position to marry, potential brides being scarce and choosy about their suitors. And the absence of a wife and family made it more likely that they would continue to spend their earnings on in-town sprees. The result was a literally vicious circle.

Among those who profited from the cowboys' recurring dissipation were the gamblers and prostitutes who flocked to the cattle towns during the shipping season, moving on during the winter or when the trade was slack. Prostitutes earned their money directly while gamblers relied on a combination of skill, house odds, and cheating to separate cowboys from their wages. One New York firm specialized in selling marked or "advantage" decks to professional gamblers for $10 a dozen or $85 a gross. Loaded ivory dice were sold in sets of nine (three high, three low, three square) for $5 apiece. Why cowboys kept coming back to the saloon gaming tables against men so equipped is puzzling, though some showed clear signs of being compulsive gamblers, easy marks for a card sharp. Other cowboys, shrewder perhaps, quit the saddle and became professional gamblers themselves.[19]

Few gamblers retired to a life of luxury. The money was sometimes good but they spent it every bit as fast as the cowboys they fleeced. The prostitutes, who often lived or associated with gamblers, spent just as recklessly. A few made money and quit the trade. Some married out, though it is hard to know how many, for they covered their tracks. But the prostitutes' more usual fate was a miserable existence copulating with sweaty strangers, earning less for their trouble as they aged. The alms-house was a common end, as was suicide by overdose or poison.[20] Many sought solace in alcohol and other drugs, typically opiates in the 1870s and 1880s and cocaine and opiates from the 1890s on.

As on the mining frontier, arguments over women and cards could quickly turn into deadly confrontations. Abbott, who witnessed several shooting scrapes in bars and sporting houses, recalled that saloon men and tinhorn gamblers were as apt to get themselves killed as cowboys. The historian Robert Dykstra, who studied newspaper reports of homicides in five booming Kansas cattle towns, confirmed Abbott's impression. He found that precisely as many cowboys were victims of homicide as men identified as gamblers.

Dykstra also found that the average incidence of homicide in the five municipalities—Abilene, Ellsworth, Wichita, Dodge City, and Caldwell—was 1.5 per town per year. This may seem a small number, but so was the average population, which did not exceed 3,000. The resulting homicide rate was quite high, 50 or more per 100,000 persons per year. Someone living in (or more likely visiting) a Kansas cattle town was ten times as likely to be murdered as a person living in an eastern city or in a midwestern farming county.

Actually, more than ten times as likely. Because Dykstra did not count all homicides outside town limits or before the towns existed as municipalities (when, at least in the case of Dodge City, there were even more killings) and because the newspaper series he used had one significant gap, the true rate was undoubtedly higher. Roger McGrath, who has reexamined Dykstra's methods and data, thinks it likely that Dodge City's actual homicide rate was in the range of that of the California mining town of Bodie, 116 per 100,000. Fort Griffin, Texas, another frontier town frequented by cowboys, buffalo hunters, and soldiers, had an even higher rate, 229 per 100,000 during its boom years in the 1870s.[21]

Fort Griffin is the perfect illustration of what happens when the biological, demographic, cultural, and social forces conducive to violence intersect in one place and time. In the 1870s the town was in the middle of the Central Texas frontier zone, an exceptionally violent region in an unusually violent state. It had a hunting, grazing, and military economy and therefore a large surplus male population, including many southern-born men who were combat veterans, sensitive about personal honor, and deeply contemptuous of other races. Family and religious life were inchoate for the transient, lower-class men, who lived and took their recreation in male groups. That recreation involved the consumption of large amounts of liquor, often in a spree pattern, and vices that could trigger sudden conflict. The conflicts were settled with deadly weapons that the combatants routinely carried. Given these circumstances, it is hardly surprising that the homicide rate was so high.

Legal Ambivalence

When differences in lethal violence are of this magnitude, homicide in Fort Griffin in the 1870s being nearly forty times as common as homicide in Boston, one is prompted to ask why the citizens put up with it. It was obvious that the spree pattern and the local vice industry were among the primary sources of violence and disorder. It was equally obvious who the culprits were. Why was the problem allowed to fester?

On this point, at least, historians are unanimous. The answer is money. A cowboy at the end of a drive had perhaps $50–$90 in his pocket, a large sum in a cash-short region. Some of his wages were bound to go to the vice parasites, but local merchants, barbers, and restaurant and hotel operators knew they would get their share, either directly from the cowboys or from the gamblers and prostitutes, who were as free-spending as their victims. Jacob Karatofsky, an immigrant dry-goods merchant who operated the Great Western Store in the heart of Abilene, understood the situation well. He sold blankets, boots, and hats to the cowboys and "fancy dress goods" to the town's prostitutes, who had expensive tastes and the wherewithal to satisfy them. When the cattle trade left

Abilene Karatofsky went with it, first to Ellsworth and then to Wichita, where business was sufficiently brisk to open two stores.[22]

The profitability of such commerce made it inexpedient to have too much law and order. The disorderly behavior of their drunken visitors was a chronic problem, but businessmen knew that if the town marshal came down too heavily the cowboys would take their cattle and their wages elsewhere. The same logic applied to the suppression of vice. Cowboys would not come to town if they could not have a good time. To deny business to the local saloons and brothels was to deny it to the dry-goods stores and banks as well.

The best that could be done was to fashion a police and court system designed to keep the lid on. Cattle-town justice, to use the term loosely, was aimed at controlling, segregating, and profiting from cowboy vice sprees, not at discouraging them. It was intended to minimize both taxpayer expense and ancillary violence, though its inconsistencies—one is tempted to call them the cultural contradictions of capitalism—made control of violence difficult.

The task fell to some of the most legendary figures in frontier history, Wild Bill Hickok, Wyatt Earp, and Bat Masterson, as well as a host of less well known peace officers. The theory was to hire someone with the pluck to stand up to criminals and drunken cowboys and the lethal skill to stop them if lesser means of coercion failed. The fight-fire-with-fire approach was reasonable enough, though it sometimes failed in application, as when Wild Bill mistakenly shot and killed another Abilene policeman. And it was of no particular use during the slack season, when the saloons were empty and the gamblers and prostitutes had gone elsewhere. Marshals were then expected to serve the taxpayers in less dramatic ways, inspecting chimneys, rounding up stray swine, and, in the improbable case of Wyatt Earp, repairing the town's sidewalks.[23]

The marshals and local judges were also expected to raise money by taxing vice. Cattle-town judicial records are full of prosecutions for operating disorderly houses, but these were merely the means of securing revenue in the form of fines. In the town of Canada, Texas, creditable prostitutes were permitted to pay deposits on their fines and then were returned to the streets to earn the balance. In Fort Worth madams simply paid up and returned to their parlor houses, regardless of the number of previous convictions. Dodge City judges afforded equally lenient treatment to prostitutes for reasons of both municipal revenue and political expediency. We know, through the voyeuristic device of manuscript census records, that several of the prostitutes were living with prominent Dodge citizens, including the mayor, two policemen, and the vice president of the local bank.[24]

Gambling arrests, another source of revenue, produced their share of politically delicate moments. A sweep of gamblers in Coffeyville, Kansas, turned up a majority of the town council. Kansas saloon owners were not subject to the indignity of fines but had to pay a substantial licensing fee, which amounted to the same thing. In Wichita the saloon license fees and other vice fines produced so much revenue that in August 1873 the city treasurer announced that no further taxation would be required to support the local government.[25]

Cattle-town courts may not have been expected to stamp out vice, but they were expected to do something about serious personal and property crime. Yet even here commercial considerations intruded upon the exercise of justice. No cowboy or cattleman was ever executed for murder in the five towns Dykstra studied. Acquittals were common, as was a form of plea bargaining in which the offender pled guilty to a lesser offense, such as assault and battery instead of attempted murder. "Under the influence of liquor" was often offered, and sometimes accepted, as an extenuating circumstance. Business calculations were paramount. When in 1874 a group of Texas cowboys deliberately killed a black laborer in Wichita, no attempt was made to apprehend them. A newspaper editor criticized the inactivity of city and county officials only to have the wrath of the town's businessmen descend upon his head. They feared that the editor would stir up the citizens against the cowboys, provoking a retaliatory boycott. Or, as Abbott put it, "They wanted our trade. That was how us cowboys got away with a lot of such stunts."[26]

Vigilantism

Lax enforcement against drunken cowboys was one thing; lax enforcement against real outlaws was quite another. Cowboy sprees were dangerous but primed the local economy. Horse thieves, cattle rustlers, and highwaymen took property and lives without conferring any offsetting benefit. The official frontier justice system, inadequate and underfunded when not actually duplicitous, failed to deter such hardened criminals. They often escaped arrest or, if apprehended, the makeshift jails in which they were detained. In 1877 some five thousand men were on the wanted list in Texas alone, not a very encouraging sign of efficiency in law enforcement.[27]

The result was extralegal movements against outlaws. Most vigilante actions were limited in scope and controlled by elites, targeted thieves who would otherwise have escaped punishment, and symbolically affirmed the values of order and property. They were, in a word, socially constructive. But vigilante actions could and did miscarry, as when they were used to arbitrarily punish racial minorities or settle personal grudges. The latter form of abuse sometimes triggered private warfare, with friends and relatives of lynch victims seeking revenge against the vigilante faction.[28]

The Central Texas range country was the epicenter of vigilantism in the two decades after the Civil War. Most of these vigilante actions (known in Texas as "mob" actions) were summary executions of accused horse and cattle thieves who were hanged or simply shot down in their jail cells. Cowboys and ranchers generally played the role of executioner, but if they were caught or accused of rustling they might be executed in turn.

Vigilantism was easily abused. The "Old Law Mob," a group active in the Fort Griffin area in the early 1870s, included a rancher who was having problems with his wife. She hired an attorney to secure a divorce. The rancher warned the attorney to leave town within twenty-four hours. The attorney demurred and was found several days later with an "O.L.M." note pinned to his dangling body. No one troubled, or perhaps dared, to bury his remains, which were still visible a year later.[29]

Vigilantism, in short, was a dangerous substitute for professional police and regular courts. It is interesting that Canada's western provinces, which had both, experienced far less violence and lynching than the American frontier states. Canadian criminals were left to the North-West Mounted Police, an efficient and highly regarded force. The Mounties were aided in the their task by the prevailing Canadian attitude toward violence, which was condemned as an American aberration having no place in the realm of peace, order, and good government.[30]

Cowboy Gun Control

The Canadian frontier had something else that was initially lacking in American cattle towns: effective gun control. It was obvious to everyone that a drunken cowboy with a pistol was a good deal more dangerous than one without. Western newspaper editors and civic leaders supported laws forbidding the carrying of pistols and other deadly weapons, mainly dirks and Bowie knives. By the early 1870s most American cattle towns had nominally outlawed the practice. Cowboys were expected to "check" their guns when they entered town, typically by exchanging them for a metal token at one of the major entry points or leaving them at the livery stable before they hit the saloons.[31]

The gun laws were a good idea but poorly enforced, especially during the 1870s, the worst decade of killing on the cattle frontier. Cowboys persisted in wearing their pistols or took to concealing them, which was even more dangerous. Their defiance of the law was both a cause and an effect of the prevailing violence: as long as there were other armed men and outlaws about, it was hard to persuade them to surrender their weapons. Their resistance was as much emotional as rational. Guns were central to the subculture, objects of ritual significance to which the cowboys had been introduced in early youth. The idea that tin-star marshals (Yankees, no less) could take them away did not sit well.[32]

The situation changed in the 1880s and 1890s. As the threat of Indians and outlaws receded and the regular police system gradually became more professional and efficient, it was harder to justify carrying personal weapons for self-defense. Responsible cattlemen like Colonel R. G. Head, the superintendent of the Prairie Land and Cattle Company, began urging their hands to forgo gun toting, which he denounced as "a pernicious and useless habit," both illegal and foolish. "If you cannot freely and finally give up your pistol," he added, "then take it off, leave it at camp or rolled up in your bedding; by doing this I am inclined to the belief that you will soon learn to appreciate the absence of such an appendage." Head's successor, Murdo McKenzie, was equally adamant against firearms, and made it a point never to carry a gun himself.[33]

Gun control, enforced by determined employers, was probably the single most potent check on homicidal violence among cowboys, more effective than the specter of the lynch mob or even Wild Bill Hickok and Wyatt Earp. Getting hanged for shooting someone was a remote prospect, but getting the sack from an angry foreman was not. Head, McKenzie, and other cattlemen who insisted that cowboys lay aside their pistols understood that their men were not usually thinking straight when they pulled the trigger and that most shootings were either accidental or due to drunkenness, gambling, or hot-headed impulse. Better, then, that they should have no gun to reach for. It was a simple and obvious means of prevention and one that seems to have worked. By 1900 most cowboys had never seen a killing, much less participated in one. Many still owned guns—they were, after all, cowboys—but kept them out of sight, stowed in a bedroll or under the bunk.[34]

The emphasis on gun control, part of the larger rationalization of the range cattle industry, was complemented by a gradual change in the composition of its employees. By the 1880s the Texans, who of all the cowboys and cattlemen were the most predisposed to use firearms and to take the law into their own hands, were gradually being replaced by easterners, midwesterners, and European immigrants. The trend was especially marked on the northern ranges, where a new class of cowboys was helping to bring greater organization and discipline to the business. The newcomers were not as inclined to use their guns promiscuously or to insist on wearing them in town.[35]

If the South exported violence as its inhabitants moved to the frontier, what happened on the northern plains during and after the 1880s was the reverse, a northern order transplant. Once again, the level of violence was not simply a function of age and gender but was influenced by the immigrants' attitudes. Any population with a surplus of young men had a built-in tendency toward trouble. But the tendency was lessened if the surplus consisted, as in this case, of an increasing number of Europeans, easterners, and farm boys trying their hand at ranching and a decreasing number of heavily armed southern men.

Cowboy Myth

The gun-toting cowboy may have been declining in numbers and influence by the 1880s, but his career as a mythic hero was only beginning. It commenced in earnest with Buffalo Bill's Wild West, a popular rodeo and historical reenactment featuring cowboys racing horses, riding steers, and lassoing broncos. When not occupied with wild animals, Buffalo Bill's cowboys repulsed Indian attacks on wagon trains and mail coaches. Allied with scouts and soldiers, the cowboys were presented as the advance troops of white civilization, heroic "rough riders" who shot it out with the exotic but menacing Indians.

William F. Cody, the show's creator and manager, was a frontier jack-of-all-trades who had achieved fame as an actor and a pulp fiction protagonist. Alert to the commercial possibilities of the public's fascination with frontier adventures, Cody launched his Wild West as a touring show in 1883. By the time of his death in 1917 the Wild West had been seen by an estimated 50 million people in a dozen countries in North America and Europe. That is, 50 million people saw the cowboy portrayed as a trick roper and Indian-fighting hero rather than a spree-prone hireling in a shrinking industry.

Buffalo Bill's Wild West was only the most spectacular vehicle of cowboy myth-making, a flourishing business that ran the gamut from hack writers like Prentiss Ingraham and Ned Buntline to real talents like the novelist Owen Wister and the painters Frederic Remington and Charles Russell. Cody's success inspired no fewer than 116 competing shows. Most were short-lived but at least one, the Miller Brothers' 101 Ranch Wild West Show, managed to last until the Great Depression. By that time the myth-making enterprise had shifted to a new and more cost-efficient medium, the motion picture.[36]

Western themes figured in movies as far back as 1903, when Edwin S. Porter released his innovative *The Great Train Robbery*. By the early 1920s Hollywood had a stable of western stars, among them William S. Hart and Tom Mix, a veteran of the Miller Brothers' show. The popularity of the western declined somewhat during the 1930s when star actors like Gene Autry were confined to "B" movies, but in 1939, Hollywood's *annus mirabilis*, the western film began a renaissance with big-budget features like *Dodge City* and *Union Pacific*. The epic westerns of the 1940s were not simply cowboy movies. They portrayed an array of frontier characters, although cattlemen and cowboys, whose colorful clothing, horses, and guns and penchant for deeds over words made them ideally suited to the action-oriented medium, remained stock figures. In films such as *American Empire* (1942) and *Red River* (1948) they were accorded central roles.[37]

The western film continued its dominance through the 1950s. Between 1950 and 1961 Hollywood studios churned out more than 1,200 films about the past, over half set in the years between 1866 and 1890. This chronological imbalance—audiences must have thought American history synonymous with the late nineteenth century—was due to the mass production of westerns. Competing media were also saturated. Publishers sold an average of 35 million paperback westerns a year. The new television networks reprised countless western movies and were soon producing their own western programs. By 1959 there were thirty running in prime time, including eight of the top ten shows. The most enduringly popular of these, *Gunsmoke*, had begun as a successful radio drama, making its television premiere in 1955. When it went off the air in 1975 it was the longest-running series in television history.[38]

Gunsmoke was the genre's last hurrah. Westerns declined in the 1960s and 1970s, becoming progressively fewer in number, more self-referential, and darker in tone. But they continued to have at least one thing in common with their predecessors: they apotheosized male violence and marginalized women and children. The mise-en-scène was a town, outpost, or ranch on the high-gender-ratio frontier, not a family farm in a demographically normal region. The basic plot, even if morally ambiguous and sympathetic to Indians, was still that of masculine corporate adventure. Individual men came together, fought for a common cause against a group of opposing men, and then went their separate ways, unless killed or snared by a woman in a romantic interlude. Gunfire and wedding bells were functionally equivalent in westerns. They both signaled that a man was about to be taken out of action, honorably in the one instance, prosaically in the other.[39]

Did the mass exposure of three generations of audiences to violent male adventurers in the guise of cowboys and other gun-toting western characters influence the level of actual violence in American society? This is an important yet frustrating question. Important because there are psychological reasons to suppose that such exposure made a difference. Frustrating because effects of mass media are difficult to isolate and measure.

Experimental studies of varying scope and ingenuity have shown the viewing of violent characters to be positively correlated with aggressive behavior, although the effect is not necessarily strong, permanent, or universal. The most pronounced effect (though weak in comparison to those of variables like alcohol abuse and family disruption) has been observed in less academically talented boys who are already relatively aggressive but who become more so after viewing rough-and-tumble episodes. Media violence, in other words, appears to serve as a trigger or an exacerbating influence rather than a primary cause of violent behavior.[40]

It may also reach deeper into our psyches. Our personalities emerge from the interaction of our genes, which are fixed and predispose us in some ways, and our social situations, which are fluid and present many possibilities for development and change. We become ourselves in no small part by emulating positive or negative figures in our social environment, something that has already been noted in connection with the behavior of men in barracks, saloons, mining camps, and other male preserves.

In the electronic age the social environment has come to mean more than flesh-and-blood people. It includes a thousand or so media personalities, the Elvis Presleys and Arnold Schwarzeneggers and Madonnas whom most of us have never met but whose images we nevertheless carry in our heads. Communication researchers have discovered that, for many people, these celebrities are socially real. People act like them, dress like them, talk like them, talk about them, talk *to* them, and even make love to them in their fantasies. As Wallace Stegner puts it, "We are not so far from our models, real and fictional, as we think."[41]

The dominant screen model for moviegoing and television-watching Americans in the mid-twentieth century was the frontier action hero, often though not always the mythic cowboy. He was personified by John Wayne, a cult star familiar to every American born before 1960. Wayne symbolized, and in his political statements explicitly affirmed, the belief that lethal means are necessary and appropriate to righteous ends. The cinematic personae of Wayne and other western stars not only legitimated gun carrying and violence, they fixed in the consciousness of an increasingly urbanized nation the whole mythic apparatus of the western range in the two decades after the Civil War. Though this realm was a sometimes violent and disproportionately male world, it became in its screen reincarnation ultraviolent and hypermasculine. The cattle frontier never closed. It just came back in technicolor.[42]

Or possibly in Southeast Asia. In many ways the best (though also the strangest) illustration of the pervasiveness of frontier myth in postwar America was the Vietnam War. The language of Vietnam GIs, young men who were more imbued with frontier imagery than any other group of Americans before or since, brimmed with cinematic clichés and western allusions. Nineteen-year-olds ate John Wayne cookies and John Wayne crackers out of C-rations they opened with their John Waynes (P-38 can openers). A John Wayne rifle was a .45-caliber service pistol—nobody could hit anything with it, but the Duke could mow them down at 300 meters. To "John Wayne it" was to attempt any foolish act of heroism. Stock short-timer advice to a cherry: Don't pull a John Wayne on me.

In Vietnam military operations had code names like Texas Star, Cochise Green, or Crazy Horse, the last featuring the Seventh Cavalry in helicopters. The deluxe Seabee bunker at Khe Sahn was called the Alamo Hilton. To "saddle up" was to head out on patrol against "the bad guys" in "Indian country" beyond the perimeter. "Dodge City" referred variously to the military complex at Tan Son Nhut; the contested valley between Charlie Ridge and Hill 55 in I Corps; or, for Navy pilots, Hanoi. "To get out of Dodge" was, generally, to leave any hostile or dangerous area.

"Cowboy" had a multiplicity of uses, usually ironic or pejorative. "The Cowboy" was Nguyen Cao Ky, the flamboyant South Vietnamese Air Force officer who served as prime minister and later as vice president. "Cowboys," plural, referred to draft-age male Vietnamese civilians; more specifically to the hoodlums and black marketeers who roamed Saigon on motorcycles, sometimes accompanied by prostitutes ("cowgirls"); or more specifically still to members of the ARVN Special Forces (LLDB) or to a new breed of U.S. Special Forces troopers who arrived after 1968. In Laos ("across the fence") cowboys were CIA paramilitary operatives, a secret Air Force helicopter unit the "Pony Express." FACs (forward air controllers) logged twelve hours a day "in the saddle." One FAC showed up dressed entirely in black—black cowboy hat, shirt, jeans, and boots—and announced that his reason for volunteering was that Laos seemed a good place to die. This was a man who had seen too many movies.[43]

Whatever their social consequences may have been, movie cowboys were very different from the genuine item. The historical cowboy was not a heroic gunfighter-avenger but an unmarried lower-class laborer who led a Jekyll-and-Hyde existence. He was a hard worker on the trail, loyal to his outfit and friends, and usually open, honest, and generous. But when he was on a spree, "drunk and dressed up and don't give a damn," he was a menace to himself and those around him.[44]

Cattle-town marshals did their best to keep serious trouble from erupting, though they were handicapped by the moral contradiction at the heart of the economic system. Open vice was profitable to their towns but attracted criminal elements along with thirsty young cowboys eager to shoot their pistols and blow their wages. The price of separating them from their money was a relatively high level of violence and disorder. Everyone in the real Dodge City understood this trade-off, which the location of the jail made explicit. It was on Front Street immediately opposite the cowboy saloons.[45]

NOTES

1. Nannie T. Alderson and Helena Huntington Smith. *A Bride Goes West* (rpt. Lincoln: University of Nebraska Press, 1969), 73; *A Compilation of the Messages and Papers of the Presidents*, vol. 11, ed. James D. Richardson (New York: Bureau of National Literature, n.d.), 4640–4641: "The Cow-Boys of the Western Plains and Their Horses," *Cheyenne Daily Leader*, 3 October 1882, rpt. in *Trailing the Cowboy: His Life and Lore as Told by Frontier Journalists*, ed. Clifford P. Westermeier (Caldwell, Idaho: Caxton Printers, 1955), 50.

2. Siberts with Walker D. Wyman, *Nothing but Prairie and Sky: Life on the Dakota Range in the Early Days* (Norman: University of Oklahoma Press, 1954), 100–101; Wallace Stegner, "Who Are the Westerners?" *American Heritage* 38 (December 1987): 36.

3. David Dary, *Cowboy Culture: A Saga of Five Centuries* (Lawrence: University Press of Kansas, 1989), 276. My brief and much simplified description of the range cattle industry draws on Dary's work and on J. Frank Dobie, *The Longhorns* (rpt. Boston: Little, Brown, 1950); Joe B. Frantz and Julian Ernest Choate Jr., *The American Cowboy* (Norman: University of Oklahoma Press, 1955); Edward Everett Dale, *The Range Cattle Industry*, rev. ed. (Norman: University of Oklahoma Press, 1960); [Joe A. Stout], "Cowboy," *Reader's Encyclopedia of the American West*, ed. Howard R. Lamar (New York: Thomas Y. Crowell, 1977), 268–270; Richard White, *"It's Your Misfortune and None of My Own": A History of the American West* (Norman: University of Oklahoma Press, 1991); Terry G. Jordan, *North American Cattle-Ranching Frontiers* (Albuquerque: University of New Mexico Press, 1993).

4. E. C. "Teddy Blue" Abbott, *We Pointed Them North: Recollections of a Cowpuncher* (New York: Farrar and Rinehart, 1939), 42.

5. *TNT: Workin' on the Railroad: Reminiscences from the Age of Steam*, ed. Richard Reinhardt (Palo Alto: American West Publishing, 1970), 95; [Stout], "Cowboy," 268; Philip Durham and Everett L. Jones, *The Negro Cowboys* (New York: Dodd, Mead, 1965), chs. 1–4. The one-seventh estimate for blacks may have been true in southeastern Texas in the years immediately after the Civil War, but if so the proportion shrank substantially during the 1870s. Cf. Jordan, *North American Cattle-Ranching Frontiers*, 214–215. Texas rate: Robert M. Ireland, "Homicide in Nineteenth Century Kentucky," *Register of the Kentucky Historical Society* 81 (1983): 134.

6. Dary, *Cowboy Culture*, 107, 209; Abbott, *We Pointed Them North*, 33.

7. Augustus L. Chetlain, *Recollections of Seventy Years* (Galena, Ill., 1899), 130–131; John E. Baur, "Cowboys and Skypilots," in *The American West and the Religious Experience*, ed. William Kramer (Los Angeles: Will Kramer, 1974), 41–70.

8. Charles Askins, *Texans, Guns and History* (New York: Winchester Press, 1970), 3, 7; *Trailing the Cowboy*, ed. Westermeier, 70–71, 72; George E. Goodfellow, "Cases of Gunshot Wound of the Abdomen Treated by Operation," *Southern California Practitioner* 4 (1889): 209–217; "The Fatal Six-Shooter Again," *Caldwell Post*, 20 July 1882, cited in *Trailing the Cowboy*, ed. Westermeier, 117; Donald Curtis Brown, "The Great Gun-Toting Controversy, 1865–1910" (Ph.D. diss., Tulane University 1983), 19, 89–91, 130, 152–153.

9. Abbott, *We Pointed Them North*, 247, 31–32.

10. *Workin' on the Railroad*, ed. Reinhardt, 96.

11. Abbott, *We Pointed Them North*, 251; Marvin E. Wolfgang, *Patterns in Criminal Homicide* (Philadelphia: University of Pennsylvania Press, 1958), 188–192, 196–197.

12. *Trailing the Cowboy*, ed. Westermeier, 25, 54; *Cowboy Life: Reconstructing an American Myth*, ed. William W. Savage Jr. (Norman: University of Oklahoma Press, 1975), 158.

13. Joseph G. McCoy, *Historic Sketches of the Cattle Trade of the West and Southwest* (Kansas City, 1874), 138–142; Abbott, *We Pointed Them North*, 256–257; *Trailing the Cowboy*, ed. Westermeier, ch. 5; W. C. Holden, "Law and Lawlessness on the Texas Frontier, 1875–1890," *SHQ* 44 (1940): 190–191; Dary, *Cowboy Culture*, 209.

14. Love quoted in John McPhee, *Rising from the Plains* (New York: Farrar, Straus, Giroux, 1986), 89. Food: Joseph R. Conlin, "Grub and Chow," in *The American West, as Seen by Europeans and Americans*, ed. Rob Kroes (Amsterdam: Free University Press, 1989), 131; McCoy, *Cattle Trade*, 137. Coffee: Winfred Blevins assisted by Ruth Valsing, *Dictionary of the American West* (New York: Facts on File, 1993), 9.

15. Abbott, *We Pointed Them North*, 145–146; Richard Erdoes, *Saloons of the Old West* (New York: Knopf, 1979), 87, 89, 150–151.

16. Dary, *Cowboy Culture*, 217; Richard F. Selcer, "Fort Worth and the Fraternity of Strange Women," *SHQ* 96 (1992): 74; Neil Larry Shumsky, "Tacit Acceptance. Respectable Americans and Segregated Prostitution, 1870–1910," *Journal of Social History* 19 (1986): 673–674.

17. Allan M. Brandt, *No Magic Bullet: A Social History of Venereal Disease in the United States since 1880* (New York: Oxford University Press, 1985), 31; Mark Thomas Connelly, *The Response to Prostitution in the Progressive Era* (Chapel Hill: University of North Carolina Press, 1980), 68, 180nn 5,6; Howard B. Woolston, *Prostitution in the United States* (rpt. Montclair, N.J.: Patterson Smith, 1980), 180, 187; Lewis Thomas, *The Youngest Science: Notes of a Medicine Watcher* (New York: Viking, 1983), 32–34, 45–46.

18. *Trailing the Cowboy*, ed. Westermeier, 33; Dary, *Cowboy Culture*, 258, 284.

19. Loaded dice: Philip D. Jordan, *Frontier Law and Order* (Lincoln; University of Nebraska Press, 1970), 54–55. Compulsive gambling: e.g., John Brown, *Twenty-Five Years a Parson in the Wild West:Being the Experience of Parson Ralph Riley* (Fall River, Mass., 1896), 55–56. Became gamblers: Julian Ralph, "A Talk with a Cowboy," *Harper's Weekly* 36 (16 April 1892): 375–376.

20. [Robert Schick], "Prostitution," *Reader's Encyclopedia of the American West*, 973; Anne M. Butler, *Daughters of Joy, Sisters of Misery: Prostitutes in the American West, 1865–90* (Urbana: University of Illinois Press, 1985), 67–68; C. Robert Haywood, *Victorian West: Class and Culture in Kansas Cattle Towns* (Lawrence: University Press of Kansas, 1991), 29–30.

21. Robert Dykstra, *The Cattle Towns* (New York: Knopf, 1968), 113, 142–148; Roger D. McGrath, "Violence and Lawlessness on the Western Frontier," in *Violence in America*, vol. 1: *The History of Crime*, ed. Ted Robert Gurr (Newbury Park, Ca.: Sage, 1989), 134–135; Robert Tyrus Cashion, "An Examination of Frontier Violence at Fort Griffin, Texas" (master's thesis, University of Texas at Arlington, 1989), 17, 55. The most commonly cited source, Don H. Biggers, *Shackelford County Sketches*, ed. Joan Farmer (Albany and Fort Griffin: Clear Fork Press, 1974), 41, reports at least fifty-five killings, including twelve lynchings, at Fort Griffin over a period of twelve years. Cashion reports "a population of approximately one-thousand and almost as many transients." I have combined the two and rounded upward to two thousand for purposes of computing the rate. A work

commonly cited to deny that the trail towns were especially violent is Frank Prassel, *The Western Peace Officer: A Legacy of Law and Order* (Norman: University of Oklahoma Press, 1972). Prassel in turn cites statistics from U.S. Census Office, *Report on the Defective, Dependent, and Delinquent Classes . . . as Returned at the Tenth Census* (1888), 566–574, to substantiate his claim that New York and other eastern cities were more violent than western towns (17). However, these data are either biased or simply wrong. Leadville officially reported no homicides in 1880, but Elliott West, as noted in Chapter 4, found fourteen in just eight months. Moreover, Prassel's table (260) contains a significant transcription error: 9,067 murders for New York in 1880 rather than 37, which is what the Census report shows.

22. Dary, *Cowboy Culture*, 201; Dykstra, *Cattle Towns*, 89–90.

23. Dykstra, *Cattle Towns*, 116–124, 131–132, 143; Cashion, "Frontier Violence," 36.

24. Butler, *Daughters of Joy*, 102–103; Selcer, "Strange Women," 65–67; Carol Leonard and Isidor Wallimann, "Prostitution and Changing Morality in the Frontier Cattle Towns of Kansas," *Kansas History* 2 (Spring 1979): 41.

25. [Alfred T. Andreas,] *History of the State of Kansas* (Chicago, 1883), 1574; Dykstra, *Cattle Towns*, 127–128, 257–259; Leonard and Wallimann, "Prostitution," 39–40.

26. Dykstra, *Cattle Towns*, 128–131; C. Robert Haywood, "Cowtown Courts: Dodge City Courts, 1876–1886," *Kansas History* 11 (1988): 24, 31–32; Abbott, *We Pointed Them North*, 31.

27. Robert M. Utley, *High Noon in Lincoln: Violence on the Western Frontier* (Albuquerque: University of New Mexico Press, 1987), 172–173; C. C. Rister, "Outlaws and Vigilantes on the Southern Plains," *Mississippi Valley Historical Review* 19 (1933): 544.

28. Richard Maxwell Brown, "The American Vigilante Tradition," in *Violence in America: Historical and Comparative Perspectives*, ed. Hugh Davis Graham and Ted Robert Gurr (New York: Bantam, 1969); Joe B. Frantz, "The Frontier Tradition: An Invitation to Violence," ibid., 140–143.

29. Cashion, "Frontier Violence," 63; Richard Maxwell Brown, *Strain of Violence: Historical Studies of American Violence and Vigilantism* (New York: Oxford University Press, 1975), 246–251.

30. David H. Breen, *The Canadian Prairie West and the Ranching Frontier, 1874–1924* (Toronto: University of Toronto Press, 1983), 85–86; Carlos A. Schwantes, "Perceptions of Violence on the Wageworkers' Frontier: An American-Canadian Comparison," *Pacific Northwest Quarterly* 77 (1986): 54–56.

31. Brown, "Gun-Toting Controversy," 17; Clark C. Spence, "The Livery Stable in the American West," *Montana* 36 (1986): 39.

32. Yankee marshals: Abbott, *We Pointed Them North*, 28.

33. Brown, "Gun-Toting Controversy," 152–164, quotations 163–164.

34. Ibid., 435–440.

35. Joseph Nimmo Jr., "The American Cow-Boy," *Harper's New Monthly Magazine* 57 (1886): 880–884; Abbott, *We Pointed Them North*, 231.

36. Don Russell, *The Lives and Legends of Buffalo Bill* (Norman: University of Oklahoma Press, 1960), 21–32; John G. Blair, "Buffalo Bill and Sitting Bull: The Wild West as Media Event," in *The American West, as Seen by Europeans and Americans*, ed. Rob Kroes (Amsterdam: Free University Press, 1989), 262–281; Richard Slotkin, *Gunfighter Nation: The Myth of the Frontier in Twentieth-Century America* (New York: Atheneum, 1992), ch. 2; Dary, *Cowboy Culture*, 333.

37. George N. Fenin and William K. Everson, *The Western: From Silents to the Seventies,*

expanded ed. (New York: Grossman, 1973); Thomas Schatz, *Hollywood Genres* (New York: Random House, 1981), 46–47; Slotkin, *Gunfighter Nation*, chs. 7–9.

38. Garth S. Jowett, "The Concept of History in American Produced Films," *Journal of Popular Culture* 3 (1970): 813; Fenin and Everson, *The Western*, ch. 16; Robert G. Athearn, *The Mythic West in Twentieth-Century America* (Lawrence: University Press of Kansas, 1986). 183; Elliott West, "Shots in the Dark: Television and the Western Myth," *Montana* 38 (1988): 72–73; Dary, *Cowboy Culture*, 335.

39. John H. Lenihan, *Showdown: Confronting Modern America in the Western Film* (Urbana: University of Illinois Press, 1980), ch. 7; Schatz, *Hollywood Genres*, 53–54, 58–63; Michael Wood, *America in the Movies or "Santa Maria, It Had Slipped My Mind"* (New York: Delta, 1975), 42–43.

40. See James Q. Wilson and Richard J. Herrnstein, *Crime and Human Nature* (New York: Simon and Schuster, 1985), ch. 13.

41. John L. Caughey, *Imaginary Social Worlds: A Cultural Approach* (Lincoln: University of Nebraska Press, 1984); Stegner, "Who Are the Westerners?" 39.

42. The John Wayne cult is discussed in Slotkin, *Gunfighter Nation*, 512ff.

43. Paraphrasing Michael Herr, *Dispatches* (New York: Knopf, 1977), 209. Language from Herr and Charles Mohr, "U.S. Special Forces: Real and on Film," *New York Times*, 20 June 1968, 49; S. L. A. Marshall, *Crimsoned Prairie: The Wars between the United States and the Plains Indians during the Winning of the West* (New York: Charles Scribner's Sons, 1972), 155; Philip D. Beidler, *American Literature and the Experience of Vietnam* (Athens: University of Georgia Press, 1982); *Dictionary of the Vietnam War*, ed. James S. Olson (Westport, Conn.: Greenwood Press, 1988); Gregory R. Clark. *Words of the Vietnam War* (Jefferson, N.C.: McFarland, 1990); Christopher Robbins, *The Ravens: The Men Who Flew in America's Secret War in Laos* (New York: Crown, 1987); and personal communication with John Olson, Lydia Fish, and Larry Wright.

44. "Festive Cowboy," in *Trailing the Cowboy*, ed. Westermeier, 53.

45. Odie B. Faulk, *Dodge City: The Most Western Town of All* (New York: Oxford University Press, 1977), 85.

Chapter Four

"Another Branch of Manly Sport"
American Rifle Games, 1840–1900

Russell S. Gilmore

Henry William Herbert, America's first sporting writer and very nearly its first sportsman, expected that before the nineteenth century ended rifles would be obsolete in the United States. The "utility and honor" of weapons disappeared with the animals they killed, so that even in 1848 rifles were rare on the East Coast and shotguns certainly would become so when the small game gave out.[1] Herbert proved no prophet. By 1900, the rifle's honor, if not its utility, had greatly advanced—had in fact turned into a cultish adulation.

Nearly all military weapons before the middle of the nineteenth century were loaded from the front, or muzzle. They also did without the helicoidal grooves, or rifling, which could spin a bullet and create real accuracy, because such grooves slowed loading. Herbert assumed that the basic military weapon would always be a smoothbore—no great wonder because American experiments with the undersized Minié bullet, which would speed the loading of rifles, had not begun when he wrote. Yet seven years later, in 1855, rifles became standard issue in the American army, bringing a revolution as important, if not as dramatic, as military breechloaders would during the Civil War. The Minié bullet (whose hollow base expanded, under the force of powder gas, to grip rifling grooves) quintupled effective range, but its potential remained unrealized. The usual view seems to have been that shooting skill, while desirable in a recruit, was only a few men's birthright. After a little desultory firing to learn the mechanics of their new weapon, most regular army companies fired no more.[2] Civilians knew even less and in 1860, at the outbreak of the first great war of the rifle, turned anxiously to the few hobbyists who could offer instruction or formed themselves into groups and together attempted to master the machine that was to be central to their lives.[3]

Early battles established that the average northerner did not sit his horse very firmly and in most other ways seemed less fit for military life than his Confederate opponent. As part of a general feeling of inadequacy, Union troops—or at

Reprinted from *Hard at Play: Leisure in America, 1840–1940*, edited by Kathryn Grover (Amherst: University of Massachusetts Press; New York: Strong Museum, 1992). Copyright © 1992 by The Strong Museum.

least Union newspapers—assumed that the enemy also shot better. In fact, the general level of marksmanship on both sides was so low as to make comparison pointless.[4] Specific complaints mentioned snipers, whose "unerring rifles" picked off Union officers. But only selected soldiers with specialized equipment served as snipers. The North had them, too, whole regiments of them, and probably those who did the most spectacular mankilling on either side served the Union as Berdan's Sharpshooters. Detached to special duty whenever opposing lines became firm, they shot from platforms in trees or carefully constructed "nests," sometimes killing from a half-mile off. The weapon for such work was heavy— occasionally too heavy to hold[5]—and fitted with a telescopic sight. The Federal Ordnance Bureau apparently purchased only a half-dozen during the whole war, but recruits to a sharpshooters' unit often brought their own, and ballistic experimenters donated privately owned "slug guns," giving up an esoteric hobby to contribute their bit to the carnage.[6]

Most Americans who knew rifles before 1861 learned either in hunting or casual targetry. Informal match shooting with rifles of the pre-Minié kind, generally considered too slow in battle, had long been commonplace, especially on the frontier. Competitors usually fired three shots apiece at twenty rods (about 110 yards), each measuring the distance of his bullet holes from the target's center with a piece of string. The shortest string won cash, whiskey, or beef. On the Atlantic Coast, an occasional "American" club[7] shot similar matches with more precise rifles for less consequential prizes. Such clubs had no military features, held no parades, and were generally inconspicuous. But they contributed many of the Civil War sharpshooters who, when they carefully squeezed triggers, expected to see men die.

The other organized bodies of American marksmen were showy and less serious but vastly more important in numbers. During the burst of enthusiasm for gorgeously uniformed volunteer militia units in the 1830s, New York firemen formed the first "target companies," the elite of which differed from the militia elite chiefly in devotion to shooting practice. At a time when state troops often served out seven-year enlistments without firing their weapons, clubs such as the Pocahontas Guards assembled "the best shooters in the city" for frequent target excursions into the suburbs and, even allowing for their casual discipline (members occasionally looted shops along the line of march), were probably more effective military units.[8] By 1850, one estimate put the members of New York City target companies at ten thousand, "thousands" of whom had volunteered for the Mexican War. Not all were firemen, because the employees of individual factories, foundries, and shipyards had begun to get up target excursions after the same pattern, and some companies formed as ward organizations.[9] At least from the 1840s, armed bands parading the streets left respectable New Yorkers uneasy, and after the Draft Riot of 1863 the Quality spoke increasingly of disarming the lower orders, or at least of subjecting those who toyed with rifles to soldierly discipline. Colonel William Conant Church of the *Army and Navy Journal* heartily wished "target companies might decline and militia companies be built up on their ruins."[10]

No one seems to have been uneasy about the other block of shooting organizations in New York City, the *Schützenbünde,* and Mayor John T. Hoffman clearly had targeteers in mind when he congratulated his Germanic brethren on establishing that "love of the rifle is not incompatible with respect for the law."[11] During the period when it was sniping at target societies, the *Army and Navy Journal* endorsed *Schützen* as serious marksmen and a complement to the militia, quoting with approval a banner motto which read, "A sharp eye and a steady hand guard our right and Fatherland."[12] (Presumably Colonel Church concluded that as the sentiment was in English, the Fatherland referred to was the United States.) Describing the 1864 meeting of the New York *Schützen* Corps, a newspaper assured its readers that efficient police and the shooters themselves patrolled the grounds so that no one need leave his family at home for fear of disturbances. Another time, *Harper's Weekly* observed that although there was "a flowing beer keg under nearly every tree . . . no man was seen to be intoxicated."[13]

The only widespread quarrel with *Schützen* riflery seems to have been over its *Gemütlichkeit,* which was offensive to some and probably seemed inappropriate to most non-Germans. The typical *Schützenfest* started with a parade of uniformed marksmen, each brilliant with ribbons and decorations. After an elaborate meal, the club president began competition by firing several shots at a traditional wooden eagle target, the first for the president, then the governor, and finally for the *Schützen* corps and himself. Each member then took a turn and claimed prizes associated with whatever bits of the eagle he dislodged. The man lucky enough to break the final fragment was *König,* immediately smothered in flowers and kisses by as many as fifty blond maidens. Gamblers liked the novelty targets, such as a full-scale iron stag pursued by an iron dog, pulled suddenly along rails from one bank of bushes to another. To hit the deer was to win five dollars; to hit the dog was to forfeit that much, as well as a twenty-five-cent match fee. The women's contest used no rifles but a lance swinging on wires and paid off in parasols, combs, and the like. Serious shooting at a minutely divided twenty-five-ring mark sometimes inspired magnificent prize lists. One "honor target" at Shell Mount Park in San Francisco offered winners twenty-five thousand dollars in goods of all sorts.[14]

But social and fraternal features of the *Schützenfeste* seemed more important to most present, because often thousands listened to the Tyrolean singers or patronized the merry-go-rounds and lottery booths while only hundreds shot. The marksmen brought their much-extended families. Grandfathers drank beer and told stories; daughters danced (with whomever took their fancy—no one had to be introduced) while their mothers sat nearby darning socks. *Schützenbünde* often had women's auxiliaries, benefit societies, secret grips, and other trappings of the lodge, though as they expanded in the years after the Civil War, they seem to have become more cosmopolitan. By the turn of the century, German maidens occasionally found themselves obliged to crown and engarland an Irishman or other non-Teuton.

Unlike target companies, which never spread beyond New York and New Jersey,[15] *Schützen* clubs flourished before 1860 in every East Coast city with a noticeable German population, and in Buffalo, Cincinnati, Chicago, Milwaukee, St. Louis, and San Francisco as well. During the eighties and nineties, midwestern federations seem to have been the most vital, and they continued to add new clubs into the present century, as did those in California. The New York *Bünde* met early competition from other ethnic social and fraternal organizations of the sort that finally displaced *Schützen* clubs altogether, but, despite complaints over apathy, the Independent Corps (one of five New York City leagues) chartered a whole steamer for members and their families attending a European contest in 1890, and the 1895 fest at Glendale Park, Long Island, proved the largest to that date. Though *Schützen* riflery declined in the twentieth century, it continued to be important until 1917, when amused tolerance of German shooting ended abruptly. Even when it had been counted harmless, Americans had never been drawn to Germany's variant on target practice, which remained ethnically narrow and in the popular mind a sort of saturnalia.[16]

Yet if more Irishmen had been willing to compete for garlands and kisses in German parks, respectable New Yorkers would have been more comfortable. Instead, during the years following the Civil War, Irish in increasing numbers assembled as frolicsome and sometimes drunken bands for target parades into the suburbs. Such affairs took on a sinister look after the 1871 Orange Riot, in which Catholic Irish, organized under the cover of a grand picnic and "target excursion," tangled with a Protestant Irish parade. Revolver shots out of the crowd brought indiscriminate return fire from National Guard regiments assigned to protect the Protestants. When the shooting ended, fifty people lay dead or dying. The Orange Riot sped modern arms into the hands of the guard and helped create the National Rifle Association to teach their use.[17]

Two months after the riot, Colonel Church formally organized the NRA in his newspaper offices, but George Wood Wingate, a New York City lawyer and guard officer, actually created it. He had been a partisan of military rifle training ever since witnessing the marksmanship of Civil War volunteers. Wingate taught a British-inspired system which had attracted almost no attention in the United States before the Orange Riot. Now other guard officers pressed him for information and help. Wingate seized the chance and soon found himself supervising construction of the NRA's splendid Creedmoor range on Long Island, intended chiefly to train the New York Guard.

While studying range construction in England and Canada, Wingate had inquired into long-range targetry and on his return helped organize the Amateur Rifle Club, sixty-two New Yorkers interested in more precise shooting than the sort intended for the militia. Alonzo Alford, a representative of the Remington Arms Company, sat as chairman of their first meeting, which elected Wingate president. The Amateur Rifle Club did nothing until Creedmoor opened officially in June 1873 and thereafter confined itself to conducting a match for a gold medal at five hundred yards, considered a great distance by American riflemen (both target companies and *Schützen* corps usually stopped at two hundred) but only half that of the most important British shooting.

In this untried state, the Amateurs accepted a challenge from the Irish victors of Great Britain's Wimbledon match who, having won by a previously unparalleled score, looked to be champions of the world.[18] New York's *Forest and Stream* called it an example of "supremest American cheek."[19] The British game of small-bore shooting had evolved from military riflery into a fiendishly complex and demanding enterprise.[20] Though huge charges drove heavy projectiles with the maximum energy available from black powder, beyond half a mile the bullets deviated wildly due to cross-winds. Changing light affected sighting. Its devotees counted small-bore riflery a science, but as practiced in Great Britain it was nearer an art, requiring delicate sensibilities and extensive practice. Arthur Blennerhassett Leech, captain of the Irish team, called it "the poetry of shooting."

Not only had no member fired at Wimbledon distances, but the Amateur Rifle Club possessed not a single weapon suitable for practice. The five-hundred-yard rifles at Creedmoor had inappropriate stocks which raised egg-sized welts on the shoulder and sights without even the crudest lateral adjustment. But George Wingate, not one to underestimate the importance of equipment, almost certainly had a promise from his friend Alford before taking up the Irish challenge. Both the Remington and Sharps arms companies came forward immediately with pledges of weapons right for the contest and together put up the five-hundred-dollar stake that the Amateur Club had agreed to post.[21] The great international rifle contest was to try not only America against Britain but the best American machine-made breechloaders against the best handmade muzzleloaders of Europe. Weapons that loaded from the rear were much more convenient, especially for military use, but seemed to be inherently less accurate than weapons whose projectiles were pushed down from the muzzle. United States devotees of the older arm prophesied disaster, pointing out that even at Creedmoor muzzleloaders had won every match that admitted them. New York's *Turf, Field and Farm* feared that the Irish would "have a competition scarcely sufficient to make it interesting."[22]

The arms argument added to an already considerable excitement. One month after the challenge, a Michigan letter writer observed that the international rifle match had become the principal subject under discussion in sporting clubs throughout the country, and *Forest and Stream*, which felt sure that riflery was to be a great national preoccupation, began a seven-part series titled, "How to Shoot at Long Range."[23] George Wingate announced that the Amateur Club had

> accepted the challenge not for ourselves alone but in behalf of the riflemen of America. We have therefore sent out a number of circulars, intended to reach all classes of individuals interested in rifle practice . . . From New Orleans, Philadelphia, Massachusetts and the far West we have received response and during the summer we may expect to see a great assembly . . . at Creedmoor.[24]

In that hope, Wingate was entirely disappointed, though national interest—at this stage largely confined to sportsmen—continued to grow, and many agonized over the low initial scores turned in with the new breechloaders.

As team captain, Wingate had tested the rifles and knew they were capable of astonishing accuracy, but he knew also that American marksmen could not equal the experienced Irish man for man. If he organized his people thoroughly and synchronized their sights, however, team members could assist each other, the best judges of wind and light going first to determine settings for the others. By the end of the summer, Wingate had rationalized rifle shooting nearly as thoroughly as Remington and Sharps rationalized rifle production. At the time of the challenge, the Chicago *Inter-Ocean*, which believed, as did nearly everyone, that the Amateurs would be trounced by the Irish, printed an editorial that in retrospect seems ironic on every count.

> While these riflemen who have carried away the shield at Wimbledon have been practicing under scientific teachers, and popping away at a bulls-eye in a carefully constructed gallery, our boys have been shooting buffaloes upon the plains or taking a wild turkey on the wing . . . It will be a contest between trained efficiency and native skill, between the dainty hand of the city and the rough grasp of the woodsman. Should the result prove contrary to our confidence in the shooting qualities of our trusty marksmen, it will be because they are unaccustomed to be trammeled by any rules, or tied down to any particular form or custom.[25]

Canadians had essayed team organization (though their system was not nearly so rigorously worked out), and Wingate almost certainly got the idea from them. They offered him another bit of help in a letter from someone identified by the editor of *Forest and Stream* as "a distinguished Canadian rifleman." Be certain, said "Royal," to "keep your oldest and coolest shot for last."

It was a fine day and a fair crowd at Creedmoor on September 26, 1874, and the excursion trains brought thousands of new spectators as telegraphs reported the United States ahead at eight hundred yards, still a little ahead at nine hundred. Clearly the Amateurs had a chance, though the Irish normally did better at the greatest range. When an American prepared to fire the final shot at one thousand yards, the match hung on it. Colonel John Bodine, unlike the other members of the team a lifelong hunter and marksman, took his position with an unperturbed air. A friend offered him some ginger beer. As Bodine reached for it, the "unpoetic" (but melodramatic) bottle exploded, driving splinters of glass into his right palm. Doctor J. B. Hamilton of the Irish team rushed to him, pronounced the wound serious, and suggested delaying the final shot. Bodine declined and took up his position with a bloodstained handkerchief around his hand. Nearly ten thousand people fanned out down the range, providing a corridor through which he made a bull's-eye.[26]

The unexpected and cliffhanging win caused a sensation. Irish team members did not go directly home but stayed to participate in a gala and then traveled west with Charles Hallock, editor of *Forest and Stream*, for prairie chicken shooting and the usual unconscionable buffalo hunt, giving the rest of the United States a chance to gape and throng. If their own exploits were not enough, the Lord Mayor of Dublin and two people with titles accompanied them. As for the Americans, a writer who wanted to obtain for the rest of sport riflery's newly acquired prestige described a remarkable shift:

The few men who met at Creedmoor . . . were of slight importance three years ago. Their doings were carelessly chronicled and respectable people who think that all sport savors of evil, only knew them to avoid them. Suddenly they are the associates of archbishops and college dignitaries and rivals of princes of the blood and ministers of state. Ah, how good it is to be a rifleman.[27]

The sensation owed something to the nation's postwar interest in and increased approval of games, but it owed more to nationalism. Representatives of the United States had achieved no such triumph over foreign opponents since 1851, when the *America* won its cup at Cowes, and this was victory not in a piddling boat race but a miniature formalized war. Prematch philippics in the sporting press demanding intense training and a win "no matter what it costs" revealed that in the minds of the writers this game involved profound psychological risks. Judge N. P. Stanton at a prematch banquet made an explicit—though of course playful—statement of the emotional investment in mock battle when he said "the representatives of two great nations are now to meet at Creedmoor with deadly weapons."[28] If, as Konrad Lorenz suggests, all sport has origins in "highly ritualized but still serious" fighting, [29] riflery must surely be closer to those origins—and therefore closer to the bone—than other contests between peoples. Perhaps it was appropriate that blood trickled down Colonel Bodine's arm as he fired the winning shot.

Though the victory had been wonderful, American sporting magazines seemed a little uncertain just whom we had beaten. The Irishmen were Great Britain's champions of course, but did they represent a middle class for whom riflery offered patriotic exercise and escape from city cares, or gentlemen of leisure such as had no counterpart in the United States? One editorial in *American Sportsman* somehow held to both views in succeeding paragraphs, but most outdoor journals favored the second characterization. Arthur Leech and his fellows did have aristocratic trappings. Photographs of the two squads show Irishmen cradling custom-built weapons and languidly sprawled in Norfolks and deer-stalker caps, while Wingate and his men look the efficient team they were, posed matter-of-factly in business suits. The Irish actually comprised two country gentlemen, three merchants, two gunmakers, and a jeweler, not an especially distinguished crew though more prosperous than better shots who had been unable to afford the trip. The typical American team member was a New Yorker, a business or professional man with officer rank from the Civil War and a current interest in the National Guard. Only in his martial experience and concerns did he differ noticeably from the Irish. The press, however, preferred to see a contest between commercial civilization and aristocracy, pointing to the fact that of the Americans, General Thomas S. Dakin alone lacked employment—and that was because he had retired from an executive career. Comparison of Remington's foreman Hepburn, the nearest thing to a working man on either team, with John Rigby, who owned the Irish gun company, allowed the claim that it was democracy's victory as well.[30]

But political philosophy got less play in the press than business civilization, perhaps because nobody doubted that a man could be a republican and a fighter—Americans had proved that to themselves a hundred years earlier. Moreover, Herbert Spencer had half convinced business that its virtues were incompatible with those of the soldier. Hence the celebration that "our clerks, merchants and men of business have shown that they are not disqualified from equality and fraternity with the gentlemen of Europe in another branch of manly sport. . . . Our capacity to be first in commerce does not militate against our being men of war, when we have something to fight for."[31] At worst, riflery promised to "keep alive in a mercenary age some spark of the old martial spirit." [32] Gentlemen, even those themselves engaged in business, frequently contrasted the discipline and self-sacrifice of military service with the greed and self-indulgence of life in the Gilded Age. And those more comfortable with the laissez-faire capitalism of the day could see shooting as the logical complement to business militant: "Though we have no privileged classes . . . whose life is the pursuit of pleasure, we can cultivate athletic and field sports, and can mingle the use of arms and the growth of physical fiber with the unpoetic but world-controlling duties of the desk and factory."[33]

American riflery successes represent an early—perhaps the first—triumph of a re-United States, but a triumph with flaws. Sporting papers of the West and Midwest complained that easterners hogged the glory, offering the example of a Chicago man who qualified for but did not shoot in the international match marking the nation's centennial. Wingate explained that the candidate had demanded one thousand dollars to participate. *Chicago Field*, the major sporting magazine published outside New York, became champion of the inland clubs, energetically disputing *Forest and Stream*'s contention that western riflemen were imaginary. What *Forest and Stream* claimed and *Chicago Field* denied was that gentlemen shooters were an East Coast phenomenon. No one doubted the existence of the hunters of the West, but their place in the nation's mythology did seem to be under attack.

Eastern newspapers printed smug accounts of city men's preeminence in riflery, the most "intellectual" of outdoor sports. The New York press even berated frontiersmen for failing to respond to Wingate's call, though few could be expected to travel two thousand miles at their own expense, especially as the best shots supported themselves precariously by hunting. If westerners would not come east, Major Henry Fulton, Creedmoor's champion, could go west, where he sought out and defeated a number of local deadeyes, much to their discomfort. Whether because of that or a more general resentment of the East's presumptuousness, W. F. Carver, a professional hunter and later a famous trick shot, hated "those Creedmoor boys." Carver told his biographer that when he and a friend came upon one hunting buffalo, they seized his rifle and threw away the breechblock.[34] Other plainsmen vented their disgust with "fancy Creedmoor target popping" in half-literate letters to the sporting press.

The reticence of marksmen in the former Confederate states created an even bigger problem than western resentment. Perhaps the members of the NRA Centennial Match election committee actually would have been willing to pay for Dudley Selph of New Orleans, the South's best long-range shot, but they never had that chance. Their letter of invitation offered him an opportunity "to revive the feelings of fraternity between North and South which we are anxious to foster,"[35] but he replied that the New Orleans team rejected his participation. He would be present to watch but not to shoot.[36] Carping from the West and aloofness in the South did not, however, keep the great small-bore matches of the 1870s from bringing national glory, especially when United States teams established a pattern of success, winning both at home and in Great Britain, in all weather, four times in a row.

There was a good deal of nativist self-congratulation. Nathaniel Southgate Shaler, the Harvard geologist who fancied American autochthons superior even at the vegetable level, observed in an essay that the inhabitants of this country excelled in the three "leading diversions of the open air, yachting, horsemanship and 'sharpshooting.' "[37] An *Army and Navy Journal* editorial later explained the win in similar terms, theorizing that the vast distances of America train eyesight to accuracy. George Wingate himself laid the rifle progress of New York Guardsmen, who in two years achieved scores the British had just attained after two decades, mostly to our "intelligence."[38] When the Amateur Club organized a return match in 1875, announcements emphasized that only native-born riflemen could try out for the team—American superiority henceforward would be even more clear-cut. During the Centennial Match a reporter saw decided contrasts between teams according to their members' place of birth. "The rapidity of the Irish fire, the slow sure aim of the Scotchmen, the steadiness of the American champions, afforded an interesting comparison of national character."[39] For many, international rifle successes proved America's special virtue.

Some preferred to emphasize the community of interest created by riflery. At first they tended to Britishers. As early as 1875, the London *Sporting Gazette* observed that while the arts of peace had not created a "bond of union" within the English-speaking world, shooting now bid fair to achieve it.[40] Because only Anglo-Saxons seemed to excel at long-range target practice, more generous or more Anglophilic Americans expanded their self-congratulation to include the rest of the race. At the very least, small-bore riflery constituted another "sweetmeat on the table of Anglo-American reconciliation."[41] Sir Henry Halford, captain of the British teams of 1877 and 1882, recalled that on his first visit Americans received him cordially, but on his second they showed real warmth. He felt certain that fondness for Britain was growing among "the thinking part" of the country (by implication, the unthinking part was Irish).[42] And as the London *Times* observed, international friendships can be cemented as private friendships are, in shared amusement—perhaps in "a slight affair like a rifle match."[43] On the eve of American involvement in the First World War, a U.S. officer recalled in *Scientific American* that Germans had never participated in "the noble sport of long range rifle shooting"[44] but stuck to their frivolous *Schützen* targetry. He attempted to explain the fact that British soldiers shot better than Germans; he suggested by his tone that a shared amusement may indeed have fostered fraternalism between the United States and Britain.

Besides revived nationalism and closer ties with the Empire, long-range riflery contributed a good deal as martial symbol and inspiration, though it had about as much direct military application as the international yacht racing to which so many compared it. Small-bore zealots required a weapon that cost half a work-ingman's yearly earnings and had to be cleaned after every shot.[45] They normally fired from contorted back positions, using delicate sights—as precise as micrometers—mounted at the buttplate. Perfection in the game demanded al-most full-time practice, as Henry Fulton, the star of the Americans, discovered to his distress.[46] Even at the height of the frenzy only a few hundred men shot seriously, and the NRA never had many to choose from when putting together a team. Faddishness probably drew most marksmen—though long-range riflery also offered peculiar psychological satisfactions.[47] Among the more clear-headed participants were National Guard officers who valued small-bore contests largely because the publicity devoted to what Leech had called the poetry of shooting greatly benefited the prose of guard recruitment.[48]

The high social class of long-range marksmen helped make their doings more newsworthy and invested the whole game with glamour. A month after the 1874 win, Chicago had the beginnings of four long-range clubs, one boasting a general, a judge, and doctor of divinity. New York's Irish Rifle Club enrolled one of the nation's leading dramatists and a famous musician, as well as several journalists, invaluable boosters. The other New York clubs also attracted luminaries, though National Guard officers predominated.[49] Upper-class men in other cities from Maine to Florida to California had clubs a year after the first international match, and even United States citizens in Peru formed a long-range squad. Most observ-ers seemed to regard the sport as not only rather nobby but notably clean and vaguely patriotic—the mayor of New York suggested that perhaps one of the city's long-range marksmen might some day pick off the general of an invading army.[50] The spillover of national interest certainly benefited the National Guard, as Wingate had hoped, but it extended much further into American life.

Before the Civil War, shooting had been regarded as the province of aristo-cratic triflers or underclass "woods loafers," but by 1875 riflery had become so worthy that it was endorsed by preachers and practiced by women. In their basements, churches set up ranges patronized by both sexes. Sporting magazines reported and welcomed such developments. "It has become quite the fashion," reported *Forest and Stream*, "for ladies to practice rifle shooting. At many fairs regular matches are shot between teams of young ladies selected according to nationality or otherwise."[51] Before 1880 several cities had all-women clubs. Target practice was a much more liberating hobby than croquet, women's first post–Civil War enthusiasm, invading a masculine prerogative and encouraging the sort of practical clothing that bicycles later required. And female participation did not render shooting a less "manly" activity in the view of American sporting journals. True, targetry cultivated masculine spirit and assertiveness, but Ameri-can women needed such qualities for self-defense, said the *Chicago Field*. The only change women brought to the game was a higher moral tone.[52] Target matches open to both sexes became a usual way to raise money for fresh air funds, hospitals, and the like.

The new wholesomeness transformed a minor American institution. Shooting galleries, the hangouts of drunks and ruffians, had existed in American cities since at least the 1830s. Except for a brief period before the Civil War when gentlemen needed to learn killing, none had attracted many respectable customers.[53] Now, though the scruffy sort persisted, several ranges in New York City appealed to serious marksmen, "the preRaphaelite school of Creedmoorites," and to less fanatic gentlemen shooters. Zettler's Gallery, opened in 1874, drew mostly purists, who used long-range rifles modified for indoor use. Conlin's, an older establishment which had been burned out with each of P. T. Barnum's unlucky museums, relocated and upgraded that same year. Its owner introduced the "safety-range," an index of the higher social class of his new customers because it required a lackey beside each marksman to load and watch for carelessness. Most of the customers of these new ranges counted as gentlemen only by comparison with earlier gallery habitués—journalists and insurance underwriters seem to have constituted a high percentage of the suddenly "huge and urgent" downtown patronage. Really prosperous shooters established private galleries, of which the New York Rifle Club may have been typical. "On entering," noted *Forest and Stream*, "the visitor is in a parlor or reception room with its piano and soft yielding carpet, its heavy window curtains, elaborate chandelier, bronzes and works of art displayed on the walls."[54] The actual shooting room was almost as sumptuous, done up in "obtrusively naturalistic Eastlake style."[55] Galleries, both plebeian and plush, constituted a purely American extension of the shooting mania. British critics dismissed them with sarcasm and counted short-range guns "vanities."[56]

Yet college galleries and short outdoor ranges seem to have helped transform both the military training promoted by the 1862 Morrill Act and student attitudes toward soldier skills. During the spring and summer before the first international match, William Conant Church exchanged worried letters with an army captain assigned to Bowdoin College, who encountered a "hornets' nest" when he attempted to teach drill.[57] The undergraduate response to military instruction usually leaned more toward indifference, yet after the first international match students at Harvard, Yale, Columbia, and a number of other universities, colleges, and schools formed rifle clubs and applied to local militia officers for training. As if to underscore the parallel between the playing fields of England and those of the United States, the club at Columbia challenged other college teams to an annual contest modeled on that between Cambridge and Oxford.[58] A few school matches held at Creedmoor with full-power military rifles attracted attention, but most undergraduates had to make do with reduced loads at short ranges. *Forest and Stream*, from the first the most passionate proponent of college riflery, thought that considerably better than nothing. Editor Charles Hallock's discussions of the intercollegiate rifle contests sponsored by his journal usually began with a homily about the cool nerves, diligence, and other manly qualities shooting conferred and praised it as a sport among other sports. But Hallock occasionally acknowledged that he hoped riflery would be the basis of a serious college program of military training. All of his prizes promoted "military shooting with military rifles."[59] In 1888 nearly fifty schools and colleges drew government ammunition and taught marksmanship. Harvard's president Charles W. Eliot proclaimed target practice the finest sport available to young men; no other had proved such a builder of coordination and self-control. Secretary of War William C. Endicott suggested raising the ammunition allowance for schools, as it might require nothing more to make shooting as popular with inland colleges as boat racing was on the seaboard.[60]

Outside the schools and the military, however, interest in target marksmanship dropped during the 1880s with the end of international small-bore contests and the growth of other sports.[61] Polo, another game promoted by James Gordon Bennett, Jr., during the 1870s, had more charm and long-term appeal for the typical member of the class that had first taken up long-range riflery. Old soldiers continued to meet for casual competition that today would be styled "plinking." In a community near Indianapolis,

> it was nothing unusual for half the merchants of the little town to shut up shop in the middle of the afternoon and, together with the lawyers, doctors and, yes, the preachers, to repair to some vacant lot and shoot impromptu matches with anything from old "pepperboxes" to the latest rifles. At that time and in that place practically all the "men" were veterans of the Civil War and this shooting business was part of their gospel.[62]

Targetry appeared in a degenerate form in the Wild West shows, which popularized trick shooting and brought fame to Annie Oakley and other adepts. William Cody contrived a set of targets connected to piano keys which allowed him to play "Yankee Doodle" with bullets, an unrivaled combination of "music, marksmanship and patriotism." Though much of the shooting at such shows was helped along with wires or was otherwise fraudulent, Americans took to it and to gimmicks such as the skating rifle match, which became surprisingly popular in the winter of 1884.[63] As interest in conventional shooting fell and real estate values rose, rifle clubs began to sell the tracts of metropolitan land that they had acquired for ranges. Galleries often became beer gardens. It was a starving time for the National Rifle Association, which died obscurely in 1892.

But it did not stay dead. The Spanish-American War brought a rush of trade to surviving city galleries, and early Boer successes against the British in South Africa persuaded many that civilian rifle experts armed with the new smokeless powder repeaters could out-soldier regulars. (A tremendous technical leap in arms occurred just before the turn of the century. Black powder, which allowed limited velocities and created great clouds of sulfurous smoke, was replaced by a new propellant that produced little smoke and burned progressively, accelerating the bullet to much higher velocities. Effective range doubled.) The present National Rifle Association, born at the turn of the century, came into an America where sporting magazines called for chairs of marksmanship at major universities and "chic summer girls" would soon crowd the shooters at the government's new National Matches. The rifle was headed toward its World War I apotheosis in the hands of Sergeant York.

Rifled arms had more than merely escaped the extinction predicted by Henry William Herbert in 1848. And yet he had been right about the disappearance of game. By the turn of the century, the sort of animals hunted with high-power rifles had nearly ceased to exist everywhere but the far West.[64] Although it had killed away its "utility," why had the rifle's "honor" so vastly increased? Target practice offered a sport justifiable in Calvinist terms, a sport chiefly improving and patriotic and only incidentally (if at all) fun. Control and repetition are essential in target shooting as in few other games. In fact, riflery with its discipline and exactitude hardly seemed recreation, even to many of the men drawn to it. Americans, unlike Germans, did not appear able to enjoy the range, reflected the sporting press, but strove on it as relentlessly as in their offices. Its partisans urged marksmanship for character building more often than for sport, and "the arm of precision" truly demanded Protestant virtues, including temperance, because alcohol and even tobacco interfered with success.[65] As for patriotism, small-bore shooters constituted at least a cadre of top-quality minutemen and perhaps a whole new weapon. Some enthusiasts expected infantry to advance under the cover of long-range rifle fire rather than artillery.[66] The rigor and patriotism of shooting did much to render sporting contests respectable during the 1870s; once respectable, such contests could take other forms with more spectator interest.

Targetry, retreating into its justification, became ever more military as the century progressed. The 1880s saw international matches between amateur soldiers replace civilian small-bore contests. During the early 1890s, marksmanship became "virtually a religion" in the United States Army.[67] And the shooting craze that arrived with the new century was almost wholly military in inspiration, even though some of its devotees saw the end of regular armies in it. All that represented the norm. In most times, few people care about target shooting outside a military context. The hugely aberrant international matches of the 1870s revealed more than a still-Calvinistic people's dalliance with mass sport. They signaled a still-sundered nation's return to self-assertion and presaged the Anglo-American alliance of our own century.

NOTES

1. Frank Forester [Henry William Herbert], *Frank Forester's Field Sports of the United States and British Provinces of North America* (New York: Stringer and Townsend, 1848), 29. Herbert, an upper-class Englishman resident in New York, wrote gunning books and essays between 1848 and 1858. Rifles had been used by specialized military units for centuries, but their bullets had to be forced down grooves rather than dropped down a smooth interior. The extra time and trouble could be justified only in units of sharpshooters.

2. Henry Heth, *The Memoirs of Henry Heth*, ed. James L. Morrison, Jr. (Westport, CT: Greenwood Press, 1974), 142; *The National Rifle Association: 1873 Annual Reports and Regulations for Rifle Practice* (New York: E. A. Kingsland and Company, 1873), 6.

3. *Forest and Stream*, 2 October 1879, 691; *Shooting and Fishing*, 16 May 1901, 95.

4. See, for example, Colonel Henry A. Gildersleeve's remarks in *Spirit of the Times*, 18 May 1876, 136. Any edge which southerners may have possessed disappeared in the lower quality of their equipment.

5. The most massive had to be fired from a bench or other rest.

6. Claud E. Fuller, *The Rifled Musket* (New York: Bonanza Books, 1968), 258; Charles Winthrop Sawyer, *Our Rifles*, vol. 3 of *Firearms in American History* (Boston: Cornhill Company, 1920), 87.

7. So called to distinguish them from the *Schützenbünde*, discussed later.

8. Augustine E. Costello, *A History of the New York Fire Department, Volunteer and Paid* (New York: Augustine E. Costello, 1887), 753. Earlier, some militia made once-a-year excursions, but the custom lapsed among them in the 1840s when semimilitary societies took it up with fervor. Colonel Emmons Clark, *History of the Seventh Regiment of New York: 1806–1889*, vol. 1 (New York: Published by the Seventh Regiment, 1890), 339.

9. Emmeline Charlotte Elizabeth Stuart-Wortley, *Travels in the United States During 1849 and 1850* (London: R. Bentley, 1851), 298–99.

10. *Army and Navy Journal*, 13 April 1867, 50. Colonel Church, a successful journalist in New York City and Washington, D.C., had established his paper in 1863, chiefly to serve the Union army's officers. By 1867, he spoke authoritatively for the military and would continue to do so through an extraordinary editorship that ended only with his death in 1917.

11. *Army and Navy Journal*, 16 May 1869, 621. Though a Tammany man, Hoffman as city judge "had done good service in punishing participants in the Draft Riot." *The Diary of George Templeton Strong: The Civil War, 1860–1865*, ed. Allan Nevins and Milton Halsey Thomas (New York: Macmillan, 1952), ix.

12. *Army and Navy Journal*, 620. *Schützen* guarded their respective parts of Germany for centuries before they brought their sport to America in the 1840s. The form had not changed appreciably since days when practice was with crossbows.

13. *New York Times*, 28 July 1864; "A German-American Fete," *Harper's Weekly*, 13 July 1895, 664.

14. *Shooting and Fishing*, 4 July 1901, 233.

15. *New York Times*, 24 April 1857. Private military societies attained considerable popularity in the South and Midwest but did not style themselves target companies. Many practiced fancy marching inspired by the Zouave drill of Colonel Elmer W. Ellsworth's Chicago troop. Theodore G. Gronert, "The First National Pastime in the Middle West," *Indiana Magazine of History* 29, 3 (September 1933): 180.

16. Newspaper accounts of *Schützenfeste* tended to be ironic, as reporters had difficulty believing that serious shooting could go on amidst such a carnival. The most native of Americans, a band of Indians, protested in war paint the fireworks set off by New York's Independent *Schützen* Corps during a fest at Lake Hopatcong, New Jersey. *Shooting and Fishing*, 7 July 1892, 215. Other Americans of old stock sometimes objected almost as strongly. *Forest and Stream*, 18 October 1888, 586.

17. "National Guard" was a term first borrowed from the French to apply to New York's volunteer militia. A militia convention in Richmond, Virginia, in 1877 created the National Guard Association. After that, the term "National Guard" was generally used

for volunteer state troops. Russell F. Weighly, *History of the United States Army* (New York: Macmillan, 1967), 282. Units were used mostly for maintaining public order (to include, frequently, strike breaking). It was not until the Dick Act of 1903 that the National Guard was effectively incorporated into the national defense.

18. Arthur Blennerhassett Leech, captain of the Irish team, had heard of neither the American NRA nor the Amateur Rifle Club, but he did know James Gordon Bennett, Jr., innovative editor of the *New York Herald*, whose bankrolling of Stanley's expedition had impressed him. Leech placed an ad in the *New York Herald* which the NRA's board of directors voted to ignore as "a mere newspaper letter" despite Wingate's pleas. Arthur B. Leech, *Irish Riflemen in America* (London: Edward Stanford, 1875), 101.

19. *Forest and Stream*, 2 August 1883, 4.

20. Modern "small-bore" shooting uses .22 rimfire cartridges at short ranges and ought not to be confused with its nineteenth-century namesake. Military weapons of the 1860s usually had bores of .50 caliber or larger. Only by comparison were .44 and .45 caliber rifles small.

21. G. W. Yale, superintendent of Sharps Rifle Company, and L. L. Hepburn, foreman of Remington's Mechanical Department, each had a place on the final team.

22. *Turf, Field and Farm*, 26 June 1874, 440.

23. *Forest and Stream*, 24 January 1874, 267.

24. *Forest and Stream*, 11 April 1874, 21.

25. Chicago *Inter-Ocean*, 28 November 1873, 2.

26. "The International Rifle Match," *Harper's Weekly*, 10 October 1874, 838.

27. *Rod and Gun*, 21 August 1875, 312. When, having won the return match, team members called on Victor Hugo in Paris, the *New York Times* (8 August 1875) counted that front-page news.

28. *Forest and Stream*, 6 April 1886, 212.

29. Konrad Lorenz, *On Aggression* (New York: Harcourt, Brace & World, 1966), 280.

30. *Rod and Gun*, 19 June 1875, 188.

31. *American Sportsman*, 10 October 1875, 91.

32. *Turf, Field and Farm*, 30 July 1875, 91.

33. *American Sportsman*, 10 October 1874, 24.

34. Not that they rejected pointless killing of buffalo, because they then chased the small herd and destroyed it in flight to educate the Creedmoor boy in western ways. Carver and Texas Jack Omohundro were guiding an Englishman at the time and apparently left the animals to rot. Raymond W. Thorp, *Spirit Gun of the West: The Story of Doc W. F. Carver* (Glendale, CA: Arthur H. Clark, 1957), 58.

35. Letter of 23 July 1877 signed by George W. Wingate, D. D. Wylie, and Joseph G. Story, printed in the *New Orleans Daily Picayune*, 30 July 1877, quoted by Dale A. Somers, *The Rise of Sports in New Orleans: 1850–1900* (Baton Rouge: Louisiana State University Press, 1972), 204.

36. *Turf, Field and Farm*, 10 August 1877, 221.

37. Nathaniel S. Shaler, "The Summing Up of the Story," in *The United States of America*, vol. 2, ed. Nathaniel S. Shaler (New York: D. Appleton, 1894), 622.

38. *Army and Navy Journal*, 18 August 1906, 1415.

39. *Spirit of the Times*, 16 September 1876, 154.

40. Quoted in *Turf, Field and Farm*, 30 July 1875, 91.

41. W. H. Nelson used this phrase to describe Sir George Otto Trevelyan's *The American Revolution*, 4 vols. (1899–1907).

42. *Forest and Stream*, 14 December 1882, 394.

43. Quoted in *Forest and Stream*, 23 September 1875, 104.

44. Edward Crossman, "German Military Rifle Practice," *Scientific American* 116, no. 5 (3 February 1917): 126.

45. One hundred dollars would buy the basic rifle. One could spend twice that much. And there were expensive accessories in addition. One dollar a day was a fair wage at the time.

46. *Army and Navy Journal*, 23 September 1876, 105.

47. Long-range riflery "imparts to him who perfects himself in the accomplishment a sense of power and self-dependence which cannot be otherwise attained. The accomplished long-range rifleman knows that the weapon he bears is a magic wand by whose power he holds at his mercy the life of any enemy, be it man or beast, that ventures in the radius of half a mile from the spot whereon he stands, and the consciousness of such power is no ordinary sensation." *Rod and Gun*, 4 September 1875, 340.

48. Wingate gave that as the reason for his own involvement. *National Guardsman*, 1 March 1878, 141.

49. *Forest and Stream*, 7 January 1875, 344.

50. *Rod and Gun*, 28 August 1875, 325.

51. *Forest and Stream*, 21 December 1876, 314.

52. *Chicago Field* 50, 19 July 1880, 300.

53. Early galleries often sold alcoholic drinks at attached refreshment stands. *Rod and Gun*, 3 April 1875, 4.

54. *Forest and Stream*, 8 April 1880, 190.

55. Ibid.

56. *Forest and Stream*, 19 March 1874, 90.

57. The Morrill Act stipulated that instruction in military tactics was to be included at land-grant colleges. In fact, such instruction could be provided by army officers to any college with 150 male students.

58. *Turf, Field and Farm*, 8 January 1875, 21.

59. *Forest and Stream*, 9 December 1875, 286.

60. Lieutenant A. C. Sharp, USA, "Military Training in Colleges," *Journal of the Military Service Institute of the United States* 8, 32 (December 1887): 411; *The Rifle*, 1 February 1888, 157; *Report of the Secretary of War*, 50th Cong., 2d sess., 1888, Ex. Doc. 1, 17. In a letter to a fellow University of Wisconsin regent that same year, an opponent of military training assumed marksmanship had become its essence. "That discipline which savors least of culture or mentality and most of brute passion and war, is being pushed most persistently and vigorously. To study classics is choice or whim—to train with a gun and know how to shoot is a requirement." George H. Paul to John C. McMynn, 7 January 1888, McMynn Papers, State Historical Society of Wisconsin, quoted by John Frank Cook, "A History of Liberal Education at the University of Wisconsin: 1862–1918" (Ph.D. diss., University of Wisconsin, 1970), 122.

61. *Turf, Field and Farm*, 30 May 1884, 418. The NRA knew well the publicity value of international small-bore contests, but foreign teams could not be tempted once they saw they had no chance to win. In 1882 and 1883 National Guardsmen and British Volunteers held practical matches, but those drew hundreds where small-bore contests had drawn thousands. *Forest and Stream* said the 1882 competition was "a military affair. . . . There were no scenes of excitement or enthusiasm" (21 September 1882, 152).

62. Herbert W. McBride, *A Rifleman Went to War* (Plantersville, SC: Small Arms Technical Publishing Company, 1935), 2.

63. *Forest and Stream* believed the fad dangerous, because shots fired while flashing over a frozen pond often went wild (14 February 1884, 40).

64. Deer began their comeback not long after 1900, thanks partly to closed seasons and partly to government and private game preserves. By the 1920s many eastern and midwestern states had more than their forests could support. James B. Trefethen, *Crusade for Wildlife* (Harrisburg, PA: Stackpole Books, 1961), 338ff.

65. "Rifle practice carries with it self-denial, sobriety, and iron nerve." *Rod and Gun*, 31 July 1875, 264.

66. *Army and Navy Journal*, 3 February 1883, 599.

67. Captain H. C. Hale, *USA*, "The New Firing Regulations for Small Arms," *Journal of the United States Infantry Association* 1, 1 (July 1904): 14.

Ambivalence and Gun Culture

Chapter Five

Guns, Politics, and Public Policy

Steven Thomas Seitz

Suppose we examine the gun control controversy in light of our discussion of open, balanced, and closed politics. This particular controversy highlights the tension between experts and democrats. In 1975, for example, Alan Otten of the *Wall Street Journal* solemnly declared that, although Senate and House committees usually like to listen to experts, they turn deaf ears to the advocates of handgun control. Otten explained that Congress believed that the National Rifle Association (NRA) and other opponents of gun control could defeat an office-holder supporting gun legislation. The NRA claims that it defeated former Senator Joseph Tydings, former Senator Joseph Clark, and several others (Otten, 1975). However, in 1977 Representative Conyers (Democrat-Michigan), Chairman of the House Subcommittee on Crime, House Judiciary Committee, requested that the General Accounting Office—the research arm of Congress—prepare a report for Congress on handgun control effectiveness. In its report delivered to Congress on February 6, 1978, the General Accounting Office recommended further legislation to restrict the availability of handguns. The Department of Justice supported the GAO recommendations (General Accounting Office, 1978).

A majority of American citizens have supported some form of handgun registration in all major polls taken since 1938. However, the federal government has enacted only two major pieces of legislation in this area, one in 1938 and the other in 1968. Both legislative enactments occurred during times of severe social unrest, the first corresponding to the organized crime violence of the 1930s and the second corresponding to the urban terrorism of the 1960s. However, in times of quiescence, when the majority of citizens appear inattentive to matters of gun control, a minority of highly organized citizens with intense views on gun control govern the course of public policy. The contours of the gun control controversy bear more than a passing resemblance to the cyclical shift in the balance of power between professionals and democrats during the twentieth century, particularly if we note that the periodic ascendancy of professionals follows the mobilization of an otherwise inattentive majority in response to a real or perceived crisis. The

Reprinted from *Structure, Law, and Power: Essays in the Sociology of Law*, Sage Research Progress Series in Criminology, ed. Paul J. Brantingham and Jack M. Kress (Thousand Oaks, Calif.: Sage, 1979), 87–95. Copyright © 1979 by Sage Publications. Reprinted by permission of Sage Publications, Inc.

Progressives, for example, mobilized support to fight the trusts and corrupt politicians. Franklin Roosevelt mobilized electoral support for bold governmental initiatives in the depressed economic sector. And Kennedy mobilized support for new initiatives in the technological race with the Soviet Union. Given these parallels, suppose we examine the gun control controversy more closely.

Cultural Heritage

One storybook truth about American history holds that the gun helped American heroes settle the West. Although more fable than fact, the tale does illustrate that the implementation of law and formal social control in the West lagged behind the pace of settlement (Kennett and Anderson, 1975: 124). This encouraged the use of guns in personalized law enforcement, and for some time after the extension of more formal mechanisms of social control, people continued to rely on their own devices for securing justice. However, the problem of guns in personalized law enforcement emerged with startling clarity in the Old South after the Civil War. The Carpetbaggers were not particularly interested in securing or maintaining a civil order comparable to the antebellum era, and the freed slaves plus poor whites found themselves in an environment into which they were not economically integrated. While some of these dispossessed people began to leave the Old South, others became little more than scavengers who rendered much of the remaining social order nasty and brutish. The general civil disorder quickly led to the widespread use of guns for equalizing justice and establishing some minimal sense of personal security in an age of enormous turmoil.

Viewed from this perspective, the gun control controversy implies a potential cleavage between cosmopolitan Americans who find little utility in the gun and an older cultural sector that continues to hold the gun in high esteem. The terrors of past social turmoil and past social insecurity still weigh heavily on many descendants of the Old South, and these cultural pockets remain unwilling to trust their lives and property to a government that once failed to provide the civil order sought by their forefathers. Among urban Americans, on the other hand, we find remnants of cultural traditions brought by emigrants from Europe to America. In Europe, the gun had been first and foremost an instrument of the upper social classes, so the lower classes who entered America had little cultural experience with the gun, particularly the handgun. And in a crowded urban environment, the handgun is a greater source of fear than a government's potential failure to maintain the proper social order, save those situations of urban unrest when residents of the metropolis, like the citizens of Detroit, rush to buy handguns for a sense of security and self-protection. But even under these crisis circumstances, urban people have been willing to register their arms, so long as governments actively enforce the same laws against those who appear to be the source of urban terror (Kennett and Anderson, 1975: 253–254). Registration, as Milton Friedman points out, might assist governments in keeping firearms out of the hands of those who are likely to use them for criminal purposes, and after the criminal event has occurred, it might assist governments in finding out who had access to firearms used in the crime (Friedman, 1962: 145).

A controversy deeply seated in cultural heritage cannot be solved by the advice of experts, because the relative effectiveness of gun control legislation, even if conclusively demonstrated, cannot compensate for the sense of fear and distrust generated by historical events like Reconstruction and subsequently amplified by myths and common wisdom passed from generation to generation. The typical professional often has little empathy for such cultural pockets, partly because such common wisdom is foreign to the professional's image of society and state, and partly because expert knowledge derives from an analysis of facts and figures that are less encumbered by family and other social forces that mold personalities and perpetuate beliefs across generations. Stated differently, the professional is more likely to think in terms of probabilities, while the ordinary men and women from such cultural pockets are more likely to construct the issue in terms of possibilities, the relative improbabilities notwithstanding. If this cultural heritage argument has some merit, then we have one potential explanation why some ordinary people prefer to keep the gun control issue in the domain of open politics, rather than deferring to the judgment of professionals.

The National Rifle Association

On March 21, 1978, the U.S. Treasury Departments' Bureau of Alcohol, Tobacco, and Firearms (ATF) issued a proposed set of updated rules regarding the regulation of firearms. The proposed rules would require that all guns manufactured in the United States bear a serial number, that gun manufacturers, importers, and dealers would submit quarterly reports on the sale and disposition of firearms, that gun dealers and others involved in firearms transactions would report theft or loss of any firearms within twenty-four hours, but that the names and addresses of individual purchasers would not be reported. Consistent with its past procedures, the National Rifle Association misrepresented the implications of these proposed regulations to its vast constituency, and the NRA mobilized a mass mailing effort that produced 300,000 letters against the ATF rules. In addition, the NRA instructed its members to write to congressmen on the House Appropriations Committee, demanding that the committee eliminate funding for the implementation of the proposed rules. Not only did the House Appropriations Committee cut funds for the new rules' implementation, but also the committee explicitly forbade ATF from initiating controversial or sensitive programs without a clear legislative mandate.

The House Appropriations Committee's action was rather stern, given the modest nature of the proposed change of rules, and given the fact that the rules did not directly affect gun consumers. Further, administrative agencies often engage in such policy elaboration, and Congress has been generally tolerant of this quasi-policy function exercised by the federal bureaucracy. In addition, the courts have enforced the need for administrative procedures guaranteeing some hearing for the impacted groups, and ATF had held a number of hearings on its proposed changes. In short, the House Appropriations Committee's response to ATF's proposals well might support the NRA's claims regarding its legislative effectiveness. If the NRA claims are valid, then we have another potential explanation why the gun control issue remains in the domain of open politics.

The Professionals

As is often the case with the federal bureaucracy, the NRA and other progun lobbyists could not keep ATF from putting the revised rules on the political agenda. In part, of course, this reflects the bureau's vested interests in the legislative mandates of 1938 and 1968. In terms of simple efficiency and effectiveness, ATF could better perform its previous legislative mandate with the revised rules it sought to implement. In addition, the ATF proposals were consistent with the spirit of the GAO report delivered to Congress in February; its proposals were consistent with the Justice Department's position that further regulation was necessary; and, the bureau did receive the support of several special interest groups favoring stricter regulation of firearms. In this bureaucratic age, it should not be surprising that governmental agencies seek more closure in the policy arenas that they are required to administer. Stated a different way, the general trend of bureaucratic policy is away from open politics and toward either balanced or closed politics. If this assessment appears reasonable, then we have one potential explanation why the NRA and its associated lobbies failed to keep the gun control matter off the political agenda in 1978. In a sense, the NRA had to expand the scope of conflict into the halls of Congress, precisely because its mass mailing effort and public testimony did not persuade ATF to rescind the proposed rule changes. Unlike the federal agencies, Congress was more responsive to the demands for an open politics in the gun control controversy, as might befit an institution of democratic representation. Without congressional intervention, ATF might have shifted the gun control issue into an arena that established some balance between professional opinion and intense public opinion mobilized by the progun lobbyists, especially given the fact that the public so mobilized constitutes only an intensely vocal minority of the citizenry.

It is against this background that we must assess Representative McClory's (Republican-Illinois) motion to reinstate funding of the ATF proposals and to delete the House Appropriation Committee's language that forbade ATF from implementing the new rules. This motion was made on June 7, 1978, just six days after the House Appropriations Committee took its action against ATF. The motion did not give the NRA time to mobilize a mass mailing campaign against members of the House, although the NRA's threat of retribution at the polls still might hold House members in line. In light of past gun control controversies, the McClory motion did not appear politically shrewd. No assassinations or urban terrorism had mobilized the otherwise inattentive majority of citizens during the Ninety-fifth Congress, several congressmen still faced stiff primary elections where the volatile progun vote might spell electoral defeat, and all the congressmen faced potentially hostile gun proponents in the general elections less than five months away. In light of existing political realities, McClory's motion would be futile.

It is clear, however, that the House vote on McClory's motion involved an issue far deeper than the modest changes proposed by ATF, particularly given the fact that the new rules would have no direct impact on ordinary citizens. The language inserted into the bill by the House Appropriations Committee made it virtually certain that, vis-à-vis ATF, the gun control matter would remain solely in the domain of open politics. McClory's motion, on the other hand, would allow part of the gun controversy to shift from the electoral arena into the bureaucratic arena. A vote for McClory's motion would help shift the gun controversy from the open politics dominated by the NRA into a more balanced accommodation of public hysteria to questions of effectiveness and efficiency.

Some Empirical Hypotheses

The June 7, 1978 vote on McClory's motion provides us with an opportunity to examine more closely the arguments presented in the previous section. The cultural heritage argument, for example, suggests that the Old South and perhaps parts of the West will stand in opposition to the more cosmopolitan areas of the Northeast, Midwest, and far West. Suppose we grant the assumption that congressmen do represent their constituents on matters of fundamental cultural importance, and suppose, in light of our cultural heritage discussion, that gun control is one such fundamental issue; then we should expect to find strong regional and socioeconomic differences between the constituencies of those representatives supporting the McClory motion and those representatives opposing the McClory motion.

The cultural heritage argument also suggests an ideological schism between those who believe in the beneficient influence of government and those who fear or distrust the powers of government. In particular, we expect that those representatives voting for McClory's motion more likely are liberal in the sense that they favor paternalistic intervention in social matters and often justify it in terms of the enlightened interests of their constituents. Those representatives opposing McClory's motion, on the other hand, should be more conservative in the sense of favoring states' rights, minimal governmental intervention, or the status quo, and often justify it in terms of the potential evils of big government and its insensitivities to common wisdom and the ethic of self-help.

By its own claims, much of the NRA's strength rests upon its ability to defeat congressmen at the polls, and on its ability to mobilize quickly its vast constituency for mass mailing campaigns. If we assume that a congressman's perception of his electoral coalition bears some minimal resemblance to the objective vote returns at election time, then we should expect that congressmen from marginal districts are more likely to oppose gun control regulations, because a campaign against them by the NRA might spell electoral defeat. Based on the NRA's first claim, therefore, we expect that congressmen from safe districts are more likely to support McClory's motion than are congressmen from marginal districts.

The NRA also claims major success in its mass mailing campaigns, arguing that it brings direct constituent pressure on the decision-making of congressmen. As proponents of such campaigns see the issue, letter writing as a form of citizen participation is one essential ingredient of participatory democracy. It is, in short, one device for keeping politics open. Controls on mass solicitations, on the other hand, particularly the registration of those soliciting mass mailings, implies some effort to gauge the spontaneity of mass mailings and thus partly offset the supposed political impact of such campaigns. Given our theoretical expectation that gun control proponents might favor a shift from open politics in the gun control controversy, and given the NRA's assertions regarding the effectiveness of its mass mailing solicitations on congressional voting, we should expect to find that gun control proponents more likely favor the registration of such solicitations than would opponents of gun legislation.

Finally, we have argued that the McClory motion involved a procedural issue far more important than the modest rules proposed by ATF. That issue centers on the degree to which the gun control controversy might be shifted into the bureaucratic arena and hence into a more balanced accommodation of public hysteria and the more sedate questions of gun control effectiveness and gun control efficiency. Our argument suggests that the gun control controversy is part of a larger syndrome of conflicts over the proper locus of policy-making and policy-elaboration along a continuum from open to closed politics. Other issues falling into this larger syndrome might include civil rights for prison inmates, the civil rights of homosexuals, and legal services for the poor. And as the 1946 debate over the inclusion of the social sciences under the National Science Foundation illustrates, this larger syndrome should reflect a conflict between the proper role of professional knowledge versus common wisdom in the political process, with the advocates of a balanced or closed politics favoring the support and use of professional knowledge and with the advocates of open politics opposing the support and use of such professional knowledge over the common wisdom.

REFERENCES

Friedman, Milton. 1962. *Capitalism and Freedom.* Chicago: University of Chicago Press.

General Accounting Office. 1978. *Handgun Control: Effectiveness and Cost. A Report to the Comptroller General of the United States.* Washington, D.C.: General Accounting Office.

Kennett, Lee B., and James L. Anderson. 1975. *The Gun in America: The Origins of a National Dilemma.* Westport, Conn.: Greenwood.

Otten, A. 1975. "Guns Do Kill People." *Wall Street Journal*, November 13, 1975, 18.

Chapter Six

The Impact of Agenda Conflict on Policy Formulation and Implementation
The Case of Gun Control

William J. Vizzard

With passage of the Brady Bill and subsequent focus on assault weapons, the issue of gun control has returned to the public spotlight. Both opponents and advocates of gun control have used the heightened interest and increased media attention to advance their cases. For those familiar with the history of gun control in the United States, the current process invokes a certain sense of *deja vu*. In addition to having the most lenient, but complex, firearms laws in the industrialized world, the United States has been unique in the level and duration of controversy over gun policy (Zimring and Hawkins, 1987; Kopel, 1992). Some have viewed this as resulting from the role that guns played in American history (Hofstadter, 1970). An examination of the policy history reveals more about the American political process than about our romance with guns. It is a history that confirms our deep commitment to pluralism and incrementalism, while raising questions regarding their utility. Rather than a politics-administration dichotomy, one discovers complex entanglements of policy formulation and implementation and a conflict over symbols and language that has produced a stalemate resembling an iron triangle in effect if not design.

History

The history of gun control can be divided into at least five distinct eras beginning with the passage of the Sullivan Law in New York in 1909 and ending with the passage of the Brady Bill in 1993. A sixth era is added by some researchers to cover the efforts of southern states to deny firearms to blacks after the Civil War (Kates, 1979).

Gun control, as a policy applicable to the general population, began in 1909 with New York State's Sullivan Law, which mandated permits for the possession of handguns. Passed in an era when the prohibition of drugs and alcoholic beverages was being widely advocated, the law was a result of these influences, as well as fear of crime and the increased population of new immigrants (Sugarmann, 1992: 171–179). New York police have used the law to deny handgun access to all but the most influential citizens, particularly in New York City. This highly restrictive approach to implementation has provided a model for control advocates and a rallying point for opponents (Vizzard, 1993: 134).

Federal Government Enters the Field

After a 1927 effort to control interstate shipment of handguns by prohibiting their shipment by mail, but not common carrier, Congress first addressed the gun issue more seriously in 1934. Attorney General Homer Cummings proposed a bill that would control all firearms, other than sporting rifles and shotguns, through a transfer tax and registration scheme modeled after the Harrison Narcotics Act. In both House and Senate hearings on the bill, it was opposed by the NRA, numerous sportsmen's associations, and the firearms industry (Leff and Leff, 1981).

A compromise was reached that excluded handguns and semi-automatic rifles from the bill (Sugarmann, 1992: 33). The National Firearms Act (NFA) was enacted in 1934 and required registration and a transfer tax only on so-called gangster-type weapons, including machine guns, silencers, and sawed-off rifles and shotguns. Although the bill had the backing of the administration and a few powerful members of Congress, southern and western lawmakers generally opposed controls and little national attention appears to have been focused on the issue (Vizzard, 1993: 174–176).

The administration continued to pursue more restrictive legislation under the interstate commerce authority. In 1938, Congress finally passed the Federal Firearms Act (FFA), which required licensing of gun dealers and their maintenance of sales records but lacked mechanics for enforcement. Hearing records indicate that the bill was primarily drafted by the NRA as an effort to prevent more restrictive legislation (Kennett and Anderson, 1975: 192–193; Sugarmann, 1992; 30). Crime rates began a decline in 1934 that would continue for almost three decades, and the limited public and congressional interest in gun control abated. Administration and enforcement of both laws were vested in the Department of Treasury, because of the underlying taxation jurisdiction of the NFA, eventually coming to rest with the Alcohol and Tobacco Tax Division of the Internal Revenue Service, where it received little attention (Vizzard, 1993: 166).

Assassinations Revive the Issue

Interest revived with the assassination of President John Kennedy and peaked with passage of the Gun Control Act (GCA) in 1968. During this period, Senator Thomas Dodd chaired hearings that examined a series of bills designed to control interstate sales of firearms and increase licensing controls on dealers. Despite strong administration support, the GCA passed by the narrowest of margins after the assassinations of Martin Luther King, Jr., and Robert Kennedy. There is substantial evidence that a sudden increase in visible public support for gun control had a significant impact on the bill's passage (Vizzard, 1993: 185–188).

Sanctions were established for dealing in firearms without a federal license, records requirements for licensed dealers became more specific, and criminal penalties were created for false recordkeeping and knowingly delivering firearms to prohibited persons, including felons. The bill set licensing fees for dealers at only $10.00 per year and did not grant any discretion in the issuance of licenses.

Although persons in the specified categories were prohibited from receiving or possessing firearms, no licensing, registration, or reporting systems were established to facilitate this end. Administrative regulations were authorized to facilitate implementation, but this process has been used very conservatively. While providing more control mechanisms than the FFA, the law still proved to be more a statement of intended policy than a framework for policy implementation.

Implementation and Reaction

During the decade following the passage of the GCA, policy implementation overshadowed formulation. Interest groups reacted to and were shaped by policy implementation, which they used to advance their efforts toward organization and, ultimately, policy formulation. The events of this period can be examined to evaluate both the incrementalist and pluralist policy models.

The Alcohol, Tobacco, and Firearms Division (ATF) was expanded and began active enforcement of the federal firearms laws. ATF, which became an independent bureau in 1972, was ill-prepared either politically or administratively to handle the task during the first years of implementation (Vizzard, 1993: 165–170). Enforcement efforts generated intense reaction from a small but vocal minority of licensed dealers and unlicensed traffickers, long used to unrestricted trafficking in guns. Enforcement had little impact on the number or availability of firearms, while providing opponents with a focus for their opposition. Opponents used an incremental model, arguing that ATF's actions were the first step toward a total ban (Hardy, 1979; Vizzard, 1993: 170–190).

Convinced that the GCA was the first step in a wave of incremental change, control advocates formed formal advocacy groups, while their congressional allies introduced a series of bills to restrict handguns under the guise of controlling Saturday Night Specials (Sherrill, 1973; Vizzard, 1993: 170–176). Opponents were energized by these forces into more intense resistance. In 1977, the leadership of the NRA was seized by its most libertarian faction, which began a campaign to discredit the GCA and its enforcers. Their primary strategy was to focus on alleged abuses in enforcement of the law and convince gun owners at large that they were at risk of future prosecution and harassment.

Opponents shifted to the offensive after they successfully forced the Carter administration to withdraw mild proposals for changes in the implementing regulations (Vizzard, 1993: 228–235). Reaction to this effort to bypass Congress and initiate policy change using administrative regulation culminated with oversight hearings of the Bureau of Alcohol, Tobacco, and Firearms in 1979 and 1980.[1] Although the administration had imposed this strategy on ATF and Treasury, they quickly abandoned the strategy and ATF, when resistance appeared (Vizzard, 1993: 180–188).

The election of Ronald Reagan as president placed in office an administration friendly to the opponents of firearms control. The immediate result was a proposal to merge the much maligned ATF with the United States Secret Service. Opponents of gun control, who had repeatedly called for ATF's elimination, quickly shifted position and opposed the merger. Real politic won out over symbolism. ATF, as a symbolic opponent, was apparently too valuable to lose.[2] Although ATF survived as a bureau, its director was replaced for the second time in three years, its budget and staffing were significantly reduced, and morale plummeted.

For most of the Reagan and Bush administrations, the opponents of controls dominated the agenda.[3] ATF shifted its attention away from commerce in firearms and concentrated almost exclusively on armed felons and drug traffickers. With this change, ATF's resources began to increase markedly as it became an integral part of the administration's war on drugs. Within the agency, the message was clear: avoid all contact with any activity perceived as gun control.

Reversing the Trend

After 1980, the primary focus of gun control opponents became the passage of the Volkmer-McClure Bill. The attack on ATF had been a key component in the strategy to pass the bill. Passed in 1986 as the Firearms Owners' Protection Act, the bill did not revoke the GCA but did dilute its already weak controls over firearms commerce. In addition, it placed constraints on future use of the implementing regulations to require dealer reporting of purchaser identity. Even before the passage of Volkmer-McClure, however, the dynamics had begun to shift again.

The optimistic view of gun control advocates that the GCA was the first of a series of incremental changes leading to strict firearms control waned throughout the 1970s. The 1982 defeat of a California initiative to prohibit handgun sales and increased congressional support for Volkmer-McClure disheartened many advocates (Vizzard, 1993: 254–258).

In the aftermath of Proposition 15, Handgun Control, Inc. (HCI) emerged as the leading force among advocates. Almost by accident, HCI encountered the issue that would revive its fortunes and influence its policy for the next decade. A small company, KTW, began marketing a Teflon-coated bullet for law enforcement use that was designed to penetrate automobiles, and NBC News presented a segment on the bullet's ability to penetrate police body armor. Although armor-piercing ammunition for handguns had been available for years and virtually all rifle bullets had the capability of defeating soft body armor, the KTW ammunition became known as "cop killer bullets," and the issue captured the imagination of the public and police organizations. Representative Mario Biaggi, a former New York police officer, advanced a bill that would control armor-piercing pistol ammunition, and the NRA immediately opposed the legislation (Davidson, 1993: 85–98).

The issue was largely ignored by ATF for two reasons. It was perceived as being of little practical importance, and the administration was clearly not desirous of being associated with gun control. Although of little significance from a practical policy perspective, the issue had significant political implications. HCI and others quickly recognized the "cop killer bullet" issue as a wedge between the NRA and the police. Their analysis was correct. This issue, closely followed by the passage of Volkmer-McClure, shifted police organizations from neutral to open support for gun control. A formula had been discovered for defeating the NRA. Rather than pursue gun control as a comprehensive policy issue, HCI would focus on limited and fairly innocuous proposals with broad symbolic appeal. Opponents would be forced to accept a control initiative or engage in opposition that would cast them as unreasonable extremists. Although the tactic broke the stalemate, it discouraged consideration of well-crafted, consistent, and comprehensive policy options, and rendered input from policy implementors largely irrelevant.

Breaking the Stalemate

The next step was the Brady Bill and a national waiting period. The majority of the population lived in states that had already enacted waiting periods. Brady fell short of most existing state laws, even prohibiting the retention of the sale information by police. It failed to address private transactions, in which most prohibited persons obtain their firearms. The political decision to use local police to check sales, rather than to require state or federal checks, has already resulted in some local sheriffs and chiefs filing suit to prevent implementation. ATF has been faced with implementing a statute complicated by state and local variations using numerous agents with whom they have little leverage.

With the passage of Brady, the political dynamics of gun control appear to have again shifted. In response, advocates moved in two directions. HCI began advancing more comprehensive policy options such as owner licensing and registration, but congressional response was lukewarm. Focus shifted to prohibition of certain assault weapons, defined more by form than function. Conceptually, such approaches face a significant problem. Assault weapons are functionally identical to semi-automatic pistols, which are also concealable. There is little practical justification for controlling the assault rifles while avoiding the politically riskier action of controlling pistols. Congress has attempted to circumvent this through controls on magazines for the pistols.[4]

Policy Dynamics of Gun Control

The dynamics of gun control policy have repeatedly been characterized in the press as those of a well-financed special interest lobby, the National Rifle Association (NRA), thwarting the desires of the majority of the population through the manipulation of key legislators. Although the NRA has played a key opposition role since 1934 and the majority of Americans appear to favor more regulatory controls than now exist, this portrayal falls far short of describing the dynamics of the issue. The elements that have molded the history of gun control policy, and likely most other policies, are far more complex than mere special interest manipulation of Congress.

At the first level of analysis, the NRA is more than simply a well-financed special interest lobby. It is a grass roots organization with widespread and intense constituent support extending beyond even its membership, with little incentive for compromise. The NRA and its allies have exercised as much control over public policy by molding public attitudes, language, and cultural paradigms as by direct influence in Congress. The NRA's strategy of seeking controversy has fostered an environment that discourages the bureaucracy from seeking solutions through experimentation in implementation or modification of existing law.

Accessing the Agenda

At an even more complex level of analysis, firearms policy reflects cultural, normative, and structural forces that are shared with other visible systemic policies. Although opponents have not kept the issue entirely off the agenda, they have been able to restrict the options considered and impact implementation strategies. Cobb and Elder (1972: 85–87) identified the four criteria for accessing the systemic political agenda as broad public awareness of the issue, consensus that it constitutes a significant problem, legitimacy as a public issue, and susceptibility to correction by government action.

Kingdon (1984: 188–200) later characterized the process as one of political entrepreneurs and policy streams that occasionally converged to open policy windows for a limited time. Underlying both works is the presumption that most policies will lack adequate constituent support to access the agenda. Only when events produce wide public awareness and support will change in systemic policy be given serious consideration. Thus the incentive is far greater to craft policy initiatives for wide appeal than for effective implementation. Expertise in policy implementation is not a critical skill, as such discussions often slow the momentum of policy adoption.

Gun control is a classic example. Since 1968, numerous policy proposals have been introduced in Congress, the press has periodically focused on the issue, and a number of presidential commissions have made recommendations for strict control, Congress has not perceived enough intensity in public support to address comprehensive controls. Public support has consistently been stronger for the concept of gun control than for specifics such as owner licensing, registration, or prohibition. It has been almost 20 years since any such proposal has been given any attention in committee and such proposals have never been on the agenda of the majority of members (Vizzard, 1993: 277–287). The bureaucracy has not been an active participant in initiating policy proposals.

Public Inaction, Private Action

In the meantime, the number of firearms has grown to well over 200 million and the number of stakeholders has vastly increased. In addition, the market has shifted from one dominated by sporting arms to one dominated by combat firearms.[5] Thus the problem has evolved while the issue hovered at the margins of the agenda, presenting policy makers with a much different environment than existed in earlier years. The primary impact of existing policies and debate has likely been an acceleration of the market, as buyers become convinced that they must act before the rules change.

Systemic Roots of Indecision

Political structure, values, and culture have all served to inhibit decisive action on gun control. Structurally, the system is designed to preclude the concentration of power, thus inhibiting decisive action (Lindblom, 1977; Oleszek, 1989; Smith, 1992; Sundquist, 1981). This is reinforced by a political culture with a strong preference for incrementalism and against collective analysis (Barber, 1984: 19–38). Advocates respond by pursuing marginal changes that undercut the argument for theory or paradigm shift, thus undercutting their own theoretical base. A bias toward the individual level of analysis favors opponents of public action, who can focus on the high costs of policies to a few impacted parties, over advocates, who pursue marginal benefits spread over the general population (Barber, 1984). The results are fragmented and inconsistent policies, often initiated after the targeted activity is well established and hardest to alter.

The Battle for Dominant Paradigms

In the case of gun control, the battle has been for control of the language and focus of cultural paradigms. Both Cobb and Elder's (1972) criteria for agenda access and Kingdon's (1984) political streams operate through the changing of prevailing public perceptions. The opposing camps in the gun control debate have attempted to define that debate by controlling its language. In doing so, they have operated at various times within four theoretical orientations. Each of these paradigms has alternate language and assumptions with specific implications for policy formulation and implementation.

Crime Control

The most conspicuous focus has been crime control. Gun control advocates have associated the high incidence of gun crime in the United States with the large number of guns and their easy access. They also focus on certain unpopular firearms and attempt to define the problem as "getting guns off the street." Opponents have countered with a variety of arguments including low crime rates in countries with high gun ownership, but the primary effort has been directed at defining firearms control as effective only on the law abiding. Their focus on language is characterized in the extreme by the phrase "when guns are outlawed, only outlaws will have guns." The historic example of alcohol prohibition is often invoked, though curiously not drug prohibition. In addition, opponents characterize gun control as the alternative to strategies such as mandatory sentencing, while defining legitimate control strategies as those that exclusively and immediately impact known criminals.

Successfully defining the goal of gun control as preventing determined criminals access to guns in a society awash with guns weakens one of the four prerequisite criteria delineated by Cobb and Elder, amenability to solution. This language presumes crime as the rational actions of a small and clearly delineated group, criminals. It assumes that this group can be easily segregated and their activities controlled through incarceration or deterrence. Opinion polls reflect substantial success by control opponents. The polls consistently reflect that even many who support gun control lack faith in its ability to reduce violent crime (Gallup Poll, 1990; Times Mirror Center for People of the Press, 1993; Wright, Rossi, and Daly, 1983: 221–240). Implementors must operate in an environment which defines legitimate policy as exclusively impacting a criminal population.

Sovereignty

The second paradigm is sovereignty. In fact, this issue is far closer to the intellectual heart of the conflict than crime control. The strongest opponents of gun control are essentially Lockian in their orientation (Knox, 1988; Tonso, 1982 and 1990). They mistrust and fear government and collective security and believe sovereignty rests with the individual citizen. They never fail to invoke the language of individual rights. The status afforded individual rights in the United States has fostered extensive use of this technique by interest groups, often on both sides of an issue as in the right to life and the right to choose. Control advocates are more accepting of collective authority and the concept of state sovereignty. Given the historical American preference for individual over collective rights, the advocates of gun control have trod lightly with this paradigm, while opponents have extolled the Second Amendment as a guarantee of an individual right to unrestricted possession of firearms. Although opponents have, to date, failed in the courts they have been far more successful at influencing language and paradigms.[6] Again, the implications for implementation are significant. Gun control is a collective and preventative strategy. Faced with political traditions that question the legitimacy of such policies by government, ATF has characterized itself as a law enforcement agency using the gun laws to impact crime and not as a gun control agency. This further delegitimizes gun control as a strategy.

Culture

If sovereignty is the intellectual heart of the controversy, culture is its normative heart. Gun control has been characterized as a conflict between cosmopolitans and traditionalists (Bruce-Biggs, 1976; Kaplan, 1981). The former are characterized as being more global in their social and political orientation, more secular, and more accepting of collective solutions. They have little experience with firearms and perceive little legitimate purpose for them. The traditionalists are more likely to have a positive view of firearms and firearms owners, the former being viewed as items for sport and self-protection and the latter being reputable citizens.[7] With half of all American homes possessing at least one firearm, the cosmopolitan view has not prevailed adequately to demonize firearms. In a society more amenable to collective action and accepting of state sovereignty, this might not be critical. The United States is not that society. By reducing legitimacy, demonization weakens the presumption of rights for the users and traffickers in a commodity, thus shifting the burden of justification to the opponents of control. This was successfully done for a time with liquor, is still the case for drugs, and is becoming so for tobacco. Successful demonization would significantly alter the dynamics of policy implementation, as evidenced by narcotics.

Public Health

Most recently, control advocates in the medical and public health community have begun to apply the language of public health to guns. To date, the impact of this approach on the public is not clear. It is clearly modeled on the experience with tobacco, seat belts, and motorcycle helmets. This approach will inevitably face the burden of shifting analysis from the individual to the collective, but it avoids the need for demonization by moving to the cost-benefit language. This paradigm may offer a more functional model for policy implementation by legitimating the language of regulation and cost-benefit analysis.

Symbols over Substance

The need for broad public acceptance and active support to move any policy leads advocates to pursue proposals based more on their symbolic impact than their expected utility in advancing the public good. As Kingdon pointed out, the policy window opens only briefly, usually through fortuitous congruence of events and the efforts of policy entrepreneurs. The probability for success is greatest in an atmosphere of crisis, often delaying action until it is least effective. Normative theories of pluralism predicted that competing forces would refine and improve policy. Incrementalist theory predicted that once adopted, the policy would evolve as needs became apparent and familiarity increased. Gun control policy has not conformed to either of these expectations.

Another Iron Triangle

Pluralist conflict has produced policy proposals crafted for political advantage and not practicality. Policies once adopted have not evolved or been refined but have provided additional impetus to pluralist conflict. The bureaucracy and legislators have been willing to avoid the conflict generated by substantive policy proposals. With advocacy groups locked in symbolic conflict largely focused on constituent support and both Congress and the bureaucracy avoiding the issue, the issue has begun to resemble a variation on the iron triangle.

The crafting of effective public policy, absent great luck, requires significant grasp of the mechanics of the field to which the policy relates and an environment that allows experimentation and adaptation. Neither of these elements are currently present for firearms control. Those that should be concerned with such issues as the mechanics of the firearms market, the role of firearms in social behavior, and options for firearms control have shown little interest. The advocacy groups are focused on political advantage with one side seeking to stir public support and the other seeking to defeat all legislation without consideration for merit. Legislative staffs have spent minimal time mastering such mundane issues, because legislators show little interest. The last potential source of knowledge and analysis, the bureaucracy, has followed the safest course of action and avoided association with significant proposals for policy change.

Prerequisite for Policy Change

In the case of gun control, the dynamics of the issue will likely change when the public's paradigms shift adequately to change the incentives and paradigms of legislators. Change could move the issue entirely off the agenda, or more likely, given demographic and crime trends, to the mainstream. If the latter occurs, several changes in the process are likely, once controls are perceived as inevitable. Advocates, more confident of their position, may focus less on symbolism and more on substance. Opponents may shift from total opposition to more active participation in the details of legislation, in hopes of producing policies least burdensome to their constituents. The bureaucracy would then likely feel secure enough to show real interest in developing proposals and crafting the details necessary for effective implementation.

Making Policy for Effective Implementation

To be effective, policies directed at public behavior must encourage widespread compliance by the majority of the population. This necessitates that the law avoid unnecessary burdens while facilitating easy enforcement. Enforcement is facilitated by simplicity, uniformity, and clear delineation between compliance and violation. Most importantly the law must be logically consistent, focused, and easily understood.

In the case of firearms, action would best have been taken before the numbers began to increase in the 1960s. Given current reality, licensing and registration are the most promising options. Registration inhibits the casual transfers that undermine any system of owner licensing. Licensing in turn, simplifies transfer controls by establishing identity and eligibility in advance. The states, using minimum federal standards, are probably the most effective jurisdiction for such action, thus leaving control of commerce primarily to the federal government. If categories of firearms are to be controlled, functional, generic definitions are preferable.[8] Assault weapons could be controlled by inclusion with machine guns and silencers under the NFA. The mechanics are familiar to many gun enthusiasts, as well as ATF, and the law has been well tested in the courts. Instead, both houses of Congress have passed bills that create new, complex, and untested procedures for controlling these firearms.

Conclusions

Gun control is only one of a multitude of policy issues facing the country. Many, such as health care, are more complex and significant. Gun control is a useful case precisely because it does not involve such massive financial interests, alter the economy, or alter most lifestyles. Problems of policy formulation and implementation are thus attributable to systemic values, culture, and structure. Those focused on policy formulation or implementation would do well to consider the critical role played by language, values, and dominant paradigms.

Although the mechanics of policy formulation do not encourage bureaucratic participation when issues are controversial, exclusion of such expertise has significant long-term implications for implementation and for the bureaucracy itself. Language and paradigms that dominate the policy debate will continue to define the dynamics of implementation. Implementation strategies will, in turn, influence the environment for future policy formulation. Incremental strategies are undercut by this process, particularly when organized interest groups oppose change.

Rather than a policy-administration dichotomy, the case of gun control reveals an interactive and highly interdependent process, although the interaction is often not planned nor well understood. The fields of public policy and administration, as well as the larger political culture, lack adequate intellectual paradigms for addressing this reality. Optimistic views of resolution through interest group interaction appear unjustified. A system that favors obstruction encourages stalemate that shifts focus from policy content to control of language and public perception.

NOTES

1. Curiously, both opponents and advocates misread the post-Watergate Congress. Advocates began a push for strict controls and opponents prepared for a fight to the death. Ironically, the new Congress proved suspicious of executive authority and was fertile ground for opponents. In addition, declining resources motivated a shift from a focus on new legislation and appropriations and toward oversight.

2. The merger required no congressional approval and was well underway when representatives of the liquor industry applied pressure on Congress to hold hearings. Language prohibiting the merger was subsequently included in the budget bill. Although the liquor industry acted quickly, the NRA appeared confused for several weeks before publicly opposing the merger.

3. Interviews with a variety of ATF and Treasury and Justice Department employees revealed that they were instructed to avoid the issue of gun control. This extended even to the research agenda of the National Institute of Justice.

4. The law as passed by Congress is similar to the assault weapon ban passed by California and the restrictions on imports imposed by ATF order. Manufacturers have easily circumvented these restrictions, which depend more on appearance than function. The effort to control ammunition magazines, first proposed by the Bush administration, is the more significant feature of the bill. From the implementation perspective this was an unfortunate strategy. Magazines are the least complicated part of a firearm to manufacture and have not been serialized. Thus, distinguishing between old legal and new illegal magazines will be impossible and magazines will be easily manufactured and distributed in the illegal market.

5. The exact number of firearms in the United States is unknown. The author has examined the work of Newton and Zimring and Wright, Rossi, and Daly and estimates made by ATF. And estimate of 200 million with a growth rate of 4 to 5 million per year is a conservative estimate. The changing nature of the market is based on ATF manufacturing figures, close observation of the market, and interviews with numerous gun dealers.

6. Although the Supreme Court has never ruled that the Second Amendment applies to private gun ownership, the perception of such a right is reflected in opinion surveys and is regularly cited by public figures.

7. Early experience is the best predictor of firearms ownership, and ownership is the best predictor of opposition to control laws.

8. The experience in California has been that police officers are often confused regarding the legal status of firearms they encounter in the field. Even persons who desire to comply with the law are sometimes unable to understand which firearms are legal and which are not. The ban on machine guns generated far less implementation problems because it made no exceptions. The NFA was more easily administered because it required those owning or acquiring the controlled firearms to first register them and obtain consent.

REFERENCES

Barber, Benjamin R. 1984. *Strong Democracy: Participatory Politics for a New Age*. Berkeley: University of California Press.

Bruce-Biggs, B. 1976. "The Great American Gun War." *The Public Interest*, vol. 45 (Fall), 37–62.

Cobb, Roger W., and Charles D. Elder. 1972. *Participation in American Politics: The Dynamics of Agenda-Building*. Baltimore: Johns Hopkins University Press.

Davidson, Osha Gray. 1993. *Under Fire: The NRA and the Battle for Gun Control*. New York: Henry Holt.

Gallup Poll. 1990. "Support for Gun Control at All Time High," vol. 55 (September 26).

Hardy, David. 1979. *The BATF War on Civil Liberties: The Assault on Gun Owners*. Bellevue, WA: Second Amendment Foundation.

Hofstadter, Richard. 1970. "America as a Gun Culture." In Richard Hofstadter and Michael Wallace, eds., *American Violence: A Documentary History*. New York: Alfred Knopf.

Kaplan, John. 1981. "The Wisdom of Gun Prohibition." *Annals, American Academy of Political and Social Science*, no. 455 (May), 11–21.

Kates, Don B. 1979. *Restricting Handguns: The Liberal Skeptics Speak Out*. Croton-on-Hudson, NY: North River Press.

Kennett, Lee, and James Anderson. 1975. *The Gun in America: The Origins of an American Dilemma*. Westport, CT: Greenwood Press.

Kingdon, John W. 1984. *Agendas, Alternatives and Public Policies*. Harper-Collins.

Knox, Neal. 1988. "The 30-Year War for Gun Ownership." *Guns and Ammo* (August).

Kopel, David B. 1992. *The Samurai, the Mountie and the Cowboy: Should America Adopt the Gun Controls of Other Democracies?* Buffalo, NY: Prometheus Books.

Leff, Carol S., and Mark H. Leff. 1981. "The Politics of Ineffectiveness: Federal Firearms Legislation, 1919–38." *Annals, American Academy of Political and Social Science*, no. 455 (May), 48–62.

Lindblom, Charles. 1977. *Politics and Markets*. New York: Basic Books.

Oleszek Walter J. 1989. *Congressional Procedures and the Policy Process*, 3rd ed. Washington, DC: Congressional Quarterly, 283–284.

Sherrill, Robert. 1973. *The Saturday Night Special and Other Guns with Which Americans Won the West, Protected Bootleg Franchises, Slew Wildlife, Robbed Countless Banks, Shot Husbands Purposely and by Mistake and Killed Presidents — Together with the Debate over Continuing Same*. New York: Charterhouse.

Smith, Steven. 1992. "The Senate in the Post Reform Era." In Roger H. Davidson, ed. *The Post Reform Congress*. College Park: University of Maryland Press.

Sugarmann, Josh. 1992. *National Rifle Association: Money, Firepower and Fear*. Washington, DC: National Press Books.

Sundquist, James L. 1981. *The Decline and Resurgence of Congress*. Washington, DC: Brookings Institution.

Times Mirror Center for the People and the Press. 1993. "Public Backs Clinton on Gun Control." December 10.

Tonso, William R. 1982. *The Gun and Society: The Social and Existential Roots of the American Attachment to Firearms*. Washington, DC: University Press.

———. 1990. *The Gun Culture and Its Enemies*. Bellevue, WA: Second Amendment Foundation.

Vizzard, William J. 1993. "Evolution of Gun Control Policy in the United States: Accessing the Public Agenda." DPA dissertation, University of Southern California.

Wright, James D., Peter H. Rossi, and Kathleen Daly. 1983. *Under the Gun: Weapons, Crime and Violence in America*. New York: Adline.

Zimring, Franklin E., and Gordon Hawkins. 1987. *The Citizen's Guide to Gun Control*. New York: MacMillan.

Chapter Seven

A Loaded Question
What Is It about Americans and Guns?

Leonard Kriegel

I have fired a gun only once in my life, hardly experience enough to qualify one as an expert on firearms. As limited as my exposure to guns has been, however, my failure to broaden that experience had nothing at all to do with moral disapproval or with the kind of righteous indignation that views an eight-year-old boy playing cops and robbers with a cap pistol as a preview of the life of a serial killer. None of us can speak with surety about alternative lives, but had circumstances been different I suspect I not only would have hunted but very probably would have enjoyed it. I might even have gone in for target shooting, a "sport" increasingly popular in New York City, where I live (like bowling, it is practiced indoors in alleys). To be truthful, I have my doubts that target shooting would really have appealed to me. But in a country in which grown men feel passionately about a game as visibly ludicrous as golf, anything is possible.

The single shot I fired didn't leave me with a traumatic hatred of or distaste for guns. Quite the opposite. I liked not only the sense of incipient skill firing that shot gave me but also the knowledge that a true marksman, like a good hitter in baseball, had to practice—and practice with a real gun. Boys on the cusp of adolescence are not usually disciplined, but they do pay attention to the demands of skill. Because I immediately recognized how difficult it would be for me to practice marksmanship, I was brought face to face with the fact that my career as a hunter was over even before it had started.

Like my aborted prospects as a major league ballplayer, my short but happy life as a hunter could be laid at the metaphorical feet of the polio virus which left me crippled at the age of eleven. Yet the one thing that continues to amaze me as I look back to that gray February afternoon when I discovered the temptation of being shooter and hunter is that I did not shoot one or the other of the two most visible targets—myself or my friend Jackie, the boy who owned the .22.

Each of us managed to fire one shot that afternoon. And when we returned to the ward in which we lived along with twenty other crippled boys between the ages of nine and thirteen, we regaled our peers with a story unashamedly embellished in the telling. As the afternoon chill faded and the narrow winter light in which we had hunted drifted toward darkness, Jackie managed to hide the .22 from ward nurses and doctors on the prowl. What neither of us attempted to hide from the other boys was our brief baptism in the world of guns.

Like me, Jackie was a Bronx boy, as ignorant about guns as I was. Both of us had been taken down with polio in the summer of '44. We had each lost the use of our legs. We were currently in wheelchairs. And we had each already spent a year and a half in the aptly named New York State Reconstruction Home, a state hospital for long-term physical rehabilitation. Neither of us had ever fired anything more lethal than a Daisy air rifle, popularly known as a BB gun—and even that, in my case at least, had been fired under adult supervision. But Jackie and I were also American claimants, our imaginations molded as much by Hollywood westerns as by New York streets. At twelve, I was a true Jeffersonian who looked upon the ownership of a six-shooter as every American's "natural" right.

To this day I don't know how Jackie got hold of that .22. He refused to tell me. And I still don't know how he got rid of it after our wheelchair hunt in the woods. For months afterward I would try to get him to promise that he and I would go hunting again, but, as if our afternoon hunt had enabled him to come to terms with his own illusions about the future (something that would take me many more years), Jackie simply shook his head and said, "That's over." I begged, wheedled, cajoled, threatened. Jackie remained obdurate. A single shot for a single hunt. It would have to be sufficient.

I never did find out whether or not I hit the raccoon. On the ride back to the ward, Jackie claimed I had. After he fired his shot, he dropped from his wheelchair and slid backward on his rump to the abandoned water pipe off the side of the dirt road into which the raccoon had leaped at the slashing crack of the .22. His hand came down on something red—a bloodstain, he excitedly suggested, as he lifted himself into his wheelchair and we turned to push ourselves back to the ward. It looked like a rust stain to me, but I didn't protest. I was quite willing to take whatever credit I could. That was around an hour after the two of us, fresh from lunch, had pushed our wheelchairs across the hospital grounds, turning west at the old road that cut through the woods and led to another state home, this one ministering to the retarded. The .22, which lay on Jackie's lap, had bounced and jostled as we maneuvered our wheelchairs across that rutted road in search of an animal—any animal would do—to shoot. The early February sky hung above us like a charcoal drawing, striations of gray slate shadings feeding our nervous expectation.

It was Jackie who first spotted the raccoon. Excited, he handed the .22 to me, a gesture spurred, I then thought, by friendship. Now I wonder whether his generosity wasn't simply self-protection. Until that moment, the .22 lying across Jackie's dead legs had been an abstraction, as much an imitation gun as the "weapons" boys in New York City constructed out of the wood frames and wood slats of fruit and vegetable crates, nails, and rubber bands—cutting up pieces of discarded linoleum and stiff cardboard to use as ammunition. I remember the feel of the .22 across my own lifeless legs, the weight of it surprisingly light, as I stared at the raccoon who eyed us curiously from in front of the broken pipe. Then I picked up the gun, aimed, and squeezed the trigger, startled not so much by the noise nor by the slight pull, but by the fact that I had actually fired at something. The sound of the shot was crisp and clean. I felt as if I had done something significant.

Jackie took the gun from me. "Okay," he said eagerly. "My turn now." The raccoon was nowhere in sight, but he aimed in the direction of the water pipe into which it had disappeared and squeezed the trigger. I heard the crack again, a freedom of music now, perhaps because we two boys had suddenly been bound to each other and had escaped, for this single winter afternoon moment, the necessary but mundane courage which dominates the everyday lives of crippled children. "Okay," I heard him cry out happily, "we're goddamn killers now."

A formidable enough hail and farewell to shooting. And certainly better than being shot at. God knows what happened to that raccoon. Probably nothing; but for me, firing that single shot was both the beginning and the end of my life as a marksman. The raccoon may have been wounded, as Jackie claimed. Perhaps it had crawled away, bleeding, to die somewhere in the woods. I doubt it. And I certainly hope I didn't hit it, although in February 1946, six months before I returned to the city and to life among the "normals," I would have taken its death as a symbolic triumph. For that was a time I needed any triumph I could find, no matter how minor. Back then it seemed natural to begin an uncertain future with a kill—even if one sensed, as I did, that my career as a hunter was already over. The future was hinting at certain demands it would make. And I was just beginning to bend into myself, to protect my inner man from being crushed by the knowledge of all I would never be able to do. Hunting would be just another deferred dream.

But guns were not a dream. Guns were real, definitive, stamped on the imagination by their functional beauty. A gun was not a phallic symbol; a gun didn't offer me revenge on polio; a gun would not bring to life dead legs or endow deferred dreams with substance. I am as willing as the next man to quarantine reality within psychology. But if a rose is no more than a rose, then tell me why a gun can't simply be a gun? Guns are not monuments to fear and aspiration any more than flowers are.

I was already fascinated by the way guns looked. I was even more fascinated by what they did and by what made people use them. Like any other twelve-year-old boy, I was absorbed by talk about guns. Six months after the end of the Second World War, boys in our ward were still engrossed by the way talking about guns entangled us in the dense underbrush of the national psyche. And no one in that ward was more immersed in weaponry than I. On the verge of adolescence, forced to seek and find adventure in my own imagination, I was captivated by guns.

It was a fascination that would never altogether die. A few weeks ago I found myself nostalgically drifting through the arms and armor galleries of the Metropolitan Museum of Art. Years ago I had often taken my young sons there. A good part of my pleasure now derived from memories pinned to the leisurely innocence of those earlier visits. As I wandered among those rich cabinets displaying ornate pistols and rifles whose carved wood stocks were embossed with gold and silver and ivory and brass, I was struck by how incredibly lovely many of these weapons were. It was almost impossible to conceive of them as serving the function they had been designed to serve. These were not machines designed to kill and maim. Created with an eye to beauty, their sense of decorative purpose was as singular as a well-designed eighteenth-century silver drinking cup. These guns in their solid display cases evoked a sense of the disciplined craftsmanship to which a man might dedicate his life.

Flintlocks, wheel locks, a magnificent pair or ivory pistols owned by Catherine the Great—all of them as beckoning to the touch of fingers, had they not been securely locked behind glass doors, as one of those small nineteenth-century engraved cameos that seem to force time itself to surrender its pleasures. I gazed longingly at a seventeenth-century wheel lock carbine, coveting it the way I might covet a drinking cup by Cellini or a small bronze horse and rider by Bologna. Its beautifully carved wooden stock had been inlaid with ivory, brass, silver, and mother-of-pearl, its pride of artisanship embossed with the name of its creator, Caspar Spät. I smiled with pleasure. Then I wandered through the galleries until I found myself in front of a case displaying eighteenth-century American flintlock rifles, all expressing the democratic spirit one finds in Louis Sullivan's buildings or Whitman's poetry or New York City playgrounds built by the WPA during the Great Depression. Their polished woods were balanced by ornately carved stag-antler powder horns, which hung like Christmas decorations beneath them. To the right was another display case devoted to long-barreled Colt revolvers; beyond that, a splendidly engraved 1894 Winchester rifle and a series of Smith & Wesson revolvers, all of them decorated by Tiffany.

And yet they were weapons, designed ultimately to do what weapons have always done—destroy. Only in those childlike posters of the 1970s did flower stems grow out of the barrel of a gun. People who shoot, like people who cook, understandably choose the best tools available. And if it is easier to hit a target with an Uzi than a homemade zip gun, chances are those who want to hit the target will feel few qualms about choosing the Uzi.

Nonetheless, these galleries are a remarkable testimony to the functional beauty of guns. Nor am I the only person who has been touched by their beauty. The problem is to define where the killing ceases and the beauty begins. At what point does a young boy's sense of adventure transform itself into the terror of blood and destruction and pain and death? I remember my sons' excitement when they toured these splendid galleries with me. (Yes doctor, I did permit them to enjoy guns. And neither became a serial killer.) These weapons helped bring us together, bound father and sons, just as going to baseball games or viewing old Chaplin movies had.

Geography may not be the sole father of morality, but one would have to be remarkably naive to ignore its claims altogether. As I write this, I can see on the table in front of me a newspaper headlining the most recent killings inflicted on New York City's anarchic populace. Firearms now rule street and schoolyard, even as the rhetoric of politicians demanding strict gun control escalates—along with the body count.

And yet I recognize that one man's fear and suffering is another man's freedom and pleasure. Here is the true morality of geography. Like it or not, we see the world against a landscape of accommodation. Guns may be displayed behind glass cases in that magnificent museum, but in the splendid park in which that museum has been set down like a crowning jewel, guns have been known to create not art but terror. Functional beauty, it turns out, does not alter purpose.

I have a friend who has lived his entire life in small towns in Maine. My friend is both a hunter and a connoisseur of guns. City streets and guns may be a volatile mix, but the Maine woods and guns apparently aren't. Rifles and pistols hang on my friends' living room wall like old family portraits. They are lived with as comfortably as a family heirloom. My friend speaks knowingly of their shape, describes each weapon lovingly, as if it possessed its own substance. He is both literate and civilized, but he would never deny that these guns are more than a possession to him. They are an altar before which he bends the knee, a right of ownership he considers inviolable, even sacrosanct. And yet my friend is not a violent man.

I, too, am not a violent man. But I am a New Yorker. And like most people who live in this city, I make certain assumptions about the value of the very indignities one faces by choosing to live here. If I didn't, I probably couldn't remain in New York. For with all of the problems it forces one to face, the moral geography of New York also breeds a determination not to give in to the daily indignities the city imposes.

During the summer of 1977, I lived within a different moral geography. I was teaching a graduate seminar on Manhood and American Culture at the University of New Mexico in Albuquerque, tracing the evolution of the American man from Ben Franklin's sturdy, middle-class acolyte to the rugged John Wayne of *Stagecoach*. Enchanted by the New Mexico landscape, I would frequently drive off to explore the small towns and brilliant canyons in whose silences ghosts still lingered. One day a friend volunteered to drive with me into the Manzano Mountains. I had announced my desire to look at the ruins of a seventeenth-century mission fort at Gran Quivira, while he wanted me to meet a man who had, by himself, built a house in those haunting, lovely mountains.

Tension between Anglos and Hispanics was strong in New Mexico in the summer of 1977. Even a stranger could feel a palpable, almost physical, struggle for political and cultural hegemony. Coming from a New York in which the growing separation of black and white was already threatening to transform everyday life into a racial battlefield, I did not feel particularly intimidated by this. Instead of black and white, New Mexico's ethnic and racial warfare would be between Anglo, Hispanic, and Indian. Mountainair, where we were to visit my friend's friend, was considered an Anglo town. Chilili, some miles up the road, was Hispanic.

My friend's friend had built his house on the outskirts of Mountainair, with a magnificent view of ponderosa pine. He was a man in his early sixties and had come to New Mexico from Virginia soon after World War II to take a job as a technical writer in a nuclear research laboratory in Albuquerque. Before the war he had done graduate work in literature at the University of Virginia, but the demands of fatherhood had decided him against finishing his doctorate. Like so many Americans before him, he had taken wife and young children to start over in the West.

In the warmth and generosity of his hospitality, however, he remained a true Southerner. As we sat and talked and laughed in the huge sun-drenched living room that opened onto that magnificent view of mountains and pines and long New Mexico sky, I could not help but feel that here was the very best of this nation—a man secure in himself, a man of liberal sympathies and a broad understanding of human behavior and a love of children and grandchildren and wife, a man who spoke perceptively of Jane Austen's novels and spoke sadly of the savage threat of drugs (his oldest son, a veteran of the war in Vietnam, was living with him, along with wife and three-year-old daughter, trying to purge the heroin addiction that threatened to wreck his life).

I remember him happily holding forth on Jane Austen's *Persuasion* when his body suddenly seemed to freeze in mid-sentence. I could hear a motor in the distance. Without another word, he turned and crossed the room. Twin double-barreled shotguns hung on the wall above the fireplace. He took one, his right hand scooping shells from a canvas bag hanging from a thong looped around a horseshoe nail banged shoulder-high into the wall. His son, the ex-Marine, grabbed the other gun and scooped shells from the same bag. Through the glassed-in cathedral living room leading to the porch, I watched the two of them stand side by side, shotguns pointed at a pickup truck already out of range. "Those bastards!" I heard my host snarl.

"We'll get 'em yet, Pop," his son said. "I swear it."

After we left to drive on to the ruins at Gran Quivira, I asked the friend who had accompanied me to explain what had happened. "A pickup truck from Chilili. Hispanics driving up the mountain to cut trees. It's illegal. But they do it anyway."

"Do the trees belong to your friend?"

"Not his trees. Not his mountain." Then he shrugged. "But it's his gun."

I angrily cast my eyes at the man and find myself staring into the twin barrels of a shotgun loosely held but pointed directly at me. It is that same summer in Albuquerque, three weeks later, and I am sitting in the driver's seat of my car, my ten-year-old son, Bruce, directly behind me. Alongside him is the eleven-year-old daughter of the man who had invited me to teach at the University of New Mexico. I have just backed my car away from a gasoline pump to allow another car to move out of the garage into the road. As the other car came out of the gas station, the man with the shotgun adroitly cut me off and maneuvered his rust-pocked yellow pickup ahead of me in line before I could get back to the gas pump.

My first reaction is irritation with my car, as if the steel and chrome were sentient and responsible. It is the same ugly gold 1971 Buick in which, five summers earlier, I had driven through a Spanish landscape remarkably similar to the New Mexico in which I now find myself. Bruce had been with me then, too, along with his older brother and mother. But it is not the Buick that attracts men with guns. Nor is it that mythical violence of American life in which European intellectuals believe so fervently. In Spain we had been stopped at a roadblock, a sandbagged machine gun aimed by one of Franco's troops perusing traffic like a farmer counting chickens in a henhouse. The soldiers had asked for passports, scowled at the children, examined the Buick as if it were an armored tank, inspecting glove compartment and trunk and wedging their hands into the spaces between seat and back. At the hotel restaurant at which we stopped for lunch twenty minutes later, we learned that two *guardia civil* had been ambushed and killed by Basque guerrillas. During Franco's last years, such acts grew more and more frequent. Spain was filled with guns and soldiers. One was always aware of the presence of soldiers patrolling the vacation beaches of the Costa del Sol—and particularly aware of their guns.

As I am aware of the shotgun now. And as I am growing aware of that same enraged sense of humiliation and helplessness that seized me as those Spanish soldiers examined car and sons and wife, their guns casually pointed at all I loved most in the world, these other lives that made my life significantly mine. "Guns don't kill, people do!" Offer that mind-deadening cliché to a man at a roadblock watching the faces of soldiers for whom the power of a gun is simply that it permits them to feel contempt for those without guns. Tell that to a man sitting in a car with two young children, contemplating doing what he knows he cannot do because the gun is in another man's hands. Both in Spain and in this New Mexico that Spain had planted in the New World like a genetic acorn breeding prerogatives of power, guns endowed men with a way to settle all questions of responsibility.

The man with the shotgun says nothing. He simply holds the weapon in his beefy hand, its muzzle casually pointed in my direction. I toy with the notion of getting out of the car and confronting him. I am angry, enraged. I don't want to give in to his rude power. Only my son and my colleague's daughter are in the back of the car. Defensively, I turn to look at them. My colleague's daughter is wide-eyed and frightened. Bruce is equally frightened, but his eyes are on me. I am his father and he expects me to do something, to say something, to alter the balance of expectation and reality. Our car was on line for gas first. To a ten-year-old, justice is a simple arithmetic.

To that ten-year-old's father it is not necessarily more complex. I could tell myself that it was insane to tell a man pointing a shotgun at me and these two children that he has broken the rules. Chances are he wouldn't have fired, would probably have responded with a shrug of the shoulders no more threatening than a confession of ignorance.

Obviously, none of this mattered. My growing sense of humiliation and rage had nothing to do with having to wait an extra minute or two while the station attendant filled the tank of the pickup. I was in no particular rush. I was simply returning home from a day-long excursion to a state park where my son and his new friend had crawled through caves and climbed rocks splashed by a warm spring. But I was facing a man with a shotgun, a man who understood that people with guns define options for themselves.

The man with the gun decides whether or not to shoot, just as he chooses where to point his gun. It is not political power that stems from the barrel of a gun, as Maoists used to proclaim so ritualistically. It is individual power, the ability to impose one's presence on the world, simply because guns always do what language only sometimes does: Guns command! Guns command attention, guns command discipline, guns command fear.

And guns bestow rights and prerogatives, even to those who have read Jane Austen and engaged the world in their own comedy of manners. There is a conditional nature to all rights. And there are obligations that should not be shunted aside. Guns are many things, some symbolic, some all too real. But in real life they are always personal and rarely playful. They measure not capacity but the obligation the bearer of the gun has to believe that power belongs not to the gun but to him. And yet were I to tell this to my friend in Maine—that sophisticated, literate, humane man—I suspect he would turn to me and say, "That's right. There's always got to be somebody's finger on the trigger."

A confession, then: I may be as fascinated by guns as my gun-owning and gun-loving friend in Maine, but were it up to me, I would rid America of its guns. I would be less verbally self-righteous about gun control than I was in the past, for I think I have begun to understand those who, like my friend in Maine, have arguments of their own in defense of guns. They are formidable arguments. Their fear matches mine, and I assume that their anguish over the safety of their children is also equal to mine. I, too, know the statistics. I can repeat, as easily as he can, that in Switzerland, where an armed citizenry is the norm, the homicide rate is far lower than in many countries that carefully control the distribution of guns to their populace. Laws are simply words on paper—unless they embody what a population wants.

There is no logic with which I can convince my gun-owning friend in Maine. But there are images I wish I could get him to focus on. Like me, he is a writer. Only I write about cities, and my friend writes about the Maine woods. He is knowledgeable about animals and rocks and trees and silence, and I am knowledgeable about stubs of grass growing between cracks in a concrete sidewalk and the pitch and pull of conflicting voices demanding recognition. I wish I could explain to him the precise configuration of that double-barreled shotgun pointing at me and those two children. Maybe then I could convince him that truth is not merely a matter of geography. Yes, guns don't kill and people do— but in the America he and I share, those people usually kill with guns.

Four years after that incident at the gas station, I was sitting with Bruce in a brasserie in Paris. It was a sunny July afternoon and we were eating lunch at a small outside table, the walls of the magisterial Invalides beckoning to us from across the street. Bruce was fourteen, and fifteen minutes earlier he had returned from his first trip alone on the Paris Metro. Suddenly a man approached, eyes menacing and bloodshot. He was short and thick, his body seemingly caked by the muscularity of a beaten-down club fighter or an unemployed stevedore. He stared at us, eyes filled with the rage of the insane. Then he flexed his muscles as if he were on exhibit as a circus strong man, cried out something—a sound I remember as a cross between gargling and choking—and disappeared just as suddenly down the street.

The incident still haunts me. The French, I suspect, are as violent as they like to claim we Americans are. But in Paris it is difficult for a man filled with rage and craziness to get hold of a gun. Not impossible, mind you, just difficult. Somewhere along the line, the French have learned not that guns don't kill and people do but that people with guns can kill. And they know what we have yet to acknowledge—that when the Furies dance in the head it's best to keep the weapons in display cases in the museum. For that, at least, I wish my friend in Maine could learn to be grateful. As I was, eating lunch with my son in Paris.

Chapter Eight

When the Time Comes to Give Up a Firearm

Judy Foreman

On the surface, they were an ordinary couple, both in their seventies and living in a Boston suburb.

But for years, the husband had been a drinker, so much so that by late life, he had brain damage. He also had a temper.

And a gun collection that terrified his wife.

Frantic that her husband could no longer handle guns safely, the wife called a counselor, who suggested she give him an ultimatum: "Either the guns go or I go."

To her dismay, he chose his guns.

Another aging gun owner was a widower in his eighties who was cared for at home, also in a Boston suburb, by his daughter.

He was demented, yet spent hours cleaning and fondling his gun, which terrified his daughter. She tried to take his weapon away, arguing gently, "Dad, you are not safe with this."

When he angrily refused, she took his ammunition instead.

Discovering this seeming treachery one night, he grabbed his gun and marched into her room. She awoke in terror to find her aging and enraged father standing over her, gun in hand.

Luckily, things turned out peacefully in these cases—the gunowners didn't kill anyone. Nor did they kill themselves, as is actually more likely, given that older white men have the highest suicide rate in the country.

In the first, the wife fled to her son's house and begged him to take his father's guns. He did, but let the older man visit often to clean them, and his mother moved back with her husband.

In the second, the daughter finally calmed her father down, then got the family doctor to persuade him to give up his gun.

But happy endings among older gunowners are not a foregone conclusion. In fact, the potential for horror is sobering, given that half the households in America now have at least one gun.

And among people over sixty-five, 29 percent own one, according to the

National Rifle Association, which bases its estimate on research from the University of Chicago.

Other researchers, using the same Chicago data, believe the rate of gun ownership among older Americans is far higher.

Mark Kaplan, assistant professor of social work at the University of Illinois at Urbana-Champaign, and his team say 80 percent of white men over sixty-five in rural areas own guns, as do 50 percent of those in cities.

To be sure, the damage inflicted on others by older men with guns is minimal, as the NRA points out. Of the more than 20,000 homicide arrests a year, only 180 involve people over sixty-five.

And some older people do use guns for self-defense. One man in California, for instance, recently shot an intruder who was beating his wife. The old man became a hero when it turned out the intruder was wanted by police for seventeen robberies.

More often, though, older men turn their guns on themselves. White men over sixty-five have the highest suicide rate in the country, far above that for white women, black men, and black women, according to the National Center for Health Statistics.

"And the rate of suicide among older white men is driven primarily by firearms," says Kaplan. Older women kill themselves with guns, too, increasingly forsaking that old standby, poisoning, but older white men are still the most vulnerable group to suicide by guns.

In fact, as a whole, white men have nearly double the suicide rate of the general population, government figures show. For those aged sixty-five to seventy-four, the rate is nearly triple. For white men over eighty-five, the rate is eight times that of the general population.

And roughly 70 percent of all white men who commit suicide use guns to do the deed; among those aged sixty-five to seventy-four, it's nearly 80 percent. In fact, just having a gun at home increases the risk of suicide, as researchers reported in the *New England Journal of Medicine* three years ago.

To be sure, there are often precipitating factors. In some cases, for instance, an older man is driven over the brink by the prospect of entering a nursing home.

One older Boston-area man packed a gun in his bag when he went to the hospital, recalls geriatric psychologist Erlene Rosowsky of Needham. Within twenty-four hours of being discharged to a nursing home, he pulled it out and shot himself.

But often, it's simple depression that makes a man pull the trigger. Older men overall are less depressed than younger men, notes Kaplan, but "there is still enough undiagnosed and untreated depression in older men to account for the suicides."

No one is suggesting that being old equals being depressed or demented, or that guns be snatched from someone just because he passes a certain birthday. That would be as silly as suggesting all old people give up drivers' licenses.

But guns, like cars, are dangerous in the wrong hands, young or old, as even the NRA knows. "Anybody who is psychologically unstable or suffering from a serious mental illness should not own a gun," acknowledges NRA spokesman Chip Walker.

And the harsh truth is that an older person doesn't have to suffer outright dementia to have normal—but significant—losses in the functioning of the brain's frontal lobes, which govern reasoning, judgment, planning, and impulse control.

"All these tend to weaken with age," says John Miner, a neuropsychologist at the Westwood Lodge Hospital, and the process often starts sooner in men. "If there are guns around, this decline in impulse control could be dangerous."

Psychologist Douglas Powell, director of behavioral science research at the Harvard University Health Services, agrees. "Guns are like any complex machinery," says Powell, who studies the process of cognitive aging. "They require judgment to operate, and judgment, we know, does decline" with age.

So what can you do if you're worried about guns in the hands of an older man whose mind may not be as strong as it once was? Just as it often falls to family members to take away car keys when an older person becomes unsafe to drive, it's often up to family members to take away guns from someone they fear is a danger to himself—or them.

This is tricky, though, because giving up a gun, like giving up driving privileges, can be very traumatic. In fact, an old man deprived of his gun may feel "a sense of loss and bewilderment," says psychologist Rosowsky. Symbolically, the gun may be a "transitional object," she says, "a tangible link with a more alive past, a connection with heightened vitality. . . . It's not just one more artifact." Furthermore, older men "never see guns as dangerous or harmful because they had them for so many years. So it becomes confusing for them when you want to take them away," she adds.

If you've tried and failed at gentle persuasion, she and others suggest, seek help from your doctor or a minister.

Even without family prodding, doctors should try harder to spot depression in older patients and ask about guns at home, says Kaplan, noting that one study showed 75 percent of older people who killed themselves had recently seen a doctor.

If the doctor or pastor can't help, try a lawyer specializing in family law, suggests Tony Keady, a lobbyist with GOAL, the Gun Owners Action League, based in Northboro. But this can be tricky, too, because a "gun is property, pure and simple," he says. Taking it away is "like taking away a car."

For guns that are collector's items, you might persuade the gun owner to give them to the Springfield Armory National Historic Site, though the armory only accepts guns that fit its mission.

As a last resort, if the gunowner is clearly lacking in mental capacity you can go to court to become his guardian and then remove the gun, says Paul Lipsitt, a Newton psychologist and lawyer. This may prove traumatic, though, as would a similar option: having the gunowner with a mental problem involuntarily committed to a hospital, then taking his gun.

Calling the police might also be an option, but if the gunowner is not "waving it around, threatening to kill you, the police won't take it away," says Boston police spokesman Robert O'Toole. "There has to be a clear and present threat. Without that you're in a bind."

Indeed you are.

But both you—and the gunowner—have a right to be safe. So if you are worried about either his safety or your own, at the very least, Rosowsky urges, "start talking about it."

Chapter Nine

Americans Love Their Guns but Fear Violence

Kathryn Kahler

When lawyer Sandy Froman is having a bad day, she steps into her backyard in the Sonoran Desert, picks up an Uzi and fires off a few rounds.

Sometimes she shoots her favorite gun, a .45 ACP Colt Commander pistol. Other times she chooses a 12-gauge shotgun to shoot at steel targets, as turkey vultures fly over the cactus and brush that fill her property on the edge of the Coronado National Forest.

"It's just fun. It's a real positive experience for me," Froman said as she gripped her pistol and aimed at a target.

Froman bought her first gun because she was afraid to stay alone in her home. Today, she and her husband, Bruce Nelson, a well-known holster maker, are genuine gun aficionados.

Froman and Nelson are like millions of Americans who love guns and have made them a part of the fabric of their lives.

At least 65 million Americans—and perhaps more than 100 million—own more than 200 million firearms. They not only own them: they revere them. In America, the love of guns and the right to keep them are integral parts of the country's social, cultural and political heritage.

Some people buy guns for protection, others for hunting or for just plain old fun. Some collect rare weapons, others search out sheer firepower. They teach their children to hunt and to shoot competitively. They oppose gun control and fiercely defend the constitutional right to bear arms.

But the dark side of this romance, critics say, is that American's passion for guns is a fatal attraction:

- A dramatic rise in murders manifests itself in endless stories of shooting deaths and assaults, and police complain they're being outgunned by criminals.
- The entertainment media celebrate America's love of guns in Western movies and in action-adventure films. Children grow up playing with toy guns and watching TV shows glorifying guns as the ultimate equalizer.

- For many urban kids, getting a gun is as much a rite of passage as it is for a boy growing up on a farm to have a gun of his own. It means they've become men.
- As the crime problem continues, more and more Americans—especially women—are arming themselves.

None of this has lessened the fury of the continuing debate over gun control. The National Rifle Association and millions of its allies oppose anything they consider might be an infringement on the public's right to own firearms, while surveys show that 80 percent of Americans favor a law requiring a waiting period before purchasing a gun. President Bush opposes gun control; President-elect Clinton supports it.

Social historians say America's gun culture goes all the way back to the birth of the nation. "We are one of the few modern countries that had a lawless frontier tradition in our history," said Ron Akers, a University of Florida sociologist. "We are one of the few societies where that is such an embedded part of our society. When white colonizers moved West, they got armed. The gun is to America what the Samurai sword is to Japan."

America has always had guns, unlike many European cultures which existed before the development of firearms in the sixteenth century and only came to know them as a new technology. Guns were essential in the colonies' winning independence from the British and settling the U.S. territories. Thomas Jefferson believed gun ownership was a political right and included it in the Bill of Rights. A century ago, a gentleman wouldn't think of going out without his gun because he would be expected to defend women and children. "Ownership of firearms is part and parcel of our culture," said Tulane University sociologist James Wright.

But in modern times, guns have become synonymous with murder and robbery. As crime has increased, gun shop owners and the National Rifle Association say more Americans—particularly young women—are buying guns and learning to shoot them. While no firm figures are available, shooting range employees say they are busier than ever, and many of their new customers are women.

"We have more violent crimes and more property crimes than most other modern industrialized societies. This creates a certain sense of threat that people feel," Akers said. "People feel they can't count on the police for protection and that it's up to me."

Fear of crime prompted Froman to buy a gun, take shooting lessons and become an expert shot. Her interest in guns grew from there. "It became more fun and less scary. . . . I was single and I met some nice single guys. Shooting expanded my horizons," she said. "I shoot guns the same way some people play golf or tennis. It's a challenge," said Froman, a litigator at a major Tucson law firm and a member of the NRA board.

Twice a year, Froman and her husband invite friends over for a party that they have glibly named the Festival of Fun, Food, Film, and Firepower. Their friends bring a covered dish and their favorite gun. They shoot, eat, and then watch a Western or *Terminator II*. One friend perches his three-year-old son on his lap outside and lets him fire his pistol just like the adults do. "It's become the social event of the century," Froman said.

Froman's friend, Elizabeth Hoffman, the associate dean at the Karl Eller Graduate School of Management in Arizona, shares a passion for guns and has become an avid game hunter. Her favorite weapons are a Citori shotgun and a 12-gauge Browning. Hoffman first became interested in hunting as a way to find a safe food supply for her husband, Brian, who is allergic to many chemicals found in processed meats. "There was something very primal about the experience of providing food and a tremendous sense of accomplishment," she said, adding that hunting also gives her time in the out of doors.

Don Burtchin, the past president of the Tucson Rod and Gun Club, grew up in Washington state where he learned to shoot as a child. He went on his first bird hunting trip at age eight and bought his first .22 caliber rifle when he was twelve. "I'd save up my money, go to the sporting goods store and take home a rifle. No one thought anything about it," Burtchin said as he loaded his 30.06 Remington Model 700 rifle at the range. Slowly, he steadied the rifle, peered through the scope, and popped the trigger.

"People in the country understand that a gun is just a tool that is useful for hunting or self defense. A gun is just a tool like a hammer. It can be used properly or improperly," he said.

For Burtchin, the appeal of guns is their craftsmanship and design, coupled with the opportunity to shoot well. He taught his daughter, now twenty-three, to learn to shoot when she was six.

Teaching young children to shoot is part of the gun tradition in America. It is common for youngsters in rural areas, particularly in the South, to learn to shoot and go on their first hunting trip before age ten.

Six-year-old Maggie Giragosian of Cheverly, Maryland, is no exception. Since she was three, her father, Jim, a former elementary school teacher turned NRA firearms instructor, has been teaching her gun safety and letting her pull the trigger while he holds the gun. "The gun is too heavy for me, so daddy holds the gun," Maggie said. "It's fun all right," she says, adding that she'll learn how to look through the site when she gets older.

Jim Giragosian said he has been teaching Maggie and her four-year-old brother about guns and gun safety. "Guns are not a subject of curiosity because they are used to them," Giragosian said. "That is part of the education process. I want her to know what to do if she is around a gun in an unsafe situation."

Dave Twigg, a former deputy sheriff turned writer, got hooked on guns by reading the history of wars. "Firearms represent freedom, a means for the individual to rise above his circumstances in terms of threats. An armed person has the means to protect their lives, their property and their loved ones. That is a significant role of firearms in American history," said Twigg, who collects antique guns and makes his own black powder ammunition. His favorite is a single-action Colt .45 made for the U.S. Cavalry in 1884.

Collectors of more modern guns gather each year at the Soldier of Fortune

Gun Show in Las Vegas. Mercenaries dressed in fatigues, law enforcement officers and gun enthusiasts who wish they'd been soldiers stroll from booth to booth looking at the latest assault weapons, high-velocity ammunition and other gun paraphernalia.

"You can find guns here that you can't find in any gun shop," said a Los Angeles grocery store clerk named Scott, a slight, unassuming man. He asked that his last name not be used.

Scott is a collector of fully automatic guns, which are banned in California. "Everything on the banned list, I want it or already have it," he said. "I'm actively violating California's gun laws." Most weekends, he drives two hours into the Mojave Desert to fire his machine guns. "I have to go where no one will bother me," he said.

Jack Arbuthnot, a professor of social psychology at Ohio University, said some people—mostly men—who buy macho guns often have low self-esteem and want to exert power and control over people.

"There's something about a gun that makes a man strut," said Hubert Williams, president of the Police Foundation and former police director in Newark, N.J.

Arbuthnot said much of the gun violence is related to men who are looking for more control and power. "How does a street bum become significant? By owning a gun," Arbuthnot said. "If you have no economic, intellectual or social power, go get a gun and they will have to listen to you. It's a quick way for someone . . . to reassert control. If you own a handgun and it gives you power, then just think what an assault weapon means in terms of power. It's mostly men, but it's not just a testosterone thing."

Among young gun users, Arbuthnot said, the main difference between kids who shoot on the farm and kids who shoot in the city is what they shoot at. "Kids on the farm shoot at animals, kids on the street shoot at people," Arbuthnot said.

Chapter Ten

The Party of Gun-Haters

Jeff Jacoby

Democrats are the party of widening government power; it stands to reason that they are the party of gun control. But when did gun control become *the* Democratic cause?

I wasn't glued to the convention in Chicago last week, but every time I turned on C-SPAN, it seemed yet another Democrat was railing against guns, demanding new restrictions, or cursing the National Rifle Association.

Just before the convention opened, President Clinton was calling for broader application of the Brady law. At a train stop in Ohio, he proposed a lifetime ban on handgun ownership by anyone convicted of a domestic-abuse misdemeanor. On Monday night, antigun crusaders Sarah and Jim Brady took the spotlight. "The Brady law," they claimed, "has stopped more than 100,000 convicted felons" from buying handguns. It hasn't, but no matter—the Bradys want more controls. "Do it," they said, "for all our children."

Tuesday: Brooklyn Rep. Charles Schumer blasts the GOP, which "said no to assault weapon ban and yes to the powerful NRA." Who, asks Mario Cuomo, "can argue today that Democrats are soft on crime after President Clinton banned assault weapons?"

Wednesday: California's Sen. Dianne Feinstein celebrates the president's "common-sense laws to keep guns out of the hands of criminals and children." Gun control laws, says Dennis Archer, the mayor of Detroit, "help us keep Uzis and AK-47s off our streets." The Democrats' general chairman, Sen. Chris Dodd, renominates Clinton for office because "the guns that deal death should not be as easy to buy as the bread that sustains life."

Thursday: Ted Kennedy takes aim at "assault-rifle-coddling" Republicans. A plan to "take guns away from the hands of people who have been convicted," Pat Schroeder promises, is just "the next step in our culture." And in the convention's final speech, Clinton boasts that the Brady law "stopped 60,000 felons, fugitives and stalkers" from getting guns (wasn't it 100,000 on Monday?). "We banned assault rifles," he adds.

Now, it doesn't come as a bolt from the blue that liberal Democrats—and the

Democrats at national conventions tend to be *very* liberal—frown on the civilian ownership of guns. They view the Second Amendment as an anachronism, to be construed as narrowly and grudgingly as possible. That more guns equals more violence is as axiomatic to them as that rain falls down, not up. They cannot understand why any reasonable person *wouldn't* want to ban handguns and semi-automatics and "assault weapons." And they are quite certain that people who enjoy firearms, or who get passionate about the right of Americans to buy and own them, are "gun nuts."

But hating guns and gun owners doesn't win elections. Liberal Democrats may find guns repellent, but don't they realize how far from the mainstream that puts them? There are more than 231 million civilian firearms in the United States. More than a third—82 million—are handguns. Nearly one out of every two U.S. households owns a gun, and the average gun household owns four. What did the Chicago Democrats hope to gain by setting their face against so many of their fellow citizens?

Or by spitting so contemptuously on the NRA? Does the Democratic Party really have no civil words for an organization of 3.5 million? Less than two years ago, Democrats were swept out of hundreds of congressional, gubernatorial and state legislative offices. It is bemusing to see a party hoping for a comeback go out of its way to heap scorn on one of the nation's largest associations.

Nineteen ninety-four should have taught Democrats that trashing gun owners is bad politics. In *Rock the House*, a book analyzing that year's elections, conservative strategist Grover Norquist says exit polls showed that gun owners were one of the two groups most likely to vote in 1994. (The other was evangelical Christians). "Anger over Clinton's passage of gun control was a key factor in defeating both Speaker Tom Foley and Judiciary Chairman Jack Brooks, and in winning the Senate seats in Oklahoma and Pennsylvania," Norquist writes. Of the 276 congressional candidates endorsed by the NRA, 221 won.

Quick to denounce intolerance in others, they revel in their own prejudice against gun owners.

In 1992, liberal legal scholar Sanford Levinson pleaded with his fellow "progressives" to start listening to the huge swath of the public that opposes unreasonable gun control. "Such a willingness to listen—and to concede that one might indeed have something to learn—is an essential first step in repairing the breach between liberal Democratic Party elites and the gun-owning constituency most suspicious of them," he wrote in the journal *Reconstruction*.

His plea, Chicago shows, fell on deaf ears. Liberal Democrats still won't listen. They still haven't figured out that most Americans don't share their fear and loathing of guns. What Americans *do* fear and loathe is violent crime—and they know that guns can make them safer.

But Democrats have a problem talking honestly about crime. Cracking down on criminals makes many of them uneasy; so they demonize guns as a substitute. It isn't a very good one. In a nation where gun ownership nears 50 percent, it isn't a very shrewd one, either.

Part II

The War over Guns
Introduction: Numbers Don't Count

As we have begun to see, nothing about guns is uncontroversial. Even seemingly objective facts give rise to dispute, making it hard to ascertain such straightforward matters as how many Americans own guns. The widely varying estimates reflect far more than the inevitable imprecision in such information gathering. Those who promote the virtues of gun ownership tend to report higher percentages of gun-owning households: the more owners there are, the more ordinary or "normal" gun ownership seems. Those alarmed by guns have a somewhat more complicated stake in the numbers game. On the one hand, advocates of gun control want to show that there are relatively few gun owners, so that stiffer regulations will not inconvenience or burden many citizens. At the same time, they must play up the menace guns pose, especially the menace that the proliferation of guns in private possession has created.

Since most evidence is based on self-reports, the heat of controversy and the paranoia at the extremes further distorts the picture. Opinion polls and attitude surveys have obvious limitations. These inherent limitations may be magnified in surveys that ask questions about guns and gun ownership. Those who possess guns illegally (e.g., convicted felons) and those who fear that information on gun ownership will facilitate gun control or confiscation initiatives by the government will be less inclined to answer questions about gun ownership candidly. Nonetheless, information on gun ownership and use derived from public opinion polls offers useful insights. In this introduction, we will draw on data from two reputable polling organizations, one academic, the other commercial.

Based at the University of Chicago, the National Opinion Research Center (NORC) has been taking the pulse of the nation on a range of issues for many decades. The results of their annual "General Social Survey" have served as benchmarks for assessing the national mood on such diverse topics as sexuality and confidence in government. In a survey conducted in the fall of 1996, 40 percent of respondents indicated the presence of at least one firearm in their household. Other polls have reported higher percentages of ownership, ranging to just over half (Hindelang et al., 1977). Gary Kleck (1997) reviewed polls dating back to 1959 and found that, although the numbers bounce around a bit, very few polls show ownership dipping below 40 percent or rising above 50 percent of all households. It thus seems fairly certain that somewhere between two-fifths and nearly half of all U.S. households contain at least one firearm.

Few of the surveys asked specifically about ownership of handguns. As a result, information on this aspect of gun ownership is more spotty. Some surveys find as many as a quarter of American households containing a handgun. The 1996 NORC survey found that 22 percent of gun-owning households owned a handgun; if true, this would mean that only about 10 percent of American households contain a handgun. Data relating to handguns have been elusive. Until the recent worries over assault weapons, handguns were the object of the most heated controversy and associated most closely with crime and mayhem. Self-reports of ownership, therefore, are likely to be understated. If the primary motive for owning a handgun is self-defense—and this is far from certain—then a 1995 CNN/Time Magazine poll finding that 29 percent of gun owners cited personal home protection as their primary reason for owning a gun would suggest that the 1996 NORC figure is probably low. Whatever the actual number, handguns are clearly owned by a small fraction of the gun-owning population and an even smaller proportion of the general population.

While gun owners have constituted a roughly steady 40 to 45 percent of American households over the past twenty-five years or so, the raw number of gun-owning households has continued to increase with the growth in population. Sales figures indicate that the number of guns in circulation has steadily risen over the course of the last century. The United States Bureau of Alcohol, Tobacco, and Firearms (BATF) estimated that between 1899 and 1993, approximately 223 million firearms (roughly evenly divided among rifles, shotguns, and handguns) became available in the United States through legal domestic manufacture or licensed import (U.S. Department of Justice, 1995, 2). There are no reliable records of how many of these guns have been seized, destroyed, or rendered inoperable by neglect, damage, or normal wear and tear. It should be noted, though, that all but the most shoddily made guns, if properly used and cared for, will last a long time. Many guns made nearly a hundred years ago are still in use or would be used were they not so valuable as collector's pieces. These ambiguities aside, we see no reason to doubt Kleck's (1991) earlier estimate that there were roughly 200 million firearms (rifles, shotguns, and handguns) in private possession by the late 1980s. Now, a decade and several million additional weapons produced and imported later, the total number of firearms in private possession likely approaches 225 million—and this may well be a conservative estimate.

Most of these firearms are rifles and shotguns primarily used for recreation: hunting and target shooting. But the popularity of handguns, judging from sales figures, has been increasing steadily in recent years. Handguns are, of course, what most of the fuss is about. Some would dearly love to ban all firearms, but this is a minority opinion even within the ranks of gun control advocates. Absent handguns (and, recently, assault rifles), the debate over the private ownership of firearms would be significantly muted. The reason is simple: handguns are the weapon of choice for criminals; they are the most commonly used weapon in domestic disputes ending in fatality; and they are the most common firearm involved in the accidental death of children.

So common are stories of tragedies involving handguns that one of the most prominent gun control advocates, Sarah Brady, speaks in medical terminology of an "epidemic of gun violence." This phrase has also been used by some physicians, most notably C. Everett Koop, the former U.S. Surgeon General, who argue that gun injuries and deaths ought to be regarded not only as a criminal matter but also an urgent public health issue. Indeed, with gun sales brisk and the stock of guns steadily rising, it would only seem logical to expect that there would be a steady rise in violent crimes, increasingly lethal domestic strife, and more tragic accidents, not to mention a rise of mayhem at the hands of disgruntled employees (or ex-employees) "going postal." Were there a tight connection between guns and violence, this would be so. But the connection is not tight.

Death rates (including accidents, homicides, and suicides) attributed to firearms have been remarkably Stable in recent years. In 1980, the firearm death rate was 14.8.per 100,000. In 1993, the last year for which these data are available, the rate had inched up to 15.6. But when this total is broken down by race and sex, a more complicated pattern emerges. For white males, the gun-related death rate was 21.1 in 1980 and 20.7 in 1993. Similarly slight declines were recorded over this same time period for white females (4.2 to 3.9) and black females (9.1 to 8.8). Only black males showed an increase, a large one at that (61.8 to 68.8) (U.S. Bureau of the Census, 1996, 103). These rates are much higher than the death rates associated with firearms in virtually all other industrialized societies, but the fact that the rates for all but African American males are declining scarcely supports the idea of an "epidemic."

Similarly, accidental deaths involving firearms have been steadily declining over the course of the century. In 1970, the accidental death rate attributable to guns was 1.2 per 100,000. In 1980, the rate had declined to 0.9, and by 1990 it dipped to 0.6, a 50 percent decline in accidental gun fatalities in twenty years (U.S. Bureau of the Census, 1996, 101) Data from 1993, again the last year for which information is available, show the rate steady at 0.6.

Violent crime involving firearms has also been declining in recent years. Most major cities have been witnessing declines in homicides and aggravated assaults with firearms, some declines quite dramatic, as in Boston and New York. Even armed robbery rates appear to be headed down. Experts are not sure why there has been so dramatic a turn around in gun-related crime, and it is by no means clear that the trend will continue. But whatever the cause and however long the trend persists, the decline is not the result of a reduction in the number of guns in circulation. While Americans are buying more guns, they seem to be using them more safely and less often outside the limits of the law. Indeed, it is only when we turn to suicide that we find guns increasingly implicated.

Suicide rates for males have been rising since the 1970s. Guns are increasingly the instrument of choice. In 1970, 58 percent of male suicides were carried out with a firearm. In 1993, the last year for which we have data, the percentage had increased to 66 percent. Suicide rates for females are lower overall than for males and guns figure less prominently for women, though gun suicides for females are up sharply, from 30 percent of all suicides in 1970 to 39 percent in 1993, a 30 percent increase in the use of guns (compared to a 14 percent increase for males). In sum, were it not for a rising suicide rate and an even more rapid rise in the use of firearms in suicides, the rates of gun death and violence associated with firearms would be declining, not rising. The only segment of our population clearly experiencing an "epidemic" of gun deaths is African American males. It hardly needs saying that this has more to do with the way we have structured race relations than it is a function of our gun policies.

Still, our gun-related death rates are clearly higher than anyone should be willing to tolerate. Much more can and should be done to accelerate the downward trend in gun violence, and special intensive efforts need to be directed at reducing the appallingly high rates of death afflicting African American males. But this is less a matter of guns than the result of a complex interaction of race, class, and gender. For the rest of the deaths associated with guns, more education about safe storage and handling of guns, especially in households with young children, would be a positive step. The Time/CNN poll referred to earlier reported, for example, that roughly 30 percent of gun owners kept a loaded gun in their home. Under pressure, some handgun manufacturers have begun to ship guns with trigger locks installed, and some states and communities have passed laws requiring the safe storage of firearms. Of course, anything that makes a firearm hard to fire reduces its usefulness for personal protection; as a result, mandatory trigger locks and safe storage laws, as reasonable as they are in the abstract, are resisted strongly by those who see guns as essential to personal protection in a world that produces unexpected and imminent dangers. In view of this, we may well have to accept the fact that "accidents happen." While each accident is heartbreakingly tragic, with the accident rate now so low, it is hard to see how gun accidents can be reduced more than marginally without moving to a total ban and confiscation program. As horrific as accidents are, it is unlikely that Americans would accept this solution.

As for violent crime, the picture is more mixed. Surprisingly, our rates of robbery and criminal assault are not all that much higher than the rates for other English-speaking nations, including England, Canada, New Zealand, and Australia (Zimring and Hawkins, 1997). We stand out however, in the death rates associated with these crimes. Our criminals are more lethal—and the reason, Zimring and Hawkins argue, is that our bad guys are well armed. But, as Daniel Polsby and Don Kates (1998) have shown, there are other ways in which our criminals differ, among them race. Since no one has come up with a plausible plan for disarming criminals (Wright, Rossi, and Daly, 1983; Kleck 1991, 1997), a growing movement has sprung up in support of "right to carry" laws that allow citizens to carry concealed weapons. The reasoning is straightforward: criminals will be deterred if they cannot assume that their potential victims are unarmed. Data on crime rates before and after states adopted right to carry laws show that violent crimes decline after the passage of such laws (Lott and Mustard 1997). In addition to pointing to the deterrent effect of guns, gun advocates also argue for stiffer penalties for those caught using guns in crimes (Kopel, 1992, 1995).

Though less comforting than the dream of a violence-free society, this may be the best we can do to cope with our armed criminals.

Suicide presents at least as complicated a challenge, not least for the irony that many of those who endorse gun control also favor an individual's right to decide when to die. In fact, in the NORC survey to which we have referred, 69 percent of those who favor stiffer gun control laws also endorse a "right to die." To be sure, as the essay by Judy Foreman in Part I makes plain, the anguish of coping with a loved one who wishes to take their life is compelling—abstract principles are one thing, one's own father is quite a different matter. We might well hope that were guns not so readily available, many suicides might be averted or at least postponed. Here too, however, the evidence is not very supportive (Kleck, 1997). In any case, with physician-assisted suicide a current subject of wrenching policy debate, linking gun control to a policy of suicide prevention will not be particularly fruitful. If, as more and more Americans seem to be concluding, we have a right to die, why then ought we not also have a right to choose the means of our exit?

So who are the people who own guns? Are they a breed apart or are they "just plain folks"? Using data from the NORC 1996 survey, we compared gun owners to those who did not own a gun. The results were predictable: poor people are far less likely than the nonpoor to possess a firearm, and many fewer blacks own guns than whites—which makes the very high rates of gun-related deaths among black males all the more striking. Gun ownership is more common among those residing in small cities and towns and in the suburbs compared to those living in large cities. Gun owners are on average somewhat better educated than their non-gun-owning peers, though this is mainly because more of the nonowning population has not completed high school. Gun owners are more politically conservative than nonowners and tend to vote Republican. They are also more likely to endorse law-and-order positions: 81 percent favor capital punishment for convicted murders, compared to only 65 percent of nonowners. But interestingly, on a range of other highly charged issues, there is little difference between owners and nonowners. For example, 40 percent of gun owners favor a woman's unlimited access to legal abortion, compared to 44 percent of nonowners. Similarly small differences appear between owners and nonowners when asked about wives working or willingness to vote for a black candidate for the presidency. The conservatism of gun owners seems closely associated with an embrace of individualism—a desire for less government activism, opposition to affirmative action, and support of free enterprise. But even here, the differences between owners and nonowners are far from overwhelming.

Small differences such as these, though, can be important precisely when groups become polarized, as on abortion and gun control. Thus, rugged individualism and cowboy versions of virtuous manhood, as well as fears of federal tyranny, become potent symbols and rallying cries for a population that feels its values and way of life under siege. Still, even though passions run deep, gun owners for the most part remain reasonable even on the matter of gun control.

The Time/CNN poll cited earlier found, for example, that 49 percent of gun owners favored stricter gun laws. Most did not favor repeal of the assault weapons ban, and fewer than half (47 percent) of the gun owners polled agreed with positions held by the NRA. Only 28 percent of gun owners reported believing that citizens needed guns to keep the government from becoming too powerful or intrusive.

Those who own guns are not a breed apart. If they were, the debate over guns would no doubt be less highly charged than it is. If gun owners were either a small fraction of the population or were in some other way "beyond the pale," sharply limiting access to guns or even contemplating confiscation might be politically acceptable. But nothing could be further from the truth. For better or worse, gun owners in the United States are not deviant (though much that has been terrible in our society has come at the hands of deviants with guns), and, as the steep decline in gun accidents indicates, they are clearly becoming more responsible in their use of firearms.

Still, our normal routines are regularly punctuated by horrific stories of disgruntled employees "going postal" or of children wreaking havoc with a firearm. It is easy to conclude that if guns could be magically made to disappear, these terrifying episodes would end. The extent of gun ownership, as we have argued, makes this understandable wish hopelessly beyond reach. To make matters worse, for all our diagnostic sophistication, we still know very little about how to predict who among us will run amok. We are appalled by senseless violence, and it is easy to imagine that with fewer guns in private hands there would be less of it. The problem is that with 200 million or more guns in our nation's homes, we cannot meaningfully reduce the availability of guns. We are thus confronted with a stark question: Are the deaths of innocents—in our homes, workplaces, and schoolyards—too high a price to pay for our liberty? This is a terrible choice, and it is one reason why the struggle over guns is so difficult to resolve.

Pro Gun

Chapter Eleven

Self-Defense
The Right and the Deterrent

Wayne LaPierre

During the emotional firestorm surrounding the 1993 murders in Florida of a German tourist near the airport in Miami and a British tourist in the rest area on I-10 near Tallahassee, TV "news magazine" programs visited juvenile detention facilities in south Florida to find out why violent juvenile predators were targeting foreign tourists.

Part of the answers were predictable, but the principal reason stunned the media and gun control proponents.

With total candor, the jailed juveniles said *they knew that tourists didn't have guns*. Since Florida allows law-abiding people to carry guns, these young criminals were afraid to attack residents. Tourists are considered easy marks; they not only have cash and expensive video and camera equipment, they are unarmed and defenseless.

Most shocking, these juveniles offenders had committed to memory—and actually recited on camera—the airline arrival schedules of flights from abroad. Their procedure is to wait near the airport and follow the tourists as they come out of the airport.

From the mouths of these young criminals came the strongest reason for allowing law-abiding people to carry firearms—protection. These juveniles may be criminals but they're not stupid—they don't want to be shot and so they avoid people who may be armed and might defend themselves.

Many have characterized criminals as fearless, but, in fact, they do fear being killed or injured by armed citizens.

Self-defense works—criminals fear armed citizens. Self-defense, the most basic of all human reactions, is triggered by the threat or fear of harm. The survival instinct is not exclusive to law-abiding people, it is just as basic to criminals.

As many as 2.45 million crimes are thwarted each year in the United States by average citizens using firearms, and in most cases the potential victim never has to fire a shot, according to a survey conducted early in 1993 by nationally recognized Florida State University criminologist Gary Kleck.[1]

The findings of Kleck's National Self-Defense Survey are consistent with a dozen previous studies which generally show that the use of guns for defensive purposes is relatively common, as well as effective. Crimes are frustrated because criminals flee when confronted with a firearm.

Kleck's study went beyond previous studies by excluding situations where respondents used a gun to investigate some suspicious noise or occurrence which turned out to be harmless. He included only defensive uses of a gun, such as when there was an actual confrontation between the intended victim and an offender.

Consider, for a moment, what the carnage on our streets and in our homes might be like if law-abiding citizens were not allowed to exercise their right to self-defense with firearms. There could potentially be as many as 2.5 million *more* crimes each year listed in the national crime data banks with an additional incalculable cost in loss of property, health, and life.

An analysis of a U.S. Justice Department victimization study found that in the categories of robbery and assault, "victims who used guns for protection were less likely either to be attacked or injured than victims who responded in any other way, including those who did not resist at all," and "victims who resisted robbers with guns . . . were less likely to lose their property. . . . When victims use guns to resist crimes, the crimes usually are disrupted and the victims are not injured."[2]

Self-defense is generally viewed today as it was in 1765 when Sir William Blackstone's *Commentaries* was first published in England. Blackstone described the use of arms for self-defense as among the "Absolute Rights of Individuals."

Blackstone's *Commentaries* is the basis of the American legal system and as such is used by the U.S. Supreme Court in its decisions involving common law and in its understanding of the roots of our constitutional rights.

But despite Blackstone's authorization of our rights to self-defense and the overwhelming proof of the deterrence of firearms, many people who exercise their right and deter violent crimes against themselves are ironically victimized and persecuted by law enforcement, the criminal justice system, or other branches of the government.

Take the case of twenty-two-year-old Rayna Ross. Ms. Ross is the Marine lance corporal who shot and killed her bayonet-wielding ex-boyfriend, Corporal Anthony Goree—also a Marine—in June of 1993. Goree had broken into her apartment at least twice before, and after further beatings, stalking, and threats, Ms. Ross finally went to military authorities and pressed charges.

The Marine Corps did little to protect Ms. Ross. They confined Goree to the brig for six days, put him on base restriction, and ordered him to stay away from Ross. Almost immediately after being released from the brig, he disobeyed orders and left the base.

The Marine Corps and civilian police couldn't find Goree, but he found Rayna Ross. Wielding a bayonet, he broke into her apartment at 3:00 A.M. and entered her bedroom, where she was sleeping with her infant daughter. Forced to defend herself and her baby, she shot and killed him with a handgun she had purchased three days before.

Remember, Ms. Ross purchased the gun only after repeated failures by the Marine Corps and civilian police to protect her.

Police ruled the act a justifiable homicide and filed no charges, but months later, to the outrage of many, the Marine Corps charged Ms. Ross with first degree murder. Forced to defend herself from the government, in this case the military, she faced a possible court-martial and life in prison.

The *Washington Times* wrote on February 22, 1994, "Why the military is weighing a murder case against her now is unclear. . . . It is also not clear why feminists haven't rallied to her cause the way they did for Lorena Bobbitt [who cut off her husband's penis]. In some respects, Ms. Ross is the dream of the politically correct: She is a black woman, a single mother and wittingly or unwittingly, a symbol of 'progress' in a putatively reactionary, hidebound (and so on) military. And no doubt that would have made a fine epitaph, except that Ms. Ross wasn't much interested in dying."

It was the National Rifle Association that came forward with legal assistance and funds to defend Ms. Ross, and stood by her until the Marine Corps finally dropped all charges against her.

But why was it all necessary? What has gone so terribly wrong with the government? Has the arrogance of power so corrupted the system that government, including the military, targets victims of crime rather than the perpetrators of crime?

There are currently no laws that prohibit self-defense, but the gun control and gun ban zealots are clearly moving in that direction. Some courts have ruled that victims have "a duty to retreat" rather than stand their ground in their own homes and defend themselves. These absurd rulings defy logic and fly in the face of the Constitution.

No would-be victim should be required to surrender his or her dignity, safety, property, or life to a criminal; no person should be required to retreat in the face of attack.

Counterattack—self-defense—has proved to be a more effective deterrent to crime than any of the laws on the books. Criminals don't fear the law—but they do fear armed citizens.

Research gathered by Professors James Wright and Peter Rossi, co-authors of "The Armed Criminal in America" in 1985, a National Institute of Justice three-year study of criminal acquisition and use of firearms in America, points to the armed citizen or threats from the armed citizen as perhaps the most effective crime deterrent in the nation.

Wright and Rossi questioned over 1,800 prisoners serving time in prisons across the nation. They found:

- 81 percent agreed that the "smart criminal" will attempt to find out if a potential victim is armed

- 74 percent felt that burglars avoided occupied dwellings for fear of being shot
- 57 percent felt that the typical criminal feared being shot by citizens more than he feared being shot by police
- 57 percent of "handgun predators" had encountered armed citizens
- 39 percent did not commit a specific crime for fear that the victim was armed
- 69 percent of "handgun predators" personally knew other criminals who were scared off or shot at by armed victims.

One glaring statistic: burglars who choose, either unintentionally or otherwise, to enter an occupied home are twice as likely to be shot or killed as they are to be caught, convicted, and imprisoned by America's criminal justice system.

While Rayna Ross actually had to shoot her gun to save her life, Sonya Dowdy did not, but both are alive today because each had a firearm and exercised the right of self-defense when attacked by a violent criminal.

Sonya Dowdy's father was deeply concerned for his daughter's safety and gave her a handgun that he had purchased on the day she was attacked. It saved her life only fifteen minutes after he had given it to her. When Ms. Dowdy went to the post office to pick up her mail, she was followed back to her car by an armed drifter who had raped a twelve-year-old girl that same day. The man told her he wouldn't hurt her but lunged toward her before she could close her car door. He stuck a .25 caliber pistol in her face and said, "I'm going to kill you, bitch!"

When he attempted to get into the back seat of the car, she pulled her gun, cocked the hammer, and said, "No, I'm going to kill you." He threw down his gun and ran. He was captured by the police four hours later.

The right of self-defense and the right to use firearms for defense of self and family are the cornerstone of individual rights enumerated in the U.S. Constitution. If the gun licensers and gun banners succeed in subverting and eroding that cornerstone—the most basic of natural rights—then surely all other individual rights will fall. The freedom of all Americans is in jeopardy.

Nationally syndicated columnist Charley Reese, in his column appearing in the *Orlando Sentinel* March 31, 1994, put it succinctly:

> It is both illogical and inconsistent for a government to say people have a right to life and a right to self-defense but no right to own the tools necessary to defend their lives.
>
> It is illogical for a government that says its police have no obligation to provide individual protection to deny people the means to protect themselves.
>
> It is immoral for a government that repeatedly releases predators to prey on people to tell those victims they cannot have a weapon for self-defense.
>
> It's stupid for a government that can't control criminals, drugs or illegal immigrants to claim it can take guns away from criminals only if honest folks will give up theirs.
>
> Gun-control proposals are also an insult. Gun control by definition affects only honest people. When a politician tells you he wants to forbid you from owning a

firearm or force you to get a license, he is telling you he doesn't trust you. That's an insult.

The government trusted me with a M-48 tank and assorted small arms when it claimed to have need of my services. It trusts common Americans with all kinds of arms when it wants them to go kill foreigners somewhere—usually for the financial benefit of some corporations.

But when the men and women take off their uniforms and return to their homes and assume responsibility for their own and their families' safety, suddenly the politicians don't trust them to own a gun. This is pure elitism. Elitists think we common folk are stupid or mad and that if we have a firearm, we are going to shoot the checkout girl at the supermarket when she makes a mistake on the register. Or, knowing what they intend for our future, maybe they fear we would shoot them.

The fact that gun control is an elitist effort at people control is easily verifiable. Go to New York or any big city and see who gets the gun permits. The small shopkeeper or the retail clerk actually exposed to crime? NO, the elite, like William F. Buckley and the publisher of *The New York Times*.

Gun control is not about guns or crime. It is about an elite that fears and despises the common people. . . .

More than ever before, politicians are clamoring to restrict Americans' constitutional right to own guns and the right of self-defense. Yet we, individually as armed citizens, are the best deterrent to violent criminal attack. We, collectively as an armed law-abiding populace, are the best protection against the taking-over of America by criminals, or, should it come to that, the tyranny of government.

[Self-defense is] justly called the primary law of nature, so it is not, neither can it be in fact, taken away by the laws of society.

—Sir William Blackstone

NOTES

1. Gordon Witkin, "Should You Own a Gun?" *U.S. News and World Report*, August 15, 1994, 27.

2. Gary Kleck. "Crime Control through the Private Use of Armed Force," *Social Problems* 15 (1): 1–21, at 7 and 9 (February 1988).

Chapter Twelve

Confessions of a Former Gun Control Supporter

Clayton E. Cramer

I started out on the other side. In 1979 I was a pacifist—the example of Mahatma Gandhi had been very persuasive. My parents had raised me to turn the other cheek when attacked, and in elementary and junior high school I had *plenty of* opportunity to put that idea into practice.

I didn't have a strong opinion about gun control, though if anyone had asked, I would have said, "Who could possibly oppose gun control?" I couldn't imagine why there might be any argument about it.

I didn't feel a need to own a gun, for I hadn't grown up around guns. My parents didn't own any guns. I didn't know any hunters, and even if I had, I probably would have kept my distance—for fear that some of their "primitive" attitudes would rub off on me.

From everything I had learned in high school, and from reading the *Los Angeles Times*, I "knew" that the Second Amendment was about the right of the National Guard to have weapons. I could see how someone might misinterpret the Second Amendment as protecting an individual right, but in any case, the Second Amendment was just history, with no relevance to my life.

Most importantly, I believed that if I didn't associate with low-lifes, I wouldn't have to worry much about crime. This was a very comforting idea, because it meant that I didn't have to worry about protecting myself. Then, between 1979 and 1981, everything I believed about violent crime, the meaning of the Second Amendment, and my personal need for a weapon dramatically changed.

Mine had been a convenient pacifism, as with many others of my generation. When I saw a man with a baseball bat threatening a teenager one night in Santa Monica, California, I had no qualms about calling the police—who were ready to use violence for a noble cause: keeping the peace. As long as *I* wasn't directly involved with the use of violence, *my* hands were clean. The man with the baseball bat was in the right, as it turned out, and the police department had three cruisers on the scene in three minutes and fifteen seconds—an impressive performance.

Reprinted from *Firing Back* by Clayton E. Cramer (Iola, Wisc.: Krause Publications, 1994), 7–10.

The End of a Convenient Pacifism

But as with most things, the passing years gave me experiences that revealed the flaws in my simplistic textbook ideology. A friend was robbed at gunpoint. Fortunately, he suffered no injuries. Handing over his wallet solved the threat, but still . . .

Things got worse. A couple I knew had just come home from dinner. Suddenly, three thugs broke down John and Linda's[1] screen door. They tied up John, beat him, then gang-raped Linda. These scum stole everything John and Linda owned, right down to their wedding pictures—which were of no value to anyone else.

These monsters were never caught—and the Los Angeles Police Department didn't even bother running the fingerprints through the FBI. As the detective responsible for the case explained to John a few months later, "It wasn't an important enough crime."

Over the next few years, I watched John and Linda struggle desperately to hold their marriage together as each battled the demons of this traumatic event. Fortunately, the time came when they could put the tragedy behind them.

Another couple I knew, Joe and Janet,[2] were awakened by three men surrounding their bed. While Joe compliantly went to another room to give them valuables, two of the thugs attempted to rape Janet. Joe fought back and was stabbed seven times. He came close to dying. Being self-employed and uninsured, Joe's medical bills put him $30,000 in debt (back when that was a lot more money than it is now).

A couple of years after graduation, I ran into Lisa, a friend from high school. Lisa's jaw was wired, making speech difficult, but she was able to tell me what happened. Two men had robbed her, after beating her so severely that they broke her jaw.

Along with these close friends, a dozen or more acquaintances and friends of friends became victims of rape and murder. The fear of being raped again haunted many of the women. Who could assure them that they were safe?

Shortly thereafter, someone burglarized my apartment, and I realized that even in a high security building I wasn't safe. What the burglar stole wasn't worth much, but he brazenly had taken time to make a meal in my kitchen—as if to say, "I'm not afraid of your coming home and catching me."

Then I met Rhonda, who is now my wife. As I, Rhonda had many friends and acquaintances who had become victims of crime. Some had confirmed the cliché, "Stay away from drug addicts and criminals, and you'll be safe." But most of the victims had been decent people minding their own business when savages attacked them.

For example, two roofers, high on heroin and intent on burglary, broke into a house. A high school acquaintance of Rhonda's walked in on the burglars—and discovered they had already raped and murdered his little sister. Then the burglars removed the young man's head with a roofing hammer.

The final event that broke my confidence in pacifism was a map showing serious crimes committed in our neighborhood during the previous three months. Rhonda and I lived in Santa Monica, a "nice" part of Los Angeles. Yet, more than a dozen rapes had been reported within four blocks of our apartment.

I began to wonder how safe we were. That three-minute police response time to the man with the bat had been an extraordinary stroke of luck. If we called the police for *our* protection, would we be so fortunate? A friend had called the Los Angeles Police Department to report a domestic disturbance one Saturday night—and waited tens of minutes before the police department answered the phone! If trouble came to our apartment, we might be on our own. There were things worse than death—such as being beaten to death with a hammer, or recovering from the emotional trauma of rape.

The Unselfish Choice: Protecting Ourselves

Rhonda didn't kid herself as I did. At her urging, we obtained licenses to carry tear gas. But over time we learned that tear gas wasn't all that effective for self-defense, and we realized something more certain was needed. As we talked about the morality of defensive violence, I came to an awesome realization: *refusing to use force was selfish.*

Rapists, murderers, and the other savages that roamed the streets of Los Angeles often had multiple victims. Refusing to defend ourselves, therefore, guaranteed not only our own suffering, but that of the next victim. Clearly, self-defense against these monsters is not a selfish act; it is an act that benefits all of civilized society. I have reason to suspect that the three savages who victimized John and Linda may have been the same trio that attacked Joe and Janet two years later. Would things have been different if John and Linda had been armed?

After many weeks of discussion, Rhonda and I made a dramatic decision: we decided to arm ourselves. I went out and bought a handgun.

I took the responsibility of gun ownership seriously. At the local library, I read through all the sections of the California Penal Code that regulated the carrying of guns, then the case law in which the courts had interpreted those statues. I was surprised to learn it was illegal to carry a gun without a permit— I hadn't even thought about it before. I was even more surprised to find that, at least where I lived, it was practically impossible to get such a permit.

Finally, I read the greatest surprise of all: California Military & Veterans Code § 120 through § 123 defined me as a member of the "unorganized militia." Wait a minute! Wasn't the "militia" the National Guard? And I couldn't recall signing up! Had I been misled about the Second Amendment?

Over the next few years I studied the subject of gun control carefully, and was surprised to find that nearly everything I thought I knew about the subject was wrong. I came to the awful realization that "conventional wisdom" about guns is almost entirely wrong, and that television and movies have greatly misled most Americans (including many gun owners) about the technical and criminological aspects of guns. After considering the way in which the mass media had misled me on this subject, I am not surprised that I automatically supported restrictive gun control laws—and that many other people do likewise.

Keep in mind, as you discuss the gun control issue, the person you are trying to persuade may be very much like I was in 1979. A well-crafted dose of the truth may go a long way toward changing that person's mind. The way you present the issue of gun rights may make today's opponent tomorrow's ally.

NOTES

1. Names changed to protect their privacy.
2. Names changed to protect their privacy.

Chapter Thirteen

A Nation of Cowards

Jeffrey R. Snyder

Our society has reached a pinnacle of self-expression and respect for individuality rare or unmatched in history. Our entire popular culture—from fashion magazines to the cinema—positively screams the matchless worth of the individual, and glories in eccentricity, nonconformity, independent judgment, and self-determination. This enthusiasm is reflected in the prevalent notion that helping someone entails increasing that person's "self-esteem"; that if a person properly values himself, he will naturally be a happy, productive, and, in some inexplicable fashion, responsible member of society.

And yet, while people are encouraged to revel in their individuality and incalculable self-worth, the media and the law enforcement establishment continually advise us that, when confronted with the threat of lethal violence, we should not resist, but simply give the attacker what he wants. If the crime under consideration is rape, there is some notable waffling on this point, and the discussion quickly moves to how the woman can change her behavior to minimize the risk of rape, and the various ridiculous, non-lethal weapons she may acceptably carry, such as whistles, keys, mace or, that weapon which really sends shivers down a rapist's spine, the portable cellular phone.

Now how can this be? How can a person who values himself so highly calmly accept the indignity of a criminal assault? How can one who believes that the essence of his dignity lies in his self-determination passively accept the forcible deprivation of that self-determination? How can he, quietly, with great dignity and poise, simply hand over the goods?

The assumption, of course, is that there is no inconsistency. The advice not to resist a criminal assault and simply hand over the goods is founded on the notion that one's life is of incalculable value, and that no amount of property is worth it. Put aside, for a moment, the outrageousness of the suggestion that a criminal who proffers lethal violence should be treated as if he has instituted a new social contract: "I will not hurt or kill you if you give me what I want." For years, feminists have labored to educate people that rape is not about sex, but about domination, degradation, and control. Evidently, someone needs to inform

Reprinted by permission of the author and *The Public Interest*, no. 113 (fall 1976): 40–56. Copyright © 1993 by National Affairs, Inc.

the law enforcement establishment and the media that kidnapping, robbery, carjacking, and assault are not about property.

Crime is not only a complete disavowal of the social contract, but also a commandeering of the victim's person and liberty. If the individual's dignity lies in the fact that he is a moral agent engaging in actions of his own will, in free exchange with others, then crime always violates the victim's dignity. It is, in fact, an act of enslavement. Your wallet, your purse, or your car may not be worth your life, but your dignity is; and if it is not worth fighting for, it can hardly be said to exist.

The Gift of Life

Although difficult for modern man to fathom, it was once widely believed that life was a gift from God, that to not defend that life when offered violence was to hold God's gift in contempt, to be a coward and to breach one's duty to one's community. A sermon given in Philadelphia in 1747 unequivocally equated the failure to defend oneself with suicide:

> He that suffers his life to be taken from him by one that hath no authority for that purpose, when he might preserve it by defense, incurs the Guilt of self murder since God hath enjoined him to seek the continuance of his life, and Nature itself teaches every creature to defend itself.

"Cowardice" and "self-respect" have largely disappeared from public discourse. In their place we are offered "self-esteem" as the bellwether of success and a proxy for dignity. "Self-respect" implies that one recognizes standards, and judges oneself worthy by the degree to which one lives up to them. "Self-esteem" simply means that one feels good about oneself. "Dignity" used to refer to the self-mastery and fortitude with which a person conducted himself in the face of life's vicissitudes and the boorish behavior of others. Now, judging by campus speech codes, dignity requires that we never encounter a discouraging word and that others be coerced into acting respectfully, evidently on the assumption that we are powerless to prevent our degradation if exposed to the demeaning behavior of others. These are signposts proclaiming the insubstantiality of our character, the hollowness of our souls.

It is impossible to address the problem of rampant crime without talking about the moral responsibility of the intended victim. Crime is rampant because the law-abiding, each of us, condone it, excuse it, permit it, submit to it. We permit and encourage it because we do not fight back, immediately, then and there, where it happens. Crime is not rampant because we do not have enough prisons, because judges and prosecutors are too soft, because the police are hamstrung with absurd technicalities. The defect is there, in our character. We are a nation of cowards and shirkers.

Do You Feel Lucky?

In 1991, when then–Attorney General Richard Thornburgh released the FBI's annual crime statistics, he noted that it is now more likely that a person will be the victim of a violent crime than that he will be in an auto accident. Despite this, most people readily believe that the existence of the police relieves them of the responsibility to take full measures to protect themselves. The police, however, are not personal bodyguards. Rather, they act as a general deterrent to crime, both by their presence and by apprehending criminals after the fact. As numerous courts have held, they have no legal obligation to protect anyone in particular. You cannot sue them for failing to prevent you from being the victim of a crime.

Insofar as the police deter by their presence, they are very, very good. Criminals take great pains not to commit a crime in front of them. Unfortunately, the corollary is that you can pretty much bet your life (and you are) that they won't be there at the moment you actually need them.

Should you ever be the victim of an assault, a robbery, or a rape, you will find it very difficult to call the police while the act is in progress, even if you are carrying a portable cellular phone. Nevertheless, you might be interested to know how long it takes them to show up. Department of Justice statistics for 1991 show that, for all crimes of violence, only 28 percent of calls are responded to within five minutes. The idea that protection is a service people can call to have delivered and expect to receive in a timely fashion is often mocked by gun owners, who love to recite the challenge, "Call for a cop, call for an ambulance, and call for a pizza. See who shows up first."

Many people deal with the problem of crime by convincing themselves that they live, work, and travel only in special "crime-free" zones. Invariably, they react with shock and hurt surprise when they discover that criminals do not play by the rules and do not respect these imaginary boundaries. If, however, you understand that crime can occur anywhere at anytime, and if you understand that you can be maimed or mortally wounded in mere seconds, you may wish to consider whether you are willing to place the responsibility for safeguarding your life in the hands of others.

Power and Responsibility

Is your life worth protecting? If so, whose responsibility is it to protect it? If you believe that it is the police's, not only are you wrong—since the courts universally rule that they have no legal obligation to do so—but you face some difficult moral quandaries. How can you rightfully ask another human being to risk his life to protect yours, when you will assume no responsibility yourself? Because that is his job and we pay him to do it? Because your life is of incalculable value, but his is only worth the $30,000 salary we pay him? If you believe it reprehensible to possess the means and will to use lethal force to repel a criminal assault, how can you call upon another to do so for you?

Do you believe that you are forbidden to protect yourself because the police are better qualified to protect you, because they know what they are doing but you're a rank amateur? Put aside that this is equivalent to believing that only concert pianists may play the piano and only professional athletes may play sports. What exactly are these special qualities possessed only by the police and beyond the rest of us mere mortals?

One who values his life and takes seriously his responsibilities to his family and community will possess and cultivate the means of fighting back, and will retaliate when threatened with death or grievous injury to himself or a loved one. He will never be content to rely solely on others for his safety, or to think he has done all that is possible by being aware of his surroundings and taking measures of avoidance. Let's not mince words: He will be armed, will be trained in the use of his weapon, and will defend himself when faced with lethal violence.

Fortunately, there is a weapon for preserving life and liberty that can be wielded effectively by almost anyone—the handgun. Small and light enough to be carried habitually, lethal, but unlike the knife or sword, not demanding great skill or strength, it truly is the "great equalizer." Requiring only hand-eye coordination and a modicum of ability to remain cool under pressure, it can be used effectively by the old and the weak against the young and the strong, by the one against the many.

The handgun is the only weapon that would give a lone female jogger a chance of prevailing against a gang of thugs intent on rape, a teacher a chance of protecting children at recess from a madman intent on massacring them, a family of tourists waiting at a mid-town subway station the means to protect themselves from a gang of teens armed with razors and knives.

But since we live in a society that by and large outlaws the carrying of arms, we are brought into the fray of the Great American Gun War. Gun control is one of the most prominent battlegrounds in our current culture wars. Yet it is unique in the half-heartedness with which our conservative leaders and pundits—our "conservative elite"—do battle, and have conceded the moral high ground to liberal gun control proponents. It is not a topic often written about, or written about with any great fervor, by William F. Buckley or Patrick Buchanan. As drug czar, William Bennett advised President Bush to ban "assault weapons." George Will is on record as recommending the repeal of the Second Amendment, and Jack Kemp is on record as favoring a ban on the possession of semiautomatic "assault weapons." The battle for gun rights is one fought predominantly by the common man. The beliefs of both our liberal and conservative elites are in fact abetting the criminal rampage through our society.

Selling Crime Prevention

By any rational measure, nearly all gun control proposals are hokum. The Brady Bill, for example, would not have prevented John Hinckley from obtaining a gun to shoot President Reagan; Hinckley purchased his weapon five months before the attack, and his medical records could not have served as a basis to deny his purchase of a gun, since medical records are not public documents filed with the police. Similarly, California's waiting period and background check did not stop Patrick Purdy from purchasing the "assault rifle" and handguns he used to massacre children during recess in a Stockton schoolyard; the felony conviction that would have provided the basis for stopping the sales did not exist, because Mr. Purdy's previous weapons violations were plea-bargained down from felonies to misdemeanors.

In the mid-sixties there was a public service advertising campaign targeted at car owners about the prevention of car theft. The purpose of the ad was to urge car owners not to leave their keys in their cars. The message was, "Don't help a good boy go bad." The implication was that, by leaving his keys in his car, the normal, law-abiding car owner was contributing to the delinquency of minors who, if they just weren't tempted beyond their limits, would be "good." Now, in those days people still had a fair sense of just who was responsible for whose behavior. The ad succeeded in enraging a goodly portion of the populace, and was soon dropped.

Nearly all of the gun control measures offered by Handgun Control, Inc. (HCI) and its ilk embody the same philosophy. They are founded on the belief that America's law-abiding gun owners are the source of the problem. With their unholy desire for firearms, they are creating a society awash in a sea of guns, thereby helping good boys go bad, and helping bad boys be badder. This laying of moral blame for violent crime at the feet of the law-abiding, and the implicit absolution of violent criminals for their misdeeds, naturally infuriates honest gun owners.

The files of HCI and other gun control organizations are filled with proposals to limit the availability of semiautomatic and other firearms to law-abiding citizens, and barren of proposals for apprehending and punishing violent criminals. It is ludicrous to expect that the proposals of HCI, or any gun control laws, will significantly curb crime. According to Department of Justice and Bureau of Alcohol, Tobacco, and Firearms (ATF) statistics, fully 90 percent of violent crimes are committed without a handgun, and 93 percent of the guns obtained by violent criminals are not obtained through the lawful purchase and sale transactions that are the object of most gun control legislation. Furthermore, the number of violent criminals is minute in comparison to the number of firearms in America—estimated by the ATF at about 200 million, approximately one-third of which are handguns. With so abundant a supply, there will always be enough guns available for those who wish to use them for nefarious ends, no matter how complete the legal prohibitions against them, or how draconian the punishment for their acquisition or use. No, the gun control proposals of HCI and other organizations are not seriously intended as crime control. Something else is at work here.

The Tyranny of the Elite

Gun control is a moral crusade against a benighted, barbaric citizenry. This is demonstrated not only by the ineffectualness of gun control in preventing crime, and by the fact that it focuses on restricting the behavior of the law-abiding rather than apprehending and punishing the guilty, but also by the execration that gun control proponents heap on gun owners and their evil instrumentality, the NRA. Gun owners are routinely portrayed as uneducated, paranoid rednecks fascinated by and prone to violence, i.e., exactly the type of person who opposes the liberal agenda and whose moral and social "re-education" is the object of liberal social policies. Typical of such bigotry is New York Gov. Mario Cuomo's famous characterization of gun-owners as "hunters who drink beer, don't vote, and lie to their wives about where they were all weekend." Similar vituperation is rained upon the NRA, characterized by Sen. Edward Kennedy as the "pusher's best friend," lampooned in political cartoons as standing for the right of children to carry firearms to school and, in general, portrayed as standing for an individual's God-given right to blow people away at will.

The stereotype is, of course, false. As criminologist and constitutional lawyer Don B. Kates, Jr., and former HCI contributor Dr. Patricia Harris have pointed out, "[s]tudies consistently show that, on the average, gun owners are better educated and have more prestigious jobs than non-owners. . . . Later studies show that gun owners are less likely than non-owners to approve of police brutality, violence against dissenters, etc."

Conservatives must understand that the antipathy many liberals have for gun owners arises in good measure from their statist utopianism. This habit of mind has nowhere been better explored than in *The Republic*. There, Plato argues that the perfectly just society is one in which an unarmed people exhibit virtue by minding their own business in the performance of their assigned functions, while the government of philosopher-kings, above the law and protected by armed guardians unquestioning in their loyalty to the state, engineers, implements, and fine-tunes the creation of that society, aided and abetted by myths that both hide and justify their totalitarian manipulation.

The Unarmed Life

When columnist Carl Rowan preaches gun control and uses a gun to defend his home, when Maryland Gov. William Donald Schaefer seeks legislation year after year to ban semiautomatic "assault weapons" whose only purpose, we are told, is to kill people, while he is at the same time escorted by state police armed with large-capacity 9mm semiautomatic pistols, it is not simple hypocrisy. It is the workings of that habit of mind possessed by all superior beings who have taken upon themselves the terrible burden of civilizing the masses and who understand, like our Congress, that laws are for other people.

The liberal elite know that they are philosopher-kings. They know that the people simply cannot be trusted; that they are incapable of just and fair self-government; that left to their own devices, their society will be racist, sexist, homophobic, and inequitable—and the liberal elite know how to fix things. They are going to help us live the good and just life, even if they have to lie to us and force us to do it. And they detest those who stand in their way.

The private ownership of firearms is a rebuke to this utopian zeal. To own firearms is to affirm that freedom and liberty are not gifts from the state. It is to reserve final judgment about whether the state is encroaching on freedom and liberty, to stand ready to defend that freedom with more than mere words, and to stand outside the state's totalitarian reach.

The Florida Experience

The elitist distrust of the people underlying the gun control movement is illustrated beautifully in HCI's campaign against a new concealed-carry law in Florida. Prior to 1987, the Florida law permitting the issuance of concealed-carry permits was administered at the county level. The law was vague, and, as a result, was subject to conflicting interpretation and political manipulation. Permits were issued principally to security personnel and the privileged few with political connections. Permits were valid only within the county of issuance.

In 1987, however, Florida enacted a uniform concealed-carry law which mandates that county authorities issue a permit to anyone who satisfies certain objective criteria. The law requires that a permit be issued to any applicant who is a resident, at least twenty-one years of age, has no criminal record, no record of alcohol or drug abuse, no history of mental illness, and provides evidence of having satisfactorily completed a firearms safety course offered by the NRA or other competent instructor. The applicant must provide a set of fingerprints, after which the authorities make a background check. The permit must be issued or denied within ninety days, is valid throughout the state, and must be renewed every three years, which provides authorities a regular means of reevaluating whether the permit holder still qualifies.

Passage of this legislation was vehemently opposed by HCI and the media. The law, they said, would lead to citizens shooting each other over everyday disputes involving fender benders, impolite behavior, and other slights to their dignity. Terms like "Florida, the Gunshine State" and "Dodge City East" were coined to suggest that the state, and those seeking passage of the law, were encouraging individuals to act as judge, jury, and executioner in a "Death Wish" society.

No HCI campaign more clearly demonstrates the elitist beliefs underlying the campaign to eradicate gun ownership. Given the qualifications required of permit holders, HCI and the media can only believe that common, law-abiding citizens are seething cauldrons of homicidal rage, ready to kill to avenge any slight to their dignity, eager to seek out and summarily execute the lawless. Only lack of immediate access to a gun restrains them and prevents the blood from flowing in the streets. They are so mentally and morally deficient that they would mistake a permit to carry a weapon in self-defense as a state-sanctioned license to kill at will.

Did the dire predictions come true? Despite the fact that Miami and Dade County have severe problems with the drug trade, the homicide rate fell in Florida following enactment of this law, as it did in Oregon following enactment of similar legislation there. There are, in addition, several documented cases of new permit holders successfully using their weapons to defend themselves. Information from the Florida Department of State shows that, from the beginning of the program in 1987 through June 1993, 160,823 permits have been issued, and only 530, or about 0.33 percent of the applicants, have been denied a permit for failure to satisfy the criteria, indicating that the law is benefitting those whom it was intended to benefit—the law-abiding. Only 16 permits, less than 1/100th of 1 percent, have been revoked due to the post-issuance commission of a crime involving a firearm.

The Florida legislation has been used as a model for legislation adopted by Oregon, Idaho, Montana, and Mississippi. There are, in addition, seven other states (Maine, North and South Dakota, Utah, Washington, West Virginia, and, with the exception of cities with a population in excess of 1 million, Pennsylvania) which provide that concealed-carry permits must be issued to law-abiding citizens who satisfy various objective criteria. Finally, no permit is required at all in Vermont. Altogether, then, there are thirteen states in which law-abiding citizens who wish to carry arms to defend themselves may do so. While no one appears to have compiled the statistics from all of these jurisdictions, there is certainly an ample data base for those seeking the truth about the trustworthiness of law-abiding citizens who carry firearms.

Other evidence also suggests that armed citizens are very responsible in using guns to defend themselves. Florida State University criminologist Gary Kleck, using surveys and other data, has determined that armed citizens defend their lives or property with firearms against criminals approximately 1 million times a year. In 98 percent of these instances, the citizen merely brandishes the weapon or fires a warning shot. Only in 2 percent of the cases do citizens actually shoot their assailants. In defending themselves with their firearms, armed citizens kill 2,000 to 3,000 criminals each year, three times the number killed by the police. A nationwide study by Kates, the constitutional lawyer and criminologist, found that only 2 percent of civilian shootings involved an innocent person mistakenly identified as a criminal. The "error rate" for the police, however, was 11 percent, over five times as high.

It is simply not possible to square the numbers above and the experience of Florida with the notions that honest, law-abiding gun owners are borderline psychopaths itching for an excuse to shoot someone, vigilantes eager to seek out and summarily execute the lawless, or incompetent fools incapable of determining when it is proper to use lethal force in defense of their lives. Nor upon reflection should these results seem surprising. Rape, robbery, and attempted murder are not typically actions rife with ambiguity or subtlety, requiring special powers of observation and great book-learning to discern. When a man pulls a knife on a woman and says, "You're coming with me," her judgment that a crime is being committed is not likely to be in error. There is little chance that she is going to shoot the wrong person. It is the police, because they are rarely at the scene of the crime when it occurs, who are more likely to find themselves in circumstances where guilt and innocence are not so clear-cut, and in which the probability for mistakes is higher.

Arms and Liberty

Classical republican philosophy has long recognized the critical relationship between personal liberty and the possession of arms by a people ready and willing to use them. Political theorists as dissimilar as Niccolo Machiavelli, Sir Thomas More, James Harrington, Algernon Sidney, John Locke, and Jean-Jacques Rousseau all shared the view that the possession of arms is vital for resisting tyranny, and that to be disarmed by one's government is tantamount to being enslaved by it. The possession of arms by the people is the ultimate warrant that government governs only with the consent of the governed. As Kates has shown, the Second Amendment is as much a product of this political philosophy as it is of the American experience in the Revolutionary War. Yet our conservative elite has abandoned this aspect of republican theory. Although our conservative pundits recognize and embrace gun owners as allies in other arenas, their battle for gun rights is desultory. The problem here is not a statist utopianism, although goodness knows that liberals are not alone in the confidence they have in the state's ability to solve society's problems. Rather, the problem seems to lie in certain cultural traits shared by our conservative and liberal elites.

One such trait is an abounding faith in the power of the word. The failure of our conservative elite to defend the Second Amendment stems in great measure from an overestimation of the power of the rights set forth in the First Amendment, and a general undervaluation of action. Implicit in calls for the repeal of the Second Amendment is the assumption that our First Amendment rights are sufficient to preserve our liberty. The belief is that liberty can be preserved as long as men freely speak their minds; that there is no tyranny or abuse that can survive being exposed in the press; and that the truth need only be disclosed for the culprits to be shamed. The people will act, and the truth shall set us, and keep us, free.

History is not kind to this belief, tending rather to support the view of Hobbes, Machiavelli, and other republican theorists that only people willing and able to defend themselves can preserve their liberties. While it may be tempting and comforting to believe that the existence of mass electronic communication has forever altered the balance of power between the state and its subjects, the belief has certainly not been tested by time, and what little history there is in the age of mass communication is not especially encouraging. The camera, radio, and press are mere tools and, like guns, can be used for good or ill. Hitler, after all, was a masterful orator, used radio to very good effect, and is well known to have pioneered and exploited the propaganda opportunities afforded by film. And then, of course, there were the Brownshirts, who knew very well how to quell dissent among intellectuals.

Polite Society

In addition to being enamored of the power of words, our conservative elite shares with liberals the notion that an armed society is just not civilized or progressive, that massive gun ownership is a blot on our civilization. This association of personal disarmament with civilized behavior is one of the great unexamined beliefs of our time.

Should you read English literature from the sixteenth through nineteenth centuries, you will discover numerous references to the fact that a gentleman, especially when out at night or traveling, armed himself with a sword or a pistol against the chance of encountering a highwayman or other such predator. This does not appear to have shocked the ladies accompanying him. True, for the most part there were no police in those days, but we have already addressed the notion that the presence of the police absolves people of the responsibility to look after their safety, and in any event the existence of the police cannot be said to have reduced crime to negligible levels.

It is by no means obvious why it is "civilized" to permit oneself to fall easy prey to criminal violence, and to permit criminals to continue unobstructed in their evil ways. While it may be that a society in which crime is so rare that no one ever needs to carry a weapon is "civilized," a society that stigmatizes the carrying of weapons by the law-abiding—because it distrusts its citizens more than it fears rapists, robbers, and murderers—certainly cannot claim this distinction. Perhaps the notion that defending oneself with lethal force is not "civilized" arises from the view that violence is always wrong, or the view that each human being is of such intrinsic worth that it is wrong to kill anyone under any circumstances. The necessary implication of these propositions, however, is that life is not worth defending. Far from being "civilized," the beliefs that counterviolence and killing are always wrong are an invitation to the spread of barbarism. Such beliefs announce loudly and clearly that those who do not respect the lives and property of others will rule over those who do.

In truth, one who believes it wrong to arm himself against criminal violence shows contempt of God's gift of life (or, in modern parlance, does not properly value himself), does not live up to his responsibilities to his family and community, and proclaims himself mentally and morally deficient, because he does not trust himself to behave responsibly. In truth, a state that deprives its law-abiding citizens of the means to effectively defend themselves is not civilized but barbarous, becoming an accomplice of murderers, rapists, and thugs and revealing its totalitarian nature by its tacit admission that the disorganized, random havoc created by criminals is far less a threat than are men and women who believe themselves free and independent, and act accordingly.

While gun control proponents and other advocates of a kinder, gentler society incessantly decry our "armed society," in truth we do not live in an armed society. We live in a society in which violent criminals and agents of the state habitually carry weapons, and in which many law-abiding citizens own firearms but do not go about armed. Department of Justice statistics indicate that 87 percent of all violent crimes occur outside the home. Essentially, although tens of millions own firearms, we are an unarmed society.

Take Back the Night

Clearly the police and the courts are not providing a significant brake on criminal activity. While liberals call for more poverty, education, and drug treatment programs, conservatives take a more direct tack. George Will advocates a massive increase in the number of police and a shift toward "community-based policing." Meanwhile, the NRA and many conservative leaders call for laws that would require violent criminals serve at least 85 percent of their sentences and would place repeat offenders permanently behind bars.

Our society suffers greatly from the beliefs that only official action is legitimate and that the state is the source of our earthly salvation. Both liberal and conservative prescriptions for violent crime suffer from the "not in my job description" school of thought regarding the responsibilities of the law-abiding citizen, and from an overestimation of the ability of the state to provide society's moral moorings. As long as law-abiding citizens assume no personal responsibility for combatting crime, liberal and conservative programs will fail to contain it.

Judging by the numerous articles about concealed-carry in gun magazines, the growing number of products advertised for such purpose, and the increase in the number of concealed-carry applications in states with mandatory-issuance laws, more and more people, including growing numbers of women, are carrying firearms for self-defense. Since there are still many states in which the issuance of permits is discretionary and in which law enforcement officials routinely deny applications, many people have been put to the hard choice between protecting their lives or respecting the law. Some of these people have learned the hard way, by being the victim of a crime, or by seeing a friend or loved one raped, robbed, or murdered, that violent crime can happen to anyone, anywhere at anytime, and that crime is not about sex or property but life, liberty, and dignity.

The laws proscribing concealed-carry of firearms by honest, law-abiding citizens breed nothing but disrespect for the law. As the Founding Fathers knew well, a government that does not trust its honest, law-abiding, taxpaying citizens with the means of self-defense is not itself worthy of trust. Laws disarming honest citizens proclaim that the government is the master, not the servant, of the people. A federal law along the lines of the Florida statute—overriding all contradictory state and local laws and acknowledging that the carrying of fire-arms by law-abiding citizens is a privilege and immunity of citizenship—is needed to correct the outrageous conduct of state and local officials operating under discretionary licensing systems.

What we certainly do not need is more gun control. Those who call for the repeal of the Second Amendment so that we can really begin controlling firearms betray a serious misunderstanding of the Bill of Rights. The Bill of Rights does not grant rights to the people, such that its repeal would legitimately confer upon government the powers otherwise proscribed. The Bill of Rights is the list of the fundamental, inalienable rights, endowed in man by his Creator, that define what it means to be a free and independent people, the rights which must exist to ensure that government governs only with the consent of the people.

At one time this was even understood by the Supreme Court. In *United States v. Cruikshank* (1876), the first case in which the Court had an opportunity to interpret the Second Amendment, it stated that the right confirmed by the Second Amendment "is not a right granted by the constitution. Neither is it in any manner dependent upon that instrument for its existence." The repeal of the Second Amendment would no more render the outlawing of firearms legitimate than the repeal of the due process clause of the Fifth Amendment would author-ize the government to imprison and kill people at will. A government that abrogates any of the Bill of Rights, with or without majoritarian approval, forever acts illegitimately, becomes tyrannical, and loses the moral right to govern.

This is the uncompromising understanding reflected in the warning that America's gun owners will not go gently into that good, utopian night: "You can have my gun when you pry it from my cold, dead hands." While liberals take this statement as evidence of the retrograde, violent nature of gun owners, we gun owners hope that liberals hold equally strong sentiments about their printing presses, word processors, and television cameras. The republic depends upon fervent devotion to all our fundamental rights.

Chapter Fourteen

Self-Defense
A Primary Civil Right

Tanya K. Metaksa

Our Founding Fathers did not create our civil liberties—the very heart and soul of our personal and national lives. They secured those liberties. They safeguarded them. The Bill of Rights is our guarantee of freedom.

Mankind and womankind had freedom of expression as a natural right. Humans had freedom of religious expression before reaching the shores of this country. Even though the right to worship had been systematically denied the human race for centuries, it was our right to assert, our right to secure.

All these great rights are ours. All these great rights are the machinery that propels this Republic. Take away one right, weaken one civil liberty, and the machine of freedom starts sputtering, tearing itself apart like an engine that's thrown a rod, grinding to a halt and leaving us stranded on the side of an abandoned road, a road patrolled only by a mob.

Conservative or liberal, Democrat or Republican, we all know it's true. Diminish freedom of the press, and we diminish democracy. Usher out the right of the people to peaceably assemble, and you usher in a police state. Abandon the safeguard against unreasonable searches and seizures, and we abandon our homes.

And then there's that Second Amendment. Could it be that the Founding Fathers, after protecting religious freedom, then set about to protect hunting? Could it be that the Founding Fathers, after safeguarding free speech and free assembly, then hastened to safeguard target shooting?

As a hunter, I can debate all night the benefits of the outdoor ethic and the role hunters play in scientific wildlife conservation. As a marksman and as an officer of an association that promotes competitive shooting, I can attest that marksmanship builds mental control and self-discipline, two characteristics we need more of in this country. But other sports build other attributes—why not safeguard gymnastics or bodybuilding? Isn't it so that sport was the furthest

Reprinted from *American Rifleman*, November 1995, 41, 74–75. Copyright © 1995 by *American Rifleman*.

thing from the minds of the Founding Fathers? They were building a country, not a country club.

Perhaps they had states' rights in mind. They wanted to protect the right of states to form militias. A collective right. If it's a right of states, where are the cases filed by states? Although they are few, Second Amendment claims are brought by individuals, not states. The courts have never struck down a single case brought by an individual citizen, because his name was not Alaska or Alabama.

And if the Founding Fathers sought to guarantee a state's right, no one uttered a word about it. If this Second Amendment safeguarded a collective right, it was the best kept secret of the eighteenth century. No known writing from the period between 1787 and 1791 even suggests that a single American entertained such a notion.

With its tap root in the British common law right of self-defense, the Second Amendment is the right that prevails when, heaven forbid, all else fails. The Second Amendment is more than an affirmation of your right to protect yourself and your family. The Second Amendment marks the property line between individual liberty and state sovereignty. The state can do all it can to assure our corporate safety, but it cannot infringe on our right to personal safety. If it does, it is not heeding the property line. It is trespassing.

When the Founding Fathers wrote those twenty-seven words, they were laying the fence line between state power and citizen's rights. Under the Second Amendment, we are not consigned the role of spectator in the struggle for freedom and safety. Under the Second Amendment, we are empowered to become what we should have been all along—an active participant with the state, a co-equal partner in the pursuit of personal and community safety.

Is the right to bear arms one of the great human rights? No. In the Second Amendment, we see preserved the greatest human right. In this amendment, we see enshrined the ultimate civil liberty—the right to defend one's own life—without which there are no rights.

Our opponents say that the courts are hostile to this right and, because of this hostility, this right is not a right, people are not people, and arms could not possibly mean arms. Yes, the courts are hostile to this right, and anyone who values civil liberties should not be surprised. Certain jurists have an aversion to certain rights. But imagine this nation if we all agreed to sit back and say, because of a court's hostility to a particular right, it is no longer a right. By that logic, we must all agree with a Supreme Court which, years ago, was hostile to the civil rights provisions of the Fourteenth Amendment. We must also all agree that people of different races should not be treated equally by their government.

From roughly the 1890s until after World War II, the Supreme Court refused to enforce the equal protection provisions of the Fourteenth Amendment and the voting rights provisions of the Fifteenth—the color-blind voting rights provisions of the Fifteenth Amendment! Care to side with the court? Or will you side with the Founding Fathers and the people as the final arbiters of our rights?

Second Amendment advocates are fond of pointing to Nazi Germany, Stalin's

Russia, Mao's China or Pol Pot's Cambodia as distant lessons of tyranny that could have been resisted by an armed citizenry. This has been a century of holocausts, from the Warsaw ghetto to the killing fields of Rwanda.

Of course, that sort of thing can never happen here. Is it intellectual cowardice that prevents us from merely asking the question about the desirability of the state having a monopoly of force? Do you become "right wing" by merely posing the question? Put another way, how can conservative Republicans claim the Second Amendment as their own? There's always been a teeter-totter relationship between the individual's delicate rights and the state's overwhelming power. Historically, hasn't it been liberal Democrats who have wanted to place the fulcrum in the position that favors the individual?

In the words of a great American: "Certainly, one of the chief guarantees of freedom under any government, no matter how popular and respected, is the right of the citizen to keep and bear arms. This is not to say that firearms should not be very carefully used and that definite rules of precaution should not be taught and enforced. But the right of the citizen to bear arms is just one more safeguard against a tyranny which now appears remote in America, but which historically has proved to be always possible."

This quote isn't from Newt Gingrich or Rush Limbaugh. It's from the exemplar of postwar American liberalism, former Vice President Hubert Humphrey. He knew then—and we know today—that we do not have tyranny in this country. The courts are open. Voting booths are open. The press, while it might sometimes appear jobless, is still on the job in America.

So, do we save the Second Amendment for a rainy day when a despot reigns? Or do we use the Second Amendment for the tiny tyrannies that claim so many lives? The tyranny of criminal attack. When you are alone. When all the speaking out on social policies doesn't matter. When all the voting and all the praying don't matter as you catch a glint of your reflection on the blade of a knife wielded by an attacker. And at the scene of this crime, as with most others, there are no police on hand. Just the victim and the predator. Just you and your attacker.

Here's a tiny tyranny that befell a Virginia woman a couple of years ago. At three a.m., Rayna Ross slept with her infant child in her garden apartment. It was fitful slumber. In the past several weeks, her former lover had attacked her, held her against her will and threatened her with a weapon. Authorities held him but later released him. He stalked her and, as he did, he wrote to her. His letters grew increasingly dark, foreshadowing what experts would later call a murder-suicide that was inevitable.

The authorities issued a warrant for his arrest. They couldn't encircle her with guards or post police officers at her doors, or follow her to and from work. They could just issue an arrest warrant.

Because Virginia employs an instantaneous computer background check for gun purchases, Ross's gun purchase was immediate. That's the system NRA is passing in state after state—it's fast, fair and effective. That's the system that the Brady waiting period evolves into in a couple of years.

Ross's purchase was not just immediate, it was also fortunate, because her attacker burst through the apartment's patio door and went after her with a huge knife at three in the morning—three days after she purchased her gun.

Had she been forced to wait, she and her child would be dead now. Another tiny tyranny—but, maybe, not so tiny to the victim.

Philip Russell Coleman worked past midnight in a Shreveport, Louisiana, liquor store and feared criminal attack. He purchased a gun under the Brady five-day waiting period. But unlike Rayna Ross, Philip Coleman will never speak out again. Coleman's gun purchase was approved August 15, 1995—three days after he was shot and killed at the liquor store in the dead of night. Another tiny tyranny, but, maybe, not so tiny to the victim.

Monroe, North Carolina, 1957. The Monroe chapter of the NAACP feared intimidation and violent attack at the hands of the Ku Klux Klan. Bravely, the Monroe NAACP members continued their civil rights struggle. They exercised their civil liberties. Their voting rights. Their right to speak out. To assemble. To associate with one another. But the Ku Klux Klan kept pushing and pushing—and they were armed, and they were illegally using those arms.

In retaliation for a resistance effort organized by the chapter's vice president, the Klan set about driving through black neighborhoods and firing guns at homes. They targeted particularly the home of the chapter vice president, Dr. Albert E. Perry.

So, the Monroe chapter of the NAACP decided to exercise another of their civil liberties—the right to keep and bear arms. In 1957, 60 members of the Monroe chapter of the NAACP affiliated with NRA and received firearms training. Many posted themselves at Dr. Perry's home. When the Klan drove into the neighborhood for another night of tyranny, they came face to face with the Second Amendment.

In the words of one participant: "An armed motorcade attacked Dr. Perry's house which is situated on the outskirts of the colored community. We shot it out with the Klan and repelled their attack and the Klan didn't have any more stomach for this type of fight. They stopped raiding our community." The terrorists failed, because one right prevailed.

Our opponents offer grim statistics and lay them at the foot of the Second Amendment. I, too, can offer those same statistics as gruesome proof of the failure of reliance on laws that do nothing more than restrict the rights of law-abiding people—from Rayna Ross to the Monroe NAACP—and do nothing to disarm criminals or thwart criminal attack.

The tragedy of crime is not only the greatest threat to our lives and property, it is the greatest threat to our civil liberties as well. Restrictions against Second Amendment rights won't restore morality, and ineffective schemes will only serve to enhance hopelessness.

If we respect the lessons taught by the tiny tyrannies in this country—and they're not tiny tyrannies at all, are they?—we will find ourselves shoulder to shoulder with our Founding Fathers.

In the Second Amendment, they lit a fire of freedom. And we can read by the light of that fire the two lessons our Founding Fathers intended—power does not belong exclusively in the hands of the state and self-defense is indeed the *primary* civil right.

Chapter Fifteen

The Second Amendment
America's First Freedom

Charlton Heston

Armed with Pride

Thank you for that very kind introduction. Some day I'll arrive at one of these events in a chariot, just to live up to your expectations. But only if some of you guys will volunteer to clean up after the horses. After all, you've been cleaning up after the Democrats for a long time.

I remember my son, when he was five, explaining to his kindergarten class what his father did for a living. "My Daddy," he said, "pretends to be people."

There have been quite a few of them. Prophets from the Old and New Testaments, a couple of Christian saints, generals of various nationalities and different centuries, several kings, three American presidents, a French cardinal and two geniuses, including Michelangelo. If you want the ceiling re-painted I'll do my best. I don't mean to boast . . . please understand. It's just that there always seem to be a lot of different fellows up here, and I'm not sure which one of them gets to talk.

So as I pondered our visit tonight it struck me: If my Creator endowed me with a talent to entertain you, to connect you somehow with the hearts and minds of these great men—if my Creator has let me spend my life helping you find emotions in these men you perhaps didn't know you could feel—then I want to use that same gift now, to re-connect you with a greatness of purpose . . . a compass for what is right, that already lives in your heart.

Dedicating the memorial at Gettysburg more than a century ago, Abraham Lincoln said of America, "We are now engaged in a great Civil War, testing whether this nation, or any nation so conceived, and so dedicated, can long endure." Lincoln was right. Friends, let me tell you: we are again engaged in a great Civil War—a cultural war that's about to hijack you right out of your own birthright. And I fear that you may no longer trust the pulsing life blood inside you that made this country rise from mud and valor into the miracle that it still is.

Let me back up. About a year ago I became a vice president of the National Rifle Association, which defines and protects the right to keep and bear arms. I ran for office, I was elected, and now I serve. I serve as a moving target for the media who've called me everything from "ridiculous" and "duped" to a "brain-injured, senile, crazy old man." I know . . . I'm pretty old, but I sure, Lord, ain't senile.

As I have stood in the crosshairs of those who want to shoot down our Second Amendment freedoms, I've realized that firearms are not the only issue . . . I am not the only target. It's much, much bigger than that.

I've come to understand that a cultural war is indeed raging across our land, storming our values, assaulting our freedoms, killing our self-confidence in who we are and what we believe.

How many of you here own a gun?

How many own a bunch of guns?

Thank you. I wonder, how many of you own guns but chose not to raise your hand?

How many almost revealed your conviction about a constitutional right, but then thought better of it?

Then you are a victim of the cultural war. You're a casualty of the cultural battle being waged against traditional American freedom of beliefs and ideas.

Now maybe you don't care much one way or the other about owning a gun.

Fair enough. But I could've asked for a show of hands of pentecostal Christians, or pro-lifers, or right-to-workers, or Promise Keepers, or school vouchers, and the result would be the same. Would you raise your hand to endorse any of those major public issues if Dan Rather were in the back of the room with a film crew? What if the same question were asked in the gym at your kids' PTA meeting?

You have been assaulted and robbed of the courage of your convictions. Your pride in who you are, and what you believe, has been ridiculed, ransacked and plundered. It may be a war without bullet or bloodshed, but there is just as much liberty lost: You and your country are less free—this, in the one country that invented freedom.

And you are not inconsequential people! You in this room, whom many would say are among the powerful people on earth, you are shamed into silence! So what other belief held in your heart will you disavow with your hand?

I remember when European Jews feared to admit their faith. The Nazis forced them to wear yellow stars as identity badges. It worked. So—what color star will they pin on gun owners' chests? How will the self-styled elite tag us? There may not be a gestapo officer on every street corner, but the influence on our culture is just as pervasive.

Now, I'm not really here to talk about the Second Amendment or the NRA but the gun issue clearly brings into focus the warfare that's going on. Rank-and-file Americans wake up every morning increasingly bewildered and confused at why their views make them lesser citizens. After enough breakfast-table TV promos hyping tattooed sex slaves on the next *Ricki Lake Show*, enough gun-glutted movies and tabloid talk shows, enough revisionist history books and prime-time ridicule of religion, enough of the TV news anchor who cocks her head, clucks her tongue and sighs about guns causing crime and finally the message begins to get through: Heaven help the God-fearing, law-abiding, Caucasian, middle class, protestant, or even worse evangelical Christian, midwest or southern or even worse rural, apparently straight or even worse admitted heterosexual, gun-owning or even worse NRA-card-carrying, average working stiff, or even, worst of all, a male working stiff, because then, not only don't you count, you're a downright nuisance, an obstacle to social progress, pal. Your tax dollars may be just as green as you hand them over, but your voice better be quiet, your opinion is less enlightened, your media access is silenced, and frankly mister, you need to wake up, wise up and learn a little something about your new America . . . and meantime, why don't you just sit down and shut up!

That's why you didn't raise your hand. That's how cultural war works. And we are losing.

This is why I've formed ARENA PAC, my very own little political action committee. And that's why, though I'm physically and financially comfortable, and have a wonderful family and grandchildren I cherish beyond measure, as well as the chances as an actor that still define my life, still I go out on the road catching redeye flights, speaking at rallies in Seattle, eating pancakes in Peoria and rubber chicken in Des Moines. Yes, indeed. Chuck Heston can find less strenuous, more glamorous things to do with his time than stump for conservative candidates out there in Anytown, U.S.A., but it's a job I can do, I believe, better than most, because most can't.

You don't see many other Hollywood luminaries speaking out for conservative causes, do you? It's not because there aren't any. It's because they can't take the heat. They dare not speak up for fear of ABC or CBS or CNN or worst of all, the IRS.

Cultural war saps the strength of our country because the personal price is simply too high to stand up for what you believe in. Today, speaking with the courage of your conviction can be so costly, the price of principle so great, that legislators won't lead, so citizens can't follow, and so there is no army to fight back. That's cultural warfare.

For instance: It's plain that our Constitution guarantees law-abiding citizens the right to own a firearm. But if I stand up and say so, why does the media assault me with such slashing derision?

Because Bill Clinton's cultural warriors want a penitential cleansing of all firearms. Millions of lawful gun owners must feel guilty for the crimes of other and seek absolution by surrendering their guns. That's what's literally underway right now, in England and Australia. Lines of submissive citizens, walking in lockstep, threatened with imprisonment, are bitterly surrendering family heirlooms, guns that won their freedom, to the blast furnace. If that fact doesn't unsettle you, then you are already anesthetized, you are already a victim of the cultural war.

So how do we get out of this mess? Moses led his people through the wilderness, but he never made it to the promised land—not even when I played him. But he did do his job—he pointed his people in the right direction.

Unlike the Ten Commandments, the Bill of Rights wasn't cut into stone tablets. But the text surely has that same righteous feel to it. It's as if you can sense the unseen hand of the almighty God guiding the sweep of a goose quill pen, while a bunch of rebellious old white guys sweated out the birth of a nation. Jefferson, Adams, Paine—they pointed the way and we made it to this promised land— the one our immigrant ancestors dreamed of, the land Abe Lincoln called "Man's last, best hope on earth." Look at me. Where else but in America could a skinny country kid named Charlton work his way out of the Michigan north woods and find a life that helps make a difference? A long time ago, my country put the gift of freedom in my hands and said, "Here kid! Make something of it." That's why I so deeply love this great nation, and the Constitution that defines it.

Just about everything I hope is good about me—who I am, what I've tried to do—can be traced back to those smoking muskets and the radical declaration of independence by those ragtag rebels. Wearing threadbare coats and marching on bleeding feet, they defeated the finest army assembled in that century, and they gave the world hope. Within them flowed an undertow of personal freedom, a relentless sense of what is right, so irresistibly strong that they simply could not abandon it.

But today's cultural warriors are trying. They're revising and rewriting these truths, yanking the Bill of Rights out of our lives like a parking ticket stuck under your windshield wiper.

They're trading traditions that are true for trends that tease us with more immediate reward. Self-gratification has displaced honor, greed has erased good taste, the desires of the moment have undermined basic morality. We are fast becoming a self-serving, boorish and arrogant people given to cultural binges, quick to dismiss anything of substance that stands in the way of our unleashed desires.

That's the culturally bereft America we see and hear in our movies, television, popular music, even I shudder to say, in our television prime time news.

We should've known what to expect when the earth shoe generation skipped into the White House with a paisley suitcase full of social experiments and revisionist history. Bill and Hillary are the product of a cultural revolution that had absolutely nothing whatsoever to do with the power of flowers. It was an adolescent uprising bent on burning bridges, not building them.

Our President's recent troubles are dramatic proof that cultural war is not a clash over the facts, or even between philosophies. It's a clash between the principled and the unprincipled.

I am not talking about whether he "did it" or "didn't do it." I am talking about people who cannot comprehend moral absolutes, and a country that seems to abide it. Here we are, two nights after the State of the Union Address, trapped in the silly spectacle of having our values measured hourly by the polls, as if the definition of the "right thing" changed like a national mood ring.

"What do you think of the President? Well, wait—after his speech, now how do you feel? Oh, wait, after the White House spin, how do you feel? But wait, after the First Lady's interview, now how do you feel?''

Behavior is judged and re-judged based not upon what's right, but upon what feels right, and to whom, at the moment. This is how cultural warriors use sexual crime to destroy their enemies. Sex between consenting adults shatters the career of a senior enlisted man, a sexual infraction wrecks the life of a corporate executive, and sexual gossip impugns the integrity of a Supreme Court nominee. Yet with the right spin by the right doctor, others are gleefully forgiven. Somewhere in this rancid mess we fight to find principle our children can understand.

But Americans shouldn't have to go to war every morning for their values. They already go to war for their families. They fight to hold down a job, raise responsible kids, make their payments, keep gas in the car, put food on the table and clothes on their backs, and still save a little to live their final days in dignity.

They prefer the America they built—where you could pray without feeling naive, love without being kinky, sing without profanity, be white without feeling guilty, own a gun without shame, and raise your hand without apology. They are the masses who find themselves under siege and long for you to get some guts, stand on principle and lead them to victory in this cultural war. They are sick and tired of national social policy that originates on Oprah, and they're ready for you to pull the plug.

Now if this all sounds a little Mosaic, my punchline is as elementary as the Golden Rule: There is only one way to win a cultural war. Do the right thing.

Triumph belongs to those who arm themselves with pride in who they are and what they believe, and then do the right thing. Not the most expedient thing, not what'll sell, not the politically correct thing, but the right thing.

And you know what? Everybody already knows what that is. You, and I, we know the right thing. President Clinton, Madonna, Louis Farrakhan, even Marilyn Manson, we all know. It's easy. You say wait a minute, you take a long look in the mirror, then into the eyes of your kids, or grandkids, and you'll know what's right.

I promised to try to reconnect you with that sense of purpose, that compass for what's right, that already lives in you. To unleash its power, you need only unbridle your pride and re-arm yourself with the raw courage of your convictions.

Our ancestors were armed with pride, and bequeathed it to us—I can prove it. If you want to feel the warm breath of freedom upon your neck . . . if you want to touch the proud pulse of liberty that beat in our founding fathers in its purest form, you can do so through the majesty of the Second Amendment right to keep and bear arms.

Because there, in that wooden stock and blued steel, is what gives the most common of common men the most uncommon of freedoms. When ordinary hands are free to own this extraordinary, symbolic tool standing for the full measure of human dignity and liberty, that's as good as it gets.

It doesn't matter whether its purpose is to defend our shores or your front door; whether the gun is a rite of passage for a young man or a tool of survival for a young woman; whether it brings meat for the table or trophies for the shelf; without respect to age, or gender, or race, or class, the Second Amendment right to keep and bear arms connects us all—with all that is right—with that sacred document: the Bill of Rights.

And no amount of oppression, no FBI, no IRS, no big government, no social engineers, no matter what and no matter who, they cannot cleave the genes we share with our founding fathers.

Remember they promised us life, liberty, and the pursuit of happiness. They didn't promise us happiness, only the chance to chase it. And being politically correct is not the way to get there. If Americans believed in political correctness, we'd still be King George's boys—subjects of the British crown. Please, seek to be politically competent, yes—politically confident and politically courageous, yes—but never politically correct.

Don't run for cover when the cultural cannons roar. Remember who you are and what you believe, and then raise your hand, stand up, and speak out. Don't be shamed or startled into lockstep conformity by seemingly powerful people.

Defeat the criminals and their apologists; oust the biased and bigoted; endure the undisciplined and unprincipled. But disavow the self-appointed social puppet masters whose relentless arrogance fuels this vicious war against so much we hold so dear. Do not yield, do not divide, do not call truce. It is your duty to muster with pride and win this cultural war.

As leaders you must do what Abraham Lincoln would do, confronted with a perverse version of what America was meant to be: Do the right thing. As Mr. Lincoln said, "With firmness in the right, as God gives us to see right, let us finish the work we are in," and then we shall save our country. I believe that says it all.

Thanks. It's been a pleasure.

Anti-Gun

Chapter Sixteen

Statement of Sarah Brady

Sarah Brady

Thank you for the opportunity to testify once again before this distinguished Subcommittee. My name is Sarah Brady. I am Vice-Chair of Handgun Control, Inc., a national citizens organization working to keep handguns out of the wrong hands. I am here today in strong support of H.R. 975, introduced by Representative Edward Feighan. . . . This legislation establishes a seven-day waiting period and allows for a background check on handgun purchasers.

Having previously testified before this Subcommittee, I know many of you are familiar with my personal experience and my involvement with this issue. It seems odd to me that it is in question whether we should act to keep handguns out of the wrong hands. For that is what this debate is about—whether we allow convicted felons to simply walk into gun stores and immediately walk out with handguns.

We already have a federal law prohibiting convicted felons, minors, people who have been adjudicated mentally ill, illegal aliens, and drug addicts from acquiring handguns. But what does that mean if we do not have the tools to enforce that law? And so I ask you today, do you believe that a convicted felon should be able to walk into a gun store and get a handgun instantly? I cannot believe that anyone could sanction that. Yet as long as we do not have a reasonable waiting period and give police the opportunity to run background checks, a convicted felon will have our seal of approval. That is why I am here today. I am making a very personal appeal to you because I believe you have a responsibility to act to keep handguns out of the hands which would misuse them. Handguns in the wrong hands result in tragedy. I do not say that theoretically. I speak from experience.

I know that you are familiar with what happened on March 30, 1981. At 2:30 P.M. that day, my husband, Jim Brady, was shot through the head by a deranged young man. Jim nearly died. The President nearly died, and two of his security men were seriously wounded.

It has been almost seven years now. March 30th marks the anniversary of the shooting. I often think about the other handgun tragedies which have taken place

Reprinted from *Taking Sides: Clashing Views on Controversial Legal Issues* by Sarah Brady (Guilford, Conn.: Dushkin, 1995), 310–21.

in these seven years that could have been prevented if there were a national waiting period. We must not wait another seven years for other tragedies to occur. We must not wait any longer. We need a national waiting period now.

John Hinckley's handguns were confiscated in October 1980 as he tried to board an airplane in Tennessee, where he was stalking President Jimmy Carter. Hinckley, a drifter, then gunless, needed to replenish his arsenal. In possession of a Texas driver's license and knowing that Texas had no waiting period or background check, Hinckley made the trip to Dallas to purchase the handgun he used to shoot my husband and the President of the United States. Hinckley no longer lived at the address he listed on the federal form he was required to complete. A simple check might have stopped him. Had police been given an opportunity to discover that Hinckley lied on the federal form, Hinckley might well have been in jail instead of on his way to Washington. Now Jim lives daily with the consequence of Hinckley's easy access to a handgun.

This bill does not change who is legally permitted to purchase a handgun. Nor does it impose a major burden on law-abiding citizens. This legislation also provides that if an individual has a legitimate, immediate need for a handgun, the waiting period can be waived by local law enforcement. Is seven days too much to ask a responsible citizen to wait when we know that so many lives are at stake? I don't think so.

Public support for a waiting period and background check is strong. A 1981 Gallup Poll found that more than 90 percent of Americans want such a law. This legislation is supported by every major law enforcement organization in the nation, many representatives of which are here today to testify in support of this bill. The American Bar Association, the American Medical Association, the AFL-CIO, and other organizations too numerous to mention, all support a federal seven-day waiting period. The 1981 Reagan Administration Task Force on Violent Crime recommended such a law. A 1985 Justice Department report states that "at minimum, the acquisition of a firearm by a felon should be somewhat more complicated than just walking into a gun shop and buying one."

While the National Rifle Association opposes this bill, it is important to note that several years ago in its own publication, the NRA stated that a waiting period would be effective as a means of "reducing crimes of passion and in preventing people with criminal records or dangerous mental illness from acquiring guns."

The NRA has flip-flopped on waiting periods and recently taken extreme positions on machine guns, cop-killer bullets, and plastic guns. Considering these extreme positions, I find it incomprehensible that any Member of Congress could trust the judgment of the NRA on a national waiting period or any legislation affecting American lives and public safety, especially when the NRA is in direct opposition to America's law enforcement community which is charged with the responsibility of protecting us.

The NRA argues that proscribed persons do not purchase their handguns over the counter and certainly will not do so if they have to submit to a waiting period. Yet, a 1985 Department of Justice study entitled "The Armed Criminal in America" found that over 20 percent of criminals obtain their handguns through gun dealers. In fact, in states with waiting period laws, many criminals and others disqualified from buying handguns have been caught trying to purchase their handguns over the counter. Law enforcement officials from across the nation report tremendous success where waiting periods are in effect.

For example, according to a police official in Memphis, Tennessee, the state's fifteen-day waiting period screens out about fifty applicants a month, most of whom have criminal records.

According to the California Department of Justice, the state's fifteen-day waiting period screened out more than 1,500 prohibited handgun purchasers in 1986. In that same year, Maryland's seven-day waiting period caught more than 700 prohibited handgun buyers.

States with waiting periods have been effective in stopping criminals before tragedy occurs, but it is unfortunate that in states without waiting periods or background checks, police do not have the same tools to prevent such tragedy.

One of the most shocking and disturbing cases of 1987 occurred in Florida in the wake of the October stock market crash. Arthur Kane purchased a handgun only forty-five minutes before murdering his Florida stock broker and wounding another. If police had been able to conduct a background check, they could have discovered that Kane was a convicted felon.

In another well-publicized event, Dwain Wallace, who had a history of mental illness, was able to instantly purchase a handgun from a Youngstown, Ohio pawnshop. Just two days later, he brandished the handgun in the Pentagon and was immediately gunned down by a Pentagon guard.

A convicted felon, Larry Dale, purchased a handgun at a Tulsa, Oklahoma gun shop, and within twenty-four hours opened fire at a grocery store, killing one customer and wounding another.

I have described a few of the many well-known cases of proscribed persons who instantly purchased their handguns over the counter without having to undergo a waiting period or background check. But for each well-known case, there are many, many more which never make the front page.

While I am not suggesting that a waiting period will stop all crime, it is obvious from these examples that we can save many lives if we want to.

The NRA claims that waiting periods do not prevent criminals from obtaining handguns because criminals will get them from other sources. But in reality, it is the states without waiting periods that are a significant source of handguns for criminals.

The Treasury's Bureau of Alcohol, Tobacco and Firearms' study of handguns used in crime found that of all the handguns used in crime in New York City, only 4 percent were purchased in New York State, which requires a background check. Virtually all the rest were from states without waiting periods or background checks. In addition, the study found that in states without waiting periods or background checks, an overwhelming majority of handguns used in crime were purchased within the same state. For example, of all the handguns used in crime in Dallas, almost 90 percent were purchased in Texas, which has no waiting period.

The NRA argues that waiting periods should be left up to the states, not the federal government. While individual states, many counties and municipalities have passed local waiting periods, a national law is critical because it will ensure that handguns are not purchased over the counter in states without waiting periods and then sold on the street in states requiring waiting periods and/or background checks.

I am ashamed that my own state of Virginia, which has no waiting period or background check, is a major source of handguns used in crime elsewhere. Just a few weeks ago, police arrested one Richmond man who reportedly purchased more than seventy guns in Virginia and then brought them into Washington, D.C. to sell on the street. Another man from the District was charged with using false identification, purchasing more than two dozen semi-automatic handguns in Virginia and selling them to District drug dealers. Unfortunately, these examples represent only the tip of the iceberg of this criminal traffic in handguns.

We can prevent needless tragedy. We can make it more difficult for criminals to get handguns. I hope that the day will come when no American family has to go through what my family has suffered. Again I ask, do you really believe that a convicted felon should be able to walk into a gun store and instantly purchase a handgun? The American people do not believe that. But until action is taken on this bill, a convicted felon purchasing a handgun will have our seal of approval.

The NRA would like to turn back the clock to the days before passage of the 1968 Gun Control Act, which has served our nation well for nearly two decades. . . .

I ask that you stand with our law enforcement community and provide the leadership that will save lives by keeping handguns out of the wrong hands.

Chapter Seventeen

Violence in America
A Public Health Emergency

C. Everett Koop, M.D., and George D. Lundberg, M.D.

Violence, according to one dictionary, is defined as "(1) exertion of any physical force so as to injure or abuse, (2) injury by or as if by distortion, infringement, or profanation, (3) intense, turbulent and often destructive action, or force." In his book *Powershift* Alvin Toffler identifies violence or the threat of violence as one of the three fundamental sources of all human power, the other two being money and knowledge. Toffler convincingly argues that these power sources influence every person and all groups including government. Of the three, violence is the lowest form of power because it can only be used to punish. Knowledge and money are far more versatile and can be used in an infinite variety of positive as well as negative or manipulative ways.[1] The violence referred to in this issue of *JAMA* is the interpersonal kind rather than such types as war or that produced by forces of nature.

Response to JAMA's *Call for Papers*

The response to a call for papers on any aspects of interpersonal violence, made last August on behalf of the editors of *JAMA* and all nine AMA specialty journals, was extraordinary.[2] *JAMA* alone received 131 topical papers for peer review and consideration. Of these, twelve appear in this issue; one relevant paper has been published in each *JAMA* since May 5, and another cluster of papers emphasizing domestic violence will appear in the June 17 issue. The specialty journals also received a great many manuscripts and published from one to twelve articles each in their June issues, in total fifty-nine. This outpouring of manuscripts not only confirms what we all know—that violence in the United States is a major issue—it underscores that violence is also a medical/public health issue, which is keenly felt by innumerable physicians and subject to medical/epidemiologic research.

The 1985 Surgeon General's Conference

One of us (C.E.K.) convened the Surgeon General's Workshop on Violence and Public Health at Leesburg, Virginia, in October 1985. The recommendations of the 150 assembled experts were reported by the Surgeon General to the Senate Committee on Children, Families, Drugs and Alcoholism.[3] Regional, state, and local workshops followed to create a new awareness of the possibilities for understanding and dealing with violence provided by multidisciplinary approaches. Pediatricians, psychiatrists, and other physicians, along with administrators and the public, were challenged to consider violence as a public health issue and to seek out its root causes and best treatments.

Seven years later, violence in our country has not diminished; instead, violence makes constant headlines. In fact, the incidence of violence has increased, especially among some groups.

- One million U.S. inhabitants die prematurely each year as the result of intentional homicide or suicide.
- From 1960 to 1980 the population of the United States increased by 26 percent; the homicide rate due to guns increased 160 percent.
- The leading cause of death in both black and white teenage boys in America is gunshot wounds.
- The number of deaths due to firearms is seven times greater in the United States than in the United Kingdom.
- The death rate from trauma in France is 66 percent that of the U.S. rate, and the rate in the Netherlands is only 39 percent.
- Armed assaults in California schools are on a sharp increase.
- One-third of students in thirty-one Illinois high schools have brought some weapons to school for self-defense.
- Suicide is the third leading cause of death among children and adolescents in the United States, a rate that has doubled in the last thirty years, the increase almost solely due to firearms.
- Of the fatalities in the 1992 Los Angeles, California, riots, the vast majority occurred as a result of gunshot wounds.

New Research in Firearm Fatalities/Deaths by Gunshot Wounds

- In this issue of *JAMA*, Fingerhut and colleagues[4,5] document extraordinarily high firearm fatality rates in many core metropolitan counties, with rates for black male and female teenagers increasing sharply in recent years to reach alarming levels.
- Saltzman et al.[6] demonstrate that firearm-associated family and intimate assaults in Atlanta, Georgia, are twelve times more likely to result in death than nonfirearm assaults.
- Weil and Hemenway[7] document in a national sample that large numbers

of handgun owners keep their guns loaded in their homes and that many loaded weapons are not locked up, even if children are in the household. This dangerous behavior seemed not to be altered with training.

• Callahan and Rivara[8] show that one-third of Seattle, Washington, high school students report easy access to handguns, 6 percent own a handgun and 6 percent of males have carried a handgun to school.

These research findings, together with other articles in these issues, and an array of related data paint a grotesque picture of a society steeped in violence, especially by firearms, and so numbed by the ubiquity and prevalence of violence as to seemingly accept it as inevitable. We do not agree. No society, including ours, need be permeated by firearm homicide. This is unacceptable. Prior solutions have not succeeded. New approaches are required. Two such are included in adjacent commentaries.[9,10]

What Now?

Regarding violence in our society as purely a sociologic matter, or one of law enforcement, has led to unmitigated failure. It is time to test further whether violence can be amenable to medical/public health interventions.

We believe violence in America to be a public health emergency, largely unresponsive to methods thus far used in its control. The solutions are very complex, but possible. We urge all persons in authority to take the following actions:

1. Support additional major research on the causes, prevention, and cures of violence.
2. Stimulate the education of all Americans about what is now known and what can now be done to address this emergency.
3. Demand legislation intended to reverse the upward trend of firearm injuries and deaths, the end result that is most out of control.

Proposed New Legislation

Automobiles, intended to be a means of transportation, when used inappropriately frequently become lethal weapons and kill human beings. Firearms are intended to be lethal weapons. When used inappropriately in peace time, they, too, frequently kill human beings.

In the state of Texas in 1990, deaths from firearms, for the first time in many decades, surpassed deaths from motor vehicles, 3,443 to 3,309, respectively, as the leading cause of injury mortality.[11] In the 1970s and 1980s, defining motor vehicle casualties as a public health issue and initiating intervention activity succeeded in reversing the upward trend of such fatalities, without banning or confiscating automobiles. We believe that comparable results can be anticipated by similarly treating gunshot wound casualties. But the decline in fatalities will not occur overnight and will require a major coordinated effort.

The right to own or operate a motor vehicle carries with it certain responsibilities. Among them are that the operator meet certain criteria:

- be a certain age and physical/mental condition;
- be identifiable as owner or operator;
- be able to demonstrate knowledge and skill in operating the motor vehicle safely;
- be subject to performance monitoring; and
- be willing to forfeit the right to operate or own a vehicle if these responsibilities are abrogated.

We propose that the right to own or operate a firearm carries with it the same prior conditions, namely, that the owner and operator of a firearm also meet specific criteria:

- be of a certain age and physical/mental condition;
- be required to demonstrate knowledge and skill in proper use of that firearm;
- be monitored in the firearm's use; and
- forfeit the right to own or operate the firearm if these conditions are abrogated.

These restrictions should apply uniformly to all firearms and to all U.S. inhabitants across all states through a system of gun registration and licensing for gun owners and users. No grandfather clauses should be allowed.

Anticipated Resistance and Support

We recognize the enormous amount of change and expense necessary to effect any major proposal such as this having to do with guns. But we believe that anything short of this proposed registration and licensing for gun ownership and use would be too little action to recommend at this time. We also believe that there is great public sentiment in support of this proposal.

A vast lobby of special interests supports the utterly unfettered ownership and use of firearms. It is certain vigorously to oppose this proposal at any cost. One of us (G.D.L.) has met with representatives of the National Rifle Association in Washington, D.C., to discuss ways to counter the acknowledged epidemic of firearm homicides. We invite that organization and any other dissenting persons and groups, to make their own rational proposals for countering this acute public health emergency of injuries and homicides, especially those occurring in young black men and women. We can wait no longer to act.

REFERENCES

1. Toffler a. *Powershift*. New York, NY: Bantam Books Inc; 1990: 2,17,38,467–469.

2. Lundberg G D, Koop C E. The AMA scientific journals—theme issues on violence: call for papers. *JAMA*. 1991;266:1126.

3. Surgeon General. *Surgeon General's Workshop on Violence and Public Health, Lessburg, Va., October 27–29, 1985*. Rockville, Md.: Office of Maternal and Child Health, Bureau of Maternal and Child Health and Resources Development, Health, Resources and Services Administration, U.S. Public Health Service, U.S. Dept. of Health and Human Services; 1986. Report to the Senate Committee on Children, Families, Drugs and Alcoholism.

4. Fingerhut L A, Ingram D D, Feldman J J. Firearm and nonfirearm homicide among persons 15 to 19 years of age: differences by level of urbanization, United States, 1979 to 1989. *JAMA*. 1992;267:3048–3053.

5. Fingerhut L A, Ingram D D, Feldman J J. Firearm homicide among black teenage males in metropolitan counties, 1983 through 1985 to 1987 through 1989. *JAMA*. 1992;267: 3054–3058.

6. Saltzman L E, Mercy J A, O'Carroll P W, Rosenberg M L, Rhodes P H. Weapon involvement and injury outcomes in family and intimate assaults. *JAMA*. 1992;267:3043–3047.

7. Weil D S, Hemenway D. Loaded guns in the home: an analysis of a national random survey of gun owners. *JAMA*. 1992;267:3033–3037.

8. Callahan C M, Rivara F P. Urban high school youth and handguns: a school-based survey. *JAMA*. 1992;267:3038–3042.

9. Rosenberg M L, O'Carroll P W, Powell K E. Let's be clear: violence is a public health problem. *JAMA*. 1992;267:3071–3072.

10. Teret S P, Wintemute G J, Beilenson P. The Firearm Fatality Reporting System: a proposal. *JAMA*. 1992;267:3073–3074.

11. Zane D F, Preece M J, Patterson P J, Svenkerud E K. Firearm-related mortality in Texas (1985–1990). *Tex Med*. 1991;87:63–65.

Chapter Eighteen

Firearms and Assault
"Guns Don't Kill People, People Kill People"

Franklin E. Zimring and Gordon Hawkins

One of the major arguments against the theory that gun control would save life is that although two-thirds of all homicides are committed with firearms, firearms controls could have no effect on homicide rates because, "human nature being what it is," homicide would continue unabated. Murderers would use the next most convenient weapon. Only the weapons used would change. If guns were eliminated from the scene, more knives, clubs, axes, pieces of pipe, blocks of wood, brass knuckles, or, for that matter, fists would be used. "Guns don't kill people, people kill people."

The classic statement of this argument may be found in Professor Marvin Wolfgang's *Patterns in Criminal Homicide* (1958):

> More than the availability of a shooting weapon is involved in homicide. Pistols and revolvers are not difficult to purchase. . . . The type of weapon used appears to be, in part, the culmination of assault intentions or events and is only superficially related to causality. To measure quantitatively the effect of the presence of firearms on the homicide rate would require knowing the number and type of homicides that would not have occurred had not the offender—or, in some cases, the victim—possessed a gun. . . . It is the contention of this observer that few homicides due to shootings could be avoided merely if a firearm were not immediately present, and that the offender would select some other weapon to achieve the same destructive goal. Probably only in those cases where a felon kills a police officer, or vice versa, would homicide be avoided in the absence of a firearm.

A more recent statement of this position can be found in Wright, Rossi, and Daly's *Under the Gun* (1983):

> Even if we were somehow able to remove all firearms from civilian possession, it is not at all clear that a substantial reduction in interpersonal violence would follow. Certainly, the violence that results from hard-core and predatory criminality would not abate by very much. Even the most ardent proponents of stricter gun laws no longer expect such laws to solve the hard-core crime problem, or even to make

much of a dent in it. There is also reason to doubt whether the "soft-core" violence, the so-called crimes of passion, would decline by very much. Stated simply, these crimes occur because some people have come to hate others, and they will continue to occur in one form or another as long as hatred persists. . . . If we could solve the problem of interpersonal hatred, it may not matter very much what we did about guns, and *unless* we solve the problem of interpersonal hatred, it may not matter very much what we do about guns. There are simply too many other objects in the world that can serve the purpose of inflicting harm on another human being. . . . Although it is true that under current conditions the large majority of gun crimes are committed with handguns (on the order, perhaps, of 70–75% of them), it definitely does *not* follow that, in the complete absence of handguns, crimes now committed with handguns would not be committed! The more plausible expectation is that they would be committed with other weaponry.

The most forcible statements of the opposing viewpoint may be found in the National Commission on the Causes and Prevention of Violence Task Force Report on Firearms and Violence and two Chicago studies of fatal and nonfatal assaults. It is pointed out that although other weapons are involved in homicide, firearms are not only the most deadly instrument of attack but also the most versatile. Firearms make some attacks possible that simply would not occur without firearms. They permit attacks at greater range and from positions of better concealment than other weapons. They also permit attacks by persons physically or psychologically unable to overpower their victim through violent physical contact. It is because of their capacity to kill instantly and from a distance that firearms are virtually the only weapon used in killing police officers.

In addition to providing greater range for the attacker, it is argued, firearms are more deadly than other weapons. The fatality rate of firearms attacks, the Task Force Report noted, was about five times higher than the fatality rate of attacks with knives, the next most dangerous weapon used in homicide. The illustrative data cited are shown in Table 18.1.

The studies also reveal that there was a substantial overlap in the circumstances involved in fatal and nonfatal assaults with guns and those committed with knives. Four out of five homicides occurred as a result of altercations over such matters as love, money, and domestic problems, and 71 percent involved acquaintances, neighbors, lovers, and family members. In short, the circumstances in which most homicides were committed suggested that they were

TABLE 18.1
Percentage of Reported Gun and Knife Attacks
Resulting in Death (Chicago, 1965–1967)

Weapons	Death as Percentage of Attacks
Knives (16,518 total attacks)	2.4
Guns (6,350 total attacks)	12.2

SOURCE: Newton and Zimring, *Firearms and Violence in American Life* (1969), Table 7-2, p. 41.

committed in a moment of rage and were not the result of a single-minded intent to kill. Planned murders involving a single-minded intent, such as gangland killings, were a spectacular but infrequent exception.

Not only did the circumstances of homicide and the relationship of victim and attacker suggest that most homicides did not involve a single-minded determination to kill, but also the choice of a gun did not appear to indicate such intent. The similarity of circumstances in which knives and guns were used suggested that the motive for an attack did not determine the weapon used. Figures obtained from the Chicago Police Department showed the similar circumstances of firearms and knife homicides as shown in Table 18.2.

Further evidence that those who used a gun were no more intent on killing than those who used knives was found in comparing the wound locations and the number of wounds as between those assaults committed with knives and those committed with guns. It was found that a greater percentage of knife attacks than gun attacks resulted in wounds to vital areas of the body—such as the head, neck, chest, abdomen, and back—where wounds were likely to be fatal. Also, many more knife attacks than gun attacks resulted in multiple wounds, suggesting that those who used the knife in those attacks had no great desire to spare the victim's life. Nevertheless, even when the comparison was controlled for the number of wounds and the body location of the most serious wound, gun assaults were far more likely to lead to death than knife assaults.

Even so, it might be contended that if gun murderers were deprived of guns they would find a way to kill as often with knives. If this were so, knife attacks in cities where guns were not so widely used would show a higher fatality rate. But analyses of cities for which the pertinent data were available revealed no such relationship. It appeared that as the number of knife attacks increased in

TABLE 18.2
Circumstance of Homicide, by Weapon (Chicago, 1967)

	Gun (Percent)	Knife (Percent)
Altercations:		
General domestic	21	25
Money	6	7
Liquor	2	8
Sex	1	3
Gambling	2	1
Triangle	5	5
Theft (alleged)	—	—
Children	2	1
Other	41	30
Armed robbery	9	9
Perversion and assault on female	2	7
Gangland	1	—
Other	2	—
Undetermined	6	4
Total	100	100
Number of cases*	265	152

* Another 93 homicides were committed with other weapons.
SOURCE: Newton and Zimring, *Firearms and Violence in American Life* (1969), Table 7-5, p. 43.

relation to the number of firearms attacks (which presumably happened where guns were less available to assailants), the proportion of knife attacks that were fatal did *not* increase relative to that proportion among gun attacks; if anything, the reverse was the case.

The conclusion that weapon dangerousness independent of any other factors had a substantial impact on the death rate from attack, which has been called the "instrumentality hypothesis," was supported by another study of violent assault in Chicago, which compared low-caliber with high-caliber firearms attacks. This study found that attacks with large-caliber firearms were far more likely to cause death than attacks by small-caliber guns that resulted in the same number of wounds to the same parts of the body.

The authors of *Under the Gun*, cited above, have disputed the conclusions drawn from the evidence presented in the Chicago studies. They dismiss the circumstantial evidence such as the motives of homicide and the frequent involvement of alcohol in killings as inconclusive on whether attacks that cause death are often ambiguously motivated. The similar demographic profiles of fatal and nonfatal attacks are not regarded as evidence that the two groups "are similar in any respect relevant to hypotheses about underlying motivations." The same conclusion apparently was applied to the similarities between victim groups.

The authors never address the possibility that chance elements determine a subsample of fatalities from the universe of those assaulted. The crucial fact that most gun killings, like most nonfatal assaults, involve only one wound is rejected as evidence against a single-minded intent to kill in favor of the conclusion that what distinguishes the hundreds of one-shot killings from thousands of one-shot nonfatal woundings in the same body location by the same sort of people is "a level of marksmanship that one would probably not expect under conditions of outrage and duress." This conclusion is reached without any evidence from the extensive literature on criminal violence.

Indeed, the only evidence offered in support of this hypothesis is drawn from the experience of one of the authors in preparing deer carcasses for home freezers. The relevance of this experience to shooting people in a homicidal situation is explained as follows:

> He is yet to encounter, over a sample of some 15–20 taken deer, even a single deer that was taken with one and only one shot. . . . [This] suggests that capable marksmen, armed with highly accurate and efficient weaponry, aiming unambiguously to kill roughly man-sized targets, are seldom able to kill their prey with a single shot. That a much higher proportion of murderers, armed with much less impressive weaponry, kill with a single shot might therefore cause us to wonder just how ambiguous the underlying motives are.

The authors do not consider the possibility that some of the marksmen, even if armed with less accurate and efficient weaponry, might not do better if they could maneuver a few of their deer into the living room. Nor do they consider the alternative hypothesis that many killers are randomly drawn from the larger pool of one-shot assaulters, or discuss why "determined" killers will often stop after one wounding when most guns have a multiple wounding capacity.

It is also curious that the sharp differences in death rates for large-caliber versus small-caliber guns assaults are not considered to be evidence that the objective dangerousness of a weapon has a significant influence on the death rate from assault. The authors briefly examine this data, and they caution that this pattern could also be explained if more determined killers chose larger-caliber guns. The evidence from the weapon caliber study that the pattern holds true even when the attacker probably did not choose the weapon is ignored.

Conclusion

The issue of instrumentality effects from guns in deadly assaults is important in its own right. It is also an instructive example of the practical and philosophical differences between the ideological forces in conflict about gun control. This dispute about instrumentality effects is not so much about the nature of the evidence available but about what that evidence means and how great the burden of proof should be.

The parable of the butchered deer carcass mentioned above seems the closest Wright and his colleagues can come to a personal background in research on criminal violence. Instead of grounding their discussion in a coherent vision of violent assault, they put forward rival hypotheses to each strand of circumstantial evidence individually, conclude that none is strict proof of instrumentality effects by itself, and assume that the cumulative impact of multiple strands of evidence is no more persuasive than any of the individual strands.

When the time came to recommend future research, the authors were prisoners of their own standards. In their report to the federal government, no further investigation of these critical issues was proposed. In their book, the authors leave the impression that nothing is known on the question of what difference guns make and nothing can be done to increase knowledge. The tone, and the level of denial, remind one of the Tobacco Institute's valiant struggle against premature conclusions on the relationship between cigarettes and lung cancer.

It should also be said that the assertion that "unless we solve the problem of interpersonal hatred it may not matter very much what we do about guns" is a nice example of the "root causes" fallacy. The essence of this argument is that if crime control measures are to be effective, they must deal with the "root causes" of crime—in this case "interpersonal hatred." Even the most effective regime of gun control would not totally eliminate homicide and on this argument could be criticized for not having dealt with the "root cause" of the problem.

REFERENCES

Newton, George D., Jr., and Franklin E. Zimring. *Firearms and Violence in American Life: A Staff Report Submitted to the National Commission on the Causes and Prevention of Violence.*

Washington, D.C.: National Commission on the Causes and Prevention of Violence, 1969.

Wolfgang, Marvin. *Patterns in Criminal Homicide.* Philadelphia: University of Pennsylvania Press, 1958.

Wright, James D., Peter H. Rossi, and Kathleen Daly. *Under the Gun: Weapons, Crime, and Violence in America.* New York: Aldine, 1983.

Zimring, Franklin E. "Is Gun Control Likely to Reduce Violent Killings?" *University of Chicago Law Review* 35 (1968): 721–737.

———. "The Medium Is the Message: Firearms Caliber as a Determinant of the Death Rate from Assault," *Journal of Legal Studies* 1 (1972): 97–123.

Chapter Nineteen

Loaded Guns in the Home
Analysis of a National Random Survey of Gun Owners

Douglas S. Weil and David Hemenway

Research that links the availability of loaded firearms to gun violence tends to be more descriptive than analytic. However, the spontaneity with which deadly violence occurs has lent support to the contention that easy access to a loaded gun may be an important risk factor for both homicide and suicide as well as unintentional shootings.

Many homicides and suicides appear to be the result of impulsive behavior. Homicides frequently occur during arguments, often domestic, when emotions run high and when one or both parties have been drinking.[1,2] Individuals who take their own lives often do so when confronting a severe but temporary crisis.[3] For example, young male suicide victims (for whom the suicide rate tripled between 1950 and 1980) were not generally depressed but acted on impulse in response to "trouble at home, in school, and with the police."[4]

The U.S. General Accounting Office (GAO) reported that 1,501 unintentional firearm deaths occurred in 1988. Over 70 percent involved a handgun, and most occurred in or near the home.[5] Several studies estimate that there are four to six nonfatal injuries for every fatal accidental shooting.[6-9] Among those killed unintentionally in 1988 were 277 children fifteen years and younger.[5] Pediatric morbidity and mortality due to accidental gunshot wounds are often the result of spontaneous happenings that occur when children find and play with a loaded gun. This fact has led researchers to suggest that failure to prevent access to these weapons may be an important risk factor for injury.[6,10-14]

As a result of the spontaneous or impulsive nature of many firearm fatalities, it is logical to expect that "a substantial portion of these events might be prevented if immediate access to lethal weapons was reduced, in particular through appropriate storage of guns and ammunition."[15] Thus, one goal of Healthy People 2000 is a 20 percent reduction in the "proportion of people who possess weapons that are inappropriately stored and therefore dangerously available."[15]

A recent national survey found that firearms were present in 46 percent of households and that one in four households had a handgun.[16] Over half of the

Reprinted courtesy of the American Medical Association from *JAMA* (June 10, 1992): 3033–37. Copyright © 1992 by the American Medical Association.

handgun owners surveyed said that their guns were currently loaded. These findings are consistent with those of a smaller study in which 55 percent of gun owners questioned claimed they always kept their weapons loaded; 10 percent said that their guns were "loaded, unlocked and within reach of children."[10]

According to virtually all experts, including the National Rifle Association and the Sporting Arms and Ammunition Manufacturer's Institute, the safe handling of a firearm requires that guns be stored unloaded in a locked area separate from the ammunition.[17,18] Many gun owners apparently do not follow this advice.

Society's ability to address the problem of firearm-related fatalities could be improved by research into the storage of guns.[8]

> We lack routinely collected information on behavioral risk factors (e.g., gun storage and accessibility to loaded weapons) that contribute to firearm associated morbidity and mortality. Information on these factors would help to establish the characteristics of persons with easy access to guns so that high-risk groups could be targeted for intervention. In addition, such information would help evaluate efforts aimed at preventing firearm injury, reducing access, and altering unsafe storage practices.[4]

This study analyzes a national random sample of gun owners to identify factors associated with keeping guns loaded. Four principal hypotheses are tested: that, all else equal, people are more likely to keep their firearms loaded if (1) the primary purpose for owning a gun is protection from crime, (2) the gun is a handgun, (3) there are no children in the household, and (4) the owner has not received instruction in the proper use of firearms.

Methods

Data Origin and Potential Sources of Bias

The data used were obtained from a random national telephone survey of gun owners 18 years and older. The survey, sponsored by *Time* magazine and Cable News Network, was conducted December 15 through 22, 1989, by Yankelovich Clancy and Shulman, Inc. Telephone numbers were randomly generated to ensure that households with both listed and unlisted numbers were included. Respondents were not identifiable to the researchers by name or address. Participants were asked a screening question; approximately one in three individuals declined to answer this screening question, with no significant drop in participation for the remaining question.

Surveys that sample the population are subject to sampling error. Results may differ from what would be obtained if the whole population were interviewed. For a survey of 600 respondents, the results are subject to an error margin of ±4 percentage points for each question because of chance variation in the sample.

Telephone surveys are subject to systematic error. Individuals without telephones or those who work unusual hours may not be represented. In 1986, 7 percent of all people in the United States (including more than 15 percent of all blacks and 27 percent of people living below the poverty line) lived in households that did not have a telephone.[19]

Registered gun owners have been shown to provide generally valid responses to questions about gun ownership.[20] However, the same may not be true for owners of unregistered weapons. Individuals who own guns illegally or for illegal purposes may be reluctant to admit ownership. Gun owners under the age of eighteen years were not surveyed.

The imprecise wording of some questions might cause measurement error or incorrect interpretation of the results. For example, respondents were asked, "Do you sometimes keep your gun loaded, always keep it loaded, or never keep it loaded?" It is not immediately clear how someone with more than one weapon would answer this question, particularly if one gun were always loaded and another never loaded.

Finally, while respondents were asked why they purchased their gun, they were not asked why they kept it loaded. A primary goal of this study is to help determine who keeps loaded weapons.

Outcome Variable

A dichotomous dependent variable was created by separating individuals who never kept their gun(s) loaded from those who did keep a gun loaded some of the time or always. A second model, which excludes individuals who sometimes kept their guns loaded, was analyzed to determine whether the predicted odds ratios were sensitive to the treatment of this intermediate response group.

Individuals who kept their gun(s) both unlocked and loaded create the greatest potential for injury. Therefore, we created an alternate dependent variable that compares people whose firearms are loaded and unlocked with all other gun owners. Our principal results were unchanged when using this variable. We report the findings of the model that uses keeping a firearm loaded as the outcome of interest so that we can show the relationship between keeping a gun locked and keeping it loaded.

Predictors

The four key indicator variables examined were (1) type of gun, (2) reason for owning a gun, (3) presence of children in the home, and (4) training in the proper use of guns. To capture the effect of gun type, respondents who owned a handgun were placed into one category, and everyone else was put into the reference group. Individuals who owned both a handgun and a long gun were placed in the handgun category.

Individuals who owned their gun(s) primarily "for protection from crime," were distinguished from the subjects in the reference group that contains all other responses (hunting, target shooting, gun collection, work, other, and not sure).

Respondents were also categorized by whether or not they lived with children. Ninety-five people could not directly be assigned to either category. However, using responses from other questions, it was possible to determine that seventy-three of these individuals lived alone and that nine were married and living only with their spouses. These eighty-two people (86 percent) were put in the "no children" category, and the rest were put in the reference group. The results of the analysis do not appreciably differ by the assignment of the remaining thirteen people.

Two questions in the survey concerned respondents' training in the use of firearms. The first asked whether the individual had been given instruction. Those who had received training were asked, "Where did you get this training—from someone you knew, from a class, from military training, or in some other way?" People who said that they received training from the military or a class were put into one category. All other individuals, including those who said that they had not received any training, were put into the reference category. Informal instruction may be more similar to military or classroom training than to a lack of training. Hence, an analysis was also conducted comparing individuals with any form of instruction in the proper use of guns with those with no training.

Background Variables

Various factors that might confound the relationship between the possession of a loaded firearm and any of the four predictors were incorporated into the model. Included among these variables were demographic characteristics such as the gun owner's age, race, sex, level of education achieved, and the region of the country where the respondent lives.

Other factors that might be associated with both the outcome and one or more predictors are the number of guns owned, whether or not they were kept locked up when not in use, and the location where they were stored (e.g., in the bedroom). Respondent's income is another potential confounder. However, 20 percent of the participants (n = 119) declined to provide information about their income, so the variable is not included in the final model. A sensitivity analysis was conducted to determine whether the presence of income in the model affects the results.

There is no established theory that suggests the functional form for many of the potential confounding variables. Alternative forms were tested to determine whether the principal results were sensitive to the way these background variables were specified. For example, the number of guns owned could be treated as a continuous or dichotomous variable. It could also be treated as several dichotomous variables. We tried various forms and none altered our results.

Multivariate logistic regression is used to estimate the odds ratio (OR) of keeping a gun loaded for individuals with a given characteristic (e.g., they were handgun owners) relative to individuals without that characteristic while simultaneously controlling for the other variables in the model.

TABLE 19.1

Crosstabulations of Possible Predictors of Private Ownership of a Loaded Gun and Associated χ^2 Statistics

Factor	No.*	Sometimes or Always Keep Gun Loaded, %	χ^2
Handgun†			
Owns a handgun	364	51	81.18‡
Does not own a handgun	227	15	
Purposes§			
Protection from crime	162	63	64.20‡
Other	432	27	
Children in house§			
No	358	42	8.11‖
Yes	236	30	
Training§			
Military or class	311	36	0.59
None or other	283	38	
Region§			
Southern¶	260	50	31.37‡
Other	334	27	
Races§			
White	523	35	6.46‖
Nonwhite	71	50	
Locked up#			
Yes	267	33	2.62**
No	319	40	
Age, y††			
≤34	228	34	1.25
≤35	361	39	
No. of guns owned§			
≤2	257	33	3.05**
≥3	337	40	
Where stored§			
Bedroom	255	39	0.61
Other	339	36	
Education††			
≤High school	320	36	0.35
>High school	296	35	

*N = 605 in the sample population.
†Fourteen observations were missing.
‡$P<.001$.
§Eleven observations were missing.
‖$P<.01$.
¶The southern region included Alabama, Arkansas, Delaware, Florida, Georgia, Kentucky, Louisiana, Maryland, Mississippi, North Carolina, Oklahoma, South Carolina, Tennessee, Texas, Virginia, and West Virginia. The other region included all remaining states. Alaska, Hawaii, and Washington, D.C., are not represented in the sample.
#Nineteen observations were missing.
**$P<.1$.
††Sixteen observations were missing.

Results

The sample consisted of 605 individuals; most were men (75 percent), few were nonwhite (12 percent). Each respondent owned at least one gun, with the majority owning more than one (77 percent). The most commonly owned type of firearm was a rifle (72 percent), while 61 percent of the respondents owned a handgun. The weapons were typically kept unloaded at all times. However, more than one-third of the gun owners kept their gun(s) loaded either all of the time (25 percent) or some of the time (12 percent). Furthermore, 53 percent of the people surveyed did not keep their firearms locked up.

Simple crosstabulations indicate that owning a handgun, purchasing the weapon for protection, and having no children in the household are all positively correlated with keeping a gun loaded; training in the proper use of firearms is not significantly correlated with the dependent variable (Table 19.1). Similar results are found in multiple logistic analysis (Table 19.2). Only 583 observations are included in this analysis, since information concerning one or more of the variables of interest is missing for twenty-two individuals.

The strongest predictor of respondents who possess a loaded firearm was the type of gun owned. Handgun owners were more than twice as likely as other individuals to keep their guns loaded at least some of the time (OR, 2.17; 95 percent confidence interval [CI], 1.67 to 2.82).

Among the people surveyed, individuals who owned their weapons primarily for protection from crime were 65 percent more likely to keep their firearms loaded than individuals who owned their guns for other purposes (OR, 1.65; 95 percent CI, 1.30 to 2.11). People who did not live with children were over 40 percent more likely to report that they kept their weapons loaded than gun owners living in households with children (OR, 1.42; 95 percent CI, 1.13 to 1.82).

Other factors associated with the maintenance of a loaded firearm are geographic location, race, and whether or not the gun was locked up when not in use. Individuals who lived in the South and those who were not white were more likely to keep their guns loaded. People who did not lock up their guns were also more likely to keep them loaded.

Of the four main hypotheses, the only one that cannot be substantiated is the proposed association between training in the proper use of guns and the likelihood that a gun will be kept loaded. In the study population, instruction did not seem to affect the probability of keeping guns loaded (OR, 0.86; 95 percent CI, 0.69 to 1.07). The result holds whether the variable is any training or only military or classroom instruction.

If the income variable is included in the model, the principal findings are unaffected. Furthermore, the results do not appreciably differ when subjects who kept their guns loaded only some of the time are excluded from the analysis.

Comment

Handguns are the most common type of firearm involved in gunshot deaths in the home, whether accidental or intentional.[12,21] The most common reason given for owning a handgun is protection from crime,[10,22] yet only a small percentage of firearm deaths in the home are the result of a incident requiring self-protection.[21,23] Unfortunately, no study seems to link specific shooting incidents with the reason for owning a gun.

TABLE 19.2

Factors Associated with Keeping a Gun Loaded*: Interpreting the Fitted Logistic

Factor	Logistic Regression Results, Odds Ratio (95% Confidence Interval)†
Handgun	
1=owns a handgun	2.17 (1.67–2.82)
0=other	
Purpose	
1=protection from crime	1.65 (1.30–2.11)
0=other	
Children living in home	
1=no	1.43 (1.13–1.82)
0=yes	
Training	
1=formal (military or other)	0.86 (0.69–1.07)
0=none or informal	
Region‡	
1=southern states	1.61 (1.31–1.98)
0=other	
Race	
1=nonwhite	1.37 (1.01–1.86)
0=white	
Locked up when stored	
1=no	1.23 (1.01–1.54)
0=yes	
Age, y§	
30s	
1=30–39	1.24 (0.92–1.66)
0=other	
40s	
1=40–49	1.10 (0.80–1.52)
0=other	
50s	
1=≥50	1.11 (0.83–1.48)
0=other	
Sex	
1=male	1.06 (0.82–1.36)
0=female	
No. of guns owned‖	
2 or 3	
1=own 2 or 3 guns	0.83 (0.62–1.11)
0=other	
4 or more	
1=own 4 or more guns	1.19 (0.88–1.62)
0=other	
Where stored	
1=bedroom	0.92 (0.75–1.14)
0=other	
Education¶	
College	
1=attended college	1.20 (0.97–1.49)
0=other	
Postgraduate	
1=have postgraduate degree	0.90 (0.54–1.48)
0=other	

*1=store gun loaded some or all of the time, 0=never store gun loaded.

†N=583 for the logistic regression result; 22 observations were missing.

‡The southern region included Alabama, Arkansas, Delaware, Florida, Georgia, Kentucky, Louisiana, Maryland, Mississippi, North Carolina, Oklahoma, South Carolina, Tennessee, Texas, Virginia, and West Virginia. The other region included all remaining states. Alaska, Hawaii, and Washington, D.C. are not represented in the sample.

§The reference group consisted of all individuals between the ages of 18 and 29 years.

‖The reference group consisted of all individuals who owned only one gun.

¶The reference group consisted of all individuals who had not been to college.

This study does not include data on shootings. However, it does link gun type and purpose of gun ownership to the likelihood of keeping a gun loaded. Handgun owners and individuals who own firearms for protection are more likely than other gun owners to keep their weapons loaded. The tendency to keep ammunition in the gun may help explain the large number of injuries associated with accidental discharges and intentional shootings not justified by self-defense needs.

Research suggests that easy access to a loaded gun may be a risk factor for accidental firearm injuries among children[11,12,14] and may be a contributing factor for adolescent suicide.[24] Among the gun owners surveyed, those with children in the home were less likely to keep their guns loaded. Nonetheless, it appears that many families with children do keep loaded guns in the home (30 percent), even though experts, such as the American Academy of Pediatrics,[13] warn of the danger.

Increased attention has been given to the potential of design modification as a way of reducing the morbidity and mortality associated with firearms discharges.[5,12,25,26] According to the GAO, two devices, a childproof safety mechanism and a mechanism that indicates whether a gun is loaded, could reduce accidental firearm fatalities by approximately 31 percent. However, noting that "a majority of the accidents . . . examined involved some violation of safe gun-handling standards," and noting the large number of weapons already privately owned, the GAO suggests the need for "proper education in the use and handling of firearms."[5]

We did not discover any study that linked instruction in the use of guns to the safe handling of these weapons by their owners. One study that looked at unintentional firearm fatalities among children did note that the victim and the gun owner (most often the victim's parent) were unlikely to have received any training in gun safety procedures.[11] Furthermore, the authors note that, even after an accident, guns often remained accessible and safety rules were not observed.

Safety instruction does not necessarily lead to the observation of safety rules. The results of this analysis indicate that training, even if provided by the military or in a formal class, is not associated with safe gun-handling procedures as they relate to keeping guns loaded. One possible explanation is that important safety information is omitted from the training. Another possible explanation is that this information is insufficiently emphasized, particularly for individuals who have purchased a firearm for protection. Unfortunately, the survey did not collect information on the specific content of the safety instruction received, so we cannot determine whether education about safe storage practices is ineffective based on this analysis.

In the study population, nonwhite individuals were more likely than whites to keep their guns loaded (OR, 1.37; 95 percent CI, 1.01 to 1.86). One possible explanation is that blacks and other racial minorities feel less secure in their homes than whites. Violent crime, such as robbery, rape, and aggravated assault, is committed against members of black households at a rate one and a half times higher than the rate among white households,[27] and nonwhites are several times more likely than whites to be homicide victims.[28]

Among the individuals surveyed, those who did not keep their weapons locked up were more likely than other individuals to keep their weapons loaded (OR, 1.23; 95 percent CI, 1.01 to 1.54). This pairing of hazardous behaviors creates the greatest risk of injury. While such behavior runs counter to the theory of risk compensation,[29] it is probably to be expected. Many people who own firearms for protection may believe they need ready access to a weapon that is both loaded and unlocked.

The South has high rates of homicide, gun homicide, and gun ownership compared with other regions of the country.[30,31] This study indicates that southerners are also more likely to keep their firearms loaded.

There are several limitations to this analysis. The information in the data set is derived from self-reports rather than observational data. This could be a problem if, for instance, respondents were unable to recall whether their guns were loaded. Indeed, the GAO report suggests that a contributing factor in many accidental firearm fatalities is the victim's belief that the gun was not loaded when it was.[5] Self-report data are also subject to inaccuracies if respondents are embarrassed to tell the truth. For example, some individuals living with small children may not want to admit to keeping a loaded gun in the house.

The generalizability of the survey may also be limited by two factors. First, racial minorities account for a small percentage of respondents. Telephone surveys tend to underrepresent low-income and minority groups, and this appears to be the case in the present study. Second, the survey excluded gun owners under eighteen years old, yet many young people own guns.

Conclusion

J. Warren Cassidy, formerly executive vice-president of the National Rifle Association, wrote that gun owners in America are "safe, sane and courteous in their use of guns."[32] The large number of gun-related assaults, homicides, suicides, and accidental shootings raises questions about this assertion. Our findings show that a significant proportion of gun owners disregard basic safety procedures. Over one-third of the gun owners surveyed kept their weapons loaded, and more than half kept them unlocked. People who owned handguns or owned their guns for protection from crime were the most likely to keep their guns loaded. The presence of children in the home was a modifying factor. However, a significant number of gun owners with children reported that their guns were neither unloaded nor locked up. One of the most interesting finding of this analysis is that instruction in the proper handling of firearms was not associated with whether a gun was kept loaded when not in use.

REFERENCES

1. Zimring FE. Is gun control likely to reduce violent killings? *Chicago Law Rev.*1968;35: 721–737.

2. Federal Bureau of Investigation. *Uniform Crime Reports for the United States, 1985.* Washington, DC: U.S. Dept. of Justice; 1986.

3. Seiden RH. Suicide prevention: a public health/public policy approach. *Omega.* 1977; 8:267–275.

4. Rosenberg ML, Mercy JA. Introduction. In: Rosenberg ML, Feneley MA, eds. *Violence in America: A Public Health Approach.* New York: Oxford University Press; 1991:3–13.

5. *Many Deaths and Injuries Caused by Firearms Could Be Prevented.* Washington, DC: U.S. General Accounting Office; 1991. Publication GAO/PEMD-91-9.

6. Rivara FP, Stapleton FB. Handguns and children: a dangerous mix. *J. Dev Behav Pediatr.* 1982; 3:35–38.

7. Jagger J, Dietz PE. Death and injury by firearms: who cares? *JAMA* 1986;255:3143–3144.

8. Cook PJ. *The Technology of Personal Violence: A Review of the Evidence Concerning the Importance of Gun Availability and Use in Violent Crime, Self Defense, and Suicide.* Washington, DC: National Academy Press. In press.

9. Wright JD, Rossi PH, Daly K. *Under the Gun: Weapons, Crime, and Violence in America.* Hawthorne, NY: Aldine Publishing Co; 1983.

10. Patterson PJ, Smith LR. Firearms in the home and child safety. *AJDC.* 1987;141:221–223.

11. Heins M, Kahn R, Bjordnal J. Gunshot wounds in children. *Am J Public Health.* 1974; 64:326–330.

12. Wintemute GJ, Teret SP, Kraus JF, Wright MA, Gretchen B. When children shoot children: 88 unintentional deaths in California. *JAMA.* 1987; 257:3107–3109.

13. Keck NJ, Istre GR, Coury DL, Jordan F, Eaton AP. Characteristics of fatal gunshot wounds in the home in Oklahoma: 1982–1983. *AJDC.* 1988;142:623–626.

14. Ordog GJ, Wasserberger J, Schatz I, et al. Gunshot wounds in children under 10 years of age: a new epidemic. *AJDC.* 1988;142:618–622.

15. *Healthy People 2000: National Health Promotion and Disease Objectives.* Washington, DC: U.S. Dept. of Health and Human Services; 1990:236. Publication PHS 91-50212.

16. *Handgun Ownership in America.* Princeton, NJ: The Gallup Organization; 1991. Distributed by the *Los Angeles Times* Syndicate, May 29, 1991.

17. Zimring FE, Hawkins G. *The Citizen's Guide to Gun Control.* New York: Macmillan, 1983.

18. *Firearms Safety Depends on You.* Riverside, CT: Sporting Arms & Ammunition Manufacturer's Association Inc; 1987.

19. Thornberry OT, Massey JT. Trends in United States telephone coverage across time and subgroups. In: Groves RM, Biemer PP, Lyberg LE, Massey JT, Nichols WL II, Waksberg J, eds. *Telephone Survey Methodology.* New York: John Wiley & Sons; 1988:25–49.

20. Kellermann AL, Rivara FP, Banton J, Reay D, Flinger CL. Validating survey responses to questions about gun ownership among owners of registered handguns. *Am J Epidemiol.* 1991; 131:1080–1084.

21. Kellermann AL, Reay DT. Protection or peril? An analysis of firearm-related deaths in the home. *N Engl J Med.* 1986;314:1557–1560.

22. Barlow B, Niemirska M, Gandhi RP. Ten years' experience with pediatric gunshot wounds. *J Pediatr Surg.* 1982;17:927–932.

23. Rushforth NB, Hirsch CS, Ford FB, Adelson L. Accidental firearm fatalities in a metropolitan county (1958–1973). *JAMA*. 1975;100:499–505.

24. Brent DA, Perper JA, Goldstein CE, et al. Risk factors for adolescent suicide: a comparison of adolescent suicide victims with suicidal inpatients. *Arch Gen Psychiatry*. 1988;45:581–588.

25. Hemenway D, Weil DS. Phasers on stun: the case for less lethal weapons. *J Policy Analysis Manage*. 1990;9:94–98.

26. Wintemute GJ, Teret SP, Kraus JF. The epidemiology of firearm deaths among residents of California. *West J Med*. 1987;46:374–377.

27. Moore M, Trojanowicz RC, Kelling GC. *Crime and Policing: Perspectives on Policy*. Washington, DC: National Institute of Justice, U.S. Dept. of Justice; 1988. Publication GPO 1988-202-045:80044.

28. *Centers for Disease Control Home Surveillance Report 1970–1978*. Atlanta: Centers for Disease Control; 1983.

29. Hemenway D. Risk compensation. In: *Prices and Choices*. Cambridge, Mass: Ballinger Publishing Co; 1988:249–258.

30. Gastil R. Violence, crime and punishment. In: Wilson CR, Ferris W, eds. *Encyclopedia of Southern Culture*. Chapel Hill: University of North Carolina Press; 1989:1469–1513.

31. *National Data Program for the Social Sciences: The NORG General Social Survey: Questions and Answers*. Chicago: University of Chicago; 1986.

32. *Time*. January 29, 1990:16.

Chapter Twenty

Political Snipers

*How the NRA Exploited Loopholes and Waged a Stealth
Campaign against the Democrats*

Robert Dreyfuss

Anybody doubting the political clout of the National Rifle Association should speak to the members of Congress—and the now former members—who supported President Clinton's ban on assault weapons as part of the 1994 crime bill. In the campaign cycle surrounding that close vote, the NRA spent some $70 million on political activities, including nearly $7 million through its political action committee, much of it targeting Democrats who had supported the measure. Although polls showed the majority of Americans approved of the weapons ban, the NRA campaign was by most accounts a success. Democrats say the NRA cost them no fewer than twenty seats, and President Clinton told one reporter that "the NRA is the reason the Republicans control the House." Speaker Newt Gingrich, meanwhile, has promised the group's service will be rewarded: "As long as I am Speaker of this House," he wrote in a letter to an NRA official, "no gun control legislation is going to move."

This is the story of how the NRA managed to accumulate so much influence over the democratic process. It is an unnerving ride through the loopholes in federal election law, which allow a powerful special interest to bring almost overwhelming force to bear in a single congressional district. It is the story of how the firearms lobby bludgeoned its opponents with slashing, near-anonymous attack commercials and buried them with bulk mailings on hot-button themes unrelated to guns. It is the story of how conservative financiers and the Republican Party used the NRA to do some of their dirty work, and the price the NRA is now extracting for those services.

This story leads to the question of how the NRA gets its money in the first place, and here, too, there is more than first meets the eye. Despite its image as a membership organization subsisting entirely on $35 membership dues, the NRA actually collects much of its money in large donations from upper-middle-class and even wealthy supporters. Big contributors, bequests, fundraising dinners, and backing from the gun industry have combined to provide the NRA with a substantial block of funds. The NRA uses that money for direct-mail solicitations, in effect converting large contributions into many smaller ones, which it then channels into political campaigns.

The GOP Cause

Over the past several years, as the NRA's PAC income has grown dramatically—from $3.7 million in 1989–90 to $5.0 million in 1991–92 and finally $6.8 million in 1993–94—its spending has tilted increasingly into the Republican column. That tendency reached peak intensity in the 1994 election cycle, with the NRA's PAC devoting 79 percent of its direct grants to Republican campaigns, along with 87 percent of its independent expenditures aimed at influencing voters. This trend coincided with the NRA's shift toward a hard-line, no-compromise stance on gun issues—the result of an insurgency led by Neal Knox, a longtime NRA radical, and Tanya Metaksa, a former Reagan-Bush aide who is now executive director of the NRA's Institute for Legislative Action (ILA) and chairman of the PAC, which is called the Political Victory Fund.

According to Metaksa, this pattern of giving represents kindred interests, not behind-the-scenes coordinating: "We're not the National Republican Association," she says. But other sources, including former NRA officials and Republican and Democratic consultants, say that during the months leading up to the Republican sweep in November 1994, the NRA closely coordinated its election strategy with Republican Party officials. According to Tom King, a Democratic political strategist who calls the NRA a "wholly owned subsidiary of the Republican Party," the Republicans provided the NRA with polling data and lists of vulnerable Democrats in order to coordinate campaigns. Indeed, in October, on the eve of the elections, Metaksa solicited contributions explicitly to help Republicans take over. In a special mailing to NRA members entitled "It's Payback Time!" Metaksa said, "Make no mistake: a revolution is afoot. Just a handful of wins in key Senate races could turn the tide," resulting in "a Republican Senate."

In addition to strategizing with the Republicans, the NRA—ostensibly a single-issue organization—was throwing its lot in with other conservative groups, many of whom had little interest in guns but shared the NRA's desire to unseat Democrats. Together, these groups pursued lower taxes, free market economics, a smaller federal government, and a cutback in safety and health regulations. The NRA's "CrimeStrike" conference last year was cosponsored by the American Conservative Union, Americans for Tax Reform, and the Cato Institute, and today the NRA remains an active member of the American Legislative Exchange Council, a public-private venture that boasts "3,000 pro–free enterprise legislators" from state capitals as members, along with most of the Fortune 500. Grover Norquist, an iconoclastic Republican ideologue and Newt Gingrich strategist who heads Americans for Tax Reform, says that the NRA played an indispensable role as a linchpin of the Republican Party alliance, which he calls "the leave-us-alone coalition." As the Republicans eyed their chances in November, says Norquist, they saw the NRA as a useful tool for undermining about fifty to seventy moderate Democrats in conservative districts.

That the NRA would work closely with the Republican Party and its supporters is no great surprise. But the fervor ran so deep that the NRA was even willing to mislead its own members on how fervently senators and congressmen supported the NRA position on guns. Going all out for a Republican sweep, the NRA fudged its traditional system of rating candidates for office. According to Joseph P. Sudbay of Handgun Control, who made a detailed study of the election for the gun-control group, the NRA gave borderline Republicans the benefit of the doubt, liberally handing out "A" ratings, while being far more hard-nosed about high ratings for Democrats. A former senior NRA official confirmed the pattern, noting "fairly glaring discrepancies" in the 1994 ratings and adding, "You can play a lot of games with that rating system."

Once the NRA made its decision to back the Republicans, the NRA's PAC followed suit, with devastating results for Democratic office seekers:

- In fifty-two House races where there was an open seat—that is, where no incumbent was running—the NRA either supported the Republican or remained neutral. In all, according to Federal Election Commission (FEC) data and the Coalition to Stop Gun Violence, the NRA spent $227,000 to help Republicans win thirty-seven of those seats.
- In the nine races for open Senate seats, the NRA backed the Republican every time, spending more than $500,000. Republicans won them all.
- Where Democratic incumbents were running, the NRA abandoned many of its traditional friends on the pretext that they voted in favor of the Clinton administration's crime bill, which contained the provision that banned certain types of semiautomatic assault weapons. Such key members as Speaker of the House Tom Foley, Representative John Dingell of Michigan, and Representative Lee Hamilton of Indiana either lost all NRA support or found themselves the target of intense NRA opposition. Foley, who had long worked with the NRA to oppose gun-control legislation, was narrowly beaten by George Nethercutt, who received more than $80,000 in NRA support in the form of independent expenditures.
- Representative Jack Brooks of Texas, another longtime NRA supporter, was chairman of the House Judiciary Committee. In mid-1994, on the eve of the House-Senate conference to assemble the final version of the crime bill, Brooks thought he had worked out a compromise with the NRA over the controversial ban on assault weapons. Rather than ban the weapons, Brooks proposed limiting the number of rounds in magazines designed for the guns, thereby restricting their firepower. That deal, worked out by NRA lobbyist James Jay Baker, a relative moderate in NRA circles, was torpedoed by Metaksa and Knox. According to an insider, Metaksa at that point wanted to use the assault weapon ban to mobilize the NRA's hard-core activist base and deliberately

wrecked chances of a compromise in order to go into the November election guns ablaze. Brooks, embittered, voted for the final crime bill and was abandoned by the NRA. His Republican successor is Steve Stockman, elected with strong support from pro-gun groups.

- The NRA's PAC concentrated more than $720,000 in independent expenditures in support of Republican Senate candidates in just six states: Tennessee, Oklahoma, Pennsylvania, Nevada, Nebraska, and North Dakota. The first three states elected four Republican senators, defeating two incumbent Senate Democrats, Harris Wofford and Jim Sasser. In Nevada, Nebraska, and North Dakota, the NRA's big-spending ways failed to bring down Democratic incumbents. In Nevada, the NRA gave $130,000 to the Republican challenger, even though the Democrat, incumbent Senator Richard Bryan, had voted consistently with the NRA during the 103rd Congress.

- The NRA vastly stepped up donations of so-called "soft money" to the Republican Party in the 1993–94 election cycle, largely through two checks totalling $275,000 to the Republican National Committee in October 1993. That infusion of cash was the NRA's contribution to successful Republican efforts to defeat New Jersey Governor Jim Florio and Virginia gubernatorial candidate Mary Sue Terry, both Democrats. The NRA also spent hundreds of thousands of dollars in independent expenditures to help beat Florio and Terry. In New Jersey, their last-minute $200,000 spending spree to fund a professional phone bank ran afoul of the state's campaign finance laws, and the NRA was fined $7,000. "They made several hundred thousand phone calls, from paid phone banks, without the opposition campaign knowing it was occurring," says Representative Robert Torricelli, who complained about the NRA's illegal spending to New Jersey authorities. "The NRA and the Republican Party . . . operate according to a single strategy."

Stealth Bombers

Perhaps nowhere in the country was the NRA-Republican alliance more evident than in Oklahoma in 1994, where the NRA caught former Representative Dave McCurdy by surprise in a closely fought race against Republican Jim Inhofe for an open Senate seat. "It was a much bigger issue than I ever would have imagined," McCurdy says, marvelling at the campaign that the NRA waged against him. First elected to Congress in 1980 in Oklahoma's fourth district, which stretches south and west from Oklahoma City to the Texas border, McCurdy had long had NRA support. But his vote in 1993 for the Brady Bill, which called for a waiting period for buying handguns, and for the ban on assault weapons in the 1994 crime bill meant that he could no longer count on NRA backing.

"I knew I was drawing the line and could not cross it," says McCurdy, who did not even bother to ask the NRA for help in 1994. Yet the ferocity of the NRA's opposition took him by surprise. The NRA's PAC spent more than $150,000 in independent expenditures to run television and newspaper advertisements and put up billboards denouncing McCurdy in addition to the $9,900 it gave directly to Inhofe, just under the maximum $10,000 allowable under FEC regulations. The NRA also spent thousands of dollars more urging its Oklahoma members to turn out for Inhofe. It was an all-out attack that turned the tide against McCurdy.

But what was crucial about the NRA's attack on McCurdy was that rarely, if ever, in their onslaught did the NRA mention the issue of guns. Instead, in keeping with the Republican candidate's strategy, the NRA bankrolled a campaign to paint McCurdy as a "Clinton clone." An NRA-sponsored television ad began with a closeup of an AIDS ribbon on a lapel, then pulled back to show that the person sporting the ribbon was none other than Dave McCurdy, who was standing behind a podium delivering a speech supporting Bill Clinton at the 1992 Democratic National Convention. The NRA also paid for billboards throughout the state reading: "No Clinton Clones. Inhofe for U.S. Senate."

McCurdy says his aides detected a clear pattern that showed that the NRA was sharing the "buys" on Oklahoma television stations with the Republican Party and the Inhofe campaign—which would have been illegal under FEC rules that require that so-called "independent" expenditures not be coordinated with any election committees. McCurdy says that his staff tried to raise the issue with the FEC, but in the heat of the election campaign, just days before the vote, it was useless. (A spokesman for Senator Inhofe said that there was no coordination between the Inhofe campaign and the NRA on television advertising.)

"I wish they had come directly on gun issues," says McCurdy. "I think I could have won on the assault weapon ban with reasonable people." But, thanks to the work of pollster Frank Luntz, who also did the polling that helped Gingrich, Representative Dick Armey, and others assemble the Contract with America, the NRA knew that few Americans got excited about reversing the ban on assault weapons. (In fact, the NRA, for all of its vaunted, no-compromise reputation, meekly submitted when Gingrich did not include a promise to repeal the assault weapons ban in the Contract.) So, rather than give McCurdy and other Democrats around the country a chance to fight back, they simply ran ads thematically coordinated with Republican campaigns.

The NRA had learned that lesson in another Oklahoma race in 1992, against Representative Mike Synar, a liberal Democrat who had been a thorn in the NRA's side for years and had repeatedly crossed oil and gas, cattle, mining, and tobacco interests. In 1992 the NRA launched a high-profile attack on Synar, spending a reported $261,000 to defeat him. In that race, the NRA also ran ads against Synar on issues that had nothing to do with guns; one print ad read, "When Mike Synar voted for flag burning, so did you." According to Tom King, the Democratic consultant who worked on the Synar campaign, the NRA's PAC routinely coordinated its work with other business PACs who wanted to oust

Synar. "They'd meet regularly, the different PACs—all the business PACs and the NRA got together and tried to beat Synar," he says. "And they met quite openly. They'd discuss strategy, what they were gonna do, how much money was needed."

But the NRA opened itself up to counterattack by making the gun issue a central part of its effort, and Synar countered by blasting the NRA as an extremist "special interest" group from Washington, out of touch with the views of most Oklahoma gun owners. Jim Brady, the namesake of the Brady Bill and a principal in Handgun Control, Inc., campaigned with Synar against the NRA. In a primary, a runoff, and the general election, Synar won each time.

The NRA vowed to continue its attack against Synar, and in 1994 it succeeded. But this time, the NRA ran a stealth campaign. Rather than adopt a high profile, the NRA quietly funded Synar's opponent in the Democratic primary, an NRA member named Virgil Cooper. "There were no full-page ads, no TV ads by the NRA," says Amy Weiss Tobe, a Synar aide. But anonymous flyers started showing up in union halls and shop floors around the district, carrying a reproduction of a nonexistent bill allegedly tied to Synar that would have banned hunting rifles. The NRA sponsored phone banks and mailings to its members in the district, but it was difficult for Synar to fight back. "It was different," says Tobe. "They were smart. It was like boxing ghosts."

"The NRA went in and went underground. And they've been more effective when they go underground than when they blatantly go in, because then they become a special interest and it can be used against them," says Tom King. In 1994, "there was nobody to fight against. It was an invisible target."

Synar lost the September 1994 primary, a stunning upset and a harbinger of the disaster that would befall the Democrats in November. It was a major victory for the coalition of Republicans, business groups, and the NRA, and it was trumpeted as such by Metaksa, who called Synar's defeat the "NRA's first scalp." But, though Metaksa told a reporter at the time that the NRA spent as much against Synar in 1994 as it did in 1992, none of that spending shows up on FEC records of campaign expenses—meaning that the NRA truly ran a stealthy, off-the-books effort that skirted FEC regulations. (Ironically, after helping Cooper to beat Synar, the NRA stayed out of Cooper's race against Republican Tom Coburn, who won. The NRA gave both Cooper and Coburn "A" ratings.)

Across the country in 1993–94, the NRA ran numerous ads that attacked Democrats on issues from taxes, the budget, health care, and education to the alliance with President Clinton. "They will write to my constituents about a business issue, a tax issue, or a spending issue, but guns are never mentioned. And often the NRA will never even identify itself," says Representative Torricelli, still burning about the 1993 Florio race. "Members of the National Rifle Association may be giving money to the organization because of a sporting purpose, but find the NRA is spending their money to attack a Democratic member on a Medicare or education issue."

"Unlike purists, they want to be effective," says Victor Kamber, a Washington public relations executive. "What they say is, 'We are using whatever the polling data show makes them vulnerable in their district. We're saying that Jim Florio is a bad guy because he raises taxes. The fact is that the voters cared about taxes, so we're going to the voters with a message about how bad this guy is.' " Thus the NRA integrated itself into the business-Republican coalition, consciously reinforcing the antitax, antigovernment message of the free marketeers that dominate the Republican right.

Lawyers, Guns, and Money

What made the NRA such a useful tool to conservatives, of course, was its ability to raise and spend vast amounts of money. In 1994 the NRA was the nation's single biggest spender on elections. But how did it raise all the cash? Although the NRA's closemouthed tradition makes answering that question somewhat difficult, interviews with many current and former NRA officials, along with experts on the pro-gun movement, provide a fairly detailed picture—a picture that looks somewhat different from the grass roots, middle-American image NRA officials have nurtured for years.

It is true that like most direct-mail operations, the bulk of the NRA's daily operating revenue comes from small contributions, averaging about $18 per donor, and from annual dues of $35. Not surprisingly, most of this money comes from the ranks of American gun owners, who at last count were some 70 million strong. But that is not the entire story. Like the Republican and Democratic parties, which tout the fact that their average giver sends them between $10 and $25, the small average can obscure the presence of large backers. The NRA maintains an additional base of big contributors, who are clearly a few income levels above the typical working-class NRA member. This list includes the nation's 20,000 gun dealers and manufacturers and a small group of wealthy conservative financiers.

According to Brad O'Leary, the NRA sustains a block of 35,000 people who contribute at least $250 per year, and another 15,000 who give the NRA $125 per year. Those 50,000 people annually kick in more than $10 million. In addition, Metaksa said in an interview that she sees a fairly steady stream of checks up to $10,000 from NRA donors and has heard that the NRA treasury sometimes receives gifts "in the five figures."

The NRA conducts a broad fundraising campaign for several of its organizations, from the NRA itself to the ILA, the NRA Foundation, and the Political Victory Fund PAC. In a column in the *American Rifleman*, the NRA's monthly, NRA President Thomas L. Washington cited a single dinner held in Corpus Christi, Texas, where 907 people donated more than $175,000 to the NRA. And the NRA recently published a list of 214 "Friends of the NRA" fundraising events scheduled between April and October 1995.

The *American Rifleman* routinely lists the names of groups and individuals around the country who give the NRA at least $1,000 at a time; until earlier this year, the magazine listed those who donated special, onetime gifts of $250 or more but dropped that practice because of space limitations. And some NRA members have left the NRA bequests in the hundreds of thousands of dollars—their parting shot, so to speak.

Finally, there is the gun industry. It has long been assumed that the NRA receives financial support from firearms dealers and manufacturers, yet Metaksa, when asked about this, replied, "Baloney. Absolutely nothing." Yet the NRA in 1993 earned $8.6 million from advertising income, largely through ads from the gun industry in NRA magazines. And the NRA has arranged with gun dealers around the country to help the NRA solicit contributions from gun buyers. According to Tom Washington's "The President's Column" in the *American Rifleman*, just one dealer—Midway Arms of Columbia, Missouri—raised more than $678,000 for the NRA in four years. "It isn't just individual volunteers who benefit our Association," wrote Washington. "Many businesses donate their time and efforts as well."

Thanks to the Federal Election Commission, those millions raised by the NRA cannot be spent on federal campaigns. The FEC carefully regulates how a PAC, in this case the Political Victory Fund (PVF) of the NRA, raises or spends its cash.

Or does it?

The answer is: It does, but not very well. There are so many loopholes in the FEC rules that an organization like the NRA can do just about anything it wants to do for political objectives. Here's how.

A glance at the NRA's PAC records on file at the FEC, provided by the Center for Responsive Politics, shows that the overwhelming bulk of the NRA's PAC money comes into the PVF in donations of less than $200. Anything more than $200 must be reported to the FEC on an itemized basis. Yet over the six-year period ending December 31, 1994, the PVF reported itemized donations of only $278,631. During the same period, the PVF raised a total of $16,499,000.

One might conclude that large donors stay away from the PVF. But the FEC is not required to verify the accuracy of the NRA's filing. The forms that the NRA fills out simply list the itemized gifts as a line item, then present a lump-sum total for the bulk of the PVF income under the nonitemized heading. Even if the FEC suspects that there is something fishy about the lopsided nature of the PVF's income, it cannot investigate on its own without evidence of wrongdoing. The FEC takes the NRA's report on faith, just as it does with every other PAC.

More important, though, the FEC does not regulate the so-called "administrative and fundraising" costs associated with a PAC. That means that the NRA can spend unlimited sums, millions of dollars, to raise PAC funds, paying for repeated mailings to the NRA's 3.4 million members—and it does not have to report a single cent of those fundraising costs to the FEC. (That is also true for all other PACs, but it is particularly important for a large organization that can harvest small contributions, as opposed to, say, a trade association with a few dozen members whose executives kick in big bucks.)

And that is exactly what the NRA does. Using its corporate treasury, which is "soft money," that is, not regulated by the FEC, the NRA in 1994 spent at least

$2 million—and probably much more—asking NRA members to contribute to the PVF. That, in turn, is what raised the PVF's $6.83 million during 1993–94. Through the science of direct mail, the NRA can estimate how much each dollar spent on soliciting donations to the PVF will bring in. So, while the FEC rules prevent a wealthy donor from giving more than $1,000 to a PAC, nothing prevents that donor from giving the NRA $5,000 in soft money, which the NRA then plows into PVF fundraising. A direct donation of $5,000 in soft money suddenly becomes $5,000, $10,000, or more in "hard money"—in other words, legally usable, reportable PAC cash.

That's not the only loophole the NRA has exploited. For example, the FEC has issued regulations saying that no association can solicit PAC money from its members unless (1) those members pay their dues and (2) those members have the right to vote for the governing body of the association. The purpose of these rules is to distinguish genuine member-controlled organizations from closely controlled direct-mail operations.

Under the NRA's bylaws, only so-called Life Members and Five Year Members, who pay larger chunks of dues at a time, have the right to vote for the NRA's 75-member board of directors—a none-too-subtle bit of class distinction. Thus, under the law, the NRA would be disallowed from soliciting the bulk of its membership, who pay only one-year dues of $35 and have no voting rights. To avoid FEC action, however, the NRA in 1994 engaged in a subterfuge so brazenly transparent that it boggles the mind. It added one position to its board to be elected at the NRA's annual meeting, to which any and all NRA members may come. Any NRA member, therefore, has the theoretical right to vote for one director, and one director only. Of course, only a minuscule portion of the NRA membership actually goes to the meeting.

This construct, laughable in its intent to subvert an FEC regulation, has not been challenged in court—yet. In the meantime, the subterfuge allows the NRA to continue to send PVF PAC mailings to its full membership and to put millions of dollars into the PVF bank account. And, by the way, the FEC conducts no audits of the NRA's membership records to determine how many members the NRA has and whether or not they are actually paying their dues.

Not-So-Independent Expenditures

Those who have found themselves in the NRA's sights, however, are generally more familiar with the organization's use of another legal loophole that allows the NRA to support candidates well beyond the limits on direct donations to campaigns.

Because the FEC cannot regulate free speech (thank goodness), the NRA—like any individual, corporation, or group—can spend unlimited amounts of money to promote its cause, even during an election, as long as the NRA does not engage in what is called "express advocacy." Express advocacy means that the

NRA must cross a fuzzy line by explicit, campaign-style promotion of a particular candidate. If a promotion crosses that line, the thinking goes, the money spent on it ought to count as a direct political contribution, thus subject to the limits set by the FEC.

But the line is so fuzzy that the NRA can run television commercials criticizing a candidate and supporting the NRA's laissez-faire attitude toward semi-automatic weapons without falling under FEC regulations at all. In the 1992 Synar race, the NRA liberally took advantage of this loophole, running one attack advertisement with "hard" PVF money blasting Synar and then, sandwiched around another commercial, following up with a second spot that used the same spokesman, Charlton Heston, yet did not mention Synar by name. That second commercial was paid for by the NRA's corporate account, not by its PAC—thus giving the NRA a double bang for its buck.

All of these loopholes, including the biggest one of all, the use of independent expenditures, were used expertly by the NRA in 1994. To put the NRA's use of independent expenditures in perspective, consider this: In 1993–94, the NRA accounted for fully one-third of all independent expenditures by all groups during the election.

Asked about the role of independent expenditures, Metaksa is unable to suppress a sly grin before the questioner even finishes. "It's a chance for the organization to put itself into the political arena," she says. "And if the purpose is to get our point of view across, then it takes more than five or ten thousand dollars, especially in a big state." Indeed—and it doesn't hurt that nobody's figured out a way to regulate those amounts. The Clinton administration's campaign finance reform bill had a provision to offset the impact of independent expenditures, by providing public subsidies for candidates victimized by them. But that bill succumbed to the threat of a Republican filibuster a few months before the 1994 election.

Self-Inflicted Wounds

Stricter campaign finance law or tougher FEC regulation of the NRA seems an unlikely possibility as long as Republicans control Congress. But the NRA's coziness with the Republican Party may yet cost the organization some loyalty among its many lower-and middle-class members, many of whom find the Republican stances on economics less appealing than the party's opposition to gun control.

In the past the NRA has been able to whipsaw organized labor, many of whose members oppose gun control. But the trade union rank-and-file is only beginning to appreciate that the NRA is an ally of bitterly anti-union legislators. Already, the AFL-CIO is launching a labor counteroffensive against the NRA. That movement is starting in the West, where key AFL-CIO state presidents and affiliates are studying the NRA's role in the 1994 elections. Don Judge, president of the Montana AFL-CIO, in a state where the NRA and the militia movement are powerful side-by-side forces, says that his organization is trying to educate union members that the candidates supported by the NRA are precisely the ones who, once in office, vote against labor on every issue from the minimum wage to right-to-work to safety and health provisions. "Many of us have decided, what have we got to lose in confronting this?" asks Judge. "The kind of people being promoted by the NRA, with rare exceptions, typically do not support the kinds of things that are important to working people, beyond the issue of gun ownership."

In Pennsylvania, the AFL-CIO was rocked by the Democrats' rout in 1994, and Rick Bloomingdale, president of the AFL-CIO there, is ready to confront the NRA. Bloomingdale points out that the NRA backed the victorious Republican Representative Tom Ridge in Pennsylvania's governor's race last year, even though Ridge had voted for the assault weapon ban in Congress in 1994. Says Bloomingdale, "We finally know what the NRA-PAC stands for: the National Republican Association." When the Pennsylvania AFL-CIO began running ads last year featuring a union member and the slogan, "I'm the NRA and I'm supporting Harris Wofford," the NRA's lawyers hit them with a cease and desist order because "I'm the NRA" is copy-righted by the organization. Adds Bloomingdale, "The same people who support the NRA are the people trying to bust unions."

A study by Professor Paul Clark of Pennsylvania State University shows that the NRA consistently backs candidates whose positions on economic issues are far to the right. "While [the NRA] claims not to take positions on overtly economic issues, the candidates they support clearly do," he says. "Significantly, they have had some success at convincing union members to support their organizations and their candidates."

Warren Cassidy, a former NRA executive vice president, card-carrying Republican, and backer of the Dole campaign, worries openly that the NRA's lurch to the right may involve a quid pro quo to support the Republicans on issues that have nothing to do with guns. "When does that quid pro quo begin to hurt your organization?" he asks. "With all the connections to a strong conservative movement, NRA got caught up in that tide and they might not be able to extricate themselves." He warns: "It isn't necessarily true that all those chits should fall to one party, the Republican Party . . . because we have always had a strong, strong, blue-collar element, both rural and urban, in the NRA. And many, many, many of these people are union members."

In addition, many former NRA board members and leaders say that the NRA is driving away its long-time friends and allies by its roughshod tactics. Oklahoma Congressman Bill Brewster, who served on the NRA's board until 1995, quietly withdrew this year. High-profile resignations by George Bush, John Dingell, and other NRA supporters have hurt the organization's political clout. Dole, who voted for the Brady Bill in 1991 (but later opposed it 1993) and now keeps the NRA at arm's length while supporting most of its agenda, is warily watching the NRA's close relationship with Senator Phil Gramm, his rival for the 1996 presidential nomination in the Republican Party.

In the meantime, NRA officials have more immediate concerns. In its single-minded fervor to defeat even the most hesitant supporters of gun control, the NRA may have recklessly stretched its spending to the breaking point. The direct-mail scheme upon which the NRA has built its empire has been costly, and the organization recently traded a sizeable chunk of its inheritance for a posh new headquarters building. All of this has led many former NRA officials to say that the organization will crash in the near future. Reports of financial difficulties have attracted the scrutiny of the Internal Revenue Service.

Still, on Capitol Hill a healthy symbiosis between the Republicans and the NRA continues to thrive. While a good number of mainstream Republicans see the NRA as a loose cannon and an organization of zealots flirting with the far right, these Republicans still want the NRA's money and grassroots army at election time, and they still worry that any misstep—even in the course of the routine give-and-take that occurs in a legislative session—could bring the NRA down on their heads.

On January 25, as Gingrich, Armey, and company moved to implement the Contract with America, the NRA convened a summit meeting in the Speaker's office. Attending were Gingrich, Armey, House Republican Conference Chairman John Boehner of Ohio, Republican Whip Tom DeLay of Texas, National Republican Conference Committee Chairman Bill Paxon of New York, and Crime Subcommittee Chairman Bill McCollum of Florida. From the NRA side, participants included Neal Knox, Tanya Metaksa, Wayne LaPierre, and, interestingly, NRA Board of Directors member Senator Larry Craig of Idaho. Following the meeting, Gingrich and the NRA announced that they had formed a "partnership" on gun issues in the House, inviting conservative Democrats like Brewster and Harold Volkmer of Missouri to join in. Shortly after that meeting, Gingrich sent Metaksa the letter promising his opposition to gun control, characterizing their meeting as "both a discussion among friends but more importantly among like-minded individuals."

Were it not for the Oklahoma City bombing, which tarred the NRA because of its association with some militia groups, Congress would likely have taken up a repeal of the assault rifle ban. The NRA worked so closely with congressional committees investigating the Waco disaster that there was no clear line between congressional and NRA staffers. And the NRA has thrown its weight around in committee action on so-called "cop killer" bullets. With the 1996 election just around the bend, it is a safe bet the Republicans will be reaching out to the NRA once again, confident that the group can accomplish its mission and willing, in exchange, to do its political bidding.

Part III

As American as Apple Pie: Guns as a Cultural Battleground
Introduction: On the Cultural Battlefield

Ambivalence toward authority appears to be as American as apple pie. Thomas Jefferson may have captured this best when he observed that a society could not remain free without regular revolutions that would cleanse the body politic of entrenched authority. The rebels from what became the Green Mountain State, Vermont, put this same sentiment in more individualistic terms: "Don't Tread on Me." Henry David Thoreau's tax resistance inspired Martin Luther King, Jr., and countless civil rights, antiwar, feminist, and labor advocates. Thoreau's distrust of established institutions was not confined to civil disobedience either: he was a staunch supporter of John Brown's campaign to overthrow slavery by force of arms.

Historian Richard Slotkin (1973, 1985, 1992) has shown how suspicion of government has been closely associated with violence, and how both have been woven deeply into the fabric of American culture—a fabric riddled with bullet holes. Americans have, it seems, always been drawn to the simplified and quick forms of "justice" that fuel our persistent romance with self-sufficiency and independence. Just as groups of vigilantes in the old West would capture, "try," and hang an alleged cattle rustler all in the same day, the modern-day Dirty Harry, to the delight of large audiences, breaks rules that he thinks give bad guys the advantage as he delivers his own version of swift and sure "justice."

Constituted authority is not always slow, deliberate, or solicitous of the peoples' rights either. The labor movement had to struggle not only against employers but also against employers' ability to mobilize the police, state militias, and even the U.S. Army to fend off workers' demands. Latter-day militias and paramilitary groups such as the Posse Comitatus organize to defend themselves (and "us") from government tyranny, typically pointing to the shootout at Ruby Ridge, Idaho, and the assault on the Branch Davidians holed up in Waco, Texas, to bolster their paranoid views.

While few Americans, fortunately, are drawn to the extremes of the so-called militias, distrust of government appears widespread. Congress routinely winds up at or near the bottom of the list in terms of peoples' reported confidence, with the presidency not far behind. Only the U.S. Supreme Court fairs rather well in this uninspiring contest, as does the U.S. Army, arguably the nation's most thoroughly integrated institution (Lipset and Schneider, 1983; Nye et al., 1997).

All in all, it would appear that we are a suspicious lot—suspicious, on the one hand, of government's ability to protect us against violence, crime, gangs, and terrorists; and, on the other, of government's inability to protect us against overzealous agents of the FBI, BATF, IRS, DEA, INS, and CIA who regularly disregard or play fast and loose with our constitutionally guaranteed freedoms.

Paradoxically, our lack of confidence in the state's ability to protect us from crime and to secure our rights leads to diametrically opposed responses. Some see the right to bear arms as a necessary bulwark, while others see easy access to firearms as the problem. In this context, suspicion grows and fears multiply, deepening the polarization.

Of course, other sources of our appetite for guns also spark increasingly sharp opposition. Southern codes of manly honor, traditions of the hunt, and inflated notions of peacekeeping in a tumultuous and dangerous world continue to feed our desire for more guns, as the chapters by James William Gibson, Richard E. Nisbett and David Cohen, and Edward C. Hansen show.

The sense of crisis that Adam Walinsky and Wendy Kaminer analyze has been produced by just such contradictory and yet mutually reinforcing forces. A simple, direct response to rising crime and the sense that public authorities are largely powerless to protect ordinary citizens is to buy a gun. Others, reading of soaring gun sales and senseless violence, plead for the state to intervene by controlling access to firearms. Having been largely frustrated in the legislative arena, gun control advocates are beginning to turn to the courts rather than the court of public opinion (see Jo-Ann Moriarty's chapter below).

Historically oppressed minorities—blacks, women, and Jews, to name three of the most obvious—have recently added their own voices to the debate over guns. The women's movement is split over the issue of self-defense. The dominant view is that women are intrinsically peacemakers (Ruddick, 1989; Gilligan, 1982) and that guns and the violence they represent are the result of male pathology (Kheel, 1995). From this persepctive, providing handguns to women and training them for armed self-defense will merely contribute to the upward spiral of violence and perhaps leave women even more exposed to victimization and brutality.

But an increasingly vocal minority claims that women are equal to men in all morally and psychologically relevant respects. They argue that women should learn to fight fire with fire: they should learn to play ice hockey, box, become fighter pilots, and to shoot guns (Quigley, 1989). And indeed, they are. Though figures are hard to come by, women are now participating alongside men on pistol and rifle ranges and on the nation's skeet and trap fields. Self-defense courses have proliferated among women of all ages, who are apparently no longer content with the notion that they should seek the protection of a doting male. For their part, gun manufacturers have retooled and are vigorously marketing "Lady Lite" revolvers and firearm accessories tailored for women. The industry reports that women represent one of their fastest growing markets.

Women are not the only ones wrestling with the onus of long-suffering passivity. With short-lived exceptions, such as the Black Panthers, African Americans continue to labor with the burden of a history not quite sufficiently marked by militant resistance. Similarly, Jews seem condemned to wonder if their fate in the diaspora would have been less the martyr's had they cleaved more closely to the example of Judas Maccabeus, the Jew whose army defeated the forces intent on destroying the Jewish temple in Jerusalem.

Of course, we will never know if slavery or anti-Semitism or male chauvinism would have been shorter lived or less heavily oppressive had the means of violence been more equally distributed. Whatever conclusions we draw, it is clear that, again and again, the strong have all too rarely been solicitous of the weak. It is therefore not surprising that there are voices within minority communities insisting that they must never again be precluded from owning guns. By contrast, it is hard to sympathize with the predominantly white and male militias: whatever indignities and failures they may have had to endure, their sense of beleaguerment is clearly excessive. For all their talk of liberty and freedom, the evidence is clear: they see guns as the means to regain a lost supremacy. Whether the militias will turn out to be merely a pathetic rear-guard defense of lost privilege or a backlash that portends a disturbing return to a repressive status quo ante remains an open question.

There is no reason, given the experience of the past century, to be sanguine. Whether it is the American Indian Movement taking up arms to protect Native Americans against FBI agents at the Pine Ridge Reservation in South Dakota, Korean shopkeepers shooting it out with looters during the 1992 riots in Los Angeles, or women gun owners enrolling in firearms education courses for personal protection, Americans continue to depend on the possession of firearms to defend themselves against antagonists of all sorts—government agents or midnight muggers, real or imagined. Whether armed women, African Americans, and Jews, among others, will prevent or pave the way to a modern-day Hobbesian hell of a war of all against all remains an open question. This is, to say the least, small comfort. But with 225 million or more guns in private hands, yearning for a disarmed citizenry as a way to achieve a "more perfect order" is hardly more comforting.

Guns as a Way of Life—Sort Of

Chapter Twenty-one

Self-Transformation in Combat and the Pleasures of Killing

James William Gibson

All the exciting escapades that characterize paramilitary movies and novels—helicopter sweeps over office buildings and enemy camps, parachute jumps into green jungles and blue oceans, manhunts up and down stairs and fire escapes—are only part of the action to which the genre title "action-adventure" refers. The true essence of para-military mythology lies in one particular action—killing.

Killing, of course, has long been a central component of much dramatic fiction. All kinds of human conflicts can readily be symbolized as a struggle between armed protagonists; even complex moral questions may be reduced to "good" versus "evil." In this sense, the New War is just a continuation of the same old morality play. However, the *act* of killing has traditionally not been very important. For the most part, the dead Indians in the Westerns, and dead Germans or Japanese in the World War II films, simply fell down and vanished from the screen. Killing in these films signified moral progress, a means to an end, not an end in itself.

In the New War, though, both the physical action of killing and its moral repercussions are radically changed. Killing is shown in detailed scenes as part of an elaborate ritual process with archaic overtones. In the modern world, when someone is killed, it is understood that his life force is no longer present on earth—whether in the Christian view of the spirit ascending to heaven or descending to hell after death, or in the atheist view of death as the final dissolution of the person.

However, the older notion of killing as "taking life" more accurately captures the New War meaning. When Dirty Harry draws his .44 Magnum down on three street punks and invites them to "make my day!" more is going on than a clever little joke. By shooting them, he absorbs their life force. It isn't just Harry's "day" that's being made; Dirty Harry himself—the warrior demigod—is being created through his kills. Similarly, when Bruce Willis in *Die Hard* manages to strangle one of the terrorists holding his wife hostage, it is the energy he absorbs from his victim that gives him the audacity to send the corpse back to his comrades with a sign attached "Now I've got a machine gun, too. Ho! Ho! Ho!" Referred to as "incorporation" in psychoanalytic theory, this fantastic appropriation of another's life force has ancient roots. As the religious-studies scholar E. O. James says, "To the primitive mind good and evil, life and death, are in the nature of materialistic entities capable of transference or expulsion by quasi-mechanical operations."[1] Of course, at its most extreme this is the logic of cannibalism: by eating the enemy's body, the warrior completes the incorporation that began with killing.

But even in less literal forms, "taking life," with its associations of transference and incorporation, is essentially a sacred act. And this is perhaps the most useful way to understand New War killings. When Dirty Harry shoots down those three punks, he does more than uphold the secular law of the modern world. He becomes a "primitive" man performing a sacred action; when the good warrior kills an evil one, he effectively transforms evil power into good power. The converse is also true: when an evil villain kills a virtuous victim, evil gains strength. Hence, no matter how secular the New War warrior may appear with his high-tech weapons and tremendous "efficient" kills, he is essentially a religious figure.

The "rites" of killing follow very specific rules. Although New War heroes like Rambo and Mack Bolan sometimes fight and kill scores of enemies in a movie or novel, not all of these killings fully qualify as sacred acts. Often the enemies simply fall down and vanish, as they do in World War II movies. There are always some scenes, though, in which the hero and villain fight face-to-face. Only through such personal combat can there be a transfer of energy from the vanquished to the victor.

When the hero and villain face each other in their final confrontation, they often engage in a short conversation or series of pronouncements before the fighting begins. Although few words are exchanged, these conversations are very important. At one level, they affirm that the fight about to take place is both personal and to the death, as when John Steele, a Vietnam veteran, addresses a drug lord in *Steele Justice* (1987): "This isn't Nam, Quan. This time only one of us is coming back. Quan, just you and me." At a second level, the verbal exchanges between hero and villain also indicate that the men in question represent two different visions of the ideal society. Quan, the leader of a Vietnamese gang in Southern California, responds to Steele's challenge by quoting the gang's totalitarian motto, "The only law is Black Tiger law." Thus, although the hero is an ex-policeman conducting his own personal war outside the corrupt establishment, he still serves as the true representative of justice.

Quan and Steele actually do have a gentlemanly duel to the death after their conversation. In many New War stories, however, there is no fair fight at all. Instead, the final confrontation between hero and villain is a scene in which the hero ceremonially executes the bad guy. Although readers and viewers already know the heinous crimes that have been committed, pronouncing sentence serves to distinguish the hero's act of murder from the villain's violent deeds. Tom

Clancy develops one of the most elaborate such ceremonies in *Red Storm Rising* when Lieutenant Edwards judges three captured Russian soldiers: "Gentlemen, you are charged under Uniform Code of Military Justice with one specification of rape and two specifications of murder. These are capital crimes. . . . Do you have anything to say in your defense? No? You are found guilty. Your sentence is death."[2] Edwards subsequently crushes the larynx of one man, causing him to suffocate ("unable to breathe, his torso bucked from side to side as his face darkened"), while a young Marine slits the throats of the other two.

In less elaborate execution ceremonies, pronouncing sentence simply indicates that the hero is in full control of himself. To kill impulsively, or to kill after yelling a savage, Indian-like war cry, would mean that the warrior has succumbed to base desires. But by uttering "Make my day!" as a warning to the villains or "Because we live here!" as the good teenage boys say before they kill their traitorous friend in *Red Dawn*, the heroes prove they are guided by a sense of justice. Sometimes the hero does not have to speak to the villain, so long as he addresses him in some way. Paul Benjamin, the hero of *Death Wish*, first fires his gun to get the attention of a culprit, then says to himself, "Well, that wasn't a miss. You son of a bitch. It was just to turn you around so you can watch me shoot you." When the suspect turns around and shows his "vicious, sneering face"—a confession of his guilt—Benjamin "steps into the light" so the intruder can see him and executes the man.[3] Thus the hero's words—even his internal monologues—establish the justice of his acts. His killings are morally sanctioned.

The hero's words are as much weapons as they are legitimation for his conduct. When he speaks to the villain, there is no real communication. Hero and villain do not come to "understand" each other better through their dialogue and so resolve their conflict. Instead, the heroic warrior's speech partially paralyzes the bad guy, rendering him more vulnerable to the next phase of the attack. In some of the ancient warrior myths, Joseph Campbell says, the most powerful man was one who "would require no physical weapon at all; the power of his magic word would suffice."[4] In the modern secular world, no hero can fight with magic words alone. Yet no contemporary warrior could win his battles without them.

Either slightly before, during, or after the death verdict has been articulated by the hero, his body hardens. At one level, there is a kind of erotic anticipation of the kill. This blending of sex and violence is most clearly expressed in Mickey Spillane's extremely popular novel, *I, the Jury*, first published in 1947. In it, detective Mike Hammer swears to find the killer of his World War II buddy, Jack Williams. (Jack had saved Mike from death at Guadalcanal and lost his right arm in the process.) Hammer finds that the killer is none other than his own beautiful blond fiancée Charlotte. When he confronts her, she takes off her clothes in an effort to save her life. Charlotte's sensuous striptease to her transparent panties—done while Hammer is accusing her of murder—is described in minute detail. Hammer's penis is undoubtedly erect when he pulls the trigger of his .45 automatic. Killing her, then, blends self-control and sadism. When, with her dying gasp, she asks, "How c-could you?," he can flatly say, "It was easy."[5]

In the New War, though, it isn't just the warrior's penis that hardens, but his whole body. Whereas the actors who played the old war and Western heros were usually big men, their flesh was only rarely exposed on the cinematic battlefield. Their bodies were not weapons. New War heroes, in contrast, must be men of steel, and the stars who portray them buffed and chiseled. Arnold Schwarzenegger was a world-class bodybuilder, while Chuck Norris and Steven Seagal were renowned martial-arts experts. Almost all of the other top male action-adventure stars have muscled physiques as well.

When movie directors and novel editors were asked why hard-bodied warriors came into fashion, some replied simply that America was on a fitness binge and the warrior of course had to be ahead of the pack. Others, like Dale Dye (a former *Soldier of Fortune* editor and technical adviser to *Platoon*), explained that the warrior's extraordinary body was necessary to make extraordinary deeds seem that more plausible:

> The "Rambo" films could not do what they wanted unless the heroes appeared superhuman. It would have been too great a stretch of the imagination otherwise. They needed a larger than life character. Well, look at the guy! Of course he could do that shit! Of course he could fire a machine gun from the hip! Of course he could lift a helicopter or haul an armored personnel carrier out of the sand with nothing but his own incredible strength![6]

Frequently the bodies of New War heroes are so strong and coordinated that they are referred to as "machines." Colonel Trautman, the Green Beret leader who serves as Rambo's father figure, calls him "a pure fighting machine." In *War Born*, Mack Bolan (often referred to as "Stony Man One"), becomes so excited when he returns to his "home" in the jungles of Vietnam that he no longer needs to eat or sleep. He is transformed into a god-like perpetual-motion machine "that feeds on the energy involved to create new energy," with eyes and ears so mechanized that whenever he spots an enemy soldier, he "locks into target acquisition" like a radar-or infrared-controlled missile.[7]

Some warriors kill with their hard bodies. In *Lethal Weapon* Mel Gibson strangles a villain with his thighs. Norris and Seagal break necks and backs with simple karate moves, their muscles bulging as they summon the strength for the executions. Other heroes have actual metal implants in their bodies to replace broken or lost limbs. Mad Max, the road warrior, has a metal brace to strengthen a wounded leg. Colonel Yukov Katzenelenbogen, of *Phoenix Force*, chooses a flesh-colored stainless-steel hand to replace the one he lost when terrorists blew up his car and killed his wife and child:

> The hand's steel fingers were slightly curled, resting naturally. When the fingers were locked straight, the hand was a two-pound sledge, capable of smashing any wood-paneled door. A glancing side blow could tear off a man's ear. A forward chop, against the sternum, could paralyze heart and lungs, kill.[8]

In techno-thriller and fighter-pilot movies such as *Top Gun* and *Iron Eagle* (1985), the steel of tanks, planes, and submarines becomes part of the bodies of the men who control them; the steel weapons become flesh. Harold Coyle describes this fusion between Folk, the gunner, and his tank in *Team Yankee*: "Folk, the loader, the cannon, and the fire control system were one complete machine, functioning automatically, efficiently, effectively."[9]

In other futuristic battle scenarios individual warriors simply don armored suits to gain tremendous power. *RoboCop* details how the brain of a critically wounded Detroit policeman is transplanted into a computerized robot to create the ideal patrol officer. In the C.A.D.S. novel series, the U.S. fighting men who survive the Soviet nuclear assault wear "immense black suits of destruction covering their bodies in protective cocoons." The "Computerized Attack Defense System" warriors were "gods of the Technological Age. Within their battle suits, their mortal bodies possessed the power of whole armies of the past."[10]

Bulging muscles and armored suits represent what psychologists call "exoskeletal defense" mechanisms, efforts to reconstruct the human body. Although bones are the hardest part of the body, they lie under layers of softer fleshy tissue and relatively fragile skin. By projecting the hard skeleton outward to the surface of the skin, the body is in fantasy made far stronger and better able to ward off threats and attacks.

The hardened bodies discussed so far fall into one of two categories. When a powerfully muscled warrior fights half-naked, his hard flesh marks his transformation into a kind of "minotaur," the legendary half-man, half-animal. He gains both the animal's power and its ability to hide. Rambo once immerses himself completely in a muddy riverbank. The entire bluff seems to move when he steps out to knife an unsuspecting Vietnamese soldier.[11] Later in the movie, he hides underwater and then leaps up in the air, like a powerful killer whale, to capture a Russian helicopter. *Soldier of Fortune* once ran a cover photograph of a man with a completely blackened face and an animal-skin bandanna over his forehead—clearly a beast of the jungle.

The second form of exoskeletal projection overcomes human weakness by transforming all human flesh into metal. The tank crews, fighter pilots, and "battle suit" wearers all fall into this second category; they, like RoboCop, are "cyborgs." Their cousins are heroes like Mack Bolan, warriors who always go into battle dressed completely in black. Black clothes are a kind of body armor: black is the color of steel, of death. At night, black hides the warrior from his many enemies. On top of these black clothes warriors wear layer upon layer of weapons and supplies. Even the head and face are frequently hidden, either by masks or by black face paint. Cyborgs often look like modern versions of medieval knights with their visors down. The body seems far away.

Either as minotaur or as cyborg, the warrior can no longer feel his skin as battle approaches. It has been transformed into nearly impenetrable body armor. At times, the hero's body armor also can make him nearly invisible to his enemies. At the very minimum, the helmet and face mask mean that the eyes of the hero cannot be seen—he has become an executioner. The enemy is thus seen and sentenced to die, but he cannot look back and establish human contact to tacitly appeal the verdict. It is a combination that can create "disbelieving hor-ror" in even the most evil of the evil ones.[12]

For decades the standard Hollywood gunfight ended with the victim collapsing with one small red dot on his chest. Rarely was there much blood. And while some old detective novels, particularly those by Mickey Spillane, featured more blood, they did not contain prolonged, graphic descriptions of killing and dying. Most New War stories, in contrast, require that the enemy body be torn open so completely that it loses human form. At minimum, the small red holes have been replaced by much larger splashes of blood, both where the bullet enters and where it exits the body.

But usually the enemy's death is much more spectacular. In *No Mercy* (1986) the mercenary hero employed as a contract agent for the CIA captures a terrorist, puts a grenade in his mouth, and then blows him apart in a ball of fire. In *Commando*, Arnold Schwarzenegger takes care of his last opponent by ramming him through the chest with a pipe that is a good four inches in diameter. Both Clint Eastwood and Chuck Norris have used antitank rockets to open up the chests of their adversaries.

In paramilitary novels, the violence is especially striking. In volume 123 of *The Executioner*, a North Vietnamese gunman fires at a woman who discovers his position: "The glass planes shattered, spearing her hands. Her face dissolved into crimson pulp and she fell out of sight."[13] In volume 39, *The New War*, Bolan shoots so that he can "feel the quick kick of the recoil in his shoulder while he watched the guy's head explode like a ripe cantaloupe smashed by a hammer."[14] Magnus Trench, the hero of *Dark Messiah*, volume 1 of *Phoenix*, has a body so hard that it kills post–World War III plague germs—the "contam" disease—upon contact. He really knows how to open up a bad guy:

> A hail of 9mm zappers destroyed the shotgunner from the waist down, tearing away his stomach, bladder, genitals, small intestines, kneecaps, and all the arteries and muscle tissue over, under and in between. Death reflexes triggered a burst, the pumpgun discharging into Badass One's own ugly face and leaving a raw, bloody mess behind as the headless, legless, faceless torso jerked forward, fountaining redly from both ends.[15]

Thus, at the moment of dying, an opponent is so thoroughly penetrated by the bullets, knives, and grenade fragments, that he completely loses control of his body. Victims are flooded with bodily fluids; they drown in their own blood, making gurgling noises as they die. It is as if violent death is a special kind of sexual release. When this orgasm comes, the body always moves uncontrollably. Legs twitch, sphincter muscles open, blood spurts from ears, noses, and mouths. Men fall to their knees, screaming, and "collapse into a heap" of shapeless flesh.[16]

Often the dead are referred to as "meat." Occasionally, though, excremental overtones are discernible. For example, the heroes frequently take special pains not to be contaminated by their victims. Jerry Ahern's protagonist in *The Defender* kills the terrorist leader (who was responsible for his family's death) with a 13 1/2-

inch knife, but the "blood spraying toward Holden's eyes" was stopped by his gas mask.[17] In *The Black Berets*, "Cowboy" kills an enemy disguised as a seductive airline stewardess in an airplane bathroom: "Cowboy then held her up till he saw that her eyes had glazed over. Then he shoved her down onto the toilet seat and returned to the first-class cabin, leaving an Out of Order sign prominently on the door."[18]

In contrast, the hero always maintains control of his body during combat. Rambo easily and comfortably fires a modified M60 machine gun with one hand while running at full speed. Dirty Harry gracefully rolls with the recoil of his .44 Magnum. Martial arts stars such as Norris and Seagal are essentially performing male dances with their victims as they kill them with their hands and legs. In the novels, this sexual connection between victor and vanquished is rendered explicitly. Tom Clancy describes Air Force Lieutenant Edwards's knifing a Russian in *Red Storm Rising* as a virtual act of rape: "Edwards rammed the knife under the man's ribs, turning his right hand within the brass-knuckled grip as he pushed the blade all the way in. The man screamed and lifted himself on his toes before falling backward, trying to get himself off the knife. Edwards withdrew and stabbed again, falling atop the man in a grotesquely sexual position."[19] Afterwards, the young Marines accompanying Edwards in their retreat across Iceland affirm his potency and call him "skipper" for the first time.

This use of sexual language and imagery to describe killing is not accidental. Editors of men's action-adventure novels acknowledge that the development of the genre was influenced by pornography. Don Pendleton actually began his career writing soft-porn novels. One editor indicated that some writers hired to write commando sagas had previous experience writing gay sadomasochistic stories. A second said that a '70s genre of pornographic novels set in the Old West became the model for action-adventure. Another editor theorized that the publishing industry had been influenced by the slow-motion killings portrayed in director Sam Peckinpah's films, such as *The Wild Bunch* and *Straw Dogs*. In his view, writers and editors said to themselves "Whoa, we can slow this down—and we can write violence like we write sex."[20]

The linkage of violence to sex also surfaced when editors speculated on why male readers enjoyed these books. The publisher of Zebra books believes these novels help men deal with their "frustrations."[21] Another editor says, "I'm not a psychologist or psychiatrist, but I always thought their basic function was to vent or sublimate feelings of violence."[22] From the editorial perspective, the "realistic" portrayal of the hero is an important piece of this dynamic. For example, Pendleton's guidebook to writers for *The Executioner* series says, "Bolan is not Flash Gordon. He is an idealized man, yes, but such men are certainly to be found beyond the comic strips. There is nothing super about Bolan except his command of self and I have known such men in real life."[23] Several other editors also mentioned their disdain of the older comic-book superheroes. The man who theorized that "we can write violence like we write sex" best described the type of hero that all the industry seemed to want. That hero is someone within reach of the male audience, someone with whom they can identify:

I think that one of the important things about the books is that the hero always be somebody that the reader can say, "Well, if I just worked out a little bit, you know, and if I thought a little harder, if I concentrated, I could do this."[24]

Readers want to identify with the hero because "they feel like some piece of their turf is being threatened," the editor explained. The problem isn't that motorcycle gangs or terrorists are camping outside the reader's front door, but that many men feel "symbolically threatened" in some way by the world. "I think it is a symbolic need and that's why the books sell—because they give the opportunity for a cathartic release."[25] The editors insist that this process of reader identification with the hero for a climatic "catharsis" is either harmless or a positive social good, but certainly other interpretations are possible.

While the paramilitary warrior's body remains hard and intact, the ruptured body of the enemy confesses its evil by exposing all its rotten spilled fluids. This pattern has an important historical precedent in the *Freikorps*. As Klaus Theweleit points out, there, too, sexuality is placed in the service of destruction as the hard, metallic bodies of heroic warriors "open up" the enemy. The *Freikorps* man's body is "poised to penetrate other bodies and mangle them in its embrace."[26] The final one-on-one duel is also a sexual climax:

> The nearest thing this man will enjoy to the utopian encounter of the lover and beloved is at the same time the most distant from it: a collision between the unbending wills of two peoples, embodied in two men in armed confrontation. They meet to kill; and the only one to "flow" is the man who dies. The holes bored in him are a signal of the murderer's own transcendence of self. His self dissipates as he melts into the blood of the man of his own kind.[27]

When the evil one's body is broken open and he "flows," the victor experiences two sensations. First, the hero notes that the other's death means that his own insecure boundaries are intact and those hardened boundaries are interpreted by him as a sign of his virtue and self-control. At the same time, the hero also experiences the pleasure—never otherwise permitted him—of merging with another as he begins to absorb the villain's life force.

The final act necessary for the heroic warrior to fully appropriate the life force of the evil ones and to transform evil into good is to burn their corpses. He must create a cleansing fire to remove the pollution created by their spilled fluids. There are so many fires in the New War that it often seems the whole world is ablaze. The very first Rambo film, *First Blood*, ends when John Rambo blows up electrical transformers and a filling station to set the small Oregon town on fire. Chuck Norris in his turn burns down the prisoner-of-war camp in *Missing in Action*. Sigourney Weaver uses a flamethrower to destroy the nest and eggs of the monster in *Aliens*. And in *Die Hard 2* (1990), Bruce Willis even manages to kill all the terrorists (who have ruined his Christmas vacation) by burning their jet airplane when it takes off.

The heat of all these fires pales next to the infernos of World War III. General Sir John Hackett sensuously describes the great conflagration of Minsk after

NATO forces launch four nuclear missiles in retaliation for the Soviet destruction of Birmingham, England. Above the city "what seemed about to form huge mushrooms was now writhing in promethean patterns, turning, twisting, and whirling" while below at ground zero, "up to 5 kilometers from the former Communist Party headquarters, everything combustible was immediately set on fire."[28] And so the putrid filth of Communism is erased.

Back in the United States, Frank Sturgis, commander of C.A.D.S., enters a post–World War III city to find "a carpet of corpses." The dead are all brown-tinted because "an army of roaches was crawling through the mouths, the eyes, the opened chests and stomachs of uncountable corpses." Worse yet, feasting rats are also celebrating victory over mankind. Sturgis orders "flame on" and his men open up with flamethrowers: "The rats were ignited instantly by the burning stream of liquid plastic that caught onto fur and claws and burned until there was nothing left."[29]

All of these New War infernos seem to be part of an archaic rite. Mircea Eliade says that in the ancient world men often used fire in their religious ceremonies for the purpose of communal purification: "The sins and faults of the individual and the community as a whole are annulled, consumed as by fire."[30] In Eliade's terms, when the New Warriors burn enemy corpses and the enemy's headquarters, they are metaphorically removing evil from the world.

But such purification rites always fail. When heroes die in the brotherhood of war, it is clear that their deaths are in the name of the "good." But when the modern-day evil ones are killed and their corpses burned, just where their spirits go is less clear. Undoubtedly the constant victory of the heroes over the enemy in the New War means that at least some of the enemy's power is transformed (incorporated) into good. But at the same time it must be remembered that in New War stories the hero's victory never results in the creation of a better society or the restoration of the original sacred order. Instead the power structure of society is still corrupt, and the hero is left living in the border zones on the frontier. Nor is he redeemed or purified by his victories. He is still a warrior who is ready for—indeed, wants—more war.

So if all the killing and burning does not empower the good gods of virtuous order, whom does it empower? There is a dark possibility here. In one of the last scenes of Sylvester Stallone's *Cobra* (1986), Stallone picks up the bad guy and rams a huge industrial hook hanging from a crane through his chest. The impaled body is then carried off into the mouth of a massive steel furnace in which fire is blazing—hell itself. It looks as if Stallone is *returning* a member of a devil-worshipping cult to the devil. The anthropologists Henri Hubert and Marcel Mauss indicate that some ancient societies made sacrifices to evil deities:

> Sacrifices of this kind were usually addressed to the infernal deities or to evil spirits. As they were charged with evil influences, it was necessary to drive them away, to cut them off from reality. It was vaguely implied that the soul of the victim, with all the maleficent powers it contained, departed to return to the world of the maleficent powers.[31]

The New War explains the persistence of evil in a similar way. If the spirit of a modern-day evil one returns to the primordial hell, then it can be reincarnated on earth in yet another form. Thus the drug dealer can come back as a Communist, the terrorist as an outlaw biker, the beastly motorcycle man can return as an angry black radical.

This makes psychological sense, of course. If the function of the enemy is to represent uncontrollable human desire, then he must be constantly reincarnated in some form or another. The mercenary leader Niles Barrabas complains that Karl Heiss, the Harvard-educated former CIA case officer who betrayed him in Vietnam, simply will not die: "Too many times in the past he had viewed the bullet-ridden or burned bodies believed to be Karl Heiss. And every time it had turned out to be a hoax; every time the man had resurfaced to do more evil."[32] Without his mirror-image—the evil one who is out of control—the hero cannot exist as the embodiment of self-control and moral purity. Without the evil one, the hero would have to acknowledge his own conflicting desires and rages and his own capacity to act immorally. Without the evil one, the hero would have to confront people who are different from him—in spirit, concerns, and values.

But such recognition is exactly what the New War warrior tries to avoid. Hero and devil are but fragments of the same human psyche, dependent upon each other for their very identity. Hence, the victory of the heroes is in large part an illusion. The New War never moves forward, never transforms society into a morally better place, never propels the hero into maturity. Killing simply makes it possible for another violent cycle to begin.

After the cleansing fires have consumed the carnal remains of the enemy and his headquarters, the hero is left alone. Sometimes he watches the fire from a distance; in other cases, he rises from the wasted ruins, covered with ashes. These fires usually destroy most if not all the evidence that good and evil confronted each other in battle. But when the heroic warrior finally leaves the battleground, the story of the struggle is indelibly inscribed in his flesh. Bullets, knives, and other weapons all leave "grazing wounds" or scars on his skin as signs of battle. American mythic heroes have always suffered these injuries but what is new here is that the hero displays his scars much more prominently than did his predecessors.

Since contemporary heroes fight wars that the power structure cannot or will not fight, they take on the public responsibilities for combating evil. Consequently, when they suffer, they suffer for all men. When the Russians capture and torture Rambo with electricity, they tie him down to a steel bed frame and spread his arms like Christ on the cross. Both Chuck Norris and Mel Gibson are captured and hung up in torture scenes. By the end of *Die Hard* (1988), Bruce Willis's bare chest is covered with blood and he limps on bare, bloody feet completely lacerated from broken glass. The symbolism in all these cases is obvious.

Yet a hero always manages to overcome his pain and transform pain into power. In the most extreme cases the hero even cauterizes his own bleeding flesh. By applying the cleansing fire to himself, the warrior stops the flow of bodily fluids and reconstructs the inviolate surface of his body armor. In *Rambo: Part 3*, for example, Rambo is shot in the shoulder while attempting to rescue Colonel Trautman from Russians in Afghanistan. He breaks open some rifle cartridges, pours gun powder into the wound channel, and lights it with a match. Flame shoots through his shoulder, sealing both the entry and exit holes with charred flesh. Although Rambo writhes on the ground in pain during the night, by dawn his full powers are regenerated. (Both the chief monsters in the *Predator* movies also have similarly good experiences with cauterization after being wounded by humans.) A scar is a small price for fixing the armor—and more-over, the warriors did it themselves, with no reliance on a doctor or nurse.

These scars function as tattoos. They are a special kind of exo-skeletal defense, namely a type of "heraldry" that in sociologist Clinton Sanders's words allows men "to symbolize their membership and indelible commitment to the group."[33] As tattoos, the scars of warriors become ways of gaining individual recognition from their peers, who know how to read the secret codes. Although the movie dialogue says nothing about scars on Rambo's breasts, Stallone (a collector of American Indian art) gave his famous character sun-dance scars. In one version of the sun dance, a ritual of the Plains Indian tribes, young men place barbed hooks under their nipples; the hooks are attached by long leather ropes to a tall pole. When the spirit reaches him after days of dancing and numbs him to pain, a man pulls back on the rope and the barbs rip open his chest. Having endured and learned to transcend pain, having written this lesson on his body and completed an important rite of passage, he can now face the world as a more powerful man.[34]

All of the great warriors are covered with such marks. Mack Bolan's body looks "like he's been hit with damn near anything that will fire or cut."[35] When the doctors in Vietnam examine Casca, the eternal mercenary, they see so many scars that "it was impossible to tell which is the oldest wound."[36] Mark Hazzard, the comic-book mercenary, has a vertical scar running both above and below the center of his right eye; the whole eye looks like a cross-haired rifle scope.[37] With these scars, the warrior proves the veracity of his war story. If and when he returns to the world, his body, emblazoned with the blood tattoos of battle, testifies to the strengths of his boundaries and the glory of his martial deeds.

At first glance, then, the warrior's state-of-the-art weaponry, hard body, and battle scars radiate male power. He is the embodiment of the masculine ideals of autonomy, integrity, physical courage, and competence. While ordinary men succumb to fear and watch from afar, he acts. He is not trapped by forces beyond his control, but instead meets and masters all challenges. His violence changes the world far more than the words and deeds of others do; his individual existence counts and he knows it.

But at second glance, a far different man appears in the hardened shell of the warrior's body. In fact, he is not really a man at all, but instead a little boy whose anger, fear, and desire are all totally beyond his control. His journey away from the family and into the war zone has not made him a man. To the contrary, far from being a path toward personal empowerment and maturity, the New War promotes psychological regression and the retreat into a solipsistic world; the New War is a playpen for men, a special one without the drag of a supervising mother.

Just as the New War warrior never grows up, so too does he prefer the play of imaginary battle that lets rage run wild to the moment when battle ends and a new sacred order is founded. The films and novels and magazine articles of paramilitary culture do not say what kind of society will be created after the enemy is vanquished. The sheer intensity of the violence in these stories tends to make the warrior's victories look like a definitive restoration of a fallen America. It's as if the end of gunfire must mean something good. But the temporary defeat of chaos is not the same thing as the recreation of a sacred order.

As in the *Freikorps* literature, nothing is created other than the pleasures of battle and the renewal of the warrior. The New War does not affirm any virtues other than warrior virtues and the nobility of male groups. Beyond that, just what the paramilitary warrior really believes in remains a mystery; many stories tell of the warriors' contempt both for the power structure and for ordinary people. Most important, there is no vision of a new society. The warriors do not go home. The war never ends.

Mythologies are created in historical contexts and no mythology can completely transcend those contexts. In the aftermath of Vietnam, the failure of the New War to imagine what a new or restored America might look like beyond the battlefield indicates a profound lack of consensus about what the United States should become. Victory over an enemy, any enemy, substitutes for the effort to establish a better society. Rambo and all his friends are fighting a death-filled holding action, and making that fight seem like the best of all possible worlds. It is truly a dark, tragic vision. Social stagnation masquerades as restoration and social progress. Psychological regression wears an armored suit of maturity. Undeveloped and emotionally dead personalities appear as the height of individualism. An aesthetic of sexual violence is presented as realism. These inversions create powerful traps. There's no easy exit from the New War.

NOTES

1. E. O. James, *Origins of Sacrifice* (Port Washington, N.Y.: Kennikat Press, 1933; reissued 1971), 184.

2. Tom Clancy, *Red Storm Rising* (New York: Berkeley, 1983), 324.

3. Brian Garfield, *Death Wish* (New York: McKay, 1972), 144.

4. Joseph Campbell, *The Hero with a Thousand Faces* (Princeton, N.J.: Princeton University Press, 1968), 88 n. 51.

5. Mickey Spillane, *I, the Jury* (New York: Dutton, 1974; Signet, 1975), 246.

6. Interview with Dale Dye in Northridge, Calif., September 1986.

7. Don Pendleton and staff writers, *War Born*, vol. 123 of *The Executioner* (Toronto: Worldwide, 1989), 166, 43.

8. Gar Wilson, *The Fury Bombs*, vol. 5 of *Phoenix Force* (Toronto: World-wide, 1983), 140.

9. Harold Coyle, *Team Yankee: A Novel of WW III* (Novato, Calif.: Presidio, 1987), 270.

10. John Sievert, *C.A.D.S. #1: Computerized Attack Defense System* (New York: Zebra, 1985), 7.

11. Arnold Schwarzenegger apparently learned this trick from Rambo, since years later, in *Predator* (1987), he too covers himself with mud to avoid the special ultraviolet eyes of the space monster.

12. Sievert, *C.A.D.S.*, 175.

13. Pendleton et al., *War Born*, 82.

14. Don Pendleton and staff writers, *The New War*, vol. 39 of *The Executioner* (Toronto: Worldwide, 1981), 30.

15. David Alexander, *Dark Messiah*, vol. 1 of *Phoenix* (New York: Leisure Books, 1987), 86.

16. Jerry Ahern, *The Battle Begins*, vol. 1 of *The Defenders* (New York: Dell, 1988), 165.

17. Ibid., 243.

18. Mike McCray, *Cold Vengeance*, vol. 2 of *The Black Berets* (New York: Dell, 1985), 108–9.

19. Tom Clancy, *Red Storm Rising* (New York: Berkeley, 1986), 320.

20. Interview, New York City, October 1986.

21. Interview with Walter Zachereis, New York City, April 23, 1986.

22. Interview, New York City, October 1986.

23. Don Pendleton, *The Executioner Series Style Guide*, no date or page number. Pendleton gave the guide to me in August 1988.

24. Interview, New York City, October 1986.

25. Ibid.

26. Klaus Theweleit, *Male Bodies: Psychoanalyzing the White Terror*, vol. 2 of *Male Fantasies*, trans. Erica Carter and Chris Turner (Minneapolis: University of Minnesota Press, 1989), 191.

27. Ibid., 276.

28. General Sir John Hackett, *The Third World War: The Untold Story* (New York: Macmillan, 1982), 311–12.

29. Sievert, *C.A.D.S.*, 244–48.

30. Mircea Eliade, *The Sacred and the Profane: The Nature of Religion*, trans. Willard R. Trask. (New York: Harcourt Brace Jovanovich, 1959), 76.

31. Henri Hubert and Marcel Mauss, *Sacrifice: Its Nature and Function*, trans. W. D. Halls (Chicago: University of Chicago Press, 1964), 38.

32. Jack Hild, *Vulture of the Horn*, vol. 10 of *SOBs: Soldiers of Barrabas* (Toronto: Worldwide, 1986), 209.

33. Clinton Sanders, *Customizing the Body: The Art and Culture of Tattooing* (Philadelphia: Temple University Press, 1989), 30.

34. Bruno Bettelheim, *Symbolic Wounds* (Glencoe, Ill.: Free Press, 1954), 88.

35. Don Pendleton and staff writers, *War Born*, vol. 123 of *The Executioner* (Toronto: Worldwide, 1989), 23.

36. Barry Sadler, *Casca: The Eternal Mercenary* (New York: Charter, 1979), 7.

37. Joe Guinto, "Childhood's End," unpublished paper, Southern Methodist University, 1988, 5.

Chapter Twenty-two

Violence and Honor in the Southern United States

Richard E. Nisbett and Dov Cohen

The U.S. South has long been viewed as a place of romance, leisure, and gentility. Southerners have been credited with warmth, expressiveness, spontaneity, close family ties, a love of music and sport, and an appreciation for the things that make life worth living—from cuisine to love.

But there has also been the claim that there is a darker strain to southern life. For several centuries, the southern United States has been regarded as more violent than the northern part of the country.[1] This belief has been shared by foreign visitors, northerners, and southerners with experience outside the South. Duels, feuds, bushwhackings, and lynchings are more frequently reported in the correspondence, autobiographies, and newspapers of the South than of the North from the eighteenth century on.[2] The rates of homicide in some areas of the South in the nineteenth century make the inner city of today look almost like a sanctuary. According to one accounting, in the plateau region of the Cumberland Mountains between 1865 and 1915, the homicide rate was 130 per 100,000[3]— more than ten times today's national homicide rate and twice as high as that of our most violent cities.

Not only homicide but also a penchant for violence in many other forms are alleged to characterize the South. The autobiographies of southerners of the eighteenth and nineteenth centuries often included accounts of severe beatings of children by parents and others.[4] And southern pastimes and games often involved violence that is as shocking to us today as it was at the time to northerners. In one game called "purring," for example, two opponents grasped each other firmly by the shoulders and began kicking each other in the shins at the starting signal. The loser was the man who released his grip first.[5] Even more horrifying to modern (and to contemporaneous northern) sensibilities was a favorite sport of frontiersmen called fighting "with no holds barred," which meant that weapons were banned but nothing else was. Contestants could and

Reprinted by permission of Westview Press from *Culture of Honor: The Psychology of Violence in the South* by Richard E. Nisbett and Dov Cohen (Boulder, Colo.: Westview Press, 1996). Copyright © 1996 by Westview Press.

did seek to maim their opponents.[6] Thus gouged-out eyes and bitten-off body parts were common outcomes of such fights.

Cases of southern violence often reflect a concern with blows to reputation or status—with "violation of personal honor"—and the tacit belief that violence is an appropriate response to such an affront. The journalist Hodding Carter has written that in the 1930s he served on a jury in Louisiana that was hearing a case concerning a man who lived next to a gas station where the hangers-on had been teasing him for some time. One day he opened fire with a shotgun, injuring two of the men and killing an innocent bystander. When Carter proposed a verdict of guilty, the other eleven jurors protested: "He ain't guilty. *He wouldn't of been much of a man if he hadn't shot them fellows.*"[7] A historian has written of the same period that it was impossible to obtain a conviction for murder in some parts of the South if the defendant had been insulted and had issued a warning that the insult had to be retracted.[8] And until the mid-1970s, Texas law held that if a man found his wife and her lover in a "compromising position" and killed them, there was no crime—only a "justifiable homicide."

The young men of the South were prepared for these violent activities by a socialization process designed to make them physically courageous and ferocious in defense of their reputations: "From an early age small boys were taught to think much of their own honor, and to be active in its defense. Honor in this society meant a pride of manhood in masculine courage, physical strength and warrior virtue. Male children were trained to defend their honor without a moment's hesitation."[9]

Even very young children were encouraged to be aggressive, learning that "they were supposed to grab for things, fight on the carpet to entertain parents, clatter their toys about, defy parental commands, and even set upon likely visitors in friendly roughhouse."[10] Children themselves rigorously enforced the code of honor. A boy who dodged a stone rather than allow himself to be hit and then respond in kind ran the risk of being ostracized by his fellows.[11]

The southerners' "expertise" in violence is reflected in their reputed success as soldiers.[12] Southerners have been alleged, at least since Tocqueville's commentary on America, to be more proficient in the arts of war than northerners and to take greater pride in their military prowess. Twentieth-century scholars have documented the southern enthusiasm for wars, their overrepresentation in the national military establishment, and their fondness for military content in preparatory schools and colleges.[13]

Explanations for Southern Violence

There are many "Souths"—the Cavalier South of seventeenth- and eighteenth-century Virginia, founded by the inheritors of the medieval knightly tradition of horsemanship and skill in battle; the mountain South, originating in eastern Appalachia and moving southward and westward decade by decade; the plantation South, based on growing cotton; and the western South, based on the herding of cattle in dry plains and hills that could sustain no other form of agriculture. Of the explanations that we will cite for southern violence, certain ones apply plausibly to some of these regions but less plausibly to others.

Four major explanations have been offered for the southern tendency to prefer violence: the higher temperature of the South and consequently the quicker tempers of southerners, the tradition of slavery, the greater poverty of the South, and the putative "culture of honor" of the South. We argue that the role of "honor" is independent of, and probably greater than, any role played by the other three.

Temperature. It has been suggested that at least a part of the violence of the South can be accounted for by the characteristically higher temperatures of the South.[14] It is indeed possible to show that variation in temperature in a locality is associated with the number of violent crimes there,[15] and we will examine the role played by temperature in the most dramatic form of violence, namely homicide.

Slavery. Slavery has long been held responsible for the violence of the South.[16] Abigail Adams was of the opinion that whites inflicted on themselves the same sort of violent treatment that they accorded their slaves.[17] Thomas Jefferson concurred, in his *Notes on Virginia*, as did many other thoughtful southerners. John Dickinson, an eighteenth-century revolutionary from the eastern shore of Maryland, believed that the institution of slavery led to southern "pride, selfishness, peevishness, violence."[18] Tocqueville also believed that slavery was responsible for the South's violence, but he emphasized, rather than the "contagion" from treatment of the slaves, the idleness encouraged by slavery:

> As [the Kentuckian] lives in an idle independence, his tastes are those of an idle man . . . and the energy which his neighbor devotes to gain turns with him to a passionate love of field sports and military exercises; he delights in violent bodily exertion, he is familiar with the use of arms, and is accustomed from a very early age to expose his life in single combat.[19]

At several points in this book we will assess the evidence for and against both aspects of slavery as explanations for southern violence.

Poverty. A third explanation for the greater violence of the South has to do with poverty. The South is poorer than any other region of the country and always has been; in each region of the country and in every sort of population unit, from rural county to large city, poverty is associated with higher homicide rates.

A variant of the economic explanation focuses not on absolute income or wealth but rather on disparities in income. Some argue that inequality in wealth breeds violence of the South both in rates of homicide and in preference for violence as a means of conflict resolution.

Violence and the Culture of Honor

We believe that the most important explanation for southern violence is that much of the South has differed from the North in a very important economic respect and that this has carried with it profound cultural consequences. Thus the southern preference for violence stems from the fact that much of the South was a lawless, frontier region settled by people whose economy was originally based on herding. As we shall see, herding societies are typically characterized by having "cultures of honor" in which a threat to property or reputation is dealt with by violence.

Virtue, Strength, and Violence

Cultures of honor have been independently invented by many of the world's societies. These cultures vary in many respects but have one element in common: The individual is prepared to protect his reputation—for probity or strength or both—by resorting to violence. Such cultures seem to be particularly likely to develop where (1) the individual is at economic risk from his fellows and (2) the state is weak or nonexistent and thus cannot prevent or punish theft of property. And those two conditions normally occur together: Herding, for example, is the main viable form of agriculture in remote areas, far from government enforcement mechanisms.

Some cultures of honor emphasize the individual's personal honesty and integrity in the sense that honor is usually meant today. That has always been one of the major meanings of the concept. Dr. Samuel Johnston, the eighteenth-century compiler of the first English dictionary, defined honor as "nobility of soul, magnanimity, and a scorn of meanness." This is "honour which derives from virtuous conduct."[20] Honor defined in those terms is prized by virtually all societies; the culture of honor, however, differs from other cultures in that its members are prepared to fight or even to kill to defend their reputations as honorable men.

The culture of honor also differs from others in an even more important respect. In addition to valuing honor defined as virtuous conduct, it values—often far more—honor defined as respect of the sort "which situates an individual socially and determines his right to precedence."[21] Honor in this sense is based not on good character but on a man's strength and power to enforce his will on others. Again, almost all societies value honor defined as precedence or status. The culture of honor differs from other cultures in that violence will be used to attain and protect this kind of honor. Honor, as we use the term in this book, is well captured by ethnographer David Mandelbaum's characterization of the Arabic and Persian word for honor—*izzat*. "It is a word often heard in men's talk, particularly when the talk is about conflict, rivalry, and struggle. It crops up as a kind of final explanation for motivation, whether for acts of aggression or beneficence."[22]

A key aspect of the culture of honor is the importance placed on the insult and the necessity to respond to it. An insult implies that the target is weak enough to be bullied. Since a reputation for strength is of the essence in the culture of honor, the individual who insults someone must be forced to retract; if the instigator refuses, he must be punished—with violence or even death. A particularly important kind of insult is one directed at female members of a man's family.

> In the Old South, as in the ancient world, "son of a bitch" or any similar epithet was a most damaging blow to male pride.... To attack his wife, mother, or sister was to assault the man himself. Outsider violence against family dependents, particularly females, was a breach not to be ignored without risk of ignominy. An impotence to deal with such wrongs carried all the weight of shame that archaic society could muster.[23]

Herding Economies and the Culture of Honor

The absence of the state makes it possible for an individual to commit violence with impunity, but it is not a sufficient condition for creating a culture that relies on violence to settle disputes. Hunting-gathering societies appear to have relatively low levels of violence, even though their members are not usually subjects of any state.[24] And farmers, even when they live in societies where the state is weak, typically are not overly concerned with their reputation for strength nor are they willing to defend it with violence.[25]

Herding and Vulnerability to Loss. There is one type of economy, however, that tends to be associated worldwide with concerns about honor and readiness to commit violence to conserve it. That is the economy based on herding of animals.[26] Together with some anthropologists, we believe that herding societies have cultures of honor for reasons having to do with the economic precariousness of herdsmen.[27] Herdsmen constantly face the possibility of loss of their entire wealth—through loss of their herds. Thus a stance of aggressiveness and willingness to kill or commit mayhem is useful in announcing their determination to protect their animals at all costs.

Herding and Sensitivity to Insults. Herdsmen adopt a stance of extreme vigilance toward any action that might imply that they are incapable of defending their property. Early in his career, in fact, the herdsman in some cultures may deliberately pick fights to show his toughness. As the ethnographer J. K. Campbell wrote of Mediterranean herding culture:

> The critical moment in the development of the young shepherd's reputation is his first quarrel. Quarrels are necessarily public. They may occur in the coffee shop, the village square, or most frequently on a grazing boundary where a curse or a stone aimed at one of his straying sheep by another shepherd is an insult which inevitably requires a violent response.[28]

Herding and the Uses of Warfare

People who herd animals usually live in places such as mountains, semideserts, and steppes, where because of the ecology, crop farming is inadequate to provide for basic food needs. They have little surplus and sometimes experience genuine want. Thus they are often tempted to take the herds of other groups. As a consequence, "theft and raiding are endemic to pastoral peoples."[29] Or, as one herdsman of the Middle East put it, "Raids are our agriculture."[30] Thus skill at warfare is valuable to a herdsman in a way that it is not to a hunter-gatherer or a farmer. It is no accident that it is the herding peoples of Europe who have been reputed to be the best soldiers over the centuries, that "to the Scots, as to the Swiss, Swedes, Albanians, Prussians and other people of Europe's margins and infertile uplands, war has been something of a national industry."[31]

In addition to the "marginal" northern Europeans, many if not most Mediterranean groups—including the traditional cultures of such peoples as the Andalusians of southern Spain, the Corsicans, Sardinians, Druze, Bedouins, Kabyle of Algeria, and Sarakatsani of Greece—are characterized as holding to a version of the culture of honor.[32] These groups all have economies that are greatly dependent on herding. Many other traditional societies of Africa[33] and the steppes of Eurasia and North America[34] also have (or had) herding economies and cultures of honor.

There are some interesting natural experiments that show that people who occupy the same general region but differ in occupation also differ in their predilections toward toughness, violence, and warfare. Anthropologist Robert Edgerton studied two neighboring tribes in East Africa, each of which included a group of herders and a group of farmers. Edgerton reported that in both tribes, the pastoralists exhibited "a syndrome that can best be described as *machismo*," whereas farmers manifested "the insistent need to get along with . . . neighbors."[35]

In North America, the Navajo and the Zuni also inhabit similar ecological niches, but the Navajo are herders and the Zuni are farmers. The Navajo are reputed to be great warriors (right up to the present—they served in large numbers and with distinction in World War II). The Zuni are more peaceable and have not been noted as warriors at any time in their history.[36]

An even better natural experiment came with the introduction of the horse to the American Indians of the Plains. Prior to the arrival of the horse, the tribes of the Plains had been relatively peaceful; after its introduction, many tribes began to behave like herders everywhere. They reckoned their wealth in terms of the number of horses they owned, they staged raids on their neighbors, and they began to glorify warfare.[37]

Herding and the Weakness of the State

Since herding usually takes place in regions where geography and low population density conspire against the ability of law enforcement officials to reach their targets, defense against enemies is left up to the individual and the small community in which he lives. For many people in such circumstances, the prevailing form of law is the feud—with the threat of deadly consequences for family members as the primary means of maintaining order. Hence it should be no surprise that the feuding societies of the world are preponderantly herding societies.[38]

The Scotch-Irish and the Herding Economy in Europe and America

What has the reputed violence of the U.S. South to do with the culture of honor as it might be evidenced by a Greek shepherd, an East African warrior, or a Navajo? In our view, a great deal.

The northern United States was settled by farmers—Puritans, Quakers, Dutch, and Germans. These people were cooperative, like farmers everywhere, and modern in their orientation toward society. They emphasized education and quickly built a civilization that included artisans, tradespeople, businesspeople, and professionals of all sorts.

In contrast, the South was settled primarily by people from the fringes of Britain—the so-called Scotch-Irish.[39] These people had always been herders because the regions where they lived—Ireland, Scotland, Wales—were not in general suitable for more-intensive forms of agriculture.[40]

The Celts and Their Descendants

The Scottish and the Irish were descendants of the Celts, who had kept cattle and pigs since prehistoric times and had never practiced large-scale agriculture.[41] Like other herding peoples, the Celts reckoned their wealth in terms of animals, not land, and were accustomed to intertribal warfare and cattle raiding.[42] The Romans feared the Celts because of their ferocity (though the Romans were not impressed with the Celts' organizational abilities). Over centuries of war, including Julius Caesar's famous battles with the Gauls, the Celts were driven into Britain. Subsequent wars—with Vikings, Danes, Angles, Saxons, and other Germanic peoples—drove them to the least hospitable fringe areas. The battles really never ceased, however, especially along the Scottish frontier with England and between the Scottish and Irish in Ulster.

One cannot know how relevant the distant past of this culture is. But it may be worth noting that the Celtic peoples did not develop the characteristics of farmers until their emigration to America.[43] They did not undergo the transformation common elsewhere in Europe from serf to peasant to bourgeois farmer. When they engaged in agriculture at all, it was generally of the horticultural or slash-and-burn variety in which a field was cultivated for three or four years and then left to lie fallow for a decade or more.[44] Such a method is the most efficient one when, as is true in most of the range of the Celtic peoples, the soil is unproductive. An important characteristic of this method of farming is that it does not encourage permanence on the land. Periodic movement was common,[45] a fact to bear in mind when one contemplates the behavior of the Scotch-Irish after they came to America.

The Scotch-Irish in the U.S. South and West

The immigration of the Scotch-Irish to North America began in the late seventeenth century and was completed by the early nineteenth century. The group was composed largely of Ulster Scots, Irish, and both lowland and highland Scots.[46] The impoverished, deeply Roman Catholic Irish who came later in the nineteenth century, as well as the Presbyterian, often highly educated Scots, were culturally very different from these earlier immigrants, who were both more secular and more inclined to violence as a means of settling disputes.[47]

Their new land, if anything, served to reinforce the herding economy practiced by the Scotch-Irish immigrants.[48] With its mountains and wide-open spaces, America, especially the Appalachians and the South, was ideally suited to the herding life and to horticulture.[49] The Scotch-Irish tended to seek out relatively unproductive lands to homestead, but even when they found themselves on highly productive land, they tended to farm in low-efficiency, horticultural fashion rather than in the more efficient agrarian manner that involves clearing the land of stumps, rotating crops, and making the sort of improvements that would have made movement away from the land hard to contemplate.[50]

The geography and low population density probably served to increase culture-of-honor tendencies in another respect as well: Because of the remoteness and ruggedness of the frontier, the law was as weak in America as it had been in Britain: "In the absence of any strong sense of order as unity, hierarchy, or social peace, backsettlers shared an idea of order as a system of retributive justice. The prevailing principle was *lex talionis*, the rule of retaliation."[51] Or, as a North Carolina proverb stated, "Every man should be sheriff on his own hearth."

The southerner, thus, was of herding origin, and herding remained a chief basis of the economy in the South for many decades. Not until the invention of the cotton gin in the early nineteenth century would there be a viable economic competitor to herding. The cotton gin made possible the plantation South. But by the early nineteenth century, the characteristic cultural forms of the Celtic herding economy were well established, and at no time in the nineteenth century did southern folkways even in the farming South converge on those of the North.[52]

NOTES

1. Gastil, 1989, p. 1473.
2. Fischer, 1989; Redfield, 1880, cited in Gastil, 1989, p. 1473.
3. Caudill, 1962, p. 46.
4. Fischer, 1989, p. 689.

5. McWhiney, 1988, p. 154.

6. Gorn, 1985, p. 20.

7. Carter, 1950, p. 50, emphasis in original.

8. Brearley, 1934.

9. Fischer, 1989, p. 690.

10. Wyatt-Brown, 1982, p. 138.

11. McWhiney, 1988, p. 203.

12. Napier, 1989.

13. May, 1989, p. 1108.

14. Anderson, 1989.

15. Anderson, 1989; Cotton, 1986; Reifman, Larrick, and Fein, 1991; Rotton and Frey, 1985.

16. Gastil, 1971.

17. Ammerman, 1989, p. 660.

18. Quoted in Wyatt-Brown, 1982, p. 153.

19. Tocqueville, [1835] 1969, p. 379.

20. Johnson, 1839.

21. Pitt-Rivers, 1965, p. 36.

22. Mandelbaum, 1988, p. 20.

23. Wyatt-Brown, 1982, p. 53.

24. Farb, [1968] 1978; O'Kelley and Carney, 1986.

25. Edgerton, 1971; Farb, [1968] 1978, pp. 121–122.

26. Edgerton, 1971, pp. 16–17; Farb, [1968] 1978, pp. 9–10; Galaty, 1991, p. 188; Lowie, 1954; Peristiany, 1965, p. 14.

27. See, for example, O'Kelley and Carney, 1986, pp. 65–81.

28. Campbell, 1965, p. 148.

29. O'Kelley and Carney, 1986, p. 65.

30. Black-Michaud, 1975, p. 199.

31. Keegan, 1944, p. 167.

32. Black-Michaud, 1975; Gilmore, 1990; Peristiany, 1965; Fisek, 1983.

33. Galaty and Bonte, 1991.

34. Lowie, 1954; Farb, [1968] 1978.

35. Edgerton, 1971, pp. 18, 297.

36. Farb, [1968] 1978, pp. 258–259.

37. Farb, [1968] 1978, p. 9–10; Lowie, 1954.

38. Black-Michaud, 1975.

39. Fischer, 1989; McWhiney, 1988; Wyatt-Brown, 1982, p. 38.

40. Blethen and Wood, 1983, p. 7.

41. Chadwick, 1970, p. 25; McWhiney, 1988, p. xxiv.

42. Corcoran, 1970, p. 25; Chadwick, 1970, p. 37.

43. Cunliffe, 1979, p. 198.

44. Blethen and Wood, 1983, p. 20.

45. McWhiney, 1988, p. 9.

46. Fischer, 1989, pp. 613–634; McWhiney, 1988, p. xli.

47. McWhiney, 1988, esp. pp. xxxvii and xli.

48. McWhiney, 1988, pp. xli ff.; Wyatt-Brown, 1982, p. 36.

49. Fitzpatrick, 1989, p. 71.

50. Blethen and Wood, 1983, p. 20.

51. Fischer, 1989, p. 765.
52. Fischer, 1989.

REFERENCES

Ammerman, D. (1989). Revolutionary era. In Wilson and Ferris (1989).

Anderson, C. A. (1989). Temperature and aggression: Ubiquitous effects of heat on occurrence of human violence. *Psychological Bulletin* 106, 74–96.

Black-Michaud, J. (1975). *Cohesive force: Feud in the Mediterranean*. Oxford: Basil Blackwell.

Blethen, T., and Wood, C., Jr. (1983). *From Ulster to Carolina: The migration of the Scotch-Irish to southwestern North Carolina*. Cullowhee, N.C.: The Mountain Heritage Center, Western Carolina University.

Brearley, H. C. (1934). The pattern of violence. In W. T. Couch, ed. *Culture in the South*. Chapel Hill: University of North Carolina Press.

Campbell, J. K. (1965). Honour and the devil. In Peristiany (1965).

Carter, H. (1950). *Southern legacy*. Baton Rouge: Louisiana State University Press.

Caudill, H. M. (1962). *Night comes to the Cumberlands*. Boston: Little, Brown.

Chadwick, N. (1970). *The Celts*. Harmondsworth, England: Penguin Books.

Corcoran, J. X. W. P. (1970). Introduction to N. Chadwick, *The Celts*. Harmondsworth, England: Penguin Books.

Cotton, J. L. (1986). Ambient temperature and violent crime. *Journal of Applied Social Psychology*, 9, 786–801.

Cunliffe, B. (1979). *The Celtic World*. New York: McGraw-Hill.

Edgerton, R. (1971). *The individual in cultural adaptation*. Berkeley: University of California Press.

Farb, P. ([1968] 1978). *Man's rise to civilization: The cultural ascent of the Indians of North America*. New York: Penguin.

Fischer, D. H. (1989). *Albion's seed: Four British folkways in America*. New York: Oxford University Press.

Fisek, G. O. (1983). Turkey: Understanding and altering family and political violence. In A. P. Goldstein and M. H. Segall, eds. *Aggression in global perspective*. New York: Pergamon.

Fitzpatrick, R. (1989). *God's frontiersmen: The Scots-Irish epic*. London: Weidenfeld and Nicolson.

Galaty, J. G. (1991). The Maasai expansion. In Galaty and Bonte (1991).

Galaty, J. G., and Bonte, P., eds. (1991). *Herders, warriors, and traders: Pastoralism in Africa*. Boulder, Colo.: Westview Press.

Gastil, R. D. (1971). Homicide and a regional culture of violence. *American Sociological Review* 36, 416–427.

——— (1989). Violence, crime and punishment. In Wilson and Ferris (1989).

Gilmore, D. D. (1990). *Manhood in the making: Cultural concepts of masculinity*. New Haven: Yale University Press.

Gorn, E. J. (1985). "Gouge, and bite, pull hair and scratch": The social significance of fighting in the southern backcountry. *American Historical Review* 90, 18–43.

Johnson, S. (1839). *Johnson's English Dictionary*. Philadelphia: Kimber and Sharpless.

Keegan, J. (1944). *Six armies in Normandy: From D-Day to the liberation of Paris*. New York: Penguin Books.

Lowie, R. H. (1954). *Indians of the plain*. New York: McGraw-Hill.

Mandelbaum, D. G. (1988). *Women's seclusion and men's honor: Sex roles in North India*. Tucson: University of Arizona Press.

May, R. E. (1989). Fighting South. In Wilson and Ferris (1989).

McWhiney, G. (1988). *Cracker culture: Celtic ways in the old South*. Tuscaloosa: University of Alabama Press.

Napier, J. (1989). Military tradition. In Wilson and Ferris (1989).

O'Kelley, C. G., and Carney, L. S. (1986). *Women and men in society*. New York: D. Van Nostrand Co.

Peristiany, J. G., ed. (1965). *Honour and shame: The values of Mediterranean society*. London: Weidenfeld and Nicolson.

Pitt-Rivers, J. (1965). Honour and social status. In Peristiany (1965).

Reifman, A. S., Larrick, R. P., and Fein, S. (1991). Temper and temperature on the diamond: The heat-aggression relationship in major league baseball. *Personality and Social Psychology Bulletin* 17, 580–585.

Rotton, J., and Frey, J. (1985). Air pollution, weather, and violent crimes: Concomitant time-series analysis of archival data. *Journal of Personality and Social Psychology* 49, 1207–1220.

Tocqueville, A. ([1835] 1969). In J. P. Mayer, ed. *Democracy in America*, trans. George Lawrence. Garden City, N.Y.: University of Chicago Press.

Wilson, C. R., and Ferris, W., eds. (1989). *Encyclopedia of southern culture*. Chapel Hill: University of North Carolina Press.

Wyatt-Brown, B. (1982). *Southern honor: Ethics and behavior in the Old South*. New York: Oxford University Press.

Chapter Twenty-three

The Great Bambi War

*Tocquevillians versus Keynesians in an
Upstate New York County*

Edward C. Hansen

A comparison of the householding strategies of two distinctive populations in Putnam County, New York, illustrates why the poorer of the two has a better chance of surviving capitalist recessions than does the richer. Like many other anthropological enterprises, this undertaking was an unintended outcome of its author's life experiences. Insufficent income led to my residence in Putnam from 1970 to 1980. At first, I had no wish to meet local people, much less to study them. In most particulars, I was part of one of the two populations: people who reside in the county, but who derive their cash income from union-scale salaries earned in New York City. As was the case with the New York City firefighters, police officers, schoolteachers, and low- to middle-level functionaries who make up the heart of this stratum, residence in Putnam County allowed me a middle-class lifestyle that I could not have afforded in the city or in the suburbs. If ever there was a fringe middle class, defined in terms of standard of living, we were it. A major human cost for the very modest home and meager yard was the fifty-mile commute to the city, undertaken either by car over bad roads or in an antediluvian train from Brewster. My own circumstances were such that I could not afford a residence in one of the nucleated settlements straddling the highways or at the railhead. What I could afford was a rundown rental property deep in the woods. My new location brought me into immediate contact with the other population of Putnam residents. Early on the second morning of my tenancy, I was jolted by a shotgun blast followed by violent but shortlived thrashing about directly outside the front door. Upon opening the door I saw that a dead and very bloody deer lay athwart the adjacent yew bushes. The second observation was yet more jarring. Less than fifteen feet from me stood the agent of the deer's undoing. Here was a stocky short fellow with exaggerated Elvis sideburns clad in greasy coveralls, shitkicker boots, and a filthy plaid cap with earflaps. Even more unsettling was his malevolent glare at me, heightened by the fact that his shotgun was pointed at my person. His words to me were: "Your house, our woods." That stated, he slung the deer over his shoulder and departed thunderously in a battered pickup truck. Even though I was a veteran ethnographer and this was a fellow American, I felt that this peremptory encounter rendered the meaning of The Other more profound than had my research and travel in the Gran Chaco, Mato Grosso, or the Catalan littoral.

My initial unnerving experience of local alterity was compounded many times over during the next several weeks. Every move I made to settle in brought me into hostile contact with similar beings who popped out of nowhere each time I turned around, to suggest, in minimalist monologues, that whatever I was doing was actually or potentially offensive to "us woodchucks." It swiftly became clear to me that (1) "woodchucks"—the semi-feral, rustic majority of the county's population—are the same people who are vulgarly and variously called pecker-woods, kickers, rednecks, or white trash elsewhere in the nation; (2) a standard model woodchuck male exhibits a style best described as Proto Masculine, that is, we are speaking of a legion of hard drinking, gun toting, violent, aggressive, male-bonded individuals for whom male sensitivity is not an issue; (3) I was now a resident of a heavily armed, very surly version of Dogpatch; and (4) if I were to enjoy economic easement and the tranquility to publish in pursuit of tenure and promotion, I should have to make some accommodation with these people, lest sheer physical survival become my major problem.

This essay is one by-product of that process of accommodation. While undergoing the rigors of adaptation, I began to realize that the conflicts between woodchucks and exurbanites had a bearing on certain key issues concerning American social stratification. Principal among them was that of social mobility, the ideological touchstone of American polity. The exurbanites measured mobility primarily in terms of first-time home ownership, however encumbered by mortgages that might be. Woodchucks held small acreages through inheritance and were concerned with stability, not mobility. In terms of standard of living, woodchucks actually enjoyed an edge over the exurbanites as they owned more substantial estates, capital equipment, and stocks of food. This is remarkable insofar as woodchucks are officially classified by both federal and state authorities as a poverty population (New York State 1990). Virtually all woodchuck families are officially unemployed for five months annually, that is, they are eligible to receive unemployment benefits during cold weather (November through March). The poverty image of the woodchuck could be bolstered by considering their salient sociometric characteristics apart from their low incomes. First, their official income derives from traditionally low-paying skills, essentially those related to the construction trades. Second, their educational levels are low for the decades 1970 to 1990; less than 50 percent held high school diplomas (Kent Board of Education 1991). Some 30 percent are functionally illiterate, and woodchuck children are notoriously poor students, truants, and the instigators of the fights that blight the reputations of local secondary schools. Yet to suggest that woodchucks, on the basis of such income data and sociometric parameters, are truly a poverty population or an emerging rural underclass (Auletta 1983) would be to embrace reification.

What begs to be explained is why woodchucks enjoy the standard of living that they do, why it is currently more secure than that of the exurbanites, and why there is such antagonism between the two strata. The strata discussed here did not emerge as a consequence of a hierarchical sorting out of local peoples via impersonal market forces operating in situ. What we have instead is the collision of two populations whose household economies were forged in different historical eras in different locales and are now enclaved together. As I shall argue below, the conflict between these two populations, which causes palpable discomfiture to each, is that between Jeffersonian/Tocquevillian yeomen and a middle class of the Keynesian compromise. Simply put, woodchucks hold productive private property, and the Keynesians reside on private property that is actually owned by banks, which entails staggering personal debts. Woodchucks assume that their property and traditional rights to forest resources are the basis of their livelihoods. They bitterly resist any intrusions of the state that might undermine these assumptions, especially when such intrusions involve raising property taxes. In a word, woodchucks are forest anarchists. By contrast, the Keynesians are creatures of government, the beneficiaries of labor struggles of the 1930s that resulted in wages having a political dimension, coupled with cheap credit.

These different historical points of economic origin and political position lie at the root of the confrontations between the two populations and express themselves in conflicts over the very definition of resources and who should have access to them. Nowhere is this clearer than in the case of deer hunting. To the woodchuck, deer is meat; to the Keynesian, it's Bambi, appealing and decorative. An effective comparison of these populations requires consideration of their respective "household resource packages," that is, the totality of activities that constitute production, consumption, and social reproduction within the home. This includes cash income, the disposition of family, kin, and network around subculturally defined resource bases, and household strategies to evade constraints and to exploit opportunities presented by the political order. To elaborate this concept, I first provide a brief history of Putnam County, and then consider the workings of woodchuck and exurbanite households.

Putnam County: Two Centuries of Official Economic Failure

One of the remarkable features of the United States is that people continue to live in areas that are economic backwaters. It is easier to explain why so many people settle in New York City, Chicago, or Los Angeles than it is to explain why others still live in Kayenta, Arizona, or Climax, Michigan, or Putnam County. Conventional wisdom asserts that a lengthy depression in agriculture commencing around 1900 led inexorably to the flow of people away from agricultural proprietorship in the countryside to wage labor employment in big cities.

Thus, in 1900, 50 percent of the American labor force was deployed in agriculture, but by 1957 the ratio had shrunk to 4 percent. By 1957, the average Iowa farmers' earnings were at roughly $2 per hour (Davidson 1990). Small wonder that so many rural people went urban. But others did not, and the question remains, Why? Were these folks simply those incapable of adapting to the new economic order, or people who rejected progress?

Putnam County offers a case in point that contradicts the conventional wisdom. The area is no stranger to economic depression. In fact it has known no other condition since the American Revolution. Here, literally, nothing has worked out well economically for two centuries. Putnam County derives its name from Colonel John Putnam, who, as head of the local militia during the revolution, was rewarded with a substantial acreage at the conclusion of hostilities, a gift that swiftly impoverished him. His reward came at the expense of the loyalist De Phillipes family, who had hoped to make money—apart from farming—by mining lead to make musket balls for the British army. The lead turned out to be of inferior quality, just as their farmland proved to be worthless (Puerrefoy 1956). There is at present not a single farm operating in Putnam County; the last one, a dairy enterprise, shut down in 1970.

Prior to 1940, most of the county's residents were classified as farmers; in the aftermath of the depression, most residents no longer farmed at all. Whenever possible, they subdivided their farms and sold tracts to local realtors, who in turn further divided and sold the properties to an increasing number of New York City dwellers seeking summer cottages. Local realtors who bought deep-woods property found little resale market; those who bought waterfront properties near the lake and reservoirs profited modestly. In fact, real estate only became a flourishing part of the county's economy after 1970 (Carmel Chamber of Commerce 1990). At present, real estate is the only viable part of the official current economy. Simply put, there is no farming, no industry; Putnam is too far from New York City for most commuters, and no large business has yet established a branch in the county. Even real estate has been a depressed economic sector for seven years of the decade 1980–1990. It is simply somewhat less depressed than other sectors.

Not surprisingly, Putnam County has been classified as an official poverty county since 1970, in spite of the fact that the area's villages are largely inhabited by refugee New York City civil servants and local businessmen whose earnings are middle income (New York State 1990). Indeed, these urban refugees have disposed of sufficient income to stimulate the development of several malls along the county's highways. The malls are the local centers of social life and consumption for the Keynesians, the focal points of weekend activities. In fine, income in New York City, a home in or near one of the small towns, and access to a mall are the key ingredients of economic and social life for the Keynesians, who constitute roughly one-third of the county's population.

Clearly, the officially poor are the woodchucks, the other two-thirds of the county's population. Virtually all of them live along the serpentine dirt roads that crisscross the low mountain, secondary forest wilderness that physically defines the county. For generations, woodchucks have tried to wrest a livelihood from this unyielding terrain. Many collapsed farm buildings, crumbled stone walls, abandoned roads, and overgrown family cemeteries testify to the failure of previous economies. Yet the numerous substantial fieldstone and wood dwellings built by woodchuck hands on retained acreages, marked by all kinds of vehicles, ruined or operative, bear witness to the woodchuck capacity for survival. In general, their survival stems from retention of family acreages, albeit reduced in size, and aggressively pressed claims to forest resources, including those to which they have no de jure property rights. The energies they expend in defending and exploiting these resources are so extensive that for woodchucks New York City, so close at hand, is not to be visited, and, via television news, becomes a metaphor for all the world's evils. In Putnam County New Yorkers are at best woodchuck cash cows; at worst, they are potentially the end of the woodchuck natural order.

The county's official poverty rating is not simply a function of the inexorable workings of extralocal economic forces. Woodchucks themselves have been active agents in the political arena promoting the persistence of official poverty. They constitute an electoral majority, and they have consistently used their voting strength to prevent the establishment of industry in the county, to block municipalities from applying for any revenue-sharing funds that might require contributions from locals, and above all, to ensure that only new properties (i.e., those that change hands) or new construction have their taxes reassessed. To woodchucks, who is elected to be mayor, or to serve on the school board, or to the post of tax assessor is more important than who is elected to be president of the United States. As long as they can control the local electoral process, woodchucks can stop both external capital investment and governmental expansion. That they have voted Republican by overwhelming margins for more than four decades underlines their perception that Republican government means less government, and therefore less local taxation, and less bureaucratic interference in their ability to protect their resource bases. Unemployment insurance is one form of government insurance that woodchucks accept, insofar as it is regarded as a cash bonus to household income; yet only 53 percent of those eligible do so. In other words, government in any form is not a benefactor but a clear and present danger.

Having established context, we turn to examine the comparative resource packages of Tocquevillians and Keynesians. It will be seen below that the conflict between the two has not only a material base, but also a related aesthetic struggle that arises over estate disposition and deer hunting. The struggle is not merely about who gets what, but also about the different cultural styles through which material goals are pursued. As simultaneously an intimate participant in the lives of both populations, an ethnologist with a profound political economy bias, and a cynic, I was struck by the fact that issues of style were more vital to all informants than those of substance on the level of discourse. I shall below offer some explanation of this seeming triumph of style over substance.

Woodchuck and Exurbanite Household Resource Packages Compared

The fundamental bases of any exurbanite's household resource package are middle-income salaries and the credit that accrues to people who earn such salaries. The salary anchor of any exurbanite family of four is at least one salary earned at union rates in New York City. Police officers, firefighters, and teachers in the city have been unionized for a long time, and their pay and benefit packets reflect that fact. A universal perception among this population is that although union-scale wages are "decent," they are insufficient to meet household consumption needs. Credit is thus a necessary bridge between need and salary shortfall. All exurbanite homes were purchased with mortgages; since 1980 there has been a dramatic increase in doubly mortgaged homes. Informants cite overextension of credit and children's college costs as the primary reasons for second mortgages. Automobiles, an absolute necessity for commuters, are purchased with either bank or dealer credit. High-ticket consumer items—stereos, washing machines, and so forth—are purchased with credit cards in the local malls, to the point where mall vendors of high-ticket items joke about being unable to identify U.S. currency. Mall consumption on the credit card–wielding exurbanite's part is commonly described as "plastic fantastic." Material life here is not about owning anything free and clear, but about enjoying consumption now with the promise to pay for such enjoyment later.

Several assumptions underlie this behavior, assumptions that have well served many post-depression Americans by their own cultural compasses, but which now threaten to annihilate them economically. Principal among these assumptions is the conviction that their salaries will steadily rise, via union salary scales, thus allowing them to convert debt into equity at least in terms of home ownership. Once they pay off the mortgage(s), the home will be theirs, at (they believe) a higher value than they paid for it. Such equity could be used for either a more comfortable retirement than that afforded by union pension alone, or to provide a modest inheritance for their children, or for some combination of both. Second, they have labored so hard at their jobs, and are willing to labor yet more to increase salaries, that they believe they are deserving of this level of consumption. The ambitious schoolteacher, firefighter, or police officer can work overtime or study to take civil service exams to achieve higher salaries faster than by simply awaiting raises accruing from union seniority. The key assumption is that wages will steadily increase, thus providing an ever-higher standard of living, both for themselves and for their children.

At present, the exurbanite's faith in these assumptions is being sorely tested by a deepening recession. Features of the recession include loss of real earning power, union bashing by Republican national administrations, the general shrinking of entitlements (e.g., health and unemployment benefits), and the reduction of the public sector workforce as debt-ridden states like New York are forced to make draconian budget cuts to balance their budgets (Blumberg 1980). The exurbanites of Putnam County are very vulnerable to these developments, especially since all their economic eggs are in the one decaying basket of unionized public sector employment. Nevertheless, exurbanites have annually out-earned woodchucks by roughly 3:1 over the period 1970–1990 (New York State 1990). Hence, it appears that if exurbanites are sweating it, then woodchucks must really be sunk. The official incomes of woodchucks seem to confirm this opinion. In 1990, a woodchuck family of four earned $16,700, while the exurbanite family of four collected $44,800. Yet cash income as recorded in governmental documents is only that which is logged in taxable transactions. Few social science analysts seem to take into account the fact that one of the most elaborate sporting contests in this society has long been that between ratepayers and governmental revenuers, even though resorting to outside coaching (accountants) is a wide-spread practice among such analysts. Although the exurbanite, unlike the analyst, may not be able to pay for a personal accountant, suffice it to say that H & R Block does very good business in Putnam County—but not among woodchucks, who operate in a host of cash and carry, off the books economies. Simply put, the tax hedge of the woodchuck is the U.S. dollar, the passage of which from one hand to the next is vastly harder to trace than the computerized payroll checks issued to the exurbanites, the latter's credit card transactions, or, for that matter, the electronic cash register recordings of mall merchants. When woodchucks sell their skills to exurbanites, they offer substantial discounts for off the books payments in cash. Few exurbanites refuse such discounts. Thus, the gap between woodchuck and exurbanite incomes is not as large as official records indicate: the exurbanites earn more money, but a substantial amount of woodchuck cash earnings is unofficial and therefore nontaxable.

Woodchucks cannot readily avail themselves of standard credit devices, as their official income is too low to qualify them for home mortgages or credit cards. But home mortgages mean little to the woodchucks, who have owned homes with sizable acreages for generations, and credit cards are not essential for their domestic consumption. Woodchucks occasionally need bank loans in order to buy capital equipment and must use their properties as collateral to secure such loans. The need to purchase a new back hoe or a bulldozer constitutes a serious household economic crisis. Yet the general lack of credit is currently a blessing in disguise for the woodchucks. Simply put, they cannot use credit to run up the staggering private debts that now threaten to sink the exurbanites.

Although woodchucks do participate to a limited extent in the official cash economy, their principal and basic economic orientation is toward household self-sufficiency. In a depression, this means simple subsistence, defined in terms of food and shelter. At the heart of the woodchuck subsistence economy is an intricate combination of family estate, forest resources, household organization, a range of specific and generalized economic skills, and extensive kin and friendship networks. Taken together, these mean that woodchuck families have a greater ability to resist economic downturns than do exurbanites. In a word, their strength is in economic diversification, a term that has meaning to the exurbanites only when they converse with the managers of their share portfolios. The dispersing of diverse eggs in diverse baskets is the key to woodchuck survival.

Let us turn to consider what these elements are, their combinations, and how these contrast with the exurbanites' resources.

The starting point of woodchuck economy is the family estate. These estates were long ago amortized; that is, they carry no debt. The size of this property ranges from 5 to 40 acres, the remainder of the 60- to 180-acre grazing farms that failed two or more generations ago. In fine, woodchucks long ago sold most of their estates to realtors in order to raise cash. Yet the 5 to 40 acres that remain are more productive than the farms ever were. All are forest properties, which are unsuitable for any form of commercial agriculture. Yet somewhere within this acreage is a half acre (or larger) garden capable of providing virtually all vegetable needs of a woodchuck family. Woodchuck wives spend long hours cultivating these gardens in the summer and preserve a wide variety of vegetables for the winter months. Potatoes and turnips are stored in antiquated but functional root cellars.

The bulk of the woodchuck estate is not farmland, but secondary forest wilderness. This is the supreme province of Man the Hunter, a.k.a. the woodchuck male. These woods are teeming with deer, the woodchucks' principal source of lean red meat. Although the official hunting season is but six weeks long, woodchucks shoot deer anytime they see a void in their half-ton freezer chests. In the ten years I lived there, I cannot recall a day unpunctuated by rifle fire and the baying of mammoth woodchuck hunting dogs. Nor are deer the only game in the woods; rabbits, guinea fowl, and pheasants also abound. The latter are tame birds bred by the New York State Conservation Commission, which turns them loose on woodchuck properties. They are not shot, but rather strangled by woodchucks who easily stalk these unwary birds. The streams, ponds, and reservoirs of the county are brimful with fish, among them the desirable smallmouth bass and German trout. Finally, the forest is a source of fuel. All woodchuck homes are essentially woodburning with limited use of fossil fuel.

In short, woodchuck households are largely self-sufficient in terms of food and fuel. In a depression, they could survive without supermarkets and fuel deliveries, but the exurbanites could not. Currently, woodchucks take modest fuel deliveries—all own modern gas furnaces, water heaters, and stoves—and do some shopping at supermarkets. The exploitation of estates and forest resources thus currently translates into a significant savings over what exurbanites must pay for food and fuel. In 1990, the average woodchuck paid about $400 for fuel and $3,100 for groceries annually. Corresponding figures for an exurbanite family were $1,900 and $10,700, respectively. Such savings go a long way toward explaining why the woodchuck standard of living in fact differs little from that of the exurbanites. Nor is it difficult to understand why both woodchuck estates and the forest are stoutly defended from encroachments by exurbanites and authorities.

Woodchuck economy is not limited to the exploitation of family estates and the woods. As I noted earlier, woodchucks depend for cash income largely on exurbanites, who are literally woodchuck cash cows, there to be milked whenever possible. Woodchucks sell their skills and labor to the exurbanites, and these are the same skills necessary to implement the woodchuck subsistence economy. A major difference between these two populations is that woodchuck economy depends upon the possession of a number of specific personal skills, of a variety of additional generalizable skills, and of a prodigious capacity for labor of all kinds. In contrast, the exurbanites depend on salaries gleaned from one profession and sometimes two, when both spouses are employed. In fine, the exurbanites are highly specialized, whereas woodchucks are flexible.

Let us inventory the repertoire of woodchuck skills. All woodchuck males practice at least one of the following crafts: carpentry, electrical repair and installations, masonry (including the use of native fieldstone, a common material used in the construction of houses, fireplaces, chimneys, and fences), plumbing, heavy equipment operation, welding, metalwork, mechanics (repairs of any form of equipment, not merely of automobiles, which virtually everyone does themselves), well drilling and maintenance (critical in a county where most water is derived from private wells), landscaping, road building (important in a county where half the roads are privately owned and maintained), and all kinds of tree work (the county is essentially a big forest). All these skills are simultaneously essential to woodchuck subsistence economy and salable to the exurbanites. At best the exurbanites are weekend do-it-yourselfers. Many are capable of painting a room, fixing a leaking faucet, planting flowers, and so forth. But when an exurbanite's home has structural damage from age or storms, when the well freezes over, or the septic tank oozes, the exurbanite contracts a woodchuck to effect repairs. What the woodchuck does for free at his own home becomes cash income when carried out at the exurbanite's place.

Possession of such skills is obviously a critical part of woodchuck household economy. More subtle are the ways in which such skills are deployed. One of the most important characteristics of woodchucks is the degree to which they manage to control their own time as households. Simply put, woodchucks try to avoid institutional arrangements of all kinds, especially routinized full-time jobs. Critical to their mode of social reproduction is the tapping of multiple resources, which are available variously in different times of the year and different hours of the day. Frequently, the pursuit of multiple resources causes conflicts in woodchuck households, which recalibrate their labor deployment on a daily, sometimes hourly basis. If you have to finish a paying construction job, but your freezer is low, do you complete the job to collect the money or bag a deer? Common complaints of the exurbanites who contract woodchuck labor are that no one can guarantee when the woodchuck craftsman will show up for work, and in what condition. The woodchuck may well have spent the night cleaning fish obtained illegally from the Hudson River, dressing out a poached deer, or brewing applejack in his garage still. If seen tapping a healing beer from his Igloo cooler—a standard 4 × 4 pickup accessory—for his breakfast, he probably had a rough night at one of the country and western boozers found along the county's back roads.

The exurbanite's lament underlines a real source of tension in woodchuck households, which boils down to this: when do you commit to the pursuit of what resources, and who will be involved in this commitment? This tension reaches a peak in warm weather months, when all resources are available simultaneously. Paid work is at its peak; fish, game, and fuel are abundant; and gardens must be tended. Woodchuck families are poorest but calmest during winters; with the onset of spring, their households become frenetic, as their resource package has to be bundled in these seven months of the year. Part of the tension stems from the fact that it is not merely a household struggling to make appropriate time commitments to gleaning diverse resources, but also that other woodchuck households with the same decision-making problems are critical to successful resolution of these problems. That is, successful woodchuck householding depends upon maintaining intricate labor exchange and barter arrangements with other woodchuck households, who are generally kin, as much as it depends upon effective exploitation of all household labor.

The complexity of labor allocation decisions regarding multiple resource exploitation injects a measure of anarchy into the daily activities of woodchuck families. It is literally impossible to solve all problems smoothly in this context. Woodchuck men frequently have trouble deciding which task is most important on any given day; woodchuck wives may be interrupted while putting up food, gardening, or helping children with homework by unanticipated visits by clients or kin, or incessant phone calls from cash clients as to the whereabouts of their husbands. Woodchuck children, particularly boys, may be pulled out of school to help their fathers at work, to garden, to cut wood, or to go fishing or hunting with dad. Woodchucks consciously weigh the value of child labor against the benefits of formal education, and do not hesitate to emphasize the former. Exurbanite children, in contrast, are a drain on the family budget. In short, the woodchucks continue to be committed to multiple resource exploitation, in spite of its tensions. There is no way that they will commit themselves or their children to dependence upon nine-to-five jobs for their livelihoods. For them, it's forest anarchy forever.

The organization of time by exurbanites is radically different. Earning a paycheck as a police officer, firefighter, or teacher involves a fundamental commitment to the forty-hour week. Police officers and firefighters average four hours a week overtime, and this is their principal means of obtaining additional money. All three jobs have professional social requirements as well; an amorphously defined but very palpable part of these jobs is collegiality. Crudely put, this means that to survive at work, the employee must hang out with other employees while he or she is officially off duty. Failure to grease social skids outside work will lead to on-the-job problems. Police officers and firefighters are notorious for after-hours bar communing (Kaprow 1991); teachers give dinner parties and picnics. These particular exurbanites have an additional time-consuming problem: the primary wage earner spends fifteen hours a week commuting to New York City.

Exurbanite time commitments are scarcely defined by jobs alone; it takes plenty of off-the-job time to fulfill the status requirements of middle-class membership. Time must be expended maintaining the appearance of one's home and its provisioning: in a word, shopping. The better part of one day each weekend is spent at the mall, most of the other in trying to put the home in order. Additionally, there are marital and familial requirements for togetherness, best addressed on weekends, since there is little other "free time," that classic oxymoron of middle-class life. Children further complicate the picture: their school, physical, and "activities" needs must be kept up to speed, lest they wind up as mall shoplifters or dopetakers, or as such poor students that they cannot get into a decent state college, or even as teenage suicides. Overcommitment to pursuit of income and status frequently means undercommitment to kids, who sometimes turn out rotten. All told, the time and money commitments of middle-class status often threaten the survival of the household.

Conclusion

Clearly, it would be folly to explain the relationships between woodchucks and exurbanites in terms of income differentials, as a pineywoods version of the unceasing struggle between poor people and the middle class. Despite the fact that exurbanites earn much more money than do woodchucks, both populations enjoy a similar standard of living. What woodchucks lack in cash income is offset by what they gain from labor exchanges, barter, and above all, the exploitation of multiple resources. To paraphrase the Bible, man—or woman—does not live by income alone. The woodchucks are certainly proof of that. Moreover, the woodchucks are more likely to survive capitalist recessions than are the exurbanites, insofar as they are well suited to live in a self-generated subsistence economy, whereas the exurbanites are absolutely dependent on cash income, credit, and governmental services for their economic and social well-being. In the current recession, these mainstays of middleclasshood are rapidly contracting, leaving the exurbanites in a much more precarious situation than the woodchucks.

Although the conflicts between the woodchucks and the exurbanites have a clear material basis—contested forest rights and divergent definitions of resources—the spirit of these conflicts cannot be understood without reference to the American Dream and its historical transformations. In a word, the woodchucks seem to have stepped right out of the pages of Jefferson's and Tocqueville's vision of the Dream, whereas the exurbanites are creatures of Bloomsbury's John Maynard Keynes, midwifed by Franklin D. Roosevelt for American consumption. In each version, private property and individual initiative occupy ideological center stage, yet the definition of property and the context of initiative are radically different in the two.

Time and space considerations permit no more than a sketch of these two visions. The Jeffersonian/Tocquevillian version foresaw a nation of modestly prosperous yeomen, economically self-sufficient by virtue of ownership of property that could generate a livelihood through prodigious household self-exploitation. In the Jeffersonian vision, American society would thus be classless, as all men would become proprietors of familial businesses. In the Tocquevillian

(1835, 1840) variant, although differences in wealth were bound to emerge, the spirit of the whole society would be profoundly democratic, to the point of vulgarity, coarseness, and rudeness. For both authors, the role of government was minimal and that of business everything. This vision was attuned to the reality that, as Dan Rose (1989) points out, the United States is the only country in the world to be founded as thirteen separate businesses. Not surprisingly, social personhood depended upon acquiring property that generated minimally a livelihood, and hopefully prosperity. Perhaps the sine qua non of property was land, as the United States remained a profoundly rural society until the end of the Civil War. From the end of the Civil War to the present, the likelihood of individual households sustaining themselves from land-based businesses has declined with each passing year, to the point where by 1980, there were roughly 11 million such businesses for 235 million Americans. Despite the conversion of Americans into a wage earning (rather than propertied) society, the political and social ideology of the country is still focused on ownership of land as an ultimate symbol of personal realization. Only the land now consists of a dwelling surrounded by grass, shrubs, and perhaps a picket fence (stockade in urban areas). Instead of generating income, it produces private indebtedness. Where once it was central to production, it is now the paramount object of national consumption. Then it offered the prospect of household independence; at present it requires dependence on government subsidies.

One of the supreme triumphs of the American political system has been the preservation of the symbol of ownership, while radically changing its content. Nowhere is this success more apparent than in the depression-era policies of the Roosevelt administrations and their successors that created the modern middle class. In their totality, these policies vitiated the downside effects of business cycles on major segments of a very contentious American polity. What evolved was an elaborate system of subsidies for different strata of the polity, which we cannot discuss here. The subsidies of concern for this essay were those concessions made to organized labor. Salient among these were the establishment of FHA mortgages, the recognition of a political dimension of wages, and the extension of consumer credit through various banking and currency reforms. Viewed through the bleak lens of classical political economy, these acts made it possible for a whole new class—the contemporary middle class—to enjoy a standard of living that it clearly did not merit through market competition. In other words, the contemporary middle class is the supreme political creation of the Roosevelt era; it is not an economic class at all, but a political artifice.

The ideological underpinnings and cultural validation of the new middle class consisted of social mobility from the working class via home and automobile ownership, plus additional credit to purchase consumer durables. The trade-off for mass consumption was increasing private indebtedness for households, an indebtedness that was relatively painless as long as government maintained subsidies and the economy continued to expand. The property of the Tocquevillians now became the home of the new middle class. Production was now converted into consumption through Keynesian economic formulae, but cultural symbols were preserved in the transformation. The conflictual coexistence of the woodchucks and the exurbanites can be best understood as the collision of old and new versions of the American Dream.

If, as Wolf (1956) proposed, the local arena is best understood as a cross-cutting manifold, a point of intersection or overlap among diverse relational fields, then Putnam County is a case in point. Here, webs of group relations, each the terminus of a distinctive set of articulations with the state and of a distinctive history, are, as Wolf suggested they could be, "wholly tangential to one another" (1956, 1065). Such a model of the local level draws much-needed attention to the cultural and stylistic aspects of intergroup conflict; cultural style is shown to be an integral part of the wider articulations and of the respective histories of the groups involved. These differences of external linkage and history influence not only how people think but also how they organize time, run households, relate to neighbors, approach local government, and respond to a deer transfixed by headlights at the side of the road.

NOTE

I wish to acknowledge a PSC-CUNY grant and a Queens College Presidential Award, which provided time and money to begin systematizing information collected between 1970 and 1980. I would like to thank Geoff Bate, Warren De Boer, Geraldine Grant, Mimi Kaprow, Sharryn Kasmir, Gloria Levitas, Dan Rose, Steve Thompson, and Brackette Williams for constructive criticism of this version of the manuscript. I owe thanks for both intellectual support for this project and a whole lot of reciprocal labor for the construction of Iron Ball Mountain to Fred and Ethel Adams, Jeremy Beckett, Howard and Peg Carpenter, Gilda and Joplin Hansen, Mo and Goo Littlejohn, Bill Dorson, Delmos Jones, Ellery McClatchy, Mervyn and Joan Meggitt, Peter and Jane Schneider, Sydel Silverman, and Eric Wolf. All are absolved from construction defects in this paper and that dwelling.

REFERENCES

Auletta, K. 1983. *The Underclass.* New York: Simon and Schuster.

Blumberg, Paul. 1980. *Inequality in an Age of Decline.* New York: Oxford University Press.

Carmel Chamber of Commerce. 1990. *Real Estate in Putnam County* Putnam, N.Y.: Chamber of Commerce.

Davidson, O. 1990. *Broken Heartland: The Rise of America's Rural Ghetto.* New York: Free Press.

Kaprow, M. 1991. "Magical Work: Firefighters in New York." *Human Organization* 50:97–103.

Kent Board of Education. 1991. *Annual Report.* Brewster, N.Y.: Southeast Lithographics.

New York State. 1990. "Employment in New York (1970–1990)." *Annual Reports.* Albany, N.Y.: Department of Labor.

Puerrefoy, D. 1956. *History of the Town of Southeast Brewster.* New York: Brewster Lithographics.

Rose, Daniel. 1989. *Patterns of American Culture: Ethnography and Estrangement*. Philadelphia: University of Pennsylvania Press.

Tocqueville, Alexis de. 1835, 1840. *Democracy in America*. New York: Vintage Books.

Wolf, Eric. 1956. "Aspects of Group Relations in a Complex Society: Mexico." *American Anthropologist* 58:1065–1078.

The Breakdown of Civil Society

Chapter Twenty-four

The Crisis of Public Order

Adam Walinsky

Numbers are useful in politics, because they are more neutral than adjectival speech and because they express magnitude—that is, they can tell us not only that we confront a danger but also what the depth and direction of the danger are. The most important numbers in America deal with violence—not the occasional terrorist violence but the terror of everyday life as it is lived by millions of citizens today, and as it threatens to become for many more of us for the rest of this century and beyond.

During his campaign and since, President Bill Clinton has spoken of a sharp decline in the strength of the nation's police forces. In the 1960s the United States as a whole had 3.3 police officers for every violent crime reported per year. In 1993 it had 3.47 violent crimes reported for every police officer. In relation to the amount of violent crime, then, we have less than one-tenth the effective police power of thirty years ago; or, in another formulation, each police officer today must deal with 11.45 times as many violent crimes as his predecessor of years gone by.

Title I of the 1994 crime bill intends to add 100,000 police officers nationally by the year 2000. (Most experts believe that far fewer new officers—perhaps 25,000—will actually be hired. For the purposes of this argument, though, let us assume the larger figure.) There are now some 554,000 officers serving on all state and local police forces; 100,000 more would be an increase of 18.4 percent. Rather than having 3.47 times as many violent crimes as police officers, we would have 2.94 times as many; or, each police officer would face not 11.45 times as many violent crimes as his predecessor but 9.7 times as many. All this assumes that the number of violent crimes will not increase over the next several years; if it does, the number of violent crimes relative to police officers will again increase.

If we wished to return to the ratio of police officers to violent crimes which gave many of us peace and security in the 1960s, we would have to add not 100,000 new police officers but about *five million*. When this number was mentioned to some Department of Justice staffers recently, they giggled; and it is understandable that the idea of such a national mobilization, such tremendous expenditures, should strike them as laughable. However, the American people are already paying out of their own pockets for an additional 1.5 million private police officers, to provide, at least in part, the protection that the public police are unable to furnish.

Private police guard office buildings, shopping malls, apartments. Businesses pay them to patrol certain down-town streets, such as those around New York's Grand Central Station and public library. And they patrol residential areas. Private patrol cars thread the streets of Los Angeles, and more than fifty applications are before the city council to close off streets so as to make those patrols more effective. Across the country much new housing is being built in gated communities, walled off and privately guarded. We are well on the way to having several million police officers, and the next decade will bring us much closer. If current trends continue, however, most of the new officers will be privately paid, available for the protection not of the citizenry as a whole—and certainly not of citizens living in the most violent ghettos and housing projects—but of the commercial and residential enclaves that can afford them. Between these enclaves there will be plenty of room to lose a country.

One Long Descending Night

People hire police officers because they are afraid—above all of violence. Their fear is occasionally a source of puzzlement and mild disdain in the press, which cannot understand why so many Americans say that crime is the nation's most urgent problem and their own greatest fear. Indeed, all through 1993 official agencies claimed that crime was declining. The FBI said that violent crime in the first six months was down 3 percent overall, and down 8 percent in the Northeast.

For crime to be down even 8 percent would mean that a precinct that had had a hundred murders in 1992 had ninety-two in 1993. But nobody came around on New Year's Day of 1993 to give everyone's memory a rinse, obliterating the horrors of the previous year. The effect is not disjunctive but cumulative. By the end of 1993, ninety-two additional people had been murdered.

Many people can also remember years before 1992, in large cities and in small. In 1960, for example, 6 murders, 4 rapes, and 16 robberies were reported in New Haven, Connecticut. In 1990 that city, with a population 14 percent smaller, had 31 murders, 168 rapes, and 1,784 robberies: robbery increased more than 100 times, or *10,000 percent*, over thirty years. In this perspective a one-year decrease of 7 percent would seem less than impressive.

New Haven is not unique. In Milwaukee in 1965 there were 27 murders, 33 rapes, and 214 robberies, and in 1990, when the city was smaller, there were 165 murders, 598 rapes, and 4,472 robberies: robbery became twenty-one times as frequent in twenty-five years. New York City in 1951 had 244 murders; every year for more than a decade it has had nearly 2,000 murders.

We experience the crime wave not as separate moments in time but as one long descending night. A loved one lost echoes in the heart for decades. Every working police officer knows the murder scene: the shocked family and neighbors, too numb yet to grieve; fear and desolation spreading to the street, the workplace, the school, the home, creating an invisible but indelible network of anguish and loss. We have experienced more than 20,000 such scenes every year for more than a decade, and few of them have been truly forgotten.

The memory of a mugging may fade but does not vanish. Nine percent of those responding to a recent poll in *New York Newsday* said that they had been mugged or assaulted in the past year. This suggests an annual total for the city of more than 600,000 muggings and assaults (remember also that many people, in poor neighborhoods especially, are assaulted more than once). That would be four times as many robberies and assaults as are reported to the police department. The Department of Justice says that not three-quarters but only half of all violent crimes go unreported: it may be that many report as having happened "last year" an incident from more than a year ago.

Nevertheless, these are stunning numbers, especially when some other common crimes are added in. Eight percent of those polled (implying 560,000 New Yorkers) said their houses or apartments had been broken into; 22 percent (1,540,000) said their cars had been broken into. In all, 42 percent (nearly three million New Yorkers) said they had been the victims of crime in 1993. And, of course, about 2,000 were murdered. This is what it means to say that crime in 1993 was down 8 percent.

In October of 1994 the Bureau of Justice Statistics reported that violent crime had not, after all, declined in 1993 but had risen by 5.6 percent.

Several years ago the Department of Justice estimated that 83 percent of all Americans would be victims of violent crime at least once in their lives. About a quarter would be victims of three or more violent crimes. We are progressing steadily toward the fulfillment of that prediction.

A Twenty-Year Fraud Exposed

Our greatest fear is of violence from a nameless, faceless stranger. Officials have always reassured citizens by stating that the great majority of murders, at any rate, are committed by a relative or an acquaintance of the victim's; a 1993 Department of Justice report said the figure for 1988 was eight out of ten.

Unfortunately, that report described only murders in which the killer was known to prosecutors and an arrest was made. It did not mention that more and more killers remain unknown and at liberty after a full police investigation; every year the police make arrests in a smaller proportion of murder cases. In our largest cities the police now make arrests in fewer than three out of five murder cases. In other words, two out of every five killers are completely untouched by the law.

When a killing is a family tragedy, or takes place between friends or acquaintances, the police make an arrest virtually every time. When the police make an arrest, they say that the crime has been "cleared"; the percentage of crimes for which they make arrests is referred to as the clearance rate. Because murder has historically been a matter principally among families and friends, the homicide clearance rate in the past was often greater than 95 percent, even in the largest cities. As late as 1965 the national homicide clearance rate was 91 percent. However, as crime has spread and changed its character over the past generation, clearance rates have steadily dropped. In the past two years the national homicide clearance rate averaged 65.5 percent. The rate in the sixty-two largest cities is 60.5 percent. In the very largest cities—those with populations over a million—the rate is 58.3 percent.

The missing killers are almost certainly not family members, friends, or neighbors. Rather, they are overwhelmingly strangers to their victims, and their acts are called "stranger murders." Here is the true arithmetic: The 40 percent of killings in which city police departments are unable to identify and arrest perpetrators must overwhelmingly be counted as stranger murders; let us assume that 90 percent of them are committed by killers unknown to the victims. That number is equivalent to 36 percent of the total of all city murders. We know that of the 60 percent of killers the police do succeed in arresting, 20 percent have murdered strangers. That is, they have committed 12 percent of all murders. As best we can count, then, at least 48 percent of city murders are now being committed by killers who are not relatives or acquaintances of the victims.

This simple arithmetic has been available to the government and its experts for years. However, the first government document to acknowledge these facts was the FBI's annual report on crime in the United States for 1993, which was released last December. The FBI now estimates that 53 percent of all homicides are being committed by strangers. For more than two decades, as homicide clearance rates have plummeted, law-enforcement agencies have continued to assure the public that four-fifths of all killings are the result of personal passions. Thus were we counseled to fear our loved ones above all, to regard the family hearth as the most dangerous place. Now that falsehood has been unmasked: the FBI tells us that actually 12 percent of all homicides take place within the family. I have heard no public official anywhere in the United States say a word about any of this.

There is another important aspect to the arithmetic: the odds facing a robber or holdup man as he decides whether to let his victim live. Again, at least 48 percent of city homicides are stranger murders, but only 12 percent of city homicides result in arrest. That is, the odds that a holdup man who kills a stranger will be arrested appear to be one in four. The Department of Justice tells us that of all those who are arrested for murder, 73 percent will be convicted of some crime; and when convicted, the killers of strangers tend to get the heaviest penalties. Nevertheless, the cumulative chances of getting clean away with the murder of a stranger are greater than 80 percent. Street thugs may be smarter than they are usually given credit for being. They do not consult government reports, but they appear to know the facts. New York bodega workers have experienced an increasing incidence of holdups ending in murder even when they have offered no resistance. Killing eliminates the possibility of witness identification.

Murder is the most frightening crime, but is the least common. Much more frequent are robbery and assault. Robbery, the forcible taking of property from the person of the victim, is the crime most likely to be committed by a stranger; 75 percent of victims are robbed by strangers. Aggravated assault, the use of a weapon or other major force with the intention of causing serious bodily harm, is the most common violent crime; 58 percent of aggravated assaults are committed by strangers.

Attacks across racial lines are a special case of crimes by strangers. Most crimes, including 80 percent of violent crimes, are committed by persons of the same race as their victims. However, the experiences of blacks and whites diverge in some respects. In cases involving a lone offender, 56 percent of white and Hispanic robbery victims report that their assailant was white or Hispanic and 40 percent that he was black. When two or more robbers commit the crime, white and Hispanic victims 38 percent of the time report them to be white or Hispanic, 46 percent of the time black, and 10 percent of the time mixed. About 8 percent of black victims, in contrast, are robbed by whites or Hispanics, and more than 85 percent by blacks, whether the offenders are alone or in groups. Blacks and whites are robbed equally—75 percent of the time—by strangers, but as these figures indicate, whites are far more likely to be robbed by strangers of a different race.

This result occurs because there are many more white people and many more white victims: 87 percent of all violent crimes are committed against whites and Hispanics. In robberies lone white offenders select white victims 96 percent of the time, and lone black offenders select white victims 62 percent of the time. White rapists select white victims 97 percent of the time; black rapists select white victims 48 percent of the time. Whites committing aggravated assault attack blacks in 3 percent of cases; blacks commit about half their assaults against whites.

When all violent crimes are taken together, 58 percent of white victims and 54 percent of black victims report that their assailant was a stranger. Citizens of all races who are fearful of random violence have good reason for their concern. Storekeepers, utility workers, police officers, and ordinary citizens out for a carton of milk or a family dinner are all increasingly at risk.

Toward a Race behind Bars

In 1990 federal, state, and local governments combined spent about $8,921 per person. According to the Department of Justice, these governments spent $299 per person—about 3.3 percent of total public expenditures—on all civil-and criminal-justice activities, including $128 per person on domestic police protection. On national defense and international relations they spent $1,383 per person.

Spending on the Armed Forces has historically risen to meet perceived threats from hostile nations, or in case of rebellion. Sharply rising crime rates have not brought equivalent increases in police forces. From 1971 to 1990, as the rates of homicide and other violent crimes soared, per person expenditures (in constant dollars) on state and local police forces increased by only 12 percent.

Spending did increase on prisons—by more than 150 percent. In 1992 state and federal prisons held 883,656 inmates (local jails held another 444,584). Out of every 100,000 residents of the United States, 344 were in prison (another 174 were in jail). Prison populations increased another 7 percent in 1993, by which year 2.9 times as many people were incarcerated as had been in 1980.

The overwhelming majority of prison inmates are male. Of the 789,700 male inmates in 1992, 51 percent, or 401,700, were black, and nearly all the remaining 388,000 white. (Here Hispanics are included in both categories; according to the Department of Justice, 93 percent of Hispanic prisoners describe themselves as white and 7 percent as black. Asians and Native Americans make up at most 2.5 percent of all prisoners.) Rates of imprisonment by race are therefore very different. In 1992, of every 100,000 white and Hispanic male residents, 372 were prisoners. Of every 100,000 black male residents, 2,678 were prisoners.

The heaviest rates of imprisonment affect men aged twenty to forty. Although the overall imprisonment rate for black men is 2,678 per 100,000, it reaches 7,210 for every 100,000 aged twenty-five to twenty-nine, and 6,299 for those aged thirty to thirty-four. At any one time 6 to 7 percent of black men at these critical ages are in state and federal prisons.

(Most arrests, and most new prison sentences, are not for violent crimes. In 1992 only 28.5 percent of offenders sentenced to state prisons had been convicted of violent offenses; 31.2 percent had been convicted of property offenses, and 30.5 percent of drug offenses. These numbers represent a major change in just over a decade: in 1980, 48.2 percent of newly sentenced offenders had been convicted of violent offenses, and only 6.8 percent of drug offenses. The Department of Justice has argued that many people convicted of nonviolent drug crimes have also committed violent offenses. But there can be no question that the police are making more drug arrests and relatively fewer arrests for violent crimes. For the past five years drug arrests have averaged one million a year, and arrests for all violent crimes combined about 600,000.)

A study was made of black men aged eighteen to thirty-four in the District of Columbia. On any given day in 1991, 15 percent of the men were in prison, 21 percent were on probation or parole, and 6 percent were being sought by the police or were on bond awaiting trial. The total thus involved with the criminal-justice system was 42 percent. The study estimated that 70 percent of black men in the District of Columbia would be arrested before the age of thirty-five, and that 85 percent would be arrested at some point in their lives.

There have been no studies of the effects of such high imprisonment rates on the wider black society—for example, on the children of prisoners. No government or private agency has suggested any way to lighten the influence of paternal and sibling imprisonment on children, or how to balance the potential value of such an effort against the need to suppress violent crimes. Although the crime bill will substantially expand prison space, no one has asked how much further we can go—whether it is possible, practically, socially, or morally, to imprison some larger proportion of the black male population at any one time.

What's Already Spoken For

In 1965 Daniel Patrick Moynihan warned that a growing proportion of black children were being born to single mothers. When such large numbers of children were abandoned by their fathers and brought up by single mothers, he said, the result was sure to be wild violence and social chaos. He was excoriated as a racist and the subject was abandoned. The national rate of illegitimacy among blacks that year was 26 percent.

It took just over a decade for the black illegitimacy rate to reach 50 percent. And in 1990, twenty-five years after Moynihan's warning, two-thirds of black children were born to single mothers, many of them teenagers. Only a third of black children lived with both parents even in the first three years of their lives. Seven percent of all black children and 5 percent of black children under the age of three were living with neither a father nor a mother in the house. The rate of illegitimacy more than doubled in one generation.

Social disorder—in its many varieties, and with the assistance of government policies—can perhaps be said to have caused the sudden collapse of family institutions and social bonds that had survived three centuries of slavery and oppression. It is at any rate certain that hundreds of thousands of the children so abandoned have become in their turn a major cause of instability. Most notably they have tended to commit crimes, especially violent crimes, out of all proportion to their numbers. Of all juveniles confined for violent offenses today, less than 30 percent grew up with both parents.

How many killers are there, and who are they? In 1990 a total of 24,932 homicides were reported. Of all killers identified by the nation's police forces and reported to the Department of Justice for that year, 43.7 percent were white and Hispanic and 54.7 percent were black. Whites made up 83.9 percent of the population that year, and blacks 12.3 percent. The rate of homicide committed by whites was thus 5.2 per 100,000, and by blacks 44.7 per 100,000—or about eight times as great. In the large counties analyzed by the Department of Justice, 62 percent of identified killers were black. This is equivalent to a black homicide rate of 50.7 per 100,000—close to ten times the rate among other citizens. Serial killers and mass murderers, however, are overwhelmingly white.

Of the urban killers identified by the Department of Justice in 1988, 90 percent were male. Virtually none were aged fourteen or younger, but 16 percent were aged fifteen to nineteen, 24 percent were twenty to twenty-four, and 20 percent were twenty-five to twenty-nine.

The white and black populations each suffered about 12,000 homicides in 1990. But the black population base is smaller, and the rate at which blacks fall victim is much higher. The victimization rate for white males was 9.0 per 100,000, and for white females 2.8 per 100,000. For black males it was an astonishing 69.2, and for black females it was 13.5. According to the Department of Justice, one out of every twenty-one black men can expect to be murdered. This is a death rate double that of American servicemen in the Second World War.

Prospects for the future are apparent in the facts known about children already born. This is what Senator Moynihan means when he says the next thirty years are "already spoken for."

We first notice the children of the ghetto when they grow muscles—at about the age of fifteen. The children born in 1965 reached their fifteenth year in 1980, and 1980 and 1981 set new records for criminal violence in the United States, as teenage and young adult blacks ripped at the fabric of life in the black inner city. Nevertheless, of all the black children who reached physical maturity in those years, three-quarters had been born to a married mother and father. Not until 1991 did we experience the arrival in their mid-teens of the first group of black youths fully half of whom had been born to single mothers—the cohort born in 1976. Criminal violence particularly associated with young men and boys reached new peaks of destruction in black communities in 1990 and 1991.

In the year 2000 the black youths born in 1985 will turn fifteen. Three-fifths of them were born to single mothers, many of whom were drug-addicted; one in fourteen will have been raised with neither parent at home; unprecedented numbers will have been subjected to beatings and other abuse; and most will have grown up amid the utter chaos pervading black city neighborhoods. It is supremely necessary to change the conditions that are producing such cohorts. But no matter what efforts we now undertake, we have already assured the creation of more very violent young men than any reasonable society can tolerate, and their numbers will grow inexorably for every one of the next twenty years.

In absolute numbers the teenage and young adult population aged fifteen to twenty-four stagnated or actually declined over the past decade. Crime has been rising because this smaller population has grown disproportionately more violent. Now it is about to get larger in size. James Fox, a dean at Northeastern University, in Boston, has shown that from 1965 to 1985 the national homicide rate tracked almost exactly the proportion of the population aged eighteen to twenty-four. Suddenly, in 1985, the two curves diverged sharply. The number of young adults as a proportion of the population declined; but the overall homicide rate went up, because among this smaller group the homicide rate increased by 65 percent in just eight years. Among those aged fourteen to seventeen, the next group of young adults, the homicide rate more than doubled. What we experienced from 1985 on was a conjunction of two terrible arrivals. One train carried the legacy of the 1970s, the children of the explosion of illegitimacy and paternal abandonment. Crack arrived on the same timetable, and unloaded at the same station.

Fox shows further that by the year 2005 the population aged fourteen to seventeen will have increased by a remarkable 23 percent. Professor John DeIulio, of Princeton University, predicts that the number of homicides may soon rise to 35,000 or 40,000 a year, with other violent offenses rising proportionally. Fox calls what we are about to witness an "epidemic" of teenage crime. He does not give a name to our present condition.

Guns

It is a commonplace that many crimes are committed with guns, particularly handguns. In 1993, 69.6 percent of all homicides were committed by gun, four-fifths of these by handgun. Guns were also used in 42.4 percent of all robberies and 25.1 percent of aggravated assaults. The total of such gun felonies reported to the police was about 571,000.

As long as surveys have asked the question, about half of all American households have answered that they own at least one gun. Patterns of ownership, however, have changed. In the 1960s weapons used primarily for sport—rifles and shotguns—made up 80 percent of the approximately 80 million guns in private hands. About 12 percent of the population reported owning one or more handguns. By 1976, with the great postwar crime wave under way, more than 21 percent of the population reported owning handguns—an increase of 75 percent. The largest increases were among nonwhites (by 99 percent), college graduates (by 147 percent), and Jews (by 679 percent, to a total of 14.8 percent reporting handgun ownership, which left them well behind Protestants but ahead of Catholics). By 1978 the estimate of total number of guns owned had increased to roughly 120 million.

In every year since, at least four million new guns have been manufactured or imported. In 1993 there were 5.1 million guns manufactured and another 2.9 million imported. Of the eight million new guns in 1993, half—3.9 million—were handguns. The current estimate is that more than 200 million guns are in private hands.

Twenty states allow any law-abiding citizen to carry a gun concealed on his or her person, and fourteen more states are actively considering such laws. In some of the states where the laws have passed, about 2 percent (Oregon and Florida) or 3 percent (Pennsylvania) of the state's population have applied for and received a permit to carry a concealed handgun at all times. There is evidence that many people own and carry handguns without permits. One 1991 survey reported that a third of all Americans own handguns, another that 7 percent carry them outside the home. A quarter of small business establishments may keep firearms for protection.

Last year the New York Times said that the city's bodegas had become "Island Under Siege," in which fifty store workers were killed in a year. It reported on Omar Rosario, the manager of a grocery store whose previous owner was killed in a holdup. Rosario prepares for work by donning a bulletproof vest and sliding a nine-millimeter semi-automatic into his waistband. When a young man with one arm hidden inside his coat enters the store, "Mr. Rosario takes out his pistol and eases it halfway into his pocket of his pants, his finger on the trigger. He faces the man and lets him see the gun in his hand. He wants to make it clear that if the young man pulls a gun, he will be killed."

Professor Gary Kleck, of Florida State University, has made a close examination of citizens' use of firearms for self-defense, including in "civilian legal defensive homicides." Self-defense is not a crime, and most defensive uses of firearms, even when criminals are killed, are not routinely reported to the FBI. On the basis of local studies Kleck estimates that at least 1,500 citizens used guns to kill criminals in 1980. This is nearly three times the number of criminals killed by the police. The Department of Justice thinks these numbers may be too high. Nevertheless, it is evident that Omar Rosario is not the only citizen with his finger on the trigger.

Beyond the Numbers

For more than twenty years the children of the ghetto have witnessed violent death as an almost routine occurrence. They have seen it on their streets, in their schools, in their families, and on TV. They have lived with constant fear. Many have come to believe that they will not live to see twenty-five. These are often children whose older brothers, friends, and uncles have taught them that only the strong and the ruthless survive. Prison does not frighten them—it is a rite of passage that a majority of their peers may have experienced. Too many have learned to kill without remorse, for a drug territory or for an insult, because of a look or a bump on the sidewalk, or just to do it: why not?

These young people have been raised in the glare of ceaseless media violence and incitement to every depravity of act and spirit. Movies may feature scores of killings in two hours' time, vying to show methods ever more horrific; many are quickly imitated on the street. Television commercials teach that a young man requires a new pair of $120 sneakers each week. Major corporations make and sell records exhorting their listeners to brutalize Koreans, rob store owners, rape women, kill the police. Ashamed and guilt-ridden, elite opinion often encourages even hoodlums to carry a sense of entitlement and grievance against society and its institutions.

These lessons are being taught to millions of children as I write and you read. They have already been taught to the age groups that will reach physical maturity during the rest of this century.

The worst lesson we have taught these benighted children I have saved for last, because it is a lesson we have also taught ourselves: We will do almost anything not to have to act to defend ourselves, our country, or our character as people of decency and strength. We have fled from our cities, virtually abandoning great institutions such as the public schools. We have permitted the spread within our country of wastelands ruled not by the Constitution and lawful authority but by the anarchic force of merciless killers. We have muted our dialogue and hidden our thoughts. We have abandoned millions of our fellow citizens—people of decency and honor trying desperately to raise their children in love and hope—to every danger and degraded assault. We have become isolated from one another, dispirited about any possibility of collective or political action to meet this menace. We shrink in fear of teenage thugs on every street. More important, we shrink even from contemplating the forceful collective action we know is required. We abandon our self-respect and our responsibility to ourselves and our posterity.

How to change all this, how to recover heart and spirit, how to save the lives and souls of millions of children, and how to save ourselves from this scourge of violent anarchy—in short, how to deal with things as they are, how to respond to the implacable and undeniable numbers: this will be the real measure and test of our political system. But more than that, it will be the measure of our own days and work, the test of our own lives and heritage.

Where Do We Start? A Modest Radicalism

In the past decade 200,000 of our citizens have been killed and millions wounded. If we assume, with the FBI, that 47 percent of them were killed by friends and family members, that leaves 106,000 dead at the hands of strangers. Ten years of war in Vietnam killed 58,000 Americans. Over an equal period we have had almost the exact equivalent of two Vietnam Wars right here at home.

Whether fighting the war or fighting against the war, participants and opponents alike engaged Vietnam with fury and passion and a desperate energy. Were we to find such energy, such passion, now, how might we use it? Where would we start?

I suggest simplicity. If your territory and your citizens are under constant deadly assault, the first thing you do is *protect them.*

To do this we need forces. We need a very large number of additional police officers: at least half a million in the next five years, and perhaps more thereafter. We do not need more private police, who protect only the circumscribed property of better-off citizens who can afford to pay; we need public police, whose mission is the protection of all citizens, and who are available for work in the ghettos and housing projects where most of the dying is taking place.

If we as a society expect black citizens to construct reasonable lives, we cannot continue to abandon so many of them and their children to criminal depredation. If we expect children to respect law and the rights of others, it would seem elementary that we must respect the law and their rights enough to keep them from getting murdered.

We need a larger police force not to imprison more of our fellow citizens but to liberate them. The police need not function as the intake valve of a criminal-justice system devoted to the production of more prison inmates, of whom we already have more than is healthy; their true role is to suppress violence and criminal activity, to protect public space that now serves as the playground and possession of the violent. The role of the police is to guard schools and homes, neighborhoods and commerce, and to protect life; they should represent the basic codes and agreements by which we live with one another. Today's vastly under-manned police forces, whose officers race from call to call, taking endless reports of crimes they were not around to prevent, do not control the streets. They do not exercise and cannot embody the authority for which we look to government. Rather, it is the most violent young men of the street who set the tone and filter the light in which the children of the city are growing. *That* is what we need at least half a million new officers just to begin to change.

Some will ask how we are to afford the $30 billion or so a year that this would cost. The question has a ready answer. We have a gross domestic product of more than $6 trillion, and a federal budget of more than $1.6 trillion. President Clinton has requested $261.4 billion for defense against foreign enemies who killed fewer than a hundred Americans in all of last year. It would be silly to suggest that the federal government should not or cannot spend an eighth as much—2 percent of even a shrunken federal budget—to defend the nation against domestic enemies who killed more than 10,000 people who were strangers to them in 1994, and who will surely kill more in every year that lies ahead.

This is not a complete program, because this is not the time for a complete program. *We have to stop the killing.* Beyond doubt we must reform welfare, minimize illegitimacy, change the schools, strengthen employment opportunities, end racism. In the midst of this war, while the killing continues, all that is just talk. And dishonest talk besides: there can be no truth to our public discussions while whites are filled with fear of black violence, and blacks live every day with the fear and bitter knowledge that they and their children have been abandoned to the rule of criminals. If some foreign enemy had invaded New England, slaughtering its people and plundering its wealth, would we be debating agri-cultural subsidies and the future of Medicaid while complaining that the deficit prevented us from enlarging the Army or buying more ammunition? Would the budget really force us to abandon New Hampshire? Why is this case different?

None of This Is Necessary

Some people will say that I propose an army of occupation. But all too many black citizens already live in territories occupied by hostile bands of brigands. How can these citizens be freed except by forces devoted to their liberation?

It is true that the police, especially in the ghettos of older cities, have often been corrupt, brutal, and ineffective, although they are almost always better than most of their critics. The remedy for bad policing is for good people to join the police force and make it better: that is why the one truly promising feature of the 1994 crime bill is the creation of a prototype Police Corps, a police ROTC that will offer four-year college scholarships to the best and most committed of our young people in return for four years of police service following their graduation. Now and for many years into the future the opportunity to give the greatest service to one's fellow citizens will be as a member of a police force—the one truly indispensable agency of a free and civil government.

Others will say—not openly, because this kind of thing is never said openly— that it's hopeless, and that the best we can hope for is that the killers will kill one another and leave the rest of us alone. Indeed, a visitor from another planet might well conclude that only such a belief could explain our society's otherwise inexplicable passivity. History should save us from such vile and horrible thoughts. Despite all vicissitudes, within two generations of Emancipation black families had achieved levels of stability and nurture comparable or superior to those of many immigrant groups. The long history of black people in America has not been one of violent or cruel conduct beyond the national norm. Rather, it is a story of great heroism and dignity, of a steady upward course from slavery to just the other day.

The collapse of the black lower class is a creation not of history but of this generation. It has been a deliberate if misguided act of government to create a welfare system that began the destruction of black family life. It was the dominant culture that desanctified morality, celebrated license, and glorified feckless-ness; as the columnist Joe Klein has observed, it is in moral conduct above all that the rich catch cold and the poor get pneumonia. It was stupidity and cowardice, along with a purposeful impulse toward justice, that led the entire governmental apparatus, the system of law enforcement and social control, to cede the black ghettos to self-rule and virtual anarchy in the 1960s and 1970s, and to abandon them entirely since. It is the evident policy of the entertainment industry to seek profit by exploiting the most degraded aspects of human and social character. None of this is necessary. All of it can be changed.

I have spoken of the need to change conditions among blacks, because they are experiencing the greatest suffering and the gravest danger today. But let none of us pretend that the bell tolls only for blacks; there is no salvation for one race alone, no hope for separate survival. At stake for all of us is the future of American cities, the promise of the American nation, and the survival of our Constitution and of American democracy itself.

Chapter Twenty-five

Crime and Community

Wendy Kaminer

Crime control is not a science; nor is it a religion, a simple matter of revealed truth, except perhaps to those who blame rising crime on the abolition of prayer in the schools. God knows whether restoring school prayer might lower the crime rate. Eighty percent of people surveyed last August believed that increasing the number of police officers would significantly decrease violent crime, and what 80 percent of the people wanted they quickly got from their elected officials: one of the most popular provisions of the new crime bill is the promise of federal dollars for 100,000 new police officers. It has intuitive, commonsense appeal. Even if the police have no direct effect on crime, many people feel safer in their presence, assuming they don't harbor suspicions of police brutality, and when people feel safer, they are more likely to venture out of their homes to make their neighborhoods safer.

The 100,000 new officers are specifically intended to help revitalize neighborhood life; they're supposed to be trained in community policing, a progressive model of police work embraced, at least rhetorically, by practically everyone. Community policing calls for a partnership of the police and local residents, and expands the focus of the police from arrests to intervention and preventive "problem solving." In its most reductive form, this approach is viewed as a shift from deploying police officers in patrol cars that randomly cruise the streets and answer calls for assistance to deploying them on the street and encouraging them to establish ongoing relationships with residents. Community policing is often described simplistically as a return to cops on the beat who are integral parts of the neighborhood.

New Age Cops

In its sophisticated form, however, community policing entails what William Bratton, formerly Boston's and now New York City's police commissioner, has called a "sea change" in the concept of policing, from reactive, "incident-oriented" law enforcement to a hybrid of enforcement and community-service work aimed at crime prevention. It envisions the demilitarization of police departments, a shifting of authority down through management to the ranks, so that cops on the street will have more discretion and can go beyond making arrests to analyzing underlying problems and responding to them with community cooperation. At its most cosmic, community policing requires teaching critical-thinking skills to people who have traditionally been taught to play by the book. Advocates of community policing stress that it is not simply a new program or strategy but a transformative new philosophy—what a New Age cop might call a paradigm shift.

Some observers are skeptical that using federal dollars to hire local police officers will facilitate community policing or enhance public safety. In general, community policing doesn't rely on increasing the numbers of police officers. It seeks to increase community participation in crime control. The idea is that police departments will become more effective not by increasing their numbers but by extending their reach into communities. The ratio of officers to citizens is, in fact, a "poor predictor of violent crime," according to Michael Smith, the president of the Vera Institute of Justice, in Manhattan. People fear street crime greatly, but while crime against strangers is rising, much violent crime still occurs between people who know each other. Private relationships need to be policed, as the history of domestic violence shows, but they need to be policed differently from holdups of convenience stores. Additional police officers will have an impact, however marginal, only in areas where the police departments are now grossly understaffed, Smith believes. In New York City "the number of new cops won't make much difference," he says. "When cutbacks reduced the number of police, the number of arrests per officer rose; crime went up and down during that period." Smith is dismissive of federal funding to hire additional officers: "The analytic work that tells you we need more cops across the board doesn't exist. It was a campaign promise."

Ronald Hampton, the executive director of the National Black Police Association, agrees that on the whole we have enough police officers; he contends that we simply don't educate or use them properly. "We need to focus on what police do, not how many of them are doing it," he says. "If I take a hundred thousand new police officers and put them through the present induction program, most of them won't end up on the street and they won't bring their heads with them if they get there. If we don't first change the philosophy of policing in this country, whatever police officers we add will fall into the black hole that exists in every police department."

Everybody talks about community policing, advocates agree, but few police departments practice it. Michael Smith calls it "rhetorical policing." Herman Goldstein, a professor of law at the University of Wisconsin, stressed last year at a Justice Department conference on community policing that the term "is widely used without any concern for its substance." He said, "Political leaders and, unfortunately, many police leaders hook onto the label for the positive images it projects but do not engage with—or invest in—the concept." Goldstein warns that if "community policing" becomes a catchall term (like "empowerment" or "codependency"), it will be regarded as a panacea for a catchall litany of urban problems. Successful implementation of community policing means fundamentally redefining both police functions and the community's expectations of the police, he says. Service-oriented policing is not intended to satisfy all the needs of communities that are "starved for social services."

If communities are apt to expect too much from community policing, many police departments are still prepared to deliver too little. The scope of the reforms that would be needed and the intensity of internal resistance to them are routinely underestimated or ignored. Hampton says that it could take up to ten years to implement community policing in a typical metropolitan police department, a task complicated by the fact that the average tenure for a police chief today is only about three years.

Mayors come and go as well, which can bring changes in policing priorities. Shortly after taking office this past January, New York City's new mayor, Rudolph Giuliani, called for a reform of the community-policing programs adopted by his predecessor, David Dinkins. Giuliani, a former prosecutor with a penchant for talking tough, criticized community policing for its focus on social services. He suggested that social service is at best an "add-on" to police work and at worst a distraction from crime control. Giuliani's remarks typified the response of law-enforcement traditionalists to new models of policing and missed the point made by advocates of community policing: that crime control includes crime prevention, which requires an understanding of a community's character and its social-service needs.

Turning the "Ship of Policing"

Community policing may be a particularly hard sell at a time when a frightened and angry public is demanding a more punitive justice system, not a more understanding one. But even in the most judicious of times community policing would be difficult to implement. The "ship of policing" will turn slowly, Commissioner Bratton cautions, because "we have to change everything we do"—recruitment, training and supervision, and militaristic management policies. Bratton says he is unaware of any program that teaches community policing "the way we would like it to be taught." There is resistance from the "old guard," who fear losing authority and control as police departments are decentralized, and there is resistance from recruits, "who come in expecting to chase people and do shoot-ups." Bratton says, "Eighty-five percent of police work is not that. The average police officer in America is never going to draw his gun in his entire career."

The image of policing is still shaped by the entertainment industry, Ronald Hampton observes. "Some recruits expect to come here and be Dirty Harry or Don Johnson. We need to shift from a spirit of adventure to a spirit of service." Hampton adds that some recruits who do enter the police academy with an ethic of service leave with a taste for authority, which they find easier to satisfy by policing racial minorities. "The way you police in an affluent white community is not the way you police in a poor black community," he says, and goes on to tell this story of a young black police officer engaged in on-the-job training in the predominantly black neighborhood where he was raised: "I asked him a few questions about his assignment. He said he was assigned to Georgetown, which is about 90 percent white, but he'd been training in a 99 percent black community. He said, 'I'm disappointed. I don't want to go to Georgetown.' He said he wanted to work where the police tell the people what to do, not where the people tell the police. That kid wouldn't have said that before he went into the police academy. Now he's calling the people he grew up with trash; he's calling them scum."

These caveats about the prospects for community policing in the near future do not necessarily mean that the federal promise of new police officers is misguided. Congressman Barney Frank asserts that the current failure to use the police force with the utmost effectiveness and efficiency is no reason not to increase its numbers. Inefficiencies are built into any bureaucracy, he observes, adding that liberals fall back on arguments about inefficiency when they have ideological objections to hiring more officers. "Do they say this about housing? Do they say we shouldn't build any more housing until we learn to use what we have efficiently? They don't say 'No more aid to poor countries unless we learn to do that efficiently' either." Bratton believes that some police departments do need additional officers, although their needs will vary. The Boston Police Department lost people over the past decade through attrition, Bratton notes; Michael Smith stresses that New York City paid for more police officers by raising taxes.

The trouble is, Michael Smith points out, that if the government allocates funds for additional officers, a city like New York will apply for them regardless of need. "Politically, you take what you can get and try to deal with the down side of the gift." What might be the down side of increasing the local police force? Additional officers making additional arrests put additional burdens on local prosecutors, defender services, courts, probation services, and jails. A change to community policing is not necessarily supposed to result in more arrests, since its focus is on prevention. But the standard measure of police effectiveness is the arrest rate, and this will not be abandoned anytime soon, despite all the talk about community policing. Senator Joseph Biden acknowledges that with an influx of new police officers "costs will go way up." (How far up, an official at the Justice Department could not say.) Perhaps in Boston the benefits will outweigh the costs. In New York they may not. More than new police officers, Michael Smith says, New York needs new drug-treatment programs.

"We Know Best"

Underlying the concern about federal funding for cops are larger questions about federal funding in general. Different localities have different public safety needs;

why should Congress decide they need more cops and not more computers ("There are police departments using dial telephones," Senator Orrin Hatch says) or better foster-care or drug-treatment services? One view emerging among many local officials, not surprisingly, favors "decategorizing" federal funding, in order to return to something like a block-grant system that would allow localities some discretion to diagnose their own problems and prescribe their own cures. Instead of allocating money for police officers, the argument goes, Congress should establish a more general, flexible fund for public safety or domestic security. New York could request drug-treatment programs, and Boston could request more police officers. At least Congress could offer localities a menu of law enforcement options, allowing them to choose one from column A and one from column B or C—more cops or computers or security guards for schools.

Attorney General Janet Reno has been obliquely advocating such decentralization for some time. In a speech to the American Bar Association last August she explained the problem of categorized funding like this: "We have created a giant federal government with many agencies designed to help people, and they come up with wonderful programs and come to the community and tell the community, 'We've got this wonderful program but, I'm sorry, you're not eligible for it. Our round grant won't fit in your square hole.' The federal government comes to communities and says, 'We can tell you how to do this; we know best.' " Communities know best, Reno and others suggest.

Perhaps. Increasing local control of federal grant money would be effective to the extent that local officials are smart, innovative, and reasonably honest. It is also true that federal control of funds is as effective as federal officials. Politics, ideology, venality, and incompetence are apt to drive programmatic priorities at the local, state, and federal levels equally. Still, it makes sense to assume that local officials in general have a better, more visceral understanding of local problems. And whether or not decentralization encourages corruption at the local level, corruption is a constant problem that requires constant monitoring at every level; a centralized design of programs may only encourage a different kind of corruption. Local officials complain privately that categorized funding encourages them to lie and vie for programs they don't really need.

There are also questions about how wisely federal officials will distribute funds. The Justice Department recently awarded a small number of community-policing grants, in some cases favoring suburbs and towns with low crime rates over more crime-ridden cities. The relatively bucolic Sandwich, Massachusetts, on Cape Cod, won out over the beleaguered city of Lynn, among other places. Indianapolis lost a grant to an affluent suburb. It doesn't make sense, the city's mayor, Stephen Goldsmith, says. "People in high-crime areas pay taxes that are then allocated, in the form of policing grants, to communities with less crime."

Goldsmith, a former prosecutor, initially welcomed the promise of new police officers. Now he is skeptical about how the Justice Department will implement it. Stressing that crime is primarily a local problem, he contends that decategorizing federal money may be the most important step the federal government could take to enhance public safety.

Federalizing Crime

That crime, like politics, is a local affair is a universally acknowledged truth. In Congress politicians, right and left, often begin discussions of crime control by pointing out that 95 percent of all crime is local. Then they explain the rationale for imposing federal penalties on whatever crime is of particular concern at the moment—carjacking and spouse abuse have been targeted recently. There are good reasons for federalizing these offenses: stolen cars and parts move in inter-state commerce; spouse abuse is still ignored in many states, and if gender-based violence is a form of discrimination, women arguably have a federal right to be free of it.

Indeed, the federalization of a great many crimes can be rationalized; an interstate nexus is rarely hard to find. (The 1964 Civil Rights Act prohibiting racial discrimination in public accommodations was based on the commerce clause of the Constitution.) Arguments about federalization tend to be more political than principled. Liberals tend to contest the federalization of criminal behavior except when civil rights are involved. Conservatives tend to oppose federalizing racial or sexual discrimination, in deference to either states' rights or a free market. People usually want the federal government to extend jurisdiction in areas in which they favor stepped-up enforcement. Or, as Congressman Barney Frank says, "People favor federalizing what they don't like and oppose federalizing what they like."

No one likes juvenile violence, which has increased dramatically and disproportionately. According to a report by Northeastern University's National Crime Analysis Program, from 1985 to 1991 the number of males aged thirteen to seventeen arrested for murder rose by more than 100 percent. Juveniles have been involved in high-profile cases (a thirteen-year-old was among those implicated in the fatal shooting of a British tourist in Florida last fall), and the spectacle of children with guns and no apparent empathy or conscience is particularly chilling. The rise in serious juvenile crime overshadows a recent modest decline in violent crime overall and accounts for much public outcry over violence. So it's not surprising that the Senate voted to federalize a great deal of juvenile crime. Amendments passed hastily by the Senate, without hearings, required that juveniles over the age of thirteen be federally prosecuted as adults for certain crimes involving firearms, federalized the possession of handguns and ammunition by juveniles, and federalized gang activity, loosely defined.

In voting for significant expansions of federal jurisdiction over juveniles, the Senate was undeterred by the absence of a federal system for prosecuting juveniles or federal correctional facilities for incarcerating them. Juvenile justice has traditionally been the province of the states. Federalizing juvenile offenses could require the establishment of a redundant federal system and could also impose additional burdens on the states, if they're required to house juveniles subject to federal prosecution. New York City's commissioner of the Department of Juvenile Justice opposed the Senate bill federalizing the possession of handguns and ammunition in the expectation that it would strain local facilities and increase delays in processing juvenile cases.

But if there are loose theoretical limits and few principled ones to extensions of federal jurisdiction, there are practical limits to what federal prosecutors, defenders, and courts can manage. Federal district courts are already swamped by drug cases that should probably be tried in state courts. It's becoming increasingly difficult to obtain a civil trial. Federal judges tend to oppose the expansion of federal jurisdiction, and the Justice Department seems wary of it as well. An official at the department asserts that some thought has been given to issuing guidelines advising federal prosecutors when to exercise jurisdiction over crimes that are federal and local concurrently. Political reasons for establishing federal jurisdiction don't necessarily translate into legal reasons for exercising it. Congress may enact a broad range of federal criminal laws that federal prosecutors may enforce only erratically, if at all—but there's no clamor yet for truth in legislating.

In recent years Congress has extended federal jurisdiction dramatically in cases involving the use or possession of firearms as well as of drugs. Whatever salutary effect this has had on gun violence has been too subtle to quantify. Liberals have long argued that instead of simply increasing penalties for the illegal use of guns, the federal government should restrict sales to the public. Last year Congress took a small practical step, or a great symbolic leap, in this direction when it passed the Brady bill, which imposes a waiting period on buyers of handguns and was signed into law by President Bill Clinton seven years after it was proposed. The Senate also passed a ban on the sale of guns to minors (which is already illegal in many states) and on the manufacture of certain assault weapons.

Sixty Million Handguns

These were not exactly controversial measures, although they were quite difficult to pass. There is strong majority support for gun control. Seventy percent of Americans want stricter gun laws, according to Gallup; nearly 90 percent of the public favors the Brady bill.

But even supporters of the Brady bill are likely to concede that it will probably have little effect overall on gun violence. Colin Ferguson, who opened fire on a crowded Long Island commuter train last December, killing six people and wounding nineteen, bought his gun in California, after undergoing a sixteen-day waiting period (the store owner added a day "for good measure" to the state's legally mandated fifteen-day period), and there's no persuasive evidence that waiting periods have decreased violent crime in states that already mandate them. A federally mandated waiting period may save a few lives, people say, and it represents a crucial, symbolic defeat for the National Rifle Association. It may also lead to more stringent gun-control laws, as advocates hope and the NRA fears, such as Senator Daniel Patrick Moynihan's proposal to tax ammunition or ban certain kinds of it. But with some 200 million firearms already at large, including 60 million handguns, there's no reason to have high hopes for traditional point-of-purchase prohibitions. Now that this initial battle for gun control has been won, it has become nearly irrelevant to the war against gun violence.

Because gun-control debates have been defined by efforts to restrict the sale of firearms in the face of NRA opposition, alternative strategies for regulating the nation's enormous stockpile of weapons have barely been considered until recently. A report published last year by the National Academy of Sciences suggests adopting some of the tactics used against drugs—focusing on illegal transactions and undesirable uses. A shift in focus away from sweeping, hotly contested bans on possession and use would at least have significant political advantages. The NRA could hardly object to attacks on the black market.

This proposal to concentrate on illegal gun markets does not equate drugs with guns, or one market with the other; nor does it necessarily imply that we should focus exclusively on the illegal supply of guns, as we have traditionally focused on the illegal supply of drugs, ignoring conditions that create the demand. But it is an acknowledgment that effective near-total prohibitions on guns are as unrealistic as prohibitions on drugs and alcohol. Given the American tradition of violent individualism, the staggering number of guns already in circulation, and the likelihood that more or less law-abiding citizens concerned with self-defense will continue to desire guns, the belief that this might someday be a gun-free country seems more and more utopian.

The failure to enact meaningful gun-control measures twenty-five or thirty years ago has made the slogan "When guns are outlawed, only outlaws will have guns" seem almost true. So far the explosion of gun violence may have increased the desire for gun control more than the desire to own guns. (Reported ownership of firearms has remained fairly stable during the past ten years, according to Gallup, while support for gun control has increased.) But the balance could shift if the violence continues; if people lose all faith in the government's ability to protect them, they will take drastic steps to protect themselves, with public approval. Last year a Louisiana jury acquitted Rodney Peairs of manslaughter after he shot and killed a Japanese exchange student who mistakenly rang his doorbell seeking a Halloween party at another address. In the belief that he was defending his home, Peairs asked no questions; the entire encounter took about one minute.

With more and more people feeling besieged, even at home, by nameless strangers, like the man who abducted and killed twelve-year-old Polly Klaas in California, studies demonstrating that keeping a gun at home nearly triples one's risk of being killed (often by someone one knows) will probably have less effect than studies linking smoking to lung cancer. Millions of people start smoking and continue to smoke because they don't really believe that lung cancer will ever attack them. Frightened people will buy guns in the belief that they will never turn them against each other. For many middle-class people who live and work in low-crime areas, fear of crime is often fear of people they don't know.

"Good Kids Have Guns"

Fear seems to play an important role in the proliferation of guns among juveniles, particularly urban minorities, according to David Kennedy, a research fellow at Harvard University's Kennedy School of Government. A recent National Institute of Justice study of male juvenile offenders and male students in inner-city high schools found that "self-protection in a hostile and violent world was the chief reason to own and carry a gun." Twenty-two percent of the students reported owning a gun. Thirty-five percent reported carrying a gun regularly or occasionally; family, friends, and illegal markets were their primary sources. A majority of students (69 percent) came from families in which men owned guns, and nearly half (45 percent) reported having been "threatened or shot at on the way to or from school." Kennedy remarks that youth culture in the inner cities is akin to prison culture: "captive, lawless, dangerous, self-regulated." Depressing as this is, he adds, it does suggest that the market for guns among juveniles may be malleable: control the fear and you control the guns, which in turn decreases the fear.

"Good kids have guns," John Silva, the director of safety and security for the Cambridge, Massachusetts, public schools, observes. "From a district attorney's perspective, a good kid would never carry a gun, but the DAs don't live in the projects. There's so much fear. Good kids who want to go to school and do the right thing—they're afraid of the gangs and the drug dealers; they want to protect themselves and their families. Good kids, bad kids—the categories don't apply anymore."

The Ideological Common Ground of "Community"

If good kids use guns, then crime is not simply a failure of character, as Ronald Reagan once claimed. Nor is it merely a failure of government—to reduce poverty and enable good people to grow. If good kids use guns, then crime is a failure of community. That, at least, is the emerging wisdom about crime.

Talk about community is beginning to dominate criminal-justice debates. Community policing, community defender services, community courts, and community "empowerment" efforts are praised for their "holistic" approach to crime. ("Holistic" is another coming word in crime control.) The concept of community is one that both liberals and conservatives can embrace. The community is a private and a public place, located somewhere between the individual and big government. It combines conservative belief in individual responsibility with liberal faith in collective, civic solutions to the individual's problems.

Politicians who want to sound progressive sometimes claim that partisan approaches to crime are giving way to a new, bipartisan pragmatism. And it is true that liberals and conservatives seem to be staking out some common ground on crime control, at least rhetorically—although the neat divisions between liberal and conservative approaches to crime have always been a little facile. Liberals focus on root causes, we always say, while conservatives focus on controlling the effects of crime. But in fact liberals have never advocated disbanding police departments, tearing down prisons, and ignoring the effects of crime while we await its cure. Nor have conservatives ignored root causes; they've just defined them differently. Every time conservative preachers and politicians rail against pornography, or the media's attack on family values, or the legitimization of homosexuality, they are addressing what they see as root causes of crime. There have even been exceptions to the liberal attachment to individual rights and the conservative attachment to authority. In the gun-control debate conservatives defended the rights of individual gun owners against liberal assertions of the need for social order.

Communitarianism has facilitated liberal appeals to order, because it finesses the conflict between individual rights and social control. Communitarians use the concept of communal "rights" to peace and security as a limit on individual rights to engage in deviant behavior. The concept is misleading: communities don't have rights under our Constitution; they have interests and a presumption of majority rule, which they're required to exercise with respect for individual rights. But the language of communal rights is politically effective; it provides liberals with a way of positing social order as a primary liberal value.

Is this common ground or merely common language? Liberals and conservatives still maintain very different notions about government's proper role in facilitating community development and instilling values in citizens. Orrin Hatch thinks that the federal government should allow each of the fifty states to develop a values curriculum for public schools, without worrying so much about strict separations of Church and State; some religious values, he says, are "generic values that help people realize there is a better way." Janet Reno talks about providing families with social services that will help ensure that every child is raised with a conscience. She talks about the need for community advocates who would help individual citizens obtain the services of their government and mediate disputes with landlords. She talks about pro bono legal work. Under the rubric of "community" Reno can call for a return to the legal-service ethic of the early 1970s while Orrin Hatch calls for government vouchers to ensure school choice, getting values into schools, and "cleaning up" television and movies. Reno does seem ready to provide the broom. It is one of the ironies of the crime debate that liberals and conservatives, while they argue over the ways to address violence directly in real life, may come together over the need to censor violence in the media.

It is fitting, however, that the media emerge as a battleground for crime prevention. Crime-control debates have always been driven by imagery. Members of Congress are used to gesturing on crime, passing laws that are less effective than expressive of an attitude toward crime (they're against it). Crime also undermines the image of America that politicians celebrate: "The American people are fundamentally decent," they intone, as if criminals were of some other species.

Violent crime became a pre-eminent problem last year not because fundamentally decent middle-class people, who set the political agenda, had an awakening of conscience. Rather, they were awakened by fear. Crime began to seem less contained in the inner cities as it spilled out onto highways, into shopping centers and suburban schools. Somehow, it seemed to take us by surprise. "How did this happen?" people ask, surveying the wreckage.

Chapter Twenty-six

The Incidence of Defensive Firearm Use by U.S. Crime Victims, 1987 through 1990

David McDowall and Brian Wiersema

Introduction

Civilian firearm ownership in the United States carries with it the cost of criminal violence. In 1990, gun-wielding offenders victimized 817,200 persons, killing 12,800 and nonfatally injuring 239,400.[1,2] Observers often cite this carnage to justify stricter gun control policies.[3]

Yet guns also may have benefits in defending against crime. Armed victims can thwart offenders, perhaps averting injuries that they would otherwise have suffered. The prospect of firearm resistance may even prevent some crimes from occurring at all. Critics of firearm control often stress these possibilities.[1]

The incidence of firearm resistance is important in comparing the crime-related costs and benefits of private guns. Criminal offenders may be less likely to obey firearm laws than are other citizens. If firearm defense is common, limiting access to guns may then make the law-abiding population more vulnerable to harm.

We used the National Crime Victimization Survey to study defensive firearm use. We were interested in the incidence of defense and the situations in which it occurred.

Methods

The National Crime Victimization Survey is a multistage probability sample of 59,000 housing units in the United States. It is conducted by the U.S. Bureau of the Census for the U.S. Bureau of Justice Statistics. Its primary use is to estimate the incidence of crime in the nation.[2,5]

Housing units remain in the National Crime Victimization Survey for three years, and residents aged twelve or older are interviewed at six-month intervals. Respondents who report an attempted or completed victimization answer de-

From *The American Journal of Public Health* 84 (December 1994): 1982–84. Reprinted by permission of *The American Journal of Public Health*.

tailed questions about the incident. The Victimization Survey gathers data on six crimes: rape, robbery, assault, burglary, personal and household larceny, and motor vehicle theft.

If victims report seeing an offender, Victimization Survey interviewers ask, "Was there anything you did or tried to do about the incident while it was going on?"[5] Victims who say that they took action then describe what they did. Interviewers code these responses into one or more of sixteen categories, including "attacked offender with gun; fired gun" and "threatened offender with gun." The interviewers continue asking "anything else?" until the victims report no further action.

The survey follows these questions with an additional probe: "Did you do anything (else) with the idea of protecting yourself or your property while the incident was going on?" Again, victims who respond affirmatively are requested to describe their activities.

Our study examined the four years from 1987 through 1990. We measured firearm protection as an attempted or completed crime in which the victim reported using a gun to attack or threaten an offender.

Our estimates are criminal incident counts, weighted to represent the population at risk.[2] The estimates for personal crimes (robbery, rape, assault, and personal larceny) represent the resident noninstitutional population of the United States, aged twelve or older. The estimates for household crimes (burglary, household larceny, and motor vehicle theft) represent the nation's housing units. We computed standard errors by using the generalized variance formulas of the U.S. Bureau of Justice Statistics.[5]

Unlike most published National Crime Victimization Survey estimates, we included series victimizations. These are three or more similar crimes that the victim cannot recall separately.[5] Because respondents cannot accurately describe each offense, we counted a series victimization as a single incident.

Results

National Crime Victimization Survey Estimates

From 1987 through 1990 there were an estimated 258,460 incidents of firearm resistance, a mean of 64,615 annually (Table 26.1). During the same period there were an estimated 143,995,448 incidents of crime. Thus, fewer than 2 victims in 1,000 defended themselves with guns.

Considering violent crimes alone, an estimated 23,011,377 rapes, robberies, and assaults occurred over the period. Victims used firearms for self-defense in 190,483 of these (47,620 per year), 0.83 percent of the total.

The estimates for defense against rape, personal larceny, and motor vehicle theft each rest on fewer than ten sample cases. The standard errors for these crimes should be cautiously interpreted, because 95 percent confidence intervals will include negative values.

National Crime Victimization Survey Estimates of Number of Self-Defensive Firearm Incidents, by Type of Crime

Type of Crime	No. of Incidents, 1987–1990	SE	Mean No. of Incidents per Year
Rape[a]	7,552	5,359	1,888.00
Robbery	30,900	9,505	7,725.00
Assault	152,031	30,290	38,007.75
Personal larceny[a]	2,056	3,581	514.00
Burglary	34,259	12,104	8,564.75
Household larceny	28,139	12,960	7,034.75
Motor vehicle theft[a]	3,523	3,660	880.75
Total	258,460	41,012	64,615.00

[a] Estimate based on fewer than 10 sample cases.

About 71 percent of the defensive incidents involved crimes by strangers (Table 26.2). The remaining incidents with known relationships were divided almost evenly between casual acquaintances and persons well known to the victim. Victims shot at offenders in 71,549 incidents (17,887 per year), 28 percent of the cases.

The National Crime Victimization Survey includes self-defense by police officers in the line of duty. Although the survey does not provide detailed occupational information, we could identify government employees who used guns to resist crimes at work. There were an estimated 50,626 such incidents over the period, about 20 percent of the protective cases. If these incidents involve police officers—as seems likely—the annual estimate of *civilian* use drops to 51,959.

Evaluation of Biases in the National Crime Victimization Survey Estimates

Assault is the least completely reported crime in the National Crime Victimization Survey, and underreporting is especially large for assaults by relatives and other nonstrangers.[5,6] If assaults involving firearm resistance are similar to other assaults, Victimization Survey estimates of gun defense will be downwardly biased.

According to our estimates, there was an annual mean of 1,886 incidents of firearm defense against assaults by friends and relatives. Although underreporting cannot be accurately measured, a rough way to gauge its effect is to weight these incidents by some correction factor.

One test of the accuracy of the National Crime Victimization Survey examined persons already known to be victims from records in police files.[7] These known victims reported to the survey only 22.2 percent of the domestic assaults recorded by the police. Applying a weight of 4.5 (that is, 1/.222) to defenses against assaults by family or friends increases the *total* annual estimate of firearm resistance to 71,216 incidents.

This "correction" is of limited value. Police records are themselves inaccurate, and other procedures would produce other results. Still, the correction empha-

TABLE 26.2

National Crime Victimization Survey Estimates of Number of Self-Defensive Firearm Incidents, by Victim-Offender Relationship and by Use of Gun

	No. of Incidents 1987–1990	SE	Mean No. of Incidents per Year
Relationship between victm and offender			
Stranger	182,368	34,452	45,592.00
Casual acquaintance	23,003	12,237	5,750.75
Well known	24,955	12,746	6,238.75
Undetermined	28,134	13,533	7,033.50
Manner in which victim used firearm			
Discharged firearm	71,549	21,581	17,887.25
Used firearm only to threaten offender	186,911	34,878	46,727.75

sizes the infrequency of firearm defense against assaults by friends or family. More extreme weighting factors would not greatly change the findings.

Popular discussions of firearm resistance often concentrate on crimes by strangers. The National Crime Victimization Survey estimate of 45,592 annual incidents involving strangers is less vulnerable to response error than is the nonstranger estimate, and it is of considerable interest by itself.

Other sampling and nonsampling errors also affect the National Crime Victimization Survey. For example, the survey may often miss individuals involved in deviant or criminal lifestyles.[8] These persons face high victimization risk, and omitting them might underestimate firearm defense. On the other hand, the Victimization Survey considers only the respondent's point of view, and in some assaults it is difficult to distinguish the victim from the offender. Here the survey might overestimate resistance.

We cannot assess the impact of these errors. Yet given the magnitude of the estimates, we believe that any bias more likely involves tens of thousands of incidents rather than hundreds of thousands.

Discussion

Cook used the National Crime Victimization Survey to examine firearm defense against burglaries, robberies, and assaults.[9] Our results are compatible with his, but they consider a wider range of crimes.

Yet our estimates are much smaller than those by Kleck, who concluded that there may be one million defensive incidents each year.[10,11] Kleck's findings are widely cited in scholarly and popular media,[12–17] and it is useful to consider his procedures.

Kleck derived his estimates from a survey that posed the following question to 1,228 registered voters:[18]

> Within the past five years have you, yourself, or another member of your household used a handgun, even if it was not fired, for self-protection or for the protection of

property at home, work, or elsewhere, excluding military service and police security work?

Four percent of the respondents reported handgun self-protection.

Kleck assumed that protective incidents were spread evenly over the five years and that households could experience only one incident. If this were true, a proportion of .008 households used handguns for protection each year. Kleck multiplied .008 by the number of households recorded in the 1980 census, and he weighted the result by estimates of national handgun and long-gun ownership. In two analyses with slightly different assumptions, Kleck computed total annual estimates of 999,068 and 783,000 incidents of firearm protection.

Unfortunately, Kleck's survey question did not confine self-defense to attempted victimizations. Merchants who arm themselves before making night bank deposits might view this as self-protection even if they have never encountered a robber. Motorists who carry guns in their cars might assert that they use the weapons for protection although they have never displayed them. Persons who have used firearms to settle arguments might believe that they have prevented assaults. In a survey of prison inmates, 63 percent of those who fired guns during crimes described their actions as self-defense.[19]

Kleck's findings rest on forty-nine respondents, and any person who reported self-defense without a victimization would noticeably influence the results. National Crime Victimization Survey interviewers ask about self-defense only when respondents report a crime, and the survey screens out acts that are not illegal. We believe that the Victimization Survey provides a stronger basis for inference than do Kleck's methods.

Implications of the National Crime Victimization Survey Estimates

The National Crime Victimization Survey estimates imply that firearms should not be disregarded as a defense against crime. From 1987 through 1990, there were an estimated 258,460 incidents of armed resistance. In 71,549 of these, victims believed themselves to be in enough peril to fire their weapons.

Yet the results also show that defensive gun use is infrequent compared with the incidence of crime. The National Crime Victimization Survey yields an estimate of 2,628,532 nonfatal gun crimes from 1987 through 1990. Adding to this the 46,319 firearm homicides over the period, gun offenses exceeded protective incidents by more than ten to one.[1,20–22]

Further, there were an estimated 500,206 National Crime Victimization Survey incidents in which the offender shot at or wounded the victim. Including homicides, criminal shootings were thus 7.6 times more frequent than were shootings in self-defense.

Altogether, our results suggest that criminals face little threat from armed victims. The probability of firearm resistance is not zero. Yet given that half of U.S. households own a gun, armed self-defense is extremely uncommon.[9] Coupled with the risks of keeping a gun for protection, these results raise questions about the collective benefits of civilian firearm ownership for crime control.[23-26]

REFERENCES

1. *Crime in the United States, 1990.* Washington, DC: Federal Bureau of Investigation; 1991.

2. *National Crime Surveys: National Sample, 1986–1991* [near-term data], Washington, DC: U.S. Bureau of Justice Statistics; 1992. Computer files. Distributed by the Interuniversity Consortium for Political and Social Research, Ann Arbor, Mich.

3. Kassirer J P. Firearms and the killing threshold. *N Engl J Med.* 1991;325:1647–1649.

4. Baker J J. Second amendment message in Los Angeles. *Am Rifleman.* 1992;140:32–35.

5. *Criminal Victimization in the United States, 1991.* Washington, DC: U.S. Bureau of Justice Statistics; 1992.

6. Skogan W G. *Issues in the Measurement of Victimization.* Washington, DC: U.S. Dept. of Justice; 1981.

7. Turner A G. The San Jose recall study. In: Lehnen R G, Skogan W G, eds. *The National Crime Survey: Working Papers,* Vol. 1. Washington, DC: U.S. Dept. of Justice; 1981.

8. Cook P J. The case of the missing victims: gunshot woundings in the National Crime Survey. *J Quant Criminology.* 1985;1:91–102.

9. Cook P J. The technology of personal violence. In: Tonry M, ed. *Crime and Justice: An Annual Review of Research,* Vol. 14. Chicago: University of Chicago Press; 1991:1–71.

10. Kleck G. Crime control through the private use of armed force. *Soc Probl.* 1988; 35:1–21.

11. Kleck G. *Point Blank: Guns and Violence in America.* New York: Aldine De Gruyter; 1991.

12. Suter E A. Firearms and the killing threshold. *N Engl J Med.* 1992;326:1159. Letter.

13. Kates D B. The value of civilian handgun possession as a deterrent to crime or a defense against crime. *Am J Criminal Law.* 1991;18:113–167.

14. Go ahead, make our day. *The New Republic.* February 22, 1988:7–9.

15. Do guns save lives? *Time.* August 12, 1988:25–26.

16. Will G F. Are we "a nation of cowards?" *Newsweek.* November 15, 1993:93–94.

17. Kopel D B. Hold your fire: gun control won't stop rising violence. *Policy Rev.* 1993; 63: 58–65.

18. *Study 1760, Violence in America* [photocopied questionnaire and marginal distributions]. Washington, DC: Peter D. Hart Research Associates, Inc; 1981.

19. Wright J D, Rossi P H. *Armed and Considered Dangerous: A Survey of Felons and Their Firearms.* New York: Aldine De Gruyter; 1986.

20. *Crime in the United States, 1987.* Washington, DC: Federal Bureau of Investigation; 1988.

21. *Crime in the United States, 1988.* Washington, DC: Federal Bureau of Investigation; 1989.

22. *Crime in the United States, 1989.* Washington, DC: Federal Bureau of Investigation; 1990.

23. Kellermann A L, Reay D T. Protection or peril? An analysis of firearm-related deaths in the home. *N Engl J Med.* 1986;314:1557–1560.

24. Wintemute G J, Teret S P, Kraus J F, Wright M A, Bradfield G. When children shoot children: 88 unintended deaths in California. *JAMA*. 1987;257:3107–3109.

25. Kellermann A L, Rivara F P, Somes G, et al. Suicide in the home in relation to gun ownership. *N Engl J Med*. 1992;327:467–472.

26. Kellermann A L, Rivara F P, Rushforth N B, et al. Gun ownership as a risk factor for homicide in the home. *N Engl J Med*. 1993;329:1084–1091.

Chapter Twenty-seven

Does Allowing Law-Abiding Citizens To Carry Concealed Handguns Save Lives?

John R. Lott, Jr.

Introduction

To gun control advocates, the logic of opposing concealed handgun laws is straightforward. If guns are introduced into a violent encounter, the probability that someone will die increases. Murders are viewed as arising from unintentional fits of rage that are quickly regretted, and simply keeping guns out of people's reach will prevent deaths. More guns are also seen as leading to more accidental gun deaths. The solution is clear: more regulation or even the complete elimination of guns.

Those who advocate letting law-abiding citizens carry concealed handguns point to polls of American citizens undertaken by organizations like the *Los Angeles Times* and Gallup showing that Americans defend themselves with guns between 764,000 and 3.6 million times each year, with the vast majority of cases simply involving people brandishing a gun to prevent attack.[1] Victims (such as women or the elderly) are most often much weaker than the criminals that attack them. Guns are seen by these advocates as the great equalizer, and allowing concealed handguns provides citizens even greater ability to defend themselves.

While cases like the 1992 incident in which a Japanese student was shot on his way to a Halloween party in Louisiana make international headlines,[2] they are rare. In another highly publicized case, a Dallas resident recently became the only Texas resident so far charged with using a permitted concealed weapon in a fatal shooting.[3] Yet, in neither case was the shooting found to be criminal.[4] The rarity of these incidents is reflected in Florida statistics: 221,443 licenses were issued between October 1, 1987, and April 30, 1994, but only eighteen crimes involving firearms were committed by those with licenses.[5] While a statewide breakdown on the nature of those crimes is not available, Dade County records indicate that four crimes involving a permitted handgun took place there be-

From the *Valparaiso University Law Review* 31 (1997): 355–63. Reprinted with permission of the *Valparaiso University Law Review*.

tween September 1987 and August 1992 and none of those cases resulted in injury.[6]

The potential defensive nature of guns is indicated by the different rates of so-called "hot burglaries," where residents are at home when the criminals strike.[7] Almost half the burglaries in Canada and Britain, which have tough gun control laws, are "hot burglaries." By contrast, the United States, with laxer restrictions, has a "hot burglary" rate of only 13 percent. Consistent with this rate, surveys of convicted felons in America reveal that they are much more worried about armed victims than they are about running into the police. This fear of potentially armed victims causes American burglars to spend more time than their foreign counterparts "casing" a house to ensure that nobody is home. Felons frequently comment in these interviews that they avoid late-night burglaries because "that's the way to get shot."[8]

A similar case exists for concealed handguns. The use of concealed handguns by some law-abiding citizens may create a positive externality for others. By the very nature of these guns being concealed, criminals are unable to tell whether the victim is armed before they strike, thus raising criminals' expected costs for committing many types of crimes

Stories of individuals using guns to defend themselves have helped motivate thirty-one states to adopt laws requiring authorities to issue, without discretion, concealed-weapons permits to qualified applicants.[9] This figure constitutes a dramatic increase from the nine states that allowed concealed weapons in 1986.[10] While many studies examine the effects of gun control,[11] and a smaller number of papers specifically address the right to carry concealed firearms,[12] these papers involve little more than either time-series or cross-sectional evidence comparing mean crime rates, and none controls for variables that normally concern economists (for example, the probability of arrest and conviction and the length of prison sentences).[13] These papers fail to recognize that it is frequently only the largest counties by population that are very restrictive when local authorities have been given discretion in granting concealed handgun permits. Therefore, state "shall issue" concealed handgun permit laws, which require permit requests be granted by the local authorities unless the individual has a criminal record or a history of significant mental illness,[14] will not alter the number of permits being issued in all counties. In other words, since rural counties generally already permit a substantial amount of concealed handguns, the effect of introducing a state law should be small in those counties.

Other papers suffer from other weaknesses. The paper by McDowall et al.,[15] which evaluates right-to-carry provisions, was widely cited in the popular press. Yet, their study suffers from many major methodological flaws: for instance, without explanation, they pick only three cities in Florida and one city each in Mississippi and Oregon (despite the provisions involving statewide laws); and they neither use the same sample period nor the same method of picking geographical areas for each of those cities.[16]

Anecdotal evidence is widely available from both sides, with the news regularly containing stories on gun violence. While defensive uses of guns are neither as dramatic nor as frequently reported, the stories have played a large role in inducing thirty-one states to gamble that concealed handguns will deter crime by guaranteeing their citizens the right to carry concealed handguns if they do not have a criminal record or histories of significant mental illness. This constitutes a dramatic increase from the nine states that allowed concealed weapons in 1986. While the effects described by both sides exist, the question is really what the net effect of such laws is: are more lives saved or lost as a result of allowing law-abiding citizens to carry concealed handguns?

Anecdotal evidence obviously cannot resolve this debate. To provide a more systematic answer, I recently completed a study with David Mustard, a graduate student at the University of Chicago, analyzing the FBI's crime statistics. Our paper uses annual cross-sectional time-series county level crime data for all 3,054 U.S. counties from 1977 to 1992 to investigate the impact of "shall issue" right-to-carry firearm laws. It is also the first paper to study the questions of deterrence using these data. While many recent crime studies employ proxies for deterrence, such as police expenditures or general levels of imprisonment, we are able to use arrest rates by type of crime, and also, for a subset of our data, conviction rates and sentence lengths by type of crime.

We also attempt to analyze a question noted but not empirically addressed in this literature: the concern over causality between increases in handgun usage and crime rates. Is it higher crime that leads to increased handgun ownership, or the reverse? The issue is more complicated than simply whether carrying concealed firearms reduces murders because there are questions such as whether criminals might substitute between different types of crimes as well as the extent to which accidental handgun deaths might increase.

The Results

The most conservative estimates show that adopting these so-called "shall issue" or nondiscretionary permit laws reduced murders by 8 percent, rapes by 5 percent, aggravated assaults by 7 percent, and robbery by 3 percent. To put it another way, if those states that did not have concealed handgun laws in 1992 had adopted them, citizens in those states would have avoided suffering approximately 1,500 murders, 4,200 rapes, over 60,000 aggravated assaults, and 12,000 robberies. Criminals do apparently respond to deterrence.

A recent National Institute of Justice study estimates the costs of different types of crime based upon lost productivity, out-of-pocket expenses such as medical bills and property losses, and losses for fear, pain, suffering, and lost quality of life.[17] While there are questions about using jury awards to measure losses such as fear, pain, suffering, and lost quality of life, the estimates provide us one method of comparing the reduction in violent crimes with the increase in property crimes. The estimated gain from allowing concealed handguns is over $5.74 billion in 1992 dollars. The reduction in violent crimes represents a gain of $6.2 billion ($4.28 billion from murder, $1.4 billion from aggravated assault, $374 million from rape, and $98 million from robbery), while the increase in property crimes represents a loss of $417 million ($343 million from auto theft, $73 million from larceny, and $1.5 million from burglary).

These estimates are probably most sensitive to the value of life used.[18] Higher estimated values of life will increase the net gains from concealed handgun use, while lower values of life will reduce the gains. To the extent that people are taking greater risks towards crime because of any increased safety produced by concealed handgun laws, these numbers will underestimate the total savings from concealed handguns.

While the initial drop in crime is frequently small, the longer the law is in effect the larger the drop in crime will be over time. Figures 27.1 and 27.2 illustrate this relationship for murder and rape.[19] This pattern closely tracks the changes in concealed handgun permits issued over time. For example, while only 33,541 permits were issued in Florida during the first year that the law was in effect, 67,043 permits had been issued by the end of the fourth year and 192,016 permits at the end of the ninth. Where county level concealed handgun permits numbers were available (Pennsylvania and Oregon), we found direct evidence that increases in the number of handgun permits reduced crime, though the relationships were not always statistically significant.

The benefits of concealed handguns are not limited to those who use a handgun in self-defense. By virtue of the fact that handguns are concealed, criminals

FIGURE 27.1
The Effect of Concealed Handgun Laws on Rape Rates

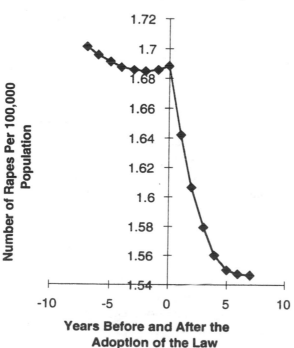

FIGURE 27.2
The Effect of Concealed Handgun Laws on Murder Rates

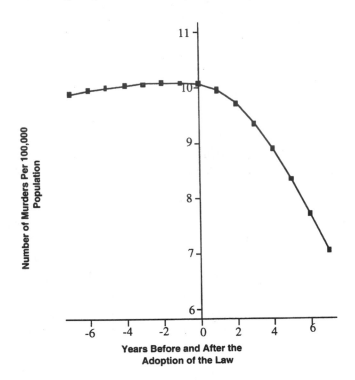

are unable to tell whether a potential victim is able to defend herself until they attack, thus making it less attractive for criminals to commit crimes where they come into direct contact with victims. Citizens who have no intention of ever carrying a concealed handgun in a sense "free ride" off the crime-fighting efforts of their fellow citizens.

Yet, while some criminals avoid crimes like robbery after concealed handgun laws are passed, they do not necessarily stop committing crime entirely. Some evidence indicated that criminals substituted crimes where the risks of confronting an armed victim are much lower. Indeed, the drawback of these laws is that while violent crimes fell, property offenses like larceny (such as stealing from unattended automobiles or vending machines) and auto theft rose.

Our study also provided some surprises. While support for strict gun control laws has usually been strongest in large cities, right-to-carry laws produced the largest drops in violent crimes in counties with the highest populations and highest crime rates. For example, in counties with populations over 200,000, concealed handgun laws produced an average drop in murder rates of over 13 percent. The half of the counties with the highest murder rates experienced over a 10 percent drop in murders. The half of the counties with the highest rape rates saw rapes fall by over 7 percent.

Concealed handguns also appear to be a great equalizer among the sexes. Murder rates decline when either more women or more men carry concealed handguns, but the effect is especially pronounced for women. An additional woman carrying a concealed handgun reduces the murder rate for women by about three to four times more than an additional man carrying a concealed handgun reduces the murder rate for men. Possibly, this arises because allowing a woman to defend herself with a concealed handgun represents a much larger change in her ability to defend herself than the change created by providing a man with a handgun.

Despite all the attention given to the 1994 Brady Law, which imposed waiting periods on gun purchases across the United States, our study is the first to provide direct evidence of the Brady Law's effect on crime rates. Using county level crime and punishment data available up through 1995 for Arizona, we find that the law's implementation is associated with both higher aggravated assault and rape rates. National data on state waiting period laws implies that there is no systematic relationship between either the presence or the length of the waiting period and the level of crime. However, there is some evidence that laws that punish criminals for using a gun in the commission of a crime reduce the number of crimes

We also found some evidence on whether permitted handguns will be used in heated disputes such as at traffic accidents. With evidence now available from thirty-one states, a few of which have had these laws for many decades, there is still only one recorded incident from earlier this year in Texas, where a permitted handgun was used in a shooting following a traffic accident. Even in that one case, a grand jury found that the shooting was in self-defense, since the driver who did the shooting did so only while he was being beaten by the other driver.

And what about accidental deaths? The number of accidental handgun deaths each year is fewer than 200. Our estimates imply that if the states without "shall issue" laws were to adopt them, the increase in accidental handgun deaths would be at most nine more deaths per year. Even the largest possible increase is quite small compared to the at least 1,500 fewer murders that would be produced.

The Effect on Youth

There is also the question of what effect concealed handgun laws have on determining which types of people are more likely to be murdered. Using the *Uniform Crime Reports Supplementary Homicide Reports* we were able to obtain annual state level data from 1977 to 1992 on the percent of victims by sex, race, and age, as well as information on whether the victim and the offender knew each other (whether they were members of the same family, knew each other but were not members of the same family, strangers, or the relationship was unknown).[20] Generally, the drop in murders that follows adoption of nondiscretionary concealed handgun laws is true across the entire range of potential victims. While the laws lower slightly the age of victims (consistent with the notion that concealed handguns deter crime against adults more than young people because only adults can legally carry concealed handguns), the effect is statistically insignificant. Possibly some of the benefits from adults carrying concealed handguns are conferred to younger people who may be protected by these adults.

Assessing the Results

How much confidence do we have in our results? No single study is likely to end the debate on concealed handguns, but ours provides the first systematic national evidence; and the almost 50,000 observations in our data set allow us to control for a range of factors that have never been accounted for in any previous study of crime, let alone any previous gun control study. By contrast, the largest prior study examined only 170 cities within a single year.[21] Among other variables, our regressions control for arrest and conviction rates, prison sentences, changes in handgun laws such as waiting periods or those imposing penalties when a gun is used in the commission of a crime, income, poverty, unemployment, and demographic changes.

Preventing law-abiding citizens from carrying handguns does not end violence, but merely makes them more vulnerable to being attacked. The very large size and strength of our results should at least give pause to those who oppose concealed handguns. Chances to relax regulations that potentially offer at least 8 percent drops in murder rates are difficult to ignore.

NOTES

1. Gary Kleck and Marc Gertz, *Armed Resistance to Crime: The Prevalence and Nature of Self-Defense with a Gun*, 86 J. CRIM. L. & CRIMINOLOGY 150, 153, 180, 180–82 (1995). Using the National Crime Victimization Survey (NCVS), Cook further states that each year there are "only" 80,000 to 82,000 defensive uses of guns during assaults, robberies, and household burglaries. *Id.* at 153. Unlike the surveys cited above, the NCVS is not a representative sample of the national population. Philip J. Cook, *The Technology of Personal Violence, in* 14 CRIME & JUST. 10, 11 n.4 (Michael Tonry ed., 1991). It is very easy to find people arguing that concealed handguns will have no deterrent effect. H. RICHARD UVILLER, VIRTUAL JUSTICE (1996) writes that, "[m]ore handguns lawfully in civilian hands will not reduce deaths from bullets and cannot stop the predators from enforcing their criminal demands and expressing their lethal purposes with the most effective tool they can get their hands on." *Id.* at 95.

2. Japan Economic Newswire, *U.S. Jury Clears Man Who Shot Japanese Student*, KYODO NEWS SERVICE, May 24, 1993; Lori Sharn, *Violence Shoots Holes in USA's Tourist Image*, USA TODAY, Sept. 9, 1993, at 2A.

3. Dawn Lewis of Texans Against Gun Violence provided a typical reaction from gun control advocates to the grand jury decision not to charge Gordon Hale. She said, "We are appalled. This law is doing what we expected, causing senseless death." Mark Potok,

Texan Says Gun Law Saved His Life 'I Did What I Thought I Had to Do,' USA TODAY, Mar. 22, 1996, at 3A. For a more recent evaluation of the Texas experience, see *Few Problems Reported After Allowing Concealed Handguns, Officers Say*, FORT WORTH STAR TELEGRAM, July 16, 1996, at A1. By the end of June 1996, more than 82,000 permits had been issued in Texas.

4. In fact, police accidentally killed 330 innocent individuals in 1993, compared to the mere 30 innocent people accidentally killed by private citizens who mistakenly believed the victim was an intruder. John R. Lott, Jr., *Now That the Brady Law Is Law, Are You Any Safer Than Before?* PHILA. INQUIRER, Feb. 1, 1994, at A9.

5. Clayton E. Cramer and David B. Kopel, *'Shall Issue': The New Wave of Concealed Handgun Permit Laws*, 62 TENN. L. REV. 679, 691 (1995). An expanded version of this paper dated 1994 is available from the Independence Institute, Golden, Colorado. Similarly, Multnomah County, Oregon, issued 11,140 permits over the period January 1990 to October 1994 and experienced five permit holders being involved in shootings, three of which were considered justified by grand juries. Bob Barnhart, *Concealed Handgun Licensing in Multnomah County* (mimeo Intelligence/Concealed Handgun Unit: Multnomah County, October 1994). Out of the other two cases, one was fired in a domestic dispute and the other was an accident that occurred while an assault rifle was being unloaded. *Id.*

6. Cramer and Kopel, *supra* note 5, at 691–92.

7. For example, see DAVID B. KOPEL, THE SAMURAI, THE MOUNTIE, AND THE COWBOY 155 (1992).

8. JAMES D. WRIGHT & PETER H. ROSSI, ARMED AND CONSIDERED DANGEROUS: A SURVEY OF FELONS AND THEIR FIREARMS 145 (1986). Wright and Rossi interviewed felony prisoners in ten state correctional systems and found that 56 percent said that criminals would not attack a potential victim who was known to be armed. *Id.* They also found evidence that criminals in those states with the highest levels of civilian gun ownership worried the most about armed victims. *Id.*

Examples of stories where people successfully defend themselves from burglaries with guns are quite common. *See, e.g., Burglar Puts 92-Year-Old in the Gun Closet and Is Shot*, N.Y. TIMES, Sept. 7, 1995, at A16; George F. Will, *Are We 'A Nation of Cowards'?*, NEWSWEEK, Nov. 15, 1993 (discussing more generally the benefits produced from an armed citizenry).

9. These states are Alabama, Alaska, Arizona, Arkansas, Connecticut, Florida, Georgia, Idaho, Indiana, Kentucky, Louisiana, Maine, Mississippi, Montana, Nevada, New Hampshire, North Carolina, North Dakota, Oklahoma, Oregon, Pennsylvania, South Carolina, South Dakota, Tennessee, Texas, Utah, Vermont, Virginia, Washington, West Virginia, and Wyoming.

10. These states were Alabama, Connecticut, Indiana, Maine, New Hampshire, North Dakota, South Dakota, Vermont, and Washington. Fourteen other states provide local discretion on whether to issue permits: California, Colorado, Delaware, Hawaii, Iowa, Louisiana, Maryland, Massachusetts, Michigan, Minnesota, New Jersey, New York, Rhode Island, and South Carolina.

11. For a survey, see Gary Kleck, *Guns and Violence: An Interpretive Review of the Field*, 1 SOC. PATH. 12 (1995).

12. *See, e.g.*, Philip J. Cook et al., *Regulating Gun Markets*, 86 J. CRIM. L. & CRIMINOLOGY 59 (1995); Cramer and Kopel, *supra* note 5; David McDowall et al., *Easing Concealed Firearms Laws: Effects on Homicide in Three States*, 86 J. CRIM. L. & CRIMINOLOGY 193 (1995); Gary Kleck and E. Britt Patterson, *The Impact of Gun Control and Gun Ownership Levels on Violence Rates*, 9 J. OF QUANTITATIVE CRIMINOLOGY 249 (1993).

13. Kleck and Patterson, *supra* note 12, at 250. All 22 gun control papers studied by Kleck use either cross-sectional state or city data or use time-series data for the entire United States or a particular city.

14. Cramer and Kopel, *supra* note 5, at 680–707.

15. McDowall et al., *supra* note 12.

16. Equally damaging, the authors appear to concede in a discussion that follows their piece that their results are highly sensitive to how they define the crimes that they study. *Id.* at 202–4. Even with their strange sample selection techniques, total murders appear to fall after the passage of concealed weapon laws. Because the authors examine only murders committed with guns, there is no attempt to control for any substitution effects that may occur between different methods of murder. For an excellent discussion of the McDowall et al. paper, see Daniel D. Polsby, *Firearms Costs, Firearms Benefits and the Limits of Knowledge*, 86 J. CRIM. L. & CRIMINOLOGY 207 (1995).

17. TED R. MILLER ET AL., VICTIM COSTS AND CONSEQUENCES: A NEW LOOK (1996).

18. MILLER ET AL., *supra* note 17, set the value of one life at about $3 million in 1992 dollars. *Id.* at 21.

19. *See* Figures 27.1 and 27.2. The figures were derived from the predicted values generated from regressions where separate time trends and those time trends squared were used before and after the implementation of the law. In estimating these regressions, we controlled for measures of income, unemployment, poverty, detailed demographic characteristics, changing arrest rates, population density, fixed year and county effects, as well as many other variables.

20. While county level data were provided in the *Supplementary Homicide Report*, matching these county observations with those used in the *Uniform Crime Reports* proved unusually difficult. A unique county identifier was used in the *Supplementary Homicide Report* and it was not consistent across years. In addition, some caution is suggested in using both the Mortality Detail Records and the *Supplementary Homicide Report* since the murder rates reported in both sources have relatively low correlations of less than .7 with the murder rates reported in *Uniform Crime Reports*. This is especially surprising for the *Supplementary Report* which is derived from the UCR.

21. Kleck and Patterson, *supra* note 12, at 256.

Chapter Twenty-eight

Should You Own a Gun?

Gordon Witkin

In a nation gripped by fear of crime, it has become an essential question: Should you buy a gun to protect yourself? More and more people are answering in the affirmative. As many as 216 million firearms are in private hands nationwide, more than double the total in 1970, and a new *U.S. News* poll reveals that fully 45 percent of gun owners, asked why they have guns, cite self-protection as one of the main reasons.

While the violent-crime rate has declined a bit over the past couple of years, it remains at historically high levels. But what has truly shaken people is the seeming randomness of crime: Carjackings, drive-by shootings and abductions in even the quietest suburbs have created the impression that everyone is vulnerable and that police cannot protect us.

The arguments for and against buying a gun for self-defense are shrill and confusing. Gun control advocates say having a gun at home represents a real danger and a false hope of safety; the National Rifle Association says a gun at home may be your last line of protection.

Each side has horror stories to support its claims. Gun opponents cite the case of Sonya Barnes of Conyers, Georgia, whose ex-husband—frequently out of town—had bought her a .357 Magnum for self-defense. Early last year, her two-year-old son found the gun and accidentally fired it into the back of his fourteen-month-old brother, leaving the younger sibling a paraplegic. Sonya got rid of the gun and now says, "I'd rather have the hell beat out of me than take another chance."

Gun proponents cite Suzanna Gratia. She was eating lunch with her parents at Luby's cafeteria in Killeen, Texas, on October 16, 1991, when a deranged man drove a truck through the front window and began shooting people. Gratia reached into her purse for her .38 revolver—then remembered she'd decided to stop carrying it, fearing she was in violation of the state's concealed-weapons law. Before the incident was over, twenty-three people were dead, including Gratia's parents. "If I'd had my weapon, I could have made a difference," she says.

But sweep away the horror stories and the quarrel over guns for self-defense boils down to the seminal researchers on the subject. Gary Kleck, a Florida State University criminology professor, says his evidence shows that millions of times each year, people use guns successfully to defend themselves. Arthur Keller-mann, director of the Center for Injury Control at Emory University's School of Public Health in Atlanta, says his studies show guns in the home are forty-three times more likely to kill a family member or friend than an intruder. The two men are quoted endlessly in the press and congressional testimony. Understand-ing their work is essential to trying to make the right choice about a deadly serious matter.

Gary Kleck

Gary Kleck seems to enjoy defying stereotypes. A native of the Chicago suburbs, he occasionally played with toy guns while growing up but otherwise has no shooting background, though he is a bit of an archery enthusiast.

Now forty-three, Kleck earned a Ph.D. in sociology from the University of Illinois and has been at Florida State since 1978. He lectures in jeans, pacing back and forth as he teaches courses in criminology and research methods. On his office door are stickers from Greenpeace, the Nature Conservancy, the Sierra Club and the Defenders of Wildlife; he freely labels himself a "tree hugger." He is also a member of Common Cause and the American Civil Liberties Union, and describes his political bent as orthodox liberal, "which means I basically think the way to reduce crime is to reduce poverty." Kleck voted for Bill Clinton, though he calls the president's positions on crime "absolutely awful." He says he has never used a gun defensively but won't say whether he owns a firearm.

Kleck got into gun research in the late 1970s because "it was an absolutely open field—somebody could really make a contribution." He produced a series of estimates on successful use of guns in self-defense. In his earlier work, Kleck extrapolated from nine surveys made between 1976 and 1990. He relied heavily on a 1981 poll of 1,228 registered voters by Peter Hart Research Associates and concluded that, excluding police and military uses, guns were used defensively against persons between 606,000 and 960,000 times per year.

In 1993, trying to refine the numbers and respond to criticism, Kleck and a colleague commissioned their own phone survey of 4,977 randomly selected households. They clarified that each defensive gun use was against a person in connection with a crime and that an actual confrontation had occurred. Extrapo-lating, Kleck concluded that guns were used in self-defense between 800,000 and 2.45 million times a year. He says the higher figure represents the respondents' most recent and reliable recollections. Rarely is anyone shot in these incidents, Kleck says; in fact, the defender fires in fewer than one in four cases. In most instances, the mere display of a weapon is sufficient to scare off the intruder.

Kleck thinks the findings have several important implications. The first is that Americans probably use guns in self-defense more often than they use guns to commit violent crimes. The Bureau of Justice Statistics estimates that about 1.1 million violent crimes were committed with guns in 1992; that is dwarfed by Kleck's estimate of up to 2.45 million defensive uses. "Gun ownership among prospective victims may well have as large a crime-*inhibiting* effect as the crime-*generating* effects of gun possession among prospective criminals," Kleck concludes in his book, *Point Blank*.

In addition, one in six survey respondents who had used a gun defensively was almost certain a life would have been lost without it—implying some 400,000 cases of guns saving lives. If even one-tenth of those people were right, says Kleck, the number of lives saved by guns would exceed the 38,000 annually lost to guns.

Kleck also contends that people who defend themselves with a gun are more likely to successfully resist the crime and less likely to be hurt. Indeed, an analysis from the annual National Crime Survey for 1979–87 showed that criminals are successful in only 14 percent of burglary attempts at occupied residences in which folks defend their property with guns—compared with a success rate of 33 percent overall. And a new study from the Bureau of Justice Statistics reveals that only one in five crime victims defending themselves with a firearm suffered injury, compared with almost half of those who defended themselves with another weapon or no weapon at all.

Kleck suspects gun ownership also has some deterrent effect. A 1986 survey of 1,900 incarcerated felons by sociologists James Wright and Peter Rossi found that 40 percent had at some time decided not to commit a crime because they believed the intended victim was armed. Three-fifths of the felons said criminals are more worried about meeting an armed victim than they are about the police. Kleck also notes that countries with far lower rates of gun ownership than the United States—like Great Britain and the Netherlands—have far higher rates of burglaries of *occupied* residences. The reason, he argues, is that the thieves have little to fear from unarmed occupants.

If all this is true, Kleck reasons, measures that reduce public gun ownership may be counterproductive. "If you take guns away from people who could have used them defensively, you're depriving them of something that would have allowed them in some cases to save lives or prevent injury," he says. He also argues that most gun control restrictions have no net effect on violence.

While other experts generally respect Kleck, several disagree sharply with the survey numbers that support his conclusions. They cite the Census Bureau's annual National Crime Victimization Survey, considered the broadest and most accurate measure of crime. Data from that survey indicate that only about 80,000 crime victims per year use firearms to defend themselves (compared with Kleck's high of 2.45 million). If that number is correct, the use of guns to commit crime would outnumber the use of guns in self-defense by about fourteen to one.

Kleck contends that the victimization survey is a poor measure of self-defense gun usage, largely because it is a nonanonymous survey, conducted by the federal government. Respondents, he says, are unlikely to talk about defensive gun use in the context of intensely personal crimes like domestic violence or rape. And since carrying a gun in public may be technically illegal, that, too, is not the kind of thing someone is going to admit to the feds. He notes that a total of ten private, anonymous surveys, including his own, all show upwards of a million self-defense uses of guns a year.

Kleck's critics admit that the victimization survey undercounts sexual assault and domestic violence. But they note that it is conducted by highly trained interviewers who return to the same households seven times over a three-year period and guarantee confidentiality. The survey, in the field for twenty years, "reflects the best thinking on how to get reliable answers to sensitive questions about crime," says Duke University public policy professor Philip Cook, a respected gun scholar. "I don't understand why people would be so much more forthcoming with Kleck's survey callers than with the government's. I find that absurd."

Another complaint is that Kleck's conclusions rest on the respondent's own, perhaps ambiguous, definition of self-defense. A report by the National Academy of Sciences' National Research Council says it may refer "to homeowners with a generalized fear of burglary . . . and even to criminals in the course of their crimes." Kleck admits this was a problem in earlier polls but says his most recent survey painstakingly fleshed out exactly what happened in each "self-defense" confrontation.

Finally, survey experts believe Kleck's work may be susceptible to "telescoping," in which memorable events are brought forward in a respondent's memory and reported as having occurred more recently than they actually did. These authorities say the national victimization survey is much less likely to suffer from telescoping problems because interviews are conducted every six months over a three-year period. Kleck accepts the point but says the telescoping would have to be massive indeed to significantly alter his conclusions.

These arguments aren't likely to be resolved anytime soon. The National Academy of Sciences panel, which conducted perhaps the most exhaustive review of the data, essentially threw up its hands and called for more research. Kleck doubts that is necessary. "Show me the evidence that I've ignored. People don't do that. They just keep speculating," he says. "But you know, an ounce of evidence outweighs a ton of maybes."

Arthur Kellermann

Unlike Kleck, Arthur Kellermann grew up with guns. There were two shotguns and a .22-caliber rifle in a rack in the kitchen in South Pittsburg, Tennessee, and his father taught Kellermann to shoot. Most of his shooting was plinking and skeet, but he also did some target practice at a YMCA summer camp. "I was familiar with long guns," he says. "We were not a handgun family."

Kellermann has not had guns in his own home for years, in part because he has a small child—a son, now six. But he notes that somehow the boy has developed a fascination with guns. "Anything longer than it is wide, he'll point and make gun sounds," sighs Kellermann.

Trained as an emergency physician, Kellermann got interested in the gun issue during a two-year fellowship in public health. The pivotal event was the fatal shooting in 1984 of rhythm-and-blues singer Marvin Gaye by his father. "My response was, 'This is crazy,' " he says. "All these guns are in people's homes, and most of the deaths that occur there apparently involve domestic disputes. Surely somebody has examined the relationship between having a gun in the home and family victimization." But he found very little research on the subject.

Kellermannn set out to fill that void and is best known for three studies that have appeared in the *New England Journal of Medicine*. In the first study, published in 1986, Kellermann and a colleague reviewed six years' worth of gunshot deaths in Seattle. About half occurred in the home where the weapon was kept. The researchers found that "for every case of self-protection homicide involving a firearm kept in the home, there were 1.3 accidental deaths, 4.6 criminal homicides and 37 suicides involving firearms"—an overall ratio of almost 43 to 1. "It may reasonably be asked," they wrote, "whether keeping firearms in the home increases a family's protection or places it in greater danger."

In 1988, Kellermann was one of nine doctors responsible for a seven-year comparison of burglaries, robberies, assaults and homicides in Seattle and in Vancouver, British Columbia, which had adopted far more restrictions on handguns. The authors found similar overall rates of crime but discovered that the risk of homicide was far greater in Seattle. "Virtually all of this excess risk," they said, "was explained by a 4.8-fold higher risk of being murdered with a handgun in Seattle." They concluded that "restricting access to handguns may reduce the rate of homicide in a community."

The most recent study was published last fall. This time, Kellermann and company studied homicides in the home in Memphis, Cleveland and Seattle over a five-year period. These households were compared with households that were not the scene of a killing but included individuals demographically similar to the victims; the idea was to identify factors affecting a family's risk of homicide in the home. Homes that contained guns were almost three times more likely to be the scene of a homicide than comparable homes without guns. "The greatest threat to the lives of household members appears to come from within," says Kellermann. He adds that the study also was capable of demonstrating a protective effect from guns but did not.

For Kellermann, the implications couldn't be clearer. The first is that a gun almost automatically makes any altercation potentially more lethal. Second, he says, "the risks of having a gun in the home substantially outweigh the benefits." His most recent study concludes that "people should be strongly discouraged from keeping guns in their homes."

Kellermann's critics argue that using death as the sole criterion for measuring the risks of gun ownership is inappropriate: The huge majority of defensive firearm uses—99 percent, critics say—involve no more than wounding, missing the target or brandishing the gun. Kellermann, they say, passes off his work as a risk-benefit analysis even though it measures risks alone. "The benefit of defensive gun ownership that would be parallel to innocent lives *lost* to guns would be innocent lives *saved* by guns," argues Kleck—conceding that "it is impossible to count the latter." In his 1986 study, Kellermann seems to admit the problem: "Studies such as ours do not include cases in which intruders are wounded or frightened away by the use or display of a firearm. A complete determination of firearm risks versus benefits would require that these figures be known."

Doubters also think Kellermann has underplayed the possibility that it may not be the guns causing the violence but the violence causing the guns. "In places where there is more violence, people will get guns for self-protection," argues Kleck. "But is it because the violence brought about gun ownership? Or is it the gun ownership that helped bring about the violence?"

Kellermann allows that the questions have some merit. But he says he made statistical adjustments to take into account a history of household violence and notes that reverse causation would have to be "enormous" to completely explain the difference in homicide rates among gun-owning households. He says, too, that if a violent atmosphere were the cause of all that gunfire, he might have found a higher risk of homicide by other means in those homes—but he didn't.

Common Ground

It comes as something of a surprise that Kleck and Kellermann actually agree on a few things—including certain gun control measures. Both, for instance, support the kind of background checks mandated by the Brady law. Such screening, says Kleck, "appears to reduce homicide and suicide."

Both men also see benefit in stricter regulation of federal firearms dealer's licenses, which require $30 and a cursory background check in many states. The number of licensees has grown 67 percent since 1975—to 245,000—outstripping the Bureau of Alcohol, Tobacco and Firearms' ability to regulate them. Only about one in four is actually a storefront business; the rest are "kitchen table" dealers who sometimes operate in violation of local laws. Proposals before Congress would hike the license fee and allow for more meaningful oversight. "It's difficult for me to imagine that society's interest is served by someone selling guns across their kitchen table," says Kellermann.

In addition, both men would bar those convicted of violent misdemeanors from buying or owning guns (current law applies only to convicted felons). Kleck points out that nearly all criminal convictions are obtained from plea bargains, which often reduce felony charges to misdemeanor versions of the same crime.

Finally, Kellermann and Kleck agree that harsher sentencing will never be the total answer to America's gun violence. "A long series of get-tough strategies have been tried, carefully evaluated and found to be either ineffective . . . or hopelessly expensive," writes Kleck.

And what about the big question: Should I buy a gun for protection? Here's

Kellermann's answer: "It's natural to want to do everything possible to defend yourself and your family. It's also natural to want to seek cover under the nearest tree in a thunderstorm. That doesn't make it a good idea." Kleck says he avoids giving advice. But in *Point Blank*, he writes: "Possession of a gun gives its owner an additional option for dealing with danger. If other sources of security are adequate, the gun does not have to be used; but where other sources fail, it can preserve bodily safety and property in at least some situations."

Even so, Kleck says, each person must evaluate other circumstances, such as the presence of children in the home or of anyone who's chronically depressed, aggressive or alcoholic. And people must consider their neighborhood's real danger; the higher the crime rate, he says, the more need for a firearm. Still, says Kleck, for most Americans, "there's little or no need for a gun for self-protection because there's so little risk of crime. People don't believe it, but it's true. You just can't convince most Americans they're not at serious risk."

Chapter Twenty-nine

Americans Losing Trust in Each Other and Institutions

Washington Post Series

Suspicion of Strangers Breeds Widespread Cynicism

RICHARD MORIN AND DAN BALZ

Janie Drake is a forty-eight-year-old Detroit mother of three who trusts almost nobody. She doesn't trust the neighborhood teenager with his low-riding pants "slopping over his behind, you know how." Not big corporations, not labor unions, not local store owners, nobody except family or longtime friends.

And like a majority of Americans, Drake said she "certainly does not" trust the government. Why should she? "If we can't trust each other, how can we trust the federal government?"

Lori Miller, eighteen, of Madison, Wisconsin, agrees that you can't be too careful these days. "There's too many people trying to hurt you financially, emotionally or physically. You never know who's the next Jeffrey Dahmer," she said. Miller too is apprehensive about the government. As she put it, "It's made up of people, isn't it?"

America is becoming a nation of suspicious strangers, and this mistrust of each other is a major reason Americans have lost confidence in the federal government and virtually every other major national institution. Every generation that has come of age since the 1950s has been more mistrusting of human nature, a transformation in the national outlook that has deeply corroded the nation's social and political life.

The relationship between how Americans view each other and how they view the government is one of the major findings of a new national survey by the *Washington Post*, Harvard University and the Kaiser Family Foundation. The survey was supplemented by two focus groups, interviews and conversations with Americans around the country, as well as with political scientists and other experts.

In the past ten years, anger at government and disgust with politicians have increased, causing voters to veer in different directions in 1992 and 1994. At the same time, political leaders, pundits and academics have issued a flurry of prescriptions to restore trust in government: Replace the current crop of politicians, return civility to the political debate in Washington, transfer power to the states or perhaps even balance the federal budget.

But the survey suggests that the sources of distrust that affect attitudes toward government—and therefore the solutions—are not so simple or nicely self-contained.

"If this were simply a matter of trust in government, then politicians could figure out what people don't like about government and political leaders and change it," said Eric Uslaner, a University of Maryland political scientist who was one of the first to identify the relationship between declining trust in human nature and attitudes toward politics and government. "But that's not the problem. The reason our politics is behaving badly is because the whole country is behaving badly."

Today, nearly two in three Americans believe that most people can't be trusted; three decades ago a majority of Americans believed that most people could be trusted. Half say most people would cheat others if they had the chance, and an equal proportion agree that "most people are looking out for themselves," the survey found.

The decline in trust in government has echoed the fall in personal trust. In 1964, three in four Americans trusted the federal government all or most of the time, a view shared by one in four persons today, according to the *Post*/Harvard/Kaiser survey.

This collapse of trust in human nature has fueled the erosion of trust in government and virtually every other institution, the survey found. Mistrustful Americans repeatedly expressed far less confidence in the federal government, the military, the Supreme Court, Congress and the Clinton administration than the dwindling numbers of Americans who were more upbeat about human nature.

Government also suffers from a lack of public confidence because of other national discontents brought about by the perceived failure of government to deal with the country's biggest problems, the survey found. Fear of crime, economic insecurity and pessimism about the lives of future generations all have separately added to the belief that government either is making things worse or is incapable of making them better.

Each of these forces also has contributed to the declining levels of participation in everything from the ballot box to the PTA to bowling leagues, giving rise to a metaphor coined by Harvard political scientist Robert Putnam, who described this new world of civic indifference as "Bowling Alone."

The new survey, one in an ongoing series examining how knowledge affects public attitudes on a broad range of subjects, also measured how much Americans know about government and politics. Here too a gloomy picture emerged. The less people know, the less likely they are to participate: They are less likely to register to vote, and if registered less likely to cast a ballot on Election Day.

And there is much Americans don't know about politics or current affairs. The overwhelming majority of those surveyed don't know the names of their elected representatives, don't know that Robert J. Dole (R-Kan.) is the Senate majority leader, don't know that the country spends far more on Medicare than it does on foreign aid. A third of all Americans, the survey found, think Congress has already passed health care reform, or aren't sure; four in ten don't know that the Republicans control Congress; and half either think the Democratic Party is more conservative politically than the GOP or don't feel they know enough to offer a guess.

But for politicians and others looking to repair the system, the other side of the coin is perhaps even more troubling: The more people know, the less confidence they have in government. Among those with high levels of knowledge about current issues or politics, 77 percent expressed only some confidence in the federal government, a view shared by 67 percent less-informed respondents. Better, but not by much.

Even those who express kind words for government have low expectations. "If they do the right thing 25 percent of the time, it's good," said Charles Merrell, a sixty-six-year-old computer programmer, from Cliffside, N.J., who has a generally positive view of government. "This is a good result."

"Mistrust of government is part of a larger problem," said John Brehm, a Duke University political scientist. "How does a president or the Congress boost people's trust in each other, or how helpful we think other people are or how trustworthy we think other people are? It's very difficult to imagine how a leader bridges those distances. That's a very pessimistic interpretation of things, I'm afraid."

This series will examine factors that explain why discontent with government in Washington has become so widespread: the knowledge gap; the insecurities fostered by a changing economy; the partisan impact of current attitudes to the problems of governing in an age of mistrust, and the decline of trust over recent generations. But at its heart, the survey suggests that the problem begins with people themselves.

Scholars like Putnam describe the generation that came of age after World War II as the last, great civic generation. Since then, every generation has been more mistrustful of human nature than the last, according to the *Post*/Harvard/Kaiser survey.

Today, a clear majority of respondents in their early twenties said they do not trust their fellow Americans, a view they share with one in four Americans over the age of sixty. "It's like living in the cave man age," said Michael Callecoat, twenty-nine, a self-employed contractor living in New Jersey with his wife and three-year-old daughter. "Nobody cares anymore. Nobody cares. They will no sooner run you down and run away than to spit in your face."

Lesvia Hernandez, twenty-three, the manager of a retail store in Windsor, Connecticut, said, "I can't trust anyone. We aren't willing to trust other people, even people who live next door to us." Hernandez said she had good reason. A few years ago a mugger stole her mother's purse. "The one who stole the purse lived next door to us," she said. "How can you trust people?"

If trust were a trait slowly acquired over a lifetime, this generation-to-generation erosion might not present such a problem for democracy. Trust, however, is acquired in early childhood, and is far more likely to diminish than to increase with age, said Wendy Rahn, a political scientist at the University of Minnesota who has done pioneering research into the causes and consequences of personal mistrust. "If the young [people] are not growing up with a sense of generalized trust, there's really not any hope that they will really develop it," Rahn said. "Trust in individuals might erode due to the events or circumstances, but if you don't have trust, you don't acquire it."

Trust in the essential goodness of others translates into what Rahn calls "a rosy glow" about America and its institutions. Mistrust of one another breeds suspicion toward government, and sometimes outright fear.

For example: The *Post*/Harvard/Kaiser survey asked people whether government actions usually end up hurting more people than they help. Two-thirds of Americans who mistrusted each other agreed with that; but the view was shared by only 29 percent of Americans who trust one another. Mistrustful Americans also were more likely to see government as a major threat to their rights and freedoms as trusting Americans.

An environment in which a majority of Americans believe that most people can't be trusted breeds attitudes that hold all politicians as corrupt, venal and self-serving, and government action as doomed to failure.

More than half of all mistrustful Americans—53 percent—strongly agree that public officials don't care "what people like me think." But only a quarter—26 percent —of trusting Americans strongly agree with that statement. Four out of ten mistrustful Americans believe that "people like me don't have any say about what the government does," but only sixteen percent of trusting Americans say that.

"Politicians call themselves public servants," said Marvin Lucas, fifty-nine, a custodial supervisor at a college in Milledgeville, Georgia. "I compare politicians with used car salesmen: say one thing, do another . . . just like most other people."

Rahn said Americans who mistrust each other believe that "the motives of people who propose solutions are always viewed as malignant and that these solutions are likely to fail or not likely to further the common good." These views sour mistrustful Americans on the political process and on politicians, and mean that virtually any attempt by political leaders or government to address national problems will be viewed with deep suspicion.

The survey found that those who mistrust other people were significantly less likely to be registered to vote or to have voted in the last two national elections. Just one-third of mistrusting Americans said they voted in 1994, compared to six in ten of those who have confidence in human nature.

Why don't people trust each other? There is no single answer. But the survey suggests that experience with crime contributes significantly to growing suspicion about the trustworthiness of others, which in turn spills over into mistrust of government.

"There was a time I would take walks at night and feel perfectly happy and enjoy myself," said Irv Sandroff, sixty-three, a retiree from the New York Board of Education who participated in one of two focus groups conducted by *Washington Post* reporters in Teaneck, New Jersey. "But I wouldn't do it anymore. I'm afraid. Literally afraid of having someone jump me. I think people are very frightened of crime and violence. And with all the other pressures on people, this makes it even worse."

The poll found that victims of violent crime were more mistrustful of other people. These crime victims also expressed less confidence in government to solve problems. "Crime has sort of a double whammy," Rahn said. "It erodes belief about human nature, which affects people's attitudes toward government. Then there is a direct effect because people hold the state responsible for maintaining public order."

"Government is seen as failing to solve the problems that touch people's lives," said Robert J. Blendon, a Harvard professor at the Kennedy School of Government and an adviser on the survey project. "At the same time, the size of government has increased as well as the taxes they pay."

He said a succession of scandals and policy failures, from Vietnam to Watergate to Whitewater, also may have contributed to diminished trust in people as well as government, giving "people less reason to trust government and more reason to mistrust each other."

Sharon Seal, forty-two, considers herself "an optimist by nature," but these days she sees "a sense of hopelessness and frustration" in people around her. Much of that, she said, comes from a sluggish and increasingly impersonal economy.

Wages have stagnated, workers change jobs frequently and downsizing corporations offer little protection even to the most loyal of employees. Many workers are doing well in the new economy, but Seal said there is a price for the changes. "There's no longer the security that comes with the job," said Seal, who works part-time for a management consulting firm in Baltimore.

Seal's observations about the public are hardly illusory, and one consequence is the erosion of confidence in the federal government. The *Post*/Harvard/Kaiser poll found that more than a third of all Americans fall into what could be called the "economically anxious" category, people who see the economy worsening, their own financial future deteriorating and who doubt their children will fare better than they have.

Dislocations in the economy, such as the recent announcement by AT&T that it would lay off 40,000 workers as part of a corporate restructuring plan, send ripples of anxiety through the labor force. More than a quarter of all those surveyed who work full-or part-time said they are "very" or "somewhat" worried they will lose their jobs within the next two years.

Not surprisingly, these economically anxious Americans have less trust in other people. Almost half of those with a pessimistic outlook about the economy distrust others, compared to less than a quarter of those who are more optimistic about the economy.

Maryland's Uslaner draws a straight line between economic well-being and trust in others. "When things look bright, as they did in the 1960s, people will trust others," he said. "When people worry about the future, fewer will trust others."

Many Americans say everything from the increased pressure to make ends meet to family breakups to concerns for personal safety robs them of the opportunity to get to know their neighbors the way earlier generations did.

"I just think people are too busy," said Kelly Gray, thirty, an office manager and single mother who lives in Lodi, New Jersey. "I come home from work and either I go to a second job or I'm running here or I'm running there. I'm going to the store. I'm cooking dinner, doing laundry. I'm taking care of my daughter. I don't have time to sit and talk in the backyard to my neighbors because my things aren't going to get done."

"I go to school like four nights a week," said Jay McCracken, thirty-four, a technical adviser who lives in Hackensack, New Jersey. "So I go from work [at] 4:30 P.M. right to school until 10:30 P.M. every night. The only time I see my kids is on weekends. So it's really tough. I don't talk to the neighbors, you know."

"If you work and you have a family, there's no time," said Angela Jacobs, of Teaneck, who is married and has two children. "So when you get in, the door is locked."

Americans who feel most pessimistic about the economy also are more likely to see the government as a threat. Almost half of them, a fifth of all Americans, say the government threatens personal freedoms. Three in five say government threatens their economic well being, and a majority of these anxious Americans say government is a major threat.

But distrust of government extends far beyond that portion of the population that is most pessimistic about the economy. That lack of confidence grows out of the perception that either government has not done enough to improve the economy or that it has actually made things worse.

An overwhelming percentage of Americans see the government as wasteful and inefficient—80 percent—and as spending tax dollars on the wrong things, 79 percent. Three in five Americans say government has not done enough to help people in need, while almost that many—55 percent—say federal taxes are too high.

"Our government is trying to take care of too much stuff that they don't know what they're doing," said Alice Blaha, sixty two, of Farmington, Minnesota. "Things broke down in not dealing with the economy."

"I think what the federal government asks of us is disproportionate to what it's willing to give back to us," said Gaymelle Dorsey, forty-four, a placement counselor for a computer school who lives in Hackensack.

A majority of Americans blame Washington for allowing U.S. jobs to go overseas and for failing to create more jobs here at home. "I think one place where the government has made a mistake is this idea of unlimited free trade," said Merrell, of Cliffside Park, New Jersey. "We've exported a lot of our jobs, especially jobs at the low end of the scale. . . . I don't say we should make ourselves a fortress, build a wall and then shut the door, but we may have gone too far."

The discontent over the economy adds to public fears about the future and to the belief that prosperity will be even more difficult to achieve for future generations. More than half of those surveyed said they are not at all confident their children will do better than they have done, a belief that also diminishes their trust in government.

Many Americans see children growing up without as many anchors in their lives, facing greater dangers to their personal security—from drugs to AIDS to street violence—and with diminished economic prospects.

Ed Hildebrandt, fifty-five, who lives in Carlstadt, New Jersey, and is retired from the U.S. Postal Service, said young people now entering the work force will not be able to buy homes or educate their children unless wages increase. "I think it's scary," he said. "When I was a kid, I went in the service, came out, got a job, wasn't afraid of working and there was enough work out there."

In the face of these challenges, government stands as a symbol of ineffectiveness. Government, said Sharon Seal, is "this big dinosaur that's mired in so many things that, even if this dinosaur might have good intentions, it's swamped by so many things and it makes it hard to move. There's this tremendous pressure for government to help people, but there are also people who are furious with government for what they see as waste and greed and inefficiencies."

Public Grows More Receptive to Anti-Government Message

THOMAS B. EDSALL

On the surface, Gregory M. Higgins would seem to be an ideal recruit for the Democratic Party. Last April, Corporate America responded to his fourteen years of loyalty and hard work with a pink slip.

Higgins, who conducts title searches, was caught in a downsizing that resulted in layoffs for 30 percent of the company's employees. He and his wife and son were forced to move from their house in suburban Cleveland to a mobile home. He's been able to find another job searching titles, but he's taken a pay cut of about one-third his old salary.

"Before I got downsized, I was saying to myself, 'Well, I'll retire with this company.' Now, I'm looking ahead, [and wondering] if I make it ten years where I am, and I'm going to be pushing fifty," said Higgins, who is thirty-eight.

Higgins, however, is anything but a Democrat. "You can almost see the black and white between the Democrats and the Republicans," he said. "John Glenn [the Democratic senator from Ohio], he's a heathen; [Rep. Louis] Stokes, he's a heathen." President Clinton, in turn, is "blasphemous."

Higgins is a Christian conservative, a part of perhaps the fastest growing constituency in American politics.

But more than that, Higgins is a part of a new political profile, whose demographic and attitudinal characteristics are reshaping the partisan and ideological tilt of the American electorate.

Married, white, male, middle-aged and religious, Higgins is the personification of the new Republican. Attitudinally, Higgins's mistrust—he does not send his son to public school and he did not want the community he lives in identified in this article—reflects a wariness that a new *Washington Post* poll found to be a dominant characteristic of the electorate.

Higgins is a part of a public that appears to be highly receptive to conservative, anti-government messages, and inclined to be hostile to liberal, pro-government themes. One of the key findings of the study of Americans' mistrust of government and politicians, conducted in cooperation with the Henry J. Kaiser Family Foundation and Harvard University, is that the Republican Party has gained a built-in advantage: the public is increasingly sympathetic to the GOP's anti-government themes and ready to believe that raising taxes to pay for federal programs is a wasteful strategy that may do more harm than good.

"The public sees the quality of life deteriorating or not improving from the 1960s, with family breakup, increased violence, a failure to produce better jobs, and, in addition, with the Cold War over, they don't see any real reduction in the risks of the possibility of a third world war. All this occurs at a time when taxes have been increasing," said Robert J. Blendon, a professor at Harvard's School of Public Health and the Kennedy School of Government who was one of the leaders of the *Post*/Kaiser/Harvard study. "The small government, low tax environment creates a real opportunity for Republicans . . . The general force of this sense of no progress is to favor the more conservative party."

"The distrust absolutely benefits the Republicans because it makes it easy to knock anything [associated with government] as guilty until proven innocent," said Samuel Popkin, a political scientist at the University of California at San Diego, who has conducted his own research on trust. "The Democrats are in the position of having to prove [whenever they try to defend a government program, or to propose new spending] that this one is an exception" to the general rule of waste and inefficiency.

The survey showed that Americans generally are becoming more distrustful of each other. More than 60 percent of the 1,514 adults interviewed last November and December agreed with the statement that "you can't be too careful in dealing with people," while 35 percent agreed that "most people can be trusted." Half of those surveyed believe "most people would try to take advantage of you if they got a chance," as opposed to believing that most people "would try to be fair."

This distrust, in turn, is inherently more damaging to the Democratic Party than to the Republican Party. Dependent for survival on winning decisive majorities of African American and Hispanic voters, Democrats need to build coalitions crossing racial and ethnic boundaries, coalitions for which trust is a crucial ingredient. But on an overall measure of trust in human nature, 40 percent of self-described Democrats were found to have low levels of trust, compared to 31 percent of Republicans. Only 24 percent of Democrats had a high level of trust in human nature, compared to 32 percent of Republicans.

The undermining of a pro-government Democratic Party is taking place on a number of fronts. Substantial segments of the public believe the federal government has hurt the economy and society in general. Nearly half said the government worsened "the difference in income between wealthy and middle-class Americans"; 37 percent said it increased the "chances that children will grow up in single-parent families"; 34 percent said federal programs worsened "the rate of violent crime." On all three of these key issues, only about 10 percent said the federal government "helped make things better."

Even for those programs for which there is substantial evidence that federal initiatives have succeeded—programs that Democrats should be able to cite to boost their case in support of other federal efforts—there is not a majority consensus recognizing these achievements.

Only 23 percent of those surveyed said federal programs have reduced the share of Americans over 65 who live in poverty, compared to 32 percent who contend the programs have "made things worse," and 39 percent who say the programs have "not had much effect either way." Similarly, in the case of the "quality of the air we breathe," only 44 percent said environmental programs have "helped make things better," while 15 percent said they made things worse, and 38 percent said there has been no change.

There is, in other words, a pervasive suspicion of the effectiveness of government spending, creating a barrier that must be surmounted every time a Democrat wants to make the case for a federal expenditure, while facilitating Republican critiques of the central government.

The glue that held together the core constituencies of the traditional Democratic coalition—blue-collar workers and union members, blacks, urban political machines based in working-class neighborhoods—was a commonality of economic interest, a shared sense of unity in the face of a Republican adversary aligned with business and corporate management. Those traditional divisions are collapsing in the face of new splits among voters.

The evidence from the *Post*/Kaiser/Harvard poll, along with data from other sources, suggests that if anything the electorate is breaking up into increasingly complex units, in which fundamental characteristics of one's identity—sex, marital status, depth of religious conviction, race—are shaping partisan allegiance.

Identity politics, as it relates to partisan politics, contrasts married people against single people; the religious against the secular; men against women; and, especially in the South, blacks against whites. For the Democratic Party, which is more heterogenous than the GOP, managing the coalition becomes increasingly difficult.

Take Juliette Gatto, thirty-two, of Ridgefield, New Jersey, and George Mercurio, sixty, of Paterson, New Jersey. They see relations between men and women in very different ways, and their politics, in turn, are very different.

"Look at single parents today. I'm one of them," Gatto said at a focus group session sponsored by the *Post*. "I don't mean anything against any men in here, but there's like no men out there anymore" who act like a man should. "You know, to go out and support a family or to pull his weight."

Gatto is inclined to support the reelection of Clinton. "He's been a good president, I believe." She views Clinton as sympathetic to the stresses and strains in her life. Single, working women like Gatto are a crucial base of support for Clinton. Divorced women lean toward the Democratic Party, which has the support of 34 percent in this constituency, while only 23 percent describe themselves as Republicans.

Mercurio, who is also divorced, said in an interview, "If a woman gives me too much nonsense, she is history." At the same focus group that Gatto participated in, Mercurio said, "The man has to be a man and the lady has to be a lady. God made them both different. The man is hard with muscles, and the woman is soft. And there is one thing: the father has to be the head of the household, to put it short."

Mercurio has fond memories from his childhood of the grandfather of the Democratic coalition, Franklin Delano Roosevelt. But he holds Clinton in disdain. "He's a do-nothing president. He doesn't make waves, he's not colorful." Mercurio describes himself as nonpartisan, but his sympathies are with conservatives. He contends, for instance, that he would like Bob Grant, a New York talk show host who makes Rush Limbaugh sound moderate, to run for president. "I just idolize him," Mercurio said.

Growing partisan differences based on gender and marital status are creating new ways of looking at the electorate. Just as it traditionally became possible to trace a steady line of increasingly strong Republican leanings and declining support for Democrats as voters moved up the income ladder, a parallel line can be drawn on the basis of marital status and gender.

One of the most Democratic groups among white voters is made up of women who have never married, among whom Democrats outnumber Republicans by better than two to one. The next most Democratic group is divorced women, 34 percent of whom call themselves Democrats compared to 23 percent who say they are Republicans. Married women split almost evenly between Democrats and Republicans.

Every parallel category of white men, in contrast, leans to the GOP. In ascending order, divorced men are 31 percent Republican, 25 percent Democratic; never married men, 34 percent Republican and 22 percent Democratic; and married men, 40 percent Republican, 25 percent Democratic.

(African American voters are so overwhelmingly Democratic—71 percent to 13 percent Republican—that there is little difference between subgroups. Hispanics, who make up about 9 percent of the population but less of the electorate, are about evenly divided between Republicans and Democrats.)

The degree to which sex and marital status are trumping traditional income divisions is reflected in the following findings from the poll. Married white men with incomes below $30,000—a largely working class, downscale group that was once reliably Democratic—now are evenly divided between Democrats and Republicans. Conversely, unmarried white women with incomes in excess of $30,000 are substantially more Democratic than Republican.

The fracturing of the electorate is emerging at another level: a partisan split is emerging among white voters separating the deeply religious of all Christian faiths—including mainline Protestants and Catholics, in addition to evangelical and born-again Christians—from those who are only moderately religious and those who are not religious at all.

"The core groups of the New Deal coalition, namely white evangelicals and white Catholics, have, to varying extents, deserted the Democratic Party," wrote political scientists Lyman A. Kellstedt, John C. Green, James L. Guth and Corwin E. Smidt in the Public Perspective. "After years of gradual disintegration, the New Deal religious coalition is now in shambles, and with it the Democratic lock on congressional and state government."

Who Will Protect Us?
Minorities and Guns

Chapter Thirty

Arms and the Woman
A Feminist Reappraisal

Mary Zeiss Stange

> This above all, to refuse to be a victim. Unless I can
> do that I can do nothing. I have to recant, give up the
> old belief that I am powerless and because of it noth-
> ing I can do will ever hurt anyone. A lie which was
> always more disastrous than the truth would have
> been.
>
> —Margaret Atwood, *Surfacing* (1972)

The "Great Equalizer," or Tool of Male Oppression?

The premise that women are helpless victims, unable to defend themselves, was entirely ignored by twelve million women who did something highly unvictimlike throughout the 1980s: they bought handguns. As violence against women reached epidemic proportions, women were not just sitting around. Quietly, carefully, with thorough training . . . while they looked after their families and tended their marriages, they were also teaching themselves to blow away potential assailants.[1]

A Lou Harris poll published in 1993 predicted that gun control might well become "the next great women's issue in the country."[2] That prediction seems to be coming true, though in ways perhaps not entirely foreseen by Harris. Millions of women are purchasing and using firearms in huge numbers, for recreational shooting and hunting, as well as for self-defense.[3] Women also comprise "one half of purely precautionary gun owners,"[4] i.e., those who own firearms solely for the purpose of self-protection. Of the approximately sixty-five to eighty million gun owners in America today, by conservative estimate seventeen million are female, and a far greater number than that have access to firearms owned by other members of their households.[5] Given current trends, there is no reason (other than severely restricting women's legal access to guns) why these numbers should not continue to grow. Guns and gun control are, indeed, women's issues of ever-increasing importance.

The above facts are liable to be unsettling to the majority of feminists who have tended to adhere to the conventional wisdom that to be feminist is to be antiviolence, and to be antiviolence is *ipso facto* to be antigun. Their argument surely has some merit; in the best of all possible worlds, women would not feel the need for lethal force to protect themselves or their children from abusers, known and unknown. However, in our violence-ridden society, most women have a legitimate reason to fear for their safety and the well-being of their loved ones.[6]

That a procontrol, or an antigun, position can be a valid component of feminist analysis surely goes without saying, given feminism's overriding concerns for values of peace and nonaggression. Yet it is equally reasonable to suggest that in a society where violence against women is so common, responsible gun use and ownership (and even, in some recreational contexts, enjoyment) among women ought to come under the purview of feminist theory as one valid option among many. Constructive dialogue is effectively blocked as long as women who argue for armed self-defense, for example, are branded as "right-wingers" or traitors to the cause of feminism.

The late poet Audre Lorde's statement that the Master's house will never be dismantled using the Master's tools[7] is often cited in feminist arguments against resorting to male-identified instruments of power, guns chief among them. There is a certain historical irony in this. In the last century, masters knew only too well the potential consequences of giving slaves access to firearms, which might become the means to their liberation. It is surely not an exaggeration to say that the antifeminist (and largely male) backlash precipitated by the film *Thelma and Louise* (1991) resonated with the same sense of nervousness at the prospect of armed and dangerous women as did the reaction of slaveholders faced with the potential of armed rebellion a hundred and fifty years earlier. It is perhaps with a sense of this historical irony that Naomi Wolf used Lorde's statement as an epigraph for her *Fire with Fire*, one of the very few feminist texts that view women arming themselves in a serious and positive light.

Yet Wolf paid for this apparent lapse in ideological consistency in the popular and feminist press. Laura Shapiro, in a *Newsweek* review of the book, castigated Wolf at some length for suggesting that women opting to arm themselves in self-defense might be a positive development.[8] Ann Jones, in *Ms.* magazine, summed up the sorry state of American society today by saying we live in "a world where popular, state-of-the-art, so-called feminist Naomi Wolf cites pistol-packin' mamas in NRA publications as splendid examples of 'pioneer feminism.' "[9] A mere three issues earlier, Wolf had shared the cover of *Ms.* with three other noted feminists, for a major feature on diversity in feminist thought.[10] That one might fall so quickly, and decisively, from grace over breaking rank on the issue of women and guns suggests that, at least as far as what may be considered "mainstream" feminism is concerned, there are some areas of theory where diversity of opinion does not apply.

It also helps to illustrate the extent of controversy with which the issue of women and guns is symbolically fraught; indeed, it is such a sensitive one in feminist circles precisely because, as we shall see below, it engages so many culturally rooted ideas and assumptions about the nature of power in the hands of women and men.

In American culture, the gun is a symbol of power—*male* power—par excellence. As David Kopel writes:

> The historical reality and the lurid mythology of the gun in America continue their struggle today. Extremists on each side are drawn to the same myth. The mythology attracts some "pro-gun" types into a swaggering world of combat fatigues and hypermasculinity. The mythology convinces other Americans that the gun is horrible and evil and even demonic. While the historical reality is more complex than either extreme will admit, America's view of the history of the gun is shaped as much by the myth as by the reality.[11]

This mythologizing of the gun as cultural symbol, owing in large part to the popular arts and news media, is further complicated by the association of firearms with sexual potency. In a *New York Times* article about Hollywood's long-standing love affair with firearms (dating back to *The Great Train Robbery* [1903]), cultural critic Jeff Silverman observed in 1993 that guns have "become sex symbols—for both men and women. . . . Guns have become increasingly eroticized and increasingly prominent."[12] Noting the flurry of "bad girl" films that followed on the heels of *Thelma and Louise*, Silverman suggests that Hollywood has finally discovered the power of a big gun (like the Remington 870 shotgun wielded both by Linda Hamilton in *Terminator 2* and Michael Douglas in *Falling Down*) to "be the new Great Equalizer." He quotes Tamra Davis, director of 1992's *Guncrazy* (which he characterizes as "a triangle involving a Lolita [Drew Barrymore], a man and a gun"): "In films like 'Point of No Return' [the American remake of *La Femme Nikita*], what I hope we see is not just women with guns but women in control. We need more cinematic images of women in control."

Of course, the woman "in control" in the above instance happened to be a hired assassin. It is the appropriation of this sort of "male power" (sexual or otherwise) which rightly concerns feminists when it is posited as a goal of some sort for women.

Yet *Thelma and Louise*, the pivotal scenes of which involve shooting a rapist in cold blood and blowing away a lecherous truckdriver's semi, received widespread feminist approbation. In the year following the film's release, "Graduate of the Thelma and Louise Finishing School" T-shirts, and "Thelma and Louise Live!" buttons were prominently displayed at women's studies conferences, and at such feminist events as the April 1992 March on Washington for reproductive rights. Something about *Thelma and Louise*'s message of fighting back against abuse struck a clear and positive feminist chord.[13]

Callie Khouri, who wrote the screenplay, told *Glamour* magazine that "Every time you see a strong female character on-screen, it's helpful because it's a validation of strength." Khouri went on to remark, however, that such screen images work precisely to the extent that audiences are able to distinguish between fantasy and reality:

> People tell me Thelma and Louise are terrible role models. . . . I say, "I know. Don't try this at home!" Movies are meant to take you places that you can't go physically, but you can go emotionally. You are not supposed to give up your identity because you see something on-screen.[14]

The notion of giving up one's sexual identity seems to lie at the heart of the opposition many women have to gun use, whether in fantasy or in fact. For example, when interviewed by the *New York Times* regarding the National Rifle Association's "Refuse To Be A Victim" women's self-defense program, Handgun Control, Inc., chairwoman Sarah Brady declared: "They prey on fear, they prey on guilt. The newest twist is 'Be assertive; do what the men are doing.' Well, no, thank you, very much, those kind of men are not men in my estimation."[15]

If guns are cultural symbols of male power, and women who take up arms in self-defense (or for whatever reason) are trying to "do what the men are doing," then these women are crossing a very treacherous line, in terms of gender roles. The fact that feminists have, for the last generation or more, been on the receiving end of charges that they are "just trying to act like men" may account, at least in part, for an uneasiness with the idea of espousing guns as symbols of female empowerment.

Any aversion to firearms founded in cultural gender stereotypes is amply supported by the advice meted out in the popular media. "Should you own a gun?" asks a typical item in *Glamour*. "The answer is probably no . . ." the piece begins, and it continues by enumerating several implicit disincentives to gun ownership, among them "Are you willing to kill someone?" and "Have you considered the likelihood of a tragic accident—for example, suppose you shot a so-called intruder who turned out to be a family member come home unexpectedly?"[16] A *Vogue* article titled "What You Know about Guns Can Kill You" even more flatly rules out firearms possession as a reasonable option for women: "The familiar argument says guns don't kill, people do. But scientists now see violence as a disease, guns as *dangerous in themselves*—and women as *especially vulnerable*."[17]

In her negative review of Wolf's *Fire with Fire*, Shapiro sarcastically strikes a warning note about Wolf's assertion that women arming themselves against abuse is a sign of so-called power feminism: "No victim feminists here by golly. (At least, not until they become victims. Studies show that having a gun at home is dangerous chiefly to the people who live there.)" An editorial in *USA Today* puts the case even more boldly. It reads, in part:

> Women of America: Watch out. The National Rifle Association is increasing its focus on you as gun owners. More of you and your children are going to die. . . . According to *The New England Journal of Medicine*, a house with a firearm is three times more likely to be the scene of a homicide, usually of a family member or friend. Those same people are 43 times more likely than an intruder to be shot. . . . Women are five times more likely to be shot dead by a spouse, boyfriend, family member or

acquaintance than an unknown assailant. . . . [A]n accessible, loaded firearm in the home is a prescription for tragedy that is regularly filled. . . . They [the NRA, in its "Refuse To Be A Victim" self-defense program] merely encourage women to add to their daily peril. That's a sure path to more gun violence, more spattered blood, and more pointless death.[18]

That these and similar messages, directed at women in the popular media, reflect a virulent antigun bias is no accident. Most of the scientific studies[19] cited again and again in the press are those championed by the antigun lobby. Indeed, until relatively recently, antigun polemicists have had a "virtual monopoly of the scholarly literature" in medicine about guns and gun use.[20]

These medical studies provide grist for the mill of antigun fundraising, much of it targeted specifically at women. A good example is an elaborate fund-solicitation mailing used by the Coalition to Stop Gun Violence in 1993. The cover letter this author received began as follows:

> Like most people, Pam thought gun violence always happened to someone else. So she was caught off guard when she was held up at gunpoint.
> And even when she gave up her purse and ran to her car, the gunmen followed and shot her dead.
> Dear Mary Stange,
> You could be next.[21]

Sarah Brady notwithstanding, the gun lobbies are not the only ones capable of preying on women's fears. The mailing went on to cite, under the heading "Frightening Gun Facts," several statistics already familiar from antigun litera-ture, including the widely discredited finding from the *New England Journal of Medicine* that a handgun "purchased for home protection" is "forty-three times more likely to be used to kill the owner, family member or friend than it is to be fired in self-defense."[22]

Of course, as feminists have tirelessly, and rightly, insisted, women's fears are legitimate enough in a society in which, according to FBI statistics one in three women will be sexually assaulted at least once during her lifetime, and a woman is beaten every sixteen seconds. What is, frankly, odd about antigun feminism in this regard is that the same analysts who routinely, and often angrily, question the factual accuracy of the way other economic and social issues pertaining to women[23] are portrayed in popular print and the electronic media, accept uncriti-cally the incessant warnings about the inherent dangers guns pose to women. They are also, in regard to gun regulation, willing to tolerate precisely the kind of government intrusion into individual behavior that they abhor, on sound feminist grounds, when it comes to such issues as sexual orientation or reproduc-tive rights.

A curious picture thus emerges in antigun feminism. In rejecting firearms as symbols of male power (the "Master's tools"), those who posit an antigun posi-tion as a sine qua non of feminism run the risk of reinforcing precisely those age-old stereotypes of female weakness and vulnerability which feminist theory seeks to dismantle. That those stereotypes are powerful—indeed, powerful enough effectively to block constructive dialogue about alternative views on women and guns—is amply borne out by a consideration of the following three cases. In each instance, an "orthodox" feminist antigun position has been maintained only at the expense of rationality and an objective consideration of the facts.

Feminist Opposition to Firearms: Three Case Studies

The Rapist in the Wilderness

An unfortunate consequence of antigun feminism is the alienation of a number of women who might otherwise identify themselves as feminists, but who have become convinced by the rhetoric that feminism is indeed reducible to "politically correct" stereotypes about it. For example, Karen McNutt, an attorney specializing in Second Amendment issues who writes for *Women & Guns* magazine, appeared to have antigun feminism in mind in a column titled "Swapping Freedom for Illusion":

> We are told that guns are an evil talisman that causes crime, accidents, and even suicides. If we can only get rid of or reduce the number of guns in our society, they preach, we will have a better community. These same self-appointed determiners of "politically correct thinking" are appalled to think that women might want to have guns.[24]

Indeed, the editors of *Ms.* magazine found the mere suggestion that gun ownership and use might be appropriate for women so ludicrous that they relegated the very existence of a publication devoted to "Women and Guns" to the level of a sick joke in *Ms's* "The Good, the Bad, and the Absurd" roundup of 1991 events.[25] They thereby wrote off not only *Women & Guns*, but its preponderantly female readership as well, lending a good deal of credence to McNutt's criticism.

Such wholesale dismissal of an entire group, in this case women gun owners and enthusiasts, can only arise from stereotyping. An excellent example of the process at work was provided a few years ago, in an exchange of viewpoints that appeared in the *Yale Law Journal*. In an article titled "The Embarrassing Second Amendment," University of Texas law professor Sanford Levinson cogently argued the case that both in terms of the original intent of its framers and of the best insights of constitutional interpretation, the Second Amendment must be construed as guaranteeing the individual right of private gun ownership.[26] He did this to some extent against his own will, since as a self-proclaimed ACLU liberal Levinson was inclined toward strict prohibitory gun regulation. Noting a relative dearth of legal literature on the Second Amendment, Levinson ventured the suggestion that the only logical way to account for the legal academy's near-silence on what had become an explosive social issue was to acknowledge that "the Amendment may be profoundly embarrassing to many who both support . . . regulation and view themselves as committed to zealous adherence to the Bill of Rights." He concluded that it appeared easier for gun-control advocates to leave the Second Amendment to stereotypical right-wing "gun nuts" and retreat to the moralistic high ground, than to confront the fact that "what it means to take rights seriously is that one will honor them even when there is significant social cost in doing so."[27] In the name of spurring "serious, engaged discussion," Levinson urged a sort of truce in which proponents of gun regulation would cease referring to their opponents as gun nuts, while gun-control opponents for their part would refrain from dismissing him and his colleagues as "bleeding heart liberals."

In a counterpoint essay, Women's Studies professor Wendy Brown, of the University of California, Santa Cruz, castigated Levinson for upholding—in the name of Constitutional law—a macho-sexist line of reasoning that "depicts man, collectively or individually, securing his autonomy, his woman and his territory with a gun."[28] Brown admitted that she was to some extent attracted by Levinson's contention that people may, for the sake of reasoned discourse, leave their prejudices about apparent differences aside. But she contended that her own social experience, as defined by feminist analysis, flew in the face of such placid acceptance of difference. To bring this point home, Brown illustrated her objection to Levinson's defense of the right to keep and bear arms with a story about her own experience.[29]

Brown recounted the dismay she and some friends felt when they returned from a week of backpacking in the High Sierras to find that her car would not start. Stranded at a remote trailhead, they were understandably relieved to discover another vehicle parked nearby. Seeking assistance, Brown encountered in it "a California sportsman making his way through a case of beer, flipping through the pages of a porn magazine and preparing to survey the area for his hunting club in anticipation of the opening of deer season." He was wearing an "NRA freedom" cap that told her that he and she were "at opposite ends of the political and cultural universe." But, "Not feeling particularly discriminating, I enlisted his aid." After two hours of concentrated labor, the man managed to get Brown's auto running, and she and her friends were on their way.

Afterward, Brown reflected that her rescuer and she were indeed opposite numbers. He had come to the high country "preparing to shoot the wildlife I came to revere, he living out of his satellite-dished Winnebago and me out of my dusty backpack, he sustained by his guns and beer, me by my Nietzsche and trail mix." His gun (or, rather, his NRA cap, since there is no evidence that he was in fact armed on this occasion) was, however, the decisive factor separating them.

> It occurred to me then, and now, that if I had run into him in those woods without my friends or a common project for us to work on, I would have been seized with one great and appropriate fear: rape. During the hours I spent with him, I had no reason to conclude that his respect for women's personhood ran any deeper than his respect for the lives of Sierra deer, and his gun could well have made the difference between an assault that my hard-won skills in self-defense could have fended off and one against which they were useless.[30]

Nothing in Brown's own tale suggests that the man had in any way threatened her. Unwittingly, she therein provided an illustration of precisely the point Levinson had been making about the futility of combating one stereotype (in this case, the beer-drinking lecherous gun nut) with another (the nonviolent nature devotee). That the former is male, the latter female, is not accidental. Quite the contrary, for Brown this fact is the heart of the matter, because of the way it points to "the differences between the social positioning and experiences of men and women in our culture." Men (especially gun-wielding sportsmen) are potential rapists, women (especially left-leaning feminists?) potential victims. Feminist analysis is in this case reduced to the facile application of an unflattering stereotype, without concern for any factual evidence which might challenge its legitimacy.

Noting that another interpreter might well have seen in Brown's experience "a wonderful story about the best of America: two strangers who disagree on practically everything, ignoring differences of politics, sex, and social and economic class, cooperating in the wilderness to solve a serious problem faced by only one of them," legal scholar Douglas Laycock supplies some of the factual information which Brown had blithely overlooked:

> There is no evidence that hunters or gun enthusiasts are disproportionately prone to rape. One study found no correlation between reported incidents of rape and the number of hunting licenses issued in a jurisdiction; another study found statistically significant negative correlations after controlling for population. A third study found no correlation between rape and the number of subscriptions to gun and hunting magazines. A fourth study found no correlation between gun ownership and attitudes toward feminism. Guns are used in only 9 percent of all rapes and attempts, and it is a reasonable guess that nearly all of these are handguns.[31]

Laycock also observes that it is instructive to consider how differently this story would have been told had Brown's car broken down in Harlem and her Good Samaritan been a young black male carrying "a gun, a beer, a porn magazine, and a boombox."

> Either her fear of rape would not have appeared in a respectable journal, or it would have appeared in a confessional tone and emphasized a very different moral. The point would have been: "He came only to help me, and I was afraid to let him; see how fear and racism distorts our whole society." The point would not have been: "I was forced to ask him for help, and it is a good thing I was not alone or he might have raped me."[32]

At a time when feminist literature on rape and sexual assault is coming increasingly under attack by interpreters who would like to write it off as simply so much antimale hysteria,[33] Brown's ungracious characterization of the man in the NRA cap is particularly unfortunate. Not only does she sound like a "victim feminist" who at heart thinks all (or most) men are rapists, she also seems utterly blind to the class snobbery implied in her anecdote. Brown also appears to be unaccountably unaware of the fact—well established in the rape literature—that the majority of rapes are committed by husbands, boyfriends, or acquaintances.

Not only would rape have been unlikely in the situation she describes, her closing suggestion that the man's very assertion of his right to keep and bear arms amounts to a form of "violation" for her suggests that she is incapable of conceiving this man to be anything other than a walking embodiment of a stereotype. This is an extraordinary amount of symbolic baggage for an NRA cap to carry.

As we shall see in the next case, the antigun lobby counts upon the NRA to evoke precisely this response in people.

"The Most Powerful and Evil Lobby in the World"

According to the Coalition to Stop Gun Violence, the National Rifle Association—"the most powerful and evil lobby in the world"—is Public Enemy No. 1. "For years the NRA has terrorized, bullied and intimidated our representatives in Washington."[34] In 1993, a group of twenty-six U.S. Congresswomen decided to take on the evil lobby. The issue was women's self-defense.

The congresswomen's charge was that the NRA was exploiting women for political and financial gain. Whatever these representatives' original objective may have been, they wound up accomplishing two things. First, they helped attract far more national media attention to the NRA's newly launched "Refuse To Be A Victim" program than it otherwise would have gotten. And, second, they put themselves on record as opposing the distribution of free information, and the offering of low-cost seminars, about women's self-defense options.

While unlikely to be confused with an aggressively profeminist organization, the NRA has paid steadily increasing attention to women's concerns in the 1990s. In January 1990, a Women's Issues and Information (WI&I) Office was established. In April of 1992 both NRA magazines (*American Hunter* and *American Rifleman*) began running a bimonthly "NRA Women's Voice" column, authored by WI&I director Liz Swasey. While the stated objectives of the WI&I office include, "to promote and publicize the association and its programs to women and to increase women's participation in hunting and shooting sports,"[35] Swasey's column regularly focused on various aspects of women's gun ownership for self-protection. The NRA's official stance relative to women and guns, emphasized in one way or another in each of Swasey's columns, is summed up as follows:

> Whether for self-protection, competitive or recreational shooting, hunting or a variety of other reasons, the decision to own a firearm is a highly personal one. And while the NRA doesn't *advocate* gun ownership for everyone, it does stand completely committed to the right of the individual to *choose*—a right guaranteed by the Constitution and reaffirmed through safe, responsible and effective firearms use.[36]

With Swasey's departure from WI&I in 1994 to head the NRA's "Crime Strike" anticrime program, and the appointment of Sonny Jones (founding editor of *Women & Guns*) to head the new Women's Personal Safety office, the NRA appeared to be consolidating its efforts to make women's issues—especially those relating to self-defense, armed or otherwise—more prominent features of the organization's overall political and social agenda.

The reasons for this move were obviously complex, and fundraising—via attracting new female members—cannot be discounted as an important motivation. However, the oft-repeated charge that this amounts to crass manipulation and exploitation of women does not necessarily follow: the NRA, after all, is an advocacy organization, and it is consistent with its mission to attract like-minded members, perhaps especially from among traditionally underrepresented constituencies. Given the marked increase in female gun ownership and use over the last decade, the NRA's vigorous interest in appealing to women makes a certain amount of practical sense.[37]

Indeed, the NRA would have to be extraordinarily sexist and stupid to ignore the significant portion of the female population that appears to be in complete agreement with the NRA's agenda. An article in *Campaigns and Elections* magazine in early 1995 analyzed exit polling results from seven different states; the pollsters had listed various organizations and asked respondents, "I'd like to know for each individual organization if that group speaks for you all of the time, most of the time or some of the time." In Idaho, Oklahoma, Tennessee, and South Carolina, the percentage of female voters who said that the NRA speaks for them "all the time" was higher than the number who said that the Democratic party or the Republican party spoke for them "all of the time."[38] In Michigan, Minnesota, and Pennsylvania, the NRA finished behind the Democrats but ahead of the Republican party for "all the time" support from female voters.[39]

In terms of outreach to women who are not necessarily in complete agreement with the NRA, the centerpiece in the NRA's women's initiative is the "Refuse To Be A Victim" program, an ambitious public information effort comprised of two major parts: a national toll-free number that provides callers with information in the form of a brochure about women's self-defense strategies, and an economically priced ($20.00) three-hour self-defense seminar taught by women. In both the brochure and the seminar, firearms are briefly mentioned as among the options available to women for self-protection. The emphasis is on women's responsibly choosing from among various alternatives, and their taking positive steps to develop a "personal safety strategy."[40]

The idea of choice at the heart of the "Refuse To Be A Victim" promotional campaign ("How to choose to refuse to be a victim") has led some critics to accuse the NRA of cynically appropriating the feminist language of reproductive rights.[41] The NRA is in something of a double-bind in this regard: it either ignores the changing roles of women and draws the charge of being insensitive to women's needs and interests, or it seeks to speak to the legitimate concerns of contemporary American women, thus risking the accusation of employing exploitative tactics. Hence, the NRA's promotional literature about the program takes pains to stress that "You won't be encouraged to own a firearm. You won't be asked to join the NRA."[42]

Rep. Nita Lowey (D-NY) and twenty-five of her House colleagues,[43] however, were not inclined to take the NRA at its word. In October 1993, shortly after the NRA had launched the "Refuse To Be A Victim" seminar program in three test cities (Miami, Houston, and Washington, D.C.), the congresswomen sent a letter to NRA president Robert Corbin demanding that NRA "immediately cease your advertising campaign aimed at the women of America." The letter read, in part:

> Under the guise of providing information about ways to increase personal safety, your four-page magazine ad[44] invites women to call an NRA hotline and join the "NRA's grassroots movement," and learn about firearms.
>
> While we enthusiastically support legitimate efforts to increase personal safety awareness, your commitment to women's safety is undermined by your continued opposition to gun control legislation that would make America safer. This ad campaign is a thinly veiled attempt by NRA to add new members and promote gun ownership by preying on women's legitimate fears of violence. Women who fear crime must not be cynically exploited as an untapped market.[45]

The letter went on to cite several bits of statistical data from "a study recently released by the *New England Journal of Medicine*"[46] and urged NRA support for the Brady Bill then pending congressional approval. It concluded, "Removing guns from our streets would certainly provide American women with more protection than the NRA."[47]

To coincide with the delivery of the letter to Corbin, Rep. Lowey announced to the press that there would be a demonstration in front of NRA's Washington headquarters. Only five of the letter's signers showed up, to be confronted by a substantial media corps, one of whom asked whether any of the demonstrators had any firsthand experience of a "Refuse To Be A Victim" seminar. None had.

Meanwhile, Tanya Metaksa, head of NRA's lobbying arm Institute for Legislative Action (ILA) also arrived, accompanied by several progun spokeswomen,[48] to hold an impromptu press conference. This quickly led to appearances by Metaksa on CNN news and Larry King's radio program, as well as the *Good Morning, America* and *Today* shows. In the first three weeks of the "Refuse To Be A Victim" program's existence, and no doubt largely owing to this national exposure, the NRA received close to five thousand requests for more information about the program.

On October 25, Metaksa, who also chairs the NRA's Women's Policy Committee, wrote a letter to the twenty-six congresswomen. Quoting their statement of "enthusiastic" support for "legitimate efforts to increase personal safety awareness," she invited them to attend the next "Refuse To Be A Victim" seminar, scheduled for October 30. The letters were hand-delivered to Capitol Hill. None of the twenty-six women replied, or attended the seminar.

The congresswomen's response would seem to be a case of the devil you don't know being better than the one you do. It was apparently easier to demonize the NRA's effort on behalf of women's self-defense than to take any substantial steps to learn about it. Those who did, such as *Washington Post* columnist Judy Mann, reported that the NRA was indeed true to its advertising when it came to not pushing guns or NRA membership at the seminars. Mann noted that she had approached the "Refuse To Be A Victim" program as a skeptic, but had retained an open mind:

> One cannot help but be somewhat skeptical about a campaign that is obviously good public relations. But the NRA didn't become the most feared lobby in the country by being out of touch with public sentiment, so it is possible that the revulsion sweeping the country over mass murder by firearms has finally gotten through to its 75-member board.

Mann came away from her investigation with an altered view of "the most evil lobby in the world"; she concluded,

> What is particularly appealing about the NRA campaign is its emphasis on the idea that there are other things women can do to ensure their safety besides getting a gun. They can refuse to be victims. This is an empowering idea. If the campaign also signals a move toward more responsible civic behavior on the part of NRA, then that should be welcomed too.[49]

Whatever one's views regarding the "deeply personal choice" of firearms ownership, an informed perspective like Mann's is clearly a more adequate response to the NRA's women's self-defense campaign than the congress-women's knee-jerk antigun hyperbole. The same tendency toward blanket condemnation, rather than objectively reasoned investigation of the issues, characterizes the next case of feminist stereotyping as well.

"Is This Power Feminism?"

In the May 1992 issue of *Women & Guns*, Sonny Jones wrote an editorial in which she blasted feminists as "progressively militant" and hypocritically out of touch with the real-life concerns of "women like you and me." Stating (inaccurately) that groups like the National Organization for Women (NOW) did not take personal safety seriously as an issue of primary importance for women, Jones (with somewhat more accuracy) castigated feminist groups for their "categorical" opposition to "gun ownership as a viable self-defense option." She concluded that the feminist movement, in essence, had nothing to offer her or her readers, who inhabit "the land of reality."[50]

Reader response to the editorial must have come as something of a shock to Jones. A significant number of *Women & Guns* readers turned out to be self-identified feminists, who reprimanded her for selling feminism short. Jones subsequently wrote, "Reaction to the May commentary on feminism just goes to show how diverse a group gun owners really are. And despite the official positions of NOW and like organizations, we all agree that self-defense is among the most important rights of all."[51] More recently, Peggy Tartaro (Jones's successor as *Women & Guns* executive editor) commented that "Women gun owners, and our readers in particular, probably skew a whole lot more liberal than either the general gun-owning population, or than the popular conception of what a gun owner is like."[52]

That this might be the case apparently never occurred to the editors of *Ms.* magazine when, relying on the popular conception of gun owners (the stereotype created largely by the media and the antigun lobby), they set out to do a special issue on women and guns. The cover of the May/June 1994 issue featured a photo of a Smith and Wesson semi-automatic pistol (casting a hot-pink shadow), with the words "Is This Power Feminism? The Push to Get Women Hooked on Guns." Inside were two articles, one by Ann Jones, author of *Women Who Kill*, titled "Living with Guns, Playing with Fire," the other by *USA Today* reporter Ellen Neuborne, under the title "Cashing In on Fear: The NRA Targets Women." That the "most evil lobby in the world" was the *bête noire* behind the *Ms.* articles was clear in the editorial comment preceding them:

> Just when we thought we were beginning to turn the tide in favor of gun control, along comes the NRA with a campaign that encourages women to exercise our right to "choose to refuse to be a victim." The new focus on women comes not because this organization supports our right to be free from rape and battery, harassment and discrimination, but because these sharpshooters are trying to seduce women into becoming dues-paying, gun-toting members with promises of power from the barrel of a gun.[53]

We have already seen that an objective consideration of the "Refuse To Be A Victim" campaign shows this not to be the case. Yet the power of a stereotype lies precisely in its ability to blind an already biased observer to what is before her very eyes. How else can one account for Neuborne's reiterating in her article every charge about the NRA's cynical manipulation of women and its progun ulterior motives, notwithstanding her own admission that in the seminar she in fact attended guns only "came up at the very end."[54] Neuborne does mount a valid, and important, criticism of NRA's approach in the campaign. The "Refuse To Be A Victim" materials all focus on what one instructor called " 'garden variety bad guys'—strangers who commit acts of violence. Stalking, domestic violence, and workplace violence—all major crime problems for women—were ignored."[55] Her criticism would have been more pointed, and carried more argumentative weight, had it not been accompanied by what has by now become the standard array of antigun statistics derived from the Kellermann studies, bolstered by an equally familiar conspiracy theory about the NRA's hidden agenda "to frighten women into buying guns."[56]

While Neuborne settles for rehashing antigun propaganda in the name of investigative journalism, Ann Jones's article presents a more problematic take on feminist opposition to women's gun ownership. Jones also questions the NRA's motives and its use of the rhetoric of choice, but she acknowledges that the question of armed self-defense might indeed occur to a reasonable woman faced with life in a violently antifeminist society.

> Women are fearful, yes. With good reason. But we're also beyond fear. We're fed up.... Women's interest in guns—such as it is—isn't just about fear. It's about fighting back.[57]

She goes on to disclose that "I know something about fighting back myself—and about the consolations of a gun." Jones had grown up hunting with her father, but gave it up at eighteen, when she shot her first deer and "the deadly and irrevocable consequence of what I was doing came home to me." However, she kept the shotgun her father had given her as a memento. Years later, on the day Martin Luther King, Jr., was assassinated, Jones borrowed a canoe and paddled into the center of a lake, where she dropped the shotgun into the water.

> I wanted to rid the world of guns and all the violence and death they seem to represent; at least I could get rid of mine. The nonviolent path of Dr. King would be my own.

Jones's symbolic resolve was to weaken twice in later life: once when, hounded by racists in the Southern town where she was teaching at an African-American college, she acquired a .38 special for self-protection, and later, when that same handgun gave her a feeling of security after she was made a victim of harassment while investigating a murder for a book she was working on. However, she eventually decided, "The threat of violence, if it makes you play by its rules, is just as deadly to the spirit as violence itself. It wasn't a gun I needed. It was courage." She disposed of the pistol.

Remarking that it saddens her now to read stories of women purchasing guns "to gain a sense of power and control . . . for I imagine them afflicted with the same incapacitating fear and the same profound anger at being made to feel afraid," Jones next recounts the story of April LaSalata. In 1988, this Long Island woman was viciously assaulted by her ex-husband, Anthony, who was charged with attempted murder as a result. When he was released on bond and the judge refused the prosecutor's request to increase bail to keep the man in jail, April LaSalata applied for a permit to carry a gun for self-protection. Her permit was denied, and within a year she was dead at thirty-four, shot twice in the head on her own doorstep, by her ex-husband.

This is an all-too-familiar scenario in American society; indeed, it is precisely the sort of data the NRA might use to build its case for women's right to armed self-defense.[58] Jones's use of it, however, defies logic. "If April LaSalata had been granted that gun permit, could she have saved herself? Maybe so. Maybe not." Jones immediately follows this equivocation by remarking, "As a practical matter, leaving the human drama aside and looking at the studies and the numbers, it doesn't make much sense to own a gun." With this cavalier dismissal of LaSalata's "human drama" (perhaps it wasn't a gun she lacked, it was courage?), Jones proceeds to recite the standard litany of "facts" derived from antigun studies.

As is the case in the Neuborne article, Jones's retreat into antigun rhetoric blunts the effect of one very solid criticism she has to make of the way gun violence is handled in our society: the fact that women who shoot men in self-defense in domestic violence situations too often receive unusually harsh prison sentences.[59] For Jones, however, it is up to the law to protect women from domestic abuse, and achieving women's safety through legal means is a job for women and men collectively. It is not, in her view, "a job to be done piecemeal by lone women, armed with pearl-handled pistols, picking off batterers and rapists one by one."

Significantly, Jones sees individual women's decisions to arm themselves as attributable, at least in part, to a widespread "mother lode of anger" among women, "a vast buildup of unrequited insults and injuries."

> Women exchange high fives in the street when Lorena Bobbitt is acquitted. Women cheer in the movie theater when Louise pulls the trigger on that scumbag wanna-be rapist in the parking lot. It's like living on an emotional fault-line; we go along calmly and then one day, boom, some little incident sets us quaking with laughter that smacks of sweet revenge.[60]

Who knows just how much anger lurks in the heart that beats beneath the "Thelma and Louise Finishing School" T-shirt, and how that anger might reasonably translate into some women's resolve to take charge of their own self-protection through responsible gun ownership? Unfortunately, Jones leaves the latter question unresolved, owing to her conviction that gun ownership inevitably represents a capitulation to male-defined institutionalized violence.

A measure of the diversity of opinion among feminists on the issue of armed self-defense did, however, emerge in the reader response to the *Ms.* antigun issue. Of the nine letters published in the September/October issue, five argued a far more balanced view of the issue of women and guns than the Jones and Neuborne articles had offered. One writer commented, "How uncharacteristically sexist for *Ms.* to treat women as a homogenous group and to portray women gun owners as in a 'panic' and as dupes of the NRA!" This self-identified gun owner (who also proclaimed her respect for women who choose not to own guns) went on to observe:

> It is ironic that on page 16 of this same issue, *Ms.* gave the armed women of the Zapatista Army of National Liberation unqualified respect and support. . . . *Ms.* apparently finds no need for an antigun stance when a worthy uprising is sanctioned and led by men.[61]

Another reader, who identified herself as an advocate of nonlethal forms of self-defense, asked:

> Instead of condescending to women with guns by viewing them as dupes of male domination, why not simply acknowledge that not all women agree on how to challenge the rape culture? Why not address gun-toting women as a competent, committed, articulate group of people with whom you disagree and then dialogue?[62]

This last question captures the essence of the problem raised by reductive feminist stereotyping of gun owners, and the general denial within feminist literature of the complexity of the issues of gun ownership and gun control. As Sanford Levinson noted, constructive dialogue can begin only when opposing sides agree to disagree with a sense of respect and mutual regard.

The most reliable factual evidence currently available in fact provides the foundation for a feminist argument in favor of women's armed self-defense. The construction of this argument, however, entails confronting and dismantling several traditional ideas about the nature of power and aggression as women and men experience them in our culture. It is to this topic we now turn in our effort toward creating the ground for constructive debate of the gun-control issue within feminism.

Women, Aggression, and the Question of Self-Defense

"When I get out of here," said Ruth Childers, whose shotgun went off by accident, "I'll never have a gun around the house again." "If I ever get out of here," countered Joyce DeVillez, "I'll never have a man around the house again."[63]

The question of women's armed self-defense is clearly more complex than what the conventional feminist reductionism of "male power" versus "female nonviolence" allows. Indeed, at issue is the very nature of women's relation to violence. D. A. Clarke, a lesbian feminist, throws considerable light on the contours of the problem in an essay titled "A Woman with a Sword: Some Thoughts on Women, Feminism and Violence." Clarke wants to call radically into question feminism's too-ready reliance upon strategies of nonviolence, especially in response to male sexual assault and battery. She acknowledges that nonviolence can indeed be a powerful form of resistance to oppression. But, she shrewdly observes, nonviolence is powerful and effective only when practiced by people who clearly *could* resort to violent force should they so choose. Women's advocacy of nonviolence tends to be ineffective, she observes,

> because women are traditionally considered incapable of violence, particularly of violence against men. . . . One of our great myths is that a "real lady" can and shall handle any difficulty, defuse any assault, without ever raising her voice or losing her manners. Female rudeness or violence in resistance to male aggression has often been taken to prove that the woman was not a lady in the first place, and therefore deserved no respect from the aggressor or sympathy from others.[64]

It may seem, at first blush, as if feminist theory would be the last place one would look to find conventional images of "femininity" or ladylike behavior. Yet, as we saw in the cases of Wendy Brown and Ann Jones above, cultural stereotypes of female vulnerability and nonaggression can all too easily slip into the guise of feminist analysis. Feminist psychologist Naomi Goldenberg sees in this tendency a real pitfall for feminism:

> For a long time, an important part of feminist ideology has been the relative innocence of women in comparison with men. As so many fine theorists argue, because women have not been the direct architects of violent institutions, they are more likely to dismantle those institutions. . . . However, if we women are to be successful at creating more humane institutions, we must not become too enamoured with a rhetoric of female purity.[65]

She cites Melanie Klein's observation that attempts to focus solely on the "positive, well-wishing efforts" of persons (male or female), without acknowledging aggression as a nasty fact of human psychology, are "doomed to failure from the beginning."[66]

Studies show that women are clearly as capable of aggression as men; gender differences in aggressive behavior arise from cultural stereotypes that are internalized at a very early age, with the result not only that girls grow up seeming "naturally" less inclined toward aggression, but also feeling more anxiety about their aggressive tendencies.[67] Girls learn very early on that aggressive behavior is not an appropriate or effective option for them.

> By the age of two, girls' aggression is much more likely to be ignored by playmates than is boys', and this lack of response is very effective in stopping behavior. Boys are overwhelmingly more successful than girls in using aggression to gain compliance from another child. So the little girl learns not only that aggression is emotionally dangerous but that it doesn't get her what she wants.[68]

Aggression comes to be identified with masculinity and male power. For a man, to be aggressive is to be in control; for a woman, it is to be out of control. Thus, the image of a woman "armed and dangerous"—the woman who can fight back when attacked—is extremely problematic, for both men and women.[69] According to psychologist and criminologist Anne Campbell:

> The very use of violence clearly casts a woman in the role of villain. Boys recognize bad guys by their refusal to follow the rules of fighting. Girls recognize bad women by their use of aggression at all. Good girls don't fight.[70]

And they certainly don't fight back.[71]

While feminist psychology has in the last generation or so made great strides in laying bare the sexist underpinnings of gender-role socialization, it has tended to do an end-run around the issue of female aggression, seeking in general to celebrate women's skills for "affiliation" and peacemaking.[72] Yet, as Campbell notes,

> By the 1970s and 1980s, women's aggression had become harder and harder to ignore. Female criminologists began to write about this taboo subject, and national surveys revealed women's high level of aggression in the home. Instead of putting a spotlight on the new findings, however, these uncomfortable events triggered the minimization phase. Men preferred not to dwell on women's aggression because it was an ugly sign of potential resistance. Women's groups colluded with them; to recognize its existence would draw attention away from men's far more lethal aggression as well as highlighting undesirably assertive qualities in a group they wanted to depict as victims. Most violent offenders were men, so women's aggression was not a serious social problem. It could be studied as a curiosity, an aberration, characteristic of very few women but not weighty enough to join the mainstream social agenda.[73]

To the extent to which female aggression remains viewed as essentially pathological, feminist arguments grounded in an ethic of nonviolent resistance are fundamentally meaningless. This is the irony that Clarke points to when she argues that nonviolence would only really make sense as a political and ethical position were more women willing to engage in violent resistance against aggression:

> If the risk involved in attacking a woman were greater, there might be fewer attacks. If women defended themselves violently, the amount of damage they were willing to do to would-be assailants would be the measure of their seriousness about the limits beyond which they would not be pushed. If more women killed husbands and boyfriends who abused them or their children, perhaps there would be less abuse. A large number of women refusing to be pushed any further would erode, however slowly, the myth of the masochistic female which threatens all our lives.[74]

Naomi Wolf strikes a similar note when she suggests that one effective strategy for rape prevention might well be publicizing the growing number of women who are armed and potentially dangerous to attackers. She writes:

> I don't want to carry a gun or endorse gun proliferation. But I am happy to benefit from publicizing the fact that an attacker's prospective victim has a good chance of being armed. . . . Our cities and towns can be plastered with announcements that read, "A hundred women in this town are trained in combat. They may be nurses, students, housewives, prostitutes, mothers. The next women to be assaulted might be one of these."[75]

Antigun feminism, of course, would argue that this is not an effective strategy for women, appealing to the conventional wisdom that it tends to be more dangerous to resist an attacker, especially to use armed resistance, [76] than it is to try to flee, to talk him out of it, or ultimately to submit. However, the commonplace idea that aggressive resistance spurs more violent attack is increasingly being called into question by empirical data.

In one major rape study conducted by Sarah Ullman and Raymond Knight of Brandeis University, two facts emerge with startling clarity. One is that women who employ forceful resistance stand a higher chance of avoiding rape than do those who attempt such nonforceful strategies as fleeing, pushing the offender away, pleading, or reasoning. The other is that nonforceful verbal strategies actually exacerbate the situation:

> Research on rapist motivation suggests that some offenders seek to feel power and control over a weaker person. . . . Such nonforceful verbal, sex-stereotypical responses (e.g., begging, pleading, and reasoning) following violent physical attacks might thus coincide with how many rapists want a woman to act.[77]

They conclude, therefore, that "women should be encouraged to scream and fight when physically attacked,"[78] rather than conform to behavior dictated by gender stereotypes.

Overall, the more violent the initial attack, the higher the chance of a woman's being raped, no matter what she does. However, Ullman and Knight argue, along with other researchers, "resistance must be at an equal level to the offender's attack to avoid rape."[79] There is simply no empirical evidence that a woman's forceful resistance makes her more likely to be raped; indeed, the evidence implies quite the opposite. Ullman and Knight focused their research on stranger rape, but suggest that there is good reason to infer that forceful self-defense strategies may work equally well in situations of acquaintance and marital rape.

Their suggestions are borne out by another study, conducted by Frances Haga and a team of researchers from North Carolina State and Virginia Commonwealth Universities. Driving their research was a question "of central concern to all women":

> What's a woman to do to defend herself, and why does whatever she actually does in her own physical defense upset people enough to seem to be always telling her she should have done something else?[80]

Utilizing a telephone survey of nearly ten thousand respondents, the researchers verified what will come as no surprise to any woman: the perception of what constitutes violent crime against a person, and that person's appropriate level of response, depends very much upon whether the perpetrator of the violence is a stranger or an acquaintance. When the attacker is a stranger, "we can envision ourselves responding with sufficient unmitigated violence to end the attack." Hence, notwithstanding the conventional prescription of nonviolent resistance, there tends to be fairly unified social support for a woman who does manage to exercise lethal force against an unknown assailant (the so-called dark stranger in sociological literature).

But, as we know, the great majority of attacks against women are not stranger rapes or random predatory violence. The woman who seeks to use forceful self-defense at home finds lacking the public approbation that would come her way, were she to have exerted the same level of resistance against a stranger. Haga and her associates locate the problem in patriarchal domestic arrangements:

> Women will continue to fear assault from strangers, but it turns out that the people actually attacking them are people known to them, where all the dynamics of ending the attack are fraught with the constraints of civilized hierarchical arrangements, second-guessing and one-ups-personship.

Haga's study amply demonstrates that the "blame the victim" reflex is alive and well in the popular mind, though in the wake of the women's movement it now takes the form less of saying the woman "brought on" the attack than of asking what she could have done (nonforcefully) to avoid it. Haga concludes:

> Intuitively, women appear to understand that half the battle of surviving physical/ sexual assault is to have conducted themselves "with common sense" for so long, with so many public witnesses and personal friends of irreproachable character that if any criminal predator crashes through the fences of common sense everyone will know that she always locked every door and it wasn't her fault. If as much energy were directed into repelling assailants as is expended in avoiding blame for being in the wrong place at the wrong time, women could be even more successful in defending themselves against predatory attack.

Prior to the telephone survey, Haga had conducted another study which she called the "Images of Fear" project, in which she sought to gauge men's and women's responses to pictorial images of gun-armed women, many of them in clear situations of danger. Noting the "unusually emotional" reactions of her respondents, Haga reports:

> People seemed to have already developed intensely held answers to the question of *whether or not women should be defending themselves at all*, and nobody seemed to be wondering who women might be arming themselves against, and with what.[81]

Ambivalence about women's armed self-defense arises both from men's and women's subjective impressions about what is appropriate female behavior, and from commonly held cultural views about women's relationship to violence. Haga and her associates concluded that:

> the growth in female gun ownership may be in response to perceived risk from predatory crime [i.e., the "dark stranger" against whom, if anyone, it is arguably all right for a woman to arm herself], while resistance to female gun-handling may be due to male perception of being at increased risk in domestic violence.

This, of course, recalls the oft-cited argument, derived from the Kellermann studies, that the presence of a gun in the home makes spousal homicide more likely. And indeed, women who kill their husbands most often use a firearm to do it.[82] Yet, submerged in the statistics is the large number of domestic violence cases in which the killing was in self-defense. As to the legitimacy of men's fears of female retaliation, Edgar Suter says of Arthur Kellermann's study of "Men, Women and Murder":

> Almost all the "spouses and domestic partners" killed by women each year are the very same men, well known to the police, often with substance abuse histories, who have been brutalizing their wives, girlfriends and children. . . . The most meaningful conclusion from this study, the conclusion missed by Kellermann and Mercy, is the tremendous restraint shown by women, that they kill so few of their contemptible abusers.[83]

That more women do not resort to killing in self-defense probably has less to do with any incapacity (real or perceived) for aggression, than with the structure of the law. Whether in situations of domestic battery or predatory violence, lethal-force self-defense is only a right under the law when the victim is threatened with death or grievous bodily harm. Recently, feminist legal theory has begun to question the role of sex-bias in self-defense law, especially with regard to when the "reasonable woman" is justified in believing she is under threat of great or lethal bodily injury.[84] However, the law has a difficult time deciding whether rape and other forms of sexual assault constitute, in themselves, grievous bodily harm.[85] University of Maryland law professor Robin West observes:

> Sexual invasion through rape is understood to be a harm, and is criminalized as such, only when it involves some other harm: today, when it is accompanied by violence that appears in a form men understand (meaning plausible threat of annihilation); in earlier times, when it was understood as theft of another man's property.[86]

As Wendy Williams of Georgetown Law School points out, thanks to gender-role stereotypes that are literally millennia old, the law continues to define rape as a sexual act (rather than an act of violence), and sex as something a man does to a woman. The male is the sexual aggressor, so the problem for police and the courts revolves around whether the woman consents, submits, or declines.[87]

This fact helps shed light on the question that emerged from Haga's "Images of Fear" study, i.e., *whether or not women should be defending themselves at all.* According to the conventional wisdom, women should look elsewhere for protection: to the men in their lives (though too many of these are the source, not the solution, of the problem), or to the police and courts. Yet the police often cannot be counted upon to provide protection for private citizens, and restraining orders against abusers and stalkers are notoriously ineffective.[88] This leads Don Kates to ask:

> How does society benefit if, instead of shooting the ex-husband who breaks into her house, a woman allows herself to be strangled because the civilized thing to do is to wait for him to be arrested for her murder? Far from advancing the cause of rational gun control, such attitudes actually retard it by creating "straw men" which aid the gun lobby in diverting attention from serious arguments for control. Unfortunately, such extreme attitudes seem to have played a major part in shaping the ideology and rhetoric of the gun control movement and have particularly influenced its analysis of defensive gun use.[89]

The same attitudes led to an astonishing arrogance on the part of some apologists for the antigun movement. Arthur Kellermann told an interviewer for *Health* magazine that "I don't think, in good conscience, I could advise a woman to get a handgun. Dial 911. Get an alarm instead."[90] This in itself is hardly a surprising comment, coming from the lead author of the several studies that drive the antigun lobby's campaign. What is rather more surprising is his admission, in the same article, that, "If you've got to resist, your chances of being hurt are less the more lethal your weapon. . . . If that were my wife, would I want her to have a thirty-eight special in her hand? . . . Yeah."[91]

Kellermann appears to be assuming here that the only sort of violence that could possibly befall his wife is random, predatory violence; hence, his reaction may be consistent with the findings of Haga's study about the sort of violent resistance permitted women in polite society.[92] The *Health* article reiterates the commonplace that "most" violent crimes occur away from home. However, random predatory violence is statistically less likely to happen to a woman than to a man.[93] As Kates has pointed out, most of the arguments typically employed by those who want to severely restrict or ban handgun use and ownership arise from middle-class, Caucasian, male experience.[94] The same is true for most of the crime reported on the evening news. Robbery, mugging, and assault—random violence for the most part, and for most individuals once-in-a-lifetime occurrences—are legitimate fears primarily for white men; thus it is only from a white male perspective that the argument that most violence occurs outside the home could make much sense as an argument against gun ownership in the home.

The claim that violence overwhelmingly occurs outside the home smacks of middle-class elitism, and—despite all protestations to the contrary—is inherently antifeminist. It erases domestic battery and acquaintance rape as crimes committed against women, cutting across all ethnic and economic categories and most usually in the home.[95] It also ignores the everyday reality of criminal violence in poor, generally nonwhite, neighborhoods and housing projects, violence which impacts nonwhite men and especially nonwhite women in disproportionate numbers.[96]

One can only marvel at the inconsistency implicit in Kellermann's allowing his wife a gun (in the abstract), while doing all he can to deprive women of the option of arming themselves against attack.[97] A kindred sort of middle-class tunnel vision is reflected in Ann Jones's reply to a question from *Ms.* regarding readers' responses to her antigun article. When asked, "What do we tell women who feel the police won't help them?" Jones responded:

> That's a good question. The alternative may be to go underground, and many women do that. . . . I got letters, too, from women who said that they managed to save themselves with a gun, and I think it's a terrible commentary on how we live now. I would suggest that women go underground, but I understand why many women don't.[98]

Exactly what kind of feminism sees the best alternative responses to male violence being either going "underground" or engaging in hand-wringing about the terrible state of things? The desire Jones shares with her colleagues at *Ms.* to imagine a better world, a world in which women could live in freedom from fear, is laudable. But what are women at risk to do in the meantime, while she and women of like persuasion debate nonviolent strategies for building that world? As Carol Ruth Silver and Don Kates remark, "musings about better solutions are of very little aid to a woman who is being strangled or beaten to death."[99] Regarding all those potential dangers of gun ownership and use repeated over and over by the antigun lobby, they go on to say:

> We find the dangers of individual choice considerably more acceptable than the arrogation of decision-making to a callous bureaucracy which sees to its own protection (and that of an influential, elite few others) while it cannot and will not provide protection to the ordinary individual to whom it denies a permit.[100]

Indeed, the gun issue for women seems to come down to the matter of choice, in the best feminist sense of that term. There is inevitably some risk involved in any choice as consequential as gun ownership; but ought not that risk be weighed by the individual woman herself, rather than by a paternalistic system that may not really understand her best interests, let alone share them? Thus, Ann Japenga summed up her investigative report on women's defensive gun ownership:

> For a woman considering this decision, the final call, in part, has to do with whether you believe people are basically reliable or unreliable. . . . This is where Kleck [Kellermann's opponent in the gun-control debate] and Kellermann really part ways. Kleck gives women credit for being able to make sound judgments. "A woman

considering whether to get a gun is in a better position than any conceivable researcher to judge the likelihood that there's someone in her household—her or anyone else—who's likely to slaughter someone," he says.[101]

As we saw at the outset, growing numbers of women are discounting conventional wisdom about female passivity, and are making informed decisions to purchase firearms today. It remains to consider who these women are, what packing a firearm means to them, and what it may mean more broadly in the context of a rapidly changing society.

Women, Firearms, and Empowerment

The real issue has to do with the use of lethal force, not with the means . . . the real issue is not the polemics of guns versus no guns; rather, for some women it is the choice of being victor or victim.[102]

Feminism is surely in some ways responsible for the large number of women who say they are arming themselves out of a deep sense that their self-protection is worth fighting for. Are these women, then, capitulating to male violence, or are they—as Wolf suggests—fighting fire with fire? Gun owner Leslita Williams, a forty-four-year-old librarian, responds this way:

So much of nonviolent philosophy was dreamed up by men who didn't have to worry about the kinds of violence women face today. . . . Everyone has to decide for herself. . . . In some ways I feel buying a gun is selling out. But the bottom line is, there is a war going on out there. You've got to do what it takes to stay alive.[103]

Williams decided to purchase a handgun ten years ago, when she and her women friends were terrorized by a rapist on the loose in their city (Athens, Georgia). Eight women, all of them "weaned on sixties-style nonviolence," enrolled in an armed self-defense course, meeting together in a consciousness-raising discussion over pizza after each class session. Ultimately, four of the women decided against arming themselves, arguing "We'd be stooping to the level of the enemy." Williams and three others judged a pacifist approach to be incongruent with the fact of a rapist at large.

Two things stand out about this anecdote. One is that it clearly exemplifies that the choice to arm oneself may certainly arise from a commitment to feminist politics and practice: that is, from the conviction that women's lives, safety, and peace of mind matter, and that it is up to women themselves to take responsibility for their own well-being. The other is that these women, in deciding either for or against gun ownership, had made an informed choice; they had not relied upon press reports or propaganda to make up their minds. As it turns out, both these facts are characteristic of women who own guns.

Hard data about women gun owners are not easy to come by. One reasonably reliable source of information is a reader survey published by *Women & Guns* magazine in 1994.[104] In light of this survey, Leslita Williams appears to be a fairly typical woman gun owner. The majority of women responding to the survey (52 percent) were middle-aged, between thirty-six and forty-nine years old, and 70 percent were married. Two-thirds had college or advanced degrees (34 percent had graduated from college, and an additional 32 percent had completed some form of postgraduate degree work);[105] by occupation they ranged from house-wives to professionals. An impressive 87 percent had taken some form of fire-arms instruction. Among reasons for gun ownership, 68 percent listed self-defense,[106] and the firearms of choice tended to be larger-caliber handguns. While only one-third of respondents had themselves been victims of serious crime, a significant 82 percent believed crime was on the increase in their locality (which tended to be rural and small town/city, probably reflecting among other things the relative difficulty of procuring firearms permits and instruction in many major population centers). Ninety-six percent were registered voters, as com-pared to 75 percent of the eligible voting population, indicative of a high level of political interest and engagement.

Interestingly, and no doubt reflecting the fact that *Women & Guns* counts among its readers a fairly large proportion of persons who might be classed not merely as gun owners, but as gun-enthusiasts,[107] the average length of time respondents had owned firearms was eleven and a half years, and on the average the women owned two or more firearms (long guns included).

In 1991, *Women & Guns* had published other survey data, collected by Fran Haga, reflecting the experience of women newer to gun ownership. Haga's sur-vey was based upon data collected during a series of women-only firearms instruction clinics offered during the summer of 1990 in Raleigh, North Caro-lina.[108] All participants in the clinics were novice shooters. They had come for instruction primarily out of concern for firearm safety and proficiency. As one woman phrased it (summarizing, Haga says, the "reasons given by the major-ity"), "I desire to become proficient in the use of my handgun. I've had little experience/exposure to handguns but have decided to consider it as an option for my personal safety."

In other key respects, however, their demographics looked much like those of the more experienced gun owners in the 1994 survey.[109] Sixty-five percent were over thirty years of age; half were heads of households. Over half (56 percent) had a college or advanced degree, and an additional 35 percent had "some college." Fifty-three percent listed their occupation as "professional," and 75 percent were registered voters.

Given the information yielded by these two surveys, it strains credulity to regard women gun owners as merely the unwitting dupes of the gun lobby. No one appears to be coercing them into considering gun ownership, and in fact their response to the prospect of firearms possession and use shows far more responsibility than that typically shown by novice, and even some experienced, male gun owners. Owing largely to ingrained cultural stereotypes, many teenage boys and adult men seem to believe that gun use should be natural, even instinc-tual, for them. Women tend to approach firearms—whether for self-protection, hunting, or recreational shooting—with far more respect, and more willingness to learn, and abide by, rules of safe handling and operation.[110]

Women also approach gun use with a somewhat greater sense of urgency than men typically do. In light not only of the violence of American society, but also of the social and cultural proscriptions against women's armed self-defense, gun ownership for women is necessarily serious business. This is particularly borne out by one hypothetical question that was included in the 1994 survey. *Women & Guns* asked its readers, "If it were illegal for you to carry a handgun for personal protection, and you felt threatened, would you carry [a gun] anyway, or obey the law?" Ninety-one percent of respondents said they would carry one anyway.[111]

What does it take to induce nine out of ten individuals in a sample of highly educated, socially responsible, and politically active women to readily imagine defying the law?[112] Tanya Metaksa has commented, relative to women's right to gun ownership, "There is a closet sisterhood of women who believe [in gun ownership] no matter what the law is."[113] Might this "closet sisterhood" be a counterpart to Ann Jones's women who opt to go "underground"? And should not all these women, who share so many fundamental concerns and experiences, be able to dialogue openly with one another?

Surely, the same sense of urgency is at work in both cases. Self-defense expert Paxton Quigley writes:

> As a former campus Vietnam War peace demonstrator and an early staff member of the first national gun-control organization, I have always championed the causes of peace and nonviolent behavior. But as a mother of two sons, I have always recognized in me a deeper, almost animal-like rage capable of causing me to do anything within my power, even kill, to protect my children. Every mother knows this undercurrent; we would die for our children, and most of us would kill to protect them. In a way, a person must know this warrior spirit is there, and can be called upon in a life-or-death crisis, even to think it would be possible to shoot someone in self-defense. If you recognize this kind of instinct in yourself, then I would say you should continue with your plans to learn self-defense skills with a gun.
>
> If, on the other hand, you have never been in touch with a feeling like that, and believe completely that you could not possibly fight back in a life-threatening crisis, do not buy a gun, whatever you do.[114]

Gun ownership is obviously not the best choice for every woman (nor for every man). But for those who approach it responsibly, it can be an empowering choice, both on the practical and on the symbolic level.

We saw early on that the gun is a potent cultural symbol of power; to a broader extent this is true of all arms. D. A. Clarke recognizes this with reference to the sword:

> A woman with a sword . . . is a powerful emblem. She is no one's property. A crime against her will be answered by her own hand. She is armed with the traditional weapon of honor and vengeance, implying both that she has a sense of personal dignity and worth, and that efforts against that dignity will be hazardous to the offending party.[115]

There is historical precedent for Clarke's assertion here. Don Kates remarks on the ancient symbolic significance of arms as signaling the status of free person·

"From Anglo-Saxon times 'the ceremony of freeing a slave included the placing in his hands of' arms 'as a symbol of new rank.' "[116] In this contextual setting, the sword or gun is no longer the "Master's tool" of oppression, but rather a sign of equality among persons.

In 1792, in the heat of the French Revolution, three hundred Parisian women presented the first of several petitions to the Legislative Assembly arguing their "natural right" to organize themselves into a unit of the National Guard. According to feminist historian Dominique Godineau:

> To be part of the armed organization of the sovereign people was one of the fundamental elements of citizenship. . . . With this demand, which would be repeated several times by 1793, these militant women laid claim to one of the rights of citizenship and thus to a place for themselves in the political sphere. Their wish to bear arms was not simply a matter of patriotic sentiment . . . it transcended sentiment to become a matter of power, of citizenship, and of equal rights for women.[117]

Then, as too frequently still, the women's request for equality on both the experiential and symbolic planes was met by the political and intellectual establishment with gasps of admonishment over the hazards inherent in inverting the "order of nature," as well as fears of the prospect that "a society destabilized by confusion of the sexes leads inevitably to chaos."[118]

Similar fears have apparently ruled gender politics in Switzerland, where "since 1291, when the people's assemblies formed circles in the village squares, and only men carrying a sword could vote, weapons have been synonymous with citizenship." David Kopel observes that "this tradition helps explain why the political and social emancipation of women has taken so much longer in Switzerland than in the rest of the Western world."[119]

The equation—actual as well as symbolic—of arms and citizenship may seem too politically charged for some tastes. Yet since the dawn of human time, men have in various ways sought to keep arms out of the hands of women. The discrete political and psychological reasons for the disarming of women fall outside the purview of this chapter. But the social consequences, in terms of women's lives and livelihoods, are all too apparent in contemporary America. So, too, as a result of the women's movement, are women's expanded options for confronting their history of disempowerment.

The traditional figure of Justice—an armed woman—is blind. When it comes to women's right to self-protection and freedom from fear, it is time to take the blindfold off that woman with a sword. Those millions of women who are taking charge of their own security, through firearms and other nonpassive means, present a forceful model of social and psychological empowerment. In the evolution of society toward genuine equality of the sexes, the "great equalizer" surely has a place.

NOTES

1. Naomi Wolf, *Fire with Fire: The New Female Power and How It Will Change the 21st Century* (New York: Random House, 1993), p. 216.

2. Associated Press report, "Support Grows for Plugging Handgun Sales," *Billings* (Montana) *Gazette*, June 4, 1993, p. 1. Harris likened the galvanizing of public opinion on the gun control issue to the earlier "crystallization of public support for abortion rights."

3. In fact, the National Sporting Goods Association reports that in the three years from 1989 to 1992, proportionally more women bought long guns for hunting or target shooting than purchased handguns. Grits Gresham, "Women Take the Field," *Sports Afield*, May 1994, p. 50. However, among women who own guns for multiple purposes, 68 percent cite self-defense as one of their reasons for arming themselves. Peggy Tartaro, "A Picture of Women Gun Owners," *Women & Guns*, March, 1994, p. 31.

In the 1980s and 1990s, the growing attention being paid to armed women has often been accompanied by the suggestion that women are arming themselves in record numbers. The precise number of armed women is not the focus of this chapter; instead, the chapter evaluates, from a feminist viewpoint, the decisions of the millions of women who have chosen to arm for protection, and the criticisms of those women by some feminists.

One recent study, conducted by the National Opinion Research Center, is widely cited for the proposition that there has not been an increase in female gun ownership. See Tom W. Smith and Robert J. Smith, "Changes in Firearms Ownership among Women, 1980–1994," paper presented at the annual meeting of the American Society of Criminology, Miami, November 1994. This paper should, perhaps, not be considered the final word on the subject. The percentage of women owning guns fluctuates wildly according to the paper's data: The percentage starts at 10.5 in 1980, increases by nearly half, to 14.5 in 1982, falls by over a third to 9.3 in 1989, again rises by half to 13.8 in 1993, and then settles off at 12.7 in 1994. Whatever the trends of female gun ownership in the last fifteen years, it seems unlikely that the period has seen two separate, major booms punctuated by one major bust that have eluded the attention of other observers and social scientists. The data do show an increase in the percentage of women owning firearms from 10.5 percent in the first year (1980) to 12.7 percent in the final year (1994). Ibid., p. 12, Table 1. Many women who may not report that they "own" a gun may use a gun formally owned by someone else in their household, such as a husband.

4. See Don Kates, *Guns, Murders and the Constitution: A Realistic Assessment of Gun Control* (San Francisco: Pacific Research Institute for Public Policy, 1990), p. 31.

5. Liz Swasey, then director of Women's Issues at the National Rifle Association, in an interview reported by Bryan Miller in "Guns and Women," *Chicago READER*, February 4, 1994, p. 11. Swasey explained that the NRA estimates there are between fifteen and twenty million women gun owners. She also noted that the National Opinion Research Center, in a recent annual survey, had reckoned that thirty-four million American women have "access to firearms."

6. See, e.g., Margaret Gordon and Stephanie Rigor, *The Female Fear: The Social Cost of Rape* (Chicago: University of Illinois Press, 1989).

7. See Audre Lorde in Cherrie Moraga and Gloria Anzaldua, eds., *This Bridge Called My Back: Writings of Radical Women of Color* (Latham, N.Y.: Kitchen Table Press, 1983).

8. Laura Shapiro, "She Enjoys Being a Girl," *Newsweek*, November 15, 1993, p. 82. It is worth noting that Wolf's discussion of women and guns occupies a total of six pages in a

353-page book, infinitesimal in comparison to the relative page-space Shapiro devoted to critiquing it.

9. Ann Jones, "Living with Guns, Playing with Fire," *Ms.*, May/June 1994, p. 44.

10. "No, Feminists Don't All Think Alike (Who Says We Have To?)," *Ms.*, September/October 1993. The other analysts featured in the round-table discussion were Gloria Steinem, bell hooks, and Urvashi Vaid; see pp. 34–43.

11. David B. Kopel, *The Samurai, the Mountie, and the Cowboy: Should America Adopt the Gun Controls of Other Democracies?* (Amherst, N.Y.: Prometheus Books, 1992), p. 346.

12. Jeff Silverman, "Romancing the Gun," *New York Times*, June 20, 1993.

13. Naomi Wolf remarks about the film's popularity among female audiences: "They were cheering the public affirmation of the part of themselves that was no longer content to just take it, whatever 'it' might be, in silence any longer." Wolf, *Fire with Fire*, p. 38.

14. "Women as Action Heroes," *Glamour*, March 1994, p. 153.

15. Melinda Henneberger, "The Small Arms Industry Comes On to Women," *New York Times*, October 24, 1993.

16. "Should You Own a Gun?" *Glamour*, January 1994, p. 44.

17. Steve Fishman, "What You Know about Guns Can Kill You," *Vogue*, October 1993, p. 142. Italics added.

18. "Targeting Women," *USA Today*, May 24, 1994, p. 12A.

19. Chief among them: A. Kellermann et al., "Gun Ownership as a Risk Factor for Homicide in the Home," *New England Journal of Medicine* 329, no. 15 (1993): 1084–91; A. Kellermann and D. Reay, "Protection or Peril? An Analysis of Firearms-Related Deaths in the Home," *New England Journal of Medicine* 314 (1986): 1557–60; A. Kellermann et al., "Suicide in the Home in Relationship to Gun Ownership," *New England Journal of Medicine* 327 (1992): 467–72; A. Kellermann and J. Mercy, "Men, Women and Murder: Gender-Specific Differences in Rates of Fatal Violence and Victimization," *Journal of Trauma* 33 (1992): 1–5; J. Sloan, A. Kellermann, et al., "Handgun Regulations, Crime, Assaults and Homicide: A Tale of Two Cities," *New England Journal of Medicine* 319 (1988): 1256–62.

For critiques of the methodological problems raised by these and other poorly reasoned antigun articles in the medical literature, see Edgar A. Suter, "Guns in the Medical Literature—A Failure of Peer Review," *Journal of the Medical Association of Georgia* 83 (March 1994): 133–48; Miguel A. Faria, "Second Opinion: Women, Guns and the Medical Literature—A Raging Debate," *Women & Guns*, October 1994, pp. 14–17, 52–53.

20. Don Kates, "The Value of Civilian Handgun Possession as a Deterrent to Crime or a Defense against Crime," *American Journal of Criminal Law* 18 (Winter 1991): 115, 130–31. Elsewhere, Kates notes some "remarkable aspects" of the firearms-related medical literature: "One is that firearms and their ownership are invariably discussed as social pathology rather than as a value-neutral phenomenon. . . . The only admissible firearms article topics in medico-public health journals are problematic: gun accidents, gun violence, gun ownership among extremist groups. . . . These things are seen as fairly representing the 50 percent of American households that contain guns. It never seems to have occurred to the gatekeepers of the medico-public health literature that gun ownership could present any issue worthy of nonproblematic or neutral study." Don Kates, "A Controlled Look at Gun Control: A White Paper on Firearms and Crime in Connection with the Author's Oral Presentation before the Select Committee of the Pennsylvania Legislature to Investigate the Use of Automatic and Semi-automatic Firearms," Harrisburg, September 20, 1994, p. 21. In the same White Paper, Kates discusses Kellermann's "adamant refusal" to share his data with other scholars who wish to evaluate it themselves (p. 47). Along similar

lines, Suter, who chairs Doctors for Integrity in Research and Public Policy, criticizes the *New England Journal of Medicine*'s "no-data-are-needed" policy: "For matters of 'fact,' it is not unusual to find third-hand citations of editorials rather than citations of primary data." See Suter, "Guns in the Medical Literature," p. 133.

21. Coalition to Stop Gun Violence, packet of promotional materials with the cover "America is bleeding to death from gun violence," mailed in the spring of 1993.

22. "Clouding the public debate, this fallacy is one of the most misused slogans of the anti-self-defense lobby." Suter, "Guns in the Medical Literature," p. 136. On this "43 percent fallacy," see David Kopel, "Peril or Protection? The Risks and Benefits of Hand-gun Prohibition," *Saint Louis University Public Law Review* 12 (1993): 285–359. In the latter article, Kopel points out that the 43 times figure "is mostly a factoid, since thirty-seven of the forty-three deaths were suicides" (p. 341). Kellermann also ignored, among other things, the facts that most gun-related accidents and homicides occur in violent house-holds, and that most often the defensive use of a firearm does not entail firing it. On the latter point, see especially Gary Kleck, *Point Blank: Guns and Violence in America* (Haw-thorne, N.Y.: Aldine de Gruyter, 1991), pp. 120–45.

23. For example, the feminization of poverty, the "glass ceiling" encountered by women in the workforce, womens' health issues, women in politics, antifeminist backlash, sexual harassment, and date rape.

24. Karen McNutt, "Legally Speaking: Swapping Freedom for Illusion," *Women & Guns*, March 1992, p. 33. On the idea that many women are reluctant to self-identify as feminists, even though they share many basic viewpoints with ideological feminism, because they are deterred by its stridency or narrow-mindedness on some issues, see also Wolf, *Fire with Fire*, pp. 57–132. Paula Kamen argues a similar point in *Feminist Fatale: Voices from the "Twentysomething" Generation Explore the Future of the "Women's Movement"* (New York: Donald I. Fine, 1991).

25. *Ms.*, January/February 1992, p. 19.

26. See Sanford Levinson, "The Embarrassing Second Amendment," *Yale Law Journal* 99 (December 1989): 637–59.

27. Ibid., p. 658.

28. Wendy Brown, "Guns, Cowboys, Philadelphia Mayors, and Civic Republicanism: On Sanford Levinson's 'The Embarrassing Second Amendment,' " *Yale Law Journal* 99 (December 1989): 661–67.

29. Ibid., pp. 666–67.

30. Brown is of course probably correct about the uselessness of her self-defense train-ing; numerous studies have shown that for aggressive resistance to succeed against sexual assault, the level of resistance must be equivalent to the level of force employed by the attacker. Significantly, the option of arming herself to forestall the sort of assault in the circumstances she imagines here does not seem to have occurred to her.

31. Douglas Laycock, "Vicious Stereotypes in Polite Society," *Constitutional Commen-tary* 8 (Summer 1991): 399, 406. For another critique of Brown's response to Levinson, see Mary Zeiss Stange, "Feminism and the Second Amendment," *Guns & Ammo Annual 1992*, pp. 6–9.

32. "Laycock, "Vicious Stereotypes in Polite Society," p. 401.

33. See, for example, Camille Paglia, *Sex, Art, and American Culture* (New York: Vintage Books, 1992); Katie Roiphe, *The Morning After: Sex, Fear and Feminism on Campus* (Boston: Little, Brown and Company, 1993); Christina Hoff Sommers, *Who Stole Feminism?* (New York: Simon and Schuster, 1994).

34. From the same fundraising literature cited above.

35. "NRA Blazes Trail for New Hunters," sidebar to Kathy Etling's "Women Afield," *American Hunter*, January 1992, p. 67.

36. NRA fact Sheet, "Women and Firearms: The Responsibilities of Choice," no date; original italics.

37. According to Kitty Beuchert, director of WI&I, as of August 1994, the NRA recorded a female membership of 116,404, up from 102,000 in December 1993, and 85,000 in December 1992. While this would appear to be a fairly small percentage of the NRA's total membership of 3.5 million, Beuchert stresses that fully one-third of the NRA's membership is signed up by initials only. There is no reliable way to "genderize" these million individuals, but—especially since women are known frequently to use initials only—it is fair to assume that many of them are female. (Telephone conversation, October 19, 1994)

38. In Tennessee, two different pollsters (Mason-Dixon and Luntz Research) asked the same question. The NRA won the Mason-Dixon poll; in the Luntz Research poll, the NRA and Democrats both received 6.2 percent "all the time" support, while Republicans received 3.5 percent.

39. Brad O'Leary, "Fire Power," *Campaigns & Elections*, December 1994/January 1995, p. 34.

40. The NRA is adamant in its insistence that this is not a "gun program." Seminar participants who do express an interest in pursuing the option of arming themselves in self-defense are directed to other NRA programs, or other training opportunities in their locality.

41. To put this accusation in perspective, it is probably fair to say that many major advertising campaigns mounted by advocacy groups in the last two or three years have also cashed in on feminist rhetoric regarding choice. The fur, tobacco, and beef industries have all promoted consumers' "right to choose" their products, and even anti-abortion groups have rallied around such mottos as "Choose Life" and "Life: What a Beautiful Choice." Both sides of the health care debate have focused on choice (of physicians and services) as a key issue, and the Libertarian party proclaims itself "pro-choice on everything."

42. Cover letter, signed by NRA Board member Susan Howard, mailed with the brochure "Refuse To Be A Victim: 42 Strategies for Personal Safety."

43. All, as it happens, Democrats: Eleanor Holmes Norton (delegate-DC), Patricia Schroeder (CO), Nancy Pelosi (CA), Lynn Woolsey (CA), Carrie Meek (FL), Nydia Velazquez (NY), Anna Eshoo (CA), Leslie Byrne (VA), Rosa DeLauro (CT), Lucille Roybal-Allard (CA), Corrine Brown (FL), Marjorie Margolies-Mezvinski (CA), Patsy Mink (HI), Louise Slaughter (NY), Lynn Schenk (CA), Barbara Kennelly (CT), Elizabeth Furse (OR), Eva Clayton (NC), Maxine Waters (CA), Eddie Bernice Johnson (TX), Cynthia McKinney (GA), Maria Cantwell (WA), Carolyn Maloney (NY), Cardiss Collins (IL), and Karen Shepherd (UT) (listed in the order in which their signatures appear on the letter). Not all members of the Congressional Women's Caucus signed the letter, of course. Those who refused included Jolene Unsoeld (WA), a progun liberal Democrat.

44. Run in regional editions of such national magazines as *People, Ladies Home Journal*, and *Woman's Day*.

45. Letter dated October 15, 1993, over the signatures of the twenty-six congresswomen. According to *Women & Guns*, the letter was originally intended to be on Congressional Women's Caucus letterhead, but owing to objections by some members of the

women's caucus was typed on standard House letterhead instead. See "New NRA 'Refuse To Be A Victim' Launched into Nationwide Orbit," *Women & Guns*, January 1994, pp. 8–9.

46. Presumably, Kellermann et al., "Gun Ownership as a Risk Factor for Homicide in the Home." The letter specified that the presence of a handgun in the home triples the chance someone will be killed there; that three-quarters of homicide victims are killed by a family member, spouse or acquaintance; and that battered women were more likely than others to be involved in a fatal shooting; all these findings have been discredited by knowledgeable critics; see discussion in endnotes above.

47. This conclusion is a blatant non sequitur, considering that all the Kellermann data cited in the preceding paragraph of the letter related to violence in the home.

48. They included Susan Brewster (wife of Bill Brewster, Democratic Congressman from Oklahoma and NRA board member), Dr. Suzanna Gratia (a survivor of the Luby's Cafeteria mass murder in Killeen, Texas), and Amy Fleming (a New Jersey woman stalked by her abusive ex-husband).

49. Judy Mann, "Annie Doesn't Have to Get a Gun," *Washington Post*, October 1, 1993, p. E3.

50. "From the Editor," *Women & Guns*, May 1992, pp. 6–7.

51. *Women & Guns*, September 1992, p. 6.

52. Telephone conversation with Peggy Tartaro, October 13, 1994. Tartaro's perception is based on a series of reader surveys, as well as the letters she receives from readers.

53. *Ms.*, May/June 1994, p. 37.

54. "Cashing In on Fear," p. 49.

55. Ibid., p. 48.

56. Ibid., p. 47. To put it bluntly, the NRA's political agenda has been anything but "hidden"; indeed, few advocacy groups are more transparent in stating their goals and objectives. It remains open to question why critics who recognize NRA's tendency toward an "all or nothing" approach to gun rights and regulation in every other area would suddenly discern a lapse into subtlety and subterfuge when it comes to women's issues.

57. Jones, "Living with Guns, Playing with Fire," p. 43.

58. In fact, "The Armed Citizen" feature that appears in each issue of the NRA's two national magazines regularly features stories about women who used firearms successfully to defend themselves against abusive ex-husbands or ex-boyfriends, frequently in stalking situations. "The Armed Citizen" is comprised of press accounts drawn from newspapers around the country.

59. Jones, "Living with Guns, Playing with Fire," p. 44. Jones does aver that spending time in prison is, at any rate, "better than being dead."

60. Jones, "Living with Guns, Playing with Fire," p. 42. It is unclear whether the "little incident" referred to here is the cutting off of part of a man's penis or the shooting to death of a would-be rapist.

61. Letter by Adriene Sere, *Ms.*, September/October 1994, p. 5.

62. Letter by Martha McCaughey, *Ms.*, September/October 1994, p. 7.

63. From Ann Jones, *Women Who Kill* (New York: Fawcett Columbine, 1980), pp. 323–24. The conversation is between two women convicted of murdering their abusers. Childers claimed her shotgun had misfired, fatally wounding her former husband; DiVillez admitted to having hired a hit man to kill her husband.

64. D. A. Clarke, "A Woman with a Sword: Some Thoughts on Women, Feminism and

Violence," in Emilie Buchwald, Paula R. Fletcher, and Martha Roth, eds., *Transforming a Rape Culture* (New York: Milkweed Editions, 1993), pp. 396–97.

65. Naomi Goldenberg, *Returning Words to Flesh: Feminism, Psychology and Religion* (Boston: Beacon Press, 1990), p. 171.

66. Ibid., p. 170.

67. See, for example, Bernice Lott, *Women's Lives: Themes and Variations in Gender Learning* (Belmont, Calif.: Brooks/Cole Publishing Company, 1987), pp. 254–55; Margaret W. Matlin, *The Psychology of Women* (Fort Worth, Tex.: Harcourt Brace Jovanovich, 1983, 1987), pp. 218–23; Jean Stockard and Miriam M. Johnson, *Sex and Gender in Society* (Englewood Cliffs, N.J.: Prentice-Hall, 1992), pp. 143–45.

68. Anne Campbell, *Men, Women, and Aggression* (New York: Basic Books, 1993), pp. 34–35.

69. See Mary Zeiss Stange, "Disarmed by Fear," *American Rifleman*, March 1992, pp. 34–37, 92.

70. Campbell, *Men, Women, and Aggression*, pp. 37–38. The bulk of Campbell's research has dealt with girls and women who deviate from the behavioral norm; her other books include *Girl Delinquents* (1981) and *The Girls in the Gang* (1984).

71. Meanwhile, violence is sometimes viewed as normative male behavior. For example, British journalist Joan Smith quotes the London judge who in 1985 sentenced a man to six years in prison after he admitted to killing his wife, chopping her body up into pieces, and scattering them around London, his defense being that she was a nag and impossible to live with: "You stand convicted of manslaughter. I will deal with you on the basis you were provoked, you lost your self-control, and that a man of reasonable self-control might have been similarly provoked and might have done what you did." See Joan Smith, *Misogynies: Reflections on Myths and Malice* (New York: Fawcett Columbine, 1989), pp. 7–9.

72. Some theorists strike a pragmatic note, observing that since aggression does not serve women's interests all that well anyway, they ought more profitably to focus their energies elsewhere; see, for example, Carol Gilligan, *In a Different Voice: Psychological Theory and Women's Development* (Cambridge, Mass.: Harvard University Press, 1982), pp. 43–47, and Jean Baker Miller, *Toward a New Psychology of Women* (Boston: Beacon Press, 1986), pp. 86–87. Others retreat into language suggesting a more transcendent essentialist perspective, in which women are viewed as literally less capable of aggression and more passive and peaceful by nature than are men; see, for example, Susan Griffin, *Woman and Nature* (New York: Harper Colophon, 1978); Mary Daly, *Gyn/Ecology: The Meta-Ethics of Radical Feminism* (Boston: Beacon Press, rev. ed. 1990); Carol Adams, *The Sexual Politics of Meat: A Feminist-Vegetarian Critical Theory* (New York: Continuum, 1990); and Andree Collard with Joyce Contrucci, *Rape of the Wild: Man's Violence against Animals and the Earth* (Bloomington: Indiana University Press, 1989). It should be noted that those theorists who have mounted the most radical arguments about the essentially pacifistic nature of female psychology are not, by training, psychologists.

73. Campbell, *Men, Women, and Aggression*, p. 143.

74. Clarke, "A Woman with a Sword," p. 401. Not surprisingly, Clarke's essay—and this particular passage—were singled out by Judith Viorst in her review of the book for the *New York Times Book Review*, November 28, 1993, as being "quite at odds with the antiviolence agenda of the book."

75. Wolf, *Fire with Fire*, p. 315. This is, among other things, a clever inversion of the antigun "you could be next" scare tactic.

76. One of the most frequently invoked arguments against women's use of guns for self-protection is that it is easy for an attacker to wrest a gun away from a victim and use it against her. Gary Kleck notes that in actuality, this is an extremely rare occurrence: at best, 1 percent of defensive uses of firearms result in the victim's loss of the firearm, and "even these few cases did not necessarily involve the offender snatching a gun out of the victim's hands." Kleck's data relate to burglaries; however, he remarks elsewhere that data regarding gun-armed resistance against rape would probably yield similar findings. See *Point Blank*, pp. 122, 126. Self-defense expert Paxton Quigley stresses the superiority of handguns over long guns in this regard; while rifles and shotguns are both more lethal than handguns, long guns are potentially easier to take away. See Paxton Quigley, *Armed and Female* (New York: St. Martin's, 1989), p. 170.

77. Sarah E. Ullman and Raymond A. Knight, "Fighting Back: Women's Resistance to Rape," *Journal of Interpersonal Violence* 7 (March 1992): 33.

78. Ibid., p. 41. See also Sarah E. Ullman and Raymond A. Knight, "The Efficacy of Women's Resistance Strategies in Rape Situations," *Psychology of Women Quarterly* 17 (1993): 23–38; P. B. Bart et al., "The Effects of Sexual Assault on Rape and Attempted Rape Victims," *Victimology* 7 (1982): 106–13; B. S. Griffin and C. T. Griffin, "Victims in Rape Confrontation," *Victimology* 6 (1981): 59–75; P. B. Bart and P. B. O'Brien, *Stopping Rape: Successful Survival Strategies* (Elmsford, N.Y.: Pergamon Press, 1985).

79. Ullman and Knight, "The Efficacy of Women's Resistance Strategies in Rape Situations," p. 35.

80. Frances O. F. Haga, Michael L. Vasu, and William V. Pelfrey, "Domestic Violence versus Predatory Assault," a paper presented in the Division on Family Violence, 1993 Annual Meeting of the American Society of Criminology, Phoenix, Arizona. All subsequent citations are to this study, the copy of which the author received from Professor Haga via electronic transmission which was not paginated.

81. From "Domestic Violence versus Predatory Assault," original emphasis. Haga presented her findings from the "Images of Fear" study at the 1992 annual meeting of the American Society of Criminology in New Orleans, and published a portion of it, "Can Pretty Girls Be Strong?" in *Women & Guns*, March 1992, pp. 10–16. Significantly, with regard to how deeply embedded are cultural ideas about the inappropriateness of women's taking aggressive action, the men and women in this study were all either gun-owners or martial-arts self-defense specialists.

82. By contrast, men who kill their girlfriends and wives tend to stab, strangle, or bludgeon them to death. See James D. Wright, "Second Thoughts about Gun Control," *The Public Interest* 91 (1988): 32.

The various studies from antigun organizations and their medical allies about the supposed inutility of women owning guns for protection tend to suffer from a common set of flaws: First, they consider a defensive gun use successful only if the criminal is shot dead, rather than merely frightened away. Second, they pretend that the only criminals who attack women are complete strangers; if a woman shoots an ex-boyfriend who is stalking her, the stalker's death is labeled a "tragic domestic homicide" that took place during "an argument," rather than lawful self-defense against a violent predator. Third, the studies undercount justifiable homicide because they look only at arrest reports, rather than final case disposition. Finally, the studies deliberately ignore the distinction between households that are at high risk for gun misuse (households containing criminals, alcoholics, and drug abusers) and all other households, for which the risks of gun misuse are quite low.

83. Suter, "Guns in the Medical Literature," p. 140.

84. See, e.g., Elizabeth M. Schneider, "The Dialectic of Rights and Politics: Perspectives from the Women's Movement," in D. Kelly Weisberg, ed., *Feminist Legal Theory: Foundations* (Philadelphia: Temple University Press, 1993), pp. 512–14, on the Wanrow case, for which Schneider was a co-counsel on appeal. (In *State* v. *Wanrow*, a Native American woman was convicted of second-degree murder in the shooting death of a white man she believed posed an immediate threat to one of her children; the jury rejected the defense's argument of self-defense—5'4" Yvonne Wanrow was on crutches with a broken leg, her child's assailant was 6'2" and intoxicated—because of the judge's instruction that an "equal force" standard be applied. The Washington State Supreme Court reversed the conviction on appeal in a landmark decision, ruling that "care must be taken to assure that our self-defense instructions afford women the right to have their conduct judged in light of the individual physical handicaps which are the product of sex-discrimination. To fail to do so is to deny the right of the individual woman involved to trial by the same rules which are applicable to male defendants.") Don Kates and Nancy Jean Engberg summarize the implications of *Wanrow* for rethinking gender-bias in self-defense law in "Deadly Force Self-Defense against Rape," *University of California-Davis Law Review* 15 (1983): 890–94. See also Sayoko Blodgett-Ford, "Do Battered Women Have a Right to Bear Arms?" *Yale Law and Policy Review* 11 (1993): 547–53, on jury instructions regarding women's right to bear arms for self-protection; and Cynthia K. Gillespie, *Justifiable Homicide: Battered Women, Self-Defense, and the Law* (Columbus: Ohio State University Press, 1989), pp. 116–18, on the limits of the applicability of the subjective standard established by *Wanrow*.

85. See Kates and Engberg, on *People* v. *Caudillo* (1978), in which the "defendant . . . was convicted of raping his victim in addition to kidnapping and robbing her. The [California Supreme Court] found that the victim suffered serious psychological and emotional trauma but only 'insubstantial' physical injuries." Kates and Engberg, "Deadly Force Self-Defense against Rape," p. 901. Ullman and Knight note that bodily injury in most sexual assaults is confined to the rape itself, not to additional "serious injury"; see "The Efficacy of Women's Resistance Strategies in Rape Situations."

86. Robin West, "Jurisprudence and Gender," in Katharine T. Bartlett and Rosanne Kennedy, eds., *Feminist Legal Theory: Readings in Law and Gender* (Boulder, Colo.: Westview Press, 1991), p. 230.

87. Wendy W. Williams, "The Equality Crisis: Some Reflections on Culture, Courts, and Feminism," in Bartlett and Kennedy, *Feminist Legal Theory*, pp. 15–34.

88. See Kleck, *Point Blank*, p. 121; also, Carol Ruth Silver and Don Kates, "Self-Defense, Handgun Ownership, and the Independence of Women in a Violent, Sexist Society," in Don Kates, ed., *Restricting Handguns: The Liberal Skeptics Speak Out* (Croton-on-Hudson, N.Y.: North River Press, 1979), pp. 144–46; and Kates, *Guns, Murders and the Constitution*, pp. 19–21. In *Warren* v. *District of Columbia* (1981), a case involving the sexual assault of three women who were held hostage for fourteen hours when the police failed to respond to their call for help, the appellate court ruled that the "government and its agents are under no general duty to provide public services, such as police protection, to any individual citizen." See Don Kates, "The Value of Civilian Handgun Possession as a Deterrent to Crime or a Defense against Crime," *American Journal of Criminal Law* 18 (Winter 1991): 123–25. In 1989, the U.S. Supreme Court applied similar logic in the *DeShaney* case, ruling that the due process clause of the Fourteenth Amendment exists to protect people from the state, not from each other. Police and other authorities are not, according to this

reasoning, required to intervene in domestic disputes, or even in crimes in progress; their responsibility is to apprehend the offender after the crime has been committed. Ann Jones addresses this problem in *Next Time She'll Be Dead: Battering and How to Stop It* (Boston: Beacon Press, 1993), but sees the solution in near-utopian reform of the legal system.

89. Kates, "The Value of Civilian Handgun Possession as a Deterrent to Crime or a Defense against Crime," pp. 126–27. Illustrating the sort of "straw men" he has in mind, Kates explains: "It is, of course, tragic when, for instance, an abused woman has to shoot to stop a current or former boyfriend or husband from beating her to death. Still, it is highly misleading to count such incidents as costs of gun ownership by misclassifying them with the very thing they prevent: murder between 'family and friends' " (p. 128). In a similar vein, Suter asks "Would it be more 'politically correct' if women or children were killed by their attackers—the common outcome when women do not defend themselves and their children with guns?" See Suter, "Guns in the Medical Literature," p. 140.

90. Ann Japenga, "Would I Be Safer with a Gun?" *Health*, March/April 1994, p. 57.

91. Ibid., pp. 59, 61.

92. It also ironically reflects the kind of violence featured in antigun fundraising literature, which thrives on images of the gun-armed "dark stranger."

93. According to Bureau of Justice statistics, women are one-third less likely to be victims of robbery or assault (rape excepted) than are men. Those women who do fall prey to random violent crime tend to belong to one or more of the following risk groups: aged 20–24 years, African-American, divorced, separated, or single; urban dwellers; never graduated from high school; and earning less than $10,000 a year.

94. Kates, *Guns, Murders and the Constitution*, pp. 34–36.

95. Alternatively, this point of view implicitly regards rape and battery as noncriminal behaviors, a fact amply borne out by the tendency for the law to regard male-on-male violence as a matter for the criminal courts, male-on-female violence being often regarded as a civil matter.

96. See Robert J. Cottrol and Raymond T. Diamond, "The Second Amendment: Toward an Afro-Americanist Reconsideration," in David B. Kopel, ed., *Guns: Who Should Have Them?* (Buffalo: Prometheus Books, 1995).

97. To his credit, for the sake of ideological consistency this apparently remains an abstract question for Kellermann. The same cannot be said for those prominent proponents of strict gun regulation who have possessed firearms for their own protection, even as they have argued against extending that privilege to other people; among gun-owning gun-prohibitionists are Dianne Feinstein (when mayor of San Francisco), journalist Carl Rowan, and *New York Times* publisher Arthur Sulzberger. See Kates, "A Controlled Look at Gun Control," p. 16; also "Elite in NYC Are Packing Heat," *Boston Globe*, January 8, 1993, p. 3.

98. "Where Do We Go from Here? An Interview with Ann Jones," *Ms.*, September/October 1994, p. 60.

99. Silver and Kates, "Self-Defense, Handgun Ownership, and the Independence of Women in a Violent, Sexist Society," p. 139.

100. Ibid., p. 143. This is a problem of particular poignancy for women, who typically have a harder time getting gun-carry permits than do men. In addition, especially for a woman in a domestic abuse situation, the imposition of a waiting period to purchase a handgun can create undue hardship, or even result in her death; see Blodgett-Ford, "Do Battered Women Have a Right to Bear Arms?" pp. 541–47.

101. Japenga, "Would I Be Safer with a Gun?" p. 61.

102. Quigley, *Armed and Female*, p. 108. Quigley had begun as a vociferous supporter of strict gun regulation, only to become disillusioned with the inefficacy of the gun-control legislation she had worked to get passed in the 1960s.

103. Japenga, "Would I Be Safer with a Gun?" p. 61.

104. Peggy Tartaro, "A Picture of Women Gun Owners," *Women & Guns*, March 1994, pp. 30–32. Based upon readers' mailing in a questionnaire, this survey was not scientific. However, because of its voluntary nature, and the fact the survey results are borne out by reader mail, Tartaro thinks the responses provide not only reliable information but information derived from the most committed women gun-owners—those who, with nothing to gain, took the time to respond. Over 400 persons responded, which provided a reasonably large sample. Eighteen percent of the responses were from men (Tartaro estimates that 16 percent of *Women & Guns*' approximately 18,000 readers are men); their responses were factored out of the figures finally reported in the magazine, so that the survey report would "show a clearer picture of women gunowners."

105. This compares quite interestingly to statistics available about male gun-owners, specifically hunters. A 1991 survey carried out by Gallup for the National Shooting Sports Foundation (NSSF) found 21 percent had had "some college," 19 percent were college graduates, and 14 percent had either some graduate work or a graduate degree. Women comprised only 7 percent of the NSSF survey sample.

106. The other reasons being recreation (21 percent), hunting (6 percent), and competition (5 percent); Tartaro notes that "in all cases where multiple reasons were checked, self-defense was one of the responses."

107. The two categories of precautionary and recreational gun use are, of course, not mutually exclusive. In fact one California woman responded, "My first gun was for defense—I found target practice so much fun that I wish I had gotten a gun years ago" ("A Picture of Women Gunowners," p. 31); hers is probably not an uncommon experience.

108. See Fran Haga, "Evolution of a Successful Handgun Clinic," *Women & Guns*, February 1991, pp. 7–12. Information is based on exit surveys collected from the seventy participants.

109. The women in Haga's sample did seem to report a rather higher incidence of victimization: 17 percent had experienced assault, burglary, abuse, or theft themselves; 28 percent had not only been victimized themselves, but also had close friends/family who were crime victims, while 19 percent had not been victimized but were close to someone who had been. Haga's survey, however, posed the question in less restrictive fashion than the 1994 survey, so the differences may be largely artificial.

110. This is corroborated by the testimony of firearms safety instructors nationwide, who consistently report that they find women and girls far more teachable than males. See the remarks by psychologist Robert Jackson of the University of Wisconsin-LaCrosse, in the conference proceedings from "Breaking Down the Barriers to Participation of Women in Angling and Hunting," University of Wisconsin-Stevens Point (August 1990), edited by and available from Professor Christine L. Thomas, College of Natural Resources, University of Wisconsin-Stevens Point.

111. Tartaro, "A Picture of Women Gunowners," p. 31. Tartaro noted regarding this question, "We have asked it in past years, with an eye toward gauging the reader's view of the entire self-defense issue. In years past, results on a similarly worded question were strikingly close" to the 1994 percentages.

112. Assuming that some of the respondents live in jurisdictions where handgun own-

ership itself may be prohibited, or permits to carry impossible or virtually so to obtain, this question was anything but hypothetical for them.

113. See Peggy Tartaro, "Tanya Metaksa Has Grassroots Lessons to Teach Washington," *Women & Guns*, June 1994, p. 54.

114. Quigley, *Armed and Female*, p. 117. Don Kates has persuasively argued that, far from it being the case that people will in the "heat of the moment" unthinkingly pick up and fire a gun wounding or killing someone irresponsibly, it is reasonable to assume that serious precautionary gun-owners in fact have a heightened sense of awareness about the power of firearms, and the ethical responsibilities attaching to their use. See Kates, "The Value of Civilian Handgun Possession as a Deterrent to Crime," pp. 149–50.

115. D. A. Clarke, "A Woman with a Sword," in *Transforming a Rape Culture*, p. 395.

116. Don Kates, "The Second Amendment and the Ideology of Self-Protection," *Constitutional Commentary* 9 (Winter 1992): 94. Kates is quoting A. V. B. Norman, *The Medieval Soldier* (New York: Thomas Crowell, 1971), p. 73.

117. Dominique Godineau, "Daughters of Liberty and Revolutionary Citizens," trans. Arthur Goldhammer, in Genevieve Fraisse and Michelle Perrot, eds., *A History of Women in the West, Volume IV: Emerging Feminism from Revolution to World War* (Cambridge, Mass.: The Belknap Press of Harvard University Press, 1993), p. 25.

118. Godineau, "Daughters of Liberty and Revolutionary Citizens," pp. 26–27. Along with the right to bear arms, French *citoyennes* also demanded, and won, the right to wear the tricolor cockade (a small ribbon, worn usually on one's hat) as an emblem of their full citizenship. The response, on the part of many men (and no doubt some women as well) was to conjure up "apocalyptic visions of women arming to murder men in a sort of Saint Bartholomew's Day Massacre." Ibid.

119. Kopel, *The Samurai, the Mountie, and the Cowboy*, p. 285. Kopel notes that today women have the same rights to purchase firearms as do men, though their participation in the national militia is still limited to noncombat roles and, although optional premilitia training is open to both sexes in high school, women are not required to undergo militia training. Ibid., pp. 282, 285, 299 n. 62.

Chapter Thirty-one

Guns Are the Tools by Which We Forge Our Liberty

Cindy Hill

I am a thirty-two-year-old woman and the mother of a precocious two-and-a-half-year-old. I have been practicing law in the fields of criminal defense, environmental protection, land use planning and other areas of public interest for nearly ten years. As an environmental activist, my interests lie in wilderness protection and the conservation of biological diversity. I am pro-choice, pro-union and support organic family farming. I'm a vegetarian. I usually (but not always) vote the Democratic ticket.

I own a gun. Several, in fact. And I belong to the National Rifle Association and the Second Amendment Foundation.

This set of circumstances confuses the marketing people to no end. When I subscribe to a vegetarian magazine, I am flooded with animal rights and anti-hunting mailings, leading directly to a spot on the handgun control fund-raising lists. My NRA membership gets me notices that I should be opposing logging industry regulation, because (so they argue) clearcuts make more deer and thus more hunting, so being pro-gun is supposed to mean being pro-clearcut.

Each "side" assumes there is a package of issues where, if I am supporting one, I'll support the rest. But my package is evidently not the same as theirs. My package is the United States Constitution and the Bill of Rights.

Liberty and democracy are precious, noble aims. America was founded on the radical notion of self-rule. The American colonies broke free, not only from the bounds of a foreign ruler, but from the concept of an inherited nobility.

Liberty is the responsibility for running this great nation. Liberty is the grave burden of stewardship; stewardship of our natural resources, our human potential, our culture and our body politic.

Liberty does not mean every citizen has the right to exploit their neighbors, our natural resources and third-world economies in order to accumulate the biggest pile of money. The responsibilities of liberty fall upon each of us as the price of the most noble of all titles, private American citizen. If we turn the obligation for our personal and national safety entirely over to standing armies, be they military or law enforcement, we are admitting that we are not responsible enough to succeed at the American experiment.

The Second Amendment of the U.S. Constitution states, in full: "A well regulated Militia, being necessary to the security of a free State, the right of the people to keep and bear Arms, shall not be infringed."

We are the people who hold the right to keep and bear Arms. We are the Militia; it is we who are necessary to the security of this free state. The term regulated doesn't mean regulations; our modern bureaucracy didn't exist in the late 1700s when the Constitution was written. A regulated Militia is a regular Army; mustered and ready to stand against infringements on our security.

If we surrender our guns out of fear of the actions of a few lawless individuals, are we not surrendering ourselves to the very forces which undermine the viability of our nation? Gun crimes should indeed be strongly punished; guns are the tools by which we forge our liberty, and their use should not be so obscenely distorted as to be turned against our own peaceful neighbors.

The mindless death of a store clerk in a robbery, or a child in a drive-by shooting, are horrible, tragic violations of our social contract.

But if in response we mount cameras, sound recorders and metal detectors at every shopping area, turn in our guns and our knives, hire more police, build bigger jails and ban meetings after dark, have we not created our own tyranny? As Noah Webster, the prominent Federalist, wrote, "before a standing army can rule, the people must be disarmed; as they are in almost every kingdom in Europe. The supreme power in America cannot enforce unjust laws by the sword; because the whole body of the people are armed." And as St. George Tucker wrote in Blackstone's Commentaries, "The right of self defense is the first law of nature. . . . Wherever . . . the right of the people to keep and bear arms is, under any color or pretext whatsoever, prohibited, liberty, if not already annihilated, is on the brink of destruction."

I will not live in a state of fear. There has always been crime; there will always be crime. In a nation like ours, with a broad spectrum of cultural influences, and a painful gulf between the wealthy and the poor, crime can be expected. When we call a group of young people wearing cool jackets a gang and cower in fear from them, we give them power over us. If we call them by their individual names, arrest and convict them in accordance with the transgressions they have each committed, we afford them the respect of being held individually responsible for their role in our society. Consequently, our society remains unweakened by the event.

Thomas Jefferson proposed public education to create an informed electorate, by which every child, every student would grow to be able to participate in the political debates of the day and shape the course of our country's future. If we each rededicate ourselves to learning and accepting the personal responsibility of liberty, the American experiment may yet succeed.

Chapter Thirty-two

Gun Control in America
A History of Discrimination against the Poor and Minorities

T. Markus Funk

One undeniable aspect of the history of gun control in the United States has been the conception that the poor, especially the non-white poor, cannot be trusted with firearms.[1] Keeping arms away from blacks had always been an issue; in fact, the first ever mention of blacks in Virginia's laws was a 1644 provision barring free blacks from owning firearms.[2] Similar to the English attitudes towards gun ownership by Catholics, who were considered to be potential subversives, black slaves and Native Americans were the suspect populations of the New World.[3]

Considering that the effect of melting-point laws is the removal of the least expensive guns from the market, and that the discussion thus far has pointed to the apparent ineffectiveness of current crime control measures, one could persuasively argue that the legislatures have a desire to keep guns out of the hands of the poor and minorities. Acceptance of the preceding arguments that melting-point laws (1) do not reduce crime, (2) actually *decrease* the likelihood of criminals being caught on the basis of their use of a handgun which passes the melting-point requirements, and (3) prevent citizens from deterring criminal activity and protecting themselves from criminals leaves few alternative explanations for the legislators' motivations. A National Institute of Justice Study found that:

> The people most likely to be deterred from acquiring a handgun by exceptionally high prices or by the nonavailability of certain kinds of handguns are not felons intent on arming themselves for criminal purposes (who can, if all else fails, steal the handgun they want), but rather poor people who have decided they need a gun to protect themselves against the felons but who find that the cheapest gun in the market costs more than they can afford to pay.[4]

As David Kopel points out, "[t]he point of banning 'cheap' guns is that people who can only afford cheap guns should not have guns. The prohibitively high price that some firearms licenses carry ($500 in Miami until recently) suggests a contemporary intent to keep guns away from lower socioeconomic groups."[5]

Melting-point laws take less expensive guns off the market, and while there is no shortage of expensive guns, poorer citizens may not be able to afford them and must make due with what they can afford. A closer look at the historical relationship between gun control and the poor in America reveals that a charge of discrimination on the part of the legislators who enacted the melting-point laws might not be too far-fetched.

An undisguised admission of the discriminatory motive underlying attempts to make handguns more expensive appears in an article on Saturday Night Specials written by gun control advocate Philip Cook:

> Individuals who would not ordinarily be able to afford an expensive gun commit a disproportionate share of violent crimes. Setting a high minimum price for handguns would be an effective means of reducing availability to precisely those groups that account for the bulk of the violent crime problem. . . . The major normative argument against a high tax is that it is *overt economic discrimination and thus unethical, or at least politically unpalatable.* . . . A high tax is not the only method of *increasing the minimum price for handguns and subtle approaches may be more acceptable politically.* One method would establish minimum standards stipulating the quality of metal and safety features of a gun. The effect of this approach would be the same as the minimum tax: to eliminate the cheapest of the domestically manufactured handguns. Unlike minimum tax, however, quality and safety standards could be justified on grounds other than economic discrimination. . . . If sufficiently high standards on safety and metal quality were adopted, the cost to manufacturers of meeting these standards would ensure a high minimum price.[6]

Early firearm laws were often enacted for the sole purpose of preventing immigrants, blacks, and other ethnic minorities from obtaining a gun.[7] Even today, police departments have a wide range of latitude in granting gun permits, yet they rarely issue them to the poor or to minority citizens.[8]

The poor are often prevented from possessing a firearm even though the poor are disproportionately victims of crime.[9] Compounding this situation is the fact that the poorer areas of cities (where most of the crime occurs) rarely get the same police protection that the more affluent areas get (where the least crime occurs).[10] As Gary Kleck puts it:

> Gun ownership costs more money than simple measures such as locking doors, having neighbors watch one's house, or avoidance behaviors such as not going out at night, but it costs less than buying and maintaining a dog, paying a security guard, or buying a burglar alarm system. Consequently, it is a self-protection measure available to many low-income people who *cannot afford more expensive alternatives.*[11]

Therefore, any gun control measure which takes cheaper guns off the market and prevents the poor from obtaining a handgun for self-defense is arguably doubly unfair. In *Delahanty v. Hinckley*, a federal district court in Washington, D.C., found that Saturday Night Special laws selectively disarm minorities.[12] The court stated:

> The fact is, of course, that while blighted areas may be some of the breeding places of crime, not all residents of [sic] are so engaged, and indeed, most persons who live there are lawabiding but have no other choice of location. But they, like their counterparts in other areas of the city, may seek to protect themselves, their families and their property against crime, and indeed, may feel an even greater need to do so since the crime rate in their community may be higher than in other areas of the city. Since one of the reasons they are likely to be living in the "ghetto" may be due to low income or employment, it is highly unlikely that they would have the resources or worth to buy an expensive handgun for self defense.[13]

Although bans on particular types of firearms have been enacted under the guise of controlling crime throughout American history, the actual effect they have often had was to disarm poor people and minorities.[14] In 1640, Virginia set up the first recorded restrictive legislation which prevented blacks from owning a firearm, and the Virginia law was said to set blacks apart from all other groups by denying them the important right and obligation of carrying a gun.[15] Legislators in the southern states not only restricted the rights of slaves, but also the rights of free blacks to bear arms. The intention was to restrict the availability of arms to both free blacks and slaves to the extent that the restrictions were consistent with the regional ideas of safety.[16]

Reflecting this attitude, Chief Justice Tawney, writing for the majority in the 1856 *Dred Scott* decision, stated that if blacks were

> entitled to the privileges and immunities of citizens, . . . [i]t would give persons of the negro race, who were recognized as citizens in any one state of the union, the right . . . to keep and bear arms wherever they went. And all of this would be done in the face of the subject race of the same color, both free and slaves, and inevitably producing discontent and insubordination among them, and endangering the peace and safety of the State.[17]

Tennessee was the first state to utilize creative melting-point style draftsmanship to prevent gun ownership by blacks in the 1870s. Tennessee barred the sale of all handguns except the "Army and Navy" guns which were already owned by ex-confederate soldiers.[18] Since the poor freedmen could not afford these expensive firearms, the "Army and Navy Law" is considered the predecessor of today's melting-point laws.[19]

After the Civil War, southerners were fearful of race war and retribution, and the mere sight of a black person with a gun was terrifying to southern whites.[20] As a result, several southern legislatures adopted comprehensive regulations which were known as the "Black Codes."[21] These codes denied the newly freed men many of the rights that whites enjoyed. In 1867, the Special Report of the Anti-Slavery Conference noted that under the Black Codes, blacks were "forbidden to own or bear firearms, and thus were rendered defenseless against assaults."[22] As an illustration of such legislation, the Mississippi Black Code contained the following provision:

Be it enacted . . . [t]hat no freedman, free negro or mulatto, not in the military . . . and not licensed to do by the board of police of his or her county, shall keep or carry fire-arms of any kind, or any ammunition, . . . and all such arms or ammunition shall be forfeited to the former.[23]

In *United States v. Cruikshank*,[24] a case which is often cited as authoritative by Handgun Control, Incorporated, and many other gun-control organizations,[25] the United States Supreme Court upheld the Ku Klux Klan's repressive actions against blacks who wanted to own guns, thus allowing the Klan and other racist groups to forcibly disarm the freedmen and impose white supremacy.[26] "Fire-arms in the Reconstruction South provided a means of political power for many. They were the symbols of the new freedom for blacks. . . . In the end, white southerners triumphed and the blacks were effectually disarmed."[27] The legislators' intent to disarm blacks also appears in the voiding of a 1941 conviction of a white man, where Florida Supreme Court Justice Buford, in his concurring opinion, stated that "[t]he Act was passed for the purpose of disarming the negro laborers. . . . [It] was never intended to be applied to the white population and in practice has never been so applied."[28]

But blacks were not the only ones whom legislators wanted to disarm; in the nineteenth century, southern states also placed restrictions on gun-ownership for certain "undesirable" whites.[29] For example, the 1911 Sullivan Law[30] was passed to keep guns out of the hands of immigrants (chiefly Italians—"[i]n the first three years of the Sullivan Law, [roughly] 70 percent of those arrested had Italian surnames").[31] Two New York newspapers reveal the mind-set which gave rise to the Sullivan Law: the *New York Tribune* grumbled about pistols found "chiefly in the pockets of ignorant and quarrelsome immigrants of law-breaking propensities,"[32] and the *New York Times* pointed out the "affinity of 'low-browed foreigners' for handguns."[33]

Tennessee Senator John K. Shields introduced a bill in the United States Congress to prohibit the shipment of pistols through the mails and by common carrier in interstate commerce.[34] The report supporting the bill that Senator Shields inserted into the Congressional Record asked: "Can not we, the dominant race, upon whom depends the enforcement of the law, so enforce the law that we will prevent the colored people from preying upon each other?"[35] In addition to blacks and foreigners, the legislators in the southern states also targeted agrarian agitators and labor organizers at the end of the nineteenth century (particularly in Alabama, in 1893, and Texas, in 1907).[36] Furthermore, heavy transaction and business taxes were imposed "on handgun sales in order to resurrect the economic barriers to [gun] ownership."[37]

Similarly, today's melting-point laws arguably reflect the old American prejudice that lower classes and minorities cannot be trusted with weapons. While the legislative bias which originated in the South may have changed in form, it apparently still exists.[38] But pro-gun groups are not the only ones to acknowledge this unfortunate reality. Gun control proponent and journalist Robert Sherrill frankly admitted that the Gun Control Act of 1968 was "passed not to control guns but to control blacks,"[39] and Barry Bruce-Briggs stated in no uncertain terms that "[i]t is difficult to escape the conclusion that the 'Saturday night special' is emphasized because it is cheap and is being sold to a particular class of people."[40] The names given to Saturday Night Specials and provisions aimed at limiting their availability provide ample evidence—the name of this gun type derived from the racist phrase "nigger-town Saturday night,"[41] and the reference is to "ghetto control" rather than gun control.[42]

Poor blacks are disproportionately the victims of crime,[43] and in 1992, black males between the ages of twenty and twenty-four were four times more likely to be victimized in a handgun crime than white males in the same age group.[44] As Stefan Tahmassebi points out:

> [Although blacks are disproportionately victimized], these citizens are often not afforded the same police protections that other more affluent and less crime ridden neighborhoods or communities enjoy. This lack of protection is especially so in the inner city urban ghettos. Firearms prohibitions discriminate against those poor and minority citizens who must rely on such arms to defend themselves from criminal activity to a much greater degree than affluent citizens living in safer and better protected communities.[45]

Victims must be able to defend themselves and their families against criminals as soon as crime strikes, and the ability to defend oneself, family, and property is more critical in the poor and minority neighborhoods, which are ravaged by crime and do not have adequate police protection.[46] Since the courts have consistently ruled that the police have no duty to protect the individual citizen,[47] and that there is "no constitutional right to be protected by the state against being murdered by criminals or madmen,"[48] citizens, regrettably, are in the position of having to defend themselves. While the deterrent effect of the police surely wards off many would-be criminals (particularly in areas where the police patrol more frequently—*i.e.*, more affluent areas), the many citizens who need *personal* protection must face the reality that the police do not and cannot function as bodyguards for ordinary people.[49] Therefore, individuals must remain responsible for their own personal protection, with the police providing only an auxiliary general deterrent.

Far from being an implement of destruction, a handgun can inspire a feeling of security and safety in a person living in this crime-ridden society.[50] And inexpensive handguns provide affordable protection to lower income individuals who are the most frequent victims of crime.[51] People who accept the preceding analysis with regard to the deterrent value of handguns and the lack of justification for melting-point laws must face the troubling prospect that melting-point laws purposefully reduce poor citizens' access to handguns, significantly impairing their ability to survive in the harsh environments in which they must subsist.

Do Melting-Point Laws Violate the Equal Protection Clause?

As discussed above, it is reasonable to suspect that covert discriminatory purposes underlie the passage of the melting-point laws and similar gun-control legislation.[52] While it is unrealistic to expect the Supreme Court, given its present composition, to rule that melting-point laws are constitutionally impermissible in the near future, it is possible to argue that the case of *Village of Arlington Heights v. Metropolitan Housing Development Corp.*[53] provides a possible framework for invalidating the legislation on the basis of racial discrimination in violation of the Fourteenth Amendment.

Arlington Heights concerned the refusal by a local zoning board to change the classification of a tract of land from single-family to multi-family. While the Seventh Circuit Court of Appeals held that the "ultimate effect" of the rezoning denial, in light of its "historical context,"[54] was racially discriminatory and, therefore, a violation of equal protection,[55] Justice Powell, writing for the majority, overturned this verdict. The Court held that "[o]fficial action will not be held unconstitutional solely because it results in a racially disproportionate impact. 'Disproportional impact is not irrelevant, but it is not the sole touchstone of an invidious racial discrimination.' "[56] A racially discriminatory intent, as evidenced by such factors as disproportionate impact, the historical background of the challenged decision, the specific antecedent events, departures from normal procedures, and contemporary statements of the decision-makers must be shown.[57] While proof of racially discriminatory intent or purpose is required to show a violation of the Equal Protection Clause, the plaintiff is not required to "prove that the challenged action rested solely on racially discriminatory purposes."[58] The Court held that "[w]hen there is a proof that a discriminatory purpose has been a *motivating factor* in the decision, this judicial deference is no longer justified."[59]

To determine whether "invidious" discriminatory purpose was a motivating factor, the court must engage in a "sensitive inquiry" into such circumstantial and direct evidence of intent as may be available, and the Court has held that the "impact of the official action[—]whether it 'bears more heavily on one race than another' [—]may provide an important starting point."[60] The Court stated that the "historical background of the decision is one evidentiary source."[61] Given the history of racist gun control legislation in the United States, a case can be made that the historical background of legislation such as the melting-point laws, the apparent lack of rational justification for the laws, and the laws' ultimate effect of making handguns less accessible to the poor lends some potency to the argument that the passage of the melting-point laws was motivated at least in part by the legislators' improper discriminatory considerations.

Of course, proof that an official decision was racially motivated does not necessarily invalidate a statute, but instead shifts the burden to the defendant to show that the "same decision would have resulted even had the impermissible purpose not been considered."[62] While it may be possible to argue that, given the apparent lack of justification for melting-point laws, the legislators would not have enacted melting-point laws in the absence of a discriminatory motive, this argument is unlikely to succeed as a practical matter, given the difficulty of proving discriminatory intent, particularly through direct evidence, on the part of the politically astute legislators.[63]

In the absence of an avowed racial motive, disproportionate impact does not trigger strict scrutiny (thus, the melting point law is tested only under the *rational relationship* test, under which it likely will stand).[64] However, if the activity at issue implicates a fundamental right,[65] courts will apply a strict scrutiny test, requiring a showing that a *compelling* need for the different treatment exists and that the means chosen are *necessary*.[66] If strict scrutiny applies, the law cannot be substantially overinclusive or underinclusive or both.[67] To find strict scrutiny applicable in the absence of a clearly racial motive or effect, however, the classification must touch on a substantive constitutional right.[68] Considering that the Second Amendment guarantees individuals the right to own arms, courts should apply strict scrutiny. And in light of the language in *Arlington* and the previous discussion of the apparent counter-productiveness of melting-point laws, the legislation appears unconstitutional.[69]

Conclusion

The justifications for melting-point laws appear to lack merit: they do not prevent ballistics and forensics experts from tracing a particular gun to a particular shooter; they do not contribute to crime reduction; they are arbitrary; and they may be motivated by discriminatory intentions. Melting-point laws, therefore, should be abandoned and legislative action should instead be aimed at reducing gun possession among persons with prior records of violence. While melting-point legislation prevents many of the nation's poorer citizens from legally protecting themselves from their dangerous environment, no convincing factual, public policy, or legal arguments justify this outcome. Although handgun violence undeniably is a serious problem in American society, preventing those who have a legal right to protect themselves with a handgun from doing so on the basis of socioeconomic considerations simply cannot be the solution. Blaming the instrument for its misuse by a minority of criminals itself seems perverse. As criminologist Gary Kleck pointed out:

> Fixating on guns seems to be, for many people, a fetish which allows [gun-control advocates] to ignore the more intransigent causes of American violence, including its dying cities, inequality, deteriorating family structure, and the all-pervasive economic and social consequences of a history of slavery and racism. . . . All parties to the crime debate would do well to give more concentrated attention to more difficult, but far more relevant, issues like how to generate more good-paying jobs for the underclass, an issue which is at the heart of the violence problem.[70]

Legislators should consider methods such as mandatory penalties for the misuse of guns in violent crimes and for the possession of stolen guns.[71] After adopting mandatory penalties for the use of a firearm in the commission of a violent crime in 1975, the murder rate in Virginia dropped 36 percent and the robbery rate dropped 24 percent in twelve years.[72] South Carolina recorded a thirty-seven percent murder rate decline between 1975 and 1987 with a similar law.[73] Other notable declines in states using mandatory penalties occurred in Arkansas (homicide rate down 32 percent in thirteen years), Delaware (homicide rate down 26 percent in fifteen years), and Montana (homicide rate down 18 percent in eleven years).[74]

Mandatory gun-training seminars are also effective.[75] Describing the differences between rural and urban gun owners, criminologist Gary Kleck stated:

> Most gun ownership is culturally patterned, linked with a rural hunting sub-culture. The culture is transmitted across generations, with gun owners being socialized by their parents into gun ownership and use from childhood. Defensive handgun owners, on the other hand, are more likely to be disconnected from any gun subcultural roots, and their gun ownership is usually not accompanied by association with other gun owners by the training in the safe handling of guns.[76]

Mandatory gun-safety training, therefore, may go far in preventing firearm accidents by training those who have no background in hunting or shooting how to use a firearm properly.

Legislators should also seriously consider proposals calling for the appointment of at least one Assistant U.S. Attorney per District who is charged with prosecuting felon-in-possession cases which involve violent offenses under 18 U.S.C. § 924.[77] Moreover, the reform and streamlining of probation revocation in such a way that those persons eligible for probation who commit violent armed felonies will have their probation revoked immediately, the creation of prison facilities that are designed solely for the purpose of ensuring that violent repeat offenders actually serve their full sentences,[78] and the establishment of a task force which can informally pressure the entertainment industry to put an end to the incessant and reckless portrayal of criminal misuse of firearms[79] are all policy proposals that present realistic alternatives to the troubling movement towards handgun prohibition.[80]

Both the Constitution and the history of the United States grant citizens the right to own a handgun. All of the states and several territories of the United States, as well as the federal government itself, recognize the sale of firearms as a lawful activity,[81] and both practical experience and empirical evidence appear to indicate that the right to own a handgun benefits society as a whole.

Some legislators, apparently due to either misinformation or personal biases (both racial and socioeconomic), have enacted melting-point laws that remove many of the lower-cost guns from the market as a method of crime prevention. Melting-point laws, however, merely bar those of lesser economic means from having a way to protect themselves against the criminals that prey on them, and such an outcome is neither fair, nor is it criminologically sound.

NOTES

1. *See* Stefan B. Tahmassebi, *Gun Control and Racism*, 2 GEO. MASON U. CIV. RTS. L. J. 67 (1991).

2. *See* WINTHROP D. JORDAN, WHITE OVER BLACK: AMERICAN ATTITUDES TOWARD THE

NEGRO, 1550–1812, at 78 (1968). *See also* Comment, *Carrying Concealed Weapons*, 15 VA. L. REG. 391–92 (1909) ("It is a matter of common knowledge that in this state and several others, the more especially in the Southern states, where the negro population is so large, that this cowardly practice of 'toting' guns has been one of the most fruitful sources of crime. . . . Let a negro board a railroad train with a quart of mean whiskey and a pistol in his grip and the chances are that there will be a murder, or at least a row, before he alights.").

3. *See* JOYCE LEE MALCOLM, TO KEEP AND BEAR ARMS 140 (1994).

4. JAMES WRIGHT & PETER ROSSI, ARMED AND CONSIDERED DANGEROUS: A SURVEY OF FELONS AND THEIR FIREARMS 238 (1986).

5. DAVID B. KOPEL, THE SAMURAI, THE MOUNTIE, AND THE COWBOY 344 (1992).

6. *See* Philip Cook, *The "Saturday Night Special": An Assessment of Alternative Definitions from a Policy Perspective*, 72 CRIM. L. & CRIMINOLOGY. 1740 (1981) (emphasis added) (citations omitted).

7. Tahmassebi, *supra* note 1, at 67. *See also* Stephen P. Halbrook, *The Jurisprudence of the Second and Fourteenth Amendments*, 4 GEO. WASH. L. REV. 1, 21–24 (1981); Raymond G. Kessler, *Gun Control and Political Power*, 5 LAW & POL'Y Q. 381 (1983).

8. *See* Tahmassebi, *supra* note 1, at 67.

9. *Id.* at 68. *See also* CHARLES MURRAY, LOSING GROUND: AMERICAN SOCIAL POLICY, 1950–1980, at 119–20 (1984).

10. *See* Tahmassebi, *supra* note 1, at 68.

11. GARY KLECK, POINT BLANK 104 (1991) (emphasis added).

12. Delahanty v. Hinckley, 686 F. Supp. 920 (D.D.C. 1986).

13. *Id.* at 928.

14. *See* Robert J. Cottrol & Raymond T. Diamond, *The Second Amendment: Towards an Afro-American Reconsideration*, 80 GEO. L. J. 309, 354–55 (1991). The notion of restricting gun ownership to the rich is nothing new, however. The English Game Act of 1609, for example, required a would-be hunter to have income from land of at least £40 a year, or a life estate of £80, or personal property worth at least £400. *See* MALCOLM, *supra* note 3, at 71–75 ("The use of an act for the preservation of game was a customary means to curb lower-class violence.").

15. JORDAN, *supra* note 2, at 78, *cited in* Tahmassebi, *supra* note 1, at 69–70.

16. *See, e.g.,* An Act Concerning Slaves, § 6, 1840 Laws of Tex. 171, 172, ch. 58 of the Texas Acts of 1850 (prohibiting slaves from using firearms altogether from 1842–1850); Act of Mar. 15, 1852, ch. 206, 1852 Laws of Miss. 328 (forbade ownership of firearms to both free blacks and slaves after 1852); Kentucky Acts of 1818, ch. 448 (providing that, should free blacks or slaves "willfully or maliciously" shoot a white person, or otherwise wound a free white person while attempting to kill another person, the slave or free black should suffer the death penalty).

17. Dred Scott v. Sandford, 60 U.S. 393, 416–17 (1856).

18. *See* KOPEL, *supra* note 40, at 336. *See also* KATES, *supra* note 138, at 14 ("Klansmen were not inconvenienced [by the legislation], having long since acquired their guns . . . , nor were the company goons, professional strike-breakers, etc., whose weapons were supplied by their corporate employers. By 1881 white supremacists were in power in the neighboring state of Arkansas and had enacted a virtually identical 'Saturday Night Special' law with virtually identical effect").

19. Kates, *supra* note 138, at 14 ("The 'Army and Navy Law' is the ancestor of today's 'Saturday Night Special' laws.").

20. *See* KOPEL, *supra* note 5, at 333.

21. *See generally* CONG. GLOBE, 39th Cong., 1st Sess. 588–891 (statement by Sen. Donelley giving examples of enacted codes).

22. *Reprinted in* HAROLD HYMAN, THE RADICAL REPUBLICANS AND RECONSTRUCTION 219 (1967), *cited in* Tahmassebi, *supra* note 1, at 71. For compelling anecdotal evidence showing the necessity for blacks to defend themselves through the use of firearms during the civil rights era, see Don B. Kates, Jr., *The Necessity of Access to Firearms by Dissenters and Minorities Whom Government Is Unwilling or Unable to Protect in* RESTRICTING HANDGUNS (1979); John R. Slater, Jr., *Civil Rights and Self-Defense*, AGAINST THE CURRENT, July/August 1988, at 23.

23. 1866 Miss. Laws ch. 23, § 1, at 165 (1865), *cited in* Tahmassebi, *supra* note 1, at 71.

24. 92 U.S. 542 (1875) (holding that the right to assemble and the right to bear arms were natural rights predating the Constitution, and that the Constitution merely gave validity to these rights. "[B]earing arms for a lawful purpose . . . is not a right granted by the Constitution."). Many feel that this decision essentially ruined the Fourteenth Amendment as a check on state abuses of human rights until its resurrection in the 1920s. *See, e.g.*, KOPEL, *supra* note 5, at 335.

25. Tahmassebi, *supra* note 1, at 75.

26. *See* KOPEL, *supra* note 5, at 335.

27. LAURENCE KENNET & JAMES L. ANDERSON, THE GUN IN AMERICA: THE ORIGINS OF A NATIONAL DILEMMA 50 (1975), *cited in* Tahmassebi, *supra* note 1, at 69.

28. Watson v. Stone, 4 So. 2d 700, 703 (Fla. 1941), *cited in* Tahmassebi, *supra* note 1, at 69.

29. *See* Don B. Kates, Jr., *Toward a History of Handgun Prohibition in the United States, in* RESTRICTING HANDGUNS: THE LIBERAL SKEPTICS SPEAK OUT 14 (Don B. Kates, Jr., ed., 1979); Tahmassebi, *supra* note 1, at 77.

30. N.Y. PENAL LAW § 1897 (Consol. 1909) (amended 1911).

31. KOPEL, *supra* note 5, at 343. *See also* Kates, *supra* note 29, at 15 ("Across the land, legislators in conservative states were importuned by business lobbyists bearing glowing endorsements of the Sullivan Law concept from such (then) arch-conservative institutions as the *New York Times* and the American Bar Association.").

32. KOPEL, *supra* note 5, at 342–43 (quoting *New York Tribune*, Nov. 19, 1903, at 6).

33. *Id.* at 343.

34. 65 CONG. REC. S3945 (daily ed. Mar. 11, 1924).

35. *Id.* § 3946.

36. *See* Tahmassebi, *supra* note 1, at 76.

37. Kates, *supra* note 29, at 15. "Moreover, in ensuing years those who ruled the South found that there were challengers other than the blacks against whom the forces of social control might have to be exerted. Agrarian agitators arose to inform poor whites that they were trading their political and economic group identity for a fraudulent racial solidarity with a false imperative of preserving white supremacy." *Id.* at 13.

38. Tahmassebi, *supra* note 1, at 80.

39. ROBERT SHERRILL, THE SATURDAY NIGHT SPECIAL 280 (1973), *cited in* Tahmassebi, *supra* note 1, at 80.

40. Barry Bruce-Briggs, *The Great American Gun War*, 45 PUB. INTEREST 37, 50 (1976).

41. *Id.*

42. *See* KLECK, *supra* note 11, at 89.

43. *See* MURRAY, *supra* note 9, at 120.

44. *See* U.S. Dep't of Justice, Guns and Crime 1 (1994).

45. Tahmassebi, *supra* note 1, at 68.

46. Don B. Kates, Jr., *Handgun Control: Prohibition Revisited*, Inquiry, Dec. 5, 1977, at 21. *See also* Kleck, *supra* note 11, at 86–87 ("Effective [Saturday Night Special] measures would disproportionately affect the law-abiding poor, since it is they who are most likely to own [Saturday Night Special] and obey the laws, and who are least likely to have the money to buy better quality, and therefore higher-priced, weapons. . . . Whereas it might not be easy for the law-abiding poor to buy a more expensive gun, few career criminals willing to assault and rob would lack the additional $50–100 it would take to purchase a gun not falling into the [Saturday Night Special] category."). The reality that criminals do not utilize the less expensive variety of handguns is underscored by the dramatic increase in the use of high quality (and high capacity) handguns during criminal episodes. Telephone interview with Richard W. Chenow, Firearms Examiner for the Chicago Police Crime Laboratory (Sept. 5, 1994).

47. *See, e.g.,* DeShaney v. Winnebago County Dep't of Social Servs., 489 U.S. 189, 196 (1989) ("[T]he Due Process Clauses generally confer no affirmative right to governmental aid, even where such aid may be necessary to secure life, liberty, or property interests."); Warren v. District of Columbia, 444 A2d 1, 3 (D.C. 1981) ("[The] government and its agents are under no general duty to provide public services, such as police protection, to any particular individual citizen."). *See also* Everton v. Willard, 468 So. 2d 936 (Fla. 1985); South v. Maryland, 59 U.S. 396 (1855).

48. Bowers v. DeVito, 686 F.2d 616, 618 (7th Cir. 1982).

49. Don B. Kates, Jr., *The Value of Civilian Arms Possession as a Deterrent to Crime or Defense Against Crime*, 18 Am. J. Crim. L. 124 (1991) ("If the circumstances permit, the police will protect a citizen in distress. But they are not legally duty bound to do even that, nor to provide any direct protection. . . . A fortiori the police have no responsibility to, and generally do not, provide personal protection to private citizens who have been threatened.").

50. *See* Note, *Handguns and Product Liability*, 97 Harv. L. Rev. 1915 (1984) ("[H]andguns provide their owners with a psychic security that cannot be easily measured.").

51. *See* Kleck, *supra* note 11, at 86.

52. Senator Daniel P. Moynihan's proposed tax on gun sales and on the purchase of ammunition is one example. *See* Gary S. Becker, *Stiffer Jail Terms Will Make Gunmen More Gun-Shy*, Business Week, February 28, 1994, at 18 (arguing that such a tax would increase the number of guns in the hands of criminals and raise the incidence of crime).

53. 429 U.S. 252 (1977).

54. Metropolitan Hous. Dev. Corp. v. Village of Arlington Heights, 517 F.2d 409, 413 (7th Cir. 1975).

55. *Id.*

56. Village of Arlington Heights v. Metropolitan Hous. Dev. Corp., 429 U.S. 252, 264–65 (1977) (citation omitted).

57. *Id.* at 253. *See also* San Antonio Indep. Sch. Dist. v. Rodriguez, 411 U.S. 1, 25 (1973) (holding that mere disproportionate impact on the poor is legal).

58. *Arlington Heights*, 429 U.S. at 265 (emphasis added).

59. *Id.* at 265–66 (emphasis added).

60. *Id.* at 266.

61. *Id.* at 267.

62. *Arlington Heights*, 429 U.S. at 271.

63. *See, e.g.,* Edward Patrick Boyle, *It's Not Easy Bein' Green: The Psychology of Racism, Environmental Discrimination, and the Argument for Modernizing Equal Protection Analysis,* 46 VAND. L. REV. 937, 939 (1993) (arguing that legislators will rarely include racist reasoning in the public record and that plaintiff is unlikely to have access to other evidentiary sources).

64. *See* JOHN E. NOWAK & RONALD D. ROTUNDA, CONSTITUTIONAL LAWS, § 14.3, at 576 (4th ed. 1991).

65. *See generally* Shapiro v. Thompson, 394 U.S. 618 (1969); Skinner v. Oklahoma *ex rel.* Williamson, 316 U.S. 535 (1942).

66. NOWAK & ROTUNDA, *supra* note 64, at 575–76 (describing the strict scrutiny test).

67. *See* Troy R. Holroyd, Comment, *Homosexuals and the Military: Integration or Discrimination?,* 8 J. CONTEMP. HEALTH L. & POL'Y 429, 441–42 (1992).

68. *See* Shapiro, 394 U.S. at 638; *Skinner,* 316 U.S. at 541. *See also* Holroyd, *supra* note 67, at 441–42.

69. This raises a question similar to whether the First Amendment could void a building code which applies to all buildings, including churches and newspapers, and which results in higher costs which may mean that poor people cannot afford to build a church or operate a newspaper. Analogy raised in letter from Don B. Kates, Jr. (Oct. 9, 1994) (on file with author).

70. Gary Kleck, *Guns and Violence: A Summary of the Field,* Paper Presented at the American Political Science Association 18 (Aug. 29, 1991), *cited in* KOPEL, *supra* note 5, at 391.

71. *See* Robert A. O'Hare, Jr. & Joroge Pedreira, *An Uncertain Right: The Second Amendment and the Assault Weapon Legislation Controversy,* 66 ST. JOHNS L. REV. 179, 204–05 (1992) (arguing that as long as "dealers can penetrate U.S. borders and reap millions of dollars in illegal profits," they will be able to arm themselves accordingly—therefore, it is not the criminal, but the law-abiding citizen who will be affected most by gun control). It follows that those who *misuse* firearms should be severely penalized and those who merely possess them should not. Becker, *supra* note 52, at 18 ("[A] state mandatory term sends a clear signal about the risk of using guns to perpetrate crimes.").

72. NRA INST. FOR LEGISLATIVE ACTION, TEN MYTHS ABOUT GUN CONTROL 21 (1989).

73. *Id.*

74. *Id.*

75. *See* David B. Kopel, *Peril or Protection? The Risks and Benefits of Handgun Prohibition,* 12 ST. LOUIS U. PUB. L. REV. 290 (1993) ("[C]itizens willing to invest some time can be schooled in defensive firearms use to at least the same level of competence as the average police officer.")

76. *See* KLECK, *supra* note 11, at 47. *See also* BRENDAN F. J. FURNISH & DWIGHT H. SMALL, THE MOUNTING THREAT OF HOME INTRUDERS 51 (1993) ("[F]irearms need not be a source of accidents if the householder and other occupants of the home are adequately trained in their proper use and care, and especially in the manner in which they are kept inaccessible to others besides the owner.").

77. ERIC C. MORGAN & DAVID B. KOPEL, THE 'ASSAULT WEAPON' PANIC 67 (1993) (Independence Institute issue paper) ("More consistent, enforcement of existing statutes would directly target criminal misuse of all firearms. State and localities could also assign prosecutors to felons perpetrating violent crimes with firearms.")

78. *Id.* ("This reform would have prevented a career criminal named Eugene Thompson from perpetrating a murder spree in the suburbs south of Denver in March 1989.").

79. *Id.* ("While a direct link between [the glamorizing of 'assault weapon' misuse in prime-time television shows such as *Riptide, 21 Jump Street,* and *Miami Vice*] and criminal violence may be difficult to establish, at least one study has linked television and movie depictions of 'assault weapons' to increased sales of those weapons.").

80. *Id.*

81. *See* BUREAU OF ALCOHOL, TOBACCO AND FIREARMS, U.S. DEP'T OF THE TREASURY, STATE LAWS AND PUBLISHED ORDINANCES—FIREARMS (1989); Gun Control Act of 1968, 18 U.S.C. §§ 921–28 (1988). The Act allows persons to engage in firearm trade upon compliance with applicable licensing procedures. *Id.* § 923. Additionally, the Act delineates exemptions from the prohibition of firearm ownership or control. *Id.* § 925.

Chapter Thirty-three

Talk at Temple Beth Shir Shalom
Friday, April 30, 1993

J. Neil Schulman

Just to introduce myself. I'm a novelist, screenwriter, and journalist. I'm also a graduate of the PC-832 reserve police training program at Rio Hondo Police Academy. I was asked to speak here tonight because I've written about firearms for the *Los Angeles Times* opinion page. I should also mention that one of my articles convinced Dennis Prager [1] to change his views about guns. And just for the record, I'm a member of the National Rifle Association, Handgun Control, Inc., and the American Civil Liberties Union. So I have all bases covered.

I'd like to start by asking you a question. How many of you can correctly quote me the Sixth Commandment?

It's not "You shall not kill" but "You shall not *murder.*"

There's a big difference between killing and murdering. Killing means purposely ending a life. Murdering means purposely ending an *innocent* life. If you kill someone who's trying to murder you or some other innocent person, that's not murder. As a matter of fact, it's a moral *requirement* to defend the innocent by killing if that's the only way you can do it.

I'm going to spend about two minutes correcting the lies you hear about guns on TV and in the newspapers.

You're told the lie that gun control will stop criminals from getting guns. The truth is that according to a Bureau of Alcohol, Tobacco, and Firearms study titled "Protecting America, Yes," criminals get 37 percent of their guns on the black market and another 34 percent from burglaries and robberies. That means that 71 percent—almost three out of every four guns a criminal uses—won't be stopped by gun control. If you pass gun restrictions, criminals will still get their guns for murder, robbery, burglary, and rape—but you won't be able to get a gun to stop them.

You're told that a gun kept in the home for protection is more likely to kill someone you know than a burglar. That's a distortion of the truth, which is that a gun kept in the home is *far* more likely to capture or chase away a burglar without having to kill anyone at all.

You're told the lie that gun accidents are killing children at unprecedented rates. The truth is that gun accidents account for less than 300 deaths of children under age fourteen each year—less than 3 percent of children's accidental deaths. Car accidents kill around 3,700 children each year, 1,200 drown, and 1,000 die in fires. In general, firearms accidents are down about 40 percent from ten years ago and down 80 percent from fifty years ago. You can thank NRA's gun safety training programs for that. If NRA's gun safety courses were taught in all schools, we could probably get it down to a quarter of that.

Yes, there are teenagers—usually gang members—murdering other teenagers with guns. But those young murderers are already forbidden by law to have guns; laws don't stop them for an instant. Matter of fact, the Bloods and the Crips are required to commit a murder to advance rank in their gangs. That's why there are so many drive-by shootings.

You hear that assault rifles are major crime guns. The California Department of Justice has admitted that was a politically motivated lie—the truth is that fewer than 2 percent of the guns used in crime fall into the prohibited categories.

I could go on refuting these lies for hours. I'm not going to bother. It's beside the real point.

Let me tell you some things you don't hear about on TV or in the newspapers. According to figures compiled from around eight different studies, private citizens in this country use a firearm about a million times each year to stop or prevent a crime.

My father is a concert violinist who was a member of the Boston Symphony Orchestra and the Metropolitan Opera Orchestra in New York. He carried a gun to protect himself in Boston and New York for fifteen years—and on around five separate occasions, carrying that gun saved him from gangs of robbers.

My father couldn't count on the police to save him, and neither can you. Under California law, which is like the laws of the rest of the country, no one in the government is legally responsible for protecting you—*no one.*

California Government Code, Section 845, states, "Neither a public entity nor a public employee is liable for failure to establish a police department or otherwise provide police protection service or, if police protection service is provided, for failure to provide sufficient police protection service."

But the California Constitution says the following in Article I, Section 1: "All people are by nature free and independent, and have certain inalienable rights, among which are those of enjoying and *defending* life and liberty; acquiring, possessing, and *protecting* property; and pursuing and obtaining *safety*, happiness, and privacy."

California law merely reflects reality: when you're attacked, the only person you can count on to protect you is *you.*

During the Los Angeles riots, police were completely unable to stop arson, shootings, and looting for three days, until another fifteen thousand army and National Guard troops showed up. A few months later, Hurricane Andrew left parts of Florida without electricity or phone for almost three months—and no one could call the police for help. A major earthquake here could do the same.

I know that some of you are thinking that the more guns you have, the more violence you have. That's another one of those lies. Switzerland has one of the lowest murder rates of anywhere on Earth. Yet the Swiss keep machine guns and anti-tank weapons in their homes, and Swiss citizens regularly carry their machine guns on bicycles and trains to the ranges where they practice. Why is it that the Swiss have hardly any murderers? The answer is simple. The Swiss take their responsibility to defend themselves very seriously. Every able-bodied male in the country is in the Swiss army or reserve and the Swiss have been eliminating their violent criminals regularly until their criminals are an endangered species.

It comes down to competition. If you're running a business today, you know that you'll go under if you don't have competitive technology. You wouldn't run an office today with typewriters when other businesses are using computers. The same is true regarding your life and property, which the criminals are in competition for. The criminals are arming themselves with 9 millimeter semi-auto pistols which can easily be smuggled in across the Mexican border. If you are going to survive, you'd better not be armed with anything less effective.

As Dennis Prager says, there are only two races of people: the decent and the indecent.' Laws should stop indecent people who use guns to commit violent crimes. That means the decent people need to be better armed than the criminals, or the criminals will win.

And that's the real issue. As Jews, we know that from the destruction of the Second Temple of Solomon two millennia ago, until 1948 when the State of Israel was created, Jews have been persecuted. Jews stopped being victimized when they took up arms and started fighting back. The first major battle was fifty years ago this month, when the Jewish militia of the Warsaw Ghetto fought a battle with the Nazi SS. Almost all the Jews in the Warsaw ghetto died in that battle, but the lesson lived on, and Jews learned they needed to fight for survival.

Jews in America have been blessed. We have been less oppressed in this country than anywhere else in modern history. But that's made a lot of us complacent and lazy.

The price of liberty is eternal vigilance. You can't count on things always being good. Jews in Germany thought they were safe because Germany was a modern, enlightened, industrialized country where they had been safe for hundreds of years. In a short twenty years that turned around. Jews in Germany submitted to Nazi gun control laws and allowed themselves to be disarmed. And because they'd lost the will to fight, a third of the Jews on this planet were murdered.

I am here to tell you that peaceful submission to evil is not only *not* a higher morality, it is not morality at all. It is a moral atrocity. Those among us who tell us to be unarmed are setting us up to be victims of the next Adolf Hitler to come to power—and if you ask me, they want us disarmed because they intend for *themselves* to be the ones in absolute power over our lives and property.

Maybe one of you is going to quote Gandhi to me about non-violent resistance. Gandhi chose that strategy in his fight to chase the British out of India because the British had already disarmed the Indians, and non-violent resistance was the only strategy Gandhi had left. Here's what Gandhi had to say about it: "Among the many misdeeds of the British rule in India, history will look upon the Act depriving a whole nation of Arms, as the blackest."

Adolf Hitler agreed with Gandhi's assessment—but from the other side. "The most foolish mistake we could possibly make," Hitler said, "would be to allow the subject races to possess arms. History shows that all conquerors who have allowed their subject races to carry arms have prepared their own downfall."

If the Jews of Germany had listened to Hitler, they might have saved Earth a Second World War.

Jews in Israel understand this. They are armed to the teeth—and have as low a murder rate as Switzerland. A few weeks ago, the Israeli Chief of Police called for all Israeli citizens to carry their guns with them at all times. Can you imagine what would have happened here if Chief Gates had done that a year ago during the LA riots?

But Israel is dependent upon the continued freedom of the United States for its own survival. If Jews in America do not actively support the right of the American people to keep and bear arms for their individual and common defense, then the American civilization is open to political dictatorship, and the next Holocaust of the Jews is just a short step behind.

We are already well down the road to Nazi Germany. Did you know that we have had the Nazi gun-control laws in America since 1968? There is strong evidence that the 1938 Nazi Weapons law was the basis for the 1968 Gun Control Act. The two laws are structurally very similar. The 1938 Nazi Weapon's Law disarmed Germany's Jewish citizens and made it possible for the democratically elected German government to murder millions of innocent people. Don't tell me it can't happen here.

Never again. Take up arms. Learn to use them properly and teach your children to use them properly. You can't have a peaceful or civilized society if good people won't fight to preserve it and practice with the weapons needed to do it.

Defend the constitutional provisions that legally protect those who keep and bear arms to preserve peace and civilization. Demand the impeachment of all government officials—police, judges, and legislators—who lie about the right to bear arms and try to disarm us. It's not the government's job to defend society from gangsters and potential dictators: it's *yours*. It's the moral responsibility of every one of us who is able to do so.

Thank you.

NOTES

1. Prager is a popular Los Angeles radio talk-show host on top-rated KABC AM. He is also a former teacher, newspaper columnist, and an author of several books on Judaism.

He is an internationally known lecturer and is considered one of the most prominent spokespersons for modern Judaism, and writes a newsletter titled *Ultimate Issues* devoted to the promotion of ethical monotheism.

2. On his radio program, Dennis attributes this paradigm to Viktor Frankl's book *Man's Search for Meaning*. I read that book years ago but didn't remember the quote until I heard it again from Dennis on a program before I gave this talk, and didn't remember the quote was from Frankl until Dennis attributed it on a subsequent program.

When Government Is the Enemy

Chapter Thirty-four

Apocalypse Now?

James Coates

> He who fights with monsters should be careful lest he
> thereby become a monster. And if thou gaze long into
> an abyss, the abyss will also gaze into thee.
> —Friedrich Nietzsche

His eyes flashing zeal for the Lord through a pair of horn-rimmed spectacles, brother Jimmy Swaggart waves a copy of the Constitution of the United States of America before his rapt audience. "This is the word of God," shouts the tremendously popular television evangelist with a mighty shake of his leonine hair that sends a halo of perspiration backlighted by klieg lights flying about his head.

And while the substance of his extraordinary sermons comes directly out of the credo of the Posse Comitatus brand of Christian Identity, Jimmy Swaggart is no cockamamie racist preacher spouting venom over some backwoods stump in the Arkansas Ozarks. He is one of the most popular evangelists in America today, the moving force behind a multimillion-dollar media empire whose message is beamed via cable television into millions of American households each week. A cousin to two highly successful musicians, rock-and-roll artist Jerry Lee Lewis and country singer Mickey Gilley, Swaggart is a magnificent showman in his own right. He pounds out hymns on a concert grand piano and sings of Jesus in a stirring molasses-thick Louisiana tenor that sets the neck hairs twitching. His followers include many blacks, and he has been known to purchase Israel bonds. Nevertheless, many of the themes voiced by this riveting proselytizer echo the sermons of Thom Robb, Bob Miles, and Richard Butler.

In common with Posse leaders such as James Wickstrom and Gordon Kahl, Swaggart views the Constitution as a divinely inspired document, and he hints darkly in his sermons that "the Beast" has attempted to corrupt that document since it was first delivered to Americans with just ten amendments, known as the Bill of Rights. Along with Identity doomsayers like Miles and Butler, the immensely popular Swaggart has warned his audiences that the "end times" are at hand and that soon one may expect the rain of nuclear missiles or other cleansing fire that will mark the period of "the Tribulations" that is to usher in the final battle of Armageddon and the Second Coming of Christ. He has made repeated references to Jews that are evocative of the same anti-Semitism documented so dramatically by Louis Harris in the backwaters of Iowa and Nebraska. He once admonished a congregation against bargaining with Jesus by warning them to remember that "Jesus is a Jew."

In tandem with so many others in today's Fundamentalist political movement, Swaggart believes that his brand of Christians with their crusade for literal interpretation of the Bible have a pressing moral duty to seize national power and impose their beliefs on the nation at large because time is now very short. He quickly became a major supporter of his fellow television evangelist Pat Robertson when Robertson announced his plans to use his own tremendously popular television empire, the Christian Broadcasting Network's 700 Club, as a platform for a possible presidential bid.

While covering Swaggart's September 1986 crusade in the national capital, Lloyd Grove of *The Washington Post* recorded an amazing conversation between the evangelist and a female reporter from Israel's largest newspaper, *Yediot Ahronot*, that dramatizes how the currently flourishing "televangelical" Christian movement is promoting the agenda of the Survival Right.

Swaggart gave the journalist a brief Cook's tour of the landscape of the future as laid out in the Book of Revelation and elsewhere:

"One day the nation of Israel will accept the Lord Jesus Christ. Several things are going to happen in the future that are cataclysmic, and most of it involves the State of Israel, to be frank with you.

"There will be a man who will rise in the Middle East not too many years from now that will project himself as the Messiah. He will say, 'I am God.' And the Jewish nation will accept him. . . . He will make a seven-year pact with Israel. In the middle of that seven-year pact—three and a half years—he will break that non-aggression treaty with Israel and will set himself up as God in Jerusalem and attack Israel, and Israel for the first time in her history will be defeated and will go to a place that you now know as Petra. It's called the Time of Jacob's Trouble. And the Bible also tells us—Zechariah does—that two-thirds of the nation of Israel will be slaughtered during that time . . .

"They're going to cry, the people of Israel, for the Messiah to come. They're going to cry. As the Bible describes it, at that hour, America will not be able to help Israel, no other nation will be able to help this little, tiny, tiny people—and they're going to cry, 'Lord! You are our only hope and if you don't come now there's no more Israel!' And that moment He's coming back. . . . He'll split the skies asunder. . . . He'll set his feet on Mount Olivet. . . . And the entire nation of Israel—those that are left—will accept the Lord. And then the Jewish people are going to become the most evangelizing, the premier nation on the face of the earth."

According to Grove's account, Swaggart then said to the Israeli journalist, "That's quite a story, isn't it?"

She replied, "It sounds scary."

It does, indeed, sound scary. But it also sounds very familiar. In fact, Swaggart had merely reiterated the same prophesies from the Book of Revelation that had fueled the anti-Papist mobs of the early nineteenth century, the Know-Nothings of the pre–Civil War years and the postwar Klan. He voiced the same chilling scenario that has driven the Survival Right everywhere, from Michael Ryan's dismal Nebraska compound to Richard Butler's infamous retreat in the Idaho panhandle.

Catholics with their Douay Version of Scripture call the final book of the New Testament by a more evocative name, the Apocalypse. To Protestants it's the Book of Revelation, the account of a series of horrific visions visited upon St. John the Divine during the waning years of his life when he was exiled as a hermit on the Aegean island of Patmos. Among today's Fundamentalists, these final twenty-two chapters of the New Testament have become the single most important biblical passage. Likewise, Revelation serves as the scriptural justification for the Survival Right, which finds in John's words both a stirring description of the chaos to come and a mandate to take every step possible to escape that chaos, a mandate to survive at all costs.

As Swaggart explained to the Israeli reporter, Revelation dwells largely on the last seven years of human history before the long-awaited Second Coming of Christ. It is a horribly violent scenario replete with strife, famine, pestilence, and war, the legendary "Four Horsemen of the Apocalypse." In the first three and a half years of the seven-year Tribulation, the dreaded Antichrist comes to power in Israel and rebuilds the temple destroyed in Jerusalem by the Romans in 70 A.D. In the second three and a half years, this leader, whose name carries the Mark of the Beast (666), defiles the temple by having his own likeness installed on the altar and plunges the world into the final confrontation between Gog and Magog, entities which most "Tribulationists" view as the United States/Israel and the Soviet Union. It is during these three and a half years that those anointed by God to survive the "end time" must hide themselves in the wilderness.

The Book of Revelation, in turn, is foreshadowed elsewhere in prophetic books of the Bible such as Daniel and Isaiah, which Apocalypse scholars have distilled into the prevailing Fundamentalist view of the so-called end time. This is the scenario that Swaggart endorses, and which has been delineated at tremendous length by best-selling writer Hal Lindsey in a series of Bantam paperbacks that have included *The Rapture, The Terminal Generation, There's a New World Coming, The 1980s: Countdown to Armageddon,* and *The Late Great Planet Earth.* This last book has sold 18 million copies, and Lindsey became one of the few authors in history to have three books simultaneously on the *New York Times* best-seller list. His blood-soaked vision of the Apocalypse, then, has reached far beyond the Survival Right, although it has had a tremendous impact on these haters as well.

Filled with a perplexing hodgepodge of symbols, John's twenty-two chapters describe the final judgment as the unrolling of a scroll with seven segments, each segment closed off with a seal. The First Seal tells of the coming of the Antichrist and of the first three and a half years before he defiles the temple. The Second Seal tells of a war in Israel which flares briefly and then dies down. The Third Seal unleashes global economic collapse, and the Fourth Seal tells of a war in which one-fourth of mankind dies. The Fifth Seal tells of a massacre in which the forces of the Antichrist set out to kill the forces of goodness. The Sixth Seal ushers in devastating earthquakes, rains of stones and fire that latter-day Tribulationists generally associate with a thermonuclear exchange. Many of the elect escape this nuclear holocaust by finding refuge in the countryside.

After the devastation come the passages of Revelation that raise the quandary of Israel for modern-day Fundamentalists. An angel arrives on the scene with a message from God to stop further torment until 144,000 Jews can be "sealed" as servants of God, 12,000 from each of the twelve tribes of Israel: all others of those tribes must perish. Many Fundamentalists, then, conclude that only 144,000 Jews, what Lindsey likes to call "144,000 Jews for Jesus," will survive the Tribulation. Hellfire, damnation and worse await all other Jews living when the end time begins.

By contrast, far more non-Jews are saved in John's lurid climactic book. He writes in Revelation (7:9–17): "I beheld and, lo, a great multitude, which no man could number, of all nations, and kindreds, and people, and tongues, stood before the throne, and before the Lamb, clothed with white robes and palms in their hands. . . . For the Lamb which is in the midst of the throne shall feed them, and shall lead them into living fountains of waters: and God shall wipe away all tears from their eyes."

With those saved wearing the white robes "washed in the blood of the Lamb," the Apocalypse continues with the Seventh Seal, which opens the way to two other sets of seven horrific catastrophes known to Fundamentalists as the Trumpet Judgments and the Bowl Judgments. The First Trumpet brings the burning of one-third of the earth's surface, the Second Trumpet is frequently interpreted as a nuclear exchange between ships on the high seas, while the Third Trumpet kills one-third of all creatures that live in the water, and the Fourth Trumpet marks a darkening of the globe much like astronomer Carl Sagan's controversial descriptions of a nuclear winter.

The Fifth Trumpet marks an infestation of bizarre locusts, which, instead of feeding on green things, eat at the tormented bodies of those who are not marked as saved on their foreheads. "And in those days shall men seek death, and shall not find it: and shall desire to die, and death shall flee from them," writes John (Revelation 9:6) in a passage evocative of Khrushchev's famous prediction that after a nuclear war the living will curse the dead out of envy. Lindsey speculates that this Fifth Trumpet foretells a biological and chemical war with the arsenals of the United States and the Soviets.

After the Sixth Trumpet blows, an army of 200 million rises in the east and slays one-third of the world's remaining population. To Lindsey, this army is the Red Chinese.

The Seventh Trumpet orders God's vengeful angels to pour seven bowls or "vials of wrath" on the already devastated planet. The first Bowl Judgment causes "noisome and grievous" sores (Lindsey says cancer) to break out on the unsaved. The Second Bowl turns the seas into blood, and the Third Bowl turns the rivers and lakes into blood. The Fourth Bowl brings scorching heat on the tormented, the Fifth Bowl creates darkness that makes the blasphemers chew out their own tongues, while the Sixth Bowl dries out the river Euphrates, bringing plague.

Finally, the Seventh Bowl summons the armies of God and of Satan to the field of Armageddon for the final battle so long awaited by so many. That battle ends with Satan being cast into a pit, heralding a period of a thousand years of peace.

Lindsey's message, as shared by Swaggart and so many other evangelists on TV and off, is essentially a millenarian one. His warning is that all of the biblical evocations of generations, of days and weeks, of epochs and eras, of begats and endings, are literal measurements of time. Further, writes Lindsey, a scholarly study of the matter shows that these biblical measurements indicate that the long-awaited end of the world will coincide roughly with the coming of the millennial year 2000. In essence, this is the same sort of millenarian concept that surfaced in Europe and the Middle East as the year 1000 A.D. approached, a time of confusion and disruption.

It is a valid but still imponderable question whether substantial numbers of people will be driven toward a new period of apocalyptic movements as the end of the second millennium actually arrives over the next decade. Certainly, as things now stand, the approach of the dreaded year 2000 can only serve to benefit the doomsayers.

Particularly important here is the universal obsession that current American Fundamentalist leaders have with the "question" of Israel, and with Jews in general. Whether the speaker is Jerry Falwell, whose Moral Majority campaign of the early 1980s was the first open effort by evangelicals to seize political power, or Ku Klux Klan chaplain Thom Robb, the focus is often the same— Israel, the Jews. The Falwells, Swaggarts, and Lindseys insist that they want above all to preserve Israel while the Robbs and Mileses say they want to see it destroyed, but both share a common obsession with the topic prompted by the same Book of Revelation.

Revelation tells them clearly that before the Apocalypse can be played out, 144,000 Jews must be converted to Christ. The Tribulation can begin only in Israel, where the Antichrist is to appear. Likewise, the final battle between Gog and Magog must happen in Israel. In a 1971 statement to the president pro tem of the California State Senate, Ronald Reagan predicted: "Ezekiel 38 and 39 says that Gog, a northern power, will invade Israel. Gog must be Russia. Most of the prophecies that had to be fulfilled before Armageddon can come have come to pass. Ezekiel said that fire and brimstone will be rained upon the enemies. That must mean that they'll be destroyed by nuclear weapons."

The resulting "pro-Semitism" voiced by so much of the Religious Right is not much more comforting than the anti-Semitism spewing from the mouths of the

Survival Right. Noting the growth of attacks against synagogues and other hostilities being visited on American Jews, Rabbi Alexander Schindler, president of the Union of American Hebrew Congregations, told an audience in San Francisco in late 1980 that it was "no coincidence that the rise of right-wing Christian fundamentalism has been accompanied by the most serious outbreak of anti-Semitism in America since the outbreak of World War II."

In their sweeping 1984 portrait of the Fundamentalist movement, *Holy Terror*, Flo Conway and Jim Siegelman note how evangelicals so often trip over their own rhetoric when paying lip service to Israel. Falwell, they recall, once tried to sugarcoat the bitter pill of pro-Semitism by telling an audience in Virginia, "A few of you here today don't like the Jew. And I know why. He can make more money accidentally than you can on purpose."

The two authors likewise observe that although Falwell's ardent support of Israel won him a medal from Israeli Prime Minister Menachem Begin, the preacher also has written in his book *Listen, America* that Jews are "spiritually blind and desperately in need of their Messiah and Saviour." Conway and Siegelman caution that "this new phenomenon of Christian 'pro-Semitism' bears close scrutiny, for it has little to do with human affection. Most Fundamentalist love for the Jews and support for Israel takes its lead from the closing chapters of the New Testament, where the prophecies of Revelation set down the conditions that must be met before Christ's Second Coming and the end of the world."

Holy Terror recalls that Jews have been forced by a lengthy history of pogroms, persecutions, and other travails to be ever vigilant for the next threat to their own survival. That awareness has made American Jewry very sensitive to every infringement on religious liberty and human freedom, since history has shown repeatedly that once intolerance is focused against one segment of society, it soon comes to bear against the Jews, no matter who was the original target.

It is painfully obvious to many Jews that the same Fundamentalist leaders who profess their undying loyalty to the State of Israel also vow perpetual enmity toward such minorities as homosexuals and atheists. It is equally disturbing to listen to the racist undertones as Fundamentalist preachers rail against government aid to the poor, to hear them sound anti-feminist themes by waxing poetic about the "sanctity of the Christian family" and call hellfire and brimstone down upon the "liberals" and "secular humanists" who have become the movement's new targets. And what are American Jews to make of the constant vows from the Religious Right to "Christianize" America?

Here it is appropriate once again to raise the question of the Smerdyakov syndrome. What sort of impression is this incessant television thundering about Armageddon and Israel and all the rest having on casual listeners? What are the chances that people who first have been softened up by the awesome persuasive powers of a Jimmy Swaggart or a Pat Robertson will then be receptive to the similar preachings of a Thom Robb or some other Identity fanatic filled with venom about the true nature of the legendary tribes of Israel so crucial to the scenarios of Revelation?

While the blatantly racist and anti-Semitic Identity preachers still struggle for airtime on public-access cable stations, marginally more mainstream evangelists are ubiquitous on the American airwaves. Pat Robertson's 700 Club, with its continual news reports from Israel and discussions about the coming end times, is available on 75 percent of the TV sets in America, according to Christian Broadcasting Network publicity materials. Jimmy Swaggart's weekly audience on the Trinity Broadcasting Network is estimated at more than 8 million in the United States and perhaps ten times that number worldwide. Falwell has claimed a television constituency of more than 25 million. Before their dramatic ouster over sexual revelations in April 1987, Jim and Tammy Bakker reached similar numbers over yet another Christian network, called PTL for Praise the Lord.

A 1985 survey by the Wichita, Kansas, *Eagle-Beacon* found that thirty television evangelists were available each week in that small city alone through its cable television system. When reporter R. Robin McDonald of the *Eagle-Beacon* sent token donations to twenty of them, the result was a deluge of 270 letters asking for more money and promoting the panoply of Fundamentalist ideologies, including repeated requests for funds to travel to Israel, money to help wounded Israeli war veterans and pleas for financing for orphanages in the Holy Land.

A 1985 survey by A. C. Nielsen, the television rating company, commissioned by Robertson's Christian Broadcasting Network, found that the evangelicals were capturing far more public attention than had been thought by scholars up to that time. The study, released at the November 1985 convention of the Society for the Scientific Study of Religion (SSSR), found that more than 61 million people, representing 40 percent of all U.S. households with TV sets, had watched one or more of the top ten syndicated religious programs for at least six minutes in February 1985.

In an address to the SSSR, the group's president, Jeffrey K. Hadden, said the Nielsen study indicates that the Fundamentalists will grow in influence over the coming decade. Hadden said, "Media access is a critical resource in a social movement and . . . the 'televangelists' have greater unrestrained access to media than any other interest group in America." He noted that Robertson alone had a faithful weekly audience of 28 million viewers.

With Robertson's impressive presence as a nationally significant political force, most analysis has focused on such questions as whether the 61 million people who sit and listen to a Jimmy Swaggart or someone like him are likely to move into Republican ranks. What is probably a far more significant question is just how receptive will these same 61 million people be when somebody comes along with the well-honed religious/political package of the Survival Right.

It doesn't take much of a crystal ball to predict a future in which fear of the AIDS epidemic creates a tremendous public animosity toward homosexuals, a future in which worsening relations with the Soviets over building the controversial Star Wars defense system leads to the sort of saber rattling that so terrified people during the 1950s and 1960s and a future in which the approach of the year 2000 may cause many to pause and reflect on the millenarian concepts being offered across the spectrum of the Religious Right.

Since 1979 the U.S. Civil Rights Commission has noted a dramatic increase in instances of serious anti-Semitic violence such as synagogue bombings, cemetery desecrations, and physical attacks. In 1979, when record keeping started, the agency found 49 such crimes. In 1984, the commission recorded 705 and in 1985, 638.

What are the prospects that these ugly incidents will increase even more as an indirect result of the efforts of sophisticated political operatives of the American right, such as direct-mail fund-raising wizard Richard Viguerie and Paul Weyrich, whose expertise in setting up Political Action Committees to promote ultra-right candidates and causes is something of a legend among political professionals of all stripes? Both men have been active to date in supporting Falwell's Moral Majority, and their efforts are widely credited with putting the country on an ideological course rightward that makes a potential Robertson candidacy far more credible than otherwise would have been conceivable. Will a further mass move to the right make those already at the farthest-right fringes even more dangerous?

As the polls concerning anti-Semitism taken by Louis Harris in early 1986 in Nebraska and Iowa illustrate, there are large segments of rural and small-town America where the growth potential of the Survival Right is considerable.

The Survival Right's own leadership concluded by the mid-1980s that conditions are particularly receptive for their credo in the five adjoining states of Wyoming, Montana, Idaho, Washington, and Oregon, a sparsely settled quarter with only tiny numbers of blacks and Jews compared with the rest of the United States. Butler moved his Church of Jesus Christ Christian to Idaho in the early 1970s, for example, after his proclamations about the divinity of Adolf Hitler and the inferiority of blacks made him extremely unpopular in Southern California, where he had collaborated for years with Identity patriarch William Potter Gale.

Many of the oaths taken by the Order members as they prepared for their fund-raising crime wave pledged their efforts to creating a "bastion" for the white race in the Pacific Northwest. Since then, largely through the leadership of school bus bomber Miles, the Survival Right has been urging its members and potential members to join in an exodus to the five states, a movement they call the Northwest Territorial Imperative.

In response to these well-publicized calls for the movement of racists into their backyards, business and social leaders in the Pacific Northwest joined forces to oppose the influx by adopting such tactics as setting up powerful Human Relations Councils in their communities. In Coeur d'Alene, Idaho, for example, the Republican-dominated local Chamber of Commerce joined forces with a well-known left-wing Catholic priest, Father Bill Wassmuth, to form a council and pursue complaints against Butler's Aryan Nations compound.

In late 1986 Wassmuth's home and several other buildings in the area were bombed and prosecutors eventually charged several of Butler's associates in the crime. David Dorr, one of several neo-Nazis charged in Idaho state courts with the bombings, had told undercover FBI informants that the attacks in Coeur d'Alene and a counterfeiting scheme in neighboring Washington had been the work of a new group that called itself Bruder Schweigen Task Force II.

When the national news media descended upon Coeur d'Alene to cover the bombings, Sandy Emerson, director of the local Chamber of Commerce, explained to many a slack-jawed journalist that of the 59,770 persons living in the county only 39 were black. "Maybe there are a handful of Jewish people here," Emerson told the author, "like maybe a half dozen." Emerson described how once he and a few other local leaders began examining the topic, they found the same sort of "ingrained" prejudice among ordinary Idaho people that Harris's poll documented in Iowa and Nebraska. He noted that the local expression most used to describe getting a bargain was to "Jew down" the seller. Bad genetic traits were ascribed to a "nigger in the woodpile," and giving up on a project was called "Japping out." With no blacks, Jews, or Japanese to complain, the slurs have become commonplace, and Butler's rhetoric in such an environment was hardly as disturbing as a drunken prospector saying "hell" or "goddamn" around the womenfolk.

But as the Idaho reformers discovered when the Order burst forth from their midst, casual bigotry all too quickly translates into real hatred. "We found out just how close the gap is between using a careless racial slur in the barroom and bombing a [synagogue]," said Emerson. Unexamined bigotry abounds in rural America, and its existence gives the haters a ready toehold.

Consider the likely impact this small masterpiece downloaded from an Aryan Nations bulletin board in Houston might have on residents of a hard-pressed farm town:

$2,304,257,900,000.00
Two trillion three hundred four billion two hundred fifty-seven million nine hundred thousand dollars in foreign aid.

According to the Library of Congress the net cost (in 1982 dollars) as of January 1, 1983, for foreign aid is the amount shown above.

Trouble meeting home and/or farm payments and taxes???

Two trillion three hundred four billion two hundred fifty-seven million nine hundred thousand dollars ($2,304,257,900,000.00) will pay cash for forty-one million eight hundred ninety-five thousand five hundred ninety eight (41,895,598) new diesel tractors at fifty-five thousand dollars ($55,000) each. Are the Orientals in Asia or Jews in Israel somehow more important to the U.S. government than working Americans?

Home or farm being foreclosed on? Trouble meeting 17 percent interest payments?

$2,304,257,900.00 will pay cold cash for 35,450,121 new houses at $65,000 each or 9,217,031 farms at $250,000 each.

At this value, the U.S. government transferred the equivalent of 35,450,121 new homes from the working American to aliens, most of whom live under communist or socialist governments. FMHA (a government agency) foreclosed on 10,000 U.S. farms in the last 15 months, putting an estimated forty thousand (four-member) American families out in the cold. Could that $2,304,257,900,000.00 have been used to help these now destitute American farmers? Simple arithmetic—that is $230,425,790.00 for each and every farm taken by "our" government from its citizens. Home foreclosures are running much higher.

If you love this country, it is time you ask yourself, "Who in the hell is this government being run for?" If you come up with the same answer that this writer did, then you have no choice but to join the "second" American Revolution. Honor demands and duty requires that we rebel against this destruction of our people by the government. For those who think we can vote the tyrants out, they should be reminded that regardless of who has been elected in the last 50 years, confiscation of the wealth of our people has gone ahead. Democrat or Republican, there has been no change. Our founding fathers, lacking success after fifteen years, gave up petitions and letter writing to the government. How about you?

"Rebellion to tyrants is obedience to God."—Thomas Jefferson

As that essay, signed with the name of the Ku Klux Klan's founder, Nathan Bedford Forrest, shows, the mood in America today is growing ever more ugly as economic conditions slip and international tensions increase. The Fundamentalist message likewise paints an ugly picture of a country in moral decay. As pastors shout their condemnation of an abortion rate approaching one in four pregnancies, others see looming disaster as the dreaded AIDS epidemic crosses over from homosexuals to the heterosexual community. A 1986 issue of *Liberty*, the magazine of the Seventh-Day Adventist Church, lamented in an article about Robertson how "America is turning into a moral outhouse. . . . The children of those who watched 'Mayberry R.F.D.,' 'Leave It to Beaver' and 'I Love Lucy' are now entertained with the sex, violence, and drugs of 'Dynasty,' 'Dallas,' and 'Miami Vice.' "

The *Liberty* article, which rejected Robertson's candidacy, nevertheless endorsed his frequent warnings that 4,000 fetuses are aborted each day and the U.S. Customs Service is seizing a massive amount of cocaine annually, which nevertheless accounts for only "a small percentage of what flows in the bloodstream of an estimated 4 million Americans. Crime is rampant, whether committed by E. F. Hutton (2,000 counts of wire and mail fraud) or James Huberty (the 1984 McDonald's restaurant massacre). Meanwhile divorce, AIDS, teenage suicides, alcoholism, and other corporate ills infest America like suppurating sores."

And while the generally pro-defense-spending Fundamentalists aren't complaining, nowhere is the departure from the moral values of even the recent past more dramatic than in the resurgence of militarism in today's popular American culture. That resurgence, of course, is very much in harmony with the styles of those in the Survival Right whose own stores of commando knives, automatic weapons, and other hardware often rival the props for such movies as *Rambo: First Blood Part II*, which grossed $75.8 million at the box office in its first twenty-three days. Likewise, blockbusters such as the 1986 hit *Top Gun* extolling the prowess of jet fighters and the 1987 television miniseries *Amerika* about a Soviet takeover of America, all serve to keep in the forefront the themes that drive the Survivalists.

A study of the sudden new phenomenon, "Militarism in America," published in 1986 by the liberal Center for Defense Information, documented a revolution in how post-Vietnam Americans react to guns and things military. The study notes, for example, that after Sylvester Stallone's Rambo movies became popular, twenty-five companies negotiated to obtain distribution rights to Rambo-related merchandise. The U.S. Army replaced its famous Uncle Sam poster with the Rambo figure clutching his machine gun and mowing down hordes of Asian attackers.

Rambo was followed by a deluge of militaristic films, including *Red Dawn*, the one about a Soviet invasion of a small Colorado town that was played over and over by Michael Ryan's Rulo, Nebraska, commune. Others have included the Chuck Norris commando movies, machine-gun operas such as *Missing in Action, Iron Eagle*, and *Invasion U.S.A.*

The CDI study found that war toy sales soared by more than 600 percent between 1982 and 1986, to over $1 billion annually. Worse, the major toy companies have joined forces with television producers to air cartoons featuring war toys, and the CDI noted that the number of cartoon series publicizing such toys jumped from zero in 1983 to ten in 1985. One popular show, for example, is based on the toy called Laser Tag, in which children strap sensors onto their chests and heads and then shoot at one another with infrared guns ("lasers") that cause the sensors to beep when hit by a light beam. These realistic toys, in turn, were developed from similar models used by military Special Forces members and others in actual training exercises; in early 1987 a teenager in California was shot to death by a sheriff's deputy who mistook the boy's Laser Tag pistol for a real weapon.

"According to the National Coalition on Television Violence, the average American child is now exposed to 250 cartoons with war themes and 800 television advertisements for war toys a year," the CDI reported. "By the age of sixteen, the average child will have watched some 200,000 hours of TV, taking in 200,000 acts of violence and 50,000 attempted murders, 33,000 of which will involve guns."

Of particular interest as far as the impact on the Survival Right is concerned is a study by the Center for Media and Public Affairs in which 500 TV shows were monitored over the past thirty years. The study found "a noticeable shift towards the use of military-style assault weaponry. Popular television series like the 'A-Team' and 'Miami Vice' promote the use of guns as necessary for survival."

And if Americans are introduced to automatics and hand grenades while still crawling about the carpet in front of the TV set, they are growing up to become avid consumers of firearms. The Justice Department estimates that U.S. citizens now own roughly 40 million revolvers and more than 100,000 registered machine guns. Estimates of unregistered machine guns, such as the one used to kill Alan Berg, run as high as 500,000, according to Michael Hancock, general counsel for the National Coalition to Ban Handguns.

Businesses like the Bullet Stop in Atlanta report doing a brisk trade renting machine guns to people who come in off the street eager to fire a burst of lead into a poster of the Ayatollah Khomeini, just as the Order members used to blast away at pictures of Menachem Begin. And the CDI has expressed particular concern that a business called National Survival Inc. runs an ongoing war game, on as many as 600 playing fields around the country, in which participants fight one another using air guns that shoot dye pellets. The game is played over courses with names like Skirmish, Combat Zone, and the Ultimate Game, the latter a reference to the short story that police in California think motivated Charles Chat Ng and Leonard Lake to hunt their victims down in the woods of Calaveras County. The CDI study found that as many as 50,000 ordinary citizens were signing up to play that "ultimate" game and others each week with National Survival Inc.

Another indication of the phenomenon cited in the CDI's study is the success of magazines like *Soldier of Fortune, SWAT, International Combat Arms* and *Firepower.* "Over 500,000 people subscribe to magazines put out by the Omega Corporation, the company that publishes *Soldier of Fortune* magazine," the report said. Indeed, Robert K. Brown's *Soldier of Fortune*, published monthly in Boulder, Colorado, and featuring a mixed bag of articles about machine guns, survivalism, and other hot modern topics, has become one of America's most successful "men's lifestyle magazines," according to Brown's publicity materials.

Each year Brown hosts a party for his magazine readers at the Sahara Hotel in Las Vegas which features a Combat Weapons Expo where as many as 5,000 visitors swap names and addresses, and buy guns, knives, blowguns, ammunition, freeze-dried food, and other survival paraphernalia—all laid out on hundreds of folding tables that fill the hotel's cavernous convention center, a room so large it once was used for Teamsters' Union national conventions. For four days hundreds of men, many of them with potbellies and bald heads, mill about the casino gaming area wearing camouflage clothing, paratroop boots and other military regalia, discussing plans to survive the coming holocaust, how to find work as hired mercenaries and other topics.

Nowhere is the Survival Right's obsession with the Bomb more obvious than at Brown's conventions. Clearly, these people have learned to live with nuclear weapons by making them part of their lore and the focus of much of their humor. One T-shirt showing an irradiated Arab reads: "Nuke Their Ass—Take the Gas." A popular poster shows a B-52 bomber flying away from a mushroom cloud rising above Moscow, with the caption: "And Then It's Miller Time." A button showing a swept-wing nuclear bomber in the same position as the famous peace symbol reads: "Drop It." Another poster depicts a 20-by-29-inch map of the United States with all likely targets for Soviet missiles marked in red so buyers can find "safe zones." Books for sale feature dozens of Survivalist topics, among them: *Survivalist's Medicine Chest, Survival Poaching, Survival Shooting, Survival Retreat, Survival Evasion and Escape, Nuclear War Survival Skills, Fallout Survival,* and *Surviving Doomsday.*

As all of the above clearly indicates, the Survival Right was not the only segment of American society turning toward heavy firepower out of nuclear anxiety during the early half of this decade. In reality, the Survivalists were part of a much larger national trend. The fact that these people became immersed in Identity religion, racism and anti-Semitism and became far more extremist than did their fellow citizens could mean simply that they are a vanguard that many more Americans will follow if, and when, things become worse than they already are.

Certainly, increased U.S.–Soviet tensions, the prospect of social panic brought on by the AIDS crisis, and the specter of the millennial year 2000 make it crucial that nobody underestimates the Survival Right as a significant potential component of the American political ethos. Indisputably the architects of this movement have left their potential converts with a very complete and complex ideology that has drawn from the most eloquent of history's hate groups to create a comprehensive world view of conspiracy, ranging from the creation of the Talmud in ancient Babylon right up to the latest board meeting at the Rockefeller Foundation. And the religious heritage passed to these Survivalists, complete with all the complicated trackings of the Lost Tribes of Israel and the interpretations of myriad Scriptures, is every bit as complex as what the local Catholic priest or Anglican pastor has to offer.

But as the examples of hatred, violence, and suffering described here illustrate, the most permanent legacy that the Survivalists offer for the future may simply be more terror and more chaos as an unknown number of potential Smerdyakovs are driven to act by the onerous background noise of Armageddon being sounded everywhere, from the Oval Office of the White House to the flickering channels on late-night television.

Certainly, as of this writing the nightmares that drive the denizens of this chapter continue. Global nuclear arsenals grow daily even as tremendous international strife compounds the sense of gloom. Economic conditions remain desperate in the farm belt, and urban defenders of hard-won civil liberties find themselves losing ground in the face of the AIDS panic. Frightened and increasingly mean-spirited people perpetuate the blight of racism everywhere, from the boroughs of New York to the backwaters of the Deep South. The millennial year is barely a decade away, and the televangelists' influence already is growing rapidly. These forces all combine to sicken the spirit of people in the mainstream just as they infect the Survivalists whose energies are so intensely focused on overcoming the chaos they believe is imminent.

The ultimate question may not be who has the Survival Sickness, but rather, who is going to survive it.

Chapter Thirty-five

They've Had Enough

Philip Weiss

A warm morning late in October, and James (Bo) Gritz stands on a mountaintop in north-central Idaho, addressing the faggot press. His words. Still, look at them: a Brit with blond hair fringing his round head—*The London Times* calling; a reporter from *People* with long hair and a goatee; the neo-beat novelist William T. Vollmann, on assignment from *Spin* magazine and accompanied by a friend, a birdlike woman with bright red lipstick and purple gloves. And there are three or four others, including a photographer from this magazine who has slipped his earring into his pocket to get under the faggot radar.

Gritz (rhymes with "bites") is long-winded. "I don't know about you, friends, but I look at everything from my guerrilla perspective," he explains, alluding to his years as a Green Beret colonel. "The Government will do a threat analysis. They'll look and say, Jiminy Christmas, this is not Waco. We're going to have to completely encircle this whole area here if we're going to control it, and as you know there's only one road. . . ."

He turns and motions over the hills to the north, toward a dirt road that winds 11 miles to the small town of Kamiah, population 1,100.

"I know what they're going to say. 'Gritz is going to have a .50-caliber up here, he's going to have cannons, he's going to have explosives in the trees.' So they're going to have to try vertical envelopment." He's referring to helicopters. "Non-habit-forming. Five thousand helicopters shot down in Vietnam. *No way!* So I think they're going to leave us alone. So we don't have to shoot at them. We don't even have to have the capability. As long as they think that there is that threat."

Gritz is talking about a place he calls Almost Heaven. It will rise right here, in northern Idaho—two hundred acres that he and his partners bought and subdivided into thirty lots that they're selling, at $3,000 an acre, to people who want to escape Government tyranny and Armageddon in the lowlands. The lots are going fast, as are those Gritz is selling on higher hilltops nearby—he calls one Shenandoah, the other Woodland Acres. Up here, with a view of the Clearwater River and Gospel Hump Wilderness Area, buyers will form a "covenant community." They will agree to stand by one another and defend one another, and maybe not pay any taxes either. "Off the umbilical," he calls it. Off the grid.

Gritz, who was briefly on the ticket with David Duke in '88 and ran for President himself in '92, is, at fifty-five, a leader of the radical right-wing survivalist movement. He quotes Scripture, prophesying end times in the next few years, times when we shall all have to accept the mark of the beast: a bar code implant in the forehead or right hand that means the cashless society is upon us, and that every transaction an individual makes will be subject to surveillance. Just as Revelation 13 describes.

"We are going to live our lives according to our ways," Gritz is saying now. "Let's say it comes down to the fact that eventually you cannot go down to the 7-Eleven and buy bread and milk and meat. Then yes, up here there's an abundance of game, and if it did come to that—and according to biblical prophecies there are times like that ahead—then we would be prepared. If it never comes, hallelujah. But personally I'm going to go off the grid, because every time I've lived off the grid, like Vietnam, I've been very happy."

Gritz does what the photographers want him to do: he props one of his black cowboy boots on a barbed-wire fence and stares off squinting and box-headed. He hugs his wife, Claudia, and walks across the land. Claudia is nearly twenty years younger than he is—she's wife No. 3—and doesn't seem like much of a survivalist. Pretty with Liz Taylor eyes, she wears two large diamonds rings on her fingers. She and Bo may be going off the grid, but Claudia is going to have a washer and dryer, a lawn.

"I'm hungry," she says. "I need to go to the bathroom, so do one more shot."

"There's a port-a-potty," one of Gritz's partners, Jerry Gillespie, tells her.

"No way," she says.

So, just one more shot. The top couple of buttons on Gritz's shirt are open, and sprigs of gray chest hair peek over his undershirt and catch the morning light, and the same sunlight takes in the valley of the Clearwater and the pale blue berries on the elderberry bushes. If you live off the grid you can make wine and pancakes with the crunchy bittersweet elderberry.

Go a half mile east. The same sunlight picks out honey-colored chinking on the log-house homestead of the first people to buy into Gritz's message and move up here: the Fullers, Dan and Barb, formerly of St. George, Utah. They are prepared for end times. They have a $20,000 solar-energy system and are storing food—stuff that looks like dried cat food and takes a long time to get used to. T.V.P.: textured vegetable protein. Taco-flavored T.V.P. Magic Barbecue T.V.P.

You get invited into their kitchen. Boy, that T.V.P. takes a while to get used to. They say Bo's got the Gospel. They say that years of study have convinced them that political collapse is a real possibility. They hand you literature from Florida that will open your eyes—*The Revelator*. In which it is written that the Anti-Christ Banksters are squeezing the life out of America in preparation for the New World Order. Shrewd goldsmiths are plotting to deceive the goyim, the goy states. Mayer Amschel Rothschild. Haym Solomon. There is a long bit from the *Protocols of the Elders of Zion.*

Dan Fuller, sixty-eight, is a retired crop-duster, and he tells you: "There are two choices. Go along with the New World Order, or change your life. They're going to decide everything about your life. Where you can work. Where you can live. Where you can go for groceries. They will tell you all of that. You're not going to be a free man, you're going to be a slave."

You're skeptical. "I don't know."

"Nothing would please me more than for it all not to be true." But, he continues, "Your clothes are not going to be yours. They're going to belong to the state."

"Who will decide?"

"World bankers."

"The Queen of England," Barb says.

"Rothschild," he says.

You say, "How will it be in the middle of winter when you have to drive down ten miles of snaking dirt road to get some milk?"

Dan shakes his head once. "Well, let me ask you this: What are you going to do when they ask you to accept the mark of the beast?

The anti-government mood that has seemingly swept the nation is nowhere more pronounced than in Idaho. This is not the state that elected Frank Church to the Senate, not any more. Idaho is sending no Democrats at all to Washington this month, and the Statehouse, which only a few years ago was roughly balanced between the two parties, now counts only 21 Democrats among its 105 members. The most powerful Democrat in the state, indeed the only Democrat holding statewide office, is J. D. Williams, the auditor. And Idaho's Republicans are not in the William Weld–Christine Whitman mold. There is Helen Chenoweth, for instance. During her successful campaign last fall to unseat Representative Larry LaRocco, a Democrat, Chenoweth declared that "white Anglo-Saxon males are an endangered species."

White Anglo-Saxons are not endangered in Idaho. The state, with a population of roughly 1,100,000, is virtually all white. The 1990 census counted about 9,000 Asians and Pacific Islanders in Idaho and slightly more than 3,000 blacks. This goes some way toward explaining why Idaho is suddenly one of the most attractive destinations for whites in flight. (A third of the state's newcomers are said to be coming from California.) So far in the 90's, only Nevada's and Arizona's population growth rates are greater than Idaho's.

"Our real estate is going nuts here because people are trying to get away from the real world," Clint Engledow, a real-estate agent in Kamiah, says. "Downtown Houston, downtown Denver, downtown Vallejo. You name it, they're fleeing. They say they're sick of drive-by shootings and fourteen-year-old orange-haired mall rats. They want to pick huckleberries and not be near any population base."

The appeal of Idaho is not simply its whiteness, though. There are good jobs in Boise, and affordable homes in suburbs here that still feel like small towns. And for those looking for a last frontier, there is the terrain. Idaho has magnificent scale, its dry Western air yielding long views of rugged river breaks and serried mountains. These vistas are preserved thanks in large part to the Federal Government. Nearly two-thirds of the state is publicly owned land, mainly national forests and wilderness.

Survivalists and conspiratorialists, Christian constitutionalists and New Age back-to-the-landers would seem to number in the several thousands in Idaho. Steve Willey, owner of Backwoods Solar Electric in Sandpoint, says he has 1,000 customers in northern Idaho, all off the grid. "There's a wide variety here that come from opposite ends philosophically to the same situation physically," Willey says. Jess Walter, a reporter for *The Spokesman-Review* in Spokane, Washington, who has done considerable reporting on survivalists, estimates that there are more than 10,000 people living off the grid, both literally and philosophically, in the hills of eastern Washington, northern Idaho, and western Montana. He has encountered a Vietnam vet who says he's hiding in the woods, a loner who shares a cabin with a grand piano, a man living in a trailer with his children and new wife, on the lam from a custody dispute, and a commune that sells food.

"If you follow a dirt road anywhere in northeast Washington or Idaho, chances are you're going to find them," he says. "They're harder to count than homeless people, because they're just gone."

In the 60's and 70's, hippies came to Idaho's empty spaces, and you can still find them growing garlic and tanning hides and holding barter fairs. And the promise of being left alone has drawn other kinds of free spirits. People like the novelist Denis Johnson, who lives near the Canadian border and who brings along bungee cords when he goes out with a chain saw so he can tourniquet himself in case of an accident.

"You come here with a vague notion of getting away from it all," Johnson says. "Then when you get out into the woods, you see how wonderful it is to be self-sufficient to any degree, how essential it is to being human. I feel I robbed myself by living in cities. The city itself is like a big baby, being supplied from outside."

Self-reliance is Idaho's byword. The landscape fosters an American romance about working out one's own fate in nature that is equal parts Thoreau and manifest destiny—and one big part pure hatred of government. Up in the mountains of the panhandle, Idahoans bring those feelings to a high art. Local newspapers are filled with laments like the one that a husband and wife, new to the state, sent to *The Clearwater Progress* in Kamiah to complain about Federal policy on land use and schooling: "We eat the bitter bread of tyranny and the cake of oppression."

For people like this, Idaho offers not only a landscape but a coherent politics, a world view: survivalism, tax protest, apocalypse, conspiracy theories. A woman in Kamiah urges you to investigate sightings of black helicopters, which, she has heard, are a sign that the United Nations is about to take over America's Armed Forces. At breakfast in the Lewis Clark Motel outside Kamiah, a retiree tells you, "In California they put a meter on your well and you get charged twice, once when it comes in and once when it flows out, as sewage," then gives you information about how to build a house from tires. And the publisher of *The Clearwater Progress*, Bill Glenn, shows you the plastic security strip they're putting into $20 bills, and says this is a step toward one world government.

Out here, there's room for such thinking, room for everything. Bo Gritz tells you that Idaho County, Idaho, is ideal for Almost Heaven because, among other things, there is only one traffic light and the citizens have rejected all efforts to impose a building code. He tells you other things too. He says that as the global tide toward world government grows stronger, "we will need a pivotal state"— Idaho as base camp.

Gritz's attraction to Idaho, his sense of having found a place here, also has to do with his role in an episode that, for Idaho's survivalists, has become a legend— one about a first taste of end times. In August 1992 a forty-four-year-old survivalist named Randall Weaver garrisoned himself and his family and a friend in a mountaintop cabin outside of Naples, Idaho, thirty miles from the Canadian border. Federal agents were moving in through the woods with a warrant for Weaver's arrest. (He had failed to appear at a trial on a gun charge in 1991.) During an unintended encounter, a deputy marshal was killed and Federal sharpshooters killed Weaver's fourteen-year-old son, Sam. The next day a sharpshooter killed Weaver's wife, Vicki, forty-three, as she stood in the doorway of the cabin holding her infant daughter. For eight days Randy Weaver huddled in his cabin with his three daughters a few feet from Vicki's body.

A vigil gathered at the base of the mountain, known as Ruby Ridge. There were neo-Nazis, tax protesters, enraged neighbors. Children held posters saying Death to ZOG—Zionist-Occupied Government. Skinheads shaved their heads in nearby Ruby Creek. The standoff ended when Bo Gritz showed up and forced himself on the hostage rescue team. He wore a special negotiator's outfit—a midnight blue jacket with epaulets that he had made for him in Thailand years before, and he eventually helped convince Weaver to give up and fight the battle in court.

The destruction of the Weaver family, and Randy Weaver's subsequent exoneration on Federal conspiracy charges, is today the parable by which many living off the grid in Idaho and elsewhere understand government's relationship to the American family. The story has the same resonance for survivalists today as confrontations between the Black Panthers and the police had for the radically alienated left in the 70's.

'Where are these people coming from that can inflict so much pain? I don't sleep at night."

Leah Balint hugs herself as she recalls the death of Vicki Weaver.

You're back at Almost Heaven. Two horses in a field. An apple tree. Leah's husband, Stewart, forty-one, in a Cochise belt buckle and a cowboy hat with a piece of polished stone, malachite or something, dangling from the band. And Leah herself walking around with just gray wool socks on her feet, a twenty-two-year-old with a fragile piping voice and clear skin and thick Venus hair. Their two small boys play with a hammer. Solar panels lean against the trailer, charging the car battery that runs their television.

They're off the grid and going further. Because Stew is engaged in the study of law. His studies began when his family lost its farm in Washington state. First he read *None Dare Call It Conspiracy*, by Gary Allen, a former speech writer for George Wallace; that opened his eyes to the designs of the international bankers who, in league with the Government, fix prices arbitrarily and cripple the nation. Now Stew is renouncing all of what he regards as his contracts with government. Driver's license. Social Security. Birth certificate. Hunting license. He has torn them up.

"The Government wasn't designed for people like us," Leah says.

She goes to the trailer and comes back out with Birkenstocks. A bird tweets from a barbed-wire fence.

"You see the magpie?"

You turn and there's a magpie perched on a wire, iridescent and strange. Meriwether Lewis was enchanted by them when he traveled here 190 years ago.

"Do you sleep at night?" she asks.

Like so many other stances of the late 60's, the back-to-the-land movement was mostly talk. People on the coasts had visions of throwing off the traces of a sick imperialist society and making a homestead, but it took a special sort to act on those beliefs and go off the grid. It wasn't people who shouted about revolution till they were hoarse. That was first chakra energy, from the groin. The true back-to-the-lander was drawing on integrative energy, higher in the body, fourth or fifth chakra.

Greg Sempel was confused by his football coaches at the University of Montana who screamed about winning and fed him twenty-one pills a day to bulk him up—but said he was wrong to smoke pot. He felt abused. He dropped out, did some ranch work—and eventually found himself on a remote hillside near Santa, Idaho, eighty miles north of Kamiah, with other hippies. He bought five acres (at $100 down, $50 a month), and melted snow for water. He formed a tree-planting co-op. It was grueling work, it tore at your back and your knees; men tended to be better cut out for it. That was a cruel truth about going back to the land; it might be saner, but it sorted out gender in a hurry. His wife, Leah, sewed quilts to exchange at the annual barter fair and gathered with the other women for home birthing.

"Ruby was born in a tepee," Leah says now, reaching for her, a friend's ten-year-old child.

"No, I was born in a bus," Ruby says.

Sheryl and Larry Nims came out to Kamiah from Portland in 1970. The land they bought had a grove of locusts in a draw, and the trees made William Blake–like silhouettes against the darkening sky. They bought a tepee for $324. They had a son they named Asa, and after he broke a pitchfork trying to pole-vault, they got him a pole and built standards out of lodgepole pines and a crossbar from a piece of thornwood. (He would later be state champ.) Sheryl farmed with horses and their hippie friends up the hill ate puppies because the Indians had done that. The Nimses found they didn't like to kill pigs or cows but they could kill goats. Goats were stupid. When it came time Larry would lead the goats they'd raised to a hollow and throw out grain for the one they'd chosen to eat that winter, and then he'd balance his rifle on a fence post 15 feet away and aim for the head. Sheryl cooked the goat and canned it, and the dogs ate the bones.

No chain saws. Chain saws were noisy, they smelled. To use one was to be fully implicated in the economy of fossil fuels. The metal blade of a crosscut saw going through the trunk of a cedar made a bright song that filled their hearts. Sheryl rode horseback and Larry walked over their land with a pruning saw hung around his neck, and they were the last people they knew who did physical eradication of weeds, pulling, no chemicals, and Sheryl wore nothing at all in the summer, even rode the horse naked. And when a surveyor came across the land one day and asked for a glass of water, Sheryl walked calmly back to the house with him in tow, naked as Eve before the fall, and got it for him in the house.

No phone. No electricity. Their lives were harder than the lives the University of Oregon had trained them for, but they were sinewy people, they liked things hard, and they abided by the frontier ethos: tolerance and distance. Everyone is escaping something. Mind your own business. Don't crowd him. Don't come on strong. Don't drop in, don't touch. A handshake means a lot more here than it does other places. Pay attention to the No Trespassing sign.

The hippies weren't the only people in northern Idaho who were convinced that society was out of whack.

There was Paul Palmer, tall and wry, who came from New Mexico in the 60's. He was an electrician by training, but now lives and farms with his family on Clear Creek, a remote spot seventeen miles from Kamiah. "After the Watts riots our feeling was that things were not right," he says. "But you don't wait for a crisis and then put up a tent in the wilderness. You go early and get prepared." For a time he pulled two of his boys from the public schools in Idaho because, he says, "a full-fledged Communist and a sex pervert" were teaching there. Meanwhile, his studies of the law convinced him that the Federal Government had grossly overstepped its limits. The income tax was voluntary, as he read the law. His refusal to file a 1040 form made it hard for him to find work.

"After my difficulties with the I.R.S., I was in the ragbag," he says. So he learned the ways of the land—how to farm with horses and dry fruit and grow beans.

Steve Majors, forty-one, came from Illinois and settled on a hillside not far from Palmer's place. He also began to read law books. "When I was farming, I began to have a conviction from God about not being on Social Security," he tells you. "You farm your land, when you're too old to farm it your son can farm it. That's your Social Security. The Government's Social Security program just didn't make sense to me. I inwardly felt the conviction that it's wrong for me to be in the system, and I better study the law to find out how best to protect myself. I started with the Bible, the basis of law in our country. The I.R.S. doesn't like my position."

A few miles down the Clearwater River in the town of Stites, (Grandpa) John Brandt sold building supplies to the hippies and said that building codes were Communism. He hung the Governor in effigy outside his store. Grandpa John had a library of literature.

You go to his store, Stites Ace Hardware. Grandpa John's having lunch. Just a minute. He finishes up and comes into his office, a big jovial man with antic eyebrows and a little mouth. Napkins his hands, talks about history.

"Hitler didn't get started on the Jews," he tells you. "He was trying to build the country up. The reason Hitler had a problem with them, there was inflation, and everything kept falling down and the Jews picked it up, for pennies on the dollar. Did you hear the expression I'm going to Jew you? That expression didn't come out of thin air. I know a lot of people got killed, but they run that Holocaust thing ragged, and that's going to stop. Now the Indians are taking that over. The Germans got credit for killing, or blame for killing, more Jews than there were at the time. Many times over. Who do you think, when we go into debt—who owns the Federal Reserve System? I've known this for at least twenty-five years. The first time people told me that, I thought, that's crazy. But they gave me books. I've spent a lot of time reading this. Roosevelt started socialism and ruined the country. I've heard one story that Eleanor shot him in the back of the head. He was with his mistress. The way this story goes—he gave away so much to the Russians, he was sick. That's normal. We know that. But he was going to confess this and she shot him, because she was a card-carrying Communist. They said it was a cerebral hemmorhage."

The hippies had their problems with the Government, too. When a D.E.A. helicopter dips over the trees on the hillsides around Santa and looks into the gardens, Hari Heath runs from his tepee, giving them the finger with one hand and waving his assault rifle with the other. Hari got to Idaho as a hippie. He still makes bows and arrows, but now he tells you how every commune he has seen fell apart because of inequities in power. Over the years he learned a lot from the right-wing survivalists and the local rednecks. He has learned that his ability to walk into a gun shop and buy anything he wants guarantees democracy.

Hari says: "The World Bank ten white guys socialist economic scam U.N. one world government? They're doing it very slowly. They know they can't pull it off if we maintain an armed population."

Larry Nims has a less alienated view of politics. He sees the American Constitution as beautifully designed. Still, as self-reliant people, he and Sheryl have self-reliant fantasies of end times. They, too, imagine the crunch, a time of bank failure, riots, social collapse. What if the dispossessed swarmed up from the lowlands? What if they came for Sheryl's canned goat and canned corn and potatoes? Would Larry be willing to shoot them?

He has met a survivalist who spoke about how you could use high land to get the drop on the hordes. And there was a way to use a handkerchief to improve your accuracy with a revolver. You wrap one corner of the handkerchief around the revolver grip, then you grip it with your hand and take the opposite corner of the handkerchief and clasp it in your teeth. Now aim the gun out from your body, strain with your mouth and your arm so you have two points of support. Here, like this. . . .

In the 1980s Idaho became strongly identified with right-wing apocalypticism. This was in large part because of the presence in the panhandle of Richard Butler, a neo-Nazi from California who bought twenty acres outside Coeur d'Alene, a short drive east of Spokane, Washington, and founded the Aryan Nations. He built a compound on his land, and it became an outpost of Christian Identity thinking, which generally holds that white Christians are the true Israelis; that blacks and other people of color are mud people, soulless animals; that Jews are the mongrelized descendants of Esau, hated by God, and that homosexuals should be exterminated. Conspiracies abound: notably, that the Government is controlled by a corrupt Babylonian system that includes the Jewish Defense League, the Anti-Defamation League of the B'nai B'rith, the Council of Foreign Relations, and the Trilateral Commission.

Today Richard Butler is seventy-five and in seeming decline, but he will spend an hour or two with you in his compound (even if you have identified yourself as a Jew). A fuzzy, crocheted swastika turns slowly in the window, his German shepherd, Bonn, rests nearby, and Butler lays out the finer points of neo-Nazi practice.

"We had a cross lighting down there—"

"Most people call it a cross burning."

"Well, Jesus Christ is the light of the world, he's the one who removes the darkness, so we call it a lighting. We don't burn the cross, we just light it."

"Gasoline?"

"No we use diesel oil. Wrap the cross in burlap. Light it, and the cross itself still stands."

"So it's the same cross year after year?"

"Oh yeah."

Ten years ago Butler was more puissant. He reached out to prisoners and other rootless young men with terrifying warnings about the crippling of the white race. Homosexuality is financed by the Jews, he'd say. That's why you never see a poor homosexual . . . Pregnant black women are coming by the millions to your neighborhood, he'd say. "Want to live in an all-white area?" Idaho beckons you. Butler and other Identity spokesmen envisioned the Idaho panhandle as the center of "a territorial imperative," a nation embracing portions of five Northwestern states in which blacks, Jews, and Indians would have few rights and face deportation or worse. In *The Politics of Righteousness*, a study of Idaho extremists, James A. Aho says Butler's training included living off the grid: "survivalist workshops, and classes in health, diet, food storage and nuclear protection."

The growing prominence of the Aryan Nations in the early 1980's presented the Coeur d'Alene community with a dilemma: leave Butler alone or come out against him. Civic leaders spoke of the state's tradition of tolerance. Ignore him and his appeal will die away. Besides, in northern Idaho his anti-Government views were widely shared.

On the other side of the debate were some Coeur d'Alene residents who organized as the Kootenai County Task Force on Human Relations. They came together in 1981 after a restaurant owned by a Jewish family was daubed with swastikas. The activists wanted to publicize Butler's message and decry it. At great personal risk—one task force leader's house was bombed as he sat in his living room—they spoke out against the Aryan Nations. And later they supported the first prosecution of an Aryan Nations follower after the man, a devotee of Hitler's, issued biblically inflected threats to a young white man whose mother had married a black man.

Inevitably Butler seeded violence. In 1984 a group linked to the Aryan Nations and calling itself the Order went on a crime spree of bank robberies and bombings and killings, notably the murder in June of that year of a Denver radio talkshow host—an outspoken liberal, and a Jew—named Alan Berg. The group's leader, Robert Jay Matthews, wrote: "I realized that white America, indeed my entire race, was headed for oblivion unless white men rose and turned the tide."

By December 1984, when Matthews died in a fiery shootout with the police on Whidbey Island in Washington, the Kootenai County Task Force was no longer lonely. Developers and the owner of several panhandle newspapers were on its side. The Nazis in the neighborhood were now a quality-of-life issue. "We had three problems," Marshall Mend, a local real-estate developer, said in *Stand Up to Hate Crimes*, a 1991 documentary celebrating the task force's first ten years. "One, our community's image was being destroyed by the media. Two, we saw minorities being discouraged from moving to the area. Three, we saw these same articles encouraging racists, bigots and other hate groups to move into our area."

Law enforcement agencies were at first rather slow to respond. The F.B.I. was "absolutely . . . behind the ball" on the Order, recalled Wayne Manis, then the special agent in charge of the F.B.I.'s Coeur d'Alene office. But officials were far better organized when a second Order group with connections to the Aryan Nations began a crime spree in 1986, setting off several bombs in the Coeur d'Alene area and threatening greater destruction: bombs for gay discos in Portland, cyanide for the water supply of Los Angeles.

"The F.B.I. did Order 1," says Tony Stewart, the current president of the Kootenai County Task Force. "Order 2 was F.B.I., A.T.F., Secret Service, the sheriff's office and the state police."

Stewart grows enthused describing this phalanx. Liberals are comfortable with government. And the Kootenai County task force worked closely with the state, helping legislators in Boise, for example, to pass far-reaching state hate crimes laws in the 1980's. Incidents of racist graffiti and harassment dropped sharply, and the hive of angry young men at the Aryan Nations began to decamp to a less sensitized region sixty miles away: the flats of Sanders County in Montana.

Coeur d'Alene began to earn recognition for its achievement. Its Mayor went to New York City in 1987 to accept a civic award from the Raoul Wallenberg Committee of the United States. The F.B.I. was all over northern Idaho; they weren't going to be surprised again. The agency, Wayne Manis says, had run up against "without a doubt the best organized and most serious terrorist threat that this country has ever seen." That the F.B.I. itself was feeling a little apocalyptic might explain the Government's actions on Ruby Ridge, the bloody standoff with the Weavers.

October: Black Hounds are baying outside. The barrel stove is going. Cougar and bear skins are draped over the couch. You're in the cabin of Jackie and Tony Brown in the hills not far from Naples, seventy miles north of Coeur d'Alene, not far from Ruby Ridge. The Browns were good friends of the Weavers.

"The Weavers were a curious blend of religious holy rollers and tactical soldiers of God, plus reactionaries," Tony says. "They reacted to things around them. So you're on the defensive, things aren't going the way you want them to do. Which is why I dropped out of the egomaniac-driven society in Oregon and followed a path of my own. But Weaver believes the Bible tells people of the knowledge and that they should expound that knowledge to their brothers and sisters. Form a body of true believers. Part of their life was sharing with people what they thought. They weren't pushy, but they thought a remnant or small group of people would bring about a new kingdom. Over the sheep type."

"The sheeple," Jackie says.

"Randy thought everyone was in for higher taxes, more restrictions, erosion of rights till you were a slave," Tony says. "One thing that sets his mental tone, he was a believer in absolute truth. I think the truth is pretty relative to what you know, two ideas can coexist. He was an idealist. The mission's right, we're going to do it."

Jackie says: "He was an all-American guy to the core. An angry, orientated farmer's kid."

In 1983, Randall Weaver was a machinist at the John Deere plant in Waterloo, Iowa. Vicki Weaver was an executive secretary. They studied religion but wanted no part of churches. He was a thin man with cavernous, troubled eyes and a strong jaw. He had trained as a Green Beret in demolitions. His wife was pretty and small, with dark hair and a wide face. She was more studious, she was the scripturalist. They were both intense, they both talked religion, they drew people to them. Don't believe me, Randall Weaver would say, according to later testimony at his trial. (Weaver declined to be interviewed.) Decide for yourself if this is the truth. But he knew it was the truth himself.

They learned that in the Idaho panhandle, they could find a mountaintop and live off the grid. There they could weather the chaos of martial law and the downfall of democracy. They would be there when the great tribulation came. Because in Matthew 24, it says, "When you see the abomination of desolation, which was spoken of by Daniel the prophet, stand in the holy place, then let them which be Judee's flee into the mountains."

They learned about the Great Illuminati that rules in Babylon, they learned

about the Trilateral Commission and Council on Foreign Relations that are pushing one world government. Which is spoken of in Revelation: "I saw a beast
rising out of the sea, with 10 horns and seven heads. . . . One of its heads seemed
to have a mortal wound, but its mortal wound was healed, and the whole earth
followed the beast with wonder." The seven heads being the G-7. And the
wounded head Germany.

In the Idaho panhandle they could home-school their three children. Home
schooling was illegal in Iowa. They would dehydrate food and arm themselves.
Because in Luke 22:36, a man is commanded to sell his cloak and buy a sword if
he have none, Randy Weaver got himself two Ruger Mini 14 semi-automatics.
And a pump-action Remington shotgun. And plenty of ammo.

The Weavers bought land on a knob 4,000 feet up in the Selkirk Mountains.
The road up was a steep, rocky, bulldozed strip that twirled and did switchbacks.
Weaver built a cabin at the top. It wasn't built to last. Did he know something?
Two-by-fours and uninsulated plywood walls. Before long the two-by-fours
began to belly. A big open room with a sleeping loft, and a shed nearby where
Vicki and the girls went when they were menstruating.

They had a rocker on the rickety back porch, and, believing themselves to be
true Israelites, they smeared the blood of a goat over their door frame to celebrate
the Passover. They had a view from that porch that could make you weep for
the power of God's hand. Washington and Montana you could see, and the plain
of the Kootenai River Valley, and the shimmering golden white shanks of the
Cabinet Mountains. Government land—but the Weavers' private view.

Vicki had visions with people's faces looming in them. She wrote a booklet
called "Feed Our Sheep," setting out what she believed to be the true Hebrew
names for things and explaining the way that Babylon had misnamed them.
Randy told people never to say God—God was dog spelled backward. They
called God Yahweh. And Jesus was Yahshua. And the sabbath was Thursday
through Friday night. Only the Judas churches had their sabbath on Sunday.

When friends would listen Vicki and Randy told them of the civil war that
was coming. Kevin Harris, a fifteen-year-old from Washington with family trouble, moved in with them, and Randy ran for sheriff of Boundary County to
restore power to the locals. "The Federal income tax is the most cunning act of
fraud that has been perpetrated against Americans since the introduction of
paper money and the credit system," he declared.

And the former executive secretary now typed letters addressed to "the Queen
of Babylon."

At least three times in the late 80's, the Weaver family drove south from their
knob to Richard Butler's campground on Hayden Lake to attend Aryan Nations
congresses. And under the dapply larches and alders and maples their children
played with other children while men wandered about in Nazi regalia talking
politics, and Butler gave out leaflets for "a nigger shoot" and hawked pamphlets
about how the Jews were plotting to enslave the white man. There were always
bikers at the congresses. Randy Weaver met a biker named Gus Magisono, 5-
foot-11, 245 pounds, in a Harley T-shirt and black boots.

The apocalypse came to the Weavers' mountain in the shape of a burly biker.

It was the fall of 1989, and Weaver was having a hard time making it off the grid, cutting wood, doing jobs for farmers. Winter was coming on; Magisono told Weaver he could make money dealing guns. They discussed the mistakes of Order 1 and Order 2, and Magisono said he needed sawed-off shotguns. Weaver said he could get him four or five a week. He had never sold a sawed-off shotgun before in his life, but he pulled his red pickup around next to Magisono's car and got his Remington pump action from a case and pointed at the barrel.

"About here." Magisono touched the barrel at thirteen inches.

A week later Weaver delivered two sawed-off shotguns, one of them the Remington. He said he hoped they went to street gangs. Magisono gave him $300, with $100 more to come.

The Government came forward. Gus Magisono was actually one Kenneth Fadeley, whom the Feds had busted for gunrunning; Fadeley was persuaded to mount a sting on Randy Weaver. The F.B.I. wanted Weaver to do the same thing: go undercover among white supremacists. Weaver refused. So he was charged with gun peddling.

Randy Weaver didn't show up for his trial. In March 1991 he became a fugitive on his mountain. Friends brought the Weavers food and gas. There came a fourth child, Elisheba, and Vicki was convinced that if Randy went down he would be killed, that they should hold the family together on top of the mountain as long as they could, come what may. The three older children carried weapons and learned to shoot them. Sam, the only boy, would shoot off his rifle in the air when strangers approached. Sam who had been home-schooled and could quote history verbatim, from the Roman era on up to the present. All the Presidents, and the Constitution too.

On August 21, 1992, Sam's dog ran barking after something in the woods and Sam and Randy and Kevin Harris went after him, guns drawn. Down through the thick forest, young tamarack and larch, cartridge casings and slash. At a trail crossing the dog came on three Federal marshals with twigs stuck in their bucket helmets and camouflage submachine guns in their hands.

"Freeze, Randy—"

Weaver cursed and ran, then the shooting began. Marshals later testified that Sam had started shooting, but another Government witness contradicted that claim. The dog was shot dead, then Sam was shot in the arm and the back. And Kevin Harris killed Deputy Marshal William Degan.

That night Harris and Weaver found Sam's body. Sam, who was not five feet tall. They carried him to the menstrual shed, took his clothes off, washed him.

Vicki was killed the next day. F.B.I. sharpshooters had gathered in the trees 100 yards from the cabin. Overnight, their orders had been changed. Flying out from Washington, D.C., Richard Rogers, commander of the hostage rescue unit of the F.B.I., had ruled that any armed adult coming out of the Weavers' cabin could be shot dead. The standard rules of engagement allowed lethal force only when the target represented a threat to another person. When Randy Weaver and Kevin Harris came out to see Sam's body, an agent named Lon T. Horiuchi shot Weaver in the upper arm. Weaver and Harris rushed back to the cabin, and Horiuchi aimed again, at Harris. This round pierced a window in the cabin's open door and hit Vicki in the head as she stood holding 10-month-old Elisheba.

Is this how the tribulation begins? A plywood cabin with three terrified girls, their mother lying dead in the kitchen, a bloody body covered with blankets.

The next day a Government robot crawled on to the crude porch. It held a loudspeaker and microphone in one claw and a shotgun in the other. Weaver refused to acknowledge it. Not till a week later did Bo Gritz talk his way in, accompanied by Vicki's friend Jackie Brown. Weaver gave her a letter signed by the family, because he thought the whole family would die. The letter acknowledged that Kevin Harris had killed William Degan, but it said the Feds had fired first.

We had run smack into a ZOG/NEW WORLD ORDER *ambush. . . . Samuel Hanson Weaver and Vicki Jean Weaver are Martyrs for Yah-Yahshua and the White Race.*

Randy surrendered the following day with Gritz at his side. In the spring of 1993 at the Federal courthouse in Boise, the Government tried Weaver and Harris on charges of conspiring to kill William Degan. But for six weeks the Government was more on trial than the defendants. Lon Horiuchi said he had missed his target on both shots. The Government admitted staging photographic evidence of bullets found on Weaver's knob and was fined $10,000 by the judge for misconduct. The defense argued simply that Randall Weaver's beliefs were his own business. The jury remained out for twenty days, then acquitted Harris of everything and Weaver of everything but failing to show up for trial. Even on the gun charge, the jury concluded that the Government had set Weaver up.

Later, Janet Reno ordered an investigation of the Justice Department's conduct with regard to the Weavers, top to bottom. The department has had a report in hand for some time, but has not released it. Last month, news reports based on leaks of the 542-page document say it is highly critical of Federal officials' strategy leading up to the shootings. Specifically, the report charges that the F.B.I.'s change in rules of engagement was imprecise and violated Vicki Weaver's constitutional rights.

Randall Weaver has moved back to Iowa. Last fall he and his three daughters sued the Government for $52 million.

In Idaho survivalists talk about Weaver's daughter Sara, what a good homemaker she was, what a good student. She has graduated from public high school in Grand Junction, Iowa, with honors, which, they say, demonstrates conclusively that home schooling works. Randy Weaver's supporters send Sara money, and Sara sends back a letter written on a word processor.

"May our Creator bless you."

What liberals there are in Idaho also talk about the Weaver children. That was the real abuse in the case, they say: the Weavers oppressed their kids, made them hostage to a feverish and paranoid ideology. Took them to an isolated mountain, made them walk around a cold knob holstered and belted with ammo. The liberals are wary of the powers of the family. To them, home schooling instills sexism—girls do traditional homemaking activities, baking bread, making dolls from corn husks, taking care of the children. Failure to regulate home schooling has made Idaho a haven for kooks and bigots, says one big panhandle paper, *The Lewiston Tribune.* The Government must step in; the Government can protect children from their families.

But what happens when the terrors of a paranoid, racist, anti-Semitic father are outdone by the violent abuses of a Government? What happens when the state shoots and kills a mother before her children? The liberal imagination fails, the liberal simply cannot conceive it.

"The Randy Weaver incident itself was not as important as the fact that people with extremist intentions were using it to make inroads into the community," a woman in the town of Bonner's Ferry, not far from the Canadian border, tells you.

"It was an aberration," Tony Stewart, the liberal activist, tells you. "He had defied a Federal court order. No one knew how the case was going to unfold. It almost had a force of its own."

Stewart gives you a videotape of Bo Gritz's last news conference up at Ruby Ridge, one he held after Randy Weaver's surrender. You play it, and watch Gritz offer a stiff-armed, slant-armed salute to the skinheads at the back. "By the way, he told me to give you guys a salute," Gritz says, referring to Weaver. "He said you knew what that is."

The skinheads heil him back.

"That was not a salute, that was a wave," Gritz is telling you. "I raised my hand like"—he gives a little wave—"it was a wave to them, I said, 'Hey guys,' and I got their attention, 'I really wanted to thank you.'"

Late at night. A room at the Lewis Clark motel. Gritz sits in a chair wearing a leather bomber jacket. His wife, Claudia, is stretched across one of two beds.

Gritz began buying land outside Kamiah early last year. He paid roughly $1,000 an acre for the 600 acres he purchased, and after putting in roads and making other improvements he offered the lots at $3,000 to $3,500 an acre for five-to 10-acre parcels. He told followers he was trying to be Noah in the time of Lot, build an ark before it was needed. He also quoted Second Corinthians 6:15 "Come out from them and be separate and touch not the unclean thing, and I will be your father and you will be my sons and my daughters."

He promoted the venture at weekend-long survivalist workshops he hosted around the country. Called Spikes (Specially Prepared Individuals for Key Events), the workshops teach people to deal with social collapse: how to pick locks, tan hides, give birth at home. Among those who show up is a friend of Gritz's who sells literature saying the Jews intend to enslave everyone else. Pressed about this association, Gritz says he is not anti-Semitic. But he tells you that until a year and a half ago he "really wondered what the truth was" about the Holocaust—whether the Jews died by premeditation or "by accident." Then he read what Hitler himself wrote about Jews in *Mein Kampf* and saw that it was premeditated.

When Gritz's plans for Almost Heaven became known last February, they caused murmured concern in and around Kamiah, even among those living off the grid. "This has been a kind of utopia," Larry Nims says. "I worried that Kamiah will become synonymous with neo-Nazism, and who will that draw?"

Seeking to allay concerns, Gritz scheduled a public meeting last August at the Kamiah High School's multipurpose room. Bill Glenn, the editor of *The Clearwater Progress*, collected questions ahead of time, and at the meeting Gritz answered fifty-one. But the gathering seemed only to solidify divisions in the community. Gritz sprinkled his answers with a soldier's language—"anal orifice," "cesspool," and "flushing your stool" cropped up in discussions of public schools, and this kind of talk bothered people. Others were upset by Gritz's comment that he hoped to work with the local members of the Nez Perce tribe, whose reservation surrounds Kamiah. The Indians, Gritz said, could teach his people how to make rope; his people could teach them how to pick locks.

Two months later, reporters from around the world gathered at Almost Heaven for an impromptu press conference, and Gritz played huckster. He talked about the occasional "light snow" the hilltop gets during the "temperate" winter. (The area gets heavy snows and the road out of Kamiah is sometimes impassable, according to residents.) Gritz asserted that he probably wouldn't make money on Almost Heaven—that his prices were well below local prices, which he said ranged from $4,500 to $10,000 an acre for raw land. This was untrue. Comparable lots of high, timbered land in the area were listed at roughly $3,200 an acre—about what Gritz was charging—and likely to sell for less.

Gritz has his supporters in Kamiah. Bill Glenn, the *Progress* editor, praised Gritz in the paper as a constitutionalist and a patriot. "All I have heard him espouse are a) common sense, b) traditional values, c) fiscal responsibility, and d) limited government," he wrote.

Glenn advised that people take a wait-and-see attitude, and that's what a lot of people seem to be doing. It's the way of the Idaho panhandle. A certain tolerance, a certain trust in those who distrust Government.

And anyway, Bo Gritz had the myth of the Weavers on his side. He had saved Randy from almost certain self-destruction. Gritz described the scene on the mountain during the meeting at the high-school multipurpose room. He told about the girls huddled in the house, and poor Vicki Weaver's body, lying in a "puddle of blood and body fluids."

The hippies who moved to Pokey Creek near Santa, Idaho, some time ago realized that they could never escape the system entirely. They even came to depend on it. A boy's health threatened by serious disease, girls touched inappropriately by a friendly man living in a tepee—their families turned to state clinics for expensive cures, to the state to put the abuser in prison.

Paul Palmer used to think about shooting marauders on his land on Clear Creek, but he has changed, too. He has come to believe in a kind of community. If people flee the cities, he imagines that his barrels of lentils and carrots stored in sand will be enough to feed them. Palmer's on the grid a little now. He got electricity from the Government, the Rural Electrification Administration. "That's socialism, yes," he says. "But you can't be a purist."

Even on the frontier, ideas of community assert themselves. The romance of self-reliance will always summon Americans, but in the end it is still a romance. Even off the grid, people find themselves connected. Randy Weaver did run for sheriff.

Sheryl and Larry Nims used to think the crunch was likely and soon. Then they got to where they felt they could handle almost any scenario, and they stopped worrying about it. Their son Asa is married now. He lives in Boise, he works in computer graphics and they're mighty proud of him.

Chapter Thirty-six

Author's Call to Arms Gets Answer

Robert George

Carolyn Chute had hoped that the first meeting of the militia she is forming to overthrow corporate America would muster the working poor she writes about in her bestselling novels.

The forty-eight-year-old Chute had publicized the inception of the Second Maine Militia as a target practice: "All of you who believe deeply that democracy can work, get your gun and your flag ready," she wrote in a manifesto that appeared last month in the editorial section of the state's largest newspaper.

Her intention was for the recruits to get acquainted, while she launched the first volley against the huge corporations she said have stolen democracy from the masses.

"CORPORATIONS ARE NOT PEOPLE," wrote the author of *The Beans of Egypt, Maine.* "You say the government is evil? Yes, yes, yes, yes. Because the government is not ours anymore."

The cure, Chute said, is to outlaw political contributions from corporations. The means, she said, is a "wicked good militia," willing to march on the state capital, picket campaign headquarters, pass out fliers and maybe even go to jail.

Bad weather on January 27 forced Chute to cancel her meeting. About thirty people showed up at her home on a remote western Maine hillside, anyway.

Few of them were poor, most were city dwellers, and none brought guns. All, however, brought their own ideas about what the militia should be, an eventuality that Chute, who repeatedly told the crowd to stay focused, had feared.

"A lot of the people who have written to me are the most opinionated people on the planet," said Chute, who had waged an editorial page battle with liberal critics objecting to her focus on guns. "They are either far to the left or far to the right, and I'm worried. I don't want them to argue."

Her militia, she said, would differ from some others that drew attention after the Oklahoma City bombing last year. She said she has focused on guns not to advocate an armed struggle, but to attract members from the countryside.

"To the people of my culture, the rural working-class people, who still have one foot in the old . . . culture, a gun, like a plow, like a canning jar, is only a tool," she wrote in response to critics. "It has come to represent one of the last instruments of our culture, and, yes, to many the only remaining emblem of their manhood."

The first supporters to arrive at her half-finished home gathered around a kettle of corn chowder. Chute stood to make a speech. Rocking nervously on the bare plywood floor, she decried the corporate "green paper nipple" that suckles the middle class and keeps it passive.

Then she urged unity of purpose and proclaimed the virtues of the working class to a punk rocker, a retired plumber, a student, an artist, a conscientious objector from the Vietnam War and a young Jewish man from Portland.

"All the ideas for fixing the system are little things, like biting the heel of Godzilla," she said. "We're thinking of bigger things, like castrating Godzilla."

People such as Chute, who is the daughter of a Cape Elizabeth electrician, and her husband, Michael, who grew up on a farm down the road, are part of a working class that has been cut out of the political process, she said.

The couple met at a turkey shoot twenty years ago, long before Chute made her name with her first novel. Michael, who keeps a row of muskets in a corner next to a small cannon, now works as caretaker for a local cemetery. She has gone on to write *Merry Men* and *Letourneau's Used Auto Parts*.

As she spoke at the meeting, he served coffee to the crowd. Then others joined the conversation.

The conscientious objector worried about the Federal Reserve having too much power and U.S. currency having too little real value. The punk rocker said he was an animal-rights activist. The old plumber spoke of the environment. A woman who drove three hours from Boston said she came because the government was too big and someone had to rein it in.

By mid-afternoon, the crowd overflowed into a rough-hewn living room, where pink fiberglass protuded from unfinished walls. They broke into small groups. Many aired earnest, long-winded complaints about the country not working.

"Thinking about the revolution, you can bet this is how it started," said Frank Hayes, a Vietnam veteran who lives in the woods north of Augusta, Maine. "It started with a bunch of people sitting around a hearth like we are."

Plans are already under way for a rally in Augusta. Two weeks ago Chute and fellow militia organizer Peter Kellman went to the state capital to scout sites for future protests—although members will pack placards, not pistols.

"Keep in mind that Europeans were holding meetings in our country for 175 years before we overthrew the king," Kellman said.

At her meeting, Chute circulated a sign-up sheet and membership cards. She asked if anyone would mind getting arrested for distributing fliers at the Maine Mall. She found no takers. But the people promised to come back for her next meeting, which was scheduled to be held yesterday.

Toward the close, Michael Chute dragged the cannon by its chain across the room and onto the porch for a ceremonial firing. He aimed toward the woods. He lit the fuse, there was a quick spout of sparks, and then *boom*. The windows shook, and the group began dispersing.

Chapter Thirty-seven

The Anti-Enviro Connection

David Helvarg

On November 14, 1994, Ellen Gray, an organizer with the Pilchuck Audubon Society in Everett, Washington, had just finished testifying at a County Council hearing in favor of a land-use ordinance to protect local streams and wetlands when a man stood up in front of her with a noose and said, "This is for you."

"We have a militia of 10,000," another man told her, "and if we can't beat you at the ballot box, we'll beat you with a bullet."

Darryl Lord, the man who brought the noose to the meeting, is an elected leader of the Snohomish County Property Rights Alliance. Another P.R.A. leader, Don Kehoe, was a featured speaker—along with John Trochmann and Bob Fletcher from the Militia of Montana—at a recent militia organizing meeting near Everett. Militia materials were also distributed at meetings where Chuck Cushman, a national leader of the anti-environmental Wise Use movement, addressed Washington property rights groups.

Although they don't agree on everything, militant members of Wise Use, property rights advocates, and members of armed militias are increasingly staking out common ground. James Nichols, for example, who's being held as a material witness in the bombing of the Oklahoma City federal building, is a member of the Michigan Property Owners Association, founded by property rights activist Zeno Budd. Budd was a featured speaker at a militia forum held in Detroit in March.

In the West the militias are using the existing Wise Use network as one of their primary recruiting bases, arguing for military resistance to the government and its "preservationist" backers, and forming three-to-six-man Autonomous Leadership Units which look and act suspiciously like terrorist cells. As of late winter 1994 local environmental activists in Washington State, New Mexico, Texas, and Montana reported receiving death threats from militia members.

Within Wise Use, the hotbed for militia organizing is the Counties Movement, which insists that county sheriffs have the right to arrest federal land managers who fail to respect the "customs and culture" of logging, mining, and grazing on public lands. The National Federal Lands Conference (N.F.L.C.) out of Boun-

Reprinted with permission from *The Nation* magazine, May 22, 1995. Copyright © 1995 by *The Nation*.

tiful, Utah, is the coordinating body for the Counties Movement. Its advisory board includes Ron Arnold, the Wise Use movement's founder and "guru," and Mark Pollot, a leading property rights attorney and former official in the Reagan Justice Department. (Pollot wrote the first presidential executive order on "regulatory takings," back in 1988.)

In its November 1994 issue, the N.F.L.C. newsletter had a cover story titled "Martial Law and Emergency Powers." It stated:

> When the federal government decides to enact martial law; and they will; the Director of FEMA becomes a virtual DICTATOR. . . . The American people will be held in bondage and can be killed on the spot with impunity: even if they are in the right. Seem far fetched? Don't be misled, there is a war going on between our heritage of freedom and our subservience.

"We're seeing incredible crossover of people and materials between Wise Use and the militias from Washington to western Montana, eastern Oregon, and northern Idaho," says Eric Ward of the Northwest Coalition Against Malicious Harassment, a Seattle-based human rights organization that was formed in 1986 in Coeur d'Alene, Idaho, to oppose white supremacists.

"They think ecosystem management is part of the New World Order" that will overrun the United States, says Jere Payton, an environmentalist in eastern Washington who recalls her first contact with a militia last year. "We looked out our window and saw a guy walking down the street of our little mountain village wearing camouflage and carrying a gun. This was right after the Militia of Montana came through and had their organizing meeting . . . Someone heard them talking about how they could 'randomly take us out.' There's a lot of loose talk about killing people in our community."

The militia movement, the largest armed expression of the ultraright since the Ku Klux Klan reached the height of its popularity in the 1920s, is united by two key themes—the right to bear arms and a conspiratorial view of government (reinforced by federal actions in the 1993 Waco assault and, earlier, by the F.B.I. killing of white separatist Randy Weaver's wife and son). Still, individual militias tend to reflect the concerns of right-wing activists in the communities where they form. For example, among some in the West the guiding belief is that land-use planning equals socialism.

This has resulted in the targeting of unarmed environmentalists, land-use planners, and federal employees of natural resource agencies. In fact, while nationally the militias have had numerous run-ins with local police, sheriffs, I.R.S. agents and others in the fifteen months since they've gone public, the majority of militia-related incidents have involved people who, one way or another, are associated with the environment.

In Kalispell, Montana, where land-use planning has become the target of anti-environmental Wise Use activists, Jess Quinn, an opponent of a building permit program, told a militia meeting, "When the hour strikes, there will be public officials dead in the streets." In New Mexico, Idaho, and Nevada, Bureau of Land Management and Forest Service agents have received death threats and been in armed standoffs with militia members. More disturbing, local politicians and sheriffs have in a number of instances taken the side of the militias.

In March three U.S. Fish and Wildlife agents investigating the shooting of a wolf in Idaho retreated from rancher Gene Hussey's land after Lemhi County Sheriff Brett Baraslou claimed their search warrant was invalid and drove off with Hussey, threatening to "go to Plan B." One of Hussey's confederates explained that Plan B meant they'd be returning with the local militia. Idaho politicians, including Senator Larry Craig and Representatives Helen Chenoweth and Mike Crapo, later expressed outrage at the *federal agents'* "harassment" of a landowner. The State Attorney General demanded that "armed federal agents" report to his office before serving any warrants.

In southern Nevada last July, Nye County Commissioner Dick Carver— backed up by an armed posse—chased two Forest Service Rangers off a road he was illegally bulldozing through the Toiyabe National Forest. "All it would have taken was for [one of the rangers] to draw a weapon," Carver later bragged, and "fifty people with sidearms would have drilled him." Carver has been a recent keynote speaker at both Wise Use and Christian Identity events. The latter is a racist religious group closely tied to both Aryan Nations and the militias.

Activities like Carver's have created an atmosphere of intimidation and violence designed to silence critics of industries involved in extracting natural resources from public lands. Some seventy counties around the country have now passed Wise Use/Counties Movement ordinances claiming local control over public lands. Last September residents of Catron County, New Mexico, which passed the first of these ordinances in 1990, formed their own militia, encouraged by their county commissioners.

"Citizens are getting tired of being tossed around and pushed to the limit by regulations," says Carl Livingston, one of the commissioners. "We want the Forest Service to know we're prepared, even though violence would be a last resort."

After Tim Tibbits, a federal wildlife biologist, went to Catron County to meet with local ranchers and talk about endangered species protections, a rancher opened his car door and told Tibbits, "If you ever come down to Catron County again, we'll blow your fucking head off."

Mike Gardner is the Forest Service district ranger for Catron. In March his office was painted with hammers and sickles. That same month the Forest Service offices in Carson City, which oversees the Toiyabe National Forest, was pipe-bombed. Seventeen months earlier the B.L.M. offices in nearby Reno were bombed during Senate debate over grazing on public lands.

A native of Oklahoma, Mike Gardner has lived in the small Catron county seat of Reserve with his wife and young kids since 1988. The local militia meets in the house next door to his.

"As far as I'm concerned, they're accomplices to what happened in Oklahoma," he says with a slow, steely drawl, like wind across barbed wire. "That's what the militias are doing, they're advocating violence and insurrection and they got the result you could expect—babies killed."

Part IV

Living with Guns—Seeking Middle Ground in the Battlefield

Introduction: Can We Live with Guns?

The theme that holds this book together is a simple one: dating from their invention some four hundred years ago, firearms have continuously sparked sharply polarized debate. The terms of this debate have changed remarkably little, despite extraordinary changes in the guns themselves as well as in the uses to which they have been put. For some, guns are little short of a blessing; for others, they are a scourge. This said, except at the outermost anti-gun extreme, it is broadly acknowledged that guns are here to stay and, like it or not, large numbers of them will remain in private hands. Indeed, it is private ownership that has been at the heart of the controversy over guns in modern times.

In societies without a tradition of widespread private ownership, the argument is whether any firearms should be privately owned. In the wake of separate incidents in which deranged men armed with semiautomatic weapons slaughtered innocents, both Australia and Great Britain have enacted broad blanket prohibitions on all sorts of firearms. When the New Labour Party, under the leadership of Tony Blair, swept parliamentary elections in Great Britain in 1997, one of the first pieces of legislation introduced was the total ban on all private ownership of handguns. It passed easily. Such sweeping legislation no doubt appeals to many Americans. But for Americans who would prefer a society with few if any guns in private hands, the problem is not simply the formidable opposition to restrictions of any kind that can be marshaled by pro-gun forces. The problem is that there are now so many guns in private hands that even if one could imagine a complete ban on all sales of new guns, it would take a century or longer for there to be any appreciable decline in the firepower in the private hands of Americans.

This fact has a profound effect on the discussion of what to do with guns. If guns are seen as the problem, banning sales of this or that firearm (assault rifles, cheap handguns) is scarcely more than a gesture, at best a weak palliative. If guns are the root of our troubles, any serious reform must go beyond banning sales and include some program of confiscation. The opponents of laws restricting access to guns understand this implicitly. This is why they see otherwise mild restrictions such as the Brady Bill as simply "the first step" on a long road to the ultimate goal of confiscation. And they take great glee when a proponent of gun control admits as much, especially when the admission seems inadvertent. This can be gleaned from the following passage from the February 1977 issue of the NRA publication *American Hunter*:

> HCI (Handgun Control, Inc.) Board Member and hardware chain owner John Hechinger fumed that a "mere" five or 10% decrease in brutal crimes wasn't enough to justify "the danger that exists when everyone carries a gun." . . . And though HCI continuously claims not to want prohibition, their long-time financial backer blurted: "We have to do away with the guns."(14)

The question that begs answering is why we, as a society, remain so thoroughly captive to extreme positions that require an almost complete suspension of common sense. With 200 million or more guns in private hands, doing away with guns is a flat impossibility. For better or worse, guns have thoroughly permeated American society. It is equally unrealistic to think that there should be no restrictions on the types of arms that may legitimately be privately owned. It is similarly wrong-headed to read into every attempt to either introduce constraints on ownership or to resist further constraints a sweeping hidden agenda of promoting gun confiscation or gun worship. The world may in fact be one vast "slippery slope," and this might mean we should all step cautiously, but surely it cannot mean that we take no steps at all. Just as surely, the slippery slope has plenty of grade changes and many plateaus from which we can consider, calmly, both where we have been and where our next steps might take us.

Having said this, we also need to acknowledge more than a little pessimism about the prospects of moving the debate over guns beyond the polarization in which it has been stalled for decades. It is not just that guns exert a powerful grip on the imagination, though this in itself makes policy formation difficult. Many Americans are deeply drawn to moralistic extremes that hold out the prospect of perfectionism and cast everyone who is less than totally committed as the enemy. The world of moral reform is filled with slippery slopes and many temptations to take first steps—the "fatal sip of beer," in the words of the Temperance movement. Violence may be as American as apple pie, but so too is the impulse to purify by prohibition.

Among our founders were men and women as convinced of their own righteousness as they were of the sinfulness of others. Their enthusiasm for reclaiming virtue from the jaws of Satan knew few bounds. Though far from simple people, they often sought simple solutions to complex problems. From the genocidal slaughter of the Pequots in the early 1600s, to the Salem witchcraft trials, to Prohibition and the current Drug-Free America crusade, our history has been punctuated by moralistic binges (Wagner, 1997).

These experiences ought to have given us pause, but they seem not to have. Whether we think of the contemporary stance of "zero tolerance" for drugs (which has made no dent whatsoever in drug traffic or use but has increased our prison population to the point where building prisons has become among the largest public works undertakings of the 1990s) or the campaign to combat teen pregnancies by promoting abstinence, Americans seem determined to go for broke. Ban this, criminalize that. The same is largely true of the ways we have grappled with the problems associated with the private ownership of guns. We have placed almost all our bets on making the possession of some firearms illegal. Very little effort has been given to making education in the safe, responsible use of firearms and certification of competency in the care and handling of firearms a condition for ownership. Only in the past few years have some commentators begun to ask why it is easier to get a permit for a firearm than it is to get a driver's license.

Moralistic binges, precisely because they demonize all who oppose or whose faith wavers, are inevitably polarizing. As in war, truth is among the first casualties. Thus, we have seen that statistics regarding gun violence and gun-related accidents are distorted and manipulated by both sides. Even modest reforms are fought over with a passion far exceeding any reasonable warrant, each side invoking their own version of the slippery slope that invests the utmost importance in the minutest of details. Divisions deepen, suspicions flourish, and communication dissolves into slogans. Under such circumstances, partisans tend to reject all efforts to find a common ground and the majority, including the majority of gun owners who recognize the need for some sorts of restrictions on access and use, finds its voice drowned out in the shouting match.

While we cannot muster optimism, some voices have begun to make themselves heard over the noise of polarized deadlock. Those trying to stake out a position somewhere between the extremes accept the fact that guns are here to stay. Even if some would prefer a society in which there were few if any firearms in private possession, "moderates" acknowledge that it is hard to imagine how sufficient political will could be mobilized for so huge an undertaking as to rid American households of their guns, even in the unlikely event that the Supreme Court would give such a move its constitutional blessing. The plain fact is that Americans in large numbers, verging on a majority, own firearms and many of them would actively or passively resist any attempt to seize them. As a result, cherished principles of civil liberties would be sorely stretched, underlining precisely the point that many gun owners insist upon: the state cannot be trusted to protect individual liberties.

We can escape this unpleasant prospect if we agree that guns, by themselves, are not the problem. Indeed, as several of the writers we include here note, there are a number of societies in which guns are even more widely dispersed than they are in the United States—Switzerland, Cuba, and Israel, for example—and in those societies rates of gun violence and crimes involving guns are quite low. Indeed, they compare favorably to societies in which private ownership of guns is heavily restricted. Our neighbor to the north, Canada, has stricter laws governing gun ownership and proportionately fewer guns in private hands than the United States, but these differences are not nearly large enough to account for their much lower rate of gun violence. For reasons yet to be completely understood, Americans and guns make a combustible combination. Just as some people cannot drink without coming to grief, so it seems Americans cannot use guns as responsibly as the Swiss or the Canadians. It may be, as some argue, that our violent past has made violence seem virtuous. In this vein, the sociologist Jack Katz (1988) has argued that a large proportion of murders are committed in the thrall of what he calls "virtuous rage": the perpetrator thinks he or she is righting some real or imagined wrong. It may also be that the combination of individualism, heavy emphasis on consumption, and the persistently high degrees of inequality that have long characterized American society has made us more fractious, more frustrated, more near the boiling point than people in other societies. Whatever the reasons, it would pay for everyone concerned about gun violence to seriously explore ways of making gun owners more responsible and a good deal less impulsive.

There are moves in this direction, though it is too early to tell if they will have an appreciable impact on gun accidents or violence. In 1996, it became possible for Texans to get a permit to carry a concealed weapon. In addition to demonstrating knowledge of the care and safe handling of a handgun and passing a background check, applicants are also required to attend a session in which participants learn basic techniques of nonviolent dispute settlement as well as how to recognize when someone (including oneself) is about to lose control (*New York Times*, November 11, 1995, A1). Though we confess some amusement contemplating a Texan intent on wearing a six-shooter on his hip having first to master the language of reconciliation and learn how to seek win-win solutions ("Remember the Alamo" indeed!) before reaching for his revolver, this approach may make far more sense than the much ballyhooed campaigns to get people to turn in their guns in exchange for twenty-five dollars or a teddy bear. Clearly we have not devoted much energy or imagination to making gun owners more careful and more thoughtful.

Some have begun to seek ways of compelling gun manufacturers to shoulder more responsibility for how their product is ultimately used. In much the same way that reformers finally were able to force auto manufacturers to equip new cars with seatbelts, air bags, and other safety features aimed at reducing deaths and injuries, there are mounting pressures on gun makers to equip their firearms with features such as trigger locks that reduce the likelihood of both accidental discharge and impulsive firing of a gun. Like the auto companies before them, manufacturers are complaining that these measures will drive up costs, hurt sales, and otherwise lead to economic ruin. Indeed, for some who propose these sorts of measures, the goal may be precisely to end the production of guns intended for private use. But that goal need not be the outcome of mandating enhanced safety features on the nation's firearms.

Safer firearms; stricter licensing standards for prospective gun owners aimed at improving the safe use, not at limiting access; greatly intensified campaigns to make firearms owners aware of the ways to improve the safe handling and storage of their guns (including harsher penalties for those found to be negligent), and programs like those being pioneered in Texas to make gun owners more adept at managing emotions and dealing nonviolently with interpersonal conflicts are all reforms that, in the aggregate, would almost certainly reduce firearms accidents. Less clear is what impact they would have on the frequency with which Americans resort to lethal force in situations where tempers flare (e.g., family arguments, jealousies, arguments between neighbors, traffic disputes), but there is no reason to believe that such policies would be completely ineffectual. Such measures are not likely to reduce violent crimes such as robbery, rape, or premeditated murder. To reduce the incidence of these sorts of crimes, we will have to look far beyond guns. In order to even begin that sort of scrutiny, though, we will need to think more clearly than we have about guns. We might start by refusing to be drawn in to the debate on the currently prevailing terms. America will never be gun-free. But our cherished liberties do not require that access to guns hinge on nothing more than money and a willing seller. Somewhere in the middle, sensible and responsible people can meet and work together to make ours a safer society. We will, in the bargain, all become freer.

Chapter Thirty-eight

America's Only Realistic Option: Promoting Responsible Gun Ownership

David B. Kopel

The prevalence of the American gun does not condemn the nation to a high violent crime rate. America's high crime level has much more to do with the absence of internal social controls than with the absence of statutory gun controls. An appropriate gun policy for America, therefore, is to encourage social control and civic virtue in gun ownership. Instead of a futile attempt to erase gun culture, there must be a conscientious effort to mold gun culture for the better.

Shaping a positive gun culture does not mean America can imitate Switzerland. Americans are harder to motivate with patriotic cries for the fatherland, especially when danger seems far away. Contrast the attitudes of the two nations' gun lobbies: Switzerland's Pro-Tell insists on mandatory citizen soldier duty and mandatory home ownership of firearms. The American NRA touts the notion of "choice" that roots a right (but not a duty) to bear arms in the American tradition of individualism.

In earlier times, America explicitly linked firearms ownership and civic responsibility. The framers of the Second Amendment envisioned a polity in which gun ownership—like voting, jury duty, and paying taxes—was one of the basic components of responsible citizenship.

The decay of the link to civic responsibility was inevitable. A society as dedicated to individualism as America could never achieve or maintain the disciplined militia culture of Switzerland. Neither Britain nor pre-Revolutionary America kept up the militia well when times were safe. While American citizen militias sometimes held their own against foreign armies, no foreign empire would have squandered its money by hiring the American militia into imperial service. Although the well-disciplined Swiss Guards were always in demand, renting the American militias would have been impossible and a waste of money anyway. And whatever the value of an armed citizenry two hundred years ago, the militia seems to have little relevance to the problems of today. Two of the purposes for gun ownership envisioned by the framers—protection against foreign invasion and overthrow of domestic tyranny—may one day be important, but appear remote now. As Supreme Court Justice Story predicted a century and a half ago, the abolition of militia training has meant that some people have no familiarity with arms. "There is certainly no small danger, that indifference may lead to disgust, and disgust to contempt; and thus gradually undermine all the protection intended by this clause of our national bill of rights."[1]

Historian Joe B. Frantz advances the case for the irrelevance of the gun culture to modern problems. He acknowledges that the frontier experience promoted important American values: individualism, mobility (both physical and social), and nationalism. These frontier virtues, including the attachment to firearms, Frantz continues, are no longer appropriate, for "direct action does not befit a nation whose problems are corporate, community, and complex."[2] Frantz is partly right. Unlike in former times, when American foreign policy consisted mostly of taking and holding as much frontier as possible, armed citizens cannot play a role in modern foreign policy. Likewise, direct action does not address acid rain control or space exploration.

Direct action can, however, make a significant contribution to the crime problem—by deterring and stopping criminals. One of the original purposes of gun ownership—defense of self and the community against crime—is as necessary as ever. On the American frontier, the law was not something in a statute book owned by the government. Law was mostly the coercive power of ordinary citizens carrying firearms and making criminal activity difficult. Today, there is a good body of scholarship to suggest that citizen gun ownership does deter crime. In polls conducted by both anti- and pro-gun firms, large numbers of Americans say they or someone in their households have actually used (i.e., fired or brandished) a gun for self-defense. The number of defensive handgun uses annually that can be derived from such totals, using conservative assumptions, is 645,000 defensive handgun uses every year.[3]

Michael Beard of the Coalition to Stop Gun Violence argues that reports of handgun-related self-defense may not be accurate. A person might hear a car backfire, jump out of bed, grab his gun, discover no danger, and report that he used a gun for self-defense. Perhaps there are many flawed reports. Still, the polling of civilians on the handgun issue is consistent with the polling of criminals. In the Wright and Rossi survey of felony offenders, three-fifths of the prisoners said that a criminal would not attack a potential victim who was known to be armed. Two-fifths of them had personally decided not to commit a crime because they thought the victim might have a gun. Criminals in states with higher civilian gun-ownership rates worried the most about armed victims.[4]

Guns in civilian hands pose a risk to criminals at least as large as the risk they face from the government. Criminologist Gary Kleck writes: "Gun use by private citizens against violent criminals and burglars is common and about as frequent as arrest, is a more prompt negative consequence of crime than legal punishment, and is more severe, at its most serious, than legal punishment. . . . Serious predatory criminals say they perceive a risk from victim gun use which is roughly comparable to that of criminal justice system actions."[5] As noted above, the National Institute of Justice study found an American burglar's chance of being sent to jail is about the same as his chance of being shot by a victim.[6]

If an armed citizenry would make even a small difference, then an armed citizenry might be a "frontier" response well suited to modern life. The rough sections of most American big cities, where the police have given up trying, are more dangerous than the nineteenth-century frontier. Law-abiding frontier folk who did not brawl in saloons had no reason to fear homicide or any other violent crime. Armed, they were secure.

The American vigilante tradition has changed, but never died, because the conditions that necessitated it have continued. Legal protection against violent crime is scarce in many American cities. In the real world of the inner cities, it is the armed citizen, not the 911 caller, who can protect the victim of a crack addict brought to a psychotic rage by desperation for money for a hit.

Attempting to erase the "frontier virtue" of gun ownership, urban policy makers may be tearing at the fabric of social cohesion. By devolving citizens of community responsibility in the use of guns, gun control and overemphasis on the police have reduced citizens' sense of responsibility for community well-being. After the Sullivan Law was passed in 1911, New Yorkers became more apathetic toward crime.[7]

Conversely, firearms owners are more inclined to assist crime victims—just as George Washington or Thomas Jefferson might have predicted. Of the "good Samaritans" who come to the aid of victims of violent crime, 81 percent are gun owners. Those gun owners are "familiar with violence, feel competent to handle it, and don't believe they will get hurt if they get involved."[8]

There is some reason, then, to consider the possibility that encouraging gun ownership might be a partial solution to the crime problem. Citizen anti-crime efforts might be especially successful if the government encouraged citizens to possess arms and offered them safety training, and the media publicized the citizens' armament.[9]

There is also an extended range of lesser possibilities for using an armed citizenry to reduce crime. A police leader might simply state that citizens are encouraged to buy arms for self-defense, doing so through proper channels, and also encouraged to undergo safety training. The statement, if publicized, might itself deter some crime.

Unarmed neighborhood watch patrols are more and more common. Armed patrols have arisen in dangerous circumstances. As noted, government encouragement can help ensure that all kinds of patrols are racially integrated, and thus help to unite diverse communities rather than dividing them.

Along with armed citizens, and (usually unarmed) citizen patrols, the police have their own role in restoring order to the cities. In recent years there has been a trend back to community-based policing. Some police forces have even experimented with police mini-stations similar to the Japanese *kzōban*.[10] Community policing may prove itself to be a cost-effective idea. But more fundamentally, community control of crime must come from within the community. Fine-tuning of external anti-crime measures from government employees is useful, but will not decide the issue.

Would an armed citizenry produce blood in the streets? Carnage was predicted in Florida after the legislature enacted a law mandating that citizens be granted "carry" licenses after a background check. In fact, the permit-holders have proven themselves highly law-abiding, as might be expected of any group of citizens who voluntarily submitted to government screening.[11] Oregon enacted a similar law in 1989. As a result, 2,200 carry permits were issued in Portland in the first seven months of 1990, compared with only 17 the previous year. Homicide fell 33 percent, the second-largest drop of any major city. [12]

A citizenry that is armed to deter and resist crime is a controversial idea that involves trusting ordinary people to possess and use deadly weapons. To favor other, less controversial, elements of a responsible gun-ownership policy, it is not necessary that one share Adam Smith's or Thomas Jefferson's favorable view of guns or people. It is simply necessary to recognize that guns cannot be eradicated from American culture; hence, a policy that promotes responsible gun use is more likely to prevent gun misuse than is a futile effort at prohibition (or semi-prohibition through bureaucratic controls).

The prospects for promoting responsible gun use are bright. America has a three-century-old tradition of gun use—in large part responsible gun use—on which to draw. Only in a few large cities has visible, responsible gun ownership by ordinary citizens been driven underground.

It is these quasi-prohibitionist cities—where the only persons seen with a gun are criminals, policemen, or television characters—that have the most to gain from responsible firearms ownership.[13]

New York City's government, after nearly a century of trying to eradicate gun culture, has succeeded instead in creating a gun culture where teenagers have no models of responsible gun users such as target match competitors. Since almost all of the one-half million to two million New Yorkers who own guns for self-defense must do so illegally and surreptitiously, they can hardly act as role models of responsible use. In a world where the only public role models are supplied by drug dealers, children learn from what they see. Far from being eradicated from New York City's culture, guns are now a must-have status symbol for many street teenagers. New York City would be better off if it had laws like modern Dodge City, Kansas, where guns may be readily purchased and used for sports and self-protection—where, perhaps partly as a result, young people are exposed to models of responsible gun ownership.

A more subtle benefit of promoting responsible gun ownership would be that the anti-gun segment of society (a more educated, urban, and pacifist group) might at least come to better understand people who own guns. A diminution in the intensity of the symbolic crusade against "demon" guns and their "sick" owners will leave the American polity more united and better able to concentrate on all social problems.[14]

Whatever the legal controls on the acquisition and handling of guns, as long as America does not choose a total prohibition, it seems that encouraging people who do own guns to handle them safely and skillfully should be agreeable to both sides of the gun debate. If guns are part of American culture, and will be for many more generations, the government should encourage responsible use.

Marksmanship

The simplest component of a "civic virtue" gun policy is marksmanship programs. People who practice shooting with their friends at target ranges are the most likely to be influenced by social models of responsible gun use. City dwellers, who may buy a gun for self-protection and never learn how to fire it safely, could particularly benefit from such a program.[15]

To require school districts to offer marksmanship programs would be an intrusion on local prerogative. On the other hand, there seems to be no downside to letting the decision about school programs remain under local control. State laws taking away such local authority should be lifted. In Illinois, the laws make it difficult or impossible even for colleges to offer target shooting as an option for student athletes.[16] Laws such as Illinois's should be reformed.

Marksmanship has a number of benefits in the context of character development in a city or school. The mental discipline leads some students to report improved ability to concentrate. Target shooting is nonsexist. Females play on the same teams as males, and regularly defeat them. The only facility needed can fit into a twenty-by-fifty-foot room. Students who have been the worst players on the junior high football team can take up marksmanship for the first time in high school and win awards. And while high school or college football players do not learn an activity that they can enjoy for the rest of their lives, target shooting, like golf, is a lifetime sport; a number of national champions have been nearly seventy years old.

Target shooting has a lower injury rate than any other sport, and fights between competitors are nonexistent. In baseball, spiked soles and beanballs are used to threaten, and sometimes inflict, serious bodily harm. Hockey, boxing, and football all involve the deliberate imposition of physical suffering on the opponent.

Thomas Jefferson advised his nephew: "Games played with a bat and ball are too violent, and stamp no character on the mind. . . . [A]s to the species of exercise, I advise the gun."[17] Were Jefferson to visit a high school shooting competition, and then a high school football game where students cheered as a player was slammed to the ground, Jefferson might think his earlier view confirmed.

The surest argument against permitting schools to offer marksmanship classes is that doing so legitimizes gun ownership. So it does. Yet even America's gun-control lobbies insist that they have no quarrel with sporting use of long guns. If there is no campaign against sporting use, and some sporting uses would reduce the injury rate in school sports, why not allow schools the choice?

Other regulations that serve solely to harass adult target shooters have no place in a rational gun-control policy. The less target shooting, the less trained and more dangerous that gun owner will be. Zoning regulations which outlaw indoor target ranges within a particular distance of a school or a church are irrational. They simply make the statement that guns are bad and should not exist near good institutions.

Likewise, there is no social benefit from laws like the one in New York City, where, according to government interpretation of the gun laws, a licensed target shooter cannot even bring a guest to a shooting range to fire a single bullet; the prospective guest must obtain his own expensive gun permit and purchase his own gun. Such a law is not a rational policy of gun control. It is bureaucratic gun prohibition, done simply to make a statement that the government heartily disapproves of anyone but the government having guns.

While airguns can be safely fired inside an apartment, New York City makes it illegal for youths to even hold an airgun in their hands, even under direct parental supervision. Thus, the city closes off one more opportunity for the children to be taught controlled, responsible gun safety.

Another simple step to encourage responsible gun use is to better allocate funds the government already spends on civilian gun use. The Pittman-Robertson Act of 1937, initiated by sportsmen, levies a federal excise tax on firearms, ammunition, and archery gear. States receive the revenue as matching funds. Hunting and associated activities get the lion's share. Putting more funds into public shooting ranges, and less into hunting, would make responsible gun training available and convenient for large numbers of urban gun owners.

Police and military target ranges, now closed to the general public, should be available to all citizens as a public resource. The typical pretext for excluding the public—fear of liability in case of an accident (despite the very low accident rate in target shooting)—could be dealt with by making government-owned ranges immune from suit.

Lastly, ranges of all types need protection from suits claiming that the noise or traffic associated with the range is a nuisance. Such suits should not be allowed if the plaintiff "came to the nuisance" by knowingly moving near an already established target range.

In short, there are numerous ways for government to promote (or at least stop impeding) target shooting and marksmanship programs. None of the suggestions requires new taxes; all of the suggestions would foster responsible gun practices and attitudes.

Safety Training

Target ranges are the best place to practice responsible gun use. Learning the theory of responsible gun use can take place in the classroom, which can be the back room of the gun store or the front room of a school. The United States already has a great deal of voluntary safety education. The National Rifle Association has trained seventeen million Americans in mature firearms handling and use. Many Californians have taken private classes entitling them to carry defensive tear gas.[18]

After mandating that all residents keep operable guns at home, Kennesaw, Georgia, offered a voluntary firearms safety program; a high percentage of the town's citizens took the course, and since the law went into effect, the town has had no firearms accidents or homicides.[19] Nancy Pywell of the University of Florida argues that schools are a good forum for gun-safety education. She also believes that the opportunity to shoot guns is a leadership experience.[20]

Elsewhere I have discussed the fierce reaction of American gun controllers against the NRA's American gun-safety comic book for children, even though the comic did not endorse gun use and simply told children that if they found a gun, they should not touch it, but instead tell an adult. Such a reaction, based on a prohibitionist mentality, is inconsistent with what even the anti-gun lobby claims are its values, and is certainly inconsistent with the rest of America's values. It is disappointing to see anti-gun citizens throw themselves into legislative battles to defeat laws to allow junior and senior high schools to offer voluntary classes in the safe use of firearms.[21]

While a citizenry armed against crime is a controversial idea for some people, the simple promotion of gun safety and responsible use, through education and marksmanship training, can be objectionable only to the gun prohibitionist.

Objections to a Civic Virtue Policy

There are a number of objections to a "civic virtue" firearms policy. The objection that guns are too dangerous for the citizenry, and must belong only to the state, works in Japan, but not in America. America has guns, and they are not going to vanish. As long as guns exist, America should encourage responsible use instead of trying to wish them out of existence. While some people would prefer a gunless society, the more realistic goal is a society that is safely armed.

A more serious problem with the government getting into the business of "responsible" or "safe" gun ownership is the possibility that the slogans can be hijacked by anti-gun administrators. The Canadian government, for example, instituted its nationwide gun-licensing program while claiming to "encourage the responsible use of guns."[22] In practice, the new law did nothing to promote responsible gun use or to reduce crime, and simply turned into a bureaucratic tool sometimes used for harassment. In the United States, groups such as Handgun Control, Inc., tout mandatory safety exams with the same enthusiasm that Jim Crow election officials touted literacy tests. A literacy requirement for voters made sense in the abstract, but racist Southern election officials turned it into a tool to prevent blacks from voting. Likewise, safety training run by police administrators who receive personal financial donations from Handgun Control, Inc., would likely be perverted into bureaucratic prohibition.[23] The Japanese police already abuse their authority to require safety training by making the training as inconvenient as possible.

Firearms owners are justifiably skeptical about any proposal propounded by the extremist groups whose members have never foregone any opportunity to eliminate as much of the American gun culture as can be destroyed at any given moment. As a result, proposals that might seem innocuous in the abstract (such as registration, licensing, or waiting periods) are fiercely resisted because the lobbies behind them usually intend them as a first step toward drastically reducing the numbers of guns in American life.[24] In the political context created by the anti-gun lobbies, mandatory government firearms training is correctly rejected by those who want to keep gun control off the slippery slope that most of the British Commonwealth is descending.

Even for a friend of responsible gun ownership, it is not clear whether a larger government role would be desirable. The New Zealand Mountain Safety Council gladly takes government checks. Yet the council's chairman cautions against making his volunteers into government workers.[25]

Yet some kind of promotion of responsible gun ownership is especially important because of the undeniable presence of irresponsible elements in the gun culture. Some of the most American traits are the most awful. The custom of shooting off guns at midnight on New Year's Eve is several centuries old,[26] and utterly indefensible in an urban society. The American image of the frontier West is the image of "Buffalo Bill" Cody. In real life, Cody slaughtered tens of thousands of bison with high-powered rifles. His "Wild West" stage show became the image of the West that America accepted as its true past. That image was grossly distorted, and so over-emphasized frontier violence that it might have been a parody. But instead of being a parody, Buffalo Bill's Wild West became the American archetype.[27]

Important parts of America's memory of its violent past are violent fiction: the always brave and virtuous militiaman who could defeat any professional army; the bloodthirsty and uncontrolled vigilante mobs; the feuding and savage Hatfields and McCoys; the Wild West. The misconnection with historical experience is indicative of a culture that in some ways is immature and irresponsible in its approach to guns and violence.

The tendency of America's affair with the gun to turn to the imaginary and the lurid is a continuing obstacle in fashioning responsible gun policy. Memory of a shoot-em-up West that never was may encourage improper and unnecessary use of deadly force in self-defense. The mistaken memory of the West may also lead policy analysts to the incorrect conclusion that more guns correlated with more violent crime, when just the opposite was true.

Yet for all the immaturity and irresponsibility in America's past, there are other examples of responsible gun use. Jim Bridger, the frontiersman who was the first white man to see the Great Salt Lake, also witnessed the wanton shooting of the bison. He was disgusted.[28] To the limited extent that government can influence popular culture, government can encourage Jim Bridger and discourage Bill Cody.

Voluntary private training has little against it, and will yield at least some benefits in safety and responsibility. In the prohibitionist strongholds, such as Washington, D.C., safety training can be a step toward a rational gun policy. Instead of prohibiting handguns, the cities should make purchases legal upon completion of safety training. Even gun carry permits should be allowed for citizens who pass both a safety test and a marksmanship test. In cities with the most extreme gun controls and worst gun crime, government support for (or at least not active hostility toward) responsible gun ownership would undo some of the damage of prohibition, which has prevented the development of a publicly visible culture of responsible gun use.

Conclusion

The details of a responsible gun policy can be decided by each state and city for itself. The examination of guns and gun culture in America and abroad seems to indicate that some type of civic virtue policy is desirable. There is little evidence that foreign gun statutes, with at best a mixed record in their own countries, would succeed in the United States. Contrary to the claims of the American gun-control movement, gun control does not deserve credit for the low crime rates in Britain, Japan, or other nations. Despite strict and sometimes draconian gun controls in other nations, guns remain readily available on the criminal black market. Gun control has not reduced crime; in fact, it has encouraged burglary. Gun registration has proven itself valueless in solving or preventing crime. Gun control has in some instances reduced gun suicide, only to see other equally deadly methods of suicide substituted.

The experiences of all the countries described in this book, including the United States, point to social control as far more important than gun control. Gun control works superbly in Japan and fairly well in most of the English-speaking British Commonwealth not because gun control directly reduces gun misuse, but because gun control validates other authoritarian features of the society. Exaltation of the police and submission to authority are values, which, when internally adopted by the citizenry, keep people out of the trouble with the law. The most important effect of gun control in Japan and the Commonwealth is that it reinforces the message that citizens must be obedient to the government. To the extent that citizens internalize that message (and everywhere except Australia and Jamaica they do), crime of all types (including gun-related crimes) is reduced.

Foreign-style gun control is doomed to failure in America. Foreign gun control comes along with searches and seizures, and with many other restrictions on civil liberties that are too intrusive for America. Gun control had done little to mature the body politic of other English-speaking nations; in the British Commonwealth and in the United States gun control is often hysterical, and often directed at already persecuted classes and races.

Foreign gun control—whether England's severe legal controls or Switzerland's strict social controls—postulates an authoritarian philosophy of government and society fundamentally at odds with the individualist and egalitarian American ethos. In the United States, the people give the law to government, not, as in almost every other country, the other way around. Even if some Americans want their nation to be more like other countries, America cannot be more like them. There are too many guns in America, and too much of an individualist gun culture in the American psyche, for imported gun control to stand a chance. Instead of transplanting foreign gun control and culture to America, a realistic American gun policy must accept the permanence of guns in American life. The encouragement of mature, responsible gun use is the policy best suited to the United States.

NOTES

1. Joseph Story, *Commentaries on the Constitution* (abridged) § 709. Story had exalted the right to bear arms as "the palladium of the liberties of a republic; since it offers a strong moral check against the usurpation and arbitary power of rulers; and will generally, if these are successful in the first instance, enable the people to resist and triumph over them." Ibid.

2. Joe B. Frantz, "The Frontier Tradition," in *Violence in America: Historical and Comparative Perspectives* (New York: Praeger, 1969), pp. 152–53.

3. Gary Kleck, "Crime Control through the Private Use of Armed Force," *Social Problems* 35 (1988): 1–21.

Kleck analyzed data collected by pollster Peter Hart for the no longer active National Alliance Against Crime. Six percent of the Hart respondents had replied "yes" to the question "Within the past five years, have you yourself or another member of your household used a handgun, even if it was not fired, for self-protection or for the protection of property at home, work, or elsewhere, excluding military service or police work?" Taking into account the number of U.S. households, and assuming that each "yes" response only related to one defensive handgun use, Kleck calculated at least 645,000 defensive handgun uses per year.

4. James D. Wright and Peter H. Rossi, *Armed and Considered Dangerous: A Survey of Felons and Their Firearms.* New York: Aldine de Gruyter. Paul Blackman, "The Armed Criminal," *American Rifleman*, August 1985, p. 35 (using the cross-tabulations from the unpublished Wright-Rossi data).

5. Kleck, "Crime Control," pp. 16–17.

6. James D. Wright, Peter Rossi, and Kathleen Daly, *Under the Gun: Weapons, Crime, and Violence in America* (Hawthorne, N.Y.: Aldine, 1983), pp. 139–40.

Anecdotal real-world experiences seem consistent with NIJ findings. In 1966 the police in Orlando, Florida, responded to a rape epidemic by embarking on a highly publicized program to train 2,500 women in firearm use. In the next year rape fell by 88 percent in Orlando (the only major city to experience a decrease that year); burglary fell by 25 percent. Not one of the 2,500 women actually ended up firing her weapon; the deterrent effect of the publicity sufficed. Five years later Orlando's rape rate was still 13 percent below the preprogram level, whereas the surrounding standard metropolitan area had suffered a 308 percent increase. Gary Kleck, "Policy Lessons from Recent Gun Control Research," *Journal of Law and Contemporary Problems* 49 (Winter 1986): 35–47; Alan S. Krug,

"The Relationship between Firearms Ownership and Crime Rates: A Statistical Analysis," *Congressional Record*, January 30, 1968, pp. H570–2.

The pattern has been repeated elsewhere, although the type of citizen arming was not on so broad and constant a scale as Orlando. During a 1974 police strike in Albuquerque armed citizens patrolled their neighborhoods and shop owners publicly armed themselves; felonies dropped significantly. Carol Ruth Silver and Donald B. Kates, Jr., "Self-Defense, Handgun Ownership, and the Independence of Women in a Violent, Sexist Society," in Donald B. Kates, Jr., ed., *Restricting Handguns: The Liberal Skeptics Speak Out* (Croton-on-Hudson, N.Y.: North River Press, 1979), p. 152.

In March 1982 Kennesaw, Georgia, enacted a law requiring householders to keep a gun at home; house burglaries fell from 65 per year to 26, and to 11 the following year. "Town to Celebrate Mandatory Arms," *New York Times*, April 11, 1987, p. 6.

Similar publicized training programs for gun-toting merchants sharply reduced robberies in stores in Highland Park, Michigan, and in New Orleans; a grocers organization's gun clinics produced the same result in Detroit. Gary Kleck and David Bordua, "The Factual Foundation for Certain Key Assumptions of Gun Control," *Law and Police Quarterly* 5 (1983): 271–98.

It should be noted, however, that when the Orlando and Kennesaw crime rates were studied in the context of long-term patterns, researchers did not find a statistically significant correlation between the change in gun policy and the crime declines. David McDowall, Alan Lizotte, and Brian Wiersman, "Deterrence Effects of Civilian Gun Ownership: An Assessment of the Quasi-Experimental Evidence," *Criminology* 29, no. 4 (November 1991): 541–59.

7. Edward F. Chandler, Member Kings County Grand Jury, letter to the Editor, "Urges Arms Law Repeal," *New York Times*, August 25, 1923, p. 6, col. 7 (if Sullivan law repealed and New Yorkers rearmed, "there would be no such thing as a daylight payroll holdup with a crowd looking on").

8. Ted L. Huston, Gilbert Geis, and Richard Wright, "The Angry Samaritans," *Psychology Today* (June 1976), p. 64.

Adam Smith found "a man incapable of defending or of revenging himself evidently wants one of the most essential parts of the character of a man." Even if a society had no fear of external invasion, Smith favored widespread training in the use of weapons "to prevent that sort of mental mutilation, deformity and wretchedness, which cowardice necessarily involves in it, from spreading themselves throughout the great body of the people." Adam Smith, *The Wealth of Nations* (New York: Random House, 1937; 1st pub. 1776), Book V, chapter I, part III, article II, p. 739.

9. The best summary of the relevant research is Donald B. Kates, Jr., "The Value of Civilian Handgun Possession as a Deterrent to Crime or a Defense against Crime," *American Journal of Criminal Law* 18, no. 2 (1991): 113–67.

10. Norval Morris, *Judicature* 72 (August–September 1988), p. 113; John F. Personos, "The Return of Officer Friendly," *Governing*, August 1989: 56–61.

11. Gary Kleck, *Point Blank*, (New York: Aldine, 1991), pp. 411–14.

12. "Portland Concealed Weapons Permits Credited with Reducing Homicide Rates," *Women & Guns*, September 1990, p. 7. Despite the headline of the cited article, it is not necessarily clear that the increase in carry permits caused the reduced homicide rate; the point is simply that more carry permits did not lead to more murders.

13. Franklin Fisher and Don Gentile, "List of Young Victims Grows," *Daily News*, September 26, 1990, p. 11.

14. One legal theorist suggests that one of the major benefits of the First Amendment's protection of almost all types of speech, no matter how repulsive, is that society is strengthened by the exercise of tolerance. Lee C. Bollinger, *The Tolerant Society* (New York: Oxford University Press, 1986).

15. Roy Innis, National Chairman of the Congress on Racial Equality, writes: "Another irony of oppressive gun control laws is that as decent citizens are forced to arm themselves illegally, they are less likely to practice and gain proficiency with the weapon." Roy Innis, "Bearing Arms for Self-Defense—A Human and Civil Right," speech, May 15, 1990, transcript, p. 3.

16. Ill. Ann. Stat, Chapter 38, § 87–2 (Smith-Hurd, 1977) (prohibition on possessing handguns without a license, with no exception for school sports).

17. John Foley, *The Jefferson Cyclopedia* (New York: Russell & Russell, 1967), p. 318.

18. "Violence in Big Cities—Behind the Surge," *U.S. News & World Report*, February 23, 1981, pp. 63, 65. Successful use of tear gas requires a difficult pinpoint shot into an oncoming attacker's eyes.

19. Patrick Carr and George W. Gardner, *Gun People* (Garden City, N.Y.: Doubleday, 1985), p. 112, quoting Kennesaw Mayor Darvis Purdy.

20. "Orlando Sessions Educate," *American Rifleman*, July 1988, p. 57.

21. California Senate Bill no. 1130, March 7, 1985; Gale Cook, "Senator Wants Schools to Teach Gun Use, Hunting," *San Francisco Examiner*, June 9, 1985, p. B4.

22. Solicitor General of Canada, *Gun Control in Canada: Working Together to Save Lives* (1978), p. 1.

23. Mandatory safety courses in Detroit and East Lansing, Michigan, charged $60, a rather high amount for the exercise of a fundamental right. The Detroit courses were only given twice a year, thereby imposing a waiting period of up to six months on gun purchasers. In 1990, the Michigan legislature preempted the field of firearms control, and abolished local ordinances like those in Detroit.

24. After the House of Representatives passed a bill for a national handgun waiting period, Representative William Clay (D-Missouri) stated: "The Brady Bill is the minimum step. . . . We need much stricter gun control and, eventually, we should bar the ownership of handguns, except in a few cases."

For more on waiting periods, see David B. Kopel, *Why Gun Waiting Periods Threaten Public Safety*, Independence Institute Issue Paper No. 4–91 (Golden, Colo.: Independence Institute, 1991), reprinted in *Congressional Record*, June 28, 1991: S9046–61 (Waiting periods and associated background checks so rarely prevent crime that the use of police resources for background checks diverts police from tasks more likely to enhance public safety. In states with waiting periods, police frequently abuse short waiting periods to turn them into lengthy waiting periods or near prohibition).

25. Bob Badland, "Firearm Safety Education in New Zealand," in *Proceedings of the International Shooting Sports Symposium* (Wellington: New Zealand Mountain Safety Council, 1981) (symposium held October 25, 1980).

26. Edward Countryman, *A People in Revolution: The American Revolution and Political Society in New York, 1760–1790* (New York: W. W. Norton, 1989), p. 178.

27. Joseph G. Rosa and Robin May, *Buffalo Bill and His Wild West* (Lawrence: University Press of Kansas, 1989).

28. Lee Kennett and James L. Anderson, *The Gun in America: The Origins of a National Dilemma* (New York: Westport Press, 1975), p. 119.

Chapter Thirty-nine

What Are the Alternatives?

Wilbur Edel

Any realistic evaluation of the gun issue must take into account several indisputable facts. First, according to a December 1993 report by the federal Bureau of Alcohol, Tobacco and Firearms, there are at least 211 million guns, including 71 million handguns, in private hands in this country. Second, thanks to the frequent use of lethal weapons in the commission of crimes, retail sales of guns purchased for personal protection are on the rise. Third, reverence for the Constitution, plus the unceasing propaganda of gun organizations, sustain the mistaken but widespread belief that the Second Amendment guarantees every individual the right to keep and bear arms. Notwithstanding this general impression, every public opinion poll taken over the past fifty years shows approximately 75 percent of the people in favor of some form of gun control. Finally, the cult of violence that pervades every aspect of American life, from daily news features to the entertainment industry to the conduct of foreign affairs, poses the greatest threat to law and order since the Civil War.[1]

The very existence of 211 million guns in a nation of 250 million people demonstrates that gun control—in the sense of a regulatory system that will provide a record of the production, distribution, sale and resale of every firearm, plus a reliable procedure for screening out would-be purchasers who are not legally entitled to own firearms—can no longer be achieved solely by the kind of legislation proposed by gun-control advocates. Those who are seriously concerned about this problem must begin to think of long-term solutions that take into consideration the country's total experience with firearms.

This is not to say that a ban on Saturday night specials and private ownership of assault weapons would not be useful. But this would be only a first step. Other important reforms are necessary. One is the development of a nationwide information network of the kind suggested by progun Representative Harley O. Staggers of West Virginia. His suggestion was to set up a "toll-free hotline that firearms dealers could contact to learn if the handgun purchaser is prohibited by federal law from possessing a handgun."[2] Offered as a substitute for the Brady bill, this measure was intended to affect handgun purchases only. However, the same system could be applied to the purchase of any firearm or any particular type of weapon.

Staggers's plan was rejected in a test vote, but it was later included in the House-Senate Conference Committee's compromise bill, which proposed putting the Brady waiting period into effect until "the national instant criminal background check system is established."[3] This took into acount the Office of Technology Assessment's estimate that it would take "five to ten years" to develop such a system.[4]

Thanks to President Bush's condemnation of the limits placed on his habeas corpus and exclusionary rule reforms, which in turn incited a progun filibuster of the compromise in the Senate, this comprehensive crime-control legislation died in 1992. Insofar as the gun-control section is concerned, a subsequent bill along the lines of the Brady-Staggers compromise was ultimately adopted and signed into law by President Clinton. When, at Clinton's urging, Congress approved the further restriction on the continued production and sale of a variety of assault weapons, it was over the strong opposition of progun organizations, whose objectives were twofold. One argument was that, at least for semiautomatic weapons, there is little to distinguish a hunting rifle from a military piece. The other was that this type of legislation is merely one step on the road to outlawing all private ownership of guns.

On the first point, they were technically correct. An ordinary repeating rifle might fire the same kind of ammunition, at the same muzzle velocity, with the same deadly effect, as a semiautomatic weapon designed for military use. But the repeater could not be mounted with a magazine holding fifty or more cartridges, and it could not be converted to fully automatic fire. Progunners insist this conversion is not easily done with semiautomatics. However, as indicated earlier, do-it-yourself manuals for converting military style semiautomatics to automatic fire are available to anyone who wishes to buy them. And as more than one hunter has pointed out, such weapons have no place in a hunter's arsenal.[5]

Further removed from reality is the repeated NRA charge that the ultimate aim of gun control advocates "is to get rid of every firearm in the hands of every law-abiding citizen in this nation."[6] Whether it is an expression of a sincere belief or merely a scare tactic to incite readers of this message to line up in opposition to any kind of control is immaterial. The fact is that only those on the outer fringe of the control faction go to this extreme. The great majority of the general public, including organizations like Handgun Control and the National Coalition to Ban Handguns, take no such position, recognizing the legitimacy of the demand for the kinds of weapons ordinarily used for hunting and target shooting. When NCBH went to court to challenge the government's policy of making surplus M-1 army rifles available to NRA members only, it was in effect demanding that sales of these guns (at cost) be open to any qualified person, whether affiliated with NRA or not.[7] Moreover, public opinion polls that show an overwhelming majority of people favoring more gun control also reveal that this desire is based on the rising crime rate and the fear for personal safety; it reflects no antipathy toward hunting and target shooting.[8]

The most far-reaching proposal would not dispossess any individual of any legitimate hunting or target-shooting weapon. It would, however, require every newly manufactured firearm to be identified by manufacturer's serial number and to be registered in the name of the dealer and/or purchaser of the weapon. This approach is no different from the one that has become traditional in dealing with automotive vehicles, with all fifty states requiring not only the registration of each vehicle but the licensing of every driver. The most ardent advocate of Second Amendment rights has yet to protest this intrusion into the private life of automobile owners. Nor is there any evidence that progunners believe dangerous drugs should be freely available without a doctor's prescription certifying to the user's need for such medication.

Legislation requiring the licensing of every gun owner and the registration of every weapon manufactured here or imported from abroad would not affect owners of the 211 million guns presently in private hands. Nor should the law be made retroactive, as the task of registering so enormous and widely distributed a quantity of weapons would be an impossible one, and the effort to do so would create so much ill will that the prospect of more effective federal control would be destroyed. Rather, the objective should be to create a mechanism that, over the long haul, would bring order out of the chaos of conflicting state laws and heretofore ineffective federal regulation.

The alternative is to muddle along with patchwork remedies that will neither reduce the number of gun-related deaths—homicidal, accidental or suicidal—nor impede the flow of firearms throughout the nation from states with few controls. And if the estimated annual increase of four million privately purchased guns continues, by the end of this decade there will be almost as many guns as people in these United States.

Another aspect of the problem is identification of persons ineligible to purchase or possess firearms. Bush's Attorney General Dick Thornburgh took a step in the direction suggested by Staggers. He did this in responding to an instruction contained in the Anti–Drug Abuse Act of 1988, which required the attorney general to report to Congress on "a system for the immediate and accurate identification of felons who attempt to purchase firearms" and "to conduct a study to determine if an effective method exists for the immediate and accurate identification of other persons who attempt to purchase firearms but are ineligible to do so because they fall into other categories created by the Gun Control Act of 1968."[9]

Some progress has been made in designing a system of criminal identification. A survey of the criminal history records of all fifty states and the District of Columbia was completed in 1991. This study revealed that 60 percent of the criminal history records maintained by state agencies are automated. As automation is adopted by other states, the Justice Department will come closer to achieving its proposed goal of establishing a system in which gun dealers can inquire by telephone or computer terminal as to the eligibility of a purchaser and receive an immediate response. The weakness of the proposed system is that it would be based upon adoption by the states of "voluntary reporting standards" recommended by the FBI. Further, it is concerned only with the identification and registration of criminals, not guns, which points up the parallel need for gun registration.

The more complex problem of identifying persons other than felons who are ineligible to purchase firearms was turned over to a private organization for study. The 1990 report of that company, the ENFORTH Corporation, found so many difficulties in establishing legally who are "unlawful users of controlled substances," or "mentally defective," or "illegal aliens," that little progress can be expected in this area.[10]

Any further discussion of the role of the Second Amendment would seem needless, except for one seemingly contradictory aspect of the general public's view of the gun problem. Notwithstanding the consistency with which the desire for stronger controls has been expressed over more than fifty years of opinion polling, the effectiveness of the gun lobby's endless repetition of the Second Amendment theme has convinced a substantial majority of people to respond affirmatively to the question, "Would you happen to know, is the right to own a gun guaranteed by the Constitution or not?" Asked this question in May 1991, 77 percent said Yes and only 9 percent said No, the remaining 14 percent either being uncertain or having no opinion.[11]

This impression was fostered not only by gun clubs but by members of national and state legislatures, most of whom, as lawyers, should know better. Indeed, it is reasonable to assume that many—especially those in Congress—do know better, being fully familiar with the series of Supreme Court decisions that refute the assertion that the Second Amendment guarantees every individual the right to keep and bear arms. Three of the five senators who signed a minority statement that helped defeat the Anti-drug, Assault Weapons Limitation Act of 1989 were lawyers with a thorough understanding of the constitutional issues. One of the three—South Carolina's Strom Thurmond—had been admitted to practice in every federal court, including the Supreme Court of the United States. Yet Thurmond joined Charles E. Grassley of Iowa, Gordon J. Humphrey of New Hampshire and lawyers Orrin Hatch of Utah and Alan K. Simpson of Wyoming in asserting that the proposed act "represents another attempt to infringe on the constitutional right to keep and bear arms."[12]

The same misstatement of fact has been heard on many occasions in the House of Representatives. Just as often, the issue is confused by a representative comparing the gun situation with some other that has no relevance whatever. In debating the choice between the Brady bill and the Staggers substitute, Robert S. Walker of Pennsylvania suggested that telling a handgun purchaser he must wait seven days before taking possession of the weapon would be like telling a newspaper editor, "If you are going to spread pornography in our society, you have to apply 7 days in advance and tell us what it is you are going to do, and then we will decide whether or not you are a criminal."[13] Later in the discussion, Representative Staggers demonstrated how easy it is to misconstrue the philosophy behind the movement for gun control. Attacking the Brady bill, he said, "A 7-day waiting period is a simplistic answer," adding, "In the same logic, if we would wait, say, 7 days to purchase cocaine, we could solve the drug problem."[14] In both cases the purpose of controlling legislation is to ensure that the purchaser is entitled to obtain and use a dangerous product. Staggers gave no indication, here or elsewhere, that he supported the view that the drug problem would be resolved by eliminating all controls over the production, sale and use of cocaine, morphine, crack and so forth. Yet this is "the same logic" that underlies his—and the gun lobby's—demand that all gun-control laws be eliminated.

Walker's assertion that the Second Amendment provides the same kind of protection for gun owners as the First Amendment does for people claiming freedom of speech is another argument frequently heard in Congress. During the debate over the choice between the Brady and Staggers bills, Representative Jolene Unsoeld of Washington spoke of "basic rights such as free speech, or free exercise of religion, a woman's right of choice or the right to keep and bear arms," as though all were equally unqualified.[15] In fact, two centuries of experience, confirmed by Supreme Court decisions, has established limits even for the freedoms guaranteed by the First Amendment. Freedom of speech, for example, does not extend to the individual who creates panic by falsely shouting "Fire" in a crowded theater. The free exercise of religion does not permit forcing worshippers to handle poisonous snakes.

These limitations are not specified in the First Amendment, but other sections of the Bill of Rights have built-in limitations. The Third Amendment's ban on quartering soldiers in private homes does not apply if in time of war laws are passed to permit such an invasion of privacy. Similarly, "the right of the people to be secure in their persons, houses, papers and effects" is conditioned by the Fourth Amendment's further provision that this applied only to "unreasonable" searches and seizures, and that a search warrant may be issued "upon probable cause, supported by Oath or affirmation, and particularly describing the place to be searched, and the persons or things to be seized." In this connection, it is interesting to note that the most vehement defenders of the right to keep and bear arms are frequently supporters of proposals—like those of President George Bush—that would weaken the Fourth Amendment by giving police greater latitude in conducting searches with or without warrants, just so long as those tactics are not used against gun owners or dealers.[16]

Just as other amendments specify the limits of their application, the Second Amendment establishes an important limit on the right to keep and bear arms by asserting that its purpose is to provide for "a well regulated Militia." The militia that was so essential to national defense during the early days of the Republic has been replaced by an enormous professional standing army of the sort that would not have been tolerated by the authors of the Second Amendment. Organizations like the National Rifle Association, the Second Amendment Foundation, and the Citizens' Committee for the Right to Keep and Bear Arms insist that the militia still exists in the National Guard and, more broadly, in an armed citizenry. But that view is no longer heard in Congress, even from members who argue against the imposition of federal gun controls. Even the NRA assumption that gun clubs help prepare people for military service carries little weight in an era in which the changing technology of war has made instruction in rifle and pistol shooting far less significant than the highly technical training required of pilots, navigators, submariners and operators of complex defense and weapons systems.

Popular acceptance of the notion that the Second Amendment guarantees everyone the right to keep and bear arms is less a barrier to legislative reform than the pervasive violence that infects American society. In a foreword to the FBI's *Uniform Crime Reports* for 1990, Director William S. Sessions wrote: "As we proceed into the 21st century, the foremost challenge of the law enforcement community is its continued success in the warfare against the escalating violent crime occurrences in the United States."[17] Disregarding the implied boast that law enforcement agencies have been winning the war against crimes of violence, the reader is struck by the acknowledgment that such activity was still on the increase near the close of an administration presumably dedicated to instilling a kinder, gentler spirit in the American way of life.

Equally alarming is the fact that most of the remaining introductory paragraphs are devoted to the growing need to devote more attention to "hate-related offenses . . . crimes motivated by prejudice against a victim's race, religion, ethnic origin or sexual orientation." The bureau's decision to begin classifying crimes under this heading was necessitated by passage of the Hate Crime Statistics Act of 1990, which Sessions says resulted from concern in Congress "that the degree of prejudice-motivated crimes in America during the 1980s had increased dramatically."[18]

No expertise in crime control is needed to demonstrate the extent to which violence has become a major force in American life. The average citizen sees the evidence in the featured story in almost every television newscast, in nearly every daily newspaper, and in the steady diet of films featuring Rambo-type heroes whose major talent is killing. And because the evidence is pressed upon the public day in and day out, it invades the minds of children as well as adults, telling them, in effect, that their world is one in which violence commands more attention, even more respect, than nonviolence, and the gun toter reigns supreme.

California provides a showcase for the way in which violence has come to dominate everyday life. In the aftermath of President Kennedy's assassination, California adopted a fifteen-day waiting period for the purchase of any concealable handgun. Following the Stockton massacre, it approved the Roberti-Roos Assault Weapons Act of 1989.[19] But in between these actions a more strict handgun control measure was defeated by a vote in which 63 percent disapproved when the proposal was put on the ballot as an initiative in the election of 1982.[20] And through this entire period the state was (and continues to be) the home of one of the country's major manufacturers of Saturday night specials.[21]

A 1992 sequence of events brought home both the accuracy of the FBI director's assessment of rising violence and the fallacy of his assertion that the war against violence is being won. In quick succession: Los Angeles police reacted to a minor misdemeanor with a savage attack on the culprit, this act by white police officers against a black suspect was given the stamp of approval by a jury selected in a white suburb far from the inner city where the arrest took place, outraged blacks went on a rampage in which lives were lost and stores looted and destroyed, and immediately the sale of guns for self-protection skyrocketed to the highest rate known to record-keeping authorities.[22]

Even as the FBI director's 1990 report was going to press, efforts were being made in New York to ban private possession of all assault weapons. Six experts were asked by the *New York Times* to suggest measures for bringing street violence under control. Four of the six simply repeated in a variety of ways the recommendations that gun laws be made more strict and/or that penalties be made more severe. One suggested that, because of the strong tie between the illegal drug trade and the many killings that trade produced, it might be desirable to consider decriminalizing the use of drugs. Only one expressed the view that "gun control alone won't help," recommending more widespread use of an experimental program that appears to reduce teenage battles by having students mediate the disputes that arise among their schoolmates.[23]

Only this last suggestion comes close to the heart of the problem, which is to wean the country away from the gun culture that has evolved to a point at which even children are led to believe that a gun brings recognition, status and fulfillment. This cannot be accomplished by legislation, although the previously recommended measures for curtailing further proliferation of privately owned weapons would put the public on notice as to the seriousness of the government's intentions.

In this connection, it is important that the laws governing the sale of guns include a provision mandating a course of training and testing for each purchaser. Here we can learn from other countries. New Zealand, for example, makes certain that every purchaser is thoroughly familiar with both the gun-control laws and the proper handling of his or her weapon, providing a detailed manual for that purpose and administering a written examination before permitting the purchase to be completed.

Change cannot be effected merely by adopting the practices of a culture different from our own, but surely we can learn from the experience of others, particularly from a country like New Zealand, whose language is the same as ours and whose pioneer background is in many ways similar to our own.

Evidence that the notion of a training requirement has gained acceptance in the United States is seen in the January 1994 monthly report of a Gallup Poll in which 89 percent of those questioned—and 82 percent of gun owners—agreed that to qualify for gun ownership gun buyers should be required to take safety classes.

Another aspect of the problem is the concept of personal responsibility and accountability on the part of gun owners. The importance of this principle has begun to penetrate the legislative mind, as in Florida. In June 1989 that state's legislature met in special session to deal with the increasing incidence of accidental shootings by children using guns that had not been properly protected by their owners. The lawmakers' reaction to this dangerous trend was made clear by their approval of a bill that states its findings in these terms:

The Legislature finds that a tragically large number of Florida children have been accidentally killed or seriously injured by negligently stored firearms; that placing firearms within the reach or easy access of children is irresponsible, encourages such accidents, and should be prohibited; and that legislative action is necessary to protect the safety of our children.

Disavowing any intent to deny adult citizens "their constitutional right to keep and bear firearms for hunting and sporting activities and for defense of self, family, home and business and as collectibles," the lawmakers made it a misdemeanor to leave a loaded firearm within easy access of a minor and a felony if the minor injures or kills someone with that weapon.[24]

The first of three cases tried under this revolutionary statute involved a fourteen-year-old boy who found his father's pistol on a closet shelf and, while showing it to a friend, accidentally shot him in the head. Although the wounded boy did not die, he lost the sight of one eye. Because of conflicting testimony as to who had loaded the gun, a jury found the father guilty of a misdemeanor rather than a felony. That decision was later upheld by a judge, who sentenced the father to six months' probation.[25]

Light as this sentence was, successful prosecution of the case set an important precedent that did not go unnoticed in other states. By mid-1993, what came to be known as "child accident prevention" laws had been passed by California, Connecticut, Illinois, Maryland, New Jersey, Wisconsin and the cities of Baltimore, Cleveland and Houston. In California, a father lost his four-year-old son when the boy killed himself with a pistol the father had left in his bedroom, still loaded, after using it to celebrate the new year. Criminally liable under the new California law, the distraught father willingly accepted a misdemeanor sentence that included an obligation to make radio and television appeals to other parents to avoid careless handling of firearms.[26]

Florida set another precedent when in the November 1990 election 84 percent of the voters approved an amendment to the state constitution that requires a three-day waiting period and a criminal background check prior to the purchase of a handgun. While state and local police expressed doubts about the deterrent effect on criminals, the fact that for the first time a state had written the waiting-period principle into its constitution indicates the degree of concern felt by the general public over the rising rate of deaths by firearms.[27]

Implementing the constitutional mandate, Florida established a requirement that gun dealers telephone for an instant computer search of criminal records at the National Crime Information Center and Florida Crime Information Center while a gun customer is in the store. According to state officials, these checks take an average of a little more than three minutes and, in the first six months of the program, revealed criminal records that resulted in rejection of 2,908 of the 108,042 requests to purchase a firearm.[28]

In some parts of the country the gun-toting tradition is so deeply rooted that acceptance of the Florida approach will be difficult to achieve. When thirteen- and fourteen-year-old gang members attended a meeting held by the mayor of Phoenix, Arizona, "with guns strapped to their hips," city officials were aghast.

They were even more perturbed to learn that the youngsters' actions were entirely legal. City authorities reacted by passing an ordinance that would bar minors from carrying guns without their parents' permission.[29] Whether or not this restriction will survive the legal challenge threatened by the NRA is, as of this writing, uncertain. The only restriction in Arizona state law affecting minors is one that prohibits the sale or gift of a firearm to a minor "without written consent of the minor's parent or legal guardian." The law says nothing that would suggest a minor does not have the same right as an adult, who in that state needs no license to carry a gun openly. Moreover, Arizona has a preemption clause that states: "A political subdivision of this state shall not require the licensing or registration of firearms or prohibit the ownership, purchase, sale or transfer of firearms."[30]

It is this kind of permissiveness in the treatment of firearms that disturbs—even frightens—many people who view the trend toward increasing violence as a serious threat to the internal security of the nation. That concern was expressed by the leaders of the medical profession in a special issue of the *Journal of the American Medical Association*. In nineteen separate articles, the journal painted a picture of violence in America that a concluding editorial characterized as "a public health emergency."[31]

Not infrequently, control advocates point to the experience of countries with strict gun laws and far lower crime rates, particularly in the homicide category, and suggest that the United States would do well to adopt their practices. But this is more easily said than done. The most powerful influence mitigating against acceptance of, for example, the British system is tradition. From the earliest period of colonization on this continent, guns were essential to the survival of the settlers. Without guns they would have been incapable of defending themselves against attacks by colonial forces of other countries and by Native Americans, who quite correctly saw these newcomers as trespassers on their lands. Without guns, and lacking the Indians' hunting skills with bow and arrow, many settlers would have starved for lack of food, particularly during the long months required to raise food crops. These two problems of defense and food supply persisted as settlers moved farther and farther west.

It is true that the early pioneers in Canada, Australia and New Zealand faced conditions that were similar in many respects to those in the United States, although in the South Pacific the British faced much less competition from the European empires that strenuously resisted their claims in North America. Other differences were equally important, particularly in Australia, which Britain used as a penal colony from the first settlement of convicts in 1788 until the last group was landed in New South Wales in 1840.

With a current population of only 17 million people and a land area almost as large as the continental United States, the vast spaces of Australia—much of it desert or rocky, arid terrain—continue to attract people of adventurous spirit. Settling initially along the eastern shore, the westward-moving pioneers have had the same need for weapons as the Americans who left the safety of the original thirteen colonies to seek opportunities farther west.

As in Australia, New Zealand settlers depended upon their weapons for both protection and food. Unlike Australia, New Zealand was never used as a penal colony. Moreover, its occupation by emigrants from the British Isles was for many years discouraged by the government. Fierce resistance by the native Maoris added to the hazards of colonization and made guns a necessity for protection as well as for hunting food.

A mountainous area the size of Colorado, New Zealand presented a challenging terrain to its colonists. Possession and use of guns came as naturally to New Zealanders as to American pioneers. Yet the island nation developed without the "wild West" tradition that in many parts of nineteenth-century America produced an atmosphere in which gun law and lynch law were not uncommon. As described earlier, twentieth-century New Zealand has developed a uniquely efficient system of control for private ownership of weapons that is probably superior to that of any other democratic nation.

Canada's development more closely parallels that of the United States. Like the United States, its early years were filled with struggles of two varieties, to establish permanent colonies in a new and hostile land, and to survive the repeated wars between England and France for domination of the area. Under these circumstances, it is understandable that guns in the hands of the settlers were as common as in the United States.

As indicated earlier, modern Canada has taken the problem of gun control far more seriously than the United States.[32] As anti-control advocates in the U.S. Congress and the White House were doing their best to water down or eliminate the modest restrictions enacted in 1968, the Canadian Parliament and Justice Department commissioned a private corporation to study the impact of its first major change in the firearms section of its criminal code. When that study showed that murders, accidents and suicides with firearms all declined after passage of the 1977 legislation, it seemed clear that statutory controls were having a beneficial effect.

Public support for this approach was widespread. A nationwide poll conducted by the *Toronto Star* indicated that 70 percent of all Canadians believed the law should be made even more restrictive. On the strength of this public support, Parliament in 1991 further strengthened its controls, among other things extending the classification of "prohibited weapon" from automatics to semi-automatics by adding to the prohibition of an automatic weapon the clause, "whether or not it has been altered to fire only one projectile with one such pressure [on the trigger]."[33]

What we learn from other countries is not the art of drafting control legislation; it is recognition of the different results that stem from an open market in gun traffic as compared with a system of controls that in no way interferes with the activities of hunters, target shooters and gun collectors, but draws a clear line between legitimate and illegitimate weaponry and between responsible and irresponsible weapon owners. Every opinion poll taken over the last half century demonstrates that the American public is aware of the need to make these distinctions. But the combination of gutlessness among many of our legislators and the fraudulent representation of the Second Amendment as a guarantee of the right ot keep and bear arms—by legislators and gun lobbyists alike—has frustrated the public will. It is tempting to propose removing this excuse by repeal of the Second Amendment as an outdated anachronism. But that would lend credence to the argument that gun-control advocates are out to destroy the Bill of Rights.

The situation is further complicated by the rising friction between ethnic and religious groups. Like a global epidemic, we read almost daily about the slaughter of Kurds by Iraqis, of Bosnians by Serbs, of Armenians by Azerbaijanis and Azerbaijanis by Armenians, of Muslims by Hindus and Hindus by Muslims, of Burundi's Hutu civilians by Tutsi soldiers. And much as we hate to admit it, the infection has made its appearance in the United States as well, though on a smaller scale.

Like AIDS, hate is a disease that is difficult to control and even more difficult to cure. It cannot be legislated out of existence. In a society that is truly free, it cannot be made illegal. It could be attacked through an educational program aimed at all ages in all segments of society. But the American educational system is not geared to such an effort. Moreover, at the high school and college levels education is commonly seen as having the more practical objective of preparing young people to meet the immediate challenges of everyday life—like earning a living and learning how to improve one's economic and social position in a highly competitive society.

One of the greatest impediments to freedom in the learning process is the attitude of leaders like the Great Communicator. As governor of California, Ronald Reagan denounced federal aid to education as "the foot in the door to federal control." On the other hand, he proposed that college faculty should be required "to be proponents of those ethical and moral standards demanded by the great majority of our society"—meaning those he preached but did little to carry out.[34]

To the extent to which ethnic, religious and racial prejudices influence choices made in providing jobs, housing, education and the luxuries of life, a listless economy and the growing disparity between rich and poor tend to foster the very prejudices that for much of this country's history kept minority ethnics and nonwhite races in inferior positions. White ethnic and religious groups such as Irish and Italian immigrants, Jews and Mormons eventually won the battle against discrimination. But the same cannot be said of nonwhites. After a period of progress beginning with the Supreme Court's 1954 decision in *Brown v. Board of Education*, the old antagonisms began to rise again. Thanks in part to twelve years of resistance to civil rights legislation by the Reagan and Bush administrations, and their efforts in support of both business and religious institutions attempting to evade the laws against discrimination, racial and religious hostilities have become more virulent. Administration toleration of business and market practices in which greed outweighed ethical considerations also encouraged a get-what-you-can-any-way-you-can attitude in all levels of society.

In the competition for recognition, political power and economic advancement, violent clashes between whites and nonwhites, between Jews and blacks and between Jews and Christians[35] occur with increasing frequency. Even among black, Hispanic and Asian groups, a 1994 survey by Louis Harris found that these minorities "resent one another almost as much as they do whites." And the murder of two Japanese students visiting Los Angeles, while not ascribed to racial animosity, reinforced opinion in Japan that the United States is a "gun society."[36]

When added to the open warfare between law enforcement agencies and both organized and unorganized crime, these ethnic animosities often extend the practice of gunplay to communities, large and small, in every part of the country. This spurs even further the demand for guns, even by normally nonviolent people, who fear for their own and their families' safety. The pity of it is that after twelve years of federal government emphasis on law and order, there is more crime, more violence, more fear than ever before. Even passage of the Brady bill had the unfortunate side effect of inducing people who never contemplated owning a gun to scurry to the nearest gunshop to secure a weapon before tighter controls could be applied.[37]

No significant change in the character of a society can occur without a change in attitude. But except where the pressures are so great as to produce a nationwide revolt, social change is a long, slow process. It took this country two centuries to arrive at a democratic society in which men and women of all races and creeds are acknowledged to be entitled to the same rights and privileges under the law. Nevertheless, the widespread poverty, competition for jobs and the divisive forces of racial, religious and ethnic animosity that encourage violence presage a bleak future—at least in the short term.

One hopeful sign is a shift in opinion regarding gun control where it counts most—in the state and local legislatures of the country. As indicated earlier, the movement to contain the proliferation of gun sales began at the grassroots level, with town and city fathers responding to the growing threat by heeding the longstanding public preference and passing laws to control the sale of firearms. State legislatures have been more reluctant to adopt such laws, but by 1993 a trend away from the laissez faire posture of the past has become noticeable. The New Jersey legislature, which in 1990 banned the private purchase of military assault-type weapons, was pressured by the NRA into reversing that action at the next session. However, despite an all-out effort by the NRA in support of repeal, the Senate failed to override Governor Florio's veto of the repeal bill. Senators who had formerly adhered strictly to the NRA point of view were swayed by repeated incidents in which innocent children, civilians and police officers had been killed by gunfire. California also banned the sale of assault weapons to the general public, followed by Connecticut, where pressure from both the NRA and Colt Manufacturing Company, a major arms producer, failed to deter state lawmakers from approving a law banning the sale of a variety of semiautomatic assault weapons, including the Colt Sporter.[38]

Significant actions were taken in other states as well. Hawaii was the first state to use a generic definition of assault weapons, although its ban applies only to assault pistols and pistol "ammunition magazines holding more than ten rounds." Both Louisiana and Missouri rejected proposals that would have permitted their citizens to carry concealed weapons. And Virginia, a major source of weapons ending up in New York, responded to pleas from New York officials by passing a law that curtails the previously unlimited purchase of guns "by the trunkful," restricting Virginia residents' purchases of guns to one a month. Even in Pennsylvania, where military-style rifles can be purchased on a walk-in basis by anyone holding an easily obtained gun permit, a Republican representative submitted a bill that would require a forty-eight-hour waiting period and background check prior to the purchase of this type of weapon. Two months later, in June 1993, Philadelphia banned further sale of military-style assault guns.[39]

Finally, a willingness to support control legislation appeared at the federal level when President Clinton told a joint session of Congress, "If you will pass the Brady bill, I'll sign it."[40] Subsequently, two government agencies that normally refrain from offering opinions on either side of a policy question came out publicly in support of a waiting period for handgun purchases. Stephen Higgins, director of the federal Bureau of Alcohol, Tobacco and Firearms (BATF), cited the Waco, Texas, shoot-out as the reason for this departure from standard practice, saying, "We've never had four agents killed on a single day before." Later that year, FBI Director William S. Sessions reversed the stand he had been obliged to take under Presidents Reagan and Bush and publicly acknowledged having sent Attorney General Janet Reno a set of proposals that included a five-day waiting period for the purchase of a handgun.[41]

Violence has become so much a part of everyday life in these United States that, as with drug use, the admonition to "just say no" will not be sufficient to produce any substantial change. Nor will gun-control legislation by itself accomplish this. The remedy—part conceptual, part economic—depends on the kind of public and private leadership that will devote whatever time and money it takes to convince both the adult and juvenile population of the need for reversing the perception, fostered by an endless stream of Rambo-type movies and war stories that focus almost exclusively on the heroics rather than the horror of mass killing, that "a nation's values and its greatness spring from the barrel of a gun."[42]

An equally compelling need is to heal the racial, religious and ethnic tensions that threaten to disrupt other efforts at recovery from the low state of morale, health and economic well-being felt by so large a segment of the population.

The task is not solely one of education, although this is crucial to success, nor is it only to reestablish a nationwide sense of harmony, but the task is to broaden opportunities for the 40 percent of American children living at the poverty level and to bring this nation back to a competitive position with other industrialized countries, most notably Germany and Japan. This also means placing as high a priority on health, education and job opportunities for all adults as on military needs and budget reduction.

Presidential candidate Franklin D. Roosevelt reminded voters in 1932 that the multitudes represented by "the forgotten man at the bottom of the economic pyramid" must be the foundation on which a nation builds its economy and its strength. Part of that building process turns on the availability of adequate educational opportunities for the forgotten man's children. Those opportunities have been made more difficult to attain by the violence that has penetrated even into the classroom. The Gun Violence Prevention Act of 1994 (S. 1882) cited this as one of the conditions that call for tighter controls, declaring: "the occurrence of gun violence in schools has resulted in a decline in the quality of education in our country and this, in turn, has an adverse impact on interstate commerce and the foreign commerce of the United States."[43]

Three-quarters of a century ago, H. G. Wells wrote, "Human history becomes more and more a race between education and catastrophe."[44] That was never more true than it is today.

NOTES

1. "200 Million Guns," 7-part series, *New York Times*, 8 March–4 April 1992; "Firepower," *Wall Street Journal*, 28 February 1992; "Los Angeles Riots Spurring Big Rise in Sales of Guns," *New York Times*, 14 May, 9 February 1992; Warren E. Berger, "The Right to Bear Arms," *Parade*, 14 January 1990, p. 4; Robert C. Byrd, "Crime Control, Not Gun Control," *Congressional Record*, 14 June 1990, S7963–64; Wayne LaPierre, "The 101st Congress Has Ended and Victory Is Ours!" *American Rifleman*, December 1990, p. 46; *The Gallup Poll*, as cited in annual volumes published since 1935; "The News at Six: TV's Grim 1994 Vision," *New York Times*, 14 June 1992; *Miami Herald*, 1 January 1994.

2. *Congressional Record* (daily), 8 May 1991, H2822, 2855–56.

3. "Violent Crime Control and Law Enforcement Act of 1991," *Conference Report 102–405* (on H. R. 3371), p. 23.

4. Cited by Representative Mel Levine of California in *Congressional Record* (daily), 8 May 1991, H2876.

5. *Field and Stream*, September 1989, pp. 16–17.

6. Joe Foss, "The President's Column," *American Rifleman*, July 1990, p. 52.

7. *Handgun Control News*, March/April 1979, p. 1. In *Gavett v. Alexander* (477 F. Supp. 1035, 1049, 1051), a federal court upheld the NCBH challenge, declaring invalid that section of the law "which requires membership in the National Rifle Association as a precondition to the purchase of Army surplus rifles" on the grounds that it "unconstitutionally deprives plaintiffs of the equal protection of the laws in violation of the Fourteenth Amendment to the Constitution."

8. *Gallup Poll*, 1990, pp. 122–26; 1991, pp. 82–84, 116–18, 135.

9. U.S. Department of Justice, *Attorney General's Program for Improving the Nation's Criminal History Records and Identifying Felons Who Attempt to Purchase Firearms* (March 1991), p. 1.

10. U.S. Department of Justice, *Identifying Persons, Other than Felons, Ineligible to Purchase Firearms: A Feasibility Study* (May 1990), p. iii.

11. *Gallup Poll*, 1991 vol., p. 118.

12. Senate Report 101–160 on S. 747, 3 October 1989, p. 16.

13. *Congressional Record* (daily), 8 May 1991, p. H819.

14. Ibid., p. H2856.

15. Ibid., 8 May 1991, p. H 2823.

16. See President Bush's proposed "good faith" exception to the rule that evidence obtained in violation of the Fourth Amendment may not be used in court, and the House Conference Report on that subject in the Violent Crime Control and Law Enforcement Act of 1991. Public Papers of the President, 15 May 1991, vol. 1, pp. 563–64; House Conference Report 102–405, 27 November 1991, p. 22.

17. U.S. Department of Justice, Federal Bureau of Investigation, *Uniform Crime Reports for the United States, 1990*, p. iii.

18. Ibid.

19. Treasury Department, BATF, *State Laws and Published Ordinances — Firearms*, 20th ed., 1994, p. 18.

20. *Washington Post*, 9 November 1982.

21. *Wall Street Journal*, 28 February 1992.

22. These events were reported by every branch of the media in gruesome detail all through the months of April and May 1992.

23. Franklin E. Zimring, "Guns, Guns Everywhere—Strategies for Arms Control," *New York Times*, 4 January 1991.

24. Florida Statutes, 90.173–74 (1991).

25. *Orlando Sentinel*, 17, 21 February, 29 March 1991.

26. *New York Times*, 31 December 1992.

27. *Orlando Sentinel*, 27 December 1991.

28. Ibid., 20 August 1991.

29. Associated Press report, Sunbury, Pa., *Daily Item*, 19 August 1992.

30. Department of the Treasury, BATF, *State Laws*, p. 5.

31. *Journal of the American Medical Association*, 10 June 1992.

32. Elizabeth Scarff, *Evaluation of the Canadian Gun Control Legislation: Executive Summary* (Ottawa: Canadian Government Publishing Center, 1983), p. 1.

33. Canadian Parliament, Bill C-117, approved 5 December 1991.

34. Ronald Reagan, *Ronald Reagan Talks to America* (Old Greenwich, Conn.: Devin Adair, 1983), p. 173.

35. Some would prefer to say Jews and non-Jews, but the fact is that most white supremacist groups parade as Christians.

36. *New York Times*, 3, 29 March 1994.

37. *New York Times*, 19 December 1993, 26 August 1994.

38. *New York Times*, 10 June 1993.

39. Handgun Control, "Progress Report," two-page flier, December 1992; "Comment: Under the Gun," *New Yorker*, 22 March 1993; *New York Times*, 26 April 1993; Sunbury, Pa., *Daily Item*, 2 April, 21 June 1993.

40. Weekly Compilation of Presidential Documents, 17 February 1993, p. 220.

41. *New Yorker*, see note 39; *New York Times*, 8 July 1993.

42. "The Media and Images of War: Perception Versus Reality," *Defense Monitor*, vol. 23, no. 4, 1994, p. 1. This entire issue is devoted to an analysis of the public impact of these factors:

- The popular interpretation of America's history "celebrates" the westward movement of the frontier through war and conquest.
- Films and television programs about war and the frontier perpetuate the myth that war and violence are the American way to achieve success.
- Post–World War II Americans, who grew up with film and television, developed the expectation that the cavalry, western lawmen, and combat

heroes always "win." Violence by "good" Americans was always portrayed as producing positive results.

- This biased view of America's past falsely mythologizes the "man with the gun" as a representative, admirable American.
- In modern war the military both creates and manages the film images the public sees. Such control can make war seem precise and largely bloodless.

43. Justification in Senate bill S.1882 (1994).
44. H. G. Wells, *The Outline of History*, chap. 15.

Chapter Forty

Lawsuit Aims at Gun Industry

Jo-Ann Moriarty

In a cramped and cluttered Wall Street office, there is the female attorney with a hair-trigger temper and the passion for a longshot.

Fifty-one stories below, in neighborhoods across the length and breadth of this city are women—wives and mothers—each of whose lives was transformed in the ruthless flash of an instant.

And in the quiet of a Connecticut suburb is a former Smith & Wesson executive who spends his days at home caring for his grammar school child.

In September, their lives will converge in a Manhattan courtroom. There the lawyer, Elisa Barnes, hopes to persuade a federal judge to let her put the firearms industry on trial for failing to do more to stem the epidemic of gun violence.

It is an epidemic that has claimed among its hundreds of thousands of victims the sons and husbands of the twenty women who are the plaintiffs in the case.

And it is Robert Hass, the former vice president of the Springfield-based gun manufacturer, whose decision to testify against the industry he served makes this case hard to dismiss as just some gun-hating women's flight of fancy.

Armed with Hass's affidavit, Barnes argues that the gun manufacturers know their method for distributing guns, while legal, in effect, "supplies a vast and uncontrolled black market, which puts guns into the hands of underage shooters."

In September, federal Judge Jack Weinstein will decide whether to dismiss the case or let it proceed to trial. And while it would seem the odds against Barnes are long, that has been the case over the course of eighteen months of pre-trial motions.

The motions have succeeded in winnowing the many strands of her attack on the gun industry, but, she believes, left the central thrust of her case intact.

If Barnes and the women she represents survive the court appearance, they will be making legal history.

"This is a new case based on an old principle. It is different from other firearms cases," said Barnes.

For two decades, lawyers have pursued product liability litigation against individual gun manufacturers. But Barnes is suing all of the nation's forty-six gun makers, as well as a number of trade associations representing the gun industry, charging them with collective negligence. The industry made slightly more than three million hand guns in 1994.

Barnes wants all gun manufacturers to limit sales to distributors who sell only to bona fide retail stores, which she said would dramatically stem black market gun sales. Now, gun manufacturers can sell to distributors who can potentially make a shipment of guns to a single licensed gun dealer with no storefront.

The gun industry thinks Barnes' case is laughable—that holding them responsible for gunfire deaths is like holding General Motors responsible for drunken driving deaths.

They say there is no legal precedent that would hold an industry liable for manufacturing and distributing a non-defective legal product.

"I am surprised it has gotten this far. All other courts have dismissed cases like this quickly. I would be surprised if it went to trial," said lawyer Anne Kimball of the Chicago law firm of Wildman, Harrold, Allen & Dixon. The firm represents five gun manufacturers, including Smith & Wesson, the world's largest manufacturer of handguns.

Kimball notes that Barnes' claim against Smith & Wesson involves a handgun that was made twenty-six years ago and legally sold and possessed for twenty years until it was stolen from a home in Mill Valley, California, four years ago. Within months, the gun was used to kill New York resident Katina Johnson's husband, David, a book editor. (Barnes said she is still researching the facts surrounding that gun.)

"She wants Smith & Wesson to be responsible for that murder and there is no precedent in the law that says Smith & Wesson is required to watch over its product for twenty years to make sure that nothing happens to it," said Kimball.

Atlanta lawyer Tim Bumann, of the firm Cozen and O'Connor, which represents another eleven gun manufacturers, said he finds Barnes' case bewildering. "I haven't any idea what it is that my clients were supposed to do to prevent the alleged injuries suffered by Mrs. Barnes' clients," said Bumann, who believes that what the case really amounts to "is an attempt through the civil system to do away with the private ownership of firearms."

And Richard Feldman, director of the Atlanta-based American Shooting Sports Council, said the real culprit in cases of gun violence is plain—"the person who pulled the trigger."

By Barnes' logic, Feldman said, everyone who contributes anything to making guns could be held responsible—"the miners who mined the ore or the smelters who made the ore into steel."

"We can keep playing this game ad nauseum," said Feldman. "We could say that the world is responsible."

Guns, he said, aren't made to kill people. "Most guns are used for sport, for punching paper in a target. In fact most guns are used for fun."

But, of course, in Western Massachusetts as elsewhere, guns are also used to kill. Officials such as Hampden County District Attorney William Bennett and

Springfield Police Chief Paula Meara worry about what Meara calls "the easy availability of guns to youths, to gangs and to family members who use them to settle arguments."

In what may be a first for the state, Bennett has indicted a Springfield man for selling the illegal handgun used in an accidental shooting May 16 that killed a fourteen-year-old Springfield boy.

"It is different than when I started twenty-seven years ago," said Holyoke Police Captain Russell Paquette. "They are shooting at anything. It is almost like a wild west mentality."

Paquette recalls a photograph police found of a fourteen-year-old boy and his girlfriend, looking like some modern, underage Bonnie and Clyde. "They look like fourteen-year-olds. She is on a cell phone. He's got his arm around her shoulder and in front of his chest, pointing up to the ceiling, is a 9-millimeter in his hand. He's got his gun. She's got her phone. All is right in the world," Paquette said.

"A lot of kids are packing (carrying guns)," said Gail Fox of Jamaica, in the Queens borough of New York. "Some for just the fun of it, a fad, like sneakers or having the best beeper."

Fox is one of the plaintiffs in the case. Two years ago, her sixteen-year-old son went to a friend's house between finishing his homework and coming home for dinner. He was gunned down within steps of his front door. She ran out to see him "on the sidewalk bleeding from the head. Police said he got caught in the crossfire."

"He wanted to be an architect. He wanted to build," said Fox. Now with a bullet lodged in his brain, he suffers nerve damage, attends special education classes and no longer plays sports.

"When I was growing up, you were safe in your neighborhood. With my son, he couldn't leave the block. Now, it's you can't leave the house," said Fox.

The Centers for Disease Control just reported a ten-year study that found guns responsible for three-quarters of the 23,720 homicides in 1994. A decade earlier, 61 percent of the homicides were caused by guns. The CDC also reported that the decade saw a 30 percent jump in the gun murders of people aged fifteen to twenty-four.

Barnes and her clients believe the gun industry ought to be held responsible because of the way it distributes its guns. Barnes, forty-three, grew up in Los Angeles but received an English degree from Barnard College and a law degree at Rutgers University (where she was editor of the law review). She now looks and sounds like the consummate New Yorker. She uses words such as "lovely" and "excellent," dripping with sarcasm, in response to criticism of her case, and flicks off personal attacks like lint from her navy blue Macy's suit.

A mother of three, Barnes was raised a Presbyterian, converted to Judaism but considers herself an agnostic. She says she became engrossed in the subject of gun violence, and increasingly enraged, reading in the newspaper on her subway ride into work each day about one teen-ager after another dying in gunfire.

"It was unspeakable to me," she recalled, noting how one of the plaintiffs described the case as "a mom thing, that only mothers would do this case and only mothers understand what the case is about."

It was a lawyer friend, who works in women's health litigation, who knew one of the mothers and brought her together with Barnes. She filed suit in January 1995, and in November, she said, Hass called her, unsolicited. "I got a phone call from this man saying that he is an ex–vice president of Smith & Wesson and he read about the case in a trade magazine," said Barnes. "I nearly dropped my socks. He gives the case the substance, the heft," said Barnes. "It is not just lawyers saying it. It's somebody who actually was in the business and making observations based on his experiences in the business. You could look at him as the key to the case."

Hass left Smith & Wesson in 1989 after eleven years as vice president of marketing and sales. One of his assignments was to make guns attractive to the female market. He was Smith & Wesson's spokesman on a variety of issues, including gun control.

His sworn statement says the present federal system of licensing gun dealers creates a much-too-loose distribution system. The present system allows un known buyers to legally bring thousands of guns into their homes away from the watchful eye of any law enforcement official.

"The company and the industry as a whole are fully aware of the extent of the criminal misuse of firearms. The company and the industry are also aware that the black market in firearms is not simply the result of stolen guns but is due to the seepage of guns into the illicit market from multiple thousands of unsupervised federal firearms licensees," Hass says in his affidavit.

"In spite of their knowledge, however, the industry's position has consistently been to take no independent action to insure responsible distribution practices," he charges.

And, Hass goes on, none of the nation's gun makers, "to my knowledge take additional steps, beyond determining the possession of a federal firearms license, to investigate, screen or supervise the wholesale distributors and retail outlets that sell their products to insure that their products are distributed responsibly."

Hass, reached last week by *The Sunday Republican* at his Connecticut home, would only say, "I have no comment. None."

Gun industry representatives say Hass is a disgruntled employee with a vindictive streak and nothing important to reveal. But Barnes portrays him as a man with a sense of moral and corporate responsibility. She adds that a law firm she will not name has agreed to represent Hass, pro bono, if the industry goes after him or his reputation in any way for his testimony.

Bill Bridgewater, spokesman for the National Alliance of Stocking Gun Dealers, believes Hass has a point when he says the firearms license system allows too many individuals to buy guns for sale. Bridgewater's North Carolina–based association represents about 19,000 gun dealers, most of them with retail stores.

He said new, tighter requirements for federal firearms licenses imposed in the 1994 crime bill have significantly reduced the number of licenses, from 260,000 three years ago to 145,382 more recently. And Bridgewater said there is a direct link between the decrease in the number of federal firearms licenses and a decline in firearms violence. "I don't think there was any question about that."

But, he said, the government, and not the industry, bears responsibility for any flaws in its licensing system, then or now. "The federal government created this black market," said Bridgewater, who rejects the idea that manufacturers are purposely supplying an illicit market as a way to expand their business.

But Kristen Rand of the National Violence Policy Center believes the gun companies are explicitly making guns favored by street criminals. She cites the TEC-9, "the No. 1 assault weapon seized by the ATF. It is intimidating. It is the assault pistol you see on TV. It has no legitimate purpose to exist."

In his affidavit, Hass says the firearms industry's response to "the proliferation of illegal firearms and the rising gun-related crime rate has been to call for stricter enforcement of criminal penalties, rather than enactment of laws that would limit access to firearms."

Feldman of the American Shooting Sports Council contends that if gun violence is still a problem, it is because the criminal justice system isn't tough enough. He said Barnes and her plaintiffs are, through the courts, "seeking to have the civil system accomplish what the criminal system has intended to do but failed the American people miserably (at doing.)"

"Exactly," says Barnes.

Springfield mother Anita Villafane doesn't know if the gun industry should be held responsible for the deaths of children. All she knows is that her oldest child, Carlos Falcon, eighteen, who would spontaneously announce, "I love life," went to meet three friends at the Kentucky Fried Chicken restaurant in Mason Square on a cold and rainy school night.

She asked him to stay home.

"He just looked at me; it was the last look he gave me," Villafane said.

A few hours later, police called Villafane to Baystate Medical Center, where she stayed the night to learn if her son would survive a bullet to his head. He and his friends had been mistaken for gang members by members of Los Solidos, a street gang.

(Recently, two of the shooters, Jason Jiles, nineteen, of Springfield, and Robert Francis, twenty, were sentenced to life in prison with no chance of parole. Louis Barrios, twenty-one, will be eligible for parole after fifteen years.)

"In the morning, the doctors came out and told me that he was brain dead, that the machines were working," said Villafane, who is not a party to the gun suit.

"At that moment, I said, 'Forget about the machines. Take his heart, his organs, his kidneys, his bones, his tissue—everything that somebody could use to live. Take it from my son.'"

The story is echoed in Tarrytown, north of New York City where another mother, Anne Cargill, and her husband raised five children. Five years ago, the couple's only son was driving with two friends on the Westside Highway on his way home from the city when he cut off a car.

Three members of the Wild Cowboys street gang were in the other car, which pulled up alongside her son's car and shot into the driver's side. Her son died instantly. His two friends, while not injured by the gunshots, have never emotionally regained their footing.

"Guns end up in the hands of teen-agers and gangs. (The gun manufacturers) send out guns anyway they want. They don't track them," said Cargill, a gun suit plaintiff who came to believe the only way things would change was if mothers such as she brought the law to bear against the industry.

"The only time you get change is when you sue them and hit them in the pocketbooks," Cargill explained. "Then, they will listen."

Chapter Forty-one

Crime Fighting's About-Face

Fox Butterfield

In the face of America's vast crime problem, liberals and conservatives have long clashed over the causes of lawlessness and what to do about it.

For liberals, crime must be traced to its roots in poverty, joblessness and racism, deep-seated social and economic ills. Nonsense, conservatives counter, the origins are cultural, stemming from the decline of the family along with the rise of welfare dependency, single motherhood and a permissive social ethos. One thing both sides agree on: there is little the police can do to reduce crime.

Taken together, these views add up to the conventional wisdom about crime that has prevailed for twenty years or more. Without profound changes in society, there isn't much anyone can do about crime in this country.

Suddenly, new facts have turned this accepted wisdom on its head. For five years, reported crime, especially murder, has been dropping sharply even though the economic plight of the inner cities and the disarray in poor families remain the same. This decline is the longest in twenty-five years, and when the final figures for 1996 are in, it is likely that the national homicide rate will fall to its lowest level since the 1960's, when an explosion of violence triggered America's modern crime problem.

No one really knows why crime is dropping. "This is a humbling time for all crime analysts," said John J. DiIulio Jr., a professor of politics and public affairs at Princeton University. "It is a puzzlement."

Still, a remarkably optimistic new view of crime prevention is emerging among experts, and their revised consensus suggests that law enforcement may make a critical difference after all, through innovative and concerted police strategies on guns, teen-agers and petty crimes. Call this the management approach.

At the same time, another new theory gaining adherents is that fighting crime is like combating an epidemic whose pattern of infection doesn't follow a tidy mathematical progression. "Acts of violence lead to further acts of violence, creating a contagion effect and a sudden jump in crime rates that is hard to explain," said John Laub, a professor of criminology at Northeastern University.

This may be what happened when the advent of crack cocaine in the mid-1980's produced a sudden, huge increase in violence.

Epidemiologists term this dramatic escalation the "tipping point." Fortunately, the same effect applies once enough measures are taken to contain the epidemic, even though the measures, by themselves, seem far less ambitious than previous efforts to attack crime at its roots.

William J. Bratton, the former New York City Police Commissioner who is credited with introducing some of the successful new law enforcement strategies, said, "I think we are now at another one of those tipping points, only on the way down."

Preliminary F.B.I. data for 1996, released this month, seem to support Mr. Bratton and underscore how mistaken the old wisdom about crime now appears. The biggest decreases in serious and violent crime last year came in the nation's largest cities, precisely those areas where traditional criminology predicted crimes would be the worst.

In the past five years, murders in New York have fallen by 50 percent, to 984 in 1996 from 1,995 in 1992. The rate also dropped in other big cities where the police have adopted new tactics: in Houston by 49 percent, Chicago by 16 percent and Boston by 62 percent.

It is difficult to overstate how different the new view of policing is. As recently as 1990, Travis Hirschi, an influential criminologist, in a book titled *A General Theory of Crime* (Stanford University Press), wrote, "No evidence exists that augmentation of police forces or equipment, differential patrol strategies or differential intensities of surveillance have any effect on crime rates."

The seeds of the new approach were sown by Mr. Bratton when he took charge of the New York City Transit Authority police in 1990. Following the advice of George Kelling, a criminologist, Mr. Bratton instituted a program of trying to head off more serious crimes by cracking down on minor ones like turnstile-jumping and panhandling. Later, as commissioner, Mr. Bratton added further elements to his management strategy, using computer-generated statistics to target crime hot spots and making his subordinates responsible for reaching crime-reduction goals, the way a businessman demands increased profits.

But, cautioned James Q. Wilson, a professor of management at the University of California at Los Angeles, improved police work is not the whole story. In Los Angeles, Professor Wilson said, "the police may not be part of the story at all," since murders have dropped there by 37 percent over the past five years despite poor police leadership, bad morale and a decline in arrests.

Instead, Professor Wilson said, it is important to note that the adult homicide rate has been declining since 1981, and that the only reason the homicide rate rose in the late 1980's was that juvenile violence tripled with the advent of crack. This form of cocaine brought youths into the drug trade and created a demand for automatic handguns. Many teen-agers suddenly wanted a gun for safety or prestige.

Unlike adult crime, teen-age crime "follows a fad-like pattern, where the changes come quickly," Professor Wilson said. Just as teen-agers' tastes in clothing are driven by trends, so was their jump into crack culture. But when they saw the cost in death, hospitalization and prison time, many turned away, he said.

Geoffrey Canada, the president of the Rheedlen Centers for Children and Families in Harlem, who counsels poor children, said he has witnessed a change among fourteen-, fifteen- and sixteen-year-olds in the past five years. The toll of death in their families, tougher police tactics and stepped-up efforts by neighborhood groups to combat violence have combined to reduce involvement in the drug trade. The drug market is still there, Mr. Canada said, but it is more stable now, back in the hands of older people who treat it like a business. "When you had fifteen-year-olds selling crack, they were wild cowboys who shot off their guns if somebody dissed them," he said.

There are several other possible explanations for the decline in murder. The development of hospital trauma centers has saved more gunshot victims from death. The ban on assault weapons and the Brady law, requiring a five-day waiting period to purchase a handgun, have made it harder for criminals to obtain guns. Longer prison sentences have removed some career criminals from the streets, though the threat of longer sentences may not actually deter crime.

Given this plenitude of possible causes, it may be that "this is a case where the whole is far greater than the sum of its parts," said Jeffrey Fagan, the director of the Center for Violence Research and Prevention at Columbia University.

This, said Professor Fagan, would also fit in the epidemiological theory of a "tipping point," where a number of small factors help reduce the epidemic faster than can be logically explained.

There is no guarantee, of course, that the drop in murder will last just because it has declined for five years. Some experts are worried that the rapidly rising popularity of methamphetamines, or speed, in the Southwest may turn it into something like crack was in the mid-1980's, an unforeseen catalyst that drives up crime rates. But the recent decrease does illustrate an important point that often gets forgotten in the shrill public debate over crime: there is nothing immutable in human nature about homicide.

Roger Lane, a historian at Haverford College, calculates the murder rate in England in the thirteenth and fourteenth centuries was at least 20 to 25 per 100,000, two to three times the 1995 American rate of 8 per 100,000.

Most of these murders took place in the countryside, where peasants, who drank beer as a daily beverage, carried knives for eating and quarterstaffs for walking on muddy roads. Quarrels between neighbors escalated into violence, with no legal authority to settle disputes.

"Whatever your prejudices, there were no guns, no blacks, no cities larger than Kokomo, Indiana," said Professor Lane, the author of a forthcoming book, *Murder in America: A History* (Ohio State University Press). "Religion, tradition, the community and attachment to the family were all powerful," he said, and hanging was the penalty for any felony.

While some criminologists remain skeptical that the current decline in crime can continue without fundamental economic and social changes, Felton Earls, a professor of child psychiatry at the Harvard School of Public Health, says he believes improved police work may help troubled neighborhoods. "This could be the leading edge of greater change," said Professor Earls, "because reduced crime brings local neighborhood life under better control."

Chapter Forty-two

Second Thoughts on the Second Amendment

Wendy Kaminer

Calmly, patiently, with considerable bravery, the instructor at the shooting range shows me how to fire the submachine gun, a MAC-11—the first real gun I have ever held. It jams repeatedly. "That's why they call it a Jam-o-matic," someone says. Finally, anticlimactically, like an idiot, I am shooting up the floor (the instructor told me to aim down). Seven or eight men standing behind me await their turns.

The fully automatic MAC-11—small, relatively lightweight, with little recoil— is less intimidating than the semi-automatic rifles, which I can't quite bring myself to use. I am anxious enough around the handguns. "Lean forward," the instructor keeps telling me, while I lean back, trying to get as far away from the gun as I can. How do thirteen-year-olds do this? I wonder, trying not to hurt myself with a huge, heavy revolver. I jump every time a shot is fired (and can't wait for the guys to stop playing with the machine gun). I can barely get the slide back on one of the semi-automatic handguns. But I'm pleased when I hit the target with the 9mm Glock, the only one of these guns I can imagine being able to use. And when someone offers me a casing from the Walther PPK I've just shot (James Bond's gun, everyone points out), I pocket it.

I've been invited to the shooting range to "observe and try out the right to bear arms in action," along with about twenty other participants in a two-day seminar on guns and the Constitution, sponsored by Academics for the Second Amendment. Funded partly by the National Rifle Association, Academics for the Second Amendment isn't exactly a collection of academic gun nuts—most of its more than five hundred members aren't academics, and its president, Joseph Olson, an NRA board member and a professor at Hamline Law School, in Minnesota, seems a rational, open-minded man. But the organization is engaged in a genteel lobbying effort to popularize what many liberals consider the gun nut's view of the Second Amendment: that it confers an individual right to bear arms, not just the right to bear arms in a well-regulated militia.

Since it was founded, in 1992, Academics for the Second Amendment has held four by-invitation-only seminars for academics who share its beliefs about the

Second Amendment—or might be persuaded to adopt them. The year before last I asked permission to attend a seminar but was turned down; last year I received an unsolicited invitation, apparently in response to an article in which I had questioned the effectiveness of traditional approaches to gun control.

Don Kates, who is a San Francisco lawyer, a gun aficionado, and the author of numerous articles on guns and the Constitution, leads the seminar energetically, taking only a little time out to show us pictures of his parrot. His approach is scatter-shot, or spray and pray. Ranging over legal, moral, and practical arguments for private gun ownership, he discusses self-defense and the deterrent effect of an armed citizenry; the correlation between guns and crime; difficulties of enforcing gun controls; bigotry against gun owners; and, finally, constitutional rights. Comments by participants are sometimes sensible and occasionally insane: one man proclaims that mothers should give guns to children who attend dangerous public schools.

"What would you do if you had a fourteen-year-old kid who felt he needed a gun for self-defense?" he asks me repeatedly.

"I'd take him out of school before giving him a gun."

But even among gun advocates there is relatively little support for the rights of juveniles to own guns, or opposition to bans on juvenile ownership. Opposition to gun prohibitions focuses on attempts to disarm more or less sane, law-abiding adults, who are deemed to be endowed with both natural and constitutional rights to self-defense against criminals and despots.

Like moral and legal claims about gun owners' rights, the practical consequences of widespread gun ownership are highly debatable. No one can say with any certainty whether it increases violence or decreases crime. Don Kates speculates that magically reducing the approximately two hundred million firearms in circulation to five million would have virtually no reductive effect on the crime rate: according to a 1983 National Institute of Justice–funded study by James D. Wright, Peter H. Rossi, and Kathleen Daly, about 1 percent of privately owned firearms are involved in criminal activity, suggesting that eliminating 99 percent of the nation's guns would not ameliorate crime. Or would it? Philip Cook, an economist at Duke University and a leading researcher on gun violence, considers Kates's speculation about the uselessness of reducing the number of guns "patently absurd." We can't predict which guns will be used in crimes, he says, even if a relatively small number are used feloniously overall. Reducing the availability of guns would raise their price and therefore reduce their accessibility, to adult felons as well as juveniles. And even if a drastic reduction in the number of guns wouldn't necessarily decrease crime, it would decrease fatalities. Guns are particularly lethal, Cook has stressed: the "fraction of serious gun assaults that result in the victim's death is much higher than that of assaults with other weapons." Since not all gun homicides reflect a clearly formulated intent to kill, Cook reasons, access to guns can increase the lethality of assaults. A decrease in the use of guns, however, might lead to an increase in nonfatal injuries. Robberies committed with guns tend to involve less violence than other robberies because the victims are less likely to resist. (Cook speculates that victims who do resist robbers armed with guns are more likely to be killed.)

Debates about gun ownership and gun control are driven more by values and ideology than by pragmatism—and hardly at all by the existing empirical research, which is complex and inconclusive. Wright, Rossi, and Daly reported that there is not even any "suggestive evidence" showing that "gun ownership . . . as a whole is, per se, an important cause of criminal violence." The evidence that guns deter criminal violence is equally insubstantial, they added, as is evidence that additional gun controls would reduce crime. Many are already in place and rarely, if ever, enforced; or they make no sense. In 1983 Wright, Rossi, and Daly concluded that the "benefits of stricter gun controls . . . are at best uncertain, and at worst close to nil."

As for legal debates about the existence of constitutional rights, empirical data is irrelevant, or at best peripheral. But the paucity of proof that gun controls lessen crime is particularly galling to people who believe that they have a fundamental right to bear arms. In theory, at least, we restrict constitutional rights only when the costs of exercising them seem unbearably high. In fact we argue continually about what those costs are: Does violence in the media cause violence in real life? Did the release of the Pentagon Papers endanger the national security? Does hate speech constitute discrimination? In the debate about firearms, however, we can't even agree on the principles that should govern restrictions on guns, because we can't agree about the right to own them.

How could we, given the importance of the competing values at stake—public safety and the right of self-defense—and the opacity of the constitutional text? The awkwardly drafted Second Amendment doesn't quite make itself clear: "A well regulated Militia, being necessary to the security of a free State, the right of the people to keep and bear Arms, shall not be infringed." Is the reference to a militia a limitation on the right to bear arms or merely an explanation of an armed citizenry's role in a government by consent? There is little dispute that one purpose of the Second Amendment was to ensure that the people would be able to resist a central government should it ever devolve into despotism. But there is little agreement about what that capacity for resistance was meant to entail—armed citizens acting under the auspices of state militias or armed citizens able to organize and act on their own. And there is virtually no consensus about the constitutional right to own a gun in the interests of individual self-defense against crime, rather than communal defense against tyranny. Is defense of the state, and of the common good, the *raison d'être* of the Second Amendment or merely one use of it?

The Supreme Court has never answered these fundamental questions about the constitutional uses of guns. It has paid scant attention to the Second Amendment, providing little guidance in the gun-control debate. Two frequently cited late-nineteenth-century cases relating to the Second Amendment were more about federalism than about the right to bear arms. *Presser v. Illinois*, decided in 1886, involved a challenge to a state law prohibiting private citizens from organizing their own military units and parades. The Court held that the Second Amendment was a limitation on federal, not state, power, reflecting the prevailing view (now discredited) that the Bill of Rights in general applied only to the federal government, not to the states. (A hundred years ago the Court did not apply the First Amendment to the states either.) *Presser* followed *U.S. v. Cruikshank,* which held that the federal government could not protect people from private infringement of their rights to assemble and bear arms. *Cruikshank,* decided in 1876, invalidated the federal convictions of participants in the lynching of two black men. This ruling, essentially concerned with limiting federal police power, is virtually irrelevant to Second Amendment debates today, although it has been cited to support the proposition that an oppressed minority has a compelling need (or a natural right) to bear arms in self-defense.

The most significant Supreme Court decision on the Second Amendment was *U.S. v. Miller* (1939), a less-than-definitive holding now cited approvingly by both sides in the gun-control debate. *Miller* involved a prosecution under the 1934 National Firearms Act. Jack Miller and his accomplice had been convicted of transporting an unregistered shotgun of less than regulation length across state lines. In striking down their Second Amendment claim and upholding their conviction, the Court noted that no evidence had been presented that a shotgun was in fact a militia weapon, providing no factual basis for a Second Amendment claim. This ruling implies that the Second Amendment could protect the right to bear arms suitable for a militia.

Advocates of gun control or prohibition like the Miller case because it makes the right to bear arms dependent on at least the possibility of service in a militia. They cite the Court's declaration that the Second Amendment was obviously intended to "assure the continuation and render possible the effectiveness" of state militias; they place less emphasis on the Court's apparent willingness to permit private citizens to possess military weapons. Citing *Miller,* a dealer at a gun show told me that the Second Amendment protects the ownership of only such devices as machine guns, Stingers, and grenade throwers. But advocates of gun ownership don't generally emphasize this awkward implication of *U.S. v. Miller* any more than their opponents do: it could lead to prohibitions on handguns. They like the *Miller* decision because it delves into the history of the Second Amendment and stresses that for the framers, the militia "comprised all males physically capable of acting in concert for the common defense."

This view of the militia as an inchoate citizens' army, not a standing body of professionals, is central to the claim that the Second Amendment protects the rights of individual civilians, not simply the right of states to organize and arm militias. And, in fact, fear and loathing of standing armies did underlie the Second Amendment, which was at least partly intended to ensure that states would be able to call up citizens in defense against a tyrannical central government. (Like the Bill of Rights in general, the Second Amendment was partly a response to concerns about federal abuses of power.) James Madison, the author of the Second Amendment, invoked in *The Federalist Papers* the potential force of a citizen militia as a guarantee against a federal military coup.

> Let a regular army, fully equal to the resources of the country, be formed; and let it be entirely at the devotion of the federal government: still it would not be going too far to say that the State governments with the people on their side would be able to repel the danger.... To [the regular army] would be opposed a militia amounting to near half a million of citizens with arms in their hands, officered by men chosen from among themselves, fighting for their common liberties and united and conducted by governments possessing their affection and confidence. It may well be doubted whether a militia thus circumstanced could ever be conquered by such a proportion of regular troops. Those who are best acquainted with the late successful resistance of this country against the British arms will be most inclined to deny the possibility of it. Besides the advantage of being armed, which the Americans possess over the people of almost every other nation, the existence of subordinate governments, to which the people are attached and by which the militia officers are appointed, forms a barrier against the enterprise of ambition, more insurmountable than any which a simple government of any form can admit of.

This passage is enthusiastically cited by advocates of the right to bear arms, because it supports their notion of the militia as the body of people, privately armed; but it's also cited by their opponents, because it suggests that the militia is activated and "conducted" by the states, and it stresses that citizens are "attached" to their local governments. The militia envisioned by Madison is not simply a "collection of unorganized, privately armed citizens," Dennis Henigan, a handgun-control advocate, has argued.

That Madison's reflections on the militia and the Supreme Court's holding in *U.S. v. Miller* can be cited with some accuracy by both sides in the debate testifies to the hybrid nature of Second Amendment rights. The Second Amendment presumes (as did the framers) that private citizens will possess private arms; Madison referred offhandedly to "the advantage of being armed, which the Americans possess." But Madison also implied that the right to bear arms is based in the obligation of citizens to band together as a militia to defend the common good, as opposed to the prerogative of citizens to take up arms individually in pursuit of self-interest and happiness.

The tension at the heart of the Second Amendment, which makes it so difficult to construe, is the tension between republicanism and liberal individualism. (To put it very simply, republicanism calls for the subordination of individual interests to the public good; liberalism focuses on protecting individuals against popular conceptions of the good.) A growing body of scholarly literature on the Second Amendment locates the right to bear arms in republican theories of governance. In a 1989 article in the *Yale Law Journal* that helped animate the Second Amendment debate, the University of Texas law professor Sanford Levinson argued that the Second Amendment confers an individual right to bear arms so that, in the republican tradition, armed citizens might rise up against an oppressive state. Wendy Brown, a professor of women's studies at the University of California at Santa Cruz, and David C. Williams, a law professor at Cornell University, have questioned the validity of a republican right to bear arms in a society that lacks the republican virtue of being willing to put communal interests first. Pro-gun activists don't generally acknowledge the challenge posed by republicanism to the individualist culture that many gun owners inhabit. They embrace republican justifications for gun ownership, stressing the use of arms in defending the community, at the same time that they stress the importance of guns in protecting individual autonomy.

Advocates of the right to bear arms often insist that the Second Amendment is rooted in both collective and individual rights of self-defense—against political oppression and crime—without recognizing how those rights conflict. The republican right to resist oppression is the right of the majority, or the people, not the right of a small religious cult in Waco, Texas, or of a few survivalist tax protesters in Idaho. The members of these groups have individual rights against the government, state and federal. (Both the American Civil Liberties Union and the NRA protested the government's actions in Waco and its attack on the survivalist Randy Weaver and his family.) But refuseniks and refugees from society are not republicans. They do not constitute the citizen militia envisioned by the framers, any more than they stand for the American community; indeed, they stand against it—withdrawing from the body politic, asserting their rights to alienation and anomie or membership in exclusionary alternative communities of their own. Republicanism can't logically be invoked in the service of libertarianism. It elevates civic virtue over individualism, consensus over dissent.

Nor can social-contract theory be readily invoked in support of a right to arm yourself in a war against street crime, despite the claims of some gun-ownership advocates. The right or power to engage in punishment or retribution is precisely what is given up when you enter an ordered civil society. The loss of self-help remedies is the price of the social contract. "God hath certainly appointed Government to restrain the partiality and violence of Men," John Locke wrote. A person may always defend his or her life when threatened, but only when there is no chance to appeal to the law. If a man points his sword at me and demands my purse, Locke explained, I may kill him. But if he steals my purse by stealth and then raises a sword to defend it, I may not use force to get it back. "My Life not being in danger, I may have the *benefit of appealing* to the Law, and have Reparation for my 100 *l.* that way."

Locke was drawing a line between self-defense and vigilantism which many gun owners would no doubt respect. Others would point to the inability of the criminal-justice system to avenge crimes and provide reparation to victims, and thus they would assert a right to engage in self-help. Social-contract theory, however, might suggest that if the government is no longer able to provide order, or justice, the remedy is not vigilantism but revolution; the utter failure of law enforcement is a fundamental breach of trust. And, in fact, there are large pockets of disaffected citizens who do not trust the government to protect them or to provide impartial justice, and who might be persuaded to rise up against it, as evidenced by the disorder that followed the 1992 acquittal of police officers who assaulted Rodney King. Was Los Angeles the scene of a riot or of an uprising?

Injustice, and the sense of oppression it spawns, are often matters of perspective—particularly today, when claims of political victimization abound and there is little consensus on the demands of public welfare. We use the term "oppression" promiscuously, to describe any instance of discrimination. In this climate of grievance and hyperbole, many acts of violence are politicized. How do we decide whether an insurrection is just? Don Kates observes that the Second Amendment doesn't exactly confer the right to resist. He says, "It gives you a right to win."

The prospect of armed resistance, however, is probably irrelevant to much public support for gun ownership, which reflects a fear of crime more than a fear or loathing of government. People don't buy guns in order to overthrow or even to thwart the government; in the belief that the police can't protect them, people buy guns to protect themselves and their families. Recognizing this, the NRA appeals to fear of crime, particularly crime against women. ("Choose to refuse to be a victim," NRA ads proclaim, showing a woman and her daughter alone in a desolate parking lot at night.) And it has countered demands for tougher gun controls not with radical individualist appeals for insurrection but with statist appeals for tougher anti-crime laws, notably stringent mandatory-minimum sentences and parole reform. There is considerable precedent for the NRA's appeal to state authority: founded after the Civil War, with the mission of teaching soldiers to shoot straight, in its early years the NRA was closely tied to the military and dependent on government largesse; until recently it drew considerable moral support from the police. Today, however, statist anti-crime campaigns are mainly matters of politics for the NRA and for gun advocates in general; laws mandating tough sentences for the criminal use of firearms defuse demands for firearm controls. Personal liberty—meaning the liberty to own guns and use them against the government if necessary—is these people's passion.

Gun advocates are apt to be extravagantly libertarian when the right to own guns is at stake. At heart many are insurrectionists—at least, they need to feel prepared. Nothing arouses their anger more, I've found, than challenges to the belief that private gun ownership is an essential check on political oppression.

During the two-day seminar held by Academics for the Second Amendment, we argue equanimously about nearly everything—crime control, constitutional rights, and the fairness and feasibility of gun controls—until I question whether, two hundred years after the Revolution, citizens armed with rifles and handguns can effectively resist the federal government. I ask, If Nixon had staged a military coup in 1974—assuming he had military support—instead of resigning the presidency, could the NRA and the nation's unaffiliated gun owners have stopped him? For the first time in two days Don Kates flares up in anger, and the room is incandescent.

"Give me one example from history of a successful government oppression of an armed populace," he demands. The FBI raid on David Koresh's compound in Waco, Texas, doesn't count, he says, because Koresh's group was a small, isolated minority. The Civil War doesn't count either. (I can't remember why.) Neither do uprisings in Malaysia and the Philippines.

People like me think it is possible to oppose the government only with nuclear weapons, Kates rages, because we're stupid; we don't understand military strategy and the effectiveness of guerrilla warfare, and we underestimate the hesitancy of troops to engage their fellow citizens in armed conflict. Millions of Americans armed only with pistols and long guns could turn a bloodless coup into a prolonged civil war.

Perhaps. I am almost persuaded that Kates might have a point, until he brings up the Holocaust.

Gun advocates sometimes point out that the Holocaust was preceded by gun-control laws that disarmed the Jews and made it easy to round them up. (In a 1994 article in *Guns and Ammo,* Jay Simkin, the president of Jews for the Preservation of Firearms Ownership, argued that gun control causes genocide. Simkin wrote that today "genocides can be prevented if civilians worldwide own military-type rifles and plenty of ammunition.") Kates doesn't go nearly this far, but he does point out that genocides are difficult to predict. At the turn of the century, he says, I would not have predicted the Holocaust, and today I can't predict what holocausts may occur in the next fifteen or fifty years. I give up. "If millions are slaughtered in the next fifty years because of gun-control laws," I declare, "let their deaths be on my head."

"It's very interesting that you say that," Kates concludes, a bit triumphantly.

Kates apologizes later for his outburst, and in a subsequent phone conversation he acknowledges that "the Holocaust was not an event where guns would have mattered; the force was overwhelming." But he adds that guns might have mattered to individual Jews who could have saved themselves had they been armed, even if the Jewish community couldn't have saved itself collectively. And guns might matter to a Croatian woman who shoots a Serbian soldier breaking into her house, he suggests; if there were a Second Amendment in Bosnia, it would protect her.

Zealots in the pro-gun camp (Kates is not among them) seem to identify with the woman defending her home to the extent that they fear attack by the federal government. "Using a national epidemic of crime and violence as their justification, media pundits and collectivist politicians are aggressively campaigning to disarm private citizens and strengthen federal law enforcement powers," proclaims a special edition of *The New American,* a magazine on sale at gun shows. After gun control, the editors suggest, the greatest threat to individual liberty is the Clinton plan for providing local police departments with federal assistance. "Is it possible that some of those who are advocating a disarmed populace and a centralized police system have totalitarian designs in mind? It is worth noting that this is exactly what happened in many countries during this century."

This can be dismissed as ravings on the fringe, but it captures in crazed form the hostility toward a powerful central government which inspired the adoption of the Second Amendment right to bear arms two hundred years ago and fuels support for it today. Advocates of First Amendment rights, who believe firmly that free speech is both a moral imperative and an instrument of democratic governance, should understand the passion of Second Amendment claims.

They should be sympathetic as well to the more dispassionate constitutional arguments of gun owners. Civil libertarians who believe that the Bill of Rights in general protects individuals have a hard time explaining why the Second Amendment protects only groups. They have a hard time reconciling their opposition to prohibitions of problematic behavior, such as drug abuse, with their support for the prohibitions of guns. (Liberals tend to demonize guns and gun owners the way conservatives tend to demonize drugs and pornography and the people who use them.) In asserting that the Second Amendment provides no individual right to bear arms or that the right provided is anachronistic and not worth its cost, civil libertarians place themselves in the awkward position of denying the existence of a constitutional right because they don't value its exercise.

The civil-libertarian principles at issue in the gun debate are made clear by the arguments of First Amendment and Second Amendment advocates, which are strikingly similar—as are the arguments their opponents use. Pornography rapes, some feminists say. Words oppress, according to advocates of censoring hate speech. "Words Kill," declared a Planned Parenthood ad following the abortion-clinic shootings in Brookline, Massachusetts, last year. And all you can say in response is "Words don't kill people; people kill people." To an anti-libertarian, the literature sold at gun shows may seem as dangerous as the guns; at a recent gun show I bought *Incendiaries*, an army manual on unconventional warfare; *Exotic Weapons: An Access Book*; *Gunrunning for Fun and Profit*; and *Vigilante Handbook*, which tells me how to harass, torture, and assassinate people. Should any of this material be censored? If it were, it would be sold on the black market; and the remedy for bad speech is good speech, First Amendment devotees point out. According to Second Amendment supporters, gun-control laws affect only law-abiding gun owners, and the best defense against armed criminals is armed victims; the remedy for the bad use of guns in violent crime is the good use of guns in self-defense.

Of course, guns do seem a bit more dangerous than books, and apart from a few anti-pornography feminists, most of us would rather be accosted by a man with a video than a man with a gun. But none of our constitutional rights are absolute. Recognizing that the Second Amendment confers an individual right to bear arms would not immunize guns from regulation; it would require that the government establish a necessity, not just a desire, to regulate. The majority of gun owners, Don Kates suggests, would be amenable to gun controls, such as waiting periods and even licensing and training requirements, if they didn't perceive them as preludes to prohibition. The irony of the Second Amendment debate is that acknowledging an individual right to bear arms might facilitate gun control more than denying it ever could.

But it will not facilitate civic engagement or the community that Americans are exhorted to seek. The civil-libertarian defense of Second Amendment rights is not a republican one. It does not derive the individual rights to bear arms from republican notions of the militia; instead it relies on traditional liberal views of personal autonomy. It is a communitarian nightmare. If the war against crime has replaced the Cold War in popular culture, a private storehouse of guns has replaced the fallout shelter in the psyche of Americans who feel besieged. Increasingly barricaded, mistrustful of their neighbors, they've sacrificed virtue to fear.

Chapter Forty-three

Ten Essential Observations on Guns in America

James D. Wright

Talk of "gun control" is very much in the air these days. Emboldened by their successes in getting the Brady Act enacted, the pro-control forces are now striking on a number of fronts: bans on various so-called assault weapons, mandatory gun registration, strict new laws against juvenile acquisition and possession of guns, and on through the list. Much current gun-control activity springs from a recent and generally successful effort to redefine gun violence mainly as a public health issue rather than a criminal justice issue.

Increasingly, the ammunition of the gun control war is data. Pro-control advocates gleefully cite studies that seem to favor their position, of which there is no shortage, and anti-control advocates do likewise. Many of the "facts" of the case are, of course, hotly disputed; so too are their implications and interpretations. Here I should like to discuss ten essential facts about guns in America that are not in dispute—ten fundamental truths that all contestants either do or should agree to—and briefly ponder the implications of each for how the problem of guns and gun violence perhaps should be approached. These facts and their implications derive from some twenty years of research and reflection on the issues.

1. *Half the households in the country own at least one gun.* So far as I have been able to determine, the first question about gun ownership asked of a national probability sample of U.S. adults was posed in 1959; a similar question asking whether anyone in the household owns a gun has since been repeated dozens of times. Over the ensuing thirty-five years, every survey has reported more or less the same result: Just about half of all U.S. households own one or more guns. This is probably not the highest gun ownership percentage among the advanced industrial societies (that honor probably goes to the Swiss), but it qualifies as a very respectable showing. We are, truly, a "gun culture."

Five important implications follow more or less unambiguously from this first essential observation.

The percentage of households owning guns has been effectively constant for nearly four decades; at the same time, the total number of guns in circulation has increased substantially, especially in the last two decades. The evident implication is that the increasing supply of guns has been absorbed by population growth, with newly formed households continuing to arm themselves at the average rate, and by the purchase of additional guns by households already owning one or more of them. In fact there is fairly solid evidence that the average number of guns owned by households owning any has increased from about three in the late 1970s to about four today.

The second implication is thus that many (and conceivably nearly all) of the new guns coming into circulation are being purchased by people who already own guns, as opposed to first-time purchases by households or individuals who previously owned no guns. I think it is also obvious that from the viewpoint of public safety, the transition from N to N + 1 guns is considerably less ominous than the transition from no guns to one gun. If this second implication is correct, it means that *most of the people in the gun shops today buying new guns already own at least one gun*, a useful point to keep in mind when pondering, for example, the alleged "cooling off" function to be served by waiting periods imposed at the point of retail sale.

Furthermore, it is frequently argued by pro-control advocates that the mere presence of guns causes people to do nutty and violent things that they would otherwise never even consider. In the academic literature on "guns as aggression-eliciting stimuli," this is called the "trigger pulls the finger" hypothesis. If there were much substance to this viewpoint, the fact that half of all U.S. households possess a gun would seem to imply that there ought to be a lot more nuttiness "out there" than we actually observe. In the face of widespread alarm about the skyrocketing homicide rate, it is important to remember that the rate is still a relatively small number of homicides (ten to fifteen or so) per hundred thousand people. If half the households own guns and the mere presence of guns incites acts of violence, then one would expect the bodies to be piled three deep, and yet they are not.

Fourth, gun ownership is normative, not deviant, behavior across vast swaths of the social landscape. In certain states and localities, it would be an odd duck indeed who did not own a gun. Surveys in some smaller southern cities, for example, have reported local gun ownership rates in excess of 90 percent.

And finally, to attempt to control crime or violence by controlling the general ownership or use of guns among the public at large is to attempt to control the behaviors of a very small fraction of the population (the criminally or violently inclined fraction) by controlling the behaviors and activities of roughly half the U.S. population. Whatever else might be said about such an approach, it is certainly not very efficient.

2. *There are 200 million guns already in circulation in the United States*, give or take a few tens of millions. It has been said, I think correctly, that firearms are the most commonly owned piece of sporting equipment in the United States, with the exception of pairs of sneakers. In any case, contestants on all sides of the gun debate generally agree that the total number of guns in circulation is on

the order of 200 million—nearly one gun for every man, woman, and child in the country.

It is not entirely clear how many acts of gun violence occur in any typical year. There are 30–35,000 deaths due to guns each year, perhaps a few hundred thousand nonfatal but injurious firearms accidents, maybe 500,000 or 600,000 chargeable gun crimes (not including crimes of illegal gun possession and carrying), and God knows how many instances in which guns are used to intimidate or prey upon one's fellow human beings. Making generous allowances all around, however, the total number of acts of accidental and intentional gun violence, whether fatal, injurious, or not, cannot be more than a couple of million, at the outside. This implies that the 200 million guns now in circulation would be sufficient to sustain roughly another century of gun violence at the current rates, even assuming that each gun was used once and only once for some nefarious purpose and that all additions to the gun supply were halted permanently and at once. Because of the large number of guns already in circulation, the violence-reductive effects of even fairly Draconian gun-control measures enacted today might well not be felt for decades.

Many recent gun-control initiatives, such as the Brady Act, are aimed at the point of retail sale of firearms and are therefore intended to reduce or in some way disrupt the flow of new guns into the domestic market. At the outside, the number of new guns coming onto the market yearly is a few million, which adds but a few percent to the existing supply. If we intend to control gun violence by reducing the availability of firearms to the general public, as many argue we should, then we have to find some workable means to confront or control the vast arsenal of guns already circulating through private hands.

Various "amnesty," "buyback," and "please turn in your guns" measures have been attempted in various jurisdictions all over the country; in one well-publicized effort, teenagers could swap guns for Toys R Us gift certificates. The success of these programs has been measured in units of several dozen or at most a few hundred relinquished firearms; the net effect on the overall supply of guns is far too trivial to even bother calculating.

3. *Most of those 200 million guns are owned for socially innocuous sport and recreational purposes.* Only about a third of the guns presently in circulation are handguns; the remainder are rifles and shotguns. When one asks gun owners why they own guns, various sport and recreational activities dominate the responses— hunting, target shooting, collecting, and the like. Even when the question is restricted to handgun owners, about 40 percent say they own the gun for sport and recreational applications, another 40 percent say they own it for self-protection, and the remaining 20 percent cite their job or occupation as the principal reason for owning a gun.

Thus for the most part, gun ownership is apparently a topic more appropriate to the sociology of leisure than to the criminology or epidemiology of violence. Many pro-control advocates look on the sporting uses of guns as atavistic, barbaric, or just plain silly. But an equally compelling case could be made against golf, which causes men to wear funny clothes, takes them away from their families, and gobbles up a lot of pretty, green, open space that would be better used as public parks. It is, of course, true that golf does not kill 35,000 people a year (although middle-aged men drop dead on the golf course quite regularly), but it is also true that the sport and recreational use of guns does not kill 35,000 people a year. There are fewer than a thousand fatal hunting accidents annually; death from skeet shooting, target practice, and such is uncounted but presumably very small. It is the violent or criminal *abuse* of guns that should concern us, and the vast majority of guns now in circulation will never be used for anything more violent or abusive than killing the furry creatures of the woods and fields.

Unfortunately, when we seek to control violence by controlling the general ownership and use of firearms among the public at large, it at least *looks* as though we think we have intuited some direct causal connection between drive-by shootings in the inner city and squirrel hunting or skeet shooting in the hinterland. In any case, this is the implication that the nation's squirrel hunters and skeet shooters often draw; frankly, is it any wonder they sometimes come to question the motives, not to mention the sanity, of anyone who would suggest such a thing?

4. *Many guns are also owned for self-defense against crime, and some are indeed used for that purpose; whether they are actually any safer or not, many people certainly seem to feel safer when they have a gun.* There is a fierce debate raging in gun advocacy circles these days over recent findings by Gary Kleck that Americans use guns to protect themselves against crime as often as one or two million times a year, which, if true, is hard to square with the common assumption of pro-control advocates that guns are not an efficacious defense against crime. Whatever the true number of self-defensive uses, about a quarter of all guns owners and about 40 percent of handgun owners cite defense against crime as the main reason they own a gun, and large percentages of those who give some other main reason will cite self-defense as a secondary reason. Gun owners and gun advocates insist that guns provide real protection, as Kleck's findings suggest; anti-gun advocates insist that the sense of security is more illusory than real.

But practically everything people do to protect themselves against crime provides only the illusion of security in that any such measure can be defeated by a sufficiently clever and motivated criminal. Dogs can be diverted or poisoned, burglar bars can be breached, home alarm systems can be subverted, chains and deadbolt locks can be cut and picked. That sales of all these items have skyrocketed in recent years is further proof—as if further proof were needed—that the fear of crime is real. Most people have also realized, correctly, that the police cannot protect them from crime. So people face the need to protect themselves and many choose to own a gun, along with taking many other measures, for this purpose. Does a society that is manifestly incapable of protecting its citizens from crime and predation really have the right or moral authority to tell people what they may and may not do to protect themselves?

Since a "sense of security" is inherently a psychological trait, it does no good to argue that the sense of security afforded by owning a gun is "just an illusion."

Psychological therapy provides an *illusion* of mental wellness even as we remain our former neurotic selves, and it is nonetheless useful. The only sensible response to the argument that guns provide only an illusion of security is, So what?

5. *The bad guys do not get their guns through customary retail channels.* Research on both adult and juvenile felons and offenders has made it obvious that the illicit firearms market is dominated, overwhelmingly, by informal swaps, trades, and purchases among family members, friends, acquaintances, and street and black-market sources. It is a rare criminal indeed who attempts to acquire a gun through a conventional over-the-counter transaction with a normal retail outlet. It is also obvious that many or most of the guns circulating through criminal hands enter the illicit market through theft from legitimate gun owners. (An aside of some possible significance: Large numbers of legitimate gun owners also obtain guns through informal "street" sources.)

As I have already noted, many efforts at gun control pertain to the initial retail sale of weapons, for example, the prohibition against gun purchases by people with felony records or alcohol or drug histories contained in the Gun Control Act of 1968, the national five-day waiting period, or various state and local permit and registration laws. Since felons rarely obtain guns through retail channels, controls imposed at the point of retail sale necessarily miss the vast majority of criminal firearms transactions. It is thus an easy prediction that the national five-day waiting period will have no effect on the acquisition of guns by criminals because that is not how the bad guys get their guns in the first place.

Having learned (now more than a decade ago) that the criminal acquisition of guns involves informal and intrinsically difficult-to-regulate transfers that are entirely independent of laws concerning registration and permits, average gun owners often conclude (whether rightly or wrongly) that such measures must therefore be intended primarily to keep tabs on them, that registration or permit requirements are "just the first step" toward outright confiscation of all privately held firearms, and that mandated registration of new gun purchases is thus an unwarranted "police state" intrusion on law-abiding citizens' constitutional rights. Reasoning in this vein often seems bizarre or even psychotic to proponents of registration or permit laws, but it is exactly this reasoning that accounts for the white-hot ferocity of the debate over guns in America today.

And similar reasoning applies to the national waiting period: Since it is well known that the bad guys do not generally obtain guns through normal retail channels, waiting periods enforced at the point of retail sale can only be aimed at thwarting the legitimate intentions of the "good guys." What conceivable crime-reductive benefit will a national five-day waiting period give us? If the answer is "probably very little," then the minds of average gun owners are free to speculate on the nefarious and conspiratorial intentions that may be harbored, consciously or not, by those who favor such a thing. The distinction between ill-considered and evil is quickly lost, and the debate over guns in America gets hotter still.

That the illicit gun market is supplied largely through theft from legitimate owners erodes any useful distinction between legitimate and illegitimate guns. Any gun that can be owned legitimately can be stolen from its legal owner and can end up in criminal hands. The effort to find some way to interdict or interfere with the criminal gun market while leaving legitimate owners pretty much alone is therefore bootless. So long as anybody can have a gun, criminals will have them too, and it is useful to remember that there are 200 million guns out there—an average of four of them in every second household.

6. *The bad guys inhabit a violent world; a gun often makes a life-or-death difference to them.* When one asks felons—either adult or juvenile—why they own and carry guns, themes of self-defense, protection, and survival dominate the responses. Very few of the bad guys say they acquire or carry guns for offensive or criminal purposes, although that is obviously how many of them get used. These men live in a very hostile and violent environment, and many of them have come to believe, no doubt correctly, that their ability to survive in that environment depends critically on being adequately armed. Thus the bad guys are highly motivated gun consumers who will not be easily dissuaded from possessing, carrying, and using guns. If sheer survival is the issue, then a gun is a bargain at practically any price. As James Q. Wilson has argued, most of the gun violence problem results from the wrong kinds of people carrying guns at the wrong time and place. The survival motive among the bad guys means exactly that the "wrong kinds of people" will be carrying guns pretty much all the time. The evident implication is that the bad guys have to be disarmed on the street if the rates of gun violence are to decline, and that implies a range of intervention strategies far removed from what gun control advocates have recently urged on the American population.

7. *Everything the bad guys do with their guns is already against the law.* That criminals will generally be indifferent to our laws would seem to follow from the definitions of the terms, but it is a lesson that we have had to relearn time and time again throughout our history. So let me stress an obvious point: Murder is already against the law, yet murderers still murder; armed robbery is against the law, yet robbers still rob. And as a matter of fact, gun acquisition by felons, whether from retail or private sources, is also already illegal, yet felons still acquire guns. Since practically everything the bad guys do with their guns is already against the law, we are entitled to wonder whether there is any new law we can pass that would persuade them to stop doing it. It is more than a little bizarre to assume that people who routinely violate laws against murder, robbery, or assault would somehow find themselves compelled to obey gun laws, whatever provisions they might contain.

8. *Demand creates it own supply.* That "demand creates its own supply" is sometimes called the First Law of Economics, and it clearly holds whether the commodity in demand is legal or illegal. So long as a demand exists, there will be profit to be made in satisfying it, and therefore it will be satisfied. In a capitalist economy, it could scarcely be otherwise. So long as people, be they criminals or average citizens, want to own guns, guns will be available for them to own. The vast arsenal of guns already out there exists in the first instance

because people who own guns like guns, the activities that guns make possible, and the sense of security that guns provide. "Supply side" approaches to the gun problem are never going to be any more effective than "supply side" approaches to the drug problem, which is to say, not at all. What alcohol and drug prohibition should have taught us (but apparently has not) is that if a demand exists and there is no legal way to satisfy it, then an illegal commerce in the commodity is spawned, and we often end up creating many more problems than we have solved.

Brazil and several European nations manufacture small arms; the Brazilian lines are relatively inexpensive but decent guns. In fundamental respects, the question whether we can disarm the American criminal population amounts to asking whether an organized criminal enterprise that successfully illegally imports hundreds of tons of Colombian cocaine into the U.S. market each year would not find the means to illegally imports hundreds of tons of handguns from Brazil. And if this is the case, then it seems more or less self-evident that the supply of firearms to the criminal population will never be reduced by enough to make an appreciable difference.

9. *Guns are neither inherently good nor inherently evil; guns, that is, do not possess teleology.* Benevolence and malevolence inhere in the motives and behaviors of people, not in the technology they possess. Any firearm is neither more nor less than a chunk of machined metal that can be put to a variety of purposes, all involving a small projectile hurtling at high velocity downrange to lodge itself in a target. We can only call this "good" when the target is appropriate and "evil" when it is not; the gun itself is immaterial to this judgment.

Gun-control advocates have a long history of singling out "bad" guns for policy attention. At one time, the emphasis was on small, cheap handguns—"Saturday Night Specials"—which were thought to be inherently "bad" because no legitimate use was thought to exist for them and because they were thought to be the preferred firearm among criminals. Both these thoughts turned out to be incorrect. Somewhat later, all handguns, regardless of their characteristics, were singled out (as by the National Coalition to Ban Handguns); most recently, the so-called military-style assault weapons are the "bad guns of the month."

Singling out certain types of guns for policy attention is almost always justified on the grounds that the type of gun in question "has no legitimate use" or "is designed only to kill." By definition, however, all guns are "designed to kill" (that is, to throw a projectile downrange to lodge in a target), and if one grants the proposition that self-defense against predation and plunder is a legitimate reason to own a gun, then all guns, regardless of their type or characteristics, have at least some potentially "legitimate" application. It seems to me, therefore, that the focus in gun-control circles on certain "bad" guns is fundamentally misplaced. When all is said and done, it is the behavior of people that we should seek to control. Any gun can be used legitimately by law-abiding people to hunt, shoot at targets, or defend themselves against crime; and likewise, any gun can be used by a criminal to prey upon and intimidate other people. Trying to sort firearms into "inherently bad" and "inherently good" categories seems fundamentally silly.

10. *Guns are important elements of our history and culture.* Attempts to control crime by regulating the ownership or use of firearms are attempts to regulate the artifacts and activities of a culture that, in its own way, is as unique as any of the myriad other cultures that comprise the American ethnic mosaic. This is the American gun culture, which remains among the least understood of any of the various subcultural strands that make up modern American society.

There is no question that a gun culture exists, one that amply fulfills any definition of a culture. The best evidence we have on its status as a culture is that the single most important predictor of whether a person owns a gun is whether his or her father owned one, which means that gun owning is a tradition transmitted across generations. Most gun owners report that there were firearms in their homes when they were growing up; this is true even of criminal gun users.

The existence and characteristics of the American gun culture have implications that rarely are appreciated. For one, gun control deals with matters that people feel strongly about, that are integral to their upbringing and their worldview. Gun-control advocates are frequently taken aback by the stridency with which their seemingly modest and sensible proposals are attacked, but from the gun culture's viewpoint, restrictions on the right to "keep and bear arms" amount to the systematic destruction of a valued way of life and are thus a form of cultural genocide.

Guns evoke powerful, emotive imagery that often stands in the way of intelligent debate. To the pro-control point of view, the gun is symbolic of much that is wrong in American culture. It symbolizes violence, aggression, and male dominance, and its use is seen as an acting out of our most regressive and infantile fantasies. To the gun culture's way of thinking, the same gun symbolizes much that is right in the culture. It symbolizes manliness, self-sufficiency, and independence, and its use is an affirmation of man's relationship to nature and to history. The "Great American Gun War," as Bruce-Briggs has described it, is far more than a contentious debate over crime and the equipment with which it is committed. It is a battle over fundamental and equally legitimate sets of values.

Scholars and criminologists who speculate on the problem of guns, crime, and violence would thus do well to look at things, at least occasionally, from the gun culture's point of view. Hardly any of the 50 million or so American families that own guns have ever harmed anyone with their guns, and virtually none ever intend to. Nearly everything these families will ever do with their firearms is both legal and largely innocuous. When, in the interests of fighting crime, we advocate restrictions on their rights to own guns, we are casting aspersions on their decency, as though we somehow hold them responsible for the crime and violence that plague this nation. It is any wonder they object, often vociferously, to such slander?

Works Cited

Cronon, William. 1983. *Changes in the Land: Indians, Colonists, and the Ecology of New England*. New York: Hill and Wang.

Faragher, John Mack. 1992. *Daniel Boone: The Life and Legend of an American Pioneer*. New York: Holt, Rinehart, and Winston.

Gilligan, Carol. 1982. *In a Different Voice: Psychological Theory and Women's Development*. Cambridge: Harvard University Press.

Gilmore, Russell S. 1975. *Crack Shots and Patriots: The National Rifle Association and America's Military-Sporting Tradition*. Ann Arbor, Mich.: University Microfilms. Ph.D. diss., Department of History, University of Wisconsin, 1974.

Gusfield, Joseph R. 1963. *Symbolic Crusade: Status Politics and the American Temperance Movement*. Urbana: University of Illinois Press.

Hindelang, M. J., et al. 1975, 1976, 1977, 1980. *Sourcebook of Criminal Justice Statistics*. Washington, D.C.: U.S. Department of Justice.

Hunter, James Davison. 1994. *Before the Shooting Begins: Searching for Democracy in America's Culture War*. New York: Free Press.

Katz, Jack. 1988. *Seductions of Crime: Moral and Sensual Attractions in Doing Evil*. New York: Basic Books.

Kheel, Marti. 1995. "License to Kill: An Ecofeminist Critique of Hunters' Discourse." In *Animals and Women: Feminist Theoretical Explorations*. Edited by Carol J. Adams and Josephine Donovan. Durham, N.C.: Duke University Press.

Kleck, Gary. 1991. *Point Blank: Guns and Violence in America*. New York: Aldine de Gruyter.
———.1997. *Targeting Guns: Firearms and Their Control*. New York: Aldine de Gruyter.

Kopel, David B. 1992. *The Samurai, the Mountie, and the Cowboy: Should America Adopt the Gun Controls of Other Democracies?* New York: Prometheus Books.
———. 1995. *Guns: Who Should Have Them?* New York: Prometheus Books.

Kruschke, Earl R. 1985. *The Right to Keep and Bear Arms: A Continuing American Dilemma*. Springfield, Ill.: Charles C. Thomas.

Lepore, Jill. 1998. *The Name of War: King Philip's War and the Origins of American Identity*. New York: Alfred A. Knopf.

Lipset, Seymour M., and William Schneider. 1983. *The Confidence Gap: Business, Labor, and Government in the Public Mind*. New York: Free Press.

Lott, John R., Jr., and David B. Mustard. 1997. "Crime, Deterrence, and the Right-to-Carry Concealed Handguns." *Journal of Legal Studies* 26, no. 1: 1–68.

Malcolm, Joyce Lee. 1994. *To Keep and Bear Arms: The Origins of an Anglo-American Right*. Cambridge: Harvard University Press.

Nye, Joseph S., Jr., Philip D. Zelikow, and David C. King, eds. 1997. *Why People Don't Trust Government*. Cambridge: Harvard University Press.

Polsby, Daniel, and Don B. Kates, Jr. 1998. "American Homicide Exceptionalism." *University of Colorado Law Review* 69, no. 4 (fall): 969–1007.

Quigley, Paxton. 1989. *Armed and Female*. New York: E. P. Dutton.

Ruddick, Sarah. 1989. *Maternal Thinking: Toward a Politics of Peace*. Boston: Beacon Press.

Slotkin, Richard. 1973. *Regeneration through Violence: The Mythology of the American Frontier 1600–1860*. Middletown, Conn.: Wesleyan University Press.

———. 1985. *Fatal Environment: The Myth of the Frontier in the Age of Industrialization, 1800–1890*. New York: Atheneum.

———. 1992. *Gunfighter Nation: The Myth of the Frontier in Twentieth-Century America*. New York: Atheneum.

Smith, Merritt Roe. 1981. "Military Entrepreneurship." In *Yankee Enterprise: The Rise of the American System of Manufactures*. Edited by Otto Mayr and Robert C. Post. Washington, D.C.: Smithsonian Institution Press.

U.S. Bureau of the Census. 1996. *Statistical Abstract of the United States: 1996* (116th edition). Washington, D.C.: Government Publications Office.

U.S. Department of Justice, Office of Justice Studies. 1995. "Guns Used in Crime." July.

Wagner, David. 1997. *The New Temperance: The American Obsession with Sin and Vice*. Boulder, Colo.: Westview.

White, Richard. 1991. *It's Your Misfortune and None of My Own: A History of the American West*. Norman: University of Oklahoma Press.

Wiebe, Robert H. 1967. *The Search for Order: 1877–1920*. New York: Hill and Wang.

Wright, James D., Peter H. Rossi, and Kathleen Daly. 1983. *Under the Gun: Weapons, Crime, and Violence in America*. New York: Aldine de Gruyter.

Zimring, Franklin E., and Gordon Hawkins. 1997. *Crime Is Not the Problem: Lethal Violence in America*. New York: Oxford University Press.

Zuckerman, Michael. 1977. "Pilgrims in the Wilderness: Community, Modernity, and the Maypole at Merry Mount." *New England Quarterly* 1, no. 2 (June): 255–275

Suggested Readings

Anderson, Jervis. 1984. *Guns in American Life*. New York: Random House.

Canada, Geoffrey. 1995. *Fist Stick Knife Gun: A Personal History of Violence in America*. Boston: Beacon Press.

Coates, James. 1987. *Armed and Dangerous: The Rise of the Survivalist Right*. New York: Hill and Wang.

Engelhardt, Tom. 1995. *The End of Victory Culture: Cold War America and the Disillusioning of a Generation*. New York: Basic Books.

Gibson, James William. 1994. *Warrior Dreams: Violence and Manhood in Post-Vietnam America*. New York: Hill and Wang.

Henigan, Dennis A., et al. 1995. *Guns and the Constitution: The Myth of the Second Amendment Protection for Firearms in America*. Northampton, Mass.: Alethcia Press.

Karl, Jonathan. 1995. *The Right to Bear Arms: The Rise of America's New Militias*. New York: HarperCollins.

Kates, Don B., Jr. 1979. *Restricting Handguns: The Liberal Skeptics Speak Out*. Croton-on-Hudson, N.Y.: North River Press.

Kates, Don B., Jr., and Gary Kleck. 1997. *Essays on Firearms and Violence*. San Francisco: Pacific Research Institute for Public Policy.

Kates, Don B., Jr., and Gary Kleck. 1997. *The Great American Gun Debate*. San Francisco: Pacific Research Institute for Public Policy.

Larsen, Erik. 1994. *Lethal Passage: The Story of a Gun*. New York: Vintage Books

Metaksa, Tanya K. 1997. *Safe, Not Sorry: Keeping Yourself and Your Family Safe in a Violent Age*. New York: HarperCollins.

Rosa, Joseph G. 1995. *Age of the Gunfighter: Men and Weapons on the Frontier, 1840–1900*. Norman: University of Oklahoma Press.

Sheley, Joseph F., and James D. Wright. 1995. *In the Line of Fire: Youth, Guns, and Violence in Urban America*. New York: Aldine de Gruyter.

Stange, Mary Zeiss. 1997. *Woman the Hunter*. Boston: Beacon Press.

Sugarmann, Josh, and Kristen Rand. 1994. *Cease Fire: A Comprehensive Study to Reduce Firearms Violence*. Washington, D.C.: Violence Policy Center.

Contributors

Stephen P. Andrews, Jr., coordinates development of youth and adult programs on environmental and natural resources issues for UC Cooperative Extension. He is currently spearheading a program to raise environmental literacy in communities throughout North-Central California. His research interests include place and culture as determinants of environmental values, environmental justice, and landscape ecology.

Dan Balz is a staff writer for the *Washington Post*. His article (with Richard Morin) appeared as part of the *Post*'s series entitled "Reality Check: The Politics of Mistrust."

Michael A. Bellesiles is an associate professor of history at Emory University and author of *Revolutionary Outlaws: Ethan Allen and the Struggle for Independence on the Early American Frontier*.

Sarah Brady is the vice chair of Handgun Control, Inc., in Washington, D.C., a public citizens' lobby working for legislative controls and government regulations on the manufacture, importation, sale, and civilian possession of handguns.

Fox Butterfield is a Pulitzer Prize–winning reporter for the *New York Times*.

James Coates joined the staff of the *Chicago Tribune* in 1967, where he has worked ever since. He has been based in Chicago; in Washington, D.C., as a Pentagon correspondent; and, since 1984, in Denver as the *Chicago Tribune*'s Western states correspondent. As an investigative reporter, Coates has covered scores of nationally significant events, including the Abscam and Koreagate scandals, the banking practices of President Carter's budget chief Bert Lance, Billy Carter's dealings with Libyan oil brokers, and the Alan Berg murder case. In addition, Coates was the reporter who discovered that the Pentagon was paying outrageously high prices for inexpensive hardware. He has received the *Chicago Tribune*'s Edward Scott Beck Award and was twice the recipient of the Raymond Clapper Award of the White House Correspondents Association. He is coauthor, with Michael Kilian, of *Heavy Losses: The Dangerous Decline of American Defense*.

Dov Cohen is assistant professor of psychology at the University of Illinois, Urbana Champaign.

David T. Courtwright is professor of history at the University of North Florida and the author of several books, including *Dark Paradise: Opiate Addiction in America before 1940.*

Clayton E. Cramer is a software engineer with a telecommunications manufacturer in Northern California. His first book, *By the Dim and Flaring Lamps: The Civil War Diary of Samuel McIvaine,* was published in 1990. He is also author of *For the Defense of Themselves and the State: The Original Intent and Judicial Interpretation of the Right to Keep and Bear Arms.*

Jan E. Dizard is the Charles Hamilton Houston Professor of American Culture at Amherst College, where he has taught sociology and American studies for the last thirty years. He is also an adjunct professor in the Animals and Public Policy Program at the Tufts University Veterinary College. He is the author of books and articles on topics including the sociology of the family, race relations, and environmental sociology. His most recent book is *Going Wild: Hunting, Animal Rights, and the Contested Meaning of Nature,* which will be reissued in 1999 in an expanded edition.

Robert Dreyfuss is a freelance writer based in Alexandria, Virginia, who specializes in politics and national security issues.

Wilbur Edel taught political science and held several senior administrative posts at Herbert H. Lehman College, City University of New York. He is the author of many books and articles on American politics.

Thomas B. Edsall is a staff writer for the *Washington Post* and coauthor, with Mary D. Edsall, of *Chain Reaction: The Impact of Race, Rights and Taxes on American Politics.*

Judy Foreman is a Wellesley graduate and a veteran of the Peace Corps (Brazil). She began a her career as a reporter with the *Boston Globe* and has been an award-winning medical and science writer for the *Boston Globe* since 1985.

T. Markus Funk is a Ph.D. candidate in law at Oxford University and a former law clerk for a federal judge. He writes extensively on a broad range of topics.

Robert George is a correspondent for the *Boston Globe.*

James William Gibson teaches sociology and history at California State University, Long Beach, and is the author of *The Perfect War: The War We Couldn't Lose and How We Did.*

Russell S. Gilmore is director of the Harbor Defense Museum in Fort Hamilton, Brooklyn, New York, and the author of *Guarding America's Front Door: Harbor Forts in Defense of New York City.* He holds a doctorate in American history from the University of Wisconsin and is a fellow of the Company of Military Historians.

Edward C. Hansen is a professor of anthropology at Queens College of the City of New York. Author of *Rural Catalonia under the Franco Regime*, his current interests focus on social class in America.

Gordon Hawkins is Senior Fellow at the Earl Warren Legal Institute at the University of California at Berkeley.

David Helvarg is a journalist and documentary producer. He is also the author of *The War against the Greens*.

David Hemenway is deputy director of the Harvard Injury Control Center and senior lecturer in the Department of Health and Policy Management, Harvard School of Public Health.

Charlton Heston, star in nearly sixty motion pictures, led the arts contingent in the 1963 Civil Rights March on Washington at which the Rev. Martin Luther King, Jr., delivered his famous "I Have A Dream" speech. He is currently the president of the National Rifle Association.

Cindy Hill, of Middlebury, Vermont, is the attorney who represented Evan Hughes in the case that overturned the Barre City gun ordinance in July 1996. Hughes was cited for carrying a loaded handgun in his car while en route to target shooting at the Barre Fish & Game Club. Hill successfully argued that the Barre City gun ordinance, which prohibited the carrying of a loaded firearm, even at home, was invalid under the Vermont Constitution.

William Hosley is curator of American Decorative Arts at the Wadsworth Atheneum in Hartford, Connecticut. He is the author of articles that have appeared in *American Heritage, Antiques*, and *Art and Antiques*.

Jeff Jacoby is an op-ed columnist for the *Boston Globe*. His twice-weekly essays, which range from foreign policy to criminal justice, are distributed nationally on the *New York Times* News Service.

Kathryn Kahler is a former writer for the Newhouse News Service and member of the U.S. Department of Education. She is currently involved with the Project for Tobacco-Free Kids.

Wendy Kaminer is a policy fellow at Radcliffe College and author of *It's All the Rage: Crime and Culture* and, most recently, *True Love Waits*.

C. Everett Koop, M.D., is chairman of the National Safe Kids Campaign in Washington, D.C., and a former Surgeon General of the United States.

David B. Kopel is research director of the Independence Institute, a free-market think tank in Golden, Colorado, and is also an associate policy analyst with the Cato Institute in Washington, D.C. Kopel is the author of numerous scholarly articles and several books on crime policy, including *The Samurai, the Mountie and the Cowboy: Should America Adopt the Gun Controls of Other Democ-*

racies?, which was named Book of the Year by the American Society of Criminology's Division of International Criminology.

Leonard Kriegel is the author of *Falling into Life,* a collection of essays.

Wayne LaPierre is executive vice president of the National Rifle Association and author of *Guns, Crime and Freedom.*

John R. Lott, Jr., is the John M. Olin Law and Economics Fellow at the University of Chicago. He was the chief economist at the United States Sentencing Commission in the late 1980s. His latest book is *More Guns, Less Crime: Understanding Crime and Gun Control Laws.*

George D. Lundberg, M.D., is a member of the American Medical Association's Scientific Publications Group in Chicago.

David McDowall works with the Violence Research Group, Department of Criminology and Criminal Justice, University of Maryland, College Park.

Tanya K. Metaksa is executive director of the National Rifle Association's Institute for Legislative Action. She is also the author of *Safe, Not Sorry.*

Jo-Ann Moriarty is a staff writer for the *Springfield Sunday Republican.*

Richard Morin is a staff writer for the *Washington Post.* His article (with Dan Balz) appeared as part of the *Post*'s series entitled "Reality Check: The Politics of Mistrust."

Robert Merrill Muth is an associate professor of natural resource policy and administration in the Department of Forestry and Wildlife Management at the University of Massachusetts, Amherst. He earned his Ph.D. in natural resource sociology through the College of Forest Resources, University of Washington in Seattle. His scientific interests focus on social conflict and natural resource policy, trapping, subsistence hunting and fishing, poaching, and the animal rights movement.

Richard E. Nisbett is Theodore M. Newcomb Distinguished Professor of Psychology and codirector of the Culture and Cognition Program at the University of Michigan.

J. Neil Schulman is an award-winning novelist, screenwriter, and writer of short fiction. He also pioneered in paperless publishing on the World Wide Web. He lectures extensively on a wide range of contemporary issues, including gun control. He is currently at work on his third novel, *Escape from Heaven.*

Steven Thomas Seitz is assistant professor in the Department of Political Science at the University of Illinois–Urbana/Champaign. His research interests include policy formation, implementation, and evaluation, with special emphasis on criminal justice policy. He is the author of *Bureaucracy, Policy, and the Public, Models of the Policy Process,* and numerous articles.

Jeffrey R. Snyder is an attorney working in Washington, D.C.

Mary Zeiss Stange is director of the Women's Studies Program and an associate professor in Religion and Women's Studies at Skidmore College and the author of *Woman the Hunter*. Her articles have appeared in the *Journal of Feminist Studies and Religion*, *Women's Studies Quarterly*, and *Commonweal*, as well as *American Hunter* and *Sports Afield*.

William J. Vizzard served as a special agent, supervisor, and manager with the Bureau of Alcohol, Tobacco, and Firearms for twenty-seven years before retiring in August 1994. He is currently assistant professor of public affairs and criminal justice at the University of Wisconsin, Oshkosh.

Adam Walinsky is a lawyer and former legislative assistant to the late Robert Kennedy. He was instrumental in shaping the 1994 Omnibus Crime Bill provisions to add citizen officers to existing police forces.

Douglas S. Weil is with the Department of Health Policy and Management, Harvard School of Public Health.

Philip Weiss is a contributing writer for the *New York Times Magazine*.

Brian Wiersema works with the Violence Research Group, Department of Criminology and Criminal Justice, University of Maryland, College Park.

Gordon Witkin is a writer for *U.S. News & World Report*.

James D. Wright is Charles and Leo Favrot Professor of Human Relations, Department of Sociology, Tulane University. He is the author of numerous journal articles and author or coauthor of more than a dozen books, including *Under the Gun: Weapons, Crime, and Violence in America*.

Franklin E. Zimring is the William F. Simon Professor of Law and Director of the Earl Warren Legal Institute at the University of California at Berkeley.